T0414286

Grading Goal Four

Grading Goal Four

Tensions, Threats, and Opportunities in the
Sustainable Development Goal on Quality Education

Edited by

Antonia Wulff

BRILL

SENSE

LEIDEN | BOSTON

All chapters in this book have undergone peer review.

The Library of Congress Cataloging-in-Publication Data is available online at http://catalog.loc.gov

Typeface for the Latin, Greek, and Cyrillic scripts: "Brill". See and download: brill.com/brill-typeface.

ISBN 978-90-04-43034-1 (paperback)
ISBN 978-90-04-43035-8 (hardback)
ISBN 978-90-04-43036-5 (e-book)

Contents

Acknowledgements

This book has benefitted from the encouragement and critical engagement of many people.

I want to start by thanking Hugh McLean for his energetic encouragement from the very beginning of this project, and the Education Support Programme of the Open Society Foundations for their backing.

This book would not have been possible without the support of Education International. My thanks go to my colleagues David Edwards, Dennis Sinyolo, Nikola Wachter, Jennifer Ulrick, and Louise Hoj Larsen, in particular.

The process was supported by a Reference Group, and I am grateful to Angeline Barrett, Aaron Benavot, Alexandra Draxler, and Anjum Halai for their guidance and invaluable advice and contributions.

I would also like to thank all the external reviewers and critical friends for their thoughtful reflections and feedback on the individual chapters. Special thanks go to Jordan Naidoo at UNESCO and Manos Antoninis at the Global Education Monitoring Report.

Finally, I must thank the authors for their respective chapters and for their engagement and contributions across chapters and to the book as a whole.

Last but not least, I am grateful to Chris Talbot for his support, which went well beyond the editorial, and to Kelly Clody for her excellent copyediting.

Figures and Tables

Figures

Tables

Abbreviations

AASU	All-African Students' Union
ACE	Africa Centres of Excellence
ACER	Australian Council for Educational Research
Action4SD	Action for Sustainable Development
ADB	Asian Development Bank
ADEA	Association for the Development of Education in Africa
AEGEE	Association des Etats Généraux des Etudiants de l'Europe
ANP	Awami National Party
ASA	Asia Students' and Youth Association
ASPBAE	Asia South Pacific Association for Basic and Adult Education
ATD 4th World	All Together in Dignity Fourth World
AU	African Union
BEST	Best Education Statistics for Improved Learning
°C	Degrees Celsius
CAMPE	Campaign for Popular Education
CANAE	Confederación Estatal de Asociaciones de Estudiantes
CARICOM	Caribbean Community
Cedefop	*Centre Européen pour le Développement de la Formation Professionnelle* [European Centre for the Development of Vocational Training]
CESR	Center for Economic and Social Rights
CFS	Canadian Federation of Students
CI	Confidence interval
CIA	Central Intelligence Agency (US)
CLADE	*Campaña Latinoamericana por el Derecho a la Educación* [Latin American Campaign for the Right to Education]
CO$_2$	Carbon dioxide
CONFEMEN	*Conférence des ministres de l'Éducation des États et gouvernements de la Francophonie* [Conference of the Ministers of Education of French-speaking countries]
COP21	Conference of Parties to the 1992 United Nations Framework Convention on Climate Change, held in Paris, 2015
COSATU	Congress of South African Trade Unions
CPD	Continuing professional development
CRPD	Convention on the Rights of Persons with Disabilities
CSA	Commonwealth Students Association
CSO	Civil society organisation
CUE	Center for Universal Education, Brookings Institution
DBE	Department of Basic Education

DESD	UN Decade of Education for Sustainable Development
DFAT	Department of Foreign Affairs and Trade (Australia)
DFID	Department for International Development (United Kingdom)
DoE	Department of Education
DOI	Digital Object Identifier
ECCE	Early childhood care and education
ECE	Early childhood education
ECHO	European Civil Protection and Humanitarian Aid Operations
ECOSOC	United Nations Economic and Social Council
ECW	Education Cannot Wait
EDS	European Democrat Students
EF	Ecological footprint
EFA	Education for All
EFA-FTI	Education for All Fast Track Initiative
EGRA	Early Grade Reading Assessment
EI	Education International
EMI	English as a medium of instruction
ESCAP	United Nations Economic and Social Commission for Asia and the Pacific
ESD	Education for Sustainable Development
ESIB	European Students' Information Bureau
ESP	Education Sector Plan
ESRC	Economic and Social Research Council (UK)
ESU	European Students' Union
EU	European Union
FDI	Foreign direct investment
FFA	Education 2030 Framework for Action
FfD	Financing for Development
FTI	Education for All Fast Track Initiative
GAD	Gender and Development
GAML	Global Alliance to Monitor Learning
GCE	Global Campaign for Education
GDP	Gross Domestic Product
GEFI	Global Education First Initiative
GEM	Global Education Monitoring
GEMR	Global Education Monitoring Report
GER	Gross Enrolment Ratio
GERM	Global Education Reform Movement
GI-ESCR	Global Initiative for Economic, Social and Cultural Rights
GIZ	*Deutsche Gesellschaft für Internationale Zusammenarbeit*
GLM	Global learning metrics
GNH	Gross National Happiness

GNI	Gross National Income
GNP	Gross National Product
GoJ	Government of Japan
GoKP	Government of Khyber Pakhtunkhwa
GoP	Government of Pakistan
GoS	Government of Sindh
GPE	Global Partnership for Education
GPI	Gender Parity Index
GSC	Education 2030 Global Steering Committee
GSV	Global Student Voice
HCETSR	High Council for Education, Training, and Scientific Research
HCI	Human Capital Index
HEC	Higher Education Commission
HLP	High-Level Plan
HLPF	High-Level Political Forum on Sustainable Development
HRW	Human Rights Watch
IADB	Inter-American Development Bank
IAEG-SDGS	Inter-agency and Expert Group on Sustainable Development Goal Indicators
IAG-EII	Inter-Agency Group on Educational Inequality Indicators
ICAE	International Council on Adult Education
ICC	International Cooperation Cambodia
ICIJ	International Consortium of Investigative Journalists
ICQN/TVSD	Inter-Country Quality Node on Technical and Vocational Skills Development
ICSU	International Council for Science
ICT	Information Communications Technology
ICTD	International Centre for Tax and Development
IEA	International Association for the Evaluation of Educational Achievement
IEAG	Independent Expert Advisory Group
IFAD	International Fund for Agricultural Development
IFFED	International Financing Facility for Education
IIEP	International Institute for Educational Planning (UNESCO)
IISD	International Institute for Sustainable Development
ILO	International Labour Organisation
ILSA	International large-scale assessment
IMF	International Monetary Fund
IPCC	Intergovernmental Panel on Climate Change
ISC	International Student Conference
ISSC	International Social Science Council

ITE	Initial teacher education
ITU	International Telecommunication Union
IUS	International Union of Students
KGB	*Komitet Gosudarstvennoy Bezopasnosti* [Committee for State Security of the Soviet Union, 1954–1991]
KoB	Kingdom of Bhutan
KoC	Kingdom of Cambodia
KoM	Kingdom of Morocco
KP	Khyber Pakhtunkhwa (Pakistan)
L1; L2	First language; second language
LAMP	Literacy Assessment and Monitoring Programme
LDCs	Least Developed Countries
LGBTIQ	Lesbian, gay, bisexual, transgender, intersex and queer/questioning
LIC	Low-income countries
LMP	Learning Metrics Partnership
LMTF	Learning Metrics Task Force
LOITASA	Language of Instruction in Tanzania and South Africa
LSA	Large-scale assessment
MAFF	Ministry of Agriculture, Forestry and Fisheries (Japan)
MDGS	Millennium Development Goals
MENA	Middle East and North Africa region
MENAP	Multilingual Education National Action Plan (Cambodia)
MFEPT	Ministry of Federal Education and Professional Training
MGIEP	Mahatma Gandhi Institute of Education for Peace and Sustainable Development
MLE	Multilingual education
MNC	Multinational corporation
MNEVT	Ministry of National Education, Vocational Training, Scientific Research and Higher Education (Morocco)
MoE	Ministry of Education
MoEYS	Ministry of Education, Youth and Sport (Cambodia)
MOI	Means of implementation
MOOC	Massive open on-line course
NDP	National Development Plan
NECC	National Education Coordinating Committee (South Africa)
NEP	National Education Policy (Pakistan)
NGO	Non-Governmental Organisation
NLSA	National large-scale assessment
NRF	National Research Foundation (South Africa)
NSO	National Union of Students in Norway
NUS-UK	UK National Union of Students

OBESSU	Organising Bureau of European School Student Unions
OCLAE	*Organización Continental Latinoamericana y Caribeña de Estudiantes* [Latin American and Caribbean Continental Student Organisation]
ODA	Official development assistance
OECD	Organisation for Economic Cooperation and Development
OHCHR	Office of the United Nations High Commissioner for Human Rights
OSF	Open Society Foundations
OWG	Open Working Group on Sustainable Development Goals
PASEC	*Programme d'Analyse des Systèmes Educatifs de la CONFEMEN* [CONFEMEN Programme for the Analysis of Education Systems]
PBS	Pakistan Bureau of Statistics
PforR	Program for Results
PIAAC	Programme for the International Assessment of Adult Competencies
PIRLS	Progress in International Reading Literacy Study
PISA	Programme for International Student Assessment
PISA-D	PISA for Development
PPPS	Public-Private Partnerships
PSO	United Nations Peace Support Operations
PTI	*Pakistan Tehreek-e-Insaf* [Pakistan Movement for Justice] (political party)
r	Pearson's correlation coefficient
RFSD	Regional Forum on Sustainable Development
Rio+20	UN Conference on Sustainable Development, 2012
RSA	Republic of South Africa
RTE	Right to Education
RTEI	Right to Education Index
RTI	Research Triangle International
SABER	Systems Approach for Better Education Results (World Bank tool)
SACMEQ	Southern and Eastern Africa Consortium for Monitoring Educational Quality
SADC	Southern African Development Community
SAIH	*Studentenes og Akademikernes Internasjonale Hjelpefond* [Students' and Academics' International Assistance Fund] (Norway)
SDGS	Sustainable Development Goals
SDSN	Sustainable Development Solutions Network
SES	Socioeconomic status
SIDS	Small Island Developing States
SSA	Sub-Saharan Africa
STEM	Science, technology, engineering and mathematics

t	Tonne
TAG	Technical Advisory Group on Education Indicators
TCC	Teacher Creativity Center (Palestine)
TCG	Technical Cooperation Group
TEI	Teacher Education Institution
THE	Times Higher Education
TIMSS	Trends in International Mathematics and Science Study
TST	Technical Support Team
TVET	Technical and vocational education and training
UIS	UNESCO Institute for Statistics
UN	United Nations
UNAPRCM	United Nations Asia-Pacific Regional Coordination Mechanism
UNCTAD	United Nations Conference on Trade and Development
UN DESA	United Nations Department for Economic and Social Affairs
UNDP	United Nations Development Programme
UNE	National Union of Students (Brazil)
UNECA	United Nations Economic Commission for Africa
UNESCO	United Nations Educational, Scientific and Cultural Organisation
UNFPA	United Nations Population Fund
UNGA	United Nations General Assembly
UNHRC	United Nations Human Rights Council
UNICEF	United Nations Children's Fund
UN MGCY	United Nations Major Group for Children and Youth
UNU-WIDER	World Institute for Development Economics Research of the United Nations University
UNV	United Nations Volunteers
UPE	Universal primary education
UPR	Universal Periodic Review
USAID	United States Agency for International Development
USSA	United States Student Association
VAT	Value-added tax
VNR	Voluntary National Review
WB	World Bank
WBG	World Bank Group
WCHE	World Conference on Higher Education
WEF	World Education Forum
WESIB	Western European Students' Information Bureau
WFP	World Food Programme
WID	Women in Development
WP	White Paper

Notes on Contributors

Joanne Ailwood
is a teacher, researcher and Associate Professor in the School of Education, University of Newcastle, Australia, and her research sits across the fields of early childhood and primary education, children and families. She has published in the fields of history and policies of education, early childhood education, and teacher education. Joanne's research is qualitative, making use of document analyses, case studies, and ethnographies. Her research is underpinned by the postfoundational theoretical perspectives of Michel Foucault and Rosi Braidotti. Joanne is a member of the Executive Leadership Board for the University of Newcastle's Centre for African Research, Engagement and Partnerships.

Stephanie Allais
is Research Chair of Skills Development and Professor of Education at the Centre for Researching Education and Labour at Wits University. Her research is located in the sociology and political economy of education, focussed on relationships between education and work. She was a fellow at the Centre for Educational Sociology at the University of Edinburgh, and prior to that, managed and conducted research into qualifications frameworks in 16 countries for the International Labour Organisation. She has worked in government, distance education, trade union education; taught high school and adult basic education and training; and led a student organisation. She served on many committees by appointment of Ministers of Education in South Africa and has been involved in numerous policy processes.

David Archer
is Head of Participation and Public Services with ActionAid, having been Head of Education for many years. In the 1990s, he developed the *Reflect* approach to adult learning and social change, which has won five UN International Literacy Prizes. Since the late 1990s, David has worked with ActionAid on human rights-based approaches to development and the building of civil society coalitions on education across Africa, Asia, and Latin America. He is Chair of the Board of the Right to Education Initiative (www.right-to-education.org), was a cofounder of the Global Campaign for Education (www.campaignforeducation.org), and is Chair of the Strategy and Impact Committee of the Global Partnership for Education (www.globalpartnership.org).

Bilal Barakat

is a researcher, lecturer, and consultant whose main research interests and expertise are in the area of educational policy modelling and statistics, including demographic, economic, and methodological aspects. Currently Senior Policy Analyst for the Global Education Monitoring Report, Bilal taught and researched these topics based principally at the Austrian Academy of Sciences. In addition, he regularly acted as a consulting expert for international development organisations. His research has been published in leading international journals and featured in major international reports, including the Intergovernmental Panel on Climate Change (IPCC). Bilal holds a Habilitation in Education and Demography from the Vienna University of Economics and Business, a DPhil in Education from the University of Oxford, and Master's degrees in Mathematics from the Universities of Cambridge and Oxford.

Aaron Benavot

is Professor of Global Education Policy in the School of Education at the University at Albany-SUNY. His scholarship has explored diverse educational issues from comparative, global, and critical perspectives – most recently, the proliferation of learning assessments; the conceptualisation and monitoring of lifelong learning; teacher enactment of mathematics curricula; and the mainstreaming of education for global citizenship and sustainable development. During the 2014–2017 period, Aaron served as Director of the Global Education Monitoring Report, an independent, evidence-based annual report published by UNESCO, which monitors global education trends and analyses progress toward international education targets in the 2030 Agenda for Sustainable Development. Aaron has also coauthored or coedited five books, including *PISA, Power, and Policy* (with H.-D. Meyer) and *School Knowledge for the Masses* (with J. Meyer and D. Kamens).

Stephanie Bengtsson

is a researcher, educator, and consultant, specialising in international education policy and planning, education in emergencies and forced displacement, teachers and teacher education, inclusive education, and the Sustainable Development Goals (SDGs) and Education for All (EFA) agenda. Currently, Stephanie is a project officer at the International Institute for Educational Planning (IIEP-UNESCO), supporting the Institute's work on crisis-sensitive planning and effective teacher management in refugee contexts. Before joining IIEP-UNESCO in 2018, Stephanie worked as a research scholar at the Wittgenstein Centre for Demography and Global Human Capital (a collaboration of IIASA,

VID/ÖAW, and WU) and as an independent education consultant. Stephanie holds a Doctorate of Education from Teachers College, Columbia University, and an MPhil in Inclusive Education from the University of Cambridge.

Carol Benson

is currently Associate Professor in International and Comparative Education at Teachers College, Columbia University. During her 30-year career, which has focussed on language issues in educational development, she has worked as a technical assistant at education ministries in multilingual countries including Guinea-Bissau, Mozambique, Bolivia, Guatemala, Vietnam, and Cambodia. As a researcher, she has contributed to published work documenting policy and practice in bi/multilingual education based on learners' own languages. Her current research interests include the role of medium of instruction in gender equity, decision-making in multilingual education policy, and the development of assessments that demonstrate the full range of learners' multilingual repertoires.

Zubeida Desai

was Dean of Education at the University of the Western Cape (UWC) in South Africa from 2007 to 2016, after which she formally retired. She is currently attached to the Department of Language Education in the Education Faculty at UWC in an extraordinary capacity. Zubeida has extensive experience working with teacher trainees, specialising in language teaching. She has published widely in the field of language in education policy and was the South African coordinator of the 10-year LOITASA Project (2002–2011), which explored the use of isiXhosa as a medium of instruction in geography, mathematics, and science in grades 4–6. She has also served on numerous advisory panels to the post-apartheid government on language policy matters.

Alexandra Draxler

is Senior Advisor to NORRAG and an education specialist. She spent many years at UNESCO and continues to work as an independent consultant for public and private entities. She was Executive Secretary of UNESCO's Delors Commission (1993–1996). She has written about technologies in education, public-private partnerships, and education policies and strategies for development. She is a member of several professional associations, is Associate Editor of the *International Journal of Educational Development*, and a Critical Friend of Education International. She has been involved for a number of years with NORRAG's programme of work, which includes critical review of EFA, the post-2015 process, and global governance.

Naureen Durrani

is a Professor at Nazarbayev University Graduate School of Education. She previously worked at the University of Sussex, Northumbria University, the University of Central Lancashire, and the University of Peshawar. Naureen's research interests lie in the social, cultural, political, and economic influences on education policy formulation and enactment, and the outcomes of education on identity formation and gender relations. Her research is underpinned by poststructural and postcolonial theories. She has published widely on identity construction and gender. Her recent publications include a coauthored book titled *Troubling Muslim Youth Identities. Nation, Religion, Gender*, published by Palgrave Macmillan. Naureen is currently leading a three-year study on gender and schooling in Kazakhstan. Contextually, her research has focussed on Pakistan, Nigeria, South Africa, Rwanda, Senegal, Occupied Palestinian Territories, Lebanon, the United Kingdom, and Kazakhstan.

Clara Fontdevila

holds a degree in sociology from the Universitat Autònoma de Barcelona and is currently a PhD candidate in the Department of Sociology at the same university, with a thesis research project on the negotiation and crafting of the post-2015 global education agenda. She has previously collaborated with Education International and the Open Society Foundations, as well as on the 2012 evaluation report of the Civil Society Education Fund. Her areas of interest are private-sector engagement in education policy, education and international development, and the global governance of education.

Viktor Grønne

spent 10 years in the Danish and European (school) student movements before graduating with a MSc in International Business and Politics from Copenhagen Business School in 2018. As first its Human Rights and Solidarity Coordinator and later a member of its Executive Committee, he represented the European Students' Union (ESU) during much of the education post-2015 negotiations between 2014 and 2016. During his years in ESU, he was also responsible for rebuilding ESU's global cooperation liaising with national and regional student movements around the world. Previously, he also represented the Danish VET students at the European level, helped establish a Danish-Zimbabwean student partnership, and acted as a youth representative in the Danish National Commission for UNESCO. He currently works for Plan Denmark.

Anjum Halai

is a Professor and international education expert with long standing experience in education in low and middle income countries like Pakistan and those in East Africa. She obtained her doctorate from Oxford University UK. She was an adjunct professor at the University of Alberta Canada (2011–2016) and a research fellow at the University of Sussex UK. Her research interests include social justice issues in education, girls' education and gender equity. She has published widely in international journals of repute and co-edited monographs and books on significant issues in education. Currently Dr. Halai is serving as Vice Provost and interim Dean Faculty of Arts and Sciences at the Aga Khan University Pakistan.

Colleen Howell

is Research Associate in the Centre for Education and International Development at the Institute of Education, University College London, working in the area of higher education. She has been extensively involved over the last 20 years in education research and policy work in South Africa, particularly focussed on issues of equity and diversity in higher education and the building of inclusive education and training systems. She has lectured and published on these issues and contributed to a number of national policy initiatives in South Africa. Between 1998 and 2014, she worked at the University of the Western Cape in Cape Town, initially as a researcher in the Centre for the Study of Higher Education and then as Director of Institutional Research in the Institutional Planning Division.

Christopher J. Johnstone

is Assistant Professor of Comparative and International Education at the University of Minnesota. His research interests focus on inclusive education, inclusive development, and international higher education. Johnstone's interest in the topic of this chapter was sparked by early career experiences as a special education and later inclusive education teacher. Johnstone's current projects include a global consultancy on inclusive education policy with UNICEF, research support for an inclusive employment project in Bhutan, and a forthcoming book on the intersection of inclusive education and inclusive development.

Mamusu Kamanda

is a senior researcher with significant experience in international development, particularly in postconflict and marginalised contexts. Her research experience ranges from international education to health and demographic population surveillance in low- and middle-income countries. Between 2014 and 2018, she worked with research institutions across sub-Saharan Africa to provide robust evidence to decision makers to support national and global development goals. In September 2018, she joined the Department for International

Development, UK, as Research and Evidence Specialist for the Middle East and North Africa (MENA) Research Hub in the Evidence Department. In this role, she champions the effective use of evidence to improve value for money and impact of programme design within country offices in the MENA region.

Hikaru Komatsu

is Research Associate at Kyoto University, Graduate School of Education. He holds a doctorate in forest sciences from the University of Tokyo. His research interests lie in the scientific and philosophical study of human–nature interactions. His most recent publications include "Refuting the OECD-World Bank Development Narrative" (in press, *Globalisation, Societies and Education*), "Stereotypes as Anglo-American Exam Ritual?" (2018, *Oxford Review of Education*), "Is Exam Hell the Cause of High Academic Achievement in East Asia?" (2018, *British Education Research Journal*), "Did the Shift to Computer-Based Testing in PISA 2015 Affect Reading Scores?" (2017, *Compare*), and "A New Global Policy Regime Founded on Invalid Statistics?" (2017, *Comparative Education*).

Allyson Krupar

is the Senior Specialist at Save the Children US in Learning Research and was formerly the Senior Associate on the Right to Education Index at RESULTS Educational Fund. She holds a PhD in Education focussed on adult education and comparative and international education from the Pennsylvania State University. Her research and work on RTEI included project management as well as data analysis and investigating how RTEI could be of use in the post-2015 education policy and programming environment. She developed the cross-cutting theme within the 2016 RTEI data to begin monitoring SDG 4.

Lizzi O. Milligan

is Lecturer in Education at the University of Bath. She obtained a PhD in Education from the University of Bristol in 2014. Her research focusses on issues of social justice, rights, and educational quality in low-income countries. She particularly explores the disjuncture between policy and practice, and the impact this has on inequalities in learning experiences and outcomes. Her recent work has considered this in relation to language of instruction, educational resources, and gender. Dr Milligan joined the editorial board of the journal *Compare* in 2016.

Palesa Molebatsi

is a doctoral student in education and development. She is based at the Centre for Researching Education and Labour in the University of the Witwatersrand's School of Education, South Africa. Palesa's role at the REAL Centre is also that of a research associate. Her research looks at the contribution that South African universities make toward the development of the South African society and economy.

Kate Moriarty

is a specialist in global education policy, advocacy, and human rights education. Kate started her career at Amnesty International, where she worked for a number of years and went on to lead human rights education globally. She has since worked for a number of NGOs, including Save the Children, the Malala Fund, and Theirworld, focussing on research and advocacy to support action on quality education for children in countries affected by conflict and crisis, girls' education, and early years education. She also worked for UNESCO as Chief of the Section of Education for Peace and Human Rights. Kate is a qualified teacher. She holds a BSc in Sociology from the London School of Economics and an MA in Politics and Development from the Institute of Latin American Studies. She has recently completed a Doctorate in International Education from the University of Sussex; her research provides a critical examination of the Sustainable Development Goal for Education (SDG 4).

Tanvir Muntasim

is working as a specialist on civil society and mutual accountability at the Global Partnership for Education (GPE) Secretariat. He provides technical advice to support stronger engagement of CSOs, teachers' organisations, and other national stakeholders in education sector policy, monitoring and management processes – including in the areas of budget tracking/education financing, effective joint sector review processes, and independent monitoring – and social accountability initiatives. Prior to joining GPE, he was the International Policy Manager, Education, for ActionAid. His role entailed monitoring and engaging with key global policy debates and policy networks on education. He previously worked for the Asia South Pacific Association for Basic and Adult Education as their Policy, Advocacy, and Campaigns Coordinator.

Lerato Posholi

is a PhD candidate and Research Associate at the Centre for Researching Education and Labour, University of the Witwatersrand, South Africa. She holds an MA in Philosophy from the University of the Witwatersrand. Her research interests are in epistemology and curriculum studies. Her PhD project broadly looks at the question of power and knowledge, and implications for curriculum.

Jeremy Rappleye

is Associate Professor at Kyoto University, Graduate School of Education. He holds a PhD from the University of Oxford. He is interested in overcoming divisions between philosophy and empirical social science, on the one hand, and Western (predominantly Anglo-American) perspectives and non-Western perspectives, on the other. His most recent publications include "Refuting the OECD-World Bank Development Narrative" (in press, *Globalisation, Societies and Education*), "Stereotypes as Anglo-American Exam Ritual?" (2018, *Oxford Review of Education*), "Is Exam Hell the Cause of High Academic Achievement in East Asia?" (2018, *British Education Research Journal*), "Did the Shift to Computer-Based Testing in PISA 2015 Affect Reading Scores?" (2017, *Compare*), and "A New Global Policy Regime Founded on Invalid Statistics?" (2017, *Comparative Education*).

Yusuf Sayed

is a global international education and development policy specialist. His research focusses on education policy formulation and implementation as it relates to concerns of equity, social justice, and transformation. Yusuf Sayed is the Professor of International Education and Development Policy at the University of Sussex and the South African Research Chair in Teacher Education, and the Founding Director of the Centre for International Teacher Education, at the Cape Peninsula University of Technology, South Africa. He is also Honorary Professor at the Institute of Social and Economic Research, Rhodes University, South Africa. Previously Yusuf was Senior Policy Analyst at the EFA Global Monitoring Report, UNESCO; Team Leader for Education and Skills, the Department for International Development UK; and Head of Department of Comparative Education at the University of the Western Cape, South Africa.

Matthew J. Schuelka

is Lecturer of Inclusive Education at the University of Birmingham. His primary area of scholarship concerns sociocultural understandings of disability and education, and a focus on design and systems of schooling for all students. Dr Schuelka has been involved in education, research, and development projects all over the world, including Zambia, Serbia, Malaysia, Japan, Denmark, India, United States, United Kingdom, and particularly in the Himalayan country of Bhutan. At the time of this writing, he is Primary Investigator on three major research projects in Bhutan for the Toyota Foundation, ERASMUS+, and the ESRC Global Challenge Research Fund.

Luke Shore

is an advisor to private foundations and impact funds. Previously, he was a Programme Officer at the Education Support Programme of the Open Society Foundations and Board Member of the Organising Bureau of European School Student Unions. He has a BA in Philosophy, Politics, and Economics from Christ Church, Oxford.

Iveta Silova

is professor and director of the Center for Advanced Studies in Global Education at Mary Lou Fulton Teachers College at Arizona State University. She holds a PhD in Comparative Education and Political Sociology from Teachers College, Columbia University. Her research focusses on globalisation and postsocialist education transformations, including intersections between postcolonialism and postsocialism after the Cold War. Iveta's most recent research engages with the decoloniality of knowledge production and being, childhood memories, ecofeminism, and environmental sustainability. Her latest books include *Childhood and Schooling in (Post)Socialist Societies: Memories of Everyday Life* (2018, coedited with Millei and Piattoeva), and *Reimagining Utopias* (2017, coedited with Sobe, Korzh, and Kovalchuk). She is a coeditor of *European Education: Issues and Studies* and an associate editor of *Education Policy Analysis Archives*.

William C. Smith

is a teaching fellow at the University of Edinburgh, and former Senior Policy Analyst at UNESCO's Global Education Monitoring Report and Thomas J. Alexander Fellow with the OECD. He holds a dual title PhD in Education Theory and Policy and Comparative International Education from Penn State University. Prior to earning his PhD, William worked for six years as a secondary social studies teacher in the United States. His research strands, which include addressing education's role in international development and the relationship between teachers, testing, and accountability, have resulted in over 30 academic and policy publications, including his edited book, *The Global Testing Culture: Shaping Education Policy, Perceptions, and Practice*.

Ghada Swadek

is a PhD candidate at the University of Minnesota. Her research focus is on inclusive education policy and practice in Morocco. She is currently involved in educational consulting specialised in supporting children with learning differences and an inclusive Arabic reading programme project. Her research interests include sociocultural understandings of inclusion and disability, inclusive education in the Middle East and North Africa (MENA), and early intervention in the MENA.

Anjela Taneja

is an education specialist with 20 years of experience with specialisation in education governance. For the last three years, she was the Head of Policy for the Global Campaign for Education, where she led the SDG processes within the Secretariat. She has worked for ActionAid, Oxfam, and CARE India, and was the Oxfam International Southern Education Lead. She is also one of the founding members of the Right to Education Forum, India's largest education network. She currently works on essential services and inequality with Oxfam India.

Elaine Unterhalter

is Professor of Education and International Development at University College London, and co-Director of CEID (the Centre for Education and International Development). She has published widely on gender and education, and on global frameworks, including the MDGs and the SDGs. Her most recent book, written with Amy North, is *Gender, Education and Global Poverty Reduction Frameworks*, published by Routledge. Elaine was joint Principal Investigator with Stephanie Allais on the project on higher education and the public good in Africa, funded by the Economic and Social Research Council, the Newton Fund, and the National Research Foundation of South Africa.

Volker Wedekind

is Associate Professor of Vocational Education in the Centre for International Education Research at the University of Nottingham and is Coordinator of the UNEVOC Centre at Nottingham. He is an honorary Associate Professor at the University of the Witwatersrand. His research has focussed on education policy from an historical-sociological perspective, on policy effect on teachers and curriculum, and more recently on vocational education policy in Africa, vocational pedagogy, and the role of vocational education for migrants. He has had extensive experience working on policy processes in South Africa as a member of a number of ministerial committees and on statutory bodies.

Joel Westheimer

is University Research Chair in Democracy and Education at the University of Ottawa and an education columnist for CBC Radio (the Canadian Broadcasting Corporation). Author, speaker, and education advocate, he grew up in New York City where he taught grades 6–8 in the NYC Public Schools. In addition to researching the role of schools in democratic societies, Westheimer studies, writes, and speaks widely on global school reform, the standards and accountability reform movements, and the politics of education and education research. His latest critically acclaimed book is *What Kind of Citizen? Educating Our Children for the Common Good*, which followed the award-winning *Pledging Allegiance: The Politics of Patriotism in America's Schools* (foreword by Howard Zinn).

Antonia Wulff

is Coordinator at Education International (EI), the world federation of teacher unions. She coordinated EI's advocacy and engagement in the intergovernmental negotiations on Agenda 2030 and is now focussing on SDG implementation, monitoring, and financing. Her work covers a broad range of policy areas related to education and the status and rights of education workers. Antonia also represents EI on the Board of the Global Campaign for Education. Prior to joining EI, Antonia managed a project on democratic education in Finland. She has a background in the student movement and is a former Board Member of the Organising Bureau of European School Student Unions and Chair of the Council of Europe Advisory Council for Youth. She has a Masters in Sociology from the University of Helsinki.

CHAPTER 1

Introduction: Bringing out the Tensions, Challenges, and Opportunities within Sustainable Development Goal 4

Antonia Wulff

For the third time in three decades, world leaders reaffirmed their promise of education for all when they adopted the Sustainable Development Goals (SDGs) in September 2015. In doing so, they pushed the deadline forward by another 15 years, but they also agreed on a stronger and broader commitment to quality and equity in education. SDG 4, 'Ensure inclusive and equitable quality education for all and promote lifelong learning', commits to progress throughout the world at all levels of education, from preprimary through to university and beyond. However, in the few years since its adoption, SDG 4 has been compromised and contested throughout its implementation. This book examines the tensions, challenges, and opportunities within SDG 4, with a view toward informing and supporting its rights-based implementation.

There were no guarantees that education would be the subject of a stand-alone goal when the discussion on a new development agenda kicked off in 2012. The Millennium Development Goals (MDGs) were viewed as an uneven success and were far from being met (UN, 2015a). The Education for All (EFA) goals were not met either and were largely unknown outside the education sector. There were also major challenges to consider, such as the climate and global financial crises, declining education and aid budgets, and rising inequality.

Whereas education was broadly considered to be one of the relatively successful MDGs, there was a more complex and sobering reality behind the global improvements in primary school enrolment and gender parity: Progress had been uneven and enrolment numbers had increased together with over-crowded and underequipped classrooms, unqualified teachers with worsening working conditions, and large disparity in both access and achievement between different groups. Patterns of inequality and exclusion had largely been reproduced, and the most marginalised communities had seen little progress (UNESCO, 2015a).

More than two decades of the EFA Agenda had left the education community impatient to learn from past mistakes and full of aspirations to take on both old persistent challenges and newly emerging ones. Alongside other sectors, the education community mobilised to secure an ambitious stand-alone goal on education within the Agenda 2030 for Sustainable Development. Beyond the inclusion of a separate goal on education within the new development agenda, there was, however, little agreement within the sector as to the specific targets to be included in the goal: how to define quality education, who should provide such education, and what minimum level of schooling should all young people in the world complete.

Rather than marking the end of these debates, the adoption of SDG 4 in September 2015 in some ways amplified tensions and diverging viewpoints within the sector. The education community continues to seek agreement on what the new agenda means in practice and what it will take to succeed. While it is ambitious and far-reaching in its targets, the agenda itself leaves much room for interpretation. The broad priorities, to which agreement was secured, are not tied to specific policies, implementation modalities, or financing arrangements, and there is minimal accountability for member states and international organisations.

Consequently, the different actors' mandates and ideological approaches are reflected in their respective SDG 4 efforts. There have been numerous attempts to reframe the agenda and alter its scope, such as deprioritising certain targets, particularly those on learning environments and teachers; denying the universality of the agenda and its relevance for rich countries; and overemphasising measurable and globally comparable learning outcomes at the expense of a broader notion of quality, which marginalises subjects that are more difficult to assess, such as education for sustainable development. This places SDG 4 implementation at the heart of tensions between an instrumentalist and rights-based approach to education.

Part of the tension arises from the fact that the SDGs simultaneously represent the world we aspire to create and the world in which we currently live. Agreed to by those in power in 2015, the agenda was bound to reproduce the power relations and imbalances of that time. Yet, the 2030 Agenda challenges the current system and its defining structural failures, pledges to rethink development as it has been understood, and opens up new opportunities for social, environmental, and economic justice. These two sides of the coin make it evermore important to reflect on the way forward, the inherent risks and opportunities, and the perverse incentives within global agendas.

Progress to date has been slow and time is tight; in fact, the age cohort that would be expected to finish upper secondary school in 2030 should already have started school! This book considers the education goal and targets as an opportunity to make desperately needed progress on education. As a point of departure, it embraces the idea that the SDGs are transformative in scope and ambition, and that they have the potential to challenge some of the pervasive forces in education, which are detailed in the final section of this chapter. In concrete terms, the book aims to support the rights-based implementation of SDG 4 in its entirety. This places the fulfilment of the right to education at the centre of all efforts to realise SDG 4 and brings with it a dual focus on the extent to which rights-holders enjoy their rights and duty-bearers deliver on their obligations.[1]

While the authors in this volume focus on different aspects of the broad education agenda, they share the value of advancing critical perspectives and rights-based approaches as part of the global conversation about SDG 4 implementation. Their analysis is firmly rooted in human rights and social justice. The chapters engage critically with SDG 4, examining its strengths and weaknesses, scrutinising the forces behind it and the challenges, tensions, and power dynamics shaping its implementation. With a decade left until the 2030 deadline, this book aims to inform, scrutinise, and create a sense of urgency. It encourages readers to contribute to ongoing deliberations and discussions, voice critical concerns, and think how best to advance rights-based perspectives. These inputs are integral to building capacity for implementation, monitoring, and evaluation of the education goal.

This introductory chapter sets the scene for the deeper analysis found in subsequent chapters. It starts with a brief overview of the MDG/EFA era and introduces the so-called post-2015 process and the deliberations around the global education goal. It then presents the new priorities in education, as captured in the goal on quality education for all. It highlights two principal challenges related to the SDGs as a whole and the broader implementation architecture. The first challenge is the limited accountability provided by the global framework for monitoring progress toward the goals. The second is the financing architecture. It then zooms in on three areas of tension and contestation within the education space: First, I discuss the equity promise within the SDGs and its implications in a context of rising inequality. Second, I examine the changing roles of both the public and the private sectors in education, and what this means for progress toward SDG 4. Third, I highlight the conflicting quests for quality education and for measurable and globally comparable learning outcomes. With these tensions in mind, I introduce the structure of the book and its individual chapters.

1   A Brief History: Formulating a New Development Agenda

In retrospect, it is hard to believe that the question at the start of the so-called post-2015 process was whether there would be an education goal at all. At that stage, there were two competing camps: Some were focused on the failure to meet the MDGs and were promoting a follow-up framework. Others had started advocating for a set of sustainable development goals in the lead-up to the United Nations (UN) Conference on Sustainable Development in 2012; that idea, which had been spearheaded by the Government of Colombia, was eventually included in the outcome document of the Conference (UNGA, 2012).

Several processes were initiated by the UN system in 2012 to inform the new development agenda, two of which in particular kickstarted the debate on what the world wanted and needed. First, the UN Secretary-General appointed a High-Level Panel of Eminent Persons on the Post-2015 Development Agenda (HLP) to advise him on a new practical but bold agenda. The HLP organised several outreach meetings, which encouraged civil society organisations (CSOs) to formulate proposals and build alliances. Second, the UN Development Programme (UNDP) launched a Global Conversation, aimed at involving people across the globe in discussion of a new set of development priorities. Under the banner of The World We Want, they carried out global, thematic, regional, and national consultations, with some 10 million people voting on their priorities in the My World Survey. A 'good education' came out as the issue that mattered the most to people across the globe (UN, 2013a, p. 8). This process also included focussed thematic discussions, including one on education.

Concurrently, negotiations on sustainable development goals had started at the UN Headquarters in New York. An Open Working Group (OWG) had been established and tasked with developing a proposal for consideration by the UN General Assembly (UNGA, 2013). When the OWG started its work in early 2012, the connections with other post-2015 processes were unclear, and few outside the sustainable development community were involved. But it soon became apparent that the OWG negotiations included the post-MDG issues too. Moreover, the OWG process was open and inclusive, encouraging civil society and other stakeholders to get involved. By mid-2014, the OWG was broadly considered the main process for formulating a new development agenda. The OWG agreed on a final proposal in July 2014, encompassing 17 sustainable development goals and 169 associated targets. For more detail on the OWG process and negotiations, see Chapter 2.

The UN General Assembly decided that the OWG proposal was to be the basis for the new development agenda, while 'other inputs' also would be considered (UNGA, 2014). The Intergovernmental Negotiations on the Post-2015 Development Agenda commenced in January 2015, aiming for the adoption of a new framework in September of that year. In addition to goals and targets, the framework was to include a declaration and an architecture for follow-up, review, and financing.

1.1   *The Education Sector's Own Post-2015 Process: Third Time Lucky?*

Discussions in the education sector began from a different starting point, since international consensus around the EFA agenda had begun in 1990, when UNESCO, UNICEF, UNDP, UNFPA, and the World Bank convened the World Conference on Education for All in Jomtien, Thailand. That conference positioned education as a development priority and agreed on an 'expanded vision of basic education', captured in the World Declaration on Education for All (World Conference on Education for All, 1990). While progress was slower than expected, the broad EFA vision was further developed at the 2000 World Education Forum in Dakar, Senegal, where six EFA goals as well as a Framework for Action were adopted, outlining strategies for implementation and transforming the agenda into something that was considered more actionable (World Education Forum, 2000).

Four months later, the UN General Assembly adopted the Millennium Declaration, pledging to eradicate extreme poverty through eight global goals. MDG 2 – the education goal – focused on universal primary education, while MDG 3 – the gender goal – was to achieve gender parity in both primary and secondary education. Within the international education community, it is commonly stated that the MDGs narrowed and skewed the EFA agenda by stealing away both attention and financing (UNESCO, 2013b). While the EFA movement was committed to a comprehensive vision of education, well beyond primary level, the MDGs focused almost exclusively on primary education. Given their overlapping ambitions, the two agendas brought about parallel but, to some extent, conflicting obligations, with member states asked to simultaneously deliver on different sets of implementation strategies and reporting duties.

As the 2015 deadline for the EFA goals was fast approaching, an extensive process was launched within the education sector to evaluate progress made and discuss new priorities and strategies. At its 2013 General Conference, UNESCO asserted its own role and that of the EFA coordination mechanisms in formulating the new education agenda, to be adopted by the World Education Forum in May 2015 and then 'embraced' by Heads of State and Government in September 2015 (UNESCO, 2013a, p. 9). The assumption was that the education sector would design and adopt the education goal to be included in the new development framework, and UNESCO proceeded accordingly.

The EFA architecture was well suited to extensive post-2015 consultation. UNESCO encouraged member states to evaluate their progress toward EFA, and more than 100 national EFA reviews formed the basis for six regional EFA 2015 Review Reports. The EFA Global Monitoring Reports 2013/14 and 2015 contributed further to a shared understanding of progress to date. The Global Education Meeting, held in Muscat, Oman, in May 2014, advanced the agenda-setting through the adoption of the Muscat Agreement, which included a proposal for an education goal with seven targets (UNESCO, 2014a). Regional Ministerial Conferences evaluated progress toward EFA and identified key challenges and priorities for education beyond 2015 ahead of the World Education Forum, which was held in Incheon, South Korea, in May 2015. Civil society consultations were organised in connection with each regional meeting, further consolidating a common vision of the education sector. The EFA Steering Committee played an active role in this regard too (Sachs-Israel, 2016).

There was an expectation that member states working within the post-EFA process would also play a role as education ambassadors within the broader post-2015 processes. At Secretariat level, UNESCO and UNICEF led the education strand and regularly shared inputs through the UN Secretariat. They also coordinated the thematic track on education as part of the UN-led conversation on The World We Want, where a good education had emerged as the top priority. The thematic track included regional meetings, an online consultation, and a Global Thematic Consultation on Education in the Post-2015 Development Agenda held in March 2013 (UN, 2013a, p. 153).

However, the many parallel tracks of the post-2015 discussions meant that the prior separation between the MDG and EFA frameworks was being reproduced. To start with, there were two parallel follow-up processes: one related to the broader post-2015 development framework and another education-focused post-2015 process. This divided the education community: While some organisations were quick to support the notion of a single post-2015 agenda, others feared that any development agenda would be unable to reflect the breadth and depth of the EFA goals, and therefore considered a separate post-EFA agenda to be necessary. There was a considerable gap between the two processes, and many found the parallel tracks problematic (Yamada, 2016).

Many within the education sector maintain that the post-EFA process had considerable influence over the formulation of SDG 4, but the parallel nature of the processes limited the impact of the post-EFA movement by framing it as an 'input' among others, rather than recognising it as the legitimate voice of the education sector. While it had been impossible to foresee the exact nature of the post-2015 process, especially the central role of the OWG, the education sector should have been more present in the overall post-MDG process (see Chapter 2). This would have made education more visible in OWG debates and allowed for a more informed and critical debate on education priorities. Moreover, it would have empowered the education community and allowed for stronger synergies and cooperation across sectors, including a more critical and thoughtful reflection on the ways in which education has to change in order to foster sustainable development.

2   An Introduction to the New Agenda: The Sustainable Development
       Goals

Addressing challenges associated with social, economic, and environmental
development, the 17 SDGs are ambitious, aspirational, and far-reaching – and
an anomaly in a world where extensive intergovernmental agreement has
become rare and policy objectives generally are expected to be evidence-
based, reasonable, and measurable. The SDGs pledge to sort out the unfinished
business of the MDGs – eradicating poverty and hunger, ensuring health and
quality education, and achieving gender equality – as well as combatting climate change, protecting oceans and ecosystems, reducing inequality within
and among countries, ensuring sustainable production and consumption, and
promoting economic growth and decent work (see Table 1.1). They set out to
transform the world by 2030, in part by asserting that sustainable development is a universal challenge, and thus a responsibility and obligation of all
countries.
    While this book considers education key to the success of Agenda 2030 as
a whole and views the SDGs as interdependent, it zooms in on the education
goal as an opportunity to make desperately needed progress on education.

3   Sustainable Development Goal 4

The education goal, SDG 4, adopted in September 2015 exceeded most expectations. The broad goal, 'Ensure inclusive and equitable quality education and
promote lifelong learning opportunities for all', is to be achieved through ten
specific targets, including three so-called means of implementation targets
(see Table 1.2). The implementation targets cover elements that are considered
essential to have in place for overall progress toward the goal to be possible.
They emerged as a consequence of the difficult negotiations over the financing
of the agenda and call for financial as well as nonfinancial means of implementation under each goal. While the education goal and its targets were expected
to go beyond the MDG promise of primary education and gender parity, SDG 4
goes beyond the scope of the EFA goals too. The most fundamental difference
is the universal nature of the agenda: all countries in the world have committed to reaching these goals.
    In practice, governments have committed to a shared level of ambition and
set of priorities. Countries are expected to translate these into national policies
and plans with specific targets, based on their contexts and their current state
of education and lifelong learning. To facilitate this, UNESCO member states[2]

TABLE 1.1   The Sustainable Development Goals (SDGS)

Number	Goals
Goal 1.	End poverty in all its forms everywhere
Goal 2.	End hunger, achieve food security and improved nutrition and promote sustainable agriculture
Goal 3.	Ensure healthy lives and promote well-being for all at all ages
Goal 4.	Ensure inclusive and equitable quality education and promote lifelong learning opportunities for all
Goal 5.	Achieve gender equality and empower all women and girls
Goal 6.	Ensure availability and sustainable management of water and sanitation for all
Goal 7.	Ensure access to affordable, reliable, sustainable and modern energy for all
Goal 8.	Promote sustained, inclusive and sustainable economic growth, full and productive employment and decent work for all
Goal 9.	Build resilient infrastructure, promote inclusive and sustainable industrialisation and foster innovation
Goal 10.	Reduce inequality within and among countries
Goal 11.	Make cities and human settlements inclusive, safe, resilient and sustainable
Goal 12.	Ensure sustainable consumption and production patterns
Goal 13.	Take urgent action to combat climate change and its impacts[a]
Goal 14.	Conserve and sustainably use the oceans, seas and marine resources for sustainable development
Goal 15.	Protect, restore and promote sustainable use of terrestrial ecosystems, sustainably manage forests, combat desertification, and halt and reverse land degradation and halt biodiversity loss
Goal 16.	Promote peaceful and inclusive societies for sustainable development, provide access to justice for all and build effective, accountable and inclusive institutions at all levels
Goal 17.	Strengthen the means of implementation and revitalise the global partnership for sustainable development

a   Acknowledging that the United Nations Framework Convention on Climate Change is the primary international, intergovernmental forum for negotiating the global response to climate change.

SOURCE: UNGA (2015b, p. 17)

adopted the Education 2030 Framework for Action (FFA) in November 2015 (WEF, 2015), following more than two years of consensus-building. It is a road-map to implementation, outlining values and principles as well as indicative strategies under each target, often specifying what is covered under each target and effectively making them more ambitious. It also provides guidance on some of the more controversial areas in education, such as private provision of education or the use of technology. Lastly, it outlines the architecture for monitoring and the set of thematic indicators. However, it is not clear to what extent governments respect the FFA, in part because there is no mechanism for monitoring and following up on its specific elements. The FFA is largely unknown outside the education sector, but one might also legitimately wonder whether it is sufficiently known within the sector and whether enough has been done to promote it.

I will not discuss each of the targets, but highlight some of their strengths and weaknesses, drawing upon the provisions within the FFA too. For the pre-cise wording of each target, see Table 1.2.

What is not included in SDG 4 is almost as important as what is. The omis-sion of early childhood education is glaring: Target 4.2 suggests that education starts at preprimary rather than early childhood level. Beyond the reference in the goal title, lifelong learning, and adult learning and education beyond lit-eracy and numeracy are excluded (for further discussion on this, see Benavot, 2018a). Furthermore, there is no target on education financing, despite the broad consensus within the education community that the lack of adequate financing was a major obstacle to EFA progress.

3.1   *"Follow-up and Review" as Opposed to Accountability*

Agenda 2030 has two serious structural flaws: the weak accountability and reporting framework, and the absence of financing commitments. There is a striking gap between the level of ambition of the goals and targets, and that of the architecture supporting and monitoring their implementation. It appears that this is the price that had to be paid for the far-reaching and ambitious goals; the adoption of a 'transformative' agenda necessitated that there be no strings attached. The so-called 'follow-up and review' – member states refused the term accountability – is 'voluntary and country-led, will take into account different national realities, capacities and levels of development, and will respect policy space and priorities' (UNGA, 2015b, paragraph 74.a). Monitor-ing at global level is based on an indicator framework and centred around the annual High-Level Political Forum on Sustainable Development, where mem-ber states come together to review progress. All of it is voluntary.

TABLE 1.2   SDG 4 and its targets. Goal 4. Ensure inclusive and equitable quality education and promote lifelong learning opportunities for all

Number	Targets
4.1	By 2030, ensure that all girls and boys complete free, equitable, and quality primary and secondary education leading to relevant and effective learning outcomes
4.2	By 2030, ensure that all girls and boys have access to quality early childhood development, care and pre-primary education so that they are ready for primary education
4.3	By 2030, ensure equal access for all women and men to affordable and quality technical, vocational and tertiary education, including university
4.4	By 2030, substantially increase the number of youth and adults who have relevant skills, including technical and vocational skills, for employment, decent jobs and entrepreneurship
4.5	By 2030, eliminate gender disparities in education and ensure equal access to all levels of education and vocational training for the vulnerable, including persons with disabilities, indigenous peoples and children in vulnerable situations
4.6	By 2030, ensure that all youth and a substantial proportion of adults, both men and women, achieve literacy and numeracy
4.7	By 2030, ensure that all learners acquire the knowledge and skills needed to promote sustainable development, including, among others, through education for sustainable development and sustainable lifestyles, human rights, gender equality, promotion of a culture of peace and non-violence, global citizenship and appreciation of cultural diversity and of culture's contribution to sustainable development
4.a	Build and upgrade education facilities that are child, disability and gender sensitive and provide safe, non-violent, inclusive and effective learning environments for all
4.b	By 2020, substantially expand globally the number of scholarships available to developing countries, in particular least developed countries, small island developing States and African countries, for enrolment in higher education, including vocational training and information and communications technology, technical, engineering and scientific programmes, in developed countries and other developing countries
4.c	By 2030, substantially increase the supply of qualified teachers, including through international cooperation for teacher training in developing countries, especially least developed countries and small island developing States

SOURCE: UNGA (2015b, p. 17)

A key component of this is the Voluntary National Review. As the name indicates, member states volunteer to review progress toward goals and targets, but also the processes, policies, and institutional mechanisms put in place to support implementation, including means of implementation and the involvement of civil society. By the end of 2019, 142 countries will have carried out voluntary national reviews. This exchange on progress as well as obstacles and challenges should allow countries to learn from each other, but is rendered difficult by the limited time available for in-depth discussion, the varying formats of the reviews presented, and the unwillingness of governments to criticise or directly challenge other governments. Given that the guidelines provided by the UN are voluntary too, countries choose what areas and aspects they review. Few reports thus far have included in-depth analysis or discussion of structural barriers; it is mostly low-income countries that have acknowledged challenges (Beisheim, 2018, p. 22). This undermines the universality of the agenda and risks reproducing hierarchies of development while ignoring systemic issues and dynamics of donor dependency. Civil society representatives tend to be the only ones asking difficult questions, and these are seldom answered.

Nevertheless, the reviews could still play an important role at the national level by pushing governments to think more holistically about the SDGs and to consider mechanisms for more effective cooperation across sectors and silos. Reviews so far have shown that a large number of countries – high- as well as low-income – have established new structures for coordination and oversight, often at the level of the government (UN DESA, 2018b). Similarly, regional structures have been established to support implementation and policy coordination.

Among the transformative elements of Agenda 2030 are its universality and its pledge to overcome silos within sustainable development. However, neither is enforced. Silos are maintained as goals are reviewed separately, and there is no framework for assessing synergies and antagonisms across goals. Beyond synergies, there is no link to rights-based monitoring efforts: despite 156 of the 169 targets having substantial linkages to human rights and labour standards, there is no effective integration of these in the review of the SDGs (Feiring & Hassler, 2016, p. 7).[3] This also means that extraterritorial human rights obligations – that is, the duties of governments to respect, protect, and fulfil human rights beyond their borders (Lusiani & Muchhala, 2015) – are ignored. A rights-based review and reporting architecture should measure the enjoyment of the right to education by rights-holders as well as the degree of compliance with human rights obligations of states. Instead, governments can report on enrolment figures without addressing the provider of education, its quality, or the costs to households. In the same vein, donor countries can count support to private fee-charging schools in recipient countries as part of its SDG implementation without having to report on its impact on communities and structures of inequality.

3.2   *Measuring and Monitoring Progress*

Accountability is further undermined by the fact that the indicators remain works in progress more than four years after the adoption of the SDGs. Member states relegated the global indicators to a technical concern and delegated their development to the UN Statistical Commission. They, in turn, established an intergovernmental expert group: the Inter-Agency Expert Group on SDG Indicators (IAEG-SDGs), charged with the daunting task of developing a single global indicator for each of the 169 targets.

But choosing what and how to measure is never neutral. As the result of political negotiations, many of the SDG targets are ambiguous and imprecise, which means that the technical task came with a de facto power to redefine the focus of targets (MacFeely, 2018). Driven by data availability and comparability as well as methodological feasibility rather than the purpose of the target, many indicators fail to measure the full scope of the target. The global indicator under Target 4.1, for instance, looks at minimum proficiency levels in numeracy and literacy as a proxy for effective and relevant learning outcomes, but fails to measure the completion of free quality primary and secondary education. There are numerous such examples (Unterhalter, 2019). This is worrying because the indicators are not simply a matter of holding governments to account but should also guide policy and help strengthen education systems.

As of April 2019, close to half of the global indicators are approved (UN, 2019). But the lack of data and conceptual and/or methodological clarity is undermining the monitoring of many goals, such as those on reducing inequality, combatting climate change, and ensuring peaceful and inclusive societies. Less than a third of the data needed to monitor progress on gender equality is available (UN Women, 2018). The greater emphasis on individual development and human rights, and the extensive disaggregation called for within Agenda 2030, are challenging for national statistical systems (MacFeely, 2018).

Indicators on which no progress has been made will be reconsidered in 2020. Additional indicators will be discussed for targets only partially covered by their indicator. While these two processes present an opportunity for better indicators, time is tight and country capacity limited. Many member states struggle with data collection, analysis, and reporting. Moreover, the average cost of all SDG 4 data has been estimated at approximately US\$1.35 million per country per year (UIS, 2018a), and SDG 4 is only one of the 17 SDGs. Furthermore, low-income countries may find themselves obliged to report on the indicators as part of reporting to donors, adding another dimension to why it is so important to get these indicators right.

According to Agenda 2030, the global indicators are to be accompanied by regional and national indicators; with few exceptions, little progress has been made on these fronts. The education sector was ahead of the global game when proposing a set of thematic education indicators, which provides a more comprehensive viewpoint on progress in education than the 11 global indicators (UIS, 2015). It is also testament to the fact that indicators, while technical, are decidedly political and thus benefit from being discussed by stakeholders. However, the methodological progress made on the thematic education indicators has been uneven, with Target 4.7 standing out as the one with least progress.

3.3   *Financing Sustainable Development – Or Reimagining the Role of the State*

Despite the consensus within the EFA community on the necessity of a financing target, and the significant civil society mobilisation during the post-2015 process, the efforts to secure an explicit commitment to education financing failed. UNESCO tried to make up for this by mobilising support for financial commitments in the Education 2030 Framework for Action, passed in November 2015. In the end, the FFA restated an older agreement on education financing, while adjusting the level of ambition to 'at least 4% to 6% of … GDP' and 'at least 15% to 20% of public expenditure' to education (WEF, 2015, p. 67). There is also an indicator on the proportion of total government spending on essential services (education, health, and social protection) under Target 1.a, on mobilising resources to end poverty.

During the SDG negotiations, the World Bank received a lot of attention for its claim that a shift from billions to trillions was necessary to achieve the SDGs, emphasising the need for private finance (World Bank, 2015a). This made for a discourse in which public responsibility and financing were framed as unfeasible and it was considered unreasonable to suggest that any government could do it on its own. Private sector participation was seen as a precondition for success, as reflected in Target 17.17, seeking 'effective public, public-private, and civil society partnerships' (UNGA, 2015b, p. 27). Blended finance and public-private partnerships (PPPs) were further championed in the Addis Ababa Action Agenda (UNGA, 2015a).

The emphasis on the amount of money needed drove attention away from the politics around the sources of financing, framing it as a mere practical arrangement. The implication is that as long as education is provided, it does not matter who the provider is. Yet the SDGs depend on political priorities and policies as much as on financing, and the sources of funding have direct consequences for the policy environment and the political architecture, including governance and the role of the state. The UN Special Rapporteur on Extreme Poverty and Human Rights recently rang the alarm bell and challenged the notion of privatisation as 'a technical solution for managing resources and reducing fiscal deficits' (UN, 2018a, p. 2). He suggested that stronger monitoring and accountability mechanisms will not be enough to mitigate the risks related to a renegotiated social contract. When private actors and organisations enter public spaces and domains of the government, there is a more ideological dynamic at play, where power is being renegotiated simply through the new role taken by the private sector and its implicit or explicit side-lining of the government. There is ample evidence pointing to the unequal sharing of risks in PPPs (see for instance Eurodad, 2018), but it is harder to evaluate the less tangible consequences of privatisation on issues such as equity and inclusion, poverty, social cohesion, or public support for taxation.

Agenda 2030 is not explicit in its articulation of the role of the state or the private sector. It simply calls on everybody to do their part. But suggesting that states and the private sector are equally important for the achievement of the SDGs is, in fact, a radical reimagining of the role of the state. One could argue that this would have been the case under the MDGs too. What has changed is the attribution of responsibility within the 2030 Agenda, the attitudes of donor nations, and the role that the private sector itself seeks to play. This new universal agenda comes with an expectation on countries to sort out their own financing, which means that many find themselves forced to look for alternative sources of funding. Moreover, public budgets are shrinking and cost-cutting efforts by governments can be observed across the globe. All of this results in a situation where the private sector is encouraged and facilitated to play a new and expanded role in public policy implementation.

3.4   *Transformation against a Capitalist Backdrop*

The SDGs set out to take two inherently incompatible ideological approaches: committing to continued economic growth while simultaneously respecting planetary boundaries and transforming the world. The collision between growth-fuelled capitalism and sustainable development is ignored, as the SDGs suggest that social, environmental, and economic goals can be reached independently from each other (Hickel, 2019). This lack of acknowledgement of the trade-offs between these competing aspirations confirms that there are strong economic and political interests at stake and suggests a lack of appreciation of the scale of the climate crisis and of the social and the environmental costs of business as usual.

The SDGs represent a tension between transformation and status quo. Adopted by the governments that were in power in 2015, the SDGs necessarily reflect the political climate and leanings of that time. Yet, there are strands that, if taken seriously, would challenge the disproportionate power and privileges of the elite. The goal on reducing inequality (SDG 10), for instance, is deeply progressive, considering the number of countries where high levels of income inequality are entrenched yet broadly accepted. The notion of reducing inequality between countries may be even more radical. It is, thus, both useful and important to remember the more progressive dimensions of the agenda and the values that underpin it. Such principles include the right to development, which, according to the 1992 *Rio Declaration on Environment and Development*, 'must be fulfilled so as to equitably meet developmental and environmental needs of present and future generations' (UNGA, 1992, p. 1). Another principle is common but differentiated responsibilities, which acknowledges that responsibilities are based on historical differences in contributions to environmental problems and the (technical and economic) capacity to tackle these. Yet another principle deals with policy space, which guarantees the autonomy of countries in determining policies and managing their economies.

These principles are fundamental in an interconnected and interdependent but profoundly unequal world – and require active defending. Whereas the negotiations on the SDGs rejected the colonial logic of development, the goals are to be implemented in a world that still is shaped by colonial structures and acutely unequal access to resources. The notion of policy space is central to the monitoring of SDG progress too: How much autonomy do the poorest countries have in making sustainable development happen? What is an adequate response to many multinational companies having a turnover that is far bigger than the GDP of whole countries?

The MDGs were part of a shift by which development was simplified into more easily digested and measured objectives, ignoring the more ideological issue of how to meet the objectives. Under the broader umbrella of MDG implementation, there was first a shift toward harmonisation and greater alignment of priorities among donor countries, and then toward more of a partnership between donor and recipient countries, principally within the context of the aid effectiveness process. The MDG era brought with it a more results-based and impact-driven understanding of aid. By reducing development to a question of efficiency, one denies the complex nature of processes of development and posits the economic side as more important, implying there is one single way forward that is more rational, suitable, and expedient.

The shift to sustainable development, however, calls for a rethinking of current models of development. It overthrows the notion of a 'developed country' both in the sense of rejecting the traditional trajectory of growth-fuelled development and asserting that no single country has figured out a way of balancing social, economic, and environmental progress.

This obliges the education sector to take a critical look at itself: is education in its current form fit for this shift to sustainable development? Throughout the post-2015 process education advocates worked to frame education as the foundation for development (UNESCO, 2013a). While education is a precondition for achieving many other development goals, causality is complex and the transformative power of education is determined by countless factors. As discussed in Chapter 3, educating girls cannot be separated from other structures, and gender equality in and through education is intrinsically linked with societal norms and structures. The intended mainstreaming and fostering of interlinkages within SDG implementation are yet to be seen, but the education sector should engage more thoughtfully with these sought-after synergies: are we willing to rethink education to the extent needed for climate justice? How can education systems support students in reflecting on their role in society and in a world that is characterised by inequality, climate crisis and human rights violations?

4   Addressing the Challenges within SDG 4

As previously mentioned, the commitment to inclusive and equitable quality education and lifelong learning opportunities within SDG 4 leaves room for different approaches, priorities, and even ideologies. The agenda calls on governments to 'sustain political leadership on education and guide the process of contextualising and implementing the SDG 4-Education 2030 goal and targets, based on national experiences and priorities' (WEF, 2015, p. 57). Such a contextualisation is a precondition for relevant, targeted, and appropriate implementation. But it also opens the door for inconsistencies and the neglect or outright undermining of dimensions of the goal. The UNESCO-driven Framework for Action aims to mitigate this by guiding the implementation, but there is little indication of it having become the normative instrument that it was designed to be. There is, however, a fundamental difference between the necessary localising of the agenda at national level and the cherry-picking within SDG 4 of some international organisations. The global education landscape is characterised by a competition for influence and authority, and the different mandates and ideological approaches of actors are naturally reflected in their respective SDG 4 efforts. Every initiative need not reflect the full scope of SDG 4, but neither can one assume that every education initiative automatically contributes to the achievement of SDG 4. More scrutiny of proposed initiatives and implementation strategies is vital for a rights-based implementation.

In fact, there have been several education initiatives that have undermined SDG 4 in its entirety in the few years since its adoption. For example, despite having signed onto the FFA, the World Bank – the largest funder of education in low-income countries – has continued to champion a narrow 'learning agenda', peppered with occasional lip service to SDG 4. The recently launched Human Capital Index posits the measurement of learning outcomes as the most urgent education priority. Through its *Systems Approach for Better Education Results* (SABER), the Bank is further pushing national governments to adopt its policy priorities, which are largely contradictory to and completely disconnected from those recommended in the FFA. For instance, the Bank's policy advice discourages governments from regulating education, setting standards for private schools, or limiting private actors and fees (Bous, 2019).

Beyond undermining the breadth of SDG 4, the Bank rejects SDG 4 and its FFA as the overarching global framework for education. As so-called knowledge-based economies grapple for growth and hunt for quick fixes and best practices in education, SDG 4 implementation is located at the heart of the tensions between an instrumentalist approach to education, where its value is determined by the economic growth that it yields, and a broader rights-based conceptualisation. Moreover, the SDGs are to be implemented in a political landscape where the UN system struggles to assert its relevance and values; UNESCO is no longer the obvious authority in education, and it is undermined by its financial situation too (Hüfner, 2017). As both the G7 and the G20 show a new interest in education, there is little to suggest that SDG 4 will be the framework for that conversation.

These differences continue to divide the education community and make implementation ever-more challenging, even if these tensions were not brought about by the SDGs as much as they simply were not resolved by the SDGs. Part of the tension derives from the fact that the 2030 Agenda does not specify the extent to which efforts have to be aligned, harmonised, or globally comparable. Several SDG targets refer to concepts within education for which there are no global standards. The most obvious example is learning outcomes and whether they should be aligned and compared at the global level. This issue should be addressed target by target, although in some cases, the global indicator framework has imposed a resolution of this dilemma that was invariably in support of convergence.

The idea for this book was born out of frustration over these divisions and particularly the misuse and misinterpretations of SDG 4 and the rejection of the FFA. The book argues that rights-based implementation of SDG 4 rests on three pillars: equitable education systems, public provision and regulation of education, and a broad conception of quality. These pillars could also be conceived of as the axes against which the tensions and contradictions are playing out.

4.1   *Going beyond Equality: Ensuring Equitable Education Systems*

A consensus emerged early in the post-2015 process on the need to reach those who had been left behind by the progress made under the MDGs and EFA goals. The aspiration of leaving no one behind quickly became the slogan for the new agenda, but little was done to define what exactly this entailed. In fact, it translated into discussions over which groups to explicitly mention rather than the ways in which structural barriers could be addressed and removed. Some have suggested that the success of the SDGs should be measured in the reduction in differences between quintiles within countries rather than the traditional comparison between countries (Lewin, 2015).

SDG 4 has been celebrated for its commitment to the universal completion of free primary and secondary education, which goes beyond the human rights obligation of making secondary education *available* and *progressively free*. The FFA goes further by specifying that it should entail the 'provision of 12 years of free, publicly funded, inclusive, equitable, quality primary and secondary education – of which at least nine years are compulsory' (WEF, 2015, p. 7). During the MDG era (2000–2015), there was frustration in the education sector over the prioritisation of primary completion over all other education challenges. One of the demands going forward was for a more balanced development of the education system as a whole, where education is understood as a continuum, and all levels benefit from policy attention and investment. But such an expansion of education requires careful attention to equity, especially as the dynamics of exclusion may differ depending on the level of education. Whereas early childhood education is broadly considered vital for overcoming differences in backgrounds of children and thus contributing to more equitable and inclusive systems, Target 4.2 aims for equal access without addressing any of the associated barriers, such as the largely privatised sector and the high costs to households (the FFA does call for at least one year of free and compulsory preprimary education). Target 4.3, on the other hand, seeks to make technical, vocational, and tertiary education affordable, implying that equity is more urgent at the level of postsecondary education. Nevertheless, Target 4.b on higher education scholarships fails to acknowledge its inherent risks related to the reproduction of patterns of privilege and marginalisation; such scholarships risk discouraging the development of the higher education sector in recipient countries, while fostering brain drain.

With the number of out-of-school children of primary school age stalling for a tenth successive year in 2017, ensuring access remains urgent (UIS, 2018a). This suggests that the structures and mechanisms of exclusion and marginalisation are deeply rooted, complex, and context-specific. The reference to equitable and inclusive education in the goal itself implies a willingness to consider targeted and differentiated measures to ensure all groups enjoy an education of comparable quality and suggests a welcome departure from the parity principle of the MDGs. Target 4.a, on disability and gender sensitive education facilities, also brings in the notion that education systems in themselves have to change, which is an important complement to Target 4.5 on eliminating gender disparities and ensuring equal access for the vulnerable. The specific reference to persons with disabilities and indigenous peoples is significant, but the narrow focus of the target itself makes it insufficient (UNGA, 2017).

Unterhalter (2019) has criticised the failure of the SDG 4 indicators to consider equity beyond parity and equal provision, which will not account for the extent to which systems in themselves may reproduce inequalities. Many have argued for learning outcomes as a proxy for equity and inclusion in education, suggesting that this would entail a shift from equality of opportunity to equality of outcome (Omoeva, Moussa, & Hatch, 2018; Center for Universal Education, Save the Children and Women Thrive Worldwide, n.d.). But whereas learning assessments can help showcase disparities, they are also likely to reproduce patterns of inequality, for instance by favouring those who are learning in their mother tongue. Most current measurements of learning also exclude the out-of-school population. Rather than increasing the number of standardised assessments, equity requires more attention to processes of teaching and learning, and how equity can be fostered and ensured in the classroom. The references to *relevant* learning outcomes in Target 4.1 call for a broader and necessary discussion on the links between the content of education and equity and inclusion, such as the inclusion of indigenous knowledge or efforts to decolonise curriculum in postcolonial contexts. But thus far, such conversations have been undermined by a more utilitarian notion of relevance, as also reflected in the global indicator on literacy and numeracy.

4.2   *Protecting a Public Good from Private Profiteers*
The hard-fought and celebrated SDG 4 commitment to free primary and secondary education has coincided with an expansion of privately provided, fee-charging education. The target is not a statement of intent to reverse this trend; as highlighted earlier, the SDG framework stays strangely silent on the question of public services. In the case of education, negotiating member states ignored the evidence pointing to public provision and regulation of education

as keys to quality and equity in education. SDG 4 suggests that the provider and arrangements are irrelevant, provided all children are in school and learning.

Since the adoption of SDG 4, there has been an impressive mobilisation of trade unions and civil society organisations against privatisation and commercialisation of and in education, and especially profit-making in education (see, for instance, Education International's Global Response[4] and the Privatisation in Education and Human Rights Consortium [Mangenot, Giannecchini, & Unsi, 2019]). Many of the private providers that have emerged in recent years are explicitly targeting poor communities, having identified a market where public services have been scarce and inadequate, public authorities largely absent, and parents anxious to secure a better future for their children. High-profile cases in Uganda (Riep and Machacek, 2016), Kenya (Education International and Kenya National Union of Teachers, 2016), and Liberia (Hook, 2017) have shown that national quality standards may be difficult to enforce in contexts with multiple and private providers of education. Moreover, they have shown that profit-making providers risk reproducing patterns of inequality by targeting different segments of society, offering a quality of education that matches the socioeconomic background of the students.

These developments are part of broader social and economic structures, which have opened up a market logic in education and a new role for the private sector (Verger, Lubienski, & Steiner-Khamsi, 2016). Sustained fiscal austerity has resulted in education budgets being cut and put public authorities under pressure to be more cost-effective through, for example, the freezing of salaries of public sector workers, the hiring of less-qualified or unqualified teachers, the closing of public schools, the introduction of education voucher schemes, and the privatisation of schools and education support services. The sustained and structural underfunding of public systems has resulted in poorer quality and systems that are struggling to keep up with changing demands. The discourse of weak public education systems sits well with the emphasis on freedom of choice; in many contexts there is a growing demand for private alternatives, often characterised by a consumerist attitude to education. The ability to choose between schools may in itself symbolise progress, and many parents are prepared to sacrifice a lot to secure the future (economic) well-being of their children. As education becomes more accessible and broadly enjoyed, a backlash often emerges in which public opinion in favour of differentiation and choice in education gains strength. The notion of education as a public good is outweighed by one of education as self-progression and personal career enhancement, and a means for social differentiation.

The role of private actors in education is likely to remain a principal source of contention throughout the SDG era. While much of the attention thus far has been on the role of the private sector, it has been estimated that 97% of the current financing gap will have to be solved through domestic resource mobilisation (International Commission on Financing Global Education Opportunity, 2016). The SDGs call on countries to strengthen their domestic resource mobilisation and capacity to collect tax, which raises the importance of debating tax justice within the education sector too, as discussed by David Archer and Tanvir Muntasim in Chapter 8. This, together with the commitment to free primary and secondary education, should bring greater focus and policy consideration to household spending on education, including better data on this key indicator of the equity of education systems.

4.3   *A Narrow Implementation of the Broad Commitment of Quality*

The third tension characterising the implementation of SDG 4 is that between a broader notion of quality education and a narrow focus on specific learning outcomes. SDG 4 is often described as a goal for quality education, and its quality commitment cuts across the different targets. While the targets on safe learning environments (4.a) and qualified teachers (4.c) focus on the inputs required for quality education, many refer to the desired outcomes of education, such as relevant and effective learning outcomes in Target 4.1; the skills for employment, decent work, and entrepreneurship in Target 4.4; and the knowledge and skills needed for sustainable development in Target 4.7.

So far, implementation of this quality commitment has been characterised by a disproportionate focus on measurable learning outcomes, specifically literacy and numeracy. The attainment of literacy and numeracy is a core component of any education system but only part of what constitutes a quality education and of what is envisaged by SDG 4. Yet, other subjects and dimensions of quality are marginalised by the emphasis on the measurability and comparability of learning outcomes. Such dimensions include pedagogy and processes of teaching and learning, behavioural as well as social and emotional learning, creativity, critical thinking, sustainable development, human rights, and a sense of social justice.

Measurement in itself is not a solution to a lack of learning, but the adoption of SDG 4 coincided with a broader push for learning metrics and large-scale assessments. This push mirrors a policy shift that has taken place in national contexts across the globe, whereby the development of education systems is increasingly driven by processes of standardisation and 'datafication', and powerful private interests (Sellar & Hogan, 2019). Such reforms build on a number of assumptions: first, the assumption that education systems currently are expensive and ineffective; second, the assumption that processes of teaching and learning can be standardised, measured, and turned into data;

and third, the assumption that the data can be used to measure the efforts and performance of students, teachers, and systems as a whole, opening them up to simplified cost-benefit analyses. In the context of results-based financing, learning outcomes are emerging as the new metric for measuring progress in education – and future economic growth. This, in turn, suggests a direct link between globally comparable assessments and learning outcomes, on the one hand, and a globally competitive nation, on the other.

Such a disproportionate emphasis on a narrow set of data points pushes systems toward global convergence and denies the importance of contextually relevant education, the complexity of processes of teaching and learning, and the expertise and professional autonomy of teachers. It undermines the broader purposes of education and themes such as arts, culture, or sustainable development. Knowledge, skills, behaviours, attitudes, and values are integral components of a quality education, but they are not easily standardised or measured. An overemphasis on the learning outcomes of individuals also shifts the attention toward individual students and teachers. This is symptomatic of the tendency to ignore patterns of inequality and perceive problems through the narrow lens of the individual, suggesting that individual effort is enough to overcome systemic, structural barriers. Structural concerns and the responsibilities of duty-bearers remain essential for discussing and assessing the quality of education, including learning.

The overemphasis on measurable learning outcomes is reflected in the methodological progress made on SDG 4 indicators. The disproportionate focus on measuring learning outcomes, narrowly defined as literacy and numeracy in the global indicator for Target 4.1, has been driven by the UNESCO Institute for Statistics, in part through the Global Alliance to Monitor Learning (GAML), which was established precisely to support the development of learning indicators and learning assessment methodologies for monitoring progress toward SDG 4 (UIS, 2017c). The same dynamic is reproduced in the financing of UIS, to which several donors have earmarked contributions specifically for measuring learning outcomes (UIS, 2017k, p. 23).

Paradoxically, the neglect of learning in the fields of human rights, climate change, and sustainable development has not been labelled a learning crisis. Progress on the indicators under Target 4.7 has been slow and underfunded compared to the abovementioned emphasis on numeracy and literacy. Yet, the quality commitment within SDG 4 should really be measured in the extent to which education systems deliver on Target 4.7 and ensure that all learners acquire the knowledge and skills needed for sustainable development and climate justice. As discussed by Joel Westheimer in Chapter 13, there are lessons in citizenship in all classrooms, regardless of whether they are labelled as such.

School will inevitably shape notions of self in relation to society and the environment. Yet, the education community has been surprisingly slow to respond to calls for education for sustainable development (ESD) and climate change education. Moreover, in its current form, ESD is largely built around the cognitive side, at the expense of the behavioural as well as social and emotional learning, limiting its depth, impact and reach – and the transformative power of education.

Moving forward, education systems have to find ways of addressing not only the science but also the politics behind the climate crisis, ensuring that students reflect on its systemic nature and seek adequate responses. Curricula, teacher training, and teaching and learning materials urgently need to be revised so as to make schools into spaces for learning about and taking action for human rights, sustainable development, and climate justice.

5   An Overview of the Chapters

While the parameters of the new global education agenda were set once the agenda was adopted in 2015, the agenda is being remade as it is implemented nationally and locally. This book aims to inform and influence those deliberations. By bringing together different voices and perspectives – academics as well as civil society advocates – this book argues for a broader understanding of the new agenda and its implications. It aims to support and inform SDG 4 advocates and activism for the right to education more broadly. As more and more initiatives are framed as contributions to the achievement of SDG 4, and the pressure to demonstrate results is mounting, a critical and principled approach to SDG 4 becomes ever-more important. Given the weak accountability framework underpinning the SDGs, it will be up to social movements, including student and teacher unions and other civil society actors, to put pressure on governments and international organisations. Thus, many of the chapters examine how the SDGs map onto and support ongoing efforts and struggles in the education sector.

While viewing the education goal as an opportunity to advance the right to education, this book takes a critical standpoint. Many of the chapters caution against the unintended consequences of global goals, highlighting areas that are ill-suited for such quantification or global comparability. Others look at the limitations of the current education paradigm, questioning the extent to which progress can be made within its parameters. One of the main messages is that the SDGs and their implementation should be analysed, criticised, and debated. This book aims to support this critical conversation, help advance rights-based perspectives, and build capacity for strengthened monitoring and critical analysis as implementation continues. It would not be possible to address all the dimensions of SDG 4 that deserve to be discussed in this volume. Both early childhood education as well as adult education and life-long learning are examples of areas that this book does not discuss explic-itly. While the authors have drawn upon work and examples from a range of countries and contexts, not all regions of the world are equally represented in these chapters. I hope that this will encourage readers to contribute to the conversation.

In Chapter 2, 'The Twists and Turns in Negotiating a Global Education Goal: A Civil Society Perspective', I set the scene by providing a critical assessment of the process leading up to the adoption of SDG 4. The education goal was nego-tiated as one of 17 SDGs, and this is the first time this process is documented and analysed. Identifying areas of consensus, contention, and controversy, I argue that understanding these dynamics is key for strategically engaging with SDG 4 and its implementation.

The book is organised according to the above mentioned axes against which the tensions and contradictions are playing out, and the first set of chapters interrogates the new commitment to *equitable* and *inclusive* education. In Chapter 3, Naureen Durrani and Anjum Halai discuss gender equality within SDG 4. They argue that the failure to consider postcolonial contexts gives rise to a disconnect between the global aspirations of the SDGs and the national realities where they are to be implemented. Drawing on case studies from Paki-stan, they caution against simplistic understandings of gender equality and particularly the power of girls' education, calling for more attention to gender *equity* and the interaction of education with social structures.

Christopher J. Johnstone, Matthew J. Schuelka, and Ghada Swadek discuss the explicit commitment to inclusive education within SDG 4 in Chapter 4. Noting that the SDGs do not provide a definition of inclusion, they explore conceptualisations of inclusion and specifically inclusive education. Drawing upon case studies in Bhutan and Morocco, they advance a rights-based under-standing of inclusion that goes well beyond parity, highlighting some chal-lenges and making recommendations.

Similarly, in Chapter 5, Lizzi O. Milligan, Zubeida Desai, and Carol Benson argue that equity must not be narrowly understood as a question of institu-tional access but broadened to include barriers such as language of instruc-tion. Discussing its impact on access to knowledge and curricula as well as engagement in processes of teaching and learning, they argue that language of instruction is a key determinant of educational equity. Drawing on examples from their own work in South Africa, Rwanda, and Cambodia, they offer solu-tions for the future.

Stephanie Allais, Elaine Unterhalter, Palesa Molebatsi, Lerato Posholi and Colleen Howell discuss the implications of the target on equal access to higher education in their chapter. Examining this equity imperative against the backdrop of universities as historically elitist institutions, and a rise in enrolments that continues to be shaped by persistent inequalities, they propose a new approach to the 'public good' role of higher education, which challenges the individualist framing of higher education.

The second set of chapters looks at the respective roles of the state and the private sector in the implementation of SDG 4, including its financing. In Chapter 7, Alexandra Draxler examines the renewed aspiration within Target 4.1 to free and equitable primary and secondary education in light of concurrent threats and attacks on public education. In 'Education for All Open for Business? Public Goods versus Private Profits', she discusses the new role of the private sector in relation to three distinct but related areas: technology in education, standardisation and benchmarking of learning, as well as the expansion of for-profit education, and argues that the SDGs facilitate a greater influence of the private sector over public policy.

In Chapter 8, David Archer and Tanvir Muntasim analyse trends in education financing and the gradual shift from external aid under the EFA and MDG regimes to domestic resource mobilisation in the SDG era. They explore what this shift means for education and call on the education community to pay closer attention to taxation and tax justice. They highlight some of the limitations of current measures and tools used in advocacy for education financing and suggest a different framework for analysing public investment in education, looking not only at the amount of money spent on education but also on its equitable allocation.

The last set of chapters is devoted to the tensions surrounding the quest for quality education. In Chapter 9, Yusuf Sayed and Kate Moriarty argue that competing conceptions of quality, notably the tensions between instrumentalist and rights-based approaches to education, characterised the process of agreeing to the education goal, and they suggest that these tensions were not resolved through the adoption of the agenda; rather, the envisaged turn to quality is jeopardised by these competing conceptions of quality.

In Chapter 10, Stephanie Bengtsson, Mamusu Kamanda, Joanne Ailwood, and Bilal Barakat provide a critical analysis of the teacher target and indicators within SDG 4, and the extent to which they advance the broader goal of equitable and inclusive quality education. They problematise the framing of teachers as simply a resource for the education sector and argue that teachers must be recognised as stakeholders and rights-holders in education, urging the education community to rethink some of the measurement strategies for Target 4.c.

In Chapter 11, Aaron Benavot and William C. Smith examine ongoing efforts to establish and legitimise global learning metrics. Looking critically at the so-called learning crisis, they discuss intended and unintended consequences of learning metrics and the extent to which they can help realise the equity and quality promises of SDG 4.

In a similar vein, in Chapter 12, Clara Fontdevila argues that SDG 4 gives more prominence and legitimacy to large-scale assessments. Acknowledging that the measurement of learning outcomes is among the most controversial elements of the new education agenda, Fontdevila explores some of the actors in the increasing institutionalisation of large-scale assessments within the global education agenda.

In Chapter 13, Joel Westheimer looks at the degree of commitment to global citizenship education within Target 4.7. Asserting that schools teach lessons in citizenship whether it is part of the curriculum or not, he problematises prevailing notions of citizenship education, such as those that promote obedient citizens and aim at maintaining status quo. Building on these, Westheimer discusses how central our conceptions of citizenship, power and democracy are to the potential transformative role of the SDGs.

Whereas Westheimer hopes for transformation of the education provided, Hikaru Komatsu, Jeremy Rappleye, and Iveta Silova question whether more and better education is what is needed. In Chapter 14, they examine what they call the possible negative interaction between progress in education and the halting of the climate crisis, challenging the view advanced by the SDGs that expanding education will lead to transformation toward environmental sustainability.

The long-awaited incorporation of technical and vocational education and training (TVET) in the global education agenda is the focus of Chapter 15. Stephanie Allais and Volker Wedekind critique the explicit, quantifiable targets associated with TVET and consider why that subsector is not easily amenable to international targets and why target-setting for TVET may have perverse or unintended consequences.

The book closes with two chapters that examine two central constituencies within the education community and their role in relation to SDG 4 efforts. Viktor Grønne and Luke Shore take as their point of departure in Chapter 16 that students are a central constituency in education and thus have a legitimate claim to be heard in debates about the future of education. They assess the role that the student movement played in defining the new education agenda, analyse the obstacles that emerged, and make recommendations about the representation of students as SDG 4 implementation gets underway.

In Chapter 17, Allyson Krupar and Anjela Taneja look at the efforts of civil society organisations to monitor the implementation of the SDGs, with a focus on the rights-based monitoring of SDG 4. They discuss the opportunities provided by the global SDG framework for national-level action, challenges arising from its weak accountability mechanisms, and unique contributions that civil society can make to effective monitoring of progress.

In conclusion, as the implementation of SDG 4 gets underway and an ever-growing number of actors and initiatives allegedly contribute to its achievement, it is becoming clear that the ambitious but broad priorities are vulnerable to cherry-picking and misrepresentation. The combination of a lack of accountability and the necessity of localising the agenda risks undermining a rights-based approach to SDG 4 and the broader defence of quality public education. As the first volume that examines early implementation efforts under SDG 4, this book calls upon the education community to engage in a more critical and thoughtful way with SDG 4 and related efforts.

Notes

1 For a detailed exploration of the meaning of the right to education, see the website of the Right to Education Initiative (https://www.right-to-education.org).
2 Three members of UNESCO are not members of the UN: Cook Islands, Niue, and Palestine. Israel, Liechtenstein, and the United States are members of the UN but not of UNESCO.
3 A noteworthy initiative to overcome this divide is the Danish Institute for Human Rights' *SDG-Human Rights Data Explorer*, a searchable database that links monitoring information from the international human rights system to the goals and targets of the 2030 Agenda: https://sdgdata.humanrights.dk.
4 https://unite4education.org/

The Twists and Turns in Negotiating a Global Education Goal: A Civil Society Perspective

Antonia Wulff

1 Introduction[1]

The crafting of the Sustainable Development Goals (SDGs) has been described as the world's most inclusive political process, with the voices of millions of people across the globe being heard, in contrast with the Millennium Development ment Goals (MDGs) that were agreed to behind closed doors. The SDGs have been praised for their ambition and courage in embracing the interlinkages of social, environmental, and economic issues (Bhattacharya & Kharas, 2015; Clarke, 2015). Conversely, they have been criticised and ridiculed for lacking clear priorities and measurable targets, and for simply being impossibly ambitious (Easterly, 2015; Hickel, 2015).

The SDGs also introduce a new set of priorities in education. Given the narrow scope of the MDGs, many working directly on advancing education were sceptical of any follow-up framework being able to respond sufficiently to their needs. The failure to reach the MDGs and the Education for All (EFA) goals, in combination with strapped public budgets, stagnating aid to education, and the limited appetite of governments for binding international agreements, had left many questioning the efficacy of another global framework (King, 2013a). At the same time, there was a great desire to get it right this time, and recommendations stemming from the MDG and EFA era provided both some initial direction and a sense of urgency (UNESCO, 2014f).

This chapter examines the making of the global education goal within the broader process of United Nations (UN) member states discussing and eventually agreeing on the 17 SDGs; it explores how education was seen and understood; what the areas of consensus, contention, and controversy were; and what happened when nonspecialists debated and decided the priorities in education. I argue that understanding these dynamics is key for strategically engaging with the SDGs and their implementation. Since the adoption of the SDGs, many attempts have been made to reinterpret and misrepresent the education goal's priorities. This chapter aims to challenge such reinterpretations by documenting the process.

The chapter does not aspire to be an objective overview of the process but rather an insider account of how the education agenda was crafted. It is based on my experiences as an education advocate, working to secure a stand-alone goal on free quality education on behalf of Education International (EI), the global federation of teacher unions. EI's engagement was fuelled by frustrations over the failure to meet earlier sets of goals, which the organisation felt reflected a lack of political will and adequate public financing, but also the failure to systematically involve teachers and their organisations. EI was determined to ensure that teachers had a voice this time around, and this became more important as the disagreements over the definition of quality were unfolding within the education sector's post-EFA process. EI profiled itself as a proponent of public education and of a broad notion of quality, encompassing quality tools and environments, as well as qualified teachers with decent terms and conditions of employment, and considered its participation vital for defending that position.

2 Getting the Process Started: The Open Working Group on Sustainable Development Goals

Numerous processes were launched in 2012 to shape the new development agenda, such as The World We Want survey (UN, 2012a) and the UN Secretary General's High-Level Panel on the Post-2015 Development Agenda (UN, 2012b). Concurrently, the Government of Colombia succeeded in its advocacy for Sustainable Development Goals. The outcome document of the UN Conference on Sustainable Development (Rio+20) Summit not only called for a set of goals but also launched the process for their design – the establishment of an *Open Working Group on Sustainable Development Goals* (OWG) with 30 members (UNGA, 2012).

The huge interest from member states – itself an indication of the OWG's importance – led to a compromise allowing countries within a regional group to share seats. Unlikely alliances (or 'troikas') were forming, such as Iran, Japan, and Nepal, or Bangladesh, the Republic of Korea, and Saudi Arabia, as 70 countries grouped together to fill the 30 seats.[2] This arrangement allowed countries to go beyond red lines put down by their regional blocs, the usual country coalitions for UN negotiations, and opened up the path for a different kind of consensus-building. These troikas made their own statements, often containing more specific suggestions than those of the regional blocs.

The OWG started its work by exploring the different elements of sustainable development through eight thematic sessions, allowing members to freely exchange views on progress made and the challenges ahead. These sessions were supported by *Issues briefs* produced by a Technical Support Team (TST) within the UN system, chaired by UNDP and the UN Department of Economic and Social Affairs (UN DESA), and with UNESCO and UNICEF leading on education; this remained the entry point for UN agencies throughout the process. Being a Rio+20 process, most countries were represented by their Ministries of Environment and/or Foreign Affairs, alongside diplomats from their respective missions to the UN in New York, while civil society participation was organised according to nine major groups.[3] The process was cochaired by the Permanent Representatives of Kenya and Hungary, Macharia Kamau and Csaba Kőrösi, respectively.

At the time, the OWG was largely unknown outside the sustainable development community. The education community was focused on its own post-2015 process, which, given the scope of this chapter, I will consider an input to the broader UN process. Arguably, the education sector was the best prepared, considering that it had had more than 20 years of a common EFA agenda, providing the education community with a Framework for Action as well as dedicated mechanisms for coordination, monitoring, and follow-up, including the EFA Steering Committee and the EFA Global Monitoring Report. Moreover, education has its own dedicated UN agency and an established global coalition of civil society organisations. This architecture provided the basis for building a robust and representative joint position, with meetings and consultations being organised to draw on the EFA lessons learned (see also Chapter 9 by Yusuf Sayed and Kate Moriarty).

3   Setting the Scene: The First OWG Session on Education (June 2013)

Education was discussed at the 4th OWG session, held in June 2013. The session brief positioned education as 'a fundamental human right and the bedrock of sustainable development' (TST, 2013, p. 1), showcased its enabling role in relation to a range of development outcomes, presented the progress made under the MDGs, and identified remaining challenges.[4]

The remaining out-of-school population was the first challenge to be faced. It was followed by the learning crisis that the EFA Global Monitoring Report had identified in 2012:

> Millions of children who go to school do not learn the basics. Out of around 650 million children of primary school age, as many as 250 million either do not reach grade 4 or, if they do, fail to attain minimum learning standards. (UNESCO, 2012b, p. 122)

Surprisingly, the brief separated learning from the structural dimensions of quality; only later in the text was it acknowledged that 'inadequate attention had been paid to the financial, human capital, and infrastructural resource constraints which undermine progress towards achieving effective learning environments for quality education', with the shortage of trained teachers as well as the stagnation of aid to education highlighted as key obstacles (TST, 2013, p. 2). While the emphasis on learning could be interpreted as a sign of feelings of urgency, EI was concerned that it had been disconnected from its causes.

The brief identified several priorities moving forward: access at all levels, equity, gender equality, relevant and measurable learning outcomes, skills and training, enabling learning environments, and sustainable financing. Interestingly, poverty and exclusion were described as 'the major markers of disadvantage' (TST, 2013, p. 2), but the direct link between costs of education and exclusion was not mentioned. This is extraordinary given the proven impact of abolishing tuition fees on enrolment figures in the MDG era. Another missing piece was the equity implications of the increasing role of nonstate actors in education. Perhaps this points to a broader problem: the briefs were effectively sales pitches for stand-alone goals, which compelled sectors to prove impact rather than engage in critical analyses.

Considering the OWG mandate, education for sustainable development was surprisingly low on the list of priorities. While the brief called for 'knowledge, skills and competencies that are linked to 21st century livelihoods and employment, and contribute to shaping attitudes and behaviors that promote social inclusion and cohesion, and environmental sustainability' (TST, 2013, p. 4), it was unclear on how and when these should be acquired. Bizarrely, the reported lack of learning only referred to literacy and numeracy.

Finally, the brief recommended merging the future development agenda with any future EFA goals, which raised questions about who had had the final say on the brief itself, as the EFA community was far from consensus at that stage. These briefs positioned UN agencies as purveyors of objective, technical advice, despite their different governance and financing arrangements, potentially ignoring biases and donor influence.

3.1   Civil Society Takes the Floor

Daily morning hearings were organised for civil society organisations (CSOs) to share their views. The process was based on the major groups self-organising: there was a steering committee of volunteers charged with selecting two presentations and eight shorter interventions for each hearing. There was no attempt to coordinate the inputs at this stage but rather ensure balanced representation in terms of gender, geography, and areas of work. Opening the hearing, the cochair, Ambassador Kamau, stressed the need to identify the 'relative importance' of education and to discuss the means of implementation (author's notes).

Education International and the Youth Coalition from Ghana had been selected to present. Calling for *universal free quality education* as the new goal, EI argued for equity as the foundation for the right to education and highlighted the financial burden – tuition fees as well as indirect costs – on households as the single greatest barrier to education, necessitating a financing target. The second key message was a rights-based approach to quality, outlining some of the necessary inputs (safe schools with adequate facilities, resources and infrastructure, a broad curriculum, qualified teachers); processes (learner-centred pedagogical practices, support for teachers); and outcomes (critical thinking, problem-solving) (Education International, 2013). The co-chair's only response was questioning where the money would come from, to which we replied, *tax justice*, while the Major Group of Children and Youth called for a cap on military expenditure (author's notes).

The Youth Coalition also highlighted the need for equity and quality but focused on the relevance of education and skills. Other topics raised were poverty (ATD 4th World, SOS Children's Villages), children's rights and inclusion (Save the Children, World Vision), and girls' education and sexual and reproductive health (International Planned Parenthood Federation). Save the Children also mentioned learning outcomes as a priority, but as part of a more holistic view of quality education (author's notes).

Although few member states were represented at the hearing (Denmark, France, Ghana, and Ireland), it was an invaluable opportunity for CSOs to present their priorities and proposals, and CSO representatives were pleased with the cochairs' summary of the inputs from civil society:

> Participants highlighted that education is at the core of sustainable development and the most effective way to poverty eradication. Education as an enabler for progress in other fields was stressed, including health and employment. Need to shift focus from the mere access to education to quality education, including adequate facilities, qualified teachers, good home-conditions, promotion of innovation, and civic mindedness, as well as measurable learning outcomes, was stressed by many. So was the need for free and equal access to education for all, including people with disabilities, children living in remote rural areas, and marginalized groups. Importance of lifelong learning was also raised.
> (OWG 4, 2013)

3.2   *The First Exchange on Priorities*

The OWG session on education opened with an external expert setting the scene. Karen Mundy, University of Toronto, articulated a powerful defence of education as a human right. While underlining that education must be directed toward the full development of human beings and respect for human rights, Mundy framed the role of the international community as one of setting-specific targets for progress, focussing on literacy as a baseline indicator of quality and equity, and the need for measuring learning outcomes. She called for early childhood and secondary education as well as skills development, and framed financing as a precondition for success, recommending targets for both national and international financing (author's notes).

The responses to Mundy's intervention were reassuring, signalling an understanding of the complexity of challenges faced in education: Ghana questioned the focus on knowledge and skills at the expense of values, attitudes, and a more holistic approach, and Pakistan queried whether it was feasible to go beyond primary education at this time. France inquired about sustainable financing, qualitative and quantitative indicators for equity and quality, the balance between the economic and the social objectives of education, and the role of new actors, such as civil society and the private sector (author's notes).

As member states then started reading their official statements, there was immediate consensus on there being both unfinished MDG business and new challenges that required action. Most countries highlighted the different groups that had been left behind thus far. In the words of the G77[5] and China: 'We must ensure that not only a greater amount [*sic*] of children are educated, but also that the education these children receive is of high quality delivered by adequately qualified teachers' (OWG 4, 2013).

As expected, a majority of countries signalled a desire to go beyond the MDG promise of primary education, but CSO representatives were positively surprised by the level of ambition. The African group called for a stand-alone goal with both quantitative and qualitative targets for primary, secondary, vocational, and tertiary education. On behalf of the Least Developed Countries (LDCs), Benin suggested universal access and completion of quality education at the same four levels. India/Pakistan/Sri Lanka emphasised skills development through technical and vocational training, alongside universal access to primary and secondary education. Another noteworthy proposal was the LDCs' call for the abolition of tuition fees (OWG 4, 2013).

Benin described how poorly trained teachers, inadequate facilities, and crowded classrooms make quality education impossible and prevent progress at all levels. The systemic factors behind the lack of quality were further elaborated upon by Zambia/Zimbabwe:

MDG 2 focused on increasing numbers within the same and existing infrastructure and more [or] less the same levels of teachers, hence increasing the pupil teacher ratio, and sometimes using untrained teachers as in community and village schools, a situation which seriously compromised quality of education. (OWG 4, 2013)

Their representative went on to propose the following solutions:

... an increase in resources to education, a shift in programming and implementation modalities to ensure corresponding infrastructure development and supportive services to improve quality, that is to areas such as teachers training, curriculum development, and school requisites or learning aids provision, should be set up. (OWG 4, 2013)

A majority of countries also addressed the necessity to look at what is being learned. In the words of Canada/Israel/US:

We clearly need much more serious attention to the quality of education and to learning outcomes. What are children learning? How are they learning? Are youth developing economically relevant skills? Are they equipping themselves with the knowledge and perspectives to be engaged and tolerant citizens? ... Schooling should provide students with transferable skills that will prepare them for today's global marketplace. Investments in science, technology, engineering, and mathematics (STEM) education are one of the most critical sources of transformation. It is equally important to ensure that entrepreneurial skills be taught as a core component of school curricula across all levels. (OWG 4, 2013)

Here education was clearly framed as a means to other ends, mostly economic development and youth employment: the African group wanted education to 'support economies' transformation and to prepare citizens for productive employment based on requirements of new labour markets', while the Caribbean community (CARICOM) called for strengthened links between education, skills training and curriculum development, and labour market demands. But many looked at all three dimensions of sustainable development and stressed 'the importance of cross-curricular integration of education for sustainable development in all subjects' (Montenegro/Slovenia) and the 'promotion of [a] culture of dialogue, tolerance, respect for human rights, environment, and cultural diversity' (Bulgaria/Croatia). The many endorsements of education for sustainable development apparently surprised the Hungarian cochair, who said that he had never thought of education as 'what makes us capable of being drivers of sustainable development'; he called it 'very deep thinking' (OWG 4, 2013; author's notes).

The broad range of issues raised by member states in their first exchange was a positive surprise. The cochairs' summary of the discussion gave a first indication of what – and whom – they perceived as important, highlighting *human rights*, *equity of access*, *quality*, and *relevance*. Education being a basic right, they concluded 'at the elementary level it should be not just affordable but free', something that had mostly been raised by civil society. But their approach to equity, quality, and relevance was reductive. They called for 'outcome-focused data if for example we want to measure not just schooling but learning for different social groups', as stressed by Karen Mundy, and 'more attention to learning outcomes in terms of literacy and numeracy', disregarding the many references to other dimensions of quality, such as qualified teachers and safe learning environments' (OWG 4, 2013).

On relevance, the cochairs exhibited a worryingly narrow view: 'For most people, getting a quality education is first and foremost about qualifying for a good job. That means learning the right things, which could include science and mathematics, entrepreneurship, [and] vocational skills" even if they then went on to recognise 'education's role in encouraging tolerance, active citizenship, and … sustainable development'. The cochairs acknowledged the wish to go beyond primary education but ignored the many calls for vocational and tertiary education from so-called developing countries, while highlighting early childhood learning as 'a firm foundation for formal schooling and lifelong learning', which had been mentioned primarily by Organisation for Economic and Development (OECD) countries. Finally, they said that 'one speaker stressed the importance of setting targets on financing – both domestic and international – to accompany an education goal'. This was an odd formulation that effectively played down the support for a financing target, given that many member states, particularly so-called developing countries, identified financing as a key challenge in past years and a precondition for success moving forward (OWG 4, 2013).

4   The First Months of Negotiations (March–April 2014)

After more than a year of thematic discussions, the OWG was finally ready to begin negotiations in March 2014.[6] The co-chairs had summarised the outcomes of these discussions in 19 Focus Areas (OWG 9, 2014), which, of course, were assumed to be stand-alone goals in disguise. Each area had a short justification for its inclusion and a number of subareas for consideration.

Education was the fourth area and introduced as a right. In theory, not much should have changed from the cochairs' summary of the 4th session in June 2013, but the scope was broader than expected, ranging from early childhood education to lifelong learning, with secondary education framed as the minimum, which implies that the UN Technical Support Team had had a say too:

Box 2.1: Focus area 4. Education (March 2014)

Everyone has a right to education, which opens up lifelong opportunities and is critical to achieving poverty eradication across generations. Achieving universal access to and quality of education is also important in promoting gender equality and empowerment of women, and in shaping values and creating the necessary skilled and productive labour force. Some areas that could be considered include: universal primary education for girls and boys, significant progress towards ensuring that every child receives at least a secondary education, and lifelong learning opportunities; ensuring equitable access to education at all levels with focus on the most marginalized; achieving high completion rates at all levels of education; ensuring effective learning outcomes at all levels and imparting knowledge and skills that match the demands of the labour market, including through vocational training; universal adult literacy; improving access to education for persons with disabilities; extending where needed opportunities for early childhood education; integrating sustainable development in education curricula, including awareness raising on how diverse cultures advance sustainable development. (UN, 2014b)

While some member states expressed concern about the number of areas, nobody questioned the inclusion of education as an area. At the same time, only a handful of countries mentioned education explicitly; it enjoyed none of the buzz that more overlooked or controversial areas had in terms of perceived urgency. In fact, education was in a bit of a double-bind, being part of the unfinished business of the MDGs, but also one of the more successful goals. No country profiled itself as an education champion, neither those on the EFA Steering Committee[7] nor the Global Education First Initiative, launched by the UN General Secretary in 2012 exactly to build support for and accelerate action on education. EI's advocacy was often met with a certain inattention or complacency; many felt that it went without saying that there would be an education goal and that it was more urgent to focus on other areas. Many gender

equality advocates, for instance, seemed tired of the singular focus on education in MDG 3, and thus were keen on putting education-related gender issues
under the education goal, so that there would be space for the 'truly urgent'
issues in the gender goal.

As the negotiation phase started, the major groups agreed to work on joint
thematic statements, in addition to their constituency-based statements. Following negotiations in a joint Google document, the parties agreed to call for
the completion of a full cycle of free quality education, from early childhood
to upper secondary education, with trained and qualified teachers and safe
learning environments, global citizenship as well as comprehensive sexuality education, and sustainable and public financing. Nobody thought that the
number of demands or level of ambition were realistic, but the participants
were determined to aim high – and frankly wanted to avoid the difficult negotiations on what or whose demand to delete.

The text of the revised Focus Areas (OWG 10, 2014), published ahead of the
10th OWG session (April 2014), was a victory in itself – as for the fourth focus
area, it included 'universal, free primary and secondary education', which
seemed to reflect the civil society proposal rather than that of any member
state. 'Universal early childhood education' and 'skills development' had been
added, but the reference to 'quality' had been removed and tertiary education
was still missing.

Box 2.2: Focus area 4. Education (April 2014)

Everyone has a right to education. Achieving universal access to quality
education is critical to poverty eradication across generations, opens up
lifelong opportunities, promotes gender equality and women's empowerment, shapes cultures, values and creates a skilled labour force. Some areas
that could be considered include:

a   universal, free primary and secondary education for girls and boys;
b   ensuring equitable access to education at all levels with focus on the
     most marginalized, including indigenous peoples, ethnic minorities,
     persons with disabilities, persons living in rural areas, and migrants;
c   achieving high completion rates at all levels of education for both girls
     and boys;
d   providing universal early childhood education;
e   ensuring effective learning outcomes at all levels and imparting knowl-
     edge and skills that match the demands of the labour market, includ-
     ing through vocational training and skills development for youth;

f   universal adult literacy and lifelong learning opportunities for all;
g   integrating sustainable development in education curricula, including
      awareness raising on how culture advances sustainable development;
h   and appropriate means of implementation (To be determined in the
      context of Focus area 18). (UN, 2014c)

While the support for a stand-alone goal on education remained high, the new format invited more specific comments from member states and differences in approaches and ambition started to become more visible. Surprisingly little was said about free education, but the African group called for affordable rather than free, which they considered to be more feasible, while Sri Lanka underlined that feasibility depends on the 'resource flow from affluent countries to developing countries'. Brazil/Nicaragua, emphasising the need to deliver on existing ODA commitments to education, called for 'conditional cash transfer schemes that combine income support with education responsibilities and health commitments', and proposed that education should be declared 'a national priority for all countries, developed and developing, keeping it shielded from cuts in national budgets'. France/Germany/Switzerland was the only northern troika to call for secured financing for education (OWG 10, 2014; author's notes).

Quality was highlighted as a priority by almost all. France/Germany/Switzerland proposed a new target: 'Improve quality of teaching & learning (Curriculums, infrastructure, training & teacher status, pupil-teacher ratios) and reduce inequalities with relevant and inclusive education programs, especially for girls' (OWG 10, 2014). Many also explicitly called for climate change to be addressed in curricula. Demands that had felt unrealistic a month earlier suddenly seemed more doable against the expanded focus area, which signalled an inclination for something more comprehensive.

EI coordinated the civil society statement on education, signed by the Major Groups of Children and Youth, Women, Indigenous Peoples, NGOs, and Workers and Trade Unions (OWG 10, 2014), reorganising the earlier demands into five targets[8] under the goal of *Ensuring the right to free, equitable, quality education and lifelong learning for all*. CSO representatives struggled to agree on the desired level of ambition for postsecondary education. Nobody aimed for universal vocational or tertiary enrolment, and considering the limited progress globally, they feared that a call for free education at all levels would seem unreasonable. Eventually, the CSOs proposed *equitable access to postsecondary and lifelong learning*.

5   Goals and Targets in the Making: Emerging Areas of Contestation
       (May 2014)

The focus areas were redrafted as goals and targets ahead of the May 2014
OWG session (OWG 11, 2014). Member states were asked to make specific suggestions, including timeframes and measurable targets, and avoid additions
unless accompanied by deletions. We feared this would mark a shift toward a
debate driven by feasibility rather than ambition.

   The proposed education goal – *Provide quality education and lifelong learning for all* – included the completion of free primary and secondary education
and safe learning environments, as civil society had proposed, but universal early childhood education had been swapped for access to preprimary
education.

**Box 2.3: Focus area 4. Education and life-long learning (May
2014) Provide quality education and life-long learning for all**

a   by 2030 ensure universal, free, equitable access to and completion of
     quality primary and secondary education for all girls and boys, leading
     to effective learning outcomes
b   ensure that persons with disabilities have access to inclusive educa-
     tion, skills development and vocational training
c   by 2030 increase by x% the proportion of children able to access and
     complete quality pre-primary education
d   by 2030 achieve universal youth and adult literacy, with particular
     attention to women and the most marginalized
e   by 2030 increase by x% the number of young and adult women and
     men with vocational training, technical, engineering and scientific
     skills
f   integrate relevant knowledge and skills in education curricula, includ-
     ing ICT skills, education for sustainable development, and awareness
     raising on culture's contribution to sustainable development
g   all schools to provide safe and healthy learning environment for all
     students Appropriate means of implementation (UN, 2014e)

By this stage of the process, the positions of member states as well as the
areas of disagreement were clear. In the following section, I elaborate on the
principal areas of contestation between member states as well as in relation to

civil society and its demands, that is: levels of education and notions of quality, learning outcomes beyond literacy and numeracy, teachers and learning environments, member state engagement with a rights-based education agenda, means of implementation, and disagreements within civil society.

5.1   *Setting the Right Level of Ambition: Levels of Education and Notions of Quality*

There was a reluctance to set specific targets beyond primary and lower secondary education. In private conversation, rich countries doubted poorer countries' ability to finance any further progress, while poor countries doubted the willingness of the rich to support their progress financially. At the same time, there was an urgency to increase enrolment at other levels. In the words of the African group: 'Research and development, capacity-building, science, technology and innovation … cannot be guaranteed by narrowing education targets to pre-primary, primary, or even secondary levels' (OWG 11, 2014). They proposed universal enrolment and completion of primary education by 2020, and 80% enrolment and completion of secondary and tertiary education by 2030, effectively lowering the ambition for secondary education while increasing it for tertiary education. But most countries seemed satisfied with the emphasis on skills in the draft target, and only a handful of countries asked for tertiary to be included. Exact targets for levels of education could be conveniently avoided by emphasising skills or equal access. Other proposals at this stage included compulsory primary education (Mexico/Peru), 'at least 10 years of basic education … in line with UNESCO's proposal' (Republic of Korea), and a separate target on universal access to lower secondary education (Pakistan) (OWG 11, 2014; author's notes).

The discussion on the levels of education was closely linked to that on the expected outcomes of and possible quality indicators at these different levels. While there had been consensus on quality education from the very beginning, it had never been defined, and at this stage of the negotiations, it was necessary to unpack the concept, particularly as the question of inputs versus outcomes was yet to be resolved.

While there were those who viewed completing a given level of education as a sufficient outcome, many argued for specifying the desired outcome of each level. Australia/Netherlands/UK wanted to 'learn the lesson from the MDGs and focus on education outcomes as well as access' and suggested one target on primary completion and 'minimum learning standards', and another one on lower secondary completion and 'recognised and measurable learning outcomes'. Further, they wanted to include upper secondary in the target on vocational and tertiary education: 'Increase the number of young and adult women and men with the skills, including upper-secondary, technical, vocational, and tertiary, that support employment and economic growth' (OWG 11, 2014).

Canada/Israel/US said that inputs should be determined at national level, and thus suggested reframing the targets according to their expected outcomes: 'All girls and boys complete free and equitable quality basic education of at least 10 years and achieve relevant learning outcomes', and 'Ensure every child, regardless of circumstance, has access to lower secondary education and increase by x% the number of girls and boys meeting standards on tasks related to reading, mathematics, and scientific literacy'. They proposed *readiness to learn* as the outcome of preprimary education (OWG 11, 2014).

While the predominantly English-speaking countries were the loudest proponents of more outcome-focused targets, there was broad consensus on the importance of 'relevant and measurable learning outcomes', in the words of G77 and China (OWG 11, 2014). But while the idea of measurable learning outcomes had a lot of traction, none of the countries addressed the question of whether these outcomes should be determined at the national or global level, that is, whether they should be the same for all countries. Most countries hid behind concepts like *relevant, minimum learning standards*, or *skills for work and life*. Bangladesh called for a balance between inputs and outcomes, and emphasised life skills as a key part of the necessary measurable learning outcomes. The Republic of Korea stated that 'there is no particular reason to limit the virtues for youth and adults only to the areas of vocational training, technical, engineering, and scientific skills' and proposed 'by 2030 [to] increase by x% those youth and adults with knowledge & skills required for work and life'. Canada/Israel/US were thus the only countries to specify which subjects to measure (OWG 11, 2014).

5.2   *Beyond Literacy and Numeracy: Educating for the Labour Market and/or Sustainable Development*

Almost all countries called for skills for work. China/Indonesia/Kazakhstan emphasised 'access to labour market' as an outcome of education; Brazil/Nicaragua suggested bridging the gap between education and labour markets by specifying that learning outcomes should be 'aligned with labour market needs', and the African group underscored the importance of vocational education and training, as well as skills development and universal youth and adult literacy. Canada/Israel/US recommended combining the target on vocational education and training with the one on relevant skills in curricula and suggested adding a reference to entrepreneurial education. Interestingly, there was no disagreement here; the problem was rather articulating the desired relationship between education and the labour market. Remarkably, civil society struggled too; there was principled opposition to an instrumental approach to education, but there was no counterproposal and little targeted advocacy (OWG 11, 2014).

The target on relevant knowledge and skills enjoyed broad support, and there were numerous additions: Denmark/Ireland/Norway called for learning 'which is relevant for the daily lives of children and adolescents, including education on human rights, life skills, and comprehensive sexuality education'. Italy/Spain/Turkey wanted to include gender equality, nonviolence, and peace in curricula; Montenegro and Slovenia suggested health as well as human rights education; and the Republic of Korea asked for global citizenship education. A new target on eliminating gender stereotypes was suggested by Denmark/Ireland/Norway as well as France/Germany/Switzerland, while Argentina/Bolivia/Ecuador proposed a broader inclusion target: 'Implement by 20xx curriculum and educational practices that promote inclusive education towards people with disabilities, indigenous people, and all other historically excluded groups, and that eliminate gender stereotypes, sexism, and homophobia in order to eliminate all forms of discrimination and racism'. Interestingly, these proposals were separated from specific levels of education, and generally considered part of the calls for learning outcomes (OWG 11, 2014).

The only proposal that met resistance was comprehensive sexuality education. It was a priority for many European governments, but the African group was against the introduction of 'contentious concepts', Egypt found references to sexual education unacceptable, and Saudi Arabia warned that such references would 'weaken the chances of adoption'. Saudi Arabia later declared it did not want 'sexual things in school' (OWG 11, 2014; author's notes).

5.3   *Enabling Quality Education: Qualified Teachers and Safe Learning Environments*

As the cochairs had not picked up on earlier references to teachers and teacher training in their draft, numerous proposals were now made: 'Improve quality education by improving professional training for competent teachers' (Italy/Spain/Turkey) and 'Promote training and support for teachers and education professionals' (China/Indonesia/Kazakhstan). Bhutan/Thailand/Vietnam suggested support and incentives for professional development, while the African group wanted to improve the 'conditions of service of educators and trainers'. EI was particularly pleased with Belarus/Serbia proposing that 'all learners are taught by qualified, professionally trained, motivated and well-supported teachers', in line with the Muscat Agreement and EI's advocacy. EI was further encouraged by cochair Kamau interrupting the debate to check whether he was right to think that there was consensus on qualified teachers as a priority.

At the same time, many countries framed qualified teachers as part of the necessary means of implementation for education (OWG 11, 2014; author's notes).

Safe and adequate learning environments were another quality dimension stressed by countries. Denmark/Ireland/Norway, for instance, called for 'an environment free from sexual harassment in schools. This should include making schools safer for girls, having a high proportion of female teachers, and adequate sanitation for both boys and girls in schools'. These calls built on lessons learned from the MDGs about obstacles to girls' education but were also a reaction to the recent abduction of hundreds of school girls in Nigeria. In line with their emphasis on outcomes, Canada/Israel/US questioned the definition of *healthy* learning environments and suggested 'ensur[ing] that all children and youth can safely access school without fear of harm, abuse, or discrimination'. To EI's surprise, several Latin American countries suggested adding 'that schools are also inclusive and respectful for both students and teachers' (Brazil/Nicaragua), but this was not supported (OWG 11, 2014).

5.4   *Delivering on Human Rights and Equity Pledges*

While many member states began their education statements with references to education as a human right and a public good, France/Germany/Switzerland went the furthest in trying to reflect this in their proposals:

> Education is a human right, a global public good, and a major driver for reducing inequalities and poverty as well as being a prerequisite for sustainable development. We propose that the choice and definition of targets under this goal be framed around the four principles of: accessibility, acceptability, adaptability, and availability. (OWG 11, 2014)

However, they never spelled out what this would mean for the proposed targets. Denmark/Ireland/Norway underlined that 'universal, free, equitable access to quality education' is consistent with the right to education, while Romania called for a rights-based approach, highlighting safe and secure environments as a precondition for access and completion (OWG 11, 2014).

There was consensus on the commitment to equity and leaving no one behind, an approach that was generally considered helpful for realising the right to education. In the words of Australia/Netherlands/UK, leaving no one behind 'requires a non-discriminatory approach that respects human rights of all. We need to ensure targets are met by all, including the special circumstances of children with disabilities, those from the lowest income quintile, and other disadvantaged groups'. Denmark/Ireland/Norway highlighted 'the urgent need to ensure access to education for children in conflict and humanitarian situations' (OWG 11, 2014).

However, *leaving no one behind* quickly became an empty slogan. In fact, its loudest proponents were also those torpedoing proposals for measures to combat (income) inequality. Perhaps the equity consensus prevailed exactly because of countries actively avoiding the discussion on what it would mean in practice. This was also the case for equitable education: any equity implications of weakened and underfunded public systems were ignored. The representative of Pakistan asked incredulously in a side meeting whether it is 'possible to have the president's son in the same school as a poor village boy'. Instead of discussing the measures required to enable this – policies that reduce structural inequalities – there was disagreement over which groups to mention, and how to refer to them; some preferred 'most vulnerable' over 'most marginalised', while others wanted to refer to populations rather than groups (author's notes).

5.5   *Making It Happen: The Question of Means of Implementation*
The means of implementation (MOI) had been a dividing line between rich and poor countries from the very beginning; the former were against goal-specific means of implementation, the latter considered them a prerequisite for the success of the new agenda. The cochairs had added 'appropriate MOI' as a placeholder under each goal, inviting member states to make suggestions.

The G77 and China called on developed countries to support efforts in developing countries through provision of financial resources, capacity-building, and technology transfer. Most G77 countries suggested a target on higher education scholarships: *Expand by x% globally the number of scholarships for students from developing countries, in particular LDCs, to enrol in higher education programmes in developed countries and other developing countries, with focus on science, engineering, and management* (OWG 11, 2014). EI's attempts to highlight the detrimental effects of such a target in terms of 'brain drain' as well as the systemic underdevelopment of the higher education sector in their own countries were falling on deaf ears; instead, some countries suggested adding scholarships for civil servants.

The LDCs made two specific proposals: 'Promote students exchange programmes, joint researches, and access to digital libraries', and 'Provide enhanced financial and technical support for LDCs to implement their national education plans and programmes with special emphasis on educational infrastructure building, including modern facilities and equipment and qualified teachers'. The latter, in particular, shows that they considered all the inputs necessary for the targets to be reached as a means of implementation. In the same vein, the African group suggested investing in learning infrastructure, alongside improving the quality and conditions of service for educators and trainers, and Brazil/Nicaragua proposed to 'improve education infrastructure in developing countries, in particular in LDCs, by 2030' (OWG 11, 2014).

While welcoming these nonfinancial means of implementation, EI was concerned about the absence of demands on financing. France/Germany/Switzerland suggested 'ensuring adequate financial and human resources to ensure quality education and lifelong learning', and Bhutan/Thailand/Vietnam asked for a global partnership to support capacity-building and training, scholarships, research and development, and transfer of knowledge. But it was civil society (Major Groups of Workers and Trade Unions, Women, Children and Youth, NGOs, and Indigenous Peoples) that kept raising education financing, requesting that, 'by 2030, sustained and sufficient financing is in place to guarantee free quality education for all, including in emergencies' (OWG 11, 2014).

5.6   *The Civil Society Contingent and Its Views*

Many civil society organisations in the education field focused primarily on the post-EFA process. At first, it was only Save the Children and Education International who worked to influence the OWG, but in the late autumn of 2013, the Global Campaign for Education (GCE) and the International Council on Adult Education (ICAE) came aboard too. Others contributing to the advocacy efforts on education included the major groups of NGOs, Women, Children and Youth, Indigenous Peoples, Workers and Trade Unions, and disability organisations. Some local and national organisations attended specific meetings, but their presence tended to depend on dedicated external funding.

Views of civil society were divergent at the start of the process, with many groups and constituencies having very specific demands. The months of forging joint statements helped build consensus on a set of common priorities: equity and quality, financing and free education, and qualified teachers and safe learning environments. But often consensus was built on a generous acceptance of each other's demands, which meant that the list of demands grew longer and longer. That process may have been to blame for the breadth of Target 4.7, for instance.[9] At the same time, CSOs were encouraged by both member states and the cochairs taking on board many of their suggestions.

The only major matter of disagreement among CSOs was the role of learning outcomes. It could be described as a battle between education and learning (for more on this, see Chapter 9). A rights-based view of education, defined by its breadth and championed by EI, GCE, and ICAE, was pitted against a focus on learning, where measurable learning outcomes were seen as the key to both equity and quality, advocated by Save the Children and a number of smaller organisations. This defining division within the education CSO community was difficult to understand for others, but the two groups organised events, mobilised for joint statements, and argued about the civil society statement at each OWG session. The emphasis on *relevant* learning outcomes was one of the many compromises made; it was understood to include literacy and numeracy as well as a broad range of subjects and indigenous knowledge, which allowed CSOs to avoid conflict and make statements in the allocated two-minute speaking slots, but also left their demands open to interpretation.

6   The Last Stretch (June–July 2014)

While the education sector had reached agreement on its own post-2015 proposal, the OWG process had moved faster than expected: once the Global Education Meeting took place, postponed from March to May 2014, and stakeholders had adopted a goal and a set of seven targets as part of the Muscat Agreement, the consensus-building process of the OWG had reached a point at which there was little appetite for accepting larger chunks of text from external processes. At the 11th OWG session, France/Germany/Switzerland had stated that 'we must ensure the coherence of the total package of targets under this goal which should be geared toward sustainable development and be closely aligned with those currently being defined in the context of the Education for All Framework for Action' (OWG 11, 2014). The identity of *we* was, however, unclear, because it was up to the member states to replace OWG formulations with those of the Muscat Agreement.

With the publication of a zero draft of the proposed SDGs and targets at its 12th session on 2 June 2014 (OWG 12, 2014; UN, 2014d), the OWG moved into a new phase. Informal sessions were organised, and focus shifted toward the more contentious issues, which meant that the education targets escaped more detailed scrutiny. In an informal discussion that I had with cochair Kamau, he expressed his surprise at anyone being concerned about the education goal, as it enjoyed, in his view, enough support to be safely adopted. Despite his reasoned focus on the bigger picture, his comments belied a lack of understanding of education policy, and more importantly, how little room the OWG process itself left for sector-specific expertise. Building political agreement was more important than the technical robustness of any single goal and its targets.

The zero draft contained a number of improvements: CSO proposals of *relevant* learning outcomes and new specific targets on teachers as well as higher education had been included, but the new formulations were weak.

> **Box 2.4: Proposed goal 4. Provide equitable and inclusive quality education and lifelong learning opportunities for all (June 2014)**
>
> 4.1 by 2030 ensure all girls and boys complete free, equitable and quality primary and secondary education leading to relevant and effective learning outcomes
> 4.2 by 2030 ensure equal access for all to affordable quality tertiary education and life-long learning
> 4.3 by 2030 increase by x% the proportion of children able to access and complete inclusive quality pre-primary education and other early childhood development programmes
> 4.4 achieve universal youth literacy and basic numeracy and an increase by x% of adult literacy and basic numeracy by 2030
> 4.5 by 2030 increase by x% the number of young and adult women and men with the skills needed for employment, including vocational training, ICT, technical, engineering and scientific skills
> 4.6 by 2030 ensure that people in vulnerable situations and marginalized people including persons with disabilities and indigenous peoples have access to inclusive education, skills development and vocational training aligned with labour market needs
> 4.7 by 2030 integrate relevant knowledge and skills in education curricula and training programs, including education for sustainable development and awareness raising on culture's contribution to sustainable development
> 4.8 by 2030 ensure that all schools and other educational institutions provide safe, healthy, non-discriminatory and inclusive learning environments for all
> 4.9 by 2030 enhance the quality of teaching through promoting training for teachers (UN, 2014d)

Civil society kept fighting for a higher level of ambition: CSOs wanted to *ensure* rather than *provide* in the goal itself, *free* rather than *affordable* higher education, and *universal* adult literacy. They also repeated their call for the Muscat teacher target – ensuring that all learners are taught by qualified, professionally trained, motivated, and well-supported teachers – and sustained and sufficient financing (OWG 12, 2014).

The EFA community made a last attempt to influence the OWG by organising a side event on the Muscat Agreement, hosted by Norway, Brazil, Argentina, UNESCO, and UNICEF. The government representatives made strong interventions, pledging to incorporate the Muscat language on teachers and financing, and Argentina consequently called for a financing target in the OWG session.

The last round of negotiations in July 2014 kicked off with some dramatic changes in the education goal: it finally included a financing target, but the targets on teacher training and scholarships had been merged. Many member states agreed with CSOs that the latter did not make sense and called for a separate target on teachers, and several countries proposed the Muscat formulation. Regrettably, many also demanded that the financing target be deleted.

Much of the action was taking place in corridors and closed meeting rooms, and it was hard to understand the logic of change at this stage. Several countries wanted to make the first nine years of education compulsory, in line with the Muscat Agreement. But this led Denmark/Ireland/Norway to propose limiting the first target to primary and lower secondary education, which would not only have excluded upper secondary from the free and universal levels of education but from the whole agenda. Informally, Norway said that universal upper secondary was unrealistic, even if it is, of course, the norm in Norway. Fortunately, it was too late for such a substantial change to be made (author's notes).

At the same time, Canada/Israel/US called for deletion of target 4.7 on integrating relevant knowledge in curricula, arguing that it was too prescriptive for countries. This was astonishing given that they had been the only troika to propose subject-specific learning outcomes to be measured under target 4.1. Nonetheless, the formulation was subsequently changed to 'ensure that all learners acquire the knowledge and skills needed to promote sustainable development' (author's notes), which raised questions about the pressure exercised behind the scenes.

Australia/Netherlands/UK suggested merging the target on vocational and tertiary education with that on skills acquisition, which made sense and was welcomed by the cochairs, but mysteriously never made it to the next draft. The battle about comprehensive sexuality education continued in a break-out group, but no compromise was ultimately found; it was too controversial and highly symbolic given the lack of earlier intergovernmental agreements.

7   Agreement on Goals and Targets

The OWG adopted the 17 goals and 169 targets unanimously in July 2014 (see Table 1.1 in Chapter 1).

Far from perfect, the education goal nevertheless exceeded our expectations; nobody had imagined as many as ten targets, ranging from the completion of free primary and secondary education, and equal access to postsecondary, including tertiary education, to targets on education for sustainable development and human rights, safe learning environments, and qualified teachers. Within the education community, the Muscat Agreement was the obvious yardstick, and the OWG measured up surprisingly well: While obvious that the goal and targets had not been crafted by education experts, they were more ambitious than the Muscat Agreement with regard to universal completion of free upper secondary and safe learning environments, for example. This had been inconceivable at the start of the post-2015 process.

But there were serious shortcomings: There was no financing target, the teacher target was weak, early childhood education was not even mentioned, and vocational and higher education were only described as *affordable.* Many formulations could have been sharper, but that in combination with the unfinished nature of some targets, such as those referring to an increase of 'x%', gave the impression that improvements were still possible – an impression that many countries seemed to share.

While almost all countries had reservations regarding the OWG outcome, the ownership of both the text and the process eased its final adoption. Instead of traditional word-by-word negotiations, the co-chairs had built a process of gradual consensus-building, adding more detail to the draft on a monthly basis, testing the waters, and incorporating the feedback. But this made for a complicated relationship with the many processes aimed at informing the post-2015 agenda. The OWG merely welcomed the different inputs and remained loyal to its own process, undermining other efforts. However, the outcomes of those other processes were often picked up by other actors and reflected in their positions, and may, thus, have influenced the OWG deliberations.

It had been impossible to foresee the OWG developing the new agenda from beginning to end, but the 'delicate balance' achieved through the OWG was considered too delicate to be touched in the subsequent intergovernmental negotiations (January–August 2015), despite persistent efforts to reduce the number of goals. Most member states wanted to change individual targets, but none of them wanted to start negotiations from scratch. It soon became clear that only targets with obvious technical flaws were likely to change, which in the case of education meant those referring to 'x%'. At the same time, the most difficult issues were yet to be agreed upon: monitoring, accountability, and means of implementation.

In these subsequent negotiations, member states rejected monitoring and accountability in favour of the ambiguous *follow-up and review,* essentially

TABLE 2.1   Evolution of the wording of the education targets during OWG negotiations, March–July 2014

	March 2014	April 2014	May 2014	June 2014	Adopted in July 2014
Title	Focus area 4. Education	Focus area 4. Education	Focus area 4. Education and lifelong learning; Provide quality education and lifelong learning for all	Proposed goal 4. Provide equitable and inclusive quality education and lifelong learning opportunities for all	Goal 4. Ensure inclusive and equitable quality education and promote lifelong learning opportunities for all
Rights-Based Approach	Everyone has a right to education, which opens up lifelong opportunities and is critical to achieving poverty eradication across generations.	Everyone has a right to education.			

(cont.)

TABLE 2.1   Evolution of the wording of the education targets during OWG negotiations, March–July 2014 (cont.)

	March 2014	April 2014	May 2014	June 2014	Adopted in July 2014
Interlinkages with other areas	[Education is] critical to achieving poverty eradication across generations. Achieving universal access to and quality of education is also important in promoting gender equality and empowerment of women, and in shaping values and creating the necessary skilled and productive labour force.	Achieving universal access to quality education is critical to poverty eradication across generations, opens up lifelong opportunities, promotes gender equality and women's empowerment, shapes cultures, and values and creates a skilled labour force.			

(cont.)

TABLE 2.1   Evolution of the wording of the education targets during OWG negotiations, March–July 2014 (*cont.*)

	March 2014	April 2014	May 2014	June 2014	Adopted in July 2014
Early childhood education	extending where needed opportunities for early childhood education	d) providing universal early childhood education	c) by 2030 increase by x% the proportion of children able to access and complete quality preprimary education	4.3 by 2030 increase by x% the proportion of children able to access and complete inclusive quality preprimary education and other early childhood development programmes	4.2 by 2030 ensure that all girls and boys have access to quality early childhood development, care and preprimary education so that they are ready for primary education
Primary and secondary education	universal primary education for girls and boys; significant progress toward ensuring that every child receives at least a secondary education	a) universal, free primary and secondary education for girls and boys	a) by 2030 ensure universal, free, equitable access to and completion of quality primary and secondary education for all girls and boys, leading to effective learning outcomes	4.1 by 2030 ensure all girls and boys complete free, equitable, and quality primary and secondary education leading to relevant and effective learning outcomes	4.1 by 2030, ensure that all girls and boys complete free, equitable, and quality primary and secondary education leading to relevant and effective learning outcomes

(*cont.*)

TABLE 2.1 Evolution of the wording of the education targets during OWG negotiations, March–July 2014 (cont.)

	March 2014	April 2014	May 2014	June 2014	Adopted in July 2014
Vocational education	... imparting knowledge and skills that match the demands of the labour market, including through vocational training	e) ... imparting knowledge and skills that match the demands of the labour market, including through vocational training and skills development for youth	e) by 2030 increase by x% the number of young and adult women and men with vocational training, technical, engineering, and scientific skills	4.5 by 2030 increase by x% the number of young and adult women and men with the skills needed for employment, including vocational training, ICT, technical, engineering, and scientific skills	4.3 by 2030 ensure equal access for all women and men to affordable quality technical, vocational, and tertiary education, including university
Higher education				4.2 by 2030 ensure equal access for all to affordable quality tertiary education and lifelong learning	4.3 by 2030 ensure equal access for all women and men to affordable quality technical, vocational, and tertiary education, including university

(cont.)

TABLE 2.1   Evolution of the wording of the education targets during OWG negotiations, March–July 2014 (*cont.*)

	March 2014	April 2014	May 2014	June 2014	Adopted in July 2014
Adult education and lifelong learning	significant progress towards ... lifelong learning opportunities; universal adult literacy	f) universal adult literacy and lifelong learning opportunities for all	d) by 2030 achieve universal youth and adult literacy, with particular attention to women and the most marginalised	4.2 by 2030 ensure equal access for all to affordable, quality tertiary education and lifelong learning 4.4 achieve universal youth literacy and basic numeracy and an increase by x% of adult literacy and basic numeracy by 2030	4.6 by 2030 ensure that all youth and at least x% of adults, both men and women, achieve literacy and numeracy
Access Versus completion	achieving high completion rates at all levels of education	c) achieving high completion rates at all levels of education for both girls and boys			

(*cont.*)

TABLE 2.1   Evolution of the wording of the education targets during OWG negotiations, March–July 2014 (cont.)

	March 2014	April 2014	May 2014	June 2014	Adopted in July 2014
Equity and Inclusion	ensuring equitable access to education at all levels with focus on the most marginalised; improving access to education for persons with disabilities	b) ensuring equitable access to education at all levels with focus on the most marginalised, including indigenous peoples, ethnic minorities, persons with disabilities, persons living in rural areas, and migrants	b) ensure that persons with disabilities have access to inclusive education, skills development, and vocational training	4.6 by 2030 ensure that people in vulnerable situations marginalised people, including persons with disabilities and indigenous peoples have access to inclusive education, skills development, and vocational training aligned with labour market needs	4.5 by 2030, eliminate gender disparities in education and ensure equal access to all levels of education and vocational training for the vulnerable, including persons with disabilities, indigenous peoples, and children in vulnerable situations
Learning Outcomes	ensuring effective learning outcomes at all levels and imparting knowledge and skills that match the demands of the labour market	e) ensuring effective learning outcomes at all levels and imparting knowledge and skills that match	a) ... quality primary and secondary education for all girls and boys, leading to	4.1 ... quality primary and secondary education leading to relevant and effective learning outcomes	4.1 ... quality primary and secondary education leading to relevant and effective learning outcomes

(cont.)

TABLE 2.1   Evolution of the wording of the education targets during OWG negotiations, March–July 2014 (cont.)

March 2014	April 2014	May 2014	June 2014	Adopted in July 2014
Learning outcomes (cont.)	the demands of the labour market, including through vocational training and skills development for youth	effective learning outcomes f) integrate relevant knowledge and skills in education curricula, including ICT skills, education for sustainable development, and awareness raising on culture's contribution to sustainable development		

(cont.)

TABLE 2.1 Evolution of the wording of the education targets during OWG negotiations, March–July 2014 (cont.)

	March 2014	April 2014	May 2014	June 2014	Adopted in July 2014
Skills	ensuring effective learning outcomes at all levels and imparting knowledge and skills that match the demands of the labour market	e) ensuring effective learning outcomes at all levels and imparting knowledge and skills that match the demands of the labour market, including through vocational training and skills development for youth	e) by 2030 increase by x% the number of young and adult women and men with vocational training, technical, engineering, and scientific skills	4.5 by 2030 increase by x% the number of young and adult women and men with the skills needed for employment, including vocational training, ICT, technical, engineering, and scientific skills	4.4 by 2030, increase by x% the number of youth and adults who have relevant skills, including technical and vocational skills, for employment, decent jobs, and entrepreneurship
Education for Sustainable Development	integrating sustainable development in education curricula, including awareness	g) integrating sustainable development in education curricula, including awareness	f) integrate relevant knowledge and skills in education curricula,	4.7 by 2030 integrate relevant knowledge and skills in education curricula and training programs, including	4.7 by 2030 ensure all learners acquire knowledge and skills needed to promote sustainable development, including among others through education

(cont.)

TABLE 2.1 Evolution of the wording of the education targets during OWG negotiations, March–July 2014 (cont.)

	March 2014	April 2014	May 2014	June 2014	Adopted in July 2014
	raising on how diverse cultures advance sustainable development.	raising on how culture advances sustainable development	including ICT skills, education for sustainable development, and awareness raising on culture's contribution to sustainable development	education for sustainable development and awareness raising on culture's contribution to sustainable development	for sustainable development and sustainable lifestyles, human rights, gender equality, promotion of a culture of peace and nonviolence, global citizenship, and appreciation of cultural diversity and of culture's contribution to sustainable development
Learning Environments			g) all schools to provide safe and healthy learning environment for all students	4.8 by 2030 ensure that all schools and other educational institutions provide safe, healthy, non-discriminatory, and inclusive learning environments for all	4.a build and upgrade education facilities that are child, disability, and gender sensitive and provide safe, nonviolent, inclusive, and effective learning environments for all

(cont.)

TABLE 2.1   Evolution of the wording of the education targets during OWG negotiations, March–July 2014 (cont.)

	March 2014	April 2014	May 2014	June 2014	Adopted in July 2014
Teachers				4.9 by 2030 enhance the quality of teaching through promoting training for teachers	4.c by 2030 increase by x% the supply of qualified teachers, including through international cooperation for teacher training in developing countries, especially LDCs and SIDS
Financing/MOI		and appropriate means of implementation (To be determined in the context of Focus area 18)	appropriate means of implementation		4.b by 2020 expand by x% globally the number of scholarships for developing countries in particular LDCs, SIDS, and African countries to enrol in higher education, including vocational training, ICT, technical, engineering, and scientific programmes in developed countries and other developing countries

making the implementation voluntary. They delegated the agreement on SDG indicators to the UN Statistical Commission, who, in turn, established a dedicated expert group. What started as a renewed partnership between governments to ensure the realisation of the SDGs quickly turned into partnerships in plural, referring mainly to partnerships with the private sector. The many CSOs campaigning against public-private partnerships and the privatisation of public services led cochair Kamau to suggest a ringfencing of public services, including education, but member states did not support this. Consequently, neither governments nor the private sector are held to account within the SDGs framework.

The contentious question of means of implementation was largely delegated to the Financing for Development process (FfD), geared toward its fourth conference in July 2015, despite the different scopes and mandates of the two processes. The overarching narrative was that the resources needed were beyond what any state could provide. The proposed formulation on nationally appropriate spending targets on essential public services, including health and education, was rejected by several member states who considered it too prescriptive – to which the Norwegian cofacilitator responded that he thought health and education would be uncontroversial. The only achievement with regard to education financing was the deletion of a paragraph asking households to use remittances to pay for education and healthcare (author's notes).

8   Conclusions

Barely had the SDGs been adopted before attempts were made to misrepresent the education goal's priorities. Some decided to exclude the means of implementation targets (4.a–c) while others framed it as an agenda for learning outcomes only. This chapter has aimed to challenge such reinterpretations by documenting the process. The danger with as broad an agenda as the SDGs is that one can pick and choose among targets, taking advantage of the room for interpretation that many targets leave. At the same time, this is an opportunity: SDG 4 requires countries to agree on what concepts such as *equitable, free,* and *quality* mean in their context and education systems, and to find ways of operationalising them.

Reflecting on what we can take away from the process as we work to realise SDG 4, I will discuss three dimensions: (i) the level of inclusion within the process, (ii) silos and incoherence within the UN system as well as at national level, and (iii) the absence of education champions.

8.1   *Inclusion in Negotiation Processes*

Whilst the OWG process was both inclusive and participatory, with open as well as webcast meetings and dedicated exchanges with civil society at every round of negotiations, it was inclusive predominantly for those who knew to follow it from the beginning and how to engage with the UN system. As a global trade union federation, Education International had access to both information and meetings through its membership in the Workers and Trade Unions Major Group. But many organisations joining toward the end of the OWG were frustrated about what they perceived as a 'done deal'.

Inclusion should also be discussed with a view to the sector-specific inputs. The education community took its time agreeing on a robust proposal, assuming that it would be respected and included by the OWG. There was a problem with the timeline – adopting the Muscat Agreement six months earlier would have allowed for targeted advocacy at the right time – but the OWG should have paid more attention to such inputs.

Considering how open the OWG process was, it is oddly difficult to trace wording back to a particular country. Many governments had pet concerns and red lines, but surprisingly few seemed to have a comprehensive vision of the new agenda. While this made it difficult to gauge how fair the cochairs were in their drafting, it also made it easier for civil society to influence the process. Once CSOs had agreement, they had considerable influence on substance as well as ambition, and many of the weakest targets reflected the absence of a common civil society proposal. Yet, CSOs could have exploited this far more had they realised how broad the scope for influence really was.

8.2   *Silos and Policy Incoherence*

Ironically, while Agenda 2030 pledges to challenge and overturn silos, the process itself was a blatant reminder of the siloed approaches within the UN system as well as national policymaking. Looking back, education was worryingly invisible at the UN headquarters. UNESCO should have prioritised education – alongside culture, on which they focused in the early days of the process – and had a stronger presence in New York, actively seeking to provide support as well as food for thought as member states engaged in discussions about development beyond 2015, for instance by organising side events in conjunction with OWG sessions. By the same token, the EFA Steering Committee could have played a more active role.

Yet, the incoherence at country-level was a more serious problem. The most extreme example of this was Ministers of Education adopting the Muscat Agreement, while their governments negotiated a different education goal within the OWG at the very same time. The fact that remarkably few member states promoted the Muscat Agreement in the OWG negotiations raised questions about national-level policy coherence and determination. It seemed as though many countries never involved their Ministries of Education in determining their OWG positions. EI's advocacy was most effective when its members (education unions and teacher organisations) shared its position with their governments, and EI followed up with the representatives at the negotiations. But in surprisingly many cases, EI's members struggled to find out exactly where their country position was determined, that is, by whom and in which ministry. This suggests a less inclusive process at the national level. In fact, civil society present at the negotiations at the UN seemed to have more access to the OWG than both national education policymakers and CSOs trying to influence their government's position.

Identifying those exercising pressure behind the scenes and on whom member states drew for advice and expertise is even harder. Many perceived UNICEF as more influential and present in New York, while UNESCO seemed to rely on individual member states to speak on its behalf. The Global Monitoring Report was a source of information throughout the process, and I suspect the World Bank and the OECD shaped the thinking of many member states. There were also significant changes in country positions – many African countries, for instance, abandoned their ambitious targets on teacher training and education financing – and one can only speculate about the extent of influence exerted by traditional donor countries. But the donors' rejection of all proposed aid and financing targets, including financial assistance for qualified teachers, did limit the scope of what was perceived to be possible. In this way, the rich countries won the battle over the means of implementation.

The absence of a financing target will have serious consequences for the success of SDG 4, and directly undermines the commitment to *leaving no one behind*. Early in the negotiations, Brazil problematised the notion of the private sector as a silver bullet and described it as an issue that will 'determine the future of [the] UN and development' (author's notes), but the question of public or private education was largely ignored. Today it would be more difficult to ignore the role of private actors and their impact on equity and quality in education in such a process; yet, we are nowhere closer to a political commitment to public education.

8.3   *Absence of Education Champions*
Providing an insight into how nonspecialists view education, the OWG signalled consistent but quiet support for education. While there were no outspoken opponents – aside from those opposed to commitments on sexuality education and financing – neither was there anyone championing education

and taking strategic ownership of the goal-in-the-making. It is hard to tell whether this was due to complacency, assuming that there would be an education goal, or a failure to understand the urgency of education progress in relation to sustainable development. What is clear, however, is that the implementation phase requires more active support, as sectors compete for financing as well as policy attention.

How countries respond to these three issues – inclusion, silos and policy incoherence, and lack of education champions – will determine the success of SDG 4. Even if few countries involved civil society at the national level in the negotiation phase, implementing the agenda requires the systematic involvement of those at the centre of education – teachers and education workers, students, and other stakeholders. At the same time, the SDGs are a much-needed reminder of the role of education in relation to other development priorities, and how investments in health and education, for instance, reinforce and support each other; the SDGs oblige governments to take a more holistic approach to education. Finally, SDG 4 opens up new spaces for countries to champion education and take the lead in making quality education for all a reality. The question is whether any country will step up to the challenge.

Notes

1 Note on sources: Representing Education International, I was a direct participant in almost all the events and meetings described and analysed in this chapter. Wherever possible, I have cited official, published documents as evidence for the statements and views presented. For some issues, I have drawn from the extensive notes that I took at each event.

2 For a list of the full membership, see https://sustainabledevelopment.un.org/post2015/owg

3 These modalities were determined by Agenda 21. The nine major groups are Women, Children and Youth, Indigenous Peoples, NGOs, Local Authorities, Workers and Trade Unions, Business and Industry, Scientific and Technological Community, and Farmers. Education International is a member of the Workers and Trade Unions group.

4 The brief was produced by UNESCO, UNICEF, UNFPA, WFP, ILO, ITU, UNV, OHCHR, PSO, UNDP, and IFAD.

5 The Group of 77 is the largest intergovernmental organisation of developing countries in the United Nations, currently representing 134 countries.

6 For a summary of how the detailed wording of the education targets evolved during the most active period of OWG negotiations (March–July 2014), see Table 2.1.

7 Composed of representatives from Member States, EFA convening agencies, EFA-
   FTI, civil society, and the private sector, the Steering Committee provided strategic
   guidance on all aspects of Education for All (UNESCO, 2011).
8 Completion of full cycle of free quality education (ECE to upper secondary education); equitable access to postsecondary and lifelong learning; trained and qualified teachers and safe learning environments; relevant quality education, including
   education for sustainable development and global citizenship; and sustained and
   sufficient financing.
9 '4.7: By 2030 ensure all learners acquire knowledge and skills needed to promote
   sustainable development, including among others through education for sustainable development and sustainable lifestyles, human rights, gender equality, promotion of a culture of peace and nonviolence, global citizenship, and appreciation of
   cultural diversity and of culture's contribution to sustainable development' (UNGA,
   2015b, p. 17).

CHAPTER 3

Gender Equality, Education, and Development: Tensions between Global, National, and Local Policy Discourses in Postcolonial Contexts

Naureen Durrani and Anjum Halai

1   Introduction

Education and gender equality remain key foci within the development agenda, particularly since the international consensus garnered through the Education for All (EFA) and Millennium Development Goals (MDGs) movements. Despite the widespread critiques of EFA and the MDGs (Dunne, 2009; Monkman & Hoffman, 2013; Unterhalter, 2012), the mobilisation they propelled led to considerable gains in widening access to education. Nevertheless, globally gender parity in enrolment remains unrealised in primary education (in over 33% of countries), lower secondary education (in 54% of countries), and upper secondary education (in 77% of countries) (UNESCO, 2016b). These disparities are mostly at the expense of girls at primary level globally, and at lower and upper secondary levels in countries with low enrolment ratios, with gender gaps much higher in countries in sub-Saharan Africa and South Asia. A majority of these countries face the contexts of postcoloniality.

Equal access to education, while essential, does not guarantee gender equality. Schools, as formal state institutions, tend to reproduce existing gender regimes and power relations rather than subvert them. Furthermore, gender and gender equality can be buzzwords that produce different interpretations across contexts and actors. Paying attention to the specificities of contexts in which gender equality discourses are interpreted, negotiated, and enacted is, therefore, crucial to understanding the construction of gender and the hope of its transformation in and through education.

We adopt a postcolonial perspective as an entry point to the proliferating literature on global gender equality policies and their enactment. Through a literature review and an empirical study of postcolonial Pakistan, we argue that global gender equality discourses tend to ignore the ways colonialism was integral to the rise of modernity in the West. The development of modern societies also saw the development of institutionalised education in forms that now underpin the promotion of mass (universal) education around the world.

These interconnections have a significant bearing on the relationship of gender and education, particularly in postcolonial contexts, where education is deployed in nation-building projects that simultaneously seek to modernise the nation by emulating the rationality, science, and technology of the colonial power in the public realm, and to keep the nation's distinction from the colonisers through the feminine. This feminine positioning involves the construction of 'authentic'/'traditional' womanhood to mark the cultural distinction of the postcolonial nation. The private/public divide that was intrinsic to Western gender relations was, thus, redoubled in contexts of postcoloniality. The collision of these competing national goals – modernity and tradition – with international policy discourses is detrimental to the realisation of gender equality.

This chapter addresses that neglect of the specificities of postcolonial settings in education and development scholarship. The next section presents our theoretical framework, covering the key concepts we deploy – nation-state, development, education, and gender. This is followed by summarising the findings of a brief literature review on the relationship of gender and education in postcolonial contexts. The next two sections first offer a description of Pakistan, the context of our empirical research, and outline the methods and data sets. We then offer key analyses from research that explored the potential of education for promoting gender equality in Pakistan. The conclusion relates the analyses back to the literature and offers implications for gender equality and the Sustainable Development Goals (SDGS).

2   Theoretical Framework

We begin with an exploration of the relationship between the nation-state and education, and the ways modernity shaped that relationship. Next, we trace the intersection of nation and gender, and the ways this relationship was shaped by colonialism. Finally, we discuss conceptualisations of gender and its location within global development and education frameworks.

2.1   *The Modern Nation-State and Education*
In a study of four postcolonial contexts, Dunne et al. (2017) demonstrate how modern values underpinned the development of the nation-state in the West. Furthermore, they discuss how the development of the nation-state was bound up with the emergence of liberal secular democracies and was premised on the supposed separation of religion and state. The term nation-state refers to

a mode of governance concerned with the protection of particular territorial boundaries alongside the governing of the people within those boundaries. Dunne et al. (2017) draw on Dean (2007) to argue that while the sovereignty of the state was recognised in Europe by the early 18th century, the conquest of the non-European world by Western nation-states went unfettered. This was justified by the discourse of modernity that sought to 'civilise' the 'barbaric' colonised nations. If the nation is an 'imagined community' discursively constituted, as argued by Anderson (1991), the establishment of a state-organised education system played a key role in forging national imaginations and the rise and spread of nations (Gellner, 1983). The emergence of state-funded schooling in modern contexts coincided with the consolidation of the modern nation-state. However, in colonial contexts, Western education was the privilege of the few and central to the creation of internal social hierarchies and division.

2.2   *Gender, Nationalism, and Colonialism*

The nation is a gendered construct, constituted through gender symbolism. Yuval-Davis and Anthias (1989) argue that women reproduce the nation biologically and sustain the boundaries of national groups through restrictions imposed on sexual relations. Women are also the main transmitters and reproducers of national culture and symbolic signifiers of national differences.

Women were central to nationalist projects in postcolonial contexts. Chatterjee (1989, p. 622) contends that the British invoked the 'oppressed' native woman as a key symbol in the discourse of the civilised West against the 'degenerative and barbaric' Indians.[1] To deal with this onslaught on their tradition, Indian nationalists resorted to a material/spiritual dichotomy. Because European countries established their dominance over non-European peoples through the material domain, which included, for example, science, technology, rational forms of economic organisation, and modern methods of statecraft, the incorporation of these characteristics in the material culture was seen as vital to overthrowing colonial subjugation. However, the spiritual inner core of the Indian culture, which Indian nationalists saw as superior to the West, had to be insulated from Western infiltration. This inner/outer distinction when applied to daily life demarcated the social space into *ghar* (the home) and *bahir* (the world), with women being the representation of *ghar,* and *bahir* being the domain of men (Chatterjee, 1989, p. 624). The nation was imagined and constituted through maintaining a balance between 'modernity' and 'tradition', with 'modernity' performed and embodied, predominantly by men, in the material/outer/public world and tradition enacted, predominantly by women, in the domain of the spiritual/inner/home. Taking up Spivak (1988), Dunne et al. (2017) contend that the symbolic significance of gender to national imaginaries leaves postcolonial women under double surveillance. Internally, they are regulated by their men and women with respect to intersecting kinship as well as national and religious norms; externally, they need to be 'rescued' from their men, including through the enforcement of international human rights regimes. Because women's rights and education feature centrally in human rights discourses, the violation of both is constituted as regressive and premodern and can offer the grounds for global interventions (Khoja-Moolji, 2017).

Chatterjee (1989) further illustrates that formal education was deployed as a key mechanism for the construction of a respectable Indian female subjectivity that fixed the essential femininity of women in terms of certain culturally visible markers of religiosity/spirituality, such as 'her dress, her eating habits, her social demeanor, her religiosity', setting her apart from Western women and women of the lower class (Chatterjee, 1989, p. 624). In the case of Muslims, as elite (*ashraf,* meaning noble) men increasingly lost their influence in the public sphere because of colonial governance, attention shifted to the home 'to redefine Muslim identity and norms of respectability' (Khoja-Moolji, 2018, p. 25). In the reconfigured colonial power relations, Muslim theologians, reformers, and nationalists saw women as 'the upholders of familial morality, domestic managers, and mothers of future citizens' (Khoja-Moolji, 2018, p. 25). Furthermore, education was seen as reforming *ashraf* women, enabling them to perform the social practices of nobility, including hard work, religiosity, and self-discipline. In other words, the iconography of woman applied to both Hindu and Muslim communities, and education sedimented class, caste, and gender hierarchies in the population.

Therefore, in postcolonial societies, while education is seen as significant to the construction of the 'ideal' woman, this idealised national female subjectivity is not necessarily aligned with the 'empowered' woman framed in global education and development discourses. Furthermore, these ideals could incorporate religious values, rather than being framed by a secular imaginary of the modern. This disconnect between the national and the international/global is a key issue in considering gender equality in the Sustainable Development agenda.

2.3   *Gender, Education, and Development*

The promotion and measurement of gender equality in education is linked to conceptualisations of gender. Unterhalter (2012) offers a distinction between 'gender' as a noun, an adjective, and a verb. Gender as a noun refers to a descriptive identification of girls/women and boys/men, as exemplified by the gender parity index (GPI) in education participation and attainment in SDG Target 4.1 on all boys and girls completing primary and secondary education (UNGA, 2015b). This theorisation of gender underpins the Women in Development (WID) framework that emphasises the entry of 'women in development, and thus girls and women into school', primarily in the interest of (economic) efficiency, but not for challenging multiple subordinations of women (Unterhalter, 2005, p. 17). Understandings of gender as a noun, despite its limitations, remain dominant in the international education and development policy landscape (Unterhalter, 2012).

Gender as an adjective is an attribute of the relationships of 'power and meaning in different sites' between men and women (Unterhalter, 2012, p. 68). An example is SDG Target 4.a: 'Build and upgrade education facilities that are child, disability, and gender sensitive and provide safe, non-violent, inclusive and effective learning environments for all' (UNGA, 2015b, p. 17). This conceptualisation focuses on the ways schools and learning processes both transform and reproduce structures of gender inequality. With respect to the relationship between gender and education, the interest is in explorations of how the curriculum and pedagogy might be gendered or how some subjects assume a gendered identity that excludes girls and women from the study of particular disciplines related to prestigious occupations. Such an understanding of gender speaks to the concerns of the Gender and Development (GAD) framework, which is interested in a more relational theorisation of gender and the removal of structural barriers to gender equality (Unterhalter, 2005).

Gender as a verb refers to the ongoing discursive construction of gender performed within the constraints of specific social contexts (Butler, 1990). Furthermore, gender is viewed as a way of structuring social practice, and therefore, intrinsically linked to other structures such as nationality, race, class, sexuality, religion, and ethnicity. Institutions, for example the state, the workplace, and the school, are considered key sites for the configuration of gender (Connell, 1995). With respect to education, the verb 'gender' refers to how girls and boys perform their gender identities within the constraints of the social context of school. The SDG 4 goals, targets, and indicators make no use of 'gender' as a verb. Theorisation of gender as a verb reveals the complicity of the WID and GAD approaches in transforming women from the Global South into objects of technical knowledge, and in the construction of white Western middle-class women as modern, free, and progressive, and women in the Global South as their 'other' (Humphreys, Undie and Dunne, 2008). From this perspective, the political and theoretical interests reside in the recognition of difference and unmasking the marginalisation of nonmainstream identities (Unterhalter, 2005).

While Unterhalter (2012) believes that all three conceptualisations of gender – noun, adjective, and verb – are limited on their own and need to complement one another, we see them as drawing on different and contradictory theoretical understandings. Gender as performative or a verb highlights the power of social construction. Gender identities are constituted by discourse and gender performances bring into being what they name – in this context, the gender binary. In other words, it is not the identity (male or female) doing the discourse but the discourse doing the gender (Butler, 1990). Treating gender as a male/female binary renders transgender and agender identities unintelligible, establishing heteronormativity and silencing nonheterosexuality. The hegemony of gender binary discourse implies that nonbinary and nonheterosexual lives 'fit no dominant frame for the human' resulting in their dehumanisation (Butler, 2004, p. 25). While the notion of performative is useful in 'troubling' and 'undoing' gender, its continued neglect in global education and development discourses is linked to the concept of development and its modern imperatives, which implies an inherent privileging of liberal theories of gender.

Against this background, global education and development discourses, while not homogenous, tend to position girls' education in the Global South as a solution to countless persistent development problems, simultaneously positioning girls as victims of poverty and 'conservative' cultural norms, and as embodying the potential to solve these very issues (Khoja-Moolji, 2015).[2] The concurrent representation of 'poor women from the South as both objects of transformation and redemption and potential entrepreneurial subjects', rather than being an aberration, is a continuity of 'colonial discourses of salvation which simultaneously infantilised its objects and imposed a moral responsibility for self-improvement on them' (Wilson, 2012, p. 68). The elevation of girls' education in the Global South as a hegemonic ideology is linked to particular social, material, and political histories, and is closely entwined with harnessing their labour in the global economy (Khoja-Moolji, 2015).

While the framing described above constrains understanding of gender equality in education by focusing on 'girls and not gender (or boys)' (Monkman and Hoffman, 2013, p. 63), Khoja-Moolji (2018, p. 4) argues that this 'global rallying around girls' education has been in relation to *specific* populations and nations in the global South', in contexts such as Pakistan, where 'poverty, terrorism, and gender-based violence' are viewed as a consequence of girls' restricted access to schooling.

3   Gender and Education in Postcolonial Contexts: Key Issues and
       Debates

Modern education was a key institution for consolidating the cognitive, moral, and political authority of colonial regimes (Topdar, 2015). Consequently, the 'childish' native was subjected to state schooling 'as part of multiple civilizing mission projects' that sought differentiated outcomes for different classes, ethnicities, and genders (Topdar, 2015, p. 3). In Canada, such colonial projects involved the forceful removal of Aboriginal children from families and their confinement in Indian Residential Schools, with a bifurcated design to separate children by gender (de Leeuw, 2009). In Sierra Leone, Leach (2008) demonstrates that since the beginning of missionary engagement, gender was the main organising basis of schooling, with the curriculum for girls centred on domestic skills and morality as a preparation for marriage. In Africa more widely, colonial education systems entrenched 'traditional Christian notions of femininity and the appropriate social roles of women', while preparing men for the economy in pursuit of capitalist colonial interests (Ricketts, 2013, p. 6).

    In the Indian context, Khoja-Moolji's (2018) archival research identifies a long-standing belief in girls' education as a key means for rescuing both girls and their nations, as reflected in the words of the Bishop of Calcutta, in 1871:

> Female education is of the utmost moment in India for religious, social, and even political reasons, there being no more effectual nurses of the fanaticism of the Musalman [Muslim] and of the superstition of the Hindoo than the women of India. (quoted in Khoja-Moolji, 2018, p. 11)

This framing of girls' education both legitimised colonial interventions to 'emancipate' Indian women, including those by white feminists (Syed and Ali, 2011) and offered Indian nationalists and social reformists opportunities to 'regulate women's bodies and mobility' (Khoja-Moolji, 2018, p. 10). The 'new' Indian woman created at the nexus of colonial and nationalist discourses became 'emancipated' to enter the public realm of school, lead other women into nationalist/freedom projects, and even take up paid employment, as long as she strictly policed the boundaries between the 'ideal' and the Western/'common' woman (Chatterjee, 1989). Khoja-Moolji (2018) and Chatterjee (1989) further highlight the class inflections of the ideological project underpinning the education of Muslim and Hindu girls, respectively, resulting in the crystallisation of group boundaries along class lines. Colonial education and social reform projects not only allowed Muslim and Hindu women from the nobility to participate in some public spaces and knowledges hitherto limited to men, but also enabled them to reinscribe their *class* status over women from lower classes, who continued to be excluded from such opportunities.

A number of studies illustrate how the 'ideal' woman is recruited in the curriculum and school practices of postcolonial contexts for the creation of the 'ideal' nation. In Pakistan, Naseem (2006) demonstrates that curriculum texts discursively constitute gendered citizens through totalisation, classification, and normalisation by excluding women visually and by fixing the meaning of the images that articulate gender in the texts. In Tanzania, school curricula seek to enable girls to become good citizens by learning the skills of accomplished home managers (Ricketts, 2013).

In addition to the official curriculum relayed through school textbooks and learning materials, the practices of schooling reproduce gender regimes through the hidden curriculum at micro and meso levels. Dunne's research in Botswana and Ghana reveals that in both contexts the informal practices of the hidden curriculum show striking similarities in the 'pervasive and inequitable gender/sexual practices within schools' (Dunne, 2007, p. 499). Likewise, a study of secondary schools in Uganda observed strong gender codes underpinned by morality and enforced and regulated by teachers and student-spy networks, resulting in the normalisation of 'compulsory heterosexuality and attendant homophobia' (Muhanguzi, Bennett, & Muhanguzi, 2011, p. 147).

Another significant theme emerging from the literature relates to the gaps between global gender goals and local/national implementation of 'empowerment' interventions on the ground. For example, Holmarsdottir, Møller Ekne, and Augestad (2011) show that South Sudan government officials comply with an array of girl-focussed interventions pushed by global development agencies, but implementation and coverage of these projects remain poor. Similarly, in Kenya, the tensions between 'national goals, competing cultural norms, and international expectations' on gender equality resulted in inconsistent gender messages in textbooks and a lack of fit between textbook messages and lived experiences, constraining students' ability to understand how gender (in) equality plays out in their lives within local communities (Foulds, 2013, p. 165).

The assumption that there is a positive relationship between education and gender equality would benefit from empirical scrutiny. As a multidimensional issue, gender equality cannot be achieved simply by expanding women's access to education and the labour market. Indeed, the study conducted by Chisamya et al. (2012) in marginalised communities in Bangladesh and Malawi found little evidence of transformation in gender relations or female empowerment despite girls' equal participation in schooling. Education interacts with social structures in complicated ways, and 'without changing social structures, education does not guarantee empowerment' (Monkman & Hoffman, 2013, p. 75). While the above example is from a postcolonial context, the illusionary belief in a direct relationship between education and emancipation also applies to Western contexts (Skelton and Francis, 2009). Nevertheless, there is often an 'orientalist' bias in the Western attribution of gender inequality to culture in postcolonial contexts, while failing to engage with culture's impact on gender inequality in the West.

In conclusion, what the preceding studies seem to suggest is that the connection between education and empowerment is rather delusional. We argue that in postcolonial contexts competing demands between nation-building goals, the harnessing of education for human capital development, international gender equality commitments, and local cultural roles considerably complicate the work of education in meeting global gender equality targets. These insights would need to be considered as the global community comes to an agreement regarding what gender equality means and how to monitor and measure progress on it.

4 Pakistan: Sociohistorical Context

Pakistan is a federation with four provinces (Punjab, Sindh, Balochistan, and Khyber Pakhtunkhwa [KP]), three territories (Azad Jammu and Kashmir, Gilgit-Baltistan, and the Federally Administered Tribal Areas), and the federal capital, Islamabad. Pakistan came into being in 1947 as a result of the partition of British India along religious lines amidst large-scale human migration, communal violence, and rape of women (Dunne et al., 2017). However, global economic and geopolitical relations continue to legitimise colonial patterns of dominance over Pakistan through global trade, terms of lending from International Monetary Fund, Western support to military regimes and *jihadi* groups in Pakistan (Kadiwal & Durrani, 2018), and more recently the 'War on Terror', which continues to incur huge human and financial losses (Durrani & Halai, 2018).

Pakistani culture is highly gender-segregated with clearly defined roles along the male/female gender binary and the exclusion of nonbinary gender identities. Many sources link the marginalisation of transgender and transsexual people in Pakistan and India to British colonial governance and their imperial project of civilising non-Western cultures (Hinchy, 2017; Khan, 2017). Precolonial India tolerated fluid gender identities, with transgender and transsexual people enjoying privileges such as land ownership, state stipends, and the possession of important positions in princely and royal courts (Khan, 2017).

Under British colonialism, the lives of transgender people became increasingly structured through modern European norms of heteronormativity. In 1860, the colonial state criminalised sodomy and carnal intercourse (Khan, 2017). British norms of gender and sexuality infiltrated the attitudes of Indian elites through British education, resulting in discrimination against transgender communities. The largely stable colonial policies of regulating transgender communities were challenged when in 2009 the Pakistani state gave the transgender community political recognition, 'identifying them as citizens of a modern state' (Khan, 2017, p. 1283).

The centrality of male/female gender binary to social life in Pakistan is strongly linked to national identity, which is constructed through religion and the military against the antagonistic non-Muslim 'other', particularly Hindu India, against whom Pakistan has fought four wars (Durrani & Halai, 2018). Gender segregation also marks the provision of school education. Government schools are the main providers of primary (grades 1–5), middle (grades 6–8), and secondary (grades 9–10) education. Currently, more than one-third of the those in education (42%) are enrolled in the private sector, with 48% enrolled in preprimary, 39% at primary, 37% at middle, 35% at secondary, and 22% at higher secondary level in private institutions (NEMIS-AEPAM, 2017). The government school system is largely gender segregated with schools for boys with male teachers and those for girls with female teachers. Parents prefer to send their daughters to girls' schools, especially at the postprimary levels.

Pakistan is a country with a significant proportion of children and young people out of school. In 2015–2016, 22.64 million out of 51.7 million children aged 5–16 were out of school, of whom 12.11 million were girls and 10.53 million boys (NEMIS-AEPAM, 2017). A gender-disaggregated analysis of key education indicators is presented in Table 3.1 for an overview, although the reliance of these statistics on gender binaries reinscribes such binaries. Table 3.1 reveals

TABLE 3.1   Pakistan – Key education indicators by gender 2012

Indicator	Female	Male
Literacy rate (Age 10+)	47%	70%
Primary school completion (15–24 Years)	58%	72%
Lower secondary completion (15–24 Years)	41%	54%
Upper secondary completion (20–29 Years)	17%	22%
Mean years of education (20–24 Years)	5.54	7.23

SOURCE: UNESCO (n.d.-b)

disparities at the expense of girls. However, income disparities are much bigger than gender, and gender intersects with household income, location (rural and urban), and region/provinces (Durrani et al., 2017; UN Women, 2018). When the intersections of gender with location and income are taken into account, gender disparities almost disappear for the richest households in urban areas, with the exception of Balochistan (UNESCO, n.d.-b).

The literature links gender disparities to supply and demand, although this resonates with human capital theory, rather than recognising the power of the sociohistorical context. On the demand side, there is a persisting pro-male bias in parental decisions to enrol and spend on education (Aslam & Kingdon, 2008). On the supply side, the number of boys' schools is proportionally greater than girls' schools across provincial levels and rural and urban areas (Durrani et al., 2017). Likewise, the supply of teachers shows an enduring shortage of female teachers for high/secondary schools, especially in science and mathematics, in remote rural areas. Provinces with the largest gender gaps in education also have the lowest proportion of female teachers (Halai and Durrani, 2018).

Over the last two decades several reform initiatives have been taken to improve girls' participation in education, including waiver of tuition fees, free distribution of textbooks, and stipends for adolescent girls (Durrani et al., 2017). However, opportunities for women in terms of access to higher education, employment, and other resources are limited. Aslam and Kingdon (2012) estimate that schooling beyond 8–10 years can counter the effects of the economically gendered culture, but in Pakistan, only one in five women has at least 10 years of education. The completion of 12 years of quality compulsory education, enshrined in SDG 4 would, therefore, help ameliorate the economic marginalisation of women in Pakistan.

The next section presents a description of our empirical case study of gender equality in education in Pakistan.

5   The Case Study of Pakistan

This study, conducted in 2015–2016, sought to explore how gender equality informs policies and perspectives in two of Pakistan's provinces – Sindh and KP – that is, how these compare with policies and perspectives at both the federal/national and global level in order to highlight areas of tensions and overlaps in relation to gender equality. The distinction between these three levels – local, national, and global – is an analytical tool to unmask persistent barriers to gender equality and illuminate ways of promoting gender equality in and through education both in Pakistan and other contexts of postcoloniality. Nevertheless, we understand that in such contexts the boundaries between the local, national, and global are blurred as contemporary relations of inequality – gender, class, religious, national, racial, and ethnic – are actively shaped by colonial and neo-colonial relations, including global imperatives in education, such as the SDGs, and the resistance they provoke.

A comparison of the southern province of Sindh and the northwestern province of KP is particularly illuminating as these have quite different historical legacies and sociodemographic compositions as summarised in Table 3.2. Sindh became part of the British Raj in 1843, receiving little attention in terms of development and 'modernisation' (Cohen, 2005). At independence, Sindh's social structures and leadership, along with a repressive feudal order, remained intact. Sindh is Pakistan's second most populous and the most urbanised province (PBS, 2017a). It has the highest proportion of non-Muslim population and is ethnolinguistically diverse, although Sindhi is the largest ethnic group (60%), followed by Urdu-language speakers (21%) (GoS, 2014).

KP was part of Punjab province after annexation by the British in 1849. In 1901 it was given the status of a province and named the North-West Frontier Province. It was renamed as Khyber Pakhtunkhwa in 2010 (GoKP, 2012). KP is the third most populous province, the least urbanised (PBS, 2017a), and the most religiously homogenous (PBS, 2017b). In terms of ethnicity, around two-thirds (74%) of KP inhabitants are Pakhtuns, who are largely governed by the

TABLE 3.2   Comparison of Sindh and Khyber Pakhtunkhwa (KP)

	Sindh	KP
Population size[a]	47.8 million national share = 23.04%	35 million national share = 14.69%
Rural/urban distribution[a]	Rural = 48% Urban = 52%	Rural = 18.7% Urban = 81.3%
Demographics[b]	Muslim = 91.31% Non-Muslim = 8.69%	Muslim = 99.44% Non-Muslim = 0.56%
GPI primary (gross enrolment rate)[c]	0.78	0.75
GPI secondary (gross enrolment rate)[c]	0.78	0.48

a SOURCE: PBS (2017A)

b SOURCE: PBS (2017B)

c SOURCE: NEMIS-AEPAM (2017)

tribal/ethnic code of *Pakhtunwali* – a highly patriarchal code requiring gender seclusion and segregation that restricts women to the domestic sphere (Dunne et al., 2017). KP is the province most affected by the Soviet invasion of Pakistan and the 'War on Terror'. In general elections, religious parties consistently manage to secure a high share of votes in the province.

Key sites for the study comprised teacher education institutions (TEIS), as teachers are central to promoting a gender transformative agenda or the sedimentation of unequal gender regimes (Halai & Durrani, 2018). A study of teacher education in Pakistan is particularly insightful, as the country has made significant investment in reforming teacher education over the last 15 years (Durrani et al., 2017). In total, five TEIs were accessed, four in Sindh and one in KP. The uneven distribution of TEIs across the two provinces reflects both the proportional size of the education sector in the two provinces and budgetary constraints. Perspectives of key stakeholders responsible for implementing the curriculum, including student-teachers, teachers, teacher educators (henceforth lecturers), and curriculum and textbook personnel, were collected (see Table 3.3). Data collection methods included individual interviews, focus group discussions, a survey with both structured and open questions, a limited number of lecture observations (see Table 3.3), and policy analysis.

The selection of sites, participants, and methods was purposeful, aiming to obtain a comprehensive picture of gender equality and education with sociocultural diversity, including social class, religion, ethnolinguistic identity, and

TABLE 3.3   Summary of participants by methods and gender

Participants	Methods	Male	Female	Total
Teachers	Focus Group	9	8	17
	Questionnaire	91	82	173
	Total	100	90	190
Student teachers	Focus Group	10	9	19
	Questionnaire	37	56	93
	Total	47	65	112
Lecturers	Interviews	12	2	14
	Classroom Observations	2	1	3
	Total	14	3	17
Curriculum experts/ Personnel	Interviews	13	11	24
International development actors	Interviews	3	9	12

TABLE 3.4   Policy texts analysed by level

Global	National	Local/Provincial
World Bank Group Gender Strategy (Fy16–23)	The White Paper 2007	Sindh Education Sector Plan (ESP) 2014–18
The Education 2030 Incheon Declaration	National Education Policy 2009	KP ESP (2010–15)
Global Education Monitoring Report 2016	National Education Policy 2017–25	KP ESP (2015–20)
Global Education Monitoring Report 2017–18	Initial Teacher Education (ITE) curriculum	Pakistan Studies Textbook in use in Sindh
	National Curriculum in Pakistan Studies[a]	Pakistan Studies Textbook in use in KP

a A compulsory and assessed subject dedicated to enhancing social cohesion and national
   unity, studied by all young people in public and private schools in grades 9 (14–15 years) and 10
   (15–16 years).

rural/urban location. Policy texts listed in Table 3.4 were critically analysed as
a prelude to our engagement with the perspectives of teachers and other key
stakeholders.

The analysis of primary data and documents focuses on gender for analytical clarity, but we understand gender as only one challenge for equality in
education. Gender intersects with other axes of marginalisation, for example, displacement and disability, the latter of which is discussed at length in
Chapter 4 by Christopher Johnstone, Matthew Schuelka, and Ghada Swadek.
We bring together data from all sources to study how gender equality was
taken up within policies and was understood by actors at local, national, and
global levels.

6   Gender Equality: Policy and Perspectives

We first present the analysis of policy documents undertaken as part of the
Pakistan case study with respect to gender equality at different levels before
reviewing the ways gender equality is understood on the ground.

6.1 *Gender Equality as Portrayed in Policy Texts*

6.1.1 Global Level

The World Bank Group's (WBG) latest gender policy framework justifies investment in women and girls as 'smart economics' in the pursuit of poverty reduction and accelerating growth through increased women's labour market participation and earnings (WBG, 2015). 'Income, employment, and assets' are seen as vital to women's empowerment and beneficial to men, children, and society as a whole (WBG, 2015, p. 12). By contrast, a lack of women' s economic empowerment is viewed as detrimental to growth, poverty reduction, and health outcomes for children, and associated with the rapid spread of HIV/AIDS and poor governance. Drawing largely on human capital theory and neoliberalism, the overriding concern of these notions of gender is to instrumentalise women, rather than transform gender relations, and to exploit their economic labour under the gloss of empowerment.

The *Education 2030: Incheon Declaration and Framework for Action* frames gender equality as central to SDG 4 and commits 'to supporting gender-sensitive policies, planning, and learning environments; mainstreaming gender issues in teacher training and curricula; and eliminating gender-based discrimination and violence in schools' (WEF, 2015, p. 8). Furthermore, it calls upon governments to review their education sector plans, budgets, curricula, textbooks, and teacher training to ensure the elimination of gender stereotypes and discrimination. Nevertheless, it acknowledges that, since gender inequality in education reflects gender norms and discrimination in the wider society, corresponding gender-sensitive policies are required in other areas if gender equality is to be achieved.

The SDGs have a more extended focus on gender equality than the MDGs, both in the stand-alone goal on gender equality, SDG 5, and the mainstreaming of gender equality into numerous other goals. With respect to SDG 4, gender equality is embedded in several indicators measured through the gender parity index: indicators 4.1.1, 4.2.1, 4.2.2, 4.3.1, 4.5.1, 4.6.1, and 4.c.1 (UIS, 2018e). (See Appendix 1 of this book for details.) While this indicator framework continues to narrow the goals, practices, and measures, the evolving discourse acknowledges that a more nuanced notion of gender equality is needed that does not equate gender with girls, that acknowledges that tackling gender asymmetries necessarily requires the engagement of men, and that takes into account how notions of masculinities and femininities impact institutional practices and norms (UNESCO, 2016b). Nevertheless, SDG Target 4.1 measures only literacy and numeracy, and does not focus on knowledge, skills, behaviour, and attitudes relevant to gender equality. Additionally, SDG 4 and 5 targets and indicators exclude those who do not fit the male/female gender binary. Finally, SDG

5 does not mention education, despite the significance of education to gender equality, and its targets only focus on women and do not include men (UNGA, 2015b, p. 18).

Despite the more nuanced understanding of gender equality, the SDG discourse tends to position girls' education as a solution to a range of development problems: 'Education, especially of girls and women, is the single most effective means of curtailing population growth, by increasing people's autonomy over fertility-related decisions and delaying pregnancy' (UNESCO, 2016b, p. 24). This instrumentalist view of girls' education frames girls as 'mothers of development' and not as 'human beings deserving of dignity and respect in their own right' (UNESCO & MGIEP, 2017).

The comparison of global gender equality policies with national level, i.e., in Pakistan, is important as UN Women (2018) have identified variations in national-level commitments to gender equality policies.

6.1.2   National Level

Historically, at national level, Pakistan's education policies have not addressed gender equality in a systematic way. As a precursor to National Education Policy (NEP) formulation, a White Paper (WP) was produced in 2007. It traces the significance accorded to gender in education policies since 1947 and notes that policies mostly paid only marginal attention to gender (Aly, 2007). Nevertheless, several education policies are cited as advocating single-sex institutions at secondary or postcompulsory education levels to address the concerns of parents, who, for sociocultural reasons, are reluctant to send daughters to coeducational schools (Aly, 2007). Increasing the number of female teachers was another policy measure recommended to encourage girls' education (Aly, 2007). The WP contends that policy rhetoric surrounding girls' schools was 'not matched with financial and social investment in the cause of female education' (Aly, 2007, p. 29).

The NEP 2009 acknowledges that disparities in access to education across 'gender, ethnic minorities, provinces, regions, and rural-urban divides' is a challenge with 'serious implications for sustainable and equitable development in the country' (GoP, MoE, 2009, p. 66). To support girls' access to schooling, the NEP 2009 recommended waiving the maximum age limit for recruiting female teachers (GoP, MoE, 2009). The most recent NEP, 2017–2025, similarly acknowledges gender disparities, alongside regional gaps and aims, and resolves 'to achieve gender parity, gender equality, and empower women and girls within [the] shortest possible time' (GoP, MFEPT, 2017, p. 13). However, the policy has no dedicated subtheme on gender, and there is no detail of strategies or actions that would be put in place to achieve the empowerment of women.

The curriculum and teacher education are key policy sites for promoting gender equality, and we look at each in turn to analyse how they address gender equality. Pakistan revised its national curriculum in 2006 in a bid to promote education quality by replacing a content-driven curriculum with a competency-based one. The revision was funded by USAID and led by the Curriculum Wing of the then Federal Ministry of Education, in consultation with the four Provincial Bureaus of Curriculum and a range of stakeholders. An additional objective of the reform was to make education purposeful by focusing the curriculum on 'important social issues' (GoP, MoE, 2009, p. 42). Gender equality is not mentioned as an area of focus. Looking specifically at the Pakistan Studies curriculum, the only specific reference to gender is the 'gender composition of population in Pakistan' (GoP, MoE, 2006, p. 13).

Alongside the overhaul of the curriculum, teacher education has received policy interventions over the last 15 years aimed at improving education quality (GoP, MoE, 2009). However, as highlighted in Chapter 9 by Yusuf Sayed and Kate Moriarty, global attention to quality has been reduced to pedagogical/technical concerns that appear to neutralise attention to issues such as gender. In the post 9/11 context of the US-led 'War on Terror', much education reform has been driven by the funding support and technical advice from international donors and development agencies, notably USAID. The revised Initial Teacher Education (ITE) curriculum positions teachers as reflective practitioners enacting critical thinking and analysis to develop their practice in order to 'facilitate the process of multiculturalism and pluralism ... to bring about social transformation' (HEC, 2010, p. 15). Although gender equality is not explicitly referred to, multiculturalism and pluralism could implicitly incorporate it. The analysis of the revised ITE curriculum revealed no dedicated module on 'gender' out of a total 45 modules covered over four years, while two modules have at least a unit or a topic relevant to gender equality. These were the 'Foundation of Education' and 'Contemporary Issues and Trends in Education' (HEC, 2010). This peripheral focus on gender equality is unlikely to support teachers effectively in promoting gender equality.

In summary, policies at national level superficially include gender equality and predominantly frame it as a matter of redistributing access to education. Gender is silenced first by technical concerns about pedagogy and second by being flattened within discourses of diversity/multiculturalism. Policies do not engage with the gender and sociocultural norms that would need to be challenged if gender equality is to be promoted in and through education.

6.1.3   Local/Provincial Level

From the national policy arena, we now move to local/provincial policies, analysing policy developments with respect to the curriculum and teacher education in Sindh and KP. While we are using the two terms – local and provincial
– interchangeably, we recognise there might be differences depending on the
positioning of the 'local' within the province.

In 2010, Pakistan devolved planning and management of education to provinces, empowering provinces to make their own education policies, including
the development of curriculum. However, all provinces have decided to keep
the 2006 curriculum, with some minor adjustments (Durrani et al., 2017). The
2006 curriculum, despite bringing some elements of internal diversity, has
largely left its gendered dimension 'untroubled' (Durrani & Halai, 2018; Halai
& Durrani 2018).

Starting with policy developments in Sindh, we analyse the Pakistan Studies textbook prescribed for use in state schools at the time of fieldwork. The
textbook portrays a gendered national imaginary established through the
exclusion of women from the historical narrative and their restriction to the
domestic sphere:

> [The] male member has acquired a unique status in Pakistani culture. He
> is the head of the family. He is the dominant member. But a woman is also
> considered an important part of the family who governs and manages all
> family affairs within the four walls. Household keeping and upbringing of
> children is [sic] entrusted to her. (Khokhar, 2013, p. 134)

Similarly, and importantly, men are excluded from the domestic sphere. The
consumption of such a policy discourse by students, both males and females,
is likely to perpetuate gender hierarchies and maintain existing gender relations, particularly as teachers in Pakistan have been reported to relay the curriculum without challenging its gendered content (Durrani, 2008).

Following devolution, Sindh has produced one Education Sector Plan (ESP)
(2014–2018) with the funding support of Global Partnership for Education
(GPE), the European Union (EU), and UNICEF. At the time of our fieldwork,
implementation of the ESP was in its infancy. The document identifies 'gender attitudes', the practice of 'early or forced marriage', and 'mother illiteracy'
(but not father illiteracy) among the main reasons behind the exclusion of a
large number of children and youth from education. In contrast to the peripheral attention to and narrow understanding of gender at the national level, the
Sindh ESP has included gender as a cross-cutting theme and recommends the

revision of teacher education policies with a 'special focus on gender sensitivity' (GoS, 2014, p. 191). It recommends:

> Provincial textbook boards shall ensure elimination of all types of gender
> biases from textbooks. Also adequate representation of females shall be
> ensured in all curriculum and textbooks review committees. (GoS, 2014,
> p. 205)

The document acknowledges the multiple and intersecting nature of gender
inequalities and recommends 'a comprehensive plan and implementation
strategy so as to meet the needs both of girls who have no/limited access to
educational provision and related opportunities, and of female teachers working in the Department of Education (including in management positions)'
(GoS, 2014, p. 245). The Sindh ESP recommends embedding gender sensitivity in classroom pedagogies, the curriculum, and overall teaching and learning
environment. Thus, the Sindh ESP appears to be more aligned with global policy discourses. The greater integration of gender equality in Sindh is to a large
extent the result of UNICEF's Conflict and Resilience programming in Pakistan
(Durrani et al., 2017), and the fact that UNICEF was also the 'Managing' Agency
for the production of the Sindh ESP (GoS, 2014, p. 12).

Since devolution, our second sampled province, KP, has produced two
ESPs for 2010–2015 and 2015–2020, respectively. The first KP ESP (2010–2015)
was developed with the technical assistance of the Deutsche Gesellschaft für
Internationale Zusammenarbeit (GIZ). It highlights a range of reasons behind
gender disparities in education, including religious conservatism and conflict
resulting from the 'War on Terror' (GoKP, 2012). The ESP claims that, while
local religious practices ignore Islamic injunctions regarding mandatory education for both men and women, the ongoing Western violent interventions in
Afghanistan and Pakistan and the ensuing militancy make girls' schools a target as they symbolise 'Westernisation' (GoKP, 2012, pp. 33, 92). The economic
rationale for girls' education underpinning the global discourse is seen as a
factor that discourages girls' education. It is argued that because most communities do not expect or want their women to have jobs, the association of
employment with education leads communities to the 'wrong conclusion'
that girls 'are not in need of education' (GoKP, 2012, p. 5). The recommended
strategies to promote girls' education speak exclusively to redistributive aims:
'incentives to increase access and participation of girls in mainstream education through free textbooks, stipends for girls at secondary level, voucher
scheme, scholarships, hostel facilities for female teachers' (GoKP, 2012, p. 39).

No substantial measure is offered to disrupt the gendered norms, for example, through the curriculum, pedagogy, or social relations in schools.

The second KP ESP (2015–2020), developed through the financial support of the UK Department for International Development (DFID) and the technical support of its implementing partner Adam Smith International, has incorporated all the SDG 4 targets and indicators, including Target 4.7, which requires the acquisition of knowledge and skills related to 'gender equality' and 'human rights'. However, it has excluded curriculum development on the grounds that the department first needs to develop a stronger institutional framework prior to introducing curriculum interventions (GoKP, 2015). Apart from the elusiveness of what a stronger institutional framework means or how and when it will be achieved, without any curricular inputs, it is hard to understand how progress toward SDG Target 4.7 can be achieved.

In the Pakistan Studies textbook authorised by the KP Textbook Board Peshawar, the national iconography again revolves around male heroes, and women's subordination is legitimised: 'In Pakistani society men have a pre-eminent position because he is [sic] responsible for the livelihood of the family' (*Pakistan Studies for Class 10th*, n.d.: 104). This reinforces the expectation that women will be in the home, rather than in employment.

In concluding this section, we draw attention to differences in the incorporation of gender equality in policy documents at different levels.

First, while the global policy discourses offer the rationale of the links between girls' education and economic growth, at the national and local level in Pakistan, policy discourses tend to overlook the contribution of women to national and household economic growth and instead to relegate women to the private/domestic sphere to establish and legitimise male dominance. The exclusive focus on the economic justification of girls' education at the global level may discourage, rather than encourage, local communities to send girls to school.

Second, while gender equality is embedded within SDG 4 targets and indicators, the national and KP policies only focus on redistributing educational access to girls, without challenging the deep-seated gendered norms and the gender stereotypes prevalent within textbooks. By contrast, the Sindh ESP offers a more integrated and nuanced approach to gender equality. However, the extent to which gender equality policy is implemented is yet to be seen. The translation of policy into practice, particularly in local contexts, is always uncertain. A lack of commitment to implementation at the local level leads to notional compliance. The commitment of KP to SDG 4, while ruling out curriculum reform, is suggestive of this. For both Sindh and KP, the extent to which any gender-related reforms will be implemented is open to question.

6.2   *Gender Equality: Issues in the Translation from Policy to Practice*
The translation of gender policies into practice is linked to how actors interpret gender equality on the ground, as well the effective monitoring of policy
implementation. This may lead to tensions or overlaps between policy as text
and policy as practice within and across the global, national, and local levels.
We explore such tensions and overlaps in the domains of school curriculum
and textbooks.

6.2.1   Global Level
The SDG agenda is not legally binding and the 'SDG follow-up and review
mechanism consists of voluntary national and non-government reporting'
(UNESCO, 2017b, p. 1). While countries are encouraged to submit their national
reviews voluntarily, only time will tell the extent to which such a country-led,
hands-off approach to promoting the 2030 Agenda is effective.

The annual Global Education Monitoring Report (GEMR), hosted and published by UNESCO, is the key mechanism for monitoring and reporting on SDG
4. Nevertheless, these reports only illuminate broad trends at best, and 'they
can misguide subsequent action' or even 'generate negative repercussions'
(DeJaeghere, 2015, p. 74). For example, an indication of gender parity in access
can wrongly transfer funds to other areas or can spark negative reactions to
programmes that exclusively focus on girls and women (DeJaeghere, 2015).

Furthermore, other markers of inequalities intersect with gender, producing
compound gender-based inequalities. The aggregate statistics of gender inequality render the most marginalised groups invisible in national statistics (UN
Women, 2018). While household wealth, ethnicity, ability, age, race, location of
residence, and migration are all important structures of inequalities, gender
identity, and sexual orientation, particularly relating to students and teachers
who claim nonbinary gender/nonheterosexual identities are precisely where
inclusion in relation to gender becomes a major challenge. Although these hidden minorities experience the most acute form of disadvantage, mainstream
policy tends to ignore them. The preceding critique highlights the significance
of complex theories of gender, as elaborated on in a previous section, which
pay attention to the performance of gender by girls, boys, and those with nonbinary gender identities.

6.2.2   National Level
Each context has its unique obstacles to policy implementation, including
policy on gender equality. In Pakistan, the curriculum revision was undertaken
with the involvement of international donors. The participation of USAID and
other international donors in the curriculum revision process, amidst the 'War

on Terror', resulted in resistance to implementation by religious and nonreligious groups (Durrani et al., 2017). Terms such as 'tolerance' became a discursive battleground for ideological wars between different groups, as recounted by a female participant in our research who worked for an international donor:

> He [a Curriculum Wing staff member] said, 'What do you mean by tolerance? ... Does it mean that somebody would attack us and we just tolerate that; attack us with drones and we tolerate them?'

At the national level, teachers were offered in-service training to support the implementation process, largely through funding and/or technical support of donors. However, new vocabulary such as 'peacebuilding' and 'anger management' was treated with suspicion. A female consultant at an international agency stated:

> [A teacher receiving training in the workshop] said, 'You have one whole chapter on controlling anger and do we really want our children to be controlled? Why are we teaching our children to be fearful?'

The control of violent masculinities or management of anger/aggression were seen by some not as promoting gender equality but as compromising the nation, as communities 'on the receiving end of strategies for gender equality are also on the receiving end of the "War on Terror"' (Purewal, 2015, p. 52). The above statements point to a major disjuncture between international education policy discourses, with their promotion of modern concepts such as tolerance and equality, and the realities of international geopolitics.

At the national level, education policy development has largely adopted a gender-blind approach (Durrani & Halai, 2018). The implementation of teacher education reforms, which have focused on technical issues of pedagogy and quality, and which deflect attention from more complex sociological concerns, has not triggered the same resistance as the curriculum. However, a main concern has been teacher educators' own capacity to promote gender equality to translate policy into practice on the ground (Durrani & Halai, 2018).

6.2.3   Provincial/Local Level

Although Sindh has been an ardent supporter of the devolution, implementation of translating the curriculum into textbooks was slow, despite the fact that the same political party, Pakistan Peoples Party, a centre-left, socialist party, has led the provincial government since 2008. Nevertheless, in early 2014, an advisory committee on curriculum and textbook reform was established with the remit to promote communication between the Bureau of Curriculum and the Textbook Board and to incorporate local context in textbooks. Discussions with actors engaged in the implementation of curriculum reform indicated a deep understanding of gendered representations in the curriculum texts. A female member of the Advisory Committee on Curriculum and Textbooks stated:

> We have to look hard to find them [women in textbooks] ... the multitude of representation that can be included, that needs to happen and to see the multiple roles women play and can play instead of confining them to childcare and housework.

There appeared to be a strong intention to shift the gendered representations of the nation in ways that could potentially promote gender equality. This entailed both excluding texts emphasising dominant masculinities and including multiple femininities. According to a male member of the Textbook Board:

> We suggested removing gender bias ... and there was too much of glamourising the military and the militarised culture. ... We raised the question why can't it be otherwise; that the girl comes [home] after playing and the mother asks the boy to go and get food for his sister.

Such voices are laudable, but the extent to which this may lead to any substantial change is a question that warrants further research using ethnographic/ qualitative case studies of relevant institutions – schools, TEIs, curriculum bureaus, and textbook boards.

There was also evidence of strong resistance to change from actors in wider society, unrelated to curriculum and textbooks. A male member of the Bureau of Curriculum stated:

> [A political-religious party] called and said that they wanted to have a meeting with us, but when they arrived ... they were fighting with us; we were shocked, and we told them, 'Please don't fight and give us your suggestions and we will look into it'.

Considering the translation of gender equality policy to classroom level, practised within TEIs in Sindh, only eight out of 266 respondents whom we surveyed indicated that there were particular modules or topics in their training that specifically dealt with gender. The subject that student teachers identified as the most important in promoting their understanding of gender equality was *Islamiat* (Islamic studies). According to a male student teacher, 'The *Islamiat* book states that Islam gives equal rights to every male and female'.

In response to other open-ended questions, both student teachers and in-service teachers indicated that *Islamiat* offers a positive model of gender equality. Lecturers concurred with this view of the significance of *Islamiat* in promoting gender equality. This contradicts dominant perceptions of the relationship between religion and gender held in secular/modern literature, which often portrays religion as necessarily antagonistic to gender equality.

An additional constraint on undoing prevailing gender stereotypes was the institutional gender regime, which, while supporting a redistributive agenda for women, offered little scope for shifting gendered norms. The hidden curriculum in teacher education institutions reproduced and perpetuated gendered norms. The 'protection' of female students from the 'gaze' of male students appeared to be a dominant practice in three out of four TEIs studied. All had enrolled male and female student teachers, but two offered a gender-segregated provision so that parents would not object to enrolling their daughters. As such, the practice was intended to redistribute access to female student teachers. Nevertheless, this practice failed to capitalise on the mixed gender environment to promote respectful and dignified social interactions across gender boundaries. Despite coeducation in the third TEI, the teacher educators strictly regulated male/female gender boundaries. This was potentially counterproductive to collaborative and communicative practices that student teachers were expected to develop and practice. A male student teacher commented:

> Initially, girls and boys behave very well, work together, but our teachers [lecturers] have made it difficult for us. If they see any male talking to a female then the teachers behave very strangely.

Stakeholders – student teachers, teachers, and lecturers – regarded education highly in the promotion of social harmony, including gender equality. Education was considered vital to nation building and to the 'desired' role of women in society 'because the [educated] girl will become a mother and will teach and train her children properly' (male teacher respondent). However, with few exceptions, there was little understanding among student teachers, teachers, and lecturers of the gendered construction of the nation or the ways gender norms are entrenched through everyday life or education. This was particularly problematic in the case of lecturers, who largely failed to recognise how gender norms were embedded in their imaginaries of social cohesion, despite showing a nuanced understanding of other markers of marginalisation – religion, ethnicity, and social class. In addition, a dominant perception among stake-holders, especially lecturers, was that gender parity in access was synonymous to gender equality, and therefore, once access is ensured there are no other issues to be dealt with. A male lecturer commented:

> In the remote areas of the interior, especially for girls, parents are not able to send their kids to schools for many reasons like secure and safe transportation. So, to encourage the parents, we have given funds to cre-ate a transport facility so the young children and girls of remote areas in interior schools can hire a vehicle on a daily basis to go to school.

Thus, gender was predominantly understood as a noun, and gender inequality was equated with issues of redistribution. The small number of stakeholders who expressed an understanding of gender as an adjective and a verb, and gender inequality as linked to structures, power asymmetries, and identities, also showed awareness of the crucial role that education plays in the repro-duction of gender inequalities. For example, according to a female teacher: 'One should not specify certain gender roles, like some professions are only for males, indoor activities are for females, these should not be part of the curriculum'. The few gender-aware respondents were predominantly, though not exclusively, female teachers and student teachers. Those who expressed agency to subvert the gender power asymmetries within their local communi-ties and schools drew on Islamic discourses, rather than on human rights or women's rights discourses. A female student teacher declared:

> When I become a teacher, I will take out all the topics from the curric-ulum that indicate gender discrimination. ... I will publish Islamic and Moral literature which will develop a sense of respect towards women among people.

In KP, the provincial government led by the Awami National Party (ANP) in the years 2008–2013 was quick to seize the opportunity offered by devolution by actively pursuing textbook revision to align textbooks with the new cur-riculum and incorporate local/Pakhtun context into textbooks. In addition, massive investment, time, and inputs were spent to produce the best possible teacher manuals that would help teachers in the delivery of the revised cur-riculum. This overall support for textbook revision, however, did not necessar-ily equate to supporting gender equality.

The textbook revision process lost momentum with the change of govern-ment in 2013. The secular, centre-left ANP was unseated by the centrist Pakistan

Tehreek-e-Insaf (PTI) and their right-wing coalition partner, Jamaat-e-Islami. As mentioned earlier, the current KP ESP, produced by the PTI and Jamaat-e-Islami government (2013–2018), has excluded curriculum and textbook revision. According to a female staff member of an international donor:

> Now the current leadership of the department has decided that they would delay working specifically on the textbooks and curriculum until the next sector plan. ... My reading of that is that it's too political for the department to deal with in the current climate.

In contrast to Sindh, where a strong intention to bring about gender equality messages in textbooks was evident, in KP, where conservative gendered norms are an essential part of the Pakhtun cultural code, expressions of gender egalitarianism were rare. For example, a member of the Textbook Board showed the manuscript of a grade 3 English textbook that depicted the picture of a girl child wearing a frock holding a microphone in her hand alongside the text, 'She is singing a song'. The member expressed amazement at the naivety of the author, saying there would be much political opposition to this on two grounds: first, the girl is wearing Western attire; second, she is engaged in an unIslamic activity (singing). Local actors largely maintained that the depiction of women should adhere strictly with their interpretation of a 'good' Muslim woman:

> Similarly, being Muslim, females should observe purdah, so the pictures shown in there, women were wearing Western attire. And we gave our recommendation that it should be replaced by the things which are according to our norms and society. (Male lecturer)

In the TEI observed in KP, gender regulation was very tight, with all core classes being single-sex, despite a coeducational organisational structure. In elective classes, with small numbers, classes were coeducational, but males and females occupied separate parts of the classroom, with a vast majority of female students veiled in and outside the classroom. The erection of spatial boundaries between male and female student teachers, while protecting females from potential gender-based violence, offered little promise for challenging gendered norms and gender inequality. There was also evidence of the attire and behaviour of female student teachers being monitored by lecturers. For example, a male lecturer admonished some female students for having long nails.

The gender regimes practised in the TEIs are bound up with different stake-holders' perceptions of the significance of education for 'perfecting' women and men for their expected roles in society. Most stakeholders – student teachers, teachers, lecturers, and policymakers – considered girls' education key to nation building. According to a male student teacher, 'Behind every great man there is a great mother. So if mothers are educated they will help bring up better children'. Girls' education was seen as central to the reproduction of national culture. The 'educated woman' was a desired identity position but not an 'emancipated' woman, who participates in the public sphere or the labour market. Her incorporation in the nation is to support the national 'man' in performing the role of provider and protector. A male textbook writer argued:

> Why do we study these topics? Because all these people are our national heroes, they sacrificed their lives for the sake of Pakistan. ... We explain each and every aspect of history, how India attacked Pakistan and these heroes at that time protected their nation; they gave up their lives but didn't let anyone invade Pakistan.

There were many overlaps and tensions in policies and perspectives across the different levels. The first overlap lies in the use of an instrumental justification for girls' education. Global, national, and local policy actors frame female education in instrumental terms, though they offer different reasons for the significance of girls' education. While global policy highlights the benefits of girls' education to the economy, national and local policy actors see education as vital to the production of the 'good' society with highly differentiated gender roles. It is not surprising therefore to see why curriculum contents dealing with gender equality have become discursive battlegrounds for ideological wars, particularly as national policy actors see the nation under siege from foreign interventions in the 'War on Terror'.

Another commonality across the global/national/provincial levels lies in the predominant association of gender equality with redistribution and gender parity and therefore with strategies promoting access and participation. This obscures the ways gender equality can remain unrealised, despite having equal numbers of males and females in educational institutions. The above overlap also associates gender equality with girls' education and, across the global, national, and provincial levels, takes attention away from the education of students with nonbinary gender identities and boys. Unless boys and men, who are dominant in the gender hierarchy, are given an education that radically seeks an egalitarian gender order, gender equality will remain an unaccomplished dream. Additionally, while global policies emphasise main-streaming gender equality across education provision, although to a lesser extent, the complete preoccupation of national and local policy actors with redistribution contributes to a neglect of how gender norms and relations are perpetuated or could be transformed through the curriculum and teacher education. Our analysis points to the limited disruptive effect of liberal theories of gender that leave it equated to male-female binaries, rather than how gender is performed.

Tensions and overlaps are also evident between the national and local levels. Although the size, influence, and remit of the national policy actors have largely diminished since devolution, there appears a strong overlap between the national and KP policy actors with respect to gender equality in the curriculum and the relationship between education and national imagination. In KP, views on gender and gender equality appeared to maintain the image of the 'ideal' Pakistani woman as a key symbol of the national imaginary in ways that have been unhelpful for promoting gender equality. Furthermore, the dominant discourses of the nation prevalent in the province worked to silence stakeholders who had the potential to undo gender. In Sindh, curriculum policy actors showed deep understanding of the gender/nation couplet and expressed the intention to undo it in ways that seemed potentially supportive of gender equality.

7   Conclusions

This chapter has engaged with the role of education in promoting gender equality in postcolonial countries through a study of the promise of national-level education reforms in promoting gender equality in Pakistan, a country with pronounced gender gaps in education at the expense of women. Comparing policy and perspectives regarding gender equality at global, national, and provincial (Sindh and KP) levels, we have identified both overlaps and tensions. While the instrumental use of girls' education is evident across levels, in contrast to the economic efficiency rationale that is predominant globally, both nationally and locally the primary purpose of girls' education is viewed as the 'perfection' of women for maintaining the nation's distinction and ensuring its cultural and biological reproduction. In a context that is at the receiving end of the 'War on Terror', gender boundaries are strictly regulated to 'protect' the ideological frontiers of the nation. Nevertheless, ruptures are also apparent between the national and the local. While the perspectives of stakeholders in KP are in alignment with the national actors in the deployment of education for maintaining and legitimising existing gender relations, curriculum actors in Sindh are largely in favour of deconstructing gender hierarchies in textbooks and promoting gender equality.

We have illustrated that educational reforms are formulated into policy and put into practice through complex and competing political and ideological interests at global, national, and local levels. We contend that global policy discourses are understood in the local and national contexts where education stakeholders negotiate their meaning and enact them in ways that make these policies intelligible to them. Furthermore, perspectives on gender equality and gender regulation vary, contributing to conflicts and tensions in the enactment of gender equality goals. These fissures raise questions regarding the sustainability of any gains made with respect to gender equality. The chapter argues that in postcolonial contexts, such as Pakistan, educational policies and their implementation work out in ways that reproduce existing gender hierarchies. In our research, opposition to these hierarchies was evident, but those opposing existing gender hierarchies have experienced aggressive attacks. Hence, a strong political will and movement driven from within Pakistan's regions and provinces would be key to making any inroads into dismantling gender inequality.

Our study offers wider implications for global policy implementation in national and local settings with respect to gender equality targets relating to SDG 4. The differences over gender equality in the two provinces under a devolved system suggest that monitoring of progress on SDG 4 targets and indicators would need to be conducted at subnational level. That would allow a fine-grained analysis, as the national macro-level data are likely to obscure multiple and overlapping (gender) inequalities, as reported by UN Women (2018). National macro-level data may also obscure tensions in policy and practice between the national and the local levels.

While we have critiqued the use of gender as a noun, if the gender parity index is to be used in the monitoring and measurement of gender equality, it must disrupt the gender binary, including nonbinary gender identities, and take into account contextually relevant markers of disadvantage to put a spotlight on the most marginalised but often invisible social groups. Such intersectional methodologies have been used in a recent report published by UN Women (UN Women, 2018), although the report has failed to disrupt the gender binary.

The expanded list of potential indicators for monitoring gender equality is a step in the right direction. Some of these indicators include the mainstreaming of gender equality in national education policies, curricula, teacher education and student assessment, and teacher and student gender-related attitudes and interactions (UIS, 2018e). However, quantitative, technical indicators of phenomena such as gender sensitivity in teacher education will say nothing about how understandings of gender might change and how practices might shift, or indeed retrench, within particular educational contexts. Global development agendas such as the SDGs rely on a preoccupation with measurement and international ranking, which often misses the most important aspects of gender equality because those aspects cannot be quantified (Unterhalter, 2017). For example, the quantification of male and female characters or visuals in textbooks or the inclusion of topics on gender equality may make it possible to rank and compare countries. But it misses important knowledge associated with gender equality, for example, features of gender relations, sexualities, and aspects of power, because these are not quantifiable. The distribution of male and female characters in texts and images frames gender as a noun and a binary, excluding nonbinary gender identities. It may say little about how gender is positioned as a verb or how texts construct gender. For example, Balagopalan (2012, pp. 320–321) notes that, in India, 'the increased numerical representation of girls in textbooks had done little in terms of altering the patriarchal and misogynist contents of these books'.

As a potential indicator for measuring gender equality, UNESCO (2016b) has proposed the percentage of teachers receiving training in gender sensitivity. As this study has identified, the capacity of teacher educators for promoting gender equality is often limited and is much neglected in educational reforms. Given that student teachers are reported to emulate their lecturers (Akyeampong et al., 2013), they are significant actors, and any training in gender sensitivity must begin with them (Durrani & Halai, 2018).

Measuring the unmeasurable would necessarily require the use of methodologies hitherto excluded in the measurement of development targets. Capturing practices in schools, classrooms, and other institutions, such as curriculum and textbook boards and teacher education institutions, may better illuminate progress toward gender equality through ethnographic and qualitative methods, particularly as these are the spaces in which policies formulated at different levels get negotiated and translated by actors on the ground. These methodologies would allow attention to how gender is performed, and therefore illuminate the possibilities of how unequal gender relations could be undone (Butler, 1990). Qualitative methodologies would be insightful in the identification of friction in the enactment of policy discourses. They may also reveal how local actors could appropriate the rather limited views of gender equality underpinning global and national policies in ways that pay specific attention to the sociocultural environment in which the school is embedded. A better understanding of the experience of gender inequalities as well as their redressal can be achieved through insights into local knowledges, experiences, and practices (DeJaeghere, 2015).

Educational interventions that seek to achieve gender equality need to be supported by laws and policies in other domains, for example, social, economic, and political, as well as the involvement of local communities (Ackerman & Scott, 2017). Working with local actors can be particularly useful in addressing the deep-rooted obstacles to girls' education. Given their credibility in local communities, they are better placed to question 'traditions, laws or social institutions that impinge on girls' rights', particularly in communities at the receiving end of global interventions linked to conflict, where 'any effort suspected to be externally driven would likely be rejected' (Ackerman & Scott, 2017, p. 135).

This chapter has argued that understandings of the nation in postcolonial contexts, such as Pakistan, transverses educational discourses in ways that sustain existing gender hierarchies. It has highlighted the limited ways in which gender is understood in policy discourses and by actors at global, national, and local levels, underscoring the need for more complex theories of gender for challenging the reproduction of gender hierarchies within education and more widely.

Notes

1   In the colonial era 'India' incorporated present day Pakistan. The discussion below relates directly to the history of the territory that became Pakistan and India after Partition in 1947.

2   International development agencies vary in their focus on gender equality and their conceptualisations pull in different directions. For example, the smart girls economic/human capital priorities of the World Bank markedly vary from the more liberal/humanist interests sometimes reflected in UN/UNESCO and SDG discourses.

Quality Education for All? The Promises and Limitations of the SDG Framework for Inclusive Education and Students with Disabilities

Christopher J. Johnstone, Matthew J. Schuelka and Ghada Swadek

1 Introduction

The Sustainable Development Goals (SDGs) reflect a contemporary vision for global development, building upon the successes and challenges of the Millennium Development Goals (MDGs) that expired in 2015. On a broad and conceptual level, the SDGs were set forth based on an agreed-upon global 'aim for a combination of economic development, environmental sustainability, and social inclusion' (Sachs, 2012, p. 2206). It was the first time that development goals integrated social, economic, and ecological dimensions within a singular framework (Griggs, 2013). The goals themselves were also developed differently as a result of a more broadly consultative process than the previous MDGs. Specifically, the SDGs were negotiated in open forum with civil society, advocacy, governmental, and scientific representatives present. This process differed from the MDG process, criticised for being overly focused on so-called 'expert opinion' and in which negotiations were conducted largely behind closed doors (Brown, 2016).

A key feature of the SDGs is the focus on the term 'inclusion'. The declaration and goals themselves contain 40 mentions of the word 'inclusive' (UNGA, 2015b), yet the term is undefined. In most cases, the term refers to 'all' – all people who have the right to access the opportunities outlined in the goals. In this chapter we draw upon two recent conceptualisations of 'rights' and 'inclusion' as a way of understanding the evolution of these concepts from the MDGs to SDGs, and as a way to identify future directions for inclusive education in the SDG era, especially in relation to children with disabilities. For the remainder of the chapter, we outline the 'plural-relational' approach to inclusive education that draws upon legal and development scholarship to conceptualize inclusive education in the SDGs.

2 Universal and Plural Rights

The United Nations organisations call for inclusive education began in 1994 with the signing of the *Salamanca Statement and Framework for Action on Special Needs Education*. This declaration called for states parties to place greater emphasis on children with special educational needs (including children with disabilities) in national education systems. According to the Framework for Action, this could be achieved inclusively. In 2006, the *Convention on the Rights of Persons with Disabilities* (UN, 2006) reinforced this commitment, again calling for inclusive education for children with disabilities. Mégret (2008) noted that the more recent commitment, which specifically focused on persons with disabilities, was one of a long line of population-specific covenants that outlined the rights of groups such as ethnic minority groups, women, children, migrant workers, and indigenous populations. The naming of specific groups in UN covenants is described by Mégret (2008, p. 495) as the 'pluralisation of human rights'.

Pluralisation, according to Mégret, requires specific efforts to adapt the language of existing global human rights as well as acknowledge the unique experiences of groups that may require the creation of new rights. Mégret holds in tension the basic, common human rights shared by all as a normative ambition with the idea that 'human rights may also be about delving deeply into issues of identity, survival, and dignity of particular groups' (Mégret, 2008, p. 496). Referring to the tension between universal and plural rights, Mégret continued:

> Even though the unity of rights captures a fundamental intuition, certain groups do need certain restatements of how rights apply to them, either because they have specific needs to enjoy their rights, different versions of the same rights, or possibly even slightly different rights. (Mégret, 2008, p. 497)

In sum, universal rights are those that may be enjoyed by all, a term frequently used in the universal sense in the MDGs. The SDGs, on the other hand, moved toward a more plural interpretation of rights, focusing on specific subgroups as target populations in discourse and for whom disaggregated data are expected in member state reports. For example, Indicator 4.5.1 requires that disability-disaggregated data be provided, to the extent possible, for all indicators. Thus, the rights of students with disabilities are conceptualised in the SDGs as a plural right. This population is subsumed under broader implications of 'all', but at the same time, disaggregation implies that this population may have particular educational needs that need to be closely monitored in national education systems.

At the same time, some of the data that are used to evaluate progress toward targets, in practice, may exclude children with disabilities. For example, targets 4.1 and 4.6 (focused on learning outcomes) will draw upon cross-national assessments, which structurally and conceptually exclude some students with disabilities (Brzyska, 2018; Schuelka, 2013a) or fail to provide appropriate accommodations. Despite limitations in data, the pluralisation of rights-based discourse in the SDGs represents a departure from the MDGs, which built upon calls for universal education. Pluralisation of educational rights, although logistically challenging in terms of evaluation, acknowledges the 'irreducible experiences of these groups in terms of rights' (Mégret, 2008, p. 498). The plural right to inclusion, then, is both concerned with the presence, participation, and achievement of all children and particularly with the educational needs of populations that have been historically marginalised (Ainscow and Miles, 2008). In the case of children with disabilities, a plural approach may begin to address the specific marginalisation of children with disabilities.

3   Theorising Inclusion in the SDGs

The pluralisation of the right to education represents a recognition of what data from both the Education for All process and the MDGs tell us – that improvements in educational access have occurred over the past three decades, but that marginalised populations remain marginalised within these mass movements. SDG 4 – in addition to naming plural rights, goes as far as identifying 'inclusion' as a solution to marginalisation, requiring nation states to 'ensure inclusive and equitable quality education and promote lifelong learning opportunities for all' (UNGA, 2015b, p. 17). The discourse of inclusive education has shifted over the past 20 years in UNESCO. In 1994, the Salamanca Framework for Action called upon schools to 'accommodate all children regardless of their physical, intellectual, emotional, social, linguistic, or other conditions'. The focus on responsiveness toward children's 'conditions' has gradually evolved into a focus on the removal of organisational and pedagogical barriers. UNESCO's web resource on inclusive education at the time of the writing of this chapter 'promotes education systems that remove the barriers limiting the participation and achievement of all learners, respect diverse needs, abilities, and characteristics and that eliminate all forms of discrimination in the learning environment' (UNESCO, n.d.-a).

Therefore, 'inclusive education' in the 21st century can be defined by two characteristics. First, it focuses on plural rights (Mégret, 2008), meaning that the concept of 'all' is held in tension with the acknowledgement that particular populations need specific attention because of historic exclusion from the benefits of universal rights. Second, inclusive education is characterised by a focus on systemic barriers that deny opportunities for presence, participation, and achievement in schools. In the context of SDG 4, metadata reporting requirements demand the evaluation of the implementation of plural rights, but these requirements face current challenges related to unavailable data.

The concept of inclusive education as a barrier-reducing activity is a challenge because, by its nature, it will require redistribution of resources, new thinking about how schools and curricula are designed, and fundamental questions about *equity* (differential resourcing of education in order to redress historic inequalities). The redistributive and transformative potential of inclusion and inclusive education, however, are equally challenged by interpretations of what the word means and how far states parties are willing to redress barriers. Sustainable development scholars Gupta and Vegelin (2016) define inclusion in economic and social terms, citing inclusion as a goal that requires structural change in how people participate in development and how scholars evaluate its outcomes. Gupta and Vegelin define 'inclusion' as

> closing the income gap between the rich and poor, eliminating discriminatory laws and implementing social protection to enhance equality. This goes beyond social protection purely to prevent people from falling below the absolute poverty line. ... It tries to tackle structural inequality through changing decision-making processes, aid, investment, and trade agreements. (Gupta & Vegelin, 2016, p. 442)

Gupta and Vegelin characterise inclusion in three ways: social inclusion, focused on participation of all in the sphere of development (Meier, 2000; Thorbecke, 2006); ecological inclusiveness, which focuses on development of ecocentric norms (Chambers and Conway, 1991); and relational inclusiveness, which focuses on issues of power and structural inequalities (Harriss-White, 2006; Mosse, 2010). Conceptualisation of inclusiveness and relevant examples are provided in Table 4.1. Gupta and Vegelin (2016) noted that only SDG 11, which focuses on inclusive and sustainable cities, met the authors' criteria for supporting all three types of inclusiveness. SDG 4 addresses both social and relational inclusion in its aims. Although some experts in inclusive education also promote inclusive schools as agents of ecological commitment (e.g.,

TABLE 4.1   Social, ecological, and relational inclusion in SDGs

SDG goal	Social inclusion	Ecological inclusion	Relational inclusion
1	End poverty everywhere	Resilience to disasters	
2	End hunger/ malnutrition	Sustainable agriculture	
3	Enhance well-being		Tobacco convention
4	Inclusive education		Gender equality, Outcome data disaggregation
5	End inequality/sexes		
6	Universal access/water	Sustainable water mgmt.	
7	Universal access/energy	Sustainable energy	
8	Employment for all	Enhance resource efficiency	
9	Inclusive industrialisation	Sustainable industrialisation	
10	Reduce inequalities		Reduce inequalities
11	Inclusive cities	Sustainable cities	Urban rural interface
12		Sustainable consumption	Control privatisation
13		Combat climate change	Clim. Ch. Response[a]
14		Sustainable marine life[b]	Clim. Ch. Response[a]
15	Sustainable livelihoods	Sustainable ecosystems	
16	Inclusive institutions		Peaceful societies
17			Global partnership, Disaggregated data

a Clim. Ch. Response refers to responsibilities of developed nations to address climate change.
b Sustainable marine life refers to both marine life and marine resources.

SOURCE: ADAPTED FROM GUPTA AND VEGELIN (2016)

Booth and Ainscow, 2016), the following paragraphs will examine social and relational inclusion examples found in the SDGs.

In terms of inclusion in education, the SDGs contain both social inclusion discourse (focus on the opportunities for participation in existing systems) and relational discourse (demonstrated by the frequent use of the term 'equitable'). Espinoza (2008) noted that educational proclamations (such as EFA, MDGs, and SDGs) frequently address equality of opportunity, meaning that students should not be discriminated against in their entry to school, but that once permitted to attend school, little is done to ensure equality of process, outputs, or outcomes. Antidiscrimination language, such as that found in the MDGs, focused on equality of opportunity.

The SDGs call for equitable education in both SDG 4 and Target 4.1. The term is also used several times in the resolution supporting the Agenda for Sustainable Development (UNGA, 2015b). Ensuring that students from marginalised groups can achieve similar results to their nonmarginalised peers requires dimensions of equitable resourcing and, more importantly, process and systems changes related to how schooling is done (Slee, 2013). Such resourcing will likely mean unequal resourcing, in favour of marginalised groups, such as children with disabilities or other special education needs (Johnstone et al., 2018). Although there is no blueprint for how states parties should consider differential resourcing in order to create inclusive systems, the acknowledgement that particular educational advantages may need to be redressed in order to promote inclusion aligns with Gupta and Vegelin's understanding of 'relational' inclusion.

4   'Plural-Relational' Inclusive Education

Our reading of the SDGs indicates that the goals are decidedly 'plural-relational' in their approach to inclusive education. SDG 4 aims to 'ensure *inclusive* and equitable quality education and promote lifelong learning for all' (emphasis added). One might, then, argue that every target and indicator has an inclusive education focus. In a majority of indicators – six, according to our analysis – 'inclusive education' is indicated by identifying the specific rights of individuals more often than a broad aim of social inclusion for all. Language in targets and the metadata used to evaluate targets focus on identifying and addressing development gaps for particular populations who have been historically marginalised (Gupta & Vegelin, 2016). Table 4.2 draws upon Mégret's (2008) and Gupta and Vegelin's (2016) work to illustrate the difference between a plural-relational approach to inclusive education and one that could be characterised as universal-social models, which are often present in practice.

SDG 4 identifies pluralistic rights by naming girls, rural children, children from the bottom fifth wealth quintile in their countries, persons with disabilities, indigenous populations, conflict-affected children, students from

TABLE 4.2   Conceptualising inclusive education

	Universal-social	Plural-relational
Population focus	All	All, with particular focus on historically marginalised
Equity/equality focus	Equal opportunity	Equity in process
Evaluative data	Access	Outcomes

developing countries, least developed countries, small island developing states, and African states as pluralistic rights bearers. Further, the disaggregated metadata for targets, coupled with calls for 'equity' imply that differential outcomes may trigger differential approaches, including new approaches to participation and performance in inclusive classrooms (UIS, 2018b).

For students with disabilities, a plural-relational approach to inclusive education represents a departure from previous educational proclamations. For example, Peters (2007) noted that the 2007 EFA global monitoring report hardly mentions children with disabilities. Anastasiou and Keller (2014) noted that a 'politics of silence' exists in the EFA discourse on disability and the education of individuals with disabilities, meaning that students with disabilities remain nameless in international discourse and ostensibly outside of what policymakers frame as 'all'. Anastasiou and Keller's cross-national study on special education – defined as educational opportunities for students with disabilities across settings; inclusive settings, resource classrooms, special schools – highlights the shortcomings of EFA approaches and implicates transnational governmental organisations for failing to recognise the educational needs of students with disabilities. The authors emphasise the lack of focus on disability as hindering the achievement of universal primary education, meaning access for all to early childhood education, literacy, and gender equity.

Miles and Singal (2010) reinforce the above critiques by first reviewing the history of EFA and its tendency to neglect children with special education needs. They further demonstrate that a tension has historically existed between EFA and inclusive education as a result of the lack of focus of EFA on particular populations, particularly children with disabilities. Furthermore, Miles and Singal suggest that the absence of individuals with disabilities from the EFA discourse is a result of a 'residual' notion that individuals with disabilities are uneducable, demonstrated by the continued presence of services in the ministries of health or ministries of social services of many counties

(Miles & Singal, 2010, p. 2). Advancing from EFA, MDG 2 was the primary goal addressing education, stating:

> To ensure that, by the year 2015, children everywhere, boys and girls alike, will be able to complete a full course of primary schooling and that girls and boys will have equal access to all levels of education. (UN, 2000, p. 20)

EFA's original language, which specifically focussed on girls, provides an interesting model for further examining the rights of children with disabilities. EFA's specific mention of girls highlights a 'plural' right (Mégret, 2008), or a right that is population-specific because of historic inequalities. By naming girls, EFA noted that 'all' is intended to be every child, but that certain children need to be highlighted for the sake of unravelling legacies of exclusion. However, EFA and later MDG 2 stopped at the focus on gendered rights to education and missed an opportunity to outline further plural rights. Girls, for example, face cross-sectional exclusions that may include language, economic class, rural residence, and disability. Although in theory, focussing on every single child in the world, the de facto definition of 'all' throughout the EFA and MDG eras ended up meaning 'most'. With the exception of girls, both proclamations failed to recognise the interplay between universal rights for all children and specific plural rights that require discursive and policy focus. By focusing on the 'universal', specific focus on the marginalisation of persons with disabilities was almost entirely absent from the MDGs (Miles & Singal, 2010). Furthermore, the synthesis of the United Nations' 2006 Convention on the Rights of Persons with Disabilities (CRPD) and the MDGs was recognised quite late in the MDG agenda (UN, 2011).

The plural-relational approach to inclusive education, specifically for children with disabilities, represents a new approach to inclusive education by the parties who negotiated the SDGs. The shift acknowledges that 'all' is a contested term and that in some places, particular children are considered ineducable or incapable of success in the classroom. The plural-relational approach to inclusive education for children with disabilities identifies the value of inclusive education, while at the *same time* recognising that this population may have unique rights and that those rights may need to be addressed through a critical examination of power structures and exclusion. At this point, the language is in place for a 2030 agenda of plural-relational inclusion, but the pragmatics of how to achieve such inclusion are still very much undetermined. The following section examines practical challenges of the plural-relational approach to inclusive education.

5   Practical Challenges

Children with disabilities are more present than ever in international education goals, primarily through the SDGs' requirement of disaggregated participation and outcomes data. However, much of the data is not available at either
national or international levels. Similarly, definitions of disability vary and are
contested across societies. The Washington Group on Disability Statistics[1] has
made inroads on instrumentation, but measurement itself is an exercise in
global diversity (for an example, see Sprunt, Hoq et al., 2017). Cappa, Petrowski,
and Njelesani (2015) identified 716 instruments in 195 countries that are currently being used to evaluate children with disabilities. Data now are scattered,
in places non-existent, and differ in degree of focus on functional, academic,
and social outcomes (Cappa et al., 2015).

Plural rights and relational inclusion strategies also carry the risk of creating stigma, which has been a historic challenge for children with disabilities.
Use of the label 'disability' in order to develop programmes, services, and supports may create 'special' programmes that stifle educational opportunities
and contradict the premise of 'inclusive education' as articulated by CRPD and
UNICEF. Although plural-relational inclusion represents an important innovation to population recognition and infrastructure of inclusive education, labels
such as 'disability' may create prejudice or serve as a rationale for exclusion in
practice.

Finally, the process of identifying marginalised populations raises new questions about who is not named as a plural-rights bearer or potential beneficiary
of relational inclusion efforts. To this end, global initiatives such as the SDGs,
their targets, and the metadata used to evaluate progress must remain flexible
and in a state of constant renewal to ensure that inclusive development both
pursues the benefits of all and recognises the particular rights and equity needs
of those for whom traditional development approaches have not succeeded.

6   Case Studies

The plural-relational approach to inclusion found in the SDGs represents a
particular approach to inclusiveness that was negotiated by participants in the
framing of the 2030 agenda. The paragraphs above have presented the great
potential for equitable inclusion that may be possible through this approach.
The above sections also outlined challenges that are likely to emerge in practice. To provide context for both the opportunities and challenges presented in
the 2030 agenda in relation to inclusive education for children with disabilities,

we present two national case studies of Bhutan and Morocco in the pages that follow. These are sites for the ongoing research of Matthew Schuelka and Ghada Swadek, which is related to inclusive education and children with disabilities, respectively.

6.1   *Bhutan*

As a country in South Asia, nestled among the peaks of the Himalayas, Bhutan stands apart from its regional neighbours. As one of the last remaining independent 'Buddhist Kingdoms', Bhutan has been attempting to guide its development path through the Buddhist-inspired philosophy of Gross National Happiness (GNH). A rejection of economic growth 'at all costs', a GNH approach has guided Bhutan toward social and economic development at a cautious, careful, and sustainable pace, and to gradually embrace rights-based approaches to social institutions such as education. Bhutan is one of the few countries not only to reach its universal primary education and gender parity targets according to EFA, but to exceed them (UNESCO, 2015b).

Despite success in EFA access indicators, Bhutan continues to face serious challenges to the quality and inclusiveness of education. In his longitudinal and ethnographic study of inclusive education and disability in Bhutan, Schuelka (2013b, 2015, 2018) finds that sociocultural and institutional barriers in Bhutan prevent the kind of systems change necessary for quality inclusive education to flourish. The Bhutanese education system features a series of high-stakes examinations and a standardised curriculum that do not allow accommodation, modification, or differentiation. The sociocultural construction of schooling in Bhutan as an elite institution has led to the internationalisation by policymakers, school leaders, teachers, and, indeed, the students themselves, of the belief that only some children have the abilities needed to 'belong' in school (Schuelka, 2018). While Bhutan has initiated a progressive and rights-based approach to special education – the National Policy on Special Educational Needs – the policy is aspirational and does not address the everyday practices of teachers in facilitating an inclusive sense of belonging for all children in the classroom (Dorji & Schuelka, 2016).

The factors and indicators of the inclusion of children with disabilities – from gross enrolment to student-teacher ratios to achievement scores – only provide a two-dimensional understanding of the experience of inclusion. Just as Sprunt, Deppeler et al. (2017) argue in their study of Fiji, the SDG indicators advance a more complex way of understanding inclusion in schools, but more needs to be done with locally and contextually relevant indicators. None of the SDG indicators ask anything of the stakeholders themselves and only focus on things that can be numerically and summarily counted for the sake of global comparability.

Narrowing the understanding of inclusion by numerical indicators alone within the SDG is problematic, particularly in a country such as Bhutan. While Bhutan has made great strides in improving its gross enrolment primary education rate to 112% (Kingdom of Bhutan [KoB], MoE, 2015), it is the actual experience of the child in the classroom that makes education inclusive or exclusive. Schuelka (2018) found numerous instances of overcrowded Bhutanese classrooms where passive learning and nonparticipation were the norm (see also Kezang Sherab et al., 2015). Students with disabilities were 'there' physically, but their learning was not being supported in that the curriculum was static and the pedagogy was content-driven. Increased student attendance does not inherently lead to a higher-quality education, nor to better educational outcomes. In fact, increasing the number of students in the classroom has been found to have a detrimental effect on inclusion and educational quality for all students (UNESCO, 2015b). In Bhutan, this is certainly the case as more and more children have entered school, but the resources and teachers available have not sufficiently caught up to meet demand. Nearly 30% of students in Bhutan do not make it to grade 10, the end of basic education (KoB, MoE, 2015), which is perhaps a better indicator of inclusive education and demonstrates the limitations of access alone as an inclusion strategy. This is captured in the SDG 4 thematic indicators (4.1.1.c and 4.1.4), but only as an outcome and not necessarily as an indication of process and practice.

Disaggregating by disability – particularly as is the case with Indicator 4.5.1 – also comes with its own conceptual problems. Determining whether or not a child has a 'disability' is inherently embedded in sociocultural understandings of human difference and education as a social institution. Disability prevalence rates are notoriously erroneous and underreported (Groce & Mont, 2017), although there has been an international effort led by the Washington Group to collect better disability data (Altman, 2016). At the national level in Bhutan, disability statistics are not collected in a sophisticated way, with even the GNH Index asking simple binary questions such as 'Do you have any of the following serious conditions, impairments or disabilities?' (Centre for Bhutan Studies and GNH Research, 2016, p. 305). This is conceptually problematic not only in Bhutan but for the SDGs as a whole, as every country will have differences in how disability data is collected and in how disability as a concept is perceived by both individuals and society.

In Bhutanese schools, many children are not labelled as being 'disabled', per se, but are otherwise struggling to cope with the curriculum and meeting learning objectives. Instead of being given a disability diagnosis and support services, these children in Bhutan are often called 'lazy' or 'slow' and left to their own devices to either overcome their learning difficulties through 'hard work and perseverance' or to fail out of the school system (Schuelka, 2018). A statistic that disaggregates by 'disability' will not solve this sociocultural issue of labelling children as 'lazy failures'. We are *not* advocating for a significant increase in disability labelling to occur in Bhutan or elsewhere; rather, we are highlighting the point that inclusive education is a systems approach that should affect the educational quality for *all* students, regardless of whether or not the institution has 'labelled' them. This is the dilemma attached to a plural-relational approach to inclusion, as argued above.

While nearly all of the SDG 4 indicators focus on macro-level statistics – participation, access, number of years, financing, etc. – there was one indicator that tentatively explored the student experience in school: 4.a.2 – Percentage of students experiencing bullying, corporal punishment, harassment, violence, sexual discrimination, and abuse (UIS, 2018b). This indicator goes beyond simply acknowledging that students with disabilities are 'there' in the classroom and begins to look into the experiences of these students. In the case of Bhutan, 4.a.2 was an important indicator of the quality of inclusion for students with disabilities. Bullying, corporal punishment, harassment, violence, sexual discrimination, and abuse were all observed phenomena in Bhutan, despite official policies against them (Schuelka, 2015, 2018). However, it seems that Indicator 4.a.2 has recently changed, as the concepts were deemed too difficult to measure (Cornu & Liu, 2018). The focus of the indicator is now on 'school violence' and narrowed only to bullying because it was methodologically easier to collect this data via a survey. A disaggregation of bullying data by disability is also not suggested (Cornu and Liu, 2018). This is a missed opportunity and indicative of how a data-driven and quantitative-indicator approach to inclusion narrows our understanding to input and outcome; rather than ecological, social, and relational inclusion (Gupta & Vegelin, 2016).

While the Education 2030 Framework for Action supports country-level leadership in forming their own contextual indicators, the universalist message is still quite clear. In the Framework, UNESCO suggests, 'The targets of SDG4-Education 2030 are specific and measurable, and contribute directly to achieving the overarching goal. They spell out a global level of ambition that should encourage countries to strive for accelerated progress' (WEF, 2015, p. 35). The national context of Bhutan suggests that the macro-scale of indicators may be too large to capture how inclusion is actually enacted in schools. Thus, we suggest that inclusive education that is specific to students with disabilities in Bhutan may be evaluated by:

- amount of time students with and without additional learning support are together (disaggregated by curricular/noncurricular);
- ratio of trained teachers to students with additional learning support;
- amount of curricular time that students with additional learning support spend with teaching assistants and unpaid volunteers;
- curricular accommodation and modification available;
- percentage of students with additional learning support in the mainstream classroom; and
- number of students that transition to higher education or meaningful employment (disaggregated by disabled/nondisabled).

Of course, in suggesting this, there remains the conceptual issue of who is and is not a 'student with additional learning support' or in other words 'disabled'. The National Policy on Special Educational Needs (KoB, MoE, 2012, pp. 6–7) in Bhutan, which is still not settled legislation as of this writing, states:

A child has Special Educational Needs if he/she:

a   *Has a significant difficulty in performing any activity compared to the majority of children of the same age;*

b   *Has a barrier which prevents or hinders her/him from making use of educational facilities of a kind generally provided for children of the same age in school;*

c   *Is gifted;*

d   *Is of school going age and falls within the definition given in (a), (b) and (c).*

This is essentially a functional definition, similar to the one used by UNICEF (2012) in conducting their Bhutan disability prevalence study, which found a prevalence rate of 21% among children aged 2–9. As of now, officially there is no policy mechanism for determining whether or not a child in a Bhutanese classroom has a 'disability' as a catalyst to receiving additional or 'special' educational services. However, recent Bhutanese educational policy guidance advocates for an inclusive education for children with 'special educational needs' (KoB, MoE, 2018). We argue that this may be a blessing in disguise, as avoiding a medicalised or pathological approach to disability labelling can be more helpful in promoting a more dynamic, inclusive system where *any* student can move in and out of receiving additional learning support based on need, context, and situation. This assertion, however, challenges the 'universalist project of comparison and technical assistance ... to those who set themselves the task of producing statistics' (Ingstad & Whyte, 2007, p. 12).

The case of Bhutan demonstrates that a rights-based inclusive education agenda, as measured by SDG indicators, may not capture how systems need to change in order for them to be considered truly inclusive. The SDGs call for equal access for children with disabilities, but in Bhutan, little is known about how inclusiveness occurs in classrooms as a matter of pedagogical and curricular practice. At the same time that Bhutan is emphasising educational access and inclusion, it also maintains a rigid, competitive, and high-stakes educational system that actively excludes and segregates children with disabilities – explicitly labelled or not. Further indicators suggested in this section, along with qualitative means of gathering information, particularly surrounding the student *experience* of being included in education, are intended to enhance the capacity of SDG 4 to promote inclusive education.

6.2   *Morocco*

Morocco is a lower-middle-income country continuing a multisectoral reform agenda set forth at the ascension to the throne of King Mohammed VI (World Bank, 2018b; Kingdom of Morocco [KoM], High Commissioner for Planning, 2015; KoM, 2012). Despite progress on the reform agenda, a persistent need for addressing the most vulnerable and marginalised populations, including children with disabilities, exists (UNESCO, 2014c). In the education sector, high student attrition and low literacy rates are pushing Morocco to embrace equity- and quality-focused educational reforms to address these gaps (Ibourk, 2016; KoM, High Council for Education, Training, and Scientific Research [HCETSR], 2015; UNESCO, 2014c; USAID, 2013). SDG 4's focus on quality and inclusion parallels Morocco's current education needs. At the same time, a drive to produce graduates with marketable skills and the complexity of SDG 4's indicators have muddied the inclusion focus in Morocco (UIS, 2018e).

In order to address ongoing exclusionary practices, Morocco committed to the SDGs and their inclusive indicators. Morocco was one of the first countries to present a Voluntary National Review, which analysed current capacity to address the SDGs, to the High-Level Political Forum on Sustainable Development (HLPF), demonstrating its preliminary commitment to the goals (KoM, 2016). The discourse found in Morocco's Voluntary National Review repeats the notion of inclusion, stating, 'Public policies will focus on being ... more inclusive ... more equitable' (KoM, 2016, p. 7) and 'without exclusion' (KoM, 2016, p. 6). National and local implementation strategies also address inclusion, but mostly at the high-level policy, governance, or quantitative level (addressing the number of 'integration classrooms', teachers trained, assistant salaries paid) rather than addressing inclusive education quality (KoM, Ministry of National Education, Vocational Training, Scientific Research, and Higher Education [MNEVT], 2017a; KoM, MNEVT, Regional Academy for Education and Vocational Training, 2017; KoM, MNEVT, 2016a, 2016b).

Some limited quality indicators have been included in educational plans at the national and regional level (supervisor/teacher trainings on specialised techniques for specific disabilities, curriculum design guides), but it is unknown whether they will be effectively implemented and evaluated for inclusionary practices (KoM, National Human Rights Council, 2015; KoM, MNEVT, Directorate of Curriculum, 2017a; KoM MNEVT, Regional Academy for Education and Vocational Training, 2017). Moreover, Morocco's financial and human resource capacity limitations hinder prospects for effective evaluation, monitoring, and data collection (Committee on the Rights of Persons with Disabilities, UN Human Rights Council [CRPD, UNHRC], 2015; KoM, 2016; Moroccan Press Agency Ecology, 2017).

In Morocco, like other low- and lower-middle-income contexts, the obstacles related to the education of marginalised populations have multisectoral root causes, ranging from lack of infrastructure, no access to prenatal and general health care, rural underdevelopment, and lack of social service capacity for linguistically diverse individuals (UNESCO, 2014c, 2018b). A variety of remedies have therefore been put in place across various ministries, government agencies, civil society, and international aid agencies, resulting in inefficient efforts and bureaucratic obstacles for those seeking support (CRPD UNHRC, 2015; UNESCO, 2014c; UNICEF, 2015). Consequently, 5% of primary school-aged children remain out of school, a large proportion of whom are children with disabilities located in urban, rural, or isolated regions of the country (UNESCO, 2014c).

One potential outcome of SDG 4 for children with disabilities in Morocco is that it will translate to meeting the access goals of the MDGs, but not necessarily the realisation of the intended 'quality' inclusive education. This is partly because Morocco's MDG experience demonstrates gaps at both the system and school level in implementation, data collection, and disaggregation, as related to marginalised populations in general and children with disabilities in particular. These gaps in foundational infrastructure for education at the systems, data, and implementation levels endure (Technical Cooperation Group [TCG], 2017; UIS, 2018c, 2018f; CRPD UNHRC, 2015; UNESCO, 2014c, 2018b). Under SDG 4, targets and indicators require new and more complex methodologies and data collection than during the MDG era. This creates feasibility obstacles for a country like Morocco that struggled to compile complete data for the MDGs (TCG, 2017; UIS, 2018c, 2018e, 2018f; CRPD UNHRC, 2015; UNESCO, 2014c; Cornu & Liu, 2018). As a result, commitment to the SDGs may bring about improvements in access for diverse populations such as children with disabilities, but quality may still be out of reach.

The reality in Morocco is that access to schools continues to be a great obstacle for many children with disabilities, despite constitutional protections, legislation, regional initiatives, and memoranda requiring registration (Myers, Pinnock, & Suresh, 2017; UNESCO, 2014c, 2018b). Families often do not know or understand where to receive support, are unclear about their rights – especially regarding education – face bureaucratic obstacles to school registration, and often must be put on waiting lists for limited spaces in centre- and school-based education programmes (Human Rights Watch [HRW], 2015; RTI International, 2016; CRPD UNHRC, 2015). Parents report that their children are often denied needed accommodations or forced to pay for supports their children require (HRW, 2015; RTI International, 2016). Historical disengagement by the Ministry of Education from meeting the needs of children with disabilities has resulted in nongovernmental organisations (NGOs) providing most services (HRW, 2015; RTI International, 2016). This situation does not provide for equitable or quality educational opportunities to and through education for children with disabilities as called for by CRPD and SDG targets 4.1, 4.5, and Indicator 4.a.1 (d) (HRW, 2015; RTI International, 2016; UIS, 2018e).

In an effort to move forward on inclusive education, the MNEVT, UNICEF, Humanity and Inclusion (formerly Handicap International), and the regional education authority partnered to conduct an evaluation and pilot programme in the Souss-Massa-Daraa region. The evaluation and pilot study found that major issues existed at the governance level, hindered by a lack of coordination between service sectors. These issues resulted in bottlenecks to schooling access, quality programmes, and financial budgets. The bottlenecks led to obstacles at the school level such as: a lack of communication and collaboration between centres and schools; school access that depended on the availability of trained teachers; a lack of specialised staff (medical and social); a lack of trained teachers in inclusive and adapted methods; and a lack of disability-friendly facilities and school transportation (UNICEF, 2014, 2015, 2016). UNICEF's evaluation also noted that attitudinal obstacles came from parents of children with and without disabilities and from teachers (UNICEF, 2014, 2016). These obstacles are those that plural-relational inclusion models seek to overcome.

Despite these challenges, evaluation of the pilot programme indicated positive results and has been used as the basis for the current national upscale of interventions for improving inclusive education. Results of the programme included: enrolment rates of children with disabilities increased to above 31%; local governments earmarked funds for inclusive education (transportation to and from school); and improved coordination with health services. Furthermore, UNICEF's evaluation indicated that pedagogical changes were adopted and approved by the MNEVT to facilitate curricular accommodations for six categories of disabilities (UNICEF, 2014, 2016). The pilot programme achievements resulted in the Ministry of Education requiring inclusion inputs in national and local education plans and budgets, such as pedagogical training for teachers and individual student monitoring.

Additionally, in the spring of 2018, testing accommodations were put into practice on national end-of-year examinations for middle school certificates and high school graduation exams (KoM, MNEVT, 2018). And as of January 2019, The High Council for Education, Training, and Scientific Research conducted a conference on 'The Right to Inclusive Education: Conceptual Shift, Changes in Practice, and Evaluation Results', presenting the council's evaluation of the state of education for children with disabilities and its support for improving inclusive education (KoM, HCETSR, 2019). The following week, the Minister of Education formally met with NGOs working for the education of children with disabilities (KoM, MNEVT, 2019). This increased momentum could be indicative of a shift in the government's willingness to directly take responsibility for the education of children with disabilities within an inclusive framework.

The positive results referred to previously could potentially lead to improved engagement beyond the access aspect of SDG 4 toward a focus on quality. However, remnants of the MoE's past lack of responsibility for meaningful inclusion for children with disabilities continues to be evident through its publications. For example, the MNEVT Directorate of Curriculum, with the support of UNICEF, developed the *Reference Framework for Curriculum Design for the Benefit of Children with Disabilities* for six disability categories, which, at first glance, seem to address SDG 4.a.1 (d) (UNICEF, 2016; KoM, MNEVT Directorate of Curriculum, 2017b). Upon closer analysis, this reference document may actually create more barriers to access. The document limits curriculum accommodations to six categories of disabilities of 'mild to moderate degree' provided that a required medical report is submitted by families. Additionally, the *Reference Framework* reinforces the role of an initial medical committee review to 'advise' families on educational placement, which may be public school-based, public centre-based, or private school-based (KoM, MNEVT, Directorate of Curriculum, 2017b). Finally, although the guide is part of the reforms to transition from 'integration classrooms' (self-contained special education classrooms in public schools usually run by NGOs) to 'inclusion classrooms' for transition into general education, the three-year limit in the 'inclusion classrooms' to gain the necessary skills for general education may lead to student removal to more restrictive placements or student attrition (KoM, MNEVT Directorate of Curriculum, 2017b; RTI International, 2016). These aspects of the *Reference Framework* are exclusionary and demonstrate limitations to education not in the spirit of SDG 4.a.1 (d) due to a lack of prerequisite legal frameworks and education system safeguards for inclusive education as required by CRPD and recommended by Morocco's Human Rights Council (UN, 2006; KoM, NHR, 2015, p. 12).

Looking at these issues through another lens, both SDG 4 (4.4) and Moroccan educational policies demonstrate a tension between 'utilitarian' aspects of education (for students to be 'employable') and broader 'transformative' education (for the common social good or education for all) (Boutieri, 2016; Brissett & Mitter, 2017). Through this confusion on the aims of education, a marginalisation of those who face barriers in attaining employable skills, such as children with disabilities, may occur. In such cases, the inclusionary vision of the SDGs, particularly tied to SDG 4, with education viewed as the key to 'leaving no one behind', may be trumped by the notion of 'relevant skills' for a global 21st-century economy (Brissett & Mitter, 2017).

Finally, the realities of financing and the geopolitical consequences of conflicts in Africa and the Middle East and North Africa (MENA) region must be discussed in the analysis of the inclusive emphasis of SDG 4 within the Moroccan context. Morocco's National Review to the HLPF reported that 'the issue of financing for development was a major challenge for negotiations, during the process leading up to the 2030 Agenda for Development' (KoM, 2016, p. 10). Morocco's status as a lower-middle-income country with international loan debt, as well as dependence on development aid, positions it as insufficient to meet the SDG agenda (World Bank Group, 2018; Myers et al., 2017). This is especially true when looking at SDG 4's complexity and that the indicators 'require new methodologies, definitions and calculation methods, as well as considerable changes to national systems reporting data' (UIS, 2018e, p. 8), which Morocco has indicated it is too financially strapped to do (KoM, 2016). This renders the inclusive aspirations of SDG 4 potentially exclusive for implementation in low- or lower-middle-income contexts. Adding to these financial pressures, Morocco has hosted an increased number of refugees and migrants from the conflicts in the MENA and various African countries attempting to move to countries of the European Union, many of whom ultimately stay in Morocco. Refugees and migrants present other marginalised populations that must be educated in order to achieve SDG 4. These economic and political conditions must be addressed realistically in order for Morocco and other Global South countries to be 'included' in achieving the SDGs' mantra, 'leave no one behind'.

In conclusion, Morocco is a country in which a transition to inclusive education is emerging. However, Morocco first has to address the rights of those that were left behind during the MDG-era through a strategy that encompasses access, equity, and quality. As with other countries in the MENA, educational planning is based on quantitative data, such as the total number of integration classrooms, integration classrooms to be added per year, and schools upgraded for accessibility (Gaad, 2011; Hadidi & Al Khateeb, 2015). Little research has been conducted and few data are available on educational effectiveness, educational considerations, and inclusive considerations most relevant to SDG 4's intention to promote equitable and quality inclusive education. As recommended for Bhutan, indicators that examine qualitative school/classroom processes and student experiences may be more useful to achieving equity and quality. The ultimate challenge for Morocco, however, may be meeting the financial obligations necessary to achieve SDG 4, without marginalising the most marginalised by prioritising education aimed at narrow visions of employability and responsiveness to market demands.

6.3   *Summary of the Case Studies*

The two case studies illustrate policy and practice at the national level. National examples (which include data from the lived classroom experiences of children) are important for two reasons. They provide a vantage point that informs broad global agendas and valuable information on the 'grain size' of national policy interventions. For example, in both Bhutan and Morocco, there appears to be a general acceptance of the plural rights of children with disabilities. At least in policy, there is a general acknowledgement of the contextualised rights that children with disabilities bear beyond those covered in universal declarations.

In both countries, however, this has historically translated into special systems of education for children with disabilities. Recent attempts at inclusion appear to align with Gupta and Vegelin's understanding of 'social inclusion' – i.e., children with disabilities are present, but may not be experiencing quality education. Such quality requires policy commitments to equity and practices that are inclusive and that provide individualised support to those who need it most. Because these two activities have historically occurred in separate environments in Bhutan, Morocco, and most UN member states, the very localised practice of how to meet the 2030 agenda requires local innovations, targets, and solutions. As it stands now, outcome data on student learning is meant to hold member states accountable to their commitments but may not be enough to support local education professionals in creating cultures of inclusive education. To do this, localised qualitative and quantitative quality indicators are needed on the front lines of inclusive education. In time, such indicators may serve as complements to global disaggregated SDG metadata.

7 Conclusion

SDG 4 represents a new era for inclusion and inclusive education. Inclusiveness is now characterised as both an acknowledgement of the unique rights of particular populations, while upholding universal rights, and a commitment to equity in education, which requires rethinking how education has always been approached by member states. In general, SDG 4 continues what was started with the MDGs by examining the outputs between sexes as a function of inclusion. However, the SDG targets and evaluative metadata are now placing greater emphasis on accountability for marginalised populations through examination of disaggregated data than ever before. As time passes, such data can be used to better understand what equity commitments need to be made on a global scale to ensure quality inclusive education for populations like children with disabilities.

In practice, such requirements will face challenges. Data collection and analysis can be expensive, the understanding of disability itself is highly localised and unstandardised, and global accountability measures have yet to catch up with new requirements. For example, universal design approaches to assessment, testing accommodations, and modifications are either non-existent or in a nascent stage for global instruments and in member states. Further, while the metadata are helpful for tracking global trends, further elaboration on what a high-quality inclusive education experience means is needed – and can possibly be accomplished through more qualitative and locally relevant indicators.

Despite these challenges, the 2030 agenda is bold in relation to inclusive education for children with disabilities. In this chapter, we have characterised the approach as plural-relational, drawing upon the human rights work of Mégret (2008) and the framing of inclusion by Gupta and Vegelin (2016). As with any global agenda, a great deal of work remains to be done at the national level and in local schools. However, three fundamental philosophical lines have been drawn by SDG 4. First, that the education of all means that special consideration must be made for those who have not historically benefited from mass educational movements. Second, because of this, equity of educational experience (rather than equality of opportunity) needs to be the focus of policy and resourcing. Finally, SDG 4 (as well as CRPD and other previous proclamations) has stated that these commitments are best accomplished through inclusive education.

Note

1   www.washingtongroup-disability.com

CHAPTER 5

A Critical Exploration of How Language-of-Instruction Choices Affect Educational Equity

Lizzi O. Milligan, Zubeida Desai and Carol Benson

1   Introduction

In many parts of the world, children are forced to sink or swim in educational systems that rely on a single dominant language as the medium of instruction. Target 4.1 of the Sustainable Development Goals (SDGs) calls for all 193 signatory countries to 'ensure that all girls and boys complete free, equitable and quality primary and secondary education leading to relevant and effective learning outcomes' by 2030, and Target 4.5 extends that mandate to 'eliminate gender disparities in education and ensure equal access to all levels of education ... for the vulnerable, including persons with disabilities, indigenous peoples and children in vulnerable situations' (UNGA, 2015b). As professionals who have spent our careers promoting quality education, we find it unacceptable that there is no specific mention of language in those targets and its essential role in providing access to literacy and quality education. In this chapter, we draw on relevant literature and case studies from Cambodia, South Africa, and Rwanda to show that Targets 4.1 and 4.5 will not be met unless more emphasis is placed on the language(s) through which learners are taught. We will argue that language(s) of instruction are either central enablers or barriers to educational equity, since it is through these languages that a learner must gain access to initial and continuing literacy as well as learn to think critically and interact with teachers and peers around curricular content.

In policy discussions about language-in-education, and about education more broadly, there is often a tendency among those promoting equity to focus on institutional access. In his seminal paper on 'epistemological access', Morrow (1993) argues that there is no guarantee that epistemological access, that is, meaningful access to the knowledge, skills, and values that are the content of the curriculum, will take place in contexts where institutional access has been broadened to be more inclusive. We define educational equity as the normative process that enables equality of educational opportunities for such epistemological access. Implicit to this is an understanding that to achieve this in practice there is no 'one size fits all' solution; rather this will entail the use of different approaches to give learners such opportunities. Equity is thus a full realisation of rights, beyond mere access to education, to include the ways that learners experience education and the outcomes that they are able to achieve.

For educational equity to be addressed, as Benson (2016) has pointed out, at least three questions must be answered about language use in the classroom: First, is the learner taught and assessed in a language s/he understands and speaks well? Second, does instruction draw on the learner's prior experiences and resources to construct new knowledge? And third, are teachers proficient in the language(s) of instruction? These questions will guide our critical exploration of language-of-instruction choices and educational equity.

2   Language-of-Instruction and National Policymaking

Globally, there are millions of children who learn in a dominant language. For many, this is a language foreign to entire populations, as is the case of Portuguese for most Mozambicans, French for most Malians, or Standard Arabic for most Moroccans. In these and other countries, there are significant portions of national populations that lack access to the dominant language, e.g., indigenous people in Cambodia for whom Khmer is a new language. The issue often goes deeper than language to include undervaluing and outright discrimination against learners whose ethnic, cultural, or economic backgrounds differ from the dominant 'norm'. In recent years, the use of English as a medium of instruction (EMI) has grown significantly in many parts of the world, driven by an assumed relationship between proficiency in a 'global' language and economic development (Casale & Posel, 2011; Dearden, 2014). Comparable drives for other dominant languages continue in parallel, revealing a second assumed relationship – that between using a language as medium of instruction and actually learning that language. This latter assumption is difficult to prove true given the large repetition, failure, and drop-out rates in systems using a foreign language of instruction, as will be discussed later. The problem is grave. A recent policy paper written for the British Council reinforces an evidence-based principle, adopted by major donors and education partners in Juba in 2012, stating that 'introducing EMI at primary level in low- or middle-income countries [for whom English is not a mother tongue] is not a policy decision or practice that should be supported' (Simpson, 2017, p. 11). The same could and should be said for Portuguese, French, and other exogenous languages still widely used in education in postcolonial countries, as well as dominant languages that are foreign to large groups of learners.

Decades of research demonstrate that the use of a dominant language as the medium of instruction negatively affects learners' ability to both learn that language and access the wider curriculum (e.g., Mohanty, 2009; Nomlomo, 2009; Brock-Utne, 2010; Heugh, 2009; Desai, 2013). The results are strikingly similar: limited access to schooling; high repetition, failure, and dropout rates; poor quality of education; and low learner self-esteem – all of which are well documented (e.g., Ball, 2010). While acknowledging that the language factor does not stand alone, Walter (2008) has found a distributional relationship between learners' access to education in their first language (L1) and level of national development, demonstrating that countries that do not provide access to L1 education experience the lowest levels of literacy and educational attainment worldwide. This evidence runs concurrent with recognition of a so-called 'learning crisis' (UNESCO, 2014f), with figures from 2014 suggesting that at least 250 million children do not have access to basic numeracy and literacy skills in any language, even by the end of grade 4 (UNESCO, 2014f). For example, the most recent Progress in International Reading Literacy Study (PIRLS) results indicate that around 78% of grade 4 learners in South Africa do not have basic reading skills by the end of the school year (Howie et al., 2017, p. 11).

Thus far we have tended to focus on the role of language in facilitating or obstructing learning. But language is also a marker of identity and as such can play an important role in influencing one's self-esteem and confidence, depending on the language(s) with which one identifies. There are resources that teachers can use in the classroom to help learners and students make the connection between their language, their identity, and their learning, and to see their language as a communicative resource. In an interesting chapter on using a multiliteracies pedagogical approach to developing texts, Cummins (2006) explores the use of multimedia to help pupils in a school in Canada to develop what he refers to as 'identity texts'. By encouraging learners to invest in their identities, they are able to develop bilingual resources. It is important that young people are proud of their identities so that learning moves seamlessly from the familiar to the less familiar.[1]

Underpinning policy assumptions about the merits of EMI is a polarisation of debates between equity and efficiency. Equity (as well as equality) has often been equated with redress and human rights, while efficiency signals economic development. The argument made is that the use of local languages 'ghettoises' learners and prevents them from being successful in an increasingly global world. The solution posited is the use of a dominant language as the medium of instruction because it will open doors for learners. Post-Apartheid South Africa is a clear example of this approach (Desai, 2000; South Africa, NECC,

1993). This line of thinking can be robustly challenged since using a dominant language as the medium of instruction has been shown in that case to be a clear obstacle to equity.

Learning in a dominant language affects the educational opportunities available to learners, particularly learners from disadvantaged backgrounds. Numerous studies have shown the negative impact on girls (Hovens, 2002; Benson, 2005) and children from lower socioeconomic groups (Fleisch, 2008; Smith, 2011), poor urban areas and remote rural areas (Benson & Wong, 2017; Evans & Cleghorn, 2012; Milligan, Clegg, & Tikly, 2016), nondominant groups (Benson & Wong, 2017), and conflict-affected areas (Dryden-Peterson, 2015). It is important to note that with increased globalisation and the movement of people, the mismatch between learners' own languages and the medium of instruction is by no means just a 'developing country problem'. Even in high-income countries, the use of a single language of instruction is problematic because it exacerbates differences between people from dominant and non-dominant social groups. However, evidence suggests that it is particularly problematic in low-income and postcolonial contexts where there is greater fracture between local and official (and usually ex-colonial) languages (Milligan & Tikly, 2016), and where the negative effects are compounded by health and safety issues, particularly for girls, as well as low levels of teacher education, content-heavy and inappropriate curricula, and lack of adequate school facilities (Benson, 2016).

Given this scenario of low educational outcomes among learners taught through an unfamiliar language, why is mother tongue–based multilingual education (or MLE) treated like such a 'hot potato' by national policymakers? The answer lies in the fact that medium-of-instruction issues are seldom resolved on pedagogical grounds, but rather on political, economic, or cultural ones. In the NEPI Report[2] on language in South Africa, the authors describe what they call 'common-sense assumptions' (South Africa, NECC, 1992). Politically, the assumption would be that a multilingual country needs a single unifying language; economically, it would be that using multiple languages is too costly; and culturally, it would be that using diverse languages could cause ethnic rivalry. All of these could be seen as representing a monolingual habitus (Gogolin, 2009), also known as a monoglossic ideology (García, 2009), meaning that people assume it is necessary to choose one single language, even though it is contrary to the nature of multilingual societies.

Each of these assumptions has been effectively challenged. On the political front, one can argue, as Bamgbose (1991) did long ago, that in a multilingual context, those citizens proficient in two (or more) languages are more integrated than those proficient in a single language, even if that language happens to be the dominant or official language. Indeed, recent research shows that jobs increasingly call for multiple language skills (Duchêne and Heller, 2012). It has been claimed that multilingualism is the true lingua franca of a globalised world (Prah & Brock-Utne, 2009; see also Benson & Elorza, 2015). The arguments on the economic front assume that a choice must be made between acquiring either a local language or a language of national or international communication. There is no disputing that in a country like South Africa, there is a need for a language like English for people to be able to interact with wider levels of society, particularly the outside world. But it is problematic to make the possibility of such interaction the basis of language-in-education policies for speakers of African languages who might never have the opportunity to go beyond their local village or township if they are denied meaningful access to education. As far as cultural arguments go, it is not only language that divides people. There are many other factors such as class inequalities, distribution of resources, and power relations that lead to rivalry between groups in a country. May takes up this point in the context of New Zealand when he defends Maori-medium education against the accusation that it is separatist and a 'retrenchment in the past' (May, 2004, p. 34). In his view, Maori-medium education is simply making available to Maori children choices that are taken for granted by majority language speakers. Despite these persuasive arguments, we continue to see dominant languages used as media of instruction in the majority of countries in the Global South, especially in the later years of primary and secondary schooling.

3   The Role of Language(s) of Instruction in SDG 4

Considering the significant evidence base presented in the previous section, it may be surprising that a review of key policy documents related to SDG 4 reveals that there is very limited attention paid to the language of instruction. In a key UNESCO publication about the SDGs entitled *Sustainable Development Begins with Education*, there is only one mention of language in a section entitled 'Education Is Essential for the Justice System to Function', which discusses how, in the case of Sierra Leone, 'many people with little education cannot use the formal court system because it operates in English ... [and] some people only speak local languages' (UNESCO, 2014e, p. 14). This is all the more disturbing because Sierra Leonean adults are typically multilingual in indigenous languages and Krio, a widely spoken lingua franca (Simons & Fennig, 2017). In the Incheon Declaration and Education 2030 Framework for Action (WEF, 2015), we see slightly more attention paid to language: it is mentioned a total of 12 times. While it is positive to see language primarily discussed in this document in relation to learners' home languages, the discussion of language is too narrowly focused on both the early years and institutional access. Language is only mentioned once in relation to learning:

> Particular attention should be paid to the role of learners' first language in becoming literate and in learning. Literacy programmes and methodologies should respond to the needs and contexts of learners, including through the provision of context-related bilingual and intercultural literacy programmes. (WEF, 2015, p. 20)

As noted in the previous section, the language issue is often seen as a deeply political and potentially contentious issue and one that often is determined primarily away from the sphere of education. This political dimension may, at least partially, explain the hesitancy with which language-related recommendations are made, as is evident in comments such as the following: Teaching and learning in the home language 'should be encouraged ... where possible' and while 'taking into account different national and subnational realities' (WEF, 2015, p. 13). No mention is made of the language of instruction for secondary education, even though Target 4.1 obliges countries to treat primary and secondary education as equally important in terms of free and compulsory access.

The failure to mention language has been addressed by professionals in the field, such as Benson (2016) and Kosonen (2017), whose background papers for the UNESCO Global Education Monitoring Reports point out language-related omissions and suggest how relevant language-related data should be collected and used to monitor educational quality. Thus far they remain suggestions, hidden in a single optional indicator in a UIS metadata document (UIS, 2018b). This single indicator (4.5.2; see Appendix 2) refers to 'the percentage of students in primary education whose first or home language is the language of instruction'. Despite the much greater emphasis on learning outcomes and a wider conceptualisation of basic education in SDG 4 more broadly, here we see language relegated to a single indicator narrowly focused on primary education and its availability, despite the intense efforts of many professional educators' negotiations.

Language is, thus, not currently recognised as an equity issue. Firstly, the focus on availability of a home language as language of instruction suggests simply equal provision. This reflects similar concerns voiced by Milligan (2014), among others, about the misguided use of gender parity measures as indicative of gender equity in the MDG era. In the same way that gender parity only reflects quantitative measures and does not address the root sociocultural gendered norms, a focus on home language availability does not allow for a more complex understanding of the ways that language of instruction can enable or disable equal opportunities to learn and so an equitable educational system. Secondly, a focus on the proportion of learners learning in a home language leads us to consider the groups of children who may not be included in that proportion. This may mean that the most marginalised become more marginalised, particularly those who do not speak the majority home language, such as refugees in an urban setting. Finally, it seems that, as with national policies, language is not seen as a key pedagogical issue. Overall, there is further need for learners to see themselves reflected in the curriculum as well as teaching and learning materials. The following sections argue for the importance of seeing language as a central factor in inclusive and equitable learning.

4   Lessons for Policy and Practice

Through exploration of recent research in South Africa, Rwanda, and Cambodia, this section of the chapter focuses on the key challenges to the achievement of SDG 4 and lessons that can be learned that will facilitate more equitable learning throughout the basic education cycle. Given the highly political nature of the language-of-instruction debate, we focus on both policy and practice. One of Desai's (2000) arguments countering objections to mother tongue–based multilingual education is that languages develop through use, and the more we use local languages, the more they will develop, thereby facilitating learning for young children. It is in this spirit that we proceed with our arguments for a multilingual approach to education and follow the argument put forward by the Asia-Pacific Multilingual Education Working group:

> We live in a multilingual world. ... Yet, most education systems ignore this multilingual reality. Equitable quality education and lifelong learning for all is only possible where education responds to and reflects the multilingual nature of the society. (Wisbey, 2016, p. 2)

In the three multilingual cases described here, there is some recognition of the potential for MLE to address equity issues. Each case provides a particular set of lessons – both positive and negative – with implications for other contexts.

4.1   *South Africa*
In terms of policy, South Africa would appear to be well ahead of other countries in recognising its multilingual realities. South Africa's language policy of

11 official languages (RSA, 1996) has been internationally acclaimed as progressive, liberal, and unique (see Adams, 1999; Deumert, Inder, & Maitra, 2005). Yet, a closer examination of language policy in practice reveals that African languages continue to be used in limited domains (Deumert et al., 2005; Mazrui & Mazrui, 1998). Nowhere is this more apparent than in education. The South African Department of Education's Language in Education Policy Document of July 1997 proclaims that schools, through their governing bodies, can choose any of the official languages as the language of learning and teaching, within the bounds of practicability. Despite such a wide choice, the reality is that most schools in African townships continue to use English as the sole medium of instruction after grade 3, particularly with regard to assessment practices (Desai, 2013; Murray, 2002; Vinjevold, 1999; Ziegler, 2013).

Despite the July 1997 policy document (RSA, DoE, 1997)[3] providing a fairly progressive framework for developing language in education policy, supposedly allowing parents (and learners) the right to choose the medium of instruction, the majority of African primary school learners find themselves at a disadvantage. Since there is no infrastructure in terms of teacher training or materials development to back parental decisions, choice becomes rather meaningless in practice. The picture that continues to emerge from schools is bleak – most learners have difficulty coping with the demands of using English as a medium in primary schools (Desai, 1999; Langenhoven, 2010; Nomlomo, 2008, 2009). Such difficulties are usually carried into high school and tertiary institutions. Even those learners who display a level of proficiency in English at what Cummins (1980, p. 175) calls the 'basic interpersonal communication skills' level, have difficulty with reading and writing tasks. Generally, the learning experience is a frustrating one for both learners and teachers. Despite this clear disjuncture between policy and practice, government officials can be overly eager to see quick results and not prepared to invest in long-term plans to address the many aspects of extending mother tongue instruction beyond the initial years. The only curriculum change has been that English is now introduced as a subject in grade 1 at schools catering to speakers of African languages (RSA, DBE, 2010a).

In light of these pedagogical concerns, the Language of Instruction in Tanzania and South Africa (LOITASA) Project – a longitudinal study spreading over three years (grades 4–6) and involving two primary schools in urban townships in the Western Cape – was undertaken. At each school, one class constituted the experimental group and the other a control group. The experimental group was taught science and geography (mathematics replaced geography in the second phase) in Xhosa while the control group was taught these subjects in English (see Brock-Utne, Desai, and Qorro, 2003, 2004, 2005, 2006; Brock-Utne, Desai, Qorro, & Pitman, 2010; Desai, Qorro, & Brock-Utne, 2010, 2013; Qorro,

Desai, & Brock-Utne, 2008, 2012, for more details on the research design and findings of the LOITASA Project). The project aimed to find out whether this switch to the mother tongue would be in the best interests of the learners for the acquisition of knowledge in science and geography (later mathematics) and development of English acquisition. Nomlomo (2008, p. 88) outlines the findings in relation to science learning as follows:

> Learners developed high self-esteem and better confidence as they participated in classroom activities in their own language. They were spontaneous in responding to teachers' questions and they could express themselves clearly in their mother tongue (isiXhosa). Their written work made more sense than their counterparts who were taught through the medium of English. They could elaborate on issues, making use of complex sentences, which showed originality and better understanding of Science concepts.

The positive impact was also seen in learning outcomes, with learners in the isiXhosa-medium class consistently outperforming their counterparts who were taught in English. For example, the pass rate in science in grade 5 for the isiXhosa class ranged from 70 to 86% (Nomlomo, 2009). This supports the work of Langenhoven, also in South Africa, who has shown that 'when pupils use their mother tongue to read and talk about a topic, they construct meaning, making sense of their world and thus generating a better understanding of scientific concepts instead of memorizing scientific facts' (Langenhoven, 2010, p. 135).

Despite these important gains made by the project, as captured in the LOITASA edited volumes (Brock-Utne et al., 2003, 2010), Desai has also reflected on the wider challenges that are presented by the South African educational context, showing that learning in both the control and experimental groups was characterised by a teacher-centred approach, with children spending most of their time listening or producing choral responses:

> Mother tongue education is a necessary but not a sufficient condition to remedy such teacher-centred approaches in the classroom, particularly in subjects such as Natural Science where it is expected that pupils' natural curiosity and higher-order thinking are to be encouraged. An intimacy with subject knowledge on the part of the teachers is needed to develop a confidence and boldness in teachers which, in turn, could lead to greater pupil involvement in learning. (Desai, 2010, p. 210)

This is a point also taken up by Cummins (2009, p. 20) when he states that 'bilingual education ... is not by itself a panacea for underachievement'. This does not mean that mother tongue–based education should not be promoted. One needs to bear in mind that the one variable that remains constant in educational research is the correlation between socioeconomic status (SES) and academic achievement. This point has recently been corroborated by the PIRLS 2016 Report on International Results in Reading. It states that, on average, students' higher reading achievement was linked to their attending schools:

- With more affluent than economically disadvantaged students
- Where a higher proportion of their peers had early reading and writing skills when entering first grade
- Where instruction was not affected by reading resource shortages. (Mullis et al., 2017, p. x)

According to PIRLS analyses, language of instruction remains an important factor and clearly furthers disadvantage. However, the issues are multifaceted, and language of instruction is not sufficient in and of itself to turn around poor academic achievement in resource-constrained poor areas.

There are a number of other clear findings from the LOITASA study. First, the tension between promoting a language of wider communication like English and local languages like isiXhosa is a tension present in many other contexts and countries. The LOITASA Project provides clear evidence of learners' competence in English not suffering as a result of extending the use of local languages as media of instruction. Second, the importance of involving local communities in supporting their children's education is a crucial factor in the project. Such parental and community support is more possible if local languages are used in education. Third, the LOITASA Project emphasises the importance of teacher training in realising the use of local languages as media of instruction. Fourth, the development of terminology in local languages was necessary. Fifth, materials had to be developed in local languages for these languages to be used as academic languages. And finally, negative attitudes toward local languages as media of instruction had to be consciously counteracted. We are aware that the LOITASA Project is not the only one looking at the role of language in learning subjects like mathematics. Phakeng has written extensively about mathematics education and language diversity (see, for example, Phakeng, 2016; Phakeng and Moschkovich, 2013). She consistently argues for a multilingual approach in teaching mathematics, so that learners can draw on their full linguistic repertoires when grappling with mathematical concepts.

4.2   *Rwanda*

While the current Rwandan policy appears to be taking a giant step away from equity in its promotion of English-medium instruction, recent research offers promising lessons for the improvement of both the quality and equity of classroom practice. In 2008, English became the medium of instruction across all levels of the Rwandan education system (Rosendal, 2011). This was modified in 2011 so that the first three years of primary schooling reverted to learning in Kinyarwanda with English a compulsory subject. While this has many similarities with language-in-education policies across East Africa and farther afield, it is remarkable in its break from the ex-colonial language and the political decision to rebrand Rwanda as an English-speaking nation (Samuelson & Freedman, 2010). While there has been attention paid to the policy shift in the academic literature (Samuelson & Freedman, 2010; Assan & Walker, 2012), much of this has focused on the political and economic rationale and implications. There has been surprisingly little written about its impact on teaching and learning opportunities in classrooms across the country.

The Improving Learner Outcomes through Language Supportive Textbooks and Pedagogy project was designed to contribute to the understanding of this impact and explore ways to support both teachers and learners toward meaningful learning opportunities when children learn in English. The focus was on learners in primary grade 4, the year when children switch to EMI learning. The project was developed from the understanding that there remain policy imperatives for many low-income countries to promote EMI, and that it is important to identify the challenges and suggest ways to enable inclusive learning in English so that children learning within these policy demands are not disadvantaged. The baseline findings, both in learner language tests and classroom observations, clearly demonstrated that learners do not have the level of English required for epistemological access to the wider curriculum (Milligan et al., 2014). Furthermore, most of the teachers observed were not proficient in the language of instruction.

Learners in these classrooms were given language-supportive textbooks, which were designed to be accessible and to develop their English. Teachers were trained in language-supportive pedagogy. Central to this is the use of the materials and associated activities to support learners to understand new concepts, in say, mathematics. Sanctioned use of Kinyarwanda was encouraged through set spoken activities and glossaries in the textbooks. This was to support learners' access to new topics, as spoken activities were designed to facilitate initial understanding and the glossary provided key vocabulary. Interviewed during the Improving Learner Outcomes through Language Supportive

Textbooks and Pedagogy project, learners spoke passionately about the difference it made to have materials that allowed the use of Kinyarwanda:

> The former books had difficult English and there were no meanings in Kinyarwanda and this made it difficult for us in rural areas to understand. But these books are easy to read and understand because they have new words explained in Kinyarwanda. This helped us increase our knowledge. (Unpublished project metadata)

This statement is particularly interesting as it highlights the potential for language-supportive textbooks to enable greater epistemological access to the wider curriculum for all children.

The study's evaluation suggests that a language-supportive approach had a significant impact both on learner outcomes and their levels of participation in the classroom (Milligan, Clegg, & Tikly, 2016). More positive test scores were witnessed across the learner groups, including those that had very low English proficiency in the pretests. Classroom observation data showed that all learners regularly engaged in speaking, writing, and reading activities, supported by both their access to their own textbook and the promotion of more activities in each lesson. Pedagogical practice witnessed in classroom observations was very different by the end of the intervention compared to that observed during the baseline study, with significantly more participation.

There are two clear findings from this study. First, it again highlights the way that language is inextricably linked with pedagogic choices in the classroom. As a Kigali teacher cited in the 2014 Education for All Global Monitoring Report eloquently explains:

> There remains no doubt that the main barrier to basic education is the forced use of English as medium of instruction. ... [It] not only impedes learning for the children, but is also a major challenge for Rwanda's teachers. Without adequate knowledge in English, teachers are unable to interact with the students, and the result is a strict chalk-and-talk structure. (UNESCO, 2014f, p. 297)

As discussed by Stephanie Bengtsson, Mamusu Kamanda, Joanne Ailwood, and Bilal Barakat in Chapter 10, and Yusuf Sayed and Kate Moriarty in Chapter 9, teacher confidence and capabilities are essential to the achievement of quality education in SDG 4. Insights from teachers from the Rwanda study clearly show the ways that teaching in a language in which they are not proficient impacts the pedagogic choices they make, which, in turn, leads to less participatory and inclusive teaching methodologies. This echoes findings from a British Council project, funded under the same Innovation for Education fund, where teachers were supported to improve their English proficiency in recognition of the limitations that their lack of English fluency placed on teaching quality (Simpson, 2013).

Second, the findings show that the debate over language of instruction does not need to conclude with an either-or decision. There are ways that classrooms can be more inclusive even when learning is happening in English, but this rests on rejection of the misguided notion that English-medium classrooms must mean complete immersion in the language of English. To develop the understanding of key concepts, children need to be able to speak, write, and read, and this can be supported by the use of Kinyarwanda, even if the education authorities insist on a policy of English as medium of instruction.

4.3   *Cambodia*

Even if the contexts are not postcolonial, Southeast Asian countries like Cambodia are also multilingual due to the presence of diverse indigenous and immigrant groups. Recently, Cambodia in particular has taken great strides toward improving access and equity in education for indigenous people through implementation of L1-based multilingual education (MLE), providing encouraging lessons for both policy and practice. The dominant language, Khmer, is spoken by the majority of the population and is the constitutionally mandated medium of instruction (Kosonen, 2013). This has long excluded speakers of an estimated 24 indigenous and other nondominant languages from accessing formal education (Simons & Fennig, 2017; CARE, 2010). In 2002–2003, working in one of the five highland provinces in the northeast where speakers of nondominant languages constitute the numerical majority, CARE International initiated a community-based schools programme of L1-based MLE as part of a larger intervention on behalf of indigenous girls and women. Working closely with provincial and national education officials and with partners such as UNICEF and the NGO International Cooperation Cambodia (ICC),[4] CARE developed a model whereby community school management committees were organised and empowered to establish their own schools. Rather than merely constructing schools, these committees made a wide range of decisions about how the schools would function, including which community members should be trained as bilingual teachers, recognising that there were few if any qualified teachers in the government system with proficiency in indigenous languages.

Beginning in two languages, Tampuen and Kreung, in six schools in the province of Ratanakiri, the programme has expanded over time to additional languages and schools in Ratanakiri and the other four highland provinces. The Ministry of Education, Youth, and Sport (MoEYS) has been integrally involved in the implementation and expansion of MLE, approving a series of legal documents and policy statements institutionalising the approach. In the 15 years since the first MLE community schools opened, five nondominant languages – Brao, Bunong, Kavet, Kreung, and Tampuen – are being used for literacy and instruction, and two others – Jarai and Kuy – are in the process of being adopted (Benson & Wong, 2017). Community teachers have been granted semiprofessional (contract) or professional (state teacher) status based on established criteria, and qualified teachers who speak Indigenous languages have been trained as bilingual teachers, expanding the number of MLE programs serving indigenous learners. Over 4,000 indigenous children were attending MLE classes in 2015 (Nowaczyk, 2015). By 2017, MLE under MoEYS had expanded to over 55 preschools and 80 primary schools throughout the five highland provinces (Benson & Wong, 2017).

Overwhelmingly positive results have been reported qualitatively in terms of parent and community satisfaction with how students are learning and teachers are teaching (e.g., Benson, 2011). A longitudinal study of learner achievement showed that MLE learners performed better in mathematics than non-MLE learners, and that there were no significant differences between MLE and non-MLE learners in L2 Khmer (Lee, Watt, & Frawley, 2015). Moreover, in northeastern Cambodia as in other contexts, it is likely that additional advantages accrue because MLE students maintain their home languages, identities, and connection to family and community, all of which are known to build learner self-esteem and facilitate learning (Ball, 2010). Assessments of L1 writing demonstrate clear advantages to MLE learners with regard to literacy skills and self-expression (Benson & Wong, 2017).

As mentioned above, the Cambodian national government has supported MLE in policy as well as practice, most recently with a 2013 *prakas* (sub-decree) and a 2015 action plan for education. The *Prakas on the Identification of Languages for Khmer* [Cambodian] *National Learners Who Are Indigenous People* (KoC, MoEYS, 2013) frees indigenous learners from the stipulation in the 2007 Education Law that Khmer be the sole language of instruction. This legal opening allows for consistency in implementing the Multilingual Education

National Action Plan (MENAP), covering the period of 2015 to 2018 (KoC, MoEYS, 2015). This plan describes a series of aims to:
- provide access to quality and relevant education for indigenous learners;
- build capacity of national and subnational education officials to manage and monitor MLE implementation;
- scale up MLE provision in the five designated provinces; and
- promote demand for quality MLE among school management committees, parents, and local authorities.

The plan also spells out a series of implementation steps, including capacity building for trainers and teachers, development of teaching and learning materials, expansion of MLE to new schools and languages, and conversion of all community schools to state schools (Benson & Wong, 2017). The MENAP along with prior documents effectively gives educational implementers in the five highland provinces the authority to expand MLE to indigenous learners.

Despite these advances, challenges remain. The most urgent may be the act that the original bilingual model adopted and enshrined in policy allows for L1 use only through grade 3, with a transition to Khmer-medium instruction by grade 4. While the policy also calls for upper primary teachers to be equipped to offer L1 support (Nowaczyk, 2015), the reality is that most trained MLE teachers are needed for placement in grades 1 through 3. There have been efforts to gain MoEYS approval for piloting a six-year MLE model that would be more theoretically sound and would potentially lead to more robust student outcomes, but thus far authorities are reluctant (Benson and Wong, 2017). Another challenge that has yet to be resolved is how to streamline government approval of orthographies for languages beyond the original five, since the additional two mentioned above have been languishing in the system for years, making it impossible to submit other languages or to move ahead with teaching and learning in those languages.

Other challenges have grown out of the very thing that makes the Cambodian case special, that is, that the government has taken ownership of important aspects of policy and implementation of MLE as developed and practised through a grassroots, community-centred programme. In the process of institutionalising MLE, and as all community schools have been converted to government schools, some of the more community-friendly aspects are falling away. One of those aspects was an alternative school calendar that conformed to the agricultural seasons when learners would be needed by their families, thus improving attendance. MLE expansion has apparently made this unworkable due to national reporting of final grades on one date for all learners in the country. Another is the conversion of the community school management committees, which were created to support MLE, into school support committees (like parent-teacher associations) like those non-MLE schools have; it is not clear if this change is in name only or if it involves loss of decision-making power for community members. Another aspect that is currently threatened is the specific teacher training done through each L1 (Personal communication with CARE staff, June 2017), which is rendered impossible due to the government's requirement of using nationally certified trainers instead of CARE-trained MLE specialists who are indigenous but not certified. Regarding this latter issue, there is reason to be hopeful for a return to effective L1-based training practices, since indigenous teachers are rapidly gaining access to higher levels of training and certification.

5   Discussion

Across the three country discussions, there are some clear wider lessons for the implementation of SDG 4. The first is that language of instruction is central to learning. Across the studies, findings show that learners achieve better outcomes when they are learning through MLE or at least through an L1-supported approach. For example, in science and mathematics, all three countries have seen significantly better results when learners' languages are part of instruction. This is consistent with findings in low-income contexts such as Cameroon (Laitin, Ramachandran, & Walter, 2016), Ethiopia (Heugh et al., 2012), and the Philippines (Walter & Dekker, 2011), and suggests that the learning of mathematics and science is facilitated by full or partial L1 instruction. Our case studies also offer clear evidence that learners are more engaged and participatory in classrooms when they understand what is going on – a fact which seems blatantly obvious, yet often eludes stakeholders and policymakers due to their histories and ideologies. While a shift to MLE should not be viewed as a panacea, for the millions of children learning in multilingual contexts, there is enough evidence to suggest that implementing MLE provides a significant step forward, not only toward more meaningful learning but also toward equitable education for all.

If we assume that meaningful learning can only take place when there is meaningful teaching, it is clear that language of instruction policy choices also have a significant impact on teacher confidence and pedagogic choices. Equitable access to materials in learners' (and teachers') own languages can also support meaningful learning. Multilingual materials have been shown to be a key resource for children's epistemological access in Rwanda. This is also being increasingly recognised in South Africa, where the Pan South African Language Board, the lexicography units for the official languages, and the

Department of Basic Education have embarked on a bilingual picture diction-
ary project for each of the nine official indigenous languages for children up
to grade 3. It is hoped that children will use the dictionaries to build on their
knowledge, but also acquire vocabulary in English (Langa, 2017). In Cambodia,
MLE classes in grades 1 through 3 have access to textbooks, which are based on
the national curriculum and relevant storybooks in the five approved indigenous languages. The goal would be to expand in the upper primary grades
to L1-based or bilingual content materials, allowing for a more theoretically
sound six-year MLE model.

In all three cases, there are clear policy and parental demands for the dominant language. In light of the evidence-based support for L1-based instruction, we would advocate for high-quality dominant language teaching. This
requires the availability of teachers who are proficient in the language and
who have the necessary material and pedagogical resources. While we have
focused on primary education, it cannot be assumed that all children will be
fluent in a dominant language before secondary school starts. Desai (2016)
has shown how home languages can facilitate learning even in university contexts. Indeed, colleges and universities are where teachers and other educational personnel are trained; they need to offer courses in both or all languages
needed for instruction.

Finally, it is clear that policy reform takes time, that parents and community
members need to be integrally involved, along with teachers, and that significant collaboration across government, NGO, and community actors is not only
desirable but also necessary. The case study from Cambodia has particularly
highlighted the effectiveness of multilevel collaboration, and it may serve as
a role model for other countries regarding how MLE for speakers of nondominant languages can be effectively implemented in practice as well as in policy.
The initial establishment of MLE as a community-based and community-
controlled form of education has given indigenous learners access to schools
and learning in languages they understand, and similarly has given indigenous
community members opportunities to be trained as teachers in their own languages. The establishment of pathways for career development has improved
conditions for community teachers and has brought qualified teachers who
speak indigenous languages into MLE classrooms (Benson & Wong, 2017). The
remarkable collaboration between the development partners and the Cambodian government has resulted in the development of structural support for
MLE implementation – something that is difficult to establish with project-
based educational innovations that have beginning and end dates. Based on
their multilevel research in communities, classrooms, and provincial and
national education offices, Benson and Wong (2017) argue that the successful

implementation of MLE in Cambodia is a testimony both to the respectful relationship built by CARE and its development partners with MoEY, and to the
demonstrated effectiveness of MLE in the target communities. This is indeed a
model that should be emulated, while respecting the historical and ideological
particularities of each context.

6   Conclusion

Based on the evidence presented in this chapter, SDG 4 will not be achieved if
education systems continue to deny quality education for all learners, which
draws on learners' own linguistic resources. Language considerations need
to be more central to the planning and delivery of quality education so that
all learners and their communities can be included, not marginalised. In this
way, language-of-instruction choice must be seen as a central enabler or disa-
bler of learner access to the curriculum. Across all of the cases discussed in
this chapter, it is apparent that there are still large groups of learners who are
not exposed to the dominant language outside of the classroom, and whose
languages need to be recognised and promoted for educational services to be
constructed to adequately meet their needs. Language policies need to reflect
inclusivity while recognising the distinctly political nature of the discussion.
Here we would like to repeat the concluding words of the NEPI Report in South
Africa, which captured the caution that needs to be exercised around choice:
'Language policy for education needs ... to be flexible without being so lais-
sez faire as to allow the perpetuation of present discriminatory practices or
ill-informed choices of alternatives to them' (South Africa, NECC, 1992, p. 93).
In other words, the state would have to play some kind of interventionist role
if we wanted present practices to change. Such intervention would need to be
backed up by investing resources in the development of local languages, which
would allow the intervention to be operationalised.

   At a time when millions of children are still being forced to learn through a
dominant language that they do not speak or understand well, where MLE is
not yet practised, it is understandable that some consider alternative strategies
that can improve the quality of learning, such as oral L1 explanations or language-supportive materials. However, the key message from this chapter is that
within discussions of educational quality, equity, and inclusion, there needs to
be greater recognition of the importance of implementing a fully developed
L1-based MLE program, where all learners are taught and assessed in languages
that they speak. More educational resources are needed in local languages, and
more teachers need relevant language-related as well as pedagogic training.

Most importantly, more advocacy at the global, national, and local levels is needed about how languages and literacies are learned to bring about policy and curriculum reform. A real commitment from all parties to recognising and using learners' own languages, and teaching the additional languages needed to access future opportunities in their societies, will contribute significantly to providing more equitable education for all.

Notes

1 See the school's website for more information: http://thornwood.peelschools.org/ Dual/
2 The NEPI (*National Education Policy Investigation*) reports were commissioned by the National Education Coordinating Committee, an umbrella body of NGOs, to provide alternative policies in 12 educational areas to assist the first post-apartheid government in South Africa.
3 There has been no formal change to the 1997 Language in Education Policy. More recent documents (RSA, DBE, 2010b) merely describe the school and district contexts with regard to home language distribution and language in education at public schools.
4 ICC had been partnering with UNESCO since 1997 on adult literacy programmes and had developed orthographies for five languages, which were approved by the Ministry of Education, Youth and Sport in 2003 for use in formal education (Nowaczyk, 2015).

CHAPTER 6

Universities, the Public Good, and the SDG 4 Vision

*Stephanie Allais, Elaine Unterhalter, Palesa Molebatsi, Lerato Posholi
and Colleen Howell*

1 Introduction

The inclusion of higher education in the Sustainable Development Goal (SDG) targets signalled a significant shift from the focus on universal primary education in the Millennium Development Goal (MDG) framework. SDG 4 expresses a vision: 'Ensure inclusive and equitable quality education and promote lifelong learning opportunities for all' (UNGA, 2015b, p. 17). This raises many issues concerning what it means for universities, which are historically associated with elites, to be inclusive and equitable, and what roles universities could and should play in society. What does quality higher education mean in the context of developing societies, or wealthy but unequal societies, or a world with growing inequality and looming environmental disasters? Given that universities serve individual learning and confer degrees, can the orientation expressed in SDG 4 to 'lifelong learning opportunities for all' sit alongside acquisition of specific and not easily accessible knowledge and skills, and promotion of highly technical areas of research?

This chapter seeks to contribute to debate on these issues, and hence look closely at the higher education components of SDG Target 4.3, using research done on the public-good role of universities in four African countries: Ghana, Kenya, Nigeria, and South Africa.[1] SDG Target 4.3 states: 'By 2030, ensure equal access for all women and men to affordable and quality technical, vocational and tertiary education, including university' (UNGA, 2015b, p. 17). The central focus of the chapter is to introduce ways to understand key terms, such as access, affordability, quality, and equality, as applied to tertiary education. To do this, we draw on views of these concepts in relation to questions about the public-good role of universities. A notion of the public good is implicit in the general SDG vision in which education is mentioned in targets for food security, women's rights, decent work, health, and equalities. In the four African countries examined, the higher education sector is relatively small, but growing at a fast pace and confronted by a range of challenges around affordability, inequalities, and who defines quality.

Contextual issues and complexities within each country call into question simply formulated targets for higher education worldwide, as envisaged in Target 4.3. While supportive of the spirit of the SDGs, which attempted to capture a vision in education that is transformative in scope and ambition (Sayed & Ahmed, 2018; Unterhalter, 2019), we review some perspectives from different settings on how the SDG policy goals may be realised. We also highlight some of the conditions that enable or hinder the possibilities for the higher education sector to contribute to the public good and the achievement of SDG 4.

Critiques of Target 4.3 have highlighted how difficult it is to assess. They question how it might guide policy given that its indicators are quite out of step with the text and aims of the target (King, 2017; Unterhalter, 2019). We concur with these comments. One of the problems with the indicators, and the direction they give to the target, is that they were developed at some distance from the contexts in which people have worked to interpret quality, equality, and public good in higher education. We discuss how indicators might help evaluate achievement of this vision and argue that for them to be effective they need to be highly context-sensitive. We propose an approach to constructing a public-good indicator that captures some of the less individualist notions of the benefits of higher education that have emerged in the four countries studied. This discussion draws out intrinsic and instrumental public-good roles of higher education and dimensions of availability, accessibility, and horizontality that are conditions for realising Target 4.3.

The chapter draws on data collected from interviews in the four countries in 2017 and 2018 to illustrate a number of conceptual points and arguments. The data were collected through interviews with a range of stakeholders associated with university systems in the countries – higher education staff, academic researchers and researchers focussed on higher education,[2] student leaders, key officials in government and administrative bodies, employers, and representatives of organisations in civil society. Key informants were interviewed about their views of the relationship between higher education and the public good.

The first section discusses some of the key contextual features of African higher education systems that are important to thinking about the SDGs. This is followed by the development of our key argument through a discussion of some issues that emanated from interviews with a range of key informants in the four countries, which foreground debates about the meanings laid out in the target of 'equal access' to 'affordable' and 'quality tertiary education'. We then present some of our initial work toward developing an indicator for the public-good role of universities and reflect on how this could contribute to thinking about indicators for Target 4.3. In the conclusion, we draw out some of the implications of the analysis for different kinds of university systems and a more context-specific interpretation of Target 4.3.

2   Situating SDG Target 4.3 in African Higher Education Systems

The 2009 UNESCO World Conference on Higher Education in Paris adopted the resolution that higher education is a public good and gave special focus to the challenges and opportunities for the revitalisation of higher education in Africa (WCHE, 2009). The resolution was adopted in the context of an enormous expansion in university participation since 1990, including across the developing world and especially in sub-Saharan Africa (SSA). While these trends are important, equally important is the persistence, in most poor countries, of historical and contemporary inequalities that complicate this picture. These inequalities continue to have a profound influence on who gains access to and progresses through higher education, and the nature of the higher education provision that is in place.

Historically, in most poor countries, universities were the domain of the elite, who were being educated for religious, professional, managerial, and administrative jobs, usually linked to projects of colonial rule. In many countries, including in Africa, increases in the number of higher education institutions coincided with gaining independence, accompanied by some associated expansion in enrolments, often linked to ideas of a developmental state (Mkandawire, 2001) and national flagship institutions (Teferra, 2016). However, the numbers of students entering and graduating from these institutions were small and generally drawn from only the highest income groups and most powerful political formations – the 'elite of African society' (Mohamedbhai, 2014, p. 6). The imperative toward increasing enrolments and strengthening national universities was severely challenged in Africa in the 1980s by structural adjustment policies, which called for state resources to be directed away from higher education to other levels of education and for increased privatisation across most higher education systems (Samoff & Carrol, 2003).

From the 1990s, however, expanding economies, the aspiration to knowledge economies, growing secondary school enrolments, and widening political participation redirected attention back to higher education and associated initiatives to expand educational provision. Although a key 1995 World Bank policy paper emphasised the importance of primary education, paving the way for the de-emphasis on higher education in the Education for All (EFA) Dakar Framework for Action and the Millennium Development Goals (MDGs), in 1997 Joseph Stiglitz was appointed Chief Economist at the World Bank and published key works on the importance of developing countries' investment in scientific research and enhancing access to global public goods (Jones, 1997; Stiglitz, 1999). In the new millennium, higher education came to be seen by multilateral organisations and governments as a key feature of participation in the knowledge economy.

This trend toward higher education expansion was evident beyond Africa as well. UNESCO data show that in 2017 the global gross enrolment ratio (GER) for tertiary education was 38%.[3] While this ratio shifts considerably across countries, from 9% in low-income countries to 77% in high-income countries, it reflects participation rates in tertiary education that have more than doubled over the last 20 years, with the fastest levels of growth having taken place across SSA (Darvas et al., 2017). However, this significant growth in tertiary enrolment in SSA has taken place from a very low base, so that in 2017 the GER for SSA was still only 9% (the same as the average for low-income countries), compared, for example, to 78% for North America and Western Europe, 51% for Latin America and the Caribbean, 51% for China, and 28% for India. In the four countries from which data for this study is drawn, significant growth is evident, although present levels of enrolment are still comparatively low within the global context. In 2016 Ghana and Kenya had GERs of 16% and 12%, up from 6% and 3%, respectively, in 2005. In South Africa, GER in higher education increased steadily from 14% in 2001 to 21% in 2016. In Nigeria, the GER increased from 6% in 1999 to 10.5% by 2010.

This expansion in enrolments, globally and within sub-Saharan Africa, has been enabled through a plurality of institutional forms. There has been growth in private and public provision, and mixtures of the two. In sub-Saharan Africa, private higher education has been especially significant in many countries, with these institutions becoming important contributors to increased student numbers and expanded higher education provision (Morley, 2014; Oanda & Jowi, 2012). It is estimated that in sub-Saharan Africa the number of private universities and colleges, including for-profit and not-for-profit institutions, mushroomed from 24 in 1990 to 468 by 2007, reaching over 1,000 in 2014 (Darvas et al., 2017). Nigeria, for example, had three private universities in 2000. This number had increased to 50 by 2011 (Bamiro, 2016) and now stands at 79 (Nigeria, National Universities Commission, 2019). Different kinds of public and private tertiary-level institutions have emerged – universities, polytechnics, community colleges, and diploma-awarding institutions linked to professional practice, social development, and industrial, agricultural, or commercial forms of work.

While these trends all indicate a substantial expansion and diversification in higher education systems across SSA, inequity is also a feature of higher education systems across the region. This is revealed by the percentages of students entering the system who manage to complete their studies and graduate, and the persistence of social and economic inequalities in determining patterns of access to higher education (Darvas et al., 2017; Morley, Leach, and Lugg, 2009; Oanda and Sall, 2016; Wangenge-Ouma, 2011), despite efforts by a number of countries to redress these historical imbalances (Schendel & McCowan, 2016; Unterhalter & Carpentier, 2010). Although researchers have drawn attention to limited data showing progression and completion in higher education in Africa (Darvas et al., 2017; Mohamedbhai, 2014), completion and graduation rates are low, with many students dropping out. Factors such as inadequate funding, myriad challenges related to poor schooling, language barriers, and inadequate levels of institutional support influence whether students manage to complete their studies (Adu-Yeboah, 2015; Breier, 2010; Mohamedbhai, 2014). Even in South Africa, with comparatively higher levels of enrolment, completion and graduation rates are low, and growth in enrolments 'has been accompanied by high failure and dropout rates', with 55% of students in universities in South Africa unlikely to complete their studies and graduate (South Africa, Council on Higher Education, 2013, p. 40).

Essack (2012) suggests that equitable access to higher education in Africa is undermined through a number of social, political, and economic factors that create and reproduce patterns of marginalisation and exclusion from the system. Socioeconomic status and household income are central to privileging 'the children of the wealthy and politically connected' (Darvas et al., 2017, p. xvi) and ensuring that, despite organisational, national, and international policy imperatives to widen participation (Morley et al., 2009), higher education across the region remains largely out of the reach of the poor. In fact, Oanda and Sall (2016) argue that, despite the dearth of reliable data, anecdotal evidence suggests that expansion may have widened disparities in access, with inequalities associated with gender, class, and geographical location remaining central to influencing access patterns.

Huge funding challenges faced by public higher education systems across the continent often amplify inequalities (Pillay, Woldegiorgis, & Knight, 2017; Teferra, 2013). These are partly related to high levels of growth and rising costs in provision. While declining state funding of higher education is a global trend, in deeply resource-constrained environments with a range of competing demands on public budgets, this challenge is especially acute. For many institutions, the consequence is often constant 'financial emergency and uncertainty' (Wangenge-Ouma, 2011, p. 171) and the absence of a stable funding base as a necessary and essential condition for both equity and excellence (Teferra, 2013). Despite the strong calls for 'free' higher education by students and other stakeholders, traditional models of taxpayer-funded provision have come under scrutiny, with some researchers arguing that such models can only sustainably fund a small number of elite universities (Oketch, 2016).

In the discussions and meetings that led to the agreement of the SDGs, there were struggles over aspects of Target 4.3. These included equal access for all, affordability, and quality tertiary education, particularly in universities (Unterhalter, 2019). But there was a lack of precision about these terms. Did *equal access* mean all should have a right to enrol in university whether or not they had passed entrance examinations, or that entrance examinations should be abolished? Did *affordable* mean free higher education, and if so, for what percentage of the population? How was *quality* higher education to be defined, given the wide variety of university mission statements? How did quality fit with the idea of the 'developmental university', an institutional form pioneered in Africa, wholly concerned with addressing social, economic, political, and human development challenges (Coleman, 1986; Nkomo & Sehoole, 2007)? How, given the difficulties of funding faced by universities and the complexities of measuring the outcomes of higher education in developing countries, was this vision to be financed and evaluated, particularly in the context of the narrowing of the quality agenda to mean only research intensity? (Boni, Lopez-Fogues, & Walker, 2016; McCowan, 2016b, 2018; Regmi, 2015; Unterhalter, Vaughan, & Smail, 2013). What were the benefits and drawbacks of seeking funding not just from historic sources such as fees and government grants, but financialised and repackaged loans, and large private sector investments? (Allais, 2017b; Mawdsley, 2018).

The global indicator for Target 4.3 focused on the '[p]articipation rate of youth and adults in formal and non-formal education and training in the previous 12 months, by sex' (see Appendix 2 of this book). This made no reference to affordability, quality, or the nature of universality, and therefore did not illuminate the target. Target 4.3 leaves much space for interpretation, and its broad priorities are not tied to any specific policies, implementation modalities, or financing arrangements. Nonetheless, the wording of the target and the selection of the global indicator suggest an approach to education as a 'quality good' that each individual needs to be able to access. We argue below that this interpretation goes against the vision of SDG 4 as outlined in the goal, which emphasises that quality is associated with inclusivity and equality. The public-good role of universities is part of an understanding of quality education. Universities' role in social development is not reducible simply to individual advancement. Considering the public-good role of universities also has implications for how affordability can be understood.

3   The Contested Meaning of Quality in Higher Education

The meaning of quality higher education is much contested (Lomas, 2002; Marginson, 2016; Schendel and McCowan, 2016). The ways in which quality, inclusion, and equality interlink and are realised in practice, particularly in contexts marked by histories of violence, dispossession, and struggles around justice, have been debated (Bhambra, Gebrial, & Nisancioglu, 2018; Boni et al., 2016; Jansen, 2017; McCowan, 2016b; Unterhalter & Carpentier, 2010). Some university rankings define quality in terms of inputs such as the level of academics' qualifications and selected outputs such as student completion time, graduate employment rates, or research intensity (Hazelkorn, 2012, 2015) and use these as metrics of accountability, performance management, or policy steering (Hazelkorn, Coates, & McCormick, 2018). Tan and Goh (2014) define quality as being concerned with what students derive from acquiring a university education, although most ways of assessing this are linked to graduate employment or employability rather than wider social benefits. These conceptions treat higher education as a machine-like process and ignore questions regarding who the students attending university are, who the lecturers are, what is being taught, and how quality might connect with equality or wider projects for social transformation.

A contested and more open-ended view of quality was evident in the data we collected, and diverse views were expressed by academics, students, professional staff, and policymakers. For some, quality was linked with universities' limitation of access to those who achieved high scores in school leaving examinations. They argued that giving admission only to high achievers would ensure a high standard of qualifications and generate high levels of research insight. In Nigeria and Ghana, the view was expressed that this goal of producing high-end knowledge and elite graduates had been compromised through massification. A different view of quality, articulated by participants in all four countries, was about widening access, understood both as participation by a wider group of students and disseminating knowledge to wider publics.

In its current expression, Target 4.3 with its stress on quality, access, and affordability reads individualistically, with an emphasis on individuals obtaining quality knowledge and skills through access to higher education. The learning outcomes of university education are not specified, in contrast with Target 4.4 which mentions skills to be acquired for 'employment, decent work and entrepreneurship' (UNGA, 2015b, p. 17).

In all four countries, informants articulated a range of ways in which universities serve society more broadly than simply enhancing individual skill acquisition or enabling individuals to obtain degrees. Generally, these broader goals were articulated in terms of contributions to the development and bet-terment of society, national development plans, or addressing inequalities and exclusions. The acquisition of skills, and participation in higher education in general, are valuable in so far as they promote the well-being or development of society more broadly rather than for the sake of individual advancement. For example, a South African academic argued, 'The role of higher education is to produce good quality graduates in those areas where the professionals in turn serve the country' (Interview, higher education researcher 1, 5 March 2018). But for some, this was not a simple input-output process, in which individuals who attended university would naturally enhance the public good, as those individuals were themselves enmeshed in relationships, which are the product of historic injustices.

Some interviewees acknowledged the individual benefits of higher education, with one arguing that universities in South Africa confer more private benefits and cannot be a public good because attending university primarily benefits the middle classes:

> If we look at South Africa now and if we look at the data on returns on investment in higher education the wage premium of people with higher education is huge. It's one of the largest in the world. (Interview, higher education researcher 1, 5 March 2018)

Another academic expressed this more pessimistically:

> It is statistically a public good just for the middle class, and it allows a small group of poor to get out of poverty, but firstly the percentage of poor that end up in higher education is miniscule: 2 to 3 percent, and the percentage of them that makes it is another 60 percent. (Interview, higher education researcher 2, 20 February 2018)

A more critical perspective was offered by a student leader at a large South African university, who argued that the public good is about benefitting the broader society:

> As a society we miss that key thing about how we help each other. Rather than focussing on just an individual, how do we grow? The system is focussed on individuals, imparting certain skills. *Rather than the bettering of broader society.* (Interview, student leader, 23 January 2018)

Two themes thus seem to weave through the discussion of quality and public good in this data. The first is how private good, namely, advancement through quality education for individuals and selective groups, is connected to public good. The second is whether there might be ways to link notions of quality higher education and public good to more fully express an idea that they co-construct decent and equitable societies.

This latter relationship was seen by many as sequentially linked with national development. For example, a representative from the Congress of South African Trade Unions (COSATU), one of South Africa's major trade union federations, argued that underfunding is preventing South African universities from contributing to developing public resources. Implicit in this is an idea of the role that universities could play in national development, were they to be better funded:

> [Underfunding is] going to set us back many decades ... in terms of our own development because if we can't develop our own human resources, how do we expect to develop our country? How do we expect to mitigate problems when a major power station ... has to be built? We have to bring artisans from Malaysia and other countries whilst we are sitting with loads and loads of unemployment. How are we going to address those problems if we do not invest largely in education and training? (Interview, COSATU official, 22 November 2018)

A sequential form of analysis, linking private gains to public good, was raised in all four countries, including through arguments that universities need to produce graduates committed to advancing the good of society through their professional work. In this form, the argument also suggested universities needed to develop knowledge that contributes to society, addressing historical injustices such as colonialism. Community engagement was seen as a necessary part of quality education and the university achieving this public-good role. An official from the South African Department of Science and Technology argued:

> The [rural] university should have programmes on monitoring water throughout the year ... You can't be doing work on things that are not contributing to development. ... You focus on local issues and through the local issues you deal with international issues because those issues could be relevant elsewhere. You begin to go national and global. (Department of Science and Technology interview, 1 December 2018)

This sense that universities' missions should be to contribute to solving local and national problems was articulated in a number of the interviews in all four countries and is one of the most common formulations of how quality higher education realises a form of public good.

But a different formulation of this relationship suggested that higher education needs to co-construct ideas of the public good and quality with different constituencies in local, national, and global communities of practice and critique. For some, particularly in South Africa, the concept of *Ubuntu*,[4] which has been applied to higher education (Letseka, 2012; Oviawe, 2016; Waghid, 2018), was linked to an expanded notion of quality.

This sense of using higher education as a setting to reformulate ideas of the public good, either critically, or through forms of practice, was raised in interviews across the four countries. However, local conditions meant that this co-construction sometimes was linked to very local struggles over resources, management, classroom practice, or approaches to student support. For example, students interviewed in Nigeria criticised the limited numbers and lack of preparation of lecturers, while the issue of decolonisation of the curriculum was a key concern in South Africa.

The claim that quality means co-construction of the public good could be seen as implying that quality education is not only measured intrinsically on academic standards or criteria internal to disciplines, but also in terms of what education can cultivate that is for society's betterment. Some reasoned that academic standards can in part be informed by this. The student representative council president of a university of technology in South Africa argued that one of the problems of the university was that

> [t]he current system keeps knowledge essentially at the top. The doors to higher education have been opened, but the highest dropout rate is young black students from disadvantaged backgrounds. When we talk about free higher education and what #Fees Must Fall is fighting for, we need students from townships and villages who can go back and tackle the issues, where it is very real to them, it's not just hypothetical. (Interview, 4 May 2018)

The COSATU representative emphasised the need for 'relevant' research that improves peoples' lives and for better communication of research findings, thus linking quality, public good, relevance, and public engagement. Here, university quality, autonomy, and public good co-construct each other. In these interpretations, the notion of quality extends considerably beyond what is learned and taught in universities, offering a wide terrain for putting Target 4.3 into practice in a direction that is oriented toward public good.

What these views of quality do not tell us, however, is how we would know whether or not a university is contributing in this way, or if its graduates are, and how measuring these aspects could or should be related to criteria within bodies of knowledge and the conduct of research (Muller, 2000; Young, 2008). There are also thorny issues about university autonomy. For example, some respondents saw aspects of quality as potentially highly compromised by the relationships and prescripts put in place in some private higher education institutions. Other interviewees emphasised similar concerns around the nature of the relationship between universities and governments.

A key feature emerging from the analysis of the data across the four countries was quality as a feature of collective possibility, not only of individual advancement. Widening participation in higher education could be a force for public and private transformation, including democratisation and personal and economic growth. But a small university system could also serve a state concerned with social services and improving the well-being of all in the society through the graduates it develops and the research it conducts. However, higher education, regardless of the size of the sector, can also contribute to the formation of elites and the practices that sustain them, and so accelerate corrosive forms of differentiation between social groups. Thus, what is co-constructed by a quality higher education system may be public bad, just as much as public good. Higher education can reproduce inequalities and arguably has done so throughout the world. This issue also surfaces in the text of SDG Target 4.3, around what meanings attach to the idea of affordable university education.

4   Access to Affordable University Education

Access and affordability are complex concepts which, like quality and public good, need to be understood in relation to particular contexts. What does affordable university education mean, and is it compatible with universal or even rising access to higher education in countries that have not managed to adequately fund universal primary education? Target 4.3 suggests affordability is a facet of quality but does not make clear whether university education is to be affordable for individuals, countries, or communities. Under what terms of social contract and evaluation of public good are these assessments made?

The inclusion of affordability in Target 4.3 is laudable, as it challenges the idea that university education is only a private good for those who can afford it. However, more and more countries are shifting to 'user fees' for university education, which place affordability under scrutiny. For some, this is a result of neo-liberal policy orientations and the shift away from universal, free service provision, but for all countries, funding mass higher education is a very different fiscal prospect compared to funding a small, elite higher education sector

(Barr, 2004; Marginson, 2016). As the numbers of students accessing university education grows, funding becomes an area of difficulty and sometimes of crisis. One response to this has been the emergence of private institutions, partly due to increased demand for higher education and partly because higher education is a growing economic sector in its own right. In many countries, governments are implementing policies that are making higher education more and more expensive for individuals, although the extent of individual contributions and the mechanisms for individual payment differ between countries (Biffl & Issac, 2002; Johnston, 2004). There is no easy policy solution to the problem of *how much* higher education should be funded from a country's public purse, and how else it should be funded.

Yet, the public-good role of universities cannot be separated from public access. In interviews in all four countries, key informants, most notably students, argued that a public good is a good that is publicly provided. As soon as higher education is treated as a commodity, it is more accessible to some members of the public than others. According to a South African trade union representative, a decommodification of higher education was needed in order both to achieve access and ensure that universities are serving the public:

> If we roll back the markets, most of the issues that are derived from education can be accessed by the society. Almost everything is in the hands of the markets and there is a huge danger with that. (Interview, COSATU official, 22 November 2018)

Other informants argued that when university education is treated as a commodity, knowledge is produced to advance the interests of the market, and students become clients or customers purchasing services or products. The public-good aspect of quality associated with higher education was bound up with understanding knowledge and pedagogic relationships, not the notion of commodity. This suggests it is necessary to think about the co-construction of the notions of quality education as a public good, together with public provision of de-commodified knowledge, funded by the state, for example, through progressive tax regimes. However, this may be problematic in the African context (Allais, 2018a; Cloete, 2016; Jansen, 2017; Motala, Vally, & Maharaj, 2018). One issue raised in the literature is fiscal erosion, which is apparent throughout Africa, both where university education is free and where it is not. The vice chancellor of a historically black university in a rural location in South Africa noted that while the public-good role of a university required widening access, the rapid expansion of the university he worked in had placed enormous burdens on institutional infrastructure, funding, student-staff ratios, and course quality. Similar comments were made by interviewees in the other countries, who stated that public higher education is underfunded, which, in the context of the levels of growth that have taken place, has had serious consequences for institutions and what they are able to provide. These comments indicate that access is not simply a matter of enrolment and that a key aspect of access requires posing the question: access to what? The social contract around public access to quality university education raises questions about affordability for institutions as well as individuals.

Informants in all four countries argued that those who benefit from higher education must pay for it. Thus, a view was expressed, linking affordability with individual benefits, and by implication, individual benefits with national development. For some, public *access*, as suggested in Target 4.3, meant a fee-based system. Some saw imposing fees as compatible with expanding access, as long as there is sufficient financial support for those who need it.

Wider meanings of access were posited by informants, including epistemological access and forms of access that challenged and transformed injustice. For example, a trade unionist in South Africa argued that access entailed examining university entrance criteria, which, in their current form, undermined an inclusive idea of the public good.

A further refinement on ideas of access was articulated, casting affordability as more of a set of social issues in which money, time, and relationships of care were implicated. This was expressed in all four countries where informants emphasised that universities needed to be decent places to work and study, and only under such conditions could they provide settings to foster public debate and build connections with an immediate geographic community. Gender-based violence on campus was raised as a serious concern in all four countries. Interviewees noted that universities are more likely to have higher levels of gender-based violence than the wider society because of the power relations between students and staff:

> Where else do you have those levels of power relations and those numbers? That unequal power relationship is magnified in this setting. For those universities that have residences there is global research that they present victim situations. You live in the space. If you are young you might not know the boundaries, you don't understand issues around consent. ... Even the boundaries between lecturers and students are not well understood on both sides. We have never had a complaint yet but there are students who have offered sexual favours for marks. There are lecturers who offer marks for sexual favours. (Interview, university gender equity officer, South Africa, 25 July 2018)

So, the power that a professor has over a student is an intense power, it's a power to define what happens for the rest of your life. It's extreme levels of power and being able to understand those kinds of powers and being able to deconstruct them and being able to make very clear choices about who is allowed to exercise that kind of power, right? Because as I said, it kills a student to be in an institution where the people who have a choice on whether you succeed or not in life are then abusive of that power and are allowed to be. (Interview, South African civil society activist, 22 November 2018)

A number of respondents in all four countries argued for the need to cultivate universities as places where public debate takes place to nurture cultural goods and public intellectuals. But, in contrast to this ideal, others pointed out that many universities are gated communities which exclude the public:

If you can't access the university physically then ... how are you going to do that? It must be a meeting place for people and ideas. (Interview, South African higher education researcher 6, 22 March 2018)

Stakeholders reasoned that it is difficult for universities to serve their immediate community when it is hard for members of a community to walk onto a campus. In South Africa, university leaders claim that they have fenced their campuses to protect staff and students from crime and violence pervasive in South Africa, an issue which is also of concern, to differing degrees, in the other countries. Some interviewees suggested that the status of a university was often signalled by its landscaped grounds and controlled access. But this too highlights the question of access to *what*, taking us back to the previous discussions on quality, and suggests other ways in which people can 'access' higher education, even if not through enrolment for degree or diploma programmes. So, for example, a student representative in South Africa suggested that his university contributes to the public good through the involvement of its management, particularly the vice chancellor, in the developmental and municipal issues of the town in which it is located. Some informants expressed a notion of engagement with the immediate material needs of the local community. In other words, access is not only immediate presence, but takes mediated forms, particularly sensitive to locale.

Access to higher education concerns the relationships between different levels of education systems. A common theme in the interviews across all the countries was that education needs to be improved at all levels – and that lack of quality schooling is a major threat to the viability of universities, including access, affordability, and quality. Quality primary and secondary education are central conditions of possibility for quality higher education. It is not surprising that a number of informants across the four countries talked of the need to fix schooling as a key to improving university education:

> When I hear about the crisis in our schooling, ... many of those teachers were produced in the last 20 years. So, why are we having the same problems in our schools? Why can't our children read properly? And it's not rocket science. Why are we having the kind of abuse of girls and women in our schools? Why are girls feeling unsafe in our schools? All of those issues, tell me? ... What kind of teaching profession are we producing? ... [T]he same can be asked of other professions. (Interview, higher education researcher 1, 5 March 2018)

An expert on schooling in South Africa argued that universities are not able to do their jobs because they are finishing the job that the primary and secondary schooling system did not do because of inadequate teaching. A student leader echoed this, suggesting that the crisis in basic education is one of the contributing factors to the crisis in higher education:

> You guys in universities are privileged already; our basic education is crumbling. ... We are privileged at university level; our basic education is my biggest concern. We are losing so many potential young people because of infrastructure in basic education, quality ... in basic education. (Interview, student leader at a small-town, historically white university, 11 December 2017)

In sum, the assumption in SDG Target 4.3 is that access to university education is about individual access, and that this is seen to be affordable by individuals, households, institutions, or nations. Target 4.b confirms this relationship with its stress on increasing the number of scholarships. Our research shows how access to quality university education is associated by some with ideas of inclusion and equity. This resonates with wider ideas about what is public, what is good, and how decommodification, conditions of work, and engagement with local needs are key dimensions of understanding equalities and inclusion.

5   Measurement and Indicators

The interviews conducted with key informants shed light on some of the complexities of the meanings of affordability, access, and quality in higher education. But, as many commentators note, the indicators for Target 4.3 close down
rather than illuminate these complexities, nuances, and perceptions of public
good and collective possibility (King, 2017; McCowan, 2018; Unterhalter, 2019).

Target 4.3 is currently to be evaluated by three indicators (UNGA, 2015b, p. 17):

4.3.1.   Participation rate of youth and adults in formal and non-formal edu-
          cation and training in the last 12-months, by sex;
4.3.2.   Gross enrolment ratio for tertiary education by sex;
4.3.3.   Participation in technical-vocational programmes (15–24 years old),
          by sex.

These indicators suggest that the expansion of enrolment is the most necessary development to capture some of the 'sense' of Target 4.3. But many elements of the focus of the target – on inclusion, affordability, and quality – are
missed. None of the three indicators deals with quality. A criticism of the GER
for tertiary education is that it is not sensitive to the age range of people participating in higher education, focusing on participation within the postsecondary school age range of a population. So, this measure does not effectively
illuminate what role access to university is playing for different demographics,
which is linked to histories of inequality. Existing metrics are not measuring
the intersections of inequalities or the forms of intervention needed to secure
equity.

To attempt to start filling these gaps, our project has proposed a dashboard
of indicators through which the complexities and nuances raised by stakeholders can be made visible. It works as a visual representation of the components
of our indicators 'at-a-glance'. This helps to better capture the public-good
character of universities by embedding the indicators in as much context as
possible. A dashboard offers a practical way of looking at data across countries,
as well as of organising qualitative and quantitative data in a meaningful way.

In developing the dashboard, we have drawn on an evaluation of existing
quantitative metrics and analysis of the qualitative data we collected. The
interview data were coded in terms of the main ideas of stakeholders regarding higher education and the public good. These ideas included the following:
higher education is only a public good under certain conditions (e.g., when
there is a conducive social contract); the public good is strongly bound to the
idea of a public sphere(s) and that the university constructs these spaces (e.g.,
through the advancement of cultural and social goods); higher education for
the public good serves the needs of society at large (e.g., by advancing human

development); and there are private and public benefits to higher education, although the private can sometimes be interwoven with the public. In terms of these views from stakeholders, conditions that enable or hinder the capacity of institutions to contribute to the public good – the conditions of possibility – were identified from the data. Some were explicit, and others implicit. These conditions were either 'external' – relating to the necessary conditions in society but outside of the higher education sector in order to facilitate the public-good role of universities – or 'internal' – relating only to the conditions necessary in the higher education sector. Some conditions of possibility were characterised as both internal and external.

Figure 6.1 provides an illustration of the proposed public-good dashboard. The first conceptual consideration is a distinction between the intrinsic and the instrumental public-good roles of higher education taken from the literature (Unterhalter et al., 2018). The intrinsic refers to the value of education as an end in itself and the experience of education for its own sake, while the instrumental has to do with higher education's value as a socially responsive institution. The interview data were organised using codes related to one of

Intrinsic Public-Good Roles

Access	Funding and provision	Deliberative space
•Gross enrolment ratio •Completion and throughput rates •Disaggregation: gender, race/ethnicity; socioeconomic background; rural/urban •Balance between public and private enrolments •Stratification	•Level of funding (percent of GDP and of government expenditure) •Balance of public/private funding •Disparities between institutions •Student/staff ratio •Staff profile •Disciplinary spread	•Academic freedom •Appointment of officials •Representation (governing councils etc.) •Student participation •Dialogical pedagogy

Instrumental PublicGood Roles

Graduate destinations	Knowledge production	Community engagement
•Rates of employment, types of employment, public and private sectors •Social enterprise/ entrepreneurship/other destinations •Disaggregation by social group •Tax contribution •Income inequalities •Political participation and civic engagement	•Research activity •Publications (Web of Science/ Scopus) •National/local/open access publications •Number of researchers per million population •Concentration/diffusion of knowledge production	•Number and type of outreach projects •Community representation in university bodies •Availability of courses for public •Public communication of research •Community use of university facilities

FIGURE 6.1   Dashboard for a public-good indicator

the two, although some stakeholders viewed the intrinsic and instrumental roles as overlapping and/or sometimes inseparable.

Also emerging from the literature and considered in the dashboard is McCowan's (2016a) framework for access, which uses three dimensions to open up the question, access to what? These are 'availability', which refers to the capacity of institutions to absorb incoming students (i.e., sufficient places so that all members of society who so desire, and who have a minimum level of preparation, can participate in higher education); 'accessibility', referring to which groups can access higher education, and how academic performance tests and tuition fees become the mechanisms determining who gets into university; and lastly, 'horizontality', which is concerned with stratification in higher education and hierarchies of prestige and quality between universities – where disadvantaged students are confined to lower quality institutions.

Out of these categories arise the six indicators displayed in Figure 6.1, labelled either intrinsic or instrumental, to make up the public-good dashboard. They cover access, funding and provision, deliberative space, graduate destinations, knowledge production, and community engagement. These categories are taken from the literature defining the key pathways through which higher education contributes to the public good in society as well as the views of stakeholders in the four African countries studied.

Only some of the indicators suggested by interviewed stakeholders can be incorporated into the dashboard, given the information resources currently available. Benchmarking tools relating to community engagement exist. Based on institutional data, these include the Higher Education Funding Council for England's regional benchmarking tool, the Russell Groups' Higher Education Community Engagement Tool in the UK, the Carnegie Foundation's Documentation Framework (2008) in the US, and the tool under development by the Conference on Community Engagement in Higher Education through the Council on Higher Education and the Joint Education Trust in South Africa (Olowu, 2012). Based on these kinds of tools for community engagement, we can see the possibility of including a 'deliberative space' indicator and asking institutions to self-report on that area. The 'deliberative space' overlaps conceptually with stakeholders' general view of the public sphere as involving critical dialogue not only within the university itself, but at what stakeholders call the 'popular level' (i.e., the community).

The dashboard under development is only a starting point to begin identifying the elements of access to quality higher education that serves a wider social transformation agenda. Our intention is not to suggest that this public-good indicator is exhaustive or without problems, but to contribute to thinking about strengthening SDG Target 4.3.

The question of measuring SDGs remains high on the agendas of many, so much so that the *Times Higher Education* (*THE*) *World University Rankings* are in the process of developing an SDG ranking system. The aim will be to assess universities' contributions to the SDGs. Metrics currently being explored include the number of graduates in health professions, the proportion of women in senior academic positions, and policies and practices regarding employment security (Bothwell, 2018). While this may look like a step forward in measuring the social justice role of universities, it is likely to present problems similar to those associated with previous *THE* rankings – not least because it remains a ranking system. Unlike the forthcoming *THE* SDG metrics, the dashboard under development through our research project is not a ranking system, but an assemblage of information that can be used by institutions and national planning systems. So, despite many possible limitations, including limited availability and reliability of data, the need to explore counterfactuals to examine the nature of contextual variables and formations of conditions of possibility, we suggest the dashboard can make a contribution toward new ways of measuring the previously unmeasured in higher education. As such it can help crystallise goals to which national systems of higher education can aspire.

6   Conclusion

Two important insights emerge from our research on higher education quality, access, and affordability in relation to the SDG Target 4.3 framework.

The first is that quality education in relation to the public-good role of universities requires movement away from an individualist focus toward the common good, to approach quality in higher education in terms of universities' contribution to wider society. The phrasing of Target 4.3, concerning 'equal access of all women and men to affordable quality higher education', allows for an interpretation that excludes this socially located sense of access to the benefits of institutions. The target can be interpreted to mean that the primary purpose of all universities is to ensure access – narrowly understood as enrolment – for all. But striving for this simplistic and individualistic goal has raised serious funding problems for most countries and could undermine other crucial roles through which universities contribute to society and which the wider framing of SDG 4 implies.

The analysis emerging from the data we collected highlights that higher education is an intrinsic good, and one that all nations should strive to provide. But what was stressed is that it is not only or even primarily an intrinsic *individual* good. We suggest that expanding higher education participation rates will not jumpstart social development. Education is a goal of social development, but in the absence of economic development, if university education becomes unaffordable, wider social development goals are placed in jeopardy.

Our findings make apparent that achieving quality higher education is linked to a range of contextual processes. In many interviews, stakeholders raised different conditions of possibility for higher education to serve the public good, and hence to be evaluated as quality. If we think of quality in terms of the public good, the conditions of possibility show how we can achieve quality education by suggesting what conditions need to be in place for higher education, whatever the form of access, to contribute to the public good.

The second insight is that this approach to quality in higher education implies measuring outputs of education somewhat differently from conventional metrics. Measurements of quality that simply tally the number of graduates produced do not reveal the significance of graduation and how graduates might contribute to a form of public good. Our proposed dashboard suggests indicators more in line with the roles for higher education associated with inclusion and equality.

Our discussion suggests interpreting Target 4.3 through the lens of the overarching SDG 4 goal with its stress on inclusion, equality, and lifelong learning, drawing out their public-good dimensions, rather than through a narrow mesh of indicators that highlight only individual access and participation. Given the many vested interests associated with an 'individual advantage' reading of access and inclusion, we consider this may well be one of the most contested issues in relation to the SDG targets. The insights we have reported from research in four African countries suggest that co-constructions of quality, inclusion, and equity in higher education are both desirable and possible.

Notes

1   The chapter draws on research conducted as part of the ESRC, Newton Fund, NRF-funded project 'Higher Education, Inequality and the Public Good: A Study in Four African Countries'. We are grateful to our fellow researchers Christine Adu-Yeboah, Samuel Fongwa, Jibrin Ibrahim, Tristan McCowan, Louise Morley, Mthobisi Ndaba, Siphelo Ngcwangu, Ibrahim Oanda, and Moses Oketch for the discussions and insight that have been associated with our three years of work together collecting and analysing data and developing a perspective on issues relating to inequalities and the public good that have informed our reflection on SDG 4 in this chapter.

2   In the citations from interviews below, we distinguish between academic staff representatives and academic experts who research higher education.

3 UNESCO defines this as the total enrolment in tertiary education, regardless of age, expressed as a percentage of the total population of the five-year age group following on from secondary school leaving. This age group may differ in different countries but is usually around 18 to 22 years. All data cited in this paragraph are drawn from the UNESCO Institute for Statistics, http://uis.unesco.org, accessed 15 February 2018.

4 *Ubuntu* is a concept used to capture the sense that 'I am because we are', which is central particularly to sub-Saharan African ethics and morality. The gist of *Ubuntu* is the connectedness and collaborations in human relationships, so that humanity is defined by the interconnections and relationships one has with other people. *Ubuntu* originates from the proverbial expressions in Sotho languages, *'Motho ke motho ka batho babang'* or in Nguni languages, *'Umuntu ngumuntu ngabantu'* (Letseka, 2012; Le Grange, 2012), translated as 'a person is a person through their relationship to others' (Swanson, 2015, p. 34; Mboti, 2015, p. 127; Metz & Gaie, 2010, p. 275). *Ubuntu* can be understood as trying to capture a communitarian essence of what it is to be human.

CHAPTER 7

Education for All Open for Business? Public Goods vs. Private Profits

Alexandra Draxler

1   Introduction

Sustainable Development Goal (SDG) 4 and its related targets (UNGA, 2015b) contain admirable commitments, although many specifics about what it will take to fulfil them must be hammered out over time and according to context. However, as analysts have pointed out, there are contradictory underlying philosophies in the goals and supporting documents, so that what is left unsaid will be a significant influence as partners make their decisions going forward (Wulff, 2017; VanderDussen Toukan, 2017; Kumi et al., 2014). The Education 2030 Declaration (World Education Forum, 2015) goes part of the way in spelling out the respective roles of the public and private sectors, but those roles are formulated somewhat inconsistently. The Declaration makes mention in six places of the crucial role of the state in regulating various aspects of education. On the other hand, the private sector is given a metaphorical seat at the public policy table throughout, similar to the overall 2030 SDG agenda, positing contradictory expectations about the role of business in the education sector. For example, the assumption that embedding market-based value judgements into goals for the future of humanity will not corrupt the latter is unproven. The assumption, which is repeated several times in Goal 17, that private funding will contribute substantially to filling any financing gap, is also unproven. Finally, the assumption that all potential partners will embrace inclusive public policies by contributing to equity is likewise unproven.

Target 4.1[1] is unambiguous about the commitment to provide *free and equitable* education for all at both primary and secondary levels, system-wide tasks for which the vast majority of private entities are structurally uncommitted and unsuited.

On the basis of both the underlying philosophical contradictions embedded in the goals, including Goal 4, and the probable practical consequences of increased private sector involvement in the provision of basic education, this chapter will examine some of the hidden benefits to the private sector that are embedded in the goals, and the way in which for-profit provision of education is likely both to distort the goals' stated objectives and hamper their achievement.

While it can be legitimately pointed out that for-profit education in developing countries is a tiny fraction of education supply, there is evidence (Steiner-Khamsi & Draxler, 2018) that market ideology is permeating public policy and action beyond the limited market-based institutions (Stiglitz, 2018). Similarly, the 'data revolution' for stimulating and benchmarking progress toward meeting the SDG goals will undoubtedly have the effect of steering policy and public management in directions that can easily be measured. We saw this with the Education for All (EFA) process (Riddell, 2007). As technology becomes a larger part of the education landscape, it would be disingenuous to imagine that policymakers would not look to the budget for teachers to find the funds to cover the additional investments needed. Finally, equity can only be assured by public authorities and a watchful citizenry. Market-based solutions are at best complements to public goods but cannot assure them.

Both development assistance and national public spending for education have declined over recent years and will likely continue to do so. Meeting the education targets would, on the contrary, require greatly increased spending, and the implication of both the agenda and background documents is that the private sector is expected to make up much of the financing gap (UNGA, 2015; International Commission on Financing Global Education Opportunity [Education Commission], 2016). Meanwhile, as David Archer and Tanvir Muntasim point out in Chapter 8, the private sector is focused principally on education supply as a business opportunity worth some US$4.4 trillion. There is no documented plan for substantial independent private financing of education that would contribute to the benchmarks of national spending. Since, historically, private investment in public education depends substantially on public subsidy (Colclough, 1996), and there is no evidence that this will change in the future, the potential for distortion of the goal through capture of public funds by private entities is real (Lewin, 2013).

The implied financing partnerships between public and private sectors laid out in the 2030 Agenda and the Addis Ababa Action Agenda (including for reaching the targets of Goal 4) are not only unrealistic but worrying in their assumption that the two sectors both prioritise the common good of all (UNGA, 2015a, 2015b). It goes without saying that governments and business have structurally different priorities, and while there are exceptions, as a rule these priorities do not seamlessly mesh into 'win-win' situations (Murgatroyd & Sahlberg, 2016). To adapt Stiglitz's image, the convergence of globalisation, technology, and market liberalisation has put the growth of inequality on steroids (Stiglitz, 2018), and this trend can only be fuelled as more and more private actors influence policy and action.

An example of convergence of interest but divergence of objectives is the push toward early childhood care and education (ECCE) expressed in Target 4.2. The Universal Declaration of Human Rights (UN, 1948) states the right to free elementary and fundamental education. It would be naïve in the extreme not to acknowledge that the fact that since ECCE is not explicitly mentioned as free, the business opportunity for expanding private and for-profit preprimary education has contributed to the motivation of private sector entities to be extremely supportive of ECCE. How they will contribute to the target, besides focussing on families with the means to pay for ECCE, is less clear.

This chapter looks at three interlocking ways by which the education goal and targets will be vulnerable because of the implicit assumption that motivations of both the public and private sectors will converge. The vulnerabilities will likely be expressed in unmet financial needs, distortion of spending for programmes, projects that cannot go to scale, and capture of public funds to support privately conceived innovations that do not have equity as their core objective. Many private sector entities have been determinedly promoting policies and practices that are primarily aimed at generating new markets and profits, and only incidentally, if at all, contributing to free and equitable education for *all*. While the SDGs themselves contain many references to the central role of the public sector in education for all, the supporting documents and institutions hedge their bets by referring frequently and insistently to things like the 'unprecedented range of public & private parties in policy creation and implementation' (OECD, 2017b). The door is everywhere open for business (Kumi et al., 2014).

The three interlocking policy trends, promoted heavily by market-oriented interests are:
- promotion of technology as a corrective for deficiencies in contemporary teaching and learning;
- internationally designed, standardised benchmarking and monitoring of learning processes and outcomes; and
- tolerance and/or encouragement of for-profit provision of both compulsory and noncompulsory education.

Each of these has its place in well-conceived and regulated education systems that aim for free and equitable education for all. But they can also engender perverse effects that challenge system-wide success of SDG 4. Many of the side effects of market-based reforms of public services, including education, take decades to emerge and then decades to correct.

Capture of public policy and funding (national and international), purportedly in the name of choice, efficiency and measurability distorts public spending, increases inequality, and progressively guts public education as it simultaneously subsidises corporate profit. The three interlocking trends seem to constitute a perfect storm for both progressively weakening the public sector and reinforcing the hold of private actors on education policies and the public purse.

The pressure to privatise significant portions of education policy and delivery, exemplified by the triad above, is gaining strength in many countries in the Global South, including for example Argentina, Brazil, India, Kenya, Liberia, Pakistan, and Peru (Verger, Fontdevila, & Zancajo, 2016), following a model heavily promoted in a handful of OECD countries and accompanied by aggressive lobbying by corporations and market-oriented philanthropies (Barkan, 2011; Martens, 2017). Many corporations describe education as one of the last lucrative economic activities that has not yet been fully mined (Gutstein, 2012; Verger et al., 2016). When Rupert Murdoch gave his speech, *Education: The Last Frontier*, to a forum in Paris, his vision was of a massive influx of technology into education processes (Murdoch, 2011). That, of course, is the gold standard for generating profit: standardisation and high volume.

A narrative of generalised failure of public education (Murgatroyd & Sahlberg, 2016; Stevenson & Wood, 2013) is used to prop up the unproven claim that market-based reforms can do better to improve access, quality, and efficiency overall. Following the view by some decision-makers and users of education that education is a positional rather than a public good, there is a real and widespread demand for ever-increasing echelons of private education and private tutoring for some parts of the population.

Standardisation of testing and therefore of classroom processes does not of itself improve learning, rather it eventually impoverishes scope, diversity, and pertinence of learning (Archer, 2014). It is, however, convenient and profitable for corporations. International benchmarking has high opportunity costs and negligible proven benefits for individual learners. The widespread use of technology in classrooms has not demonstrated cost-effectiveness in learning (Glewwe & Krafft, 2014) so much as its lucrative nature for technology industries. Recent funding trends and donor policies are resulting in backtracking from the objective of free universal basic education toward a model that shifts costs to households who are willing or constrained to pay.

Over the last few years, a rich and informative body of scholarly analysis has emerged on the subject of private sector involvement in education, which is called variously, privatisation, marketisation, the global education reform movement (GERM), and the global education industry, among others (Verger et al., 2016; Barkan, 2018; Aslam, Rawal, & Saeed, 2017; Steiner-Khamsi & Draxler, 2018). This chapter's purpose is to use a summary overview of the topic to attempt to tease out what marketisation may mean for progress toward SDGs.

As with privatisation of other public services, perverse effects are not immediate but build up over time. In countries such as the USA and the UK, where market-based reforms go back to the 1980s, there is ample research about negative side effects: inequality in spending and outcomes is growing, teacher disaffection is high, and teacher shortages are widespread.

The subject of market-based reform of education is highly ideologically fraught and, in the end, places in opposition two different philosophies on the purpose of education. These opposing philosophies exist uneasily side-by-side in the SDGs (VanderDussen Toukan, 2017). The shift in power relationships between governments and nonstate actors, which is currently accelerating, will threaten the optimistic assumption that with good will all actors can work together for a better educational world.

2   Some Side Effects of Learner-Centred Philosophies of Education

During the 1960s, two very different visions of education converged on a key belief, which is that teachers are significant obstacles to needed evolutions in education. Philosophers such as Bourdieu (1970), Freire (1970), Illich (1971), and Reimer (1971) claimed that schooling and teachers contribute to perpetuating social reproduction, inequality, and submissiveness. For these thinkers, reworking education processes to pass on to learners more initiative and control was therefore logically the only path to individual empowerment, liberation from a conservative past, and creation of social mobility.

Human capital theorists (Becker, 1993; Schultz, 1961) and subsequent advocates of an economically utilitarian conception of education also saw teachers as obstacles rather than mediators for progress, but from a different angle. For them, since education processes focused on practical outcomes and the creation of human capital for mainly economic ends, one necessarily should look at free human interaction in classrooms with suspicion. In this view, teacher-controlled pedagogy seemed to be the frail and random element of the learning process. The logical shift to making education more predictable and therefore closer to manufacturing in nature would necessarily involve intervening in teacher autonomy. The fact that stricter controls could also reduce the required level of qualifications, and therefore costs, was not always openly acknowledged as a desirable by-product of reform. Following on this logic, with learning evaluated increasingly as a 'set of distinct, measurable competencies', teachers can be reduced to being 'deliverers of agreed upon curriculum' (Murgatroyd & Sahlberg, 2016, p. 3).

These two threads obviously run through very different ideological visions of education. They nevertheless seem each to have contributed to an implicit contemporary position that the outcomes of education are principally the responsibility of the individual teacher and learner. On the one hand, shifting responsibility toward individuals can indeed be viewed as a form of liberation from hierarchical and conformist governance mechanisms, which has long been the mainstream view of philosophers of education, including the radical philosophers of the 1960s and 1970s. However, the same shift can facilitate putting too much responsibility, and even blame, on teachers and learners for inequalities of achievement that are directly attributable to factors outside the school system, such as socioeconomic status, financing, health, segregation, language of instruction, and so on. Calls for individualised learning have arrived simultaneously in many countries with the use of standardised tests to measure competencies, which limit the impact of individualisation. In other words, when predictability and measurability in the learning process are judged to be the best guarantors of quality, blame can be assigned for failure to meet predefined standards. Inevitably a pernicious hierarchy of winners and losers is established, with the losers being the culprits.

Beginning principally in the United States several decades ago and now spreading in both wealthy and poorer countries, the narrative of failing schools has developed into a commonly accepted truth (United States, National Commission on Excellence in Education, 1983; Ravitch, 2013; Barkan, 2018). It has been used both to shift attention away from the extra-school factors that lead to low results and high dropout, and to promote the notion that the solution is for parents to be able to shop around for private or public schools deemed by them to be preferable, paid for in various ways by public money. This market-based notion of 'choice' has been successfully promoted as a method of improving education generally, in spite of the fact that there is no evidence that this is happening (Musset, 2012).

So, we are facing tolerance of the Darwinian view that competition and a free market will do the education job better than public policies, and that success and failure in learning achievement can be explained by individual choices and effort. Although simultaneously reducing the agency of teachers through more scripted materials and standardising testing could seem to be in conflict with individual responsibility, it fits in neatly with the manufacturing approach whereby processes and outcomes are standardised, and quality control of the line workers (teachers) and the final product (graduates) is a process of rejecting items that are dissimilar to the desired result. Hardly coincidentally, such a view of education also presents the optimum business model for supply of services at every level (Davis, 2016).

3   Technologies in Education

Since the 1960s, successive technological advances have been touted as providing needed solutions for almost every perceived educational problem, whether related to inputs, processes, or outcomes. They are proposed as means of enhancing access in situations of teacher shortage, freeing learning from the constraints of space and time, making learning materials more reliable through standardisation, making evaluations comparable, individualising learning, limiting the roles of teachers in the name of eliminating human error, across-the-board management, and of course promising cost-effectiveness (Draxler & Haddad, 2002). Many of these solutions are conceived along the line of manufacturing models, with the technologies enabling a reliable, uniform, and predictable outcome, that is, acquisition by learners of a set of measurable and predefined skills. The range of products developed and sold to schools and universities has been very broad as technologies have evolved: radio and 'interactive' radio, overhead projectors, various types of recording equipment, television, whiteboards, computers, tablets, and smart phones. Distance, online, and blended learning have come to occupy a significant place in the higher education landscape and are poised to make inroads in basic and postbasic education all over the world.

Based on the self-evident observation that some teachers do not perform according to legitimate expectations of time on task, relationships with learners, and quality of instruction, the notion of using technologies to compensate has appeal. Teacher salaries are by far the principal recurrent cost of education. However, a rich literature of research shows that the principal in-school factor influencing learning outcomes is qualified and motivated teachers (EFA GMR Team, 2015). Similarly, massive open online courses (MOOCs) and similar offerings have dramatically high dropout rates unless they are combined with tutoring by humans (Laurillard & Kennedy, 2017). For-profit higher education institutions, including virtual ones, use a business model based on reducing personnel costs and increasing numbers of students. No studies show long-term, across-the-board gains in learning outcomes from the use of technologies in classrooms in countries where they are most widely used (OECD, 2016b).

Education is one of the last relatively untapped sources of profit for large corporations. Historically, education has been a fragmented, labour-intensive activity with the main private sector opportunities being infrastructure and learning materials in the form of textbooks. While profit can be extracted from both, technological progress has opened the possibility of the production of huge volumes of standardised learning materials. The education technology market in the US is worth over US$8 billion and growing. With less than 2% digitisation worldwide, the latest estimate of the worth of the market is already US$5.2 trillion (United States, Department of Education Office of Planning Evaluation and Policy Development, 2010).

Although technologies are now ubiquitous in schools and universities in wealthy countries, so far, little of the promise has materialised,[2] and certainly educational spending has not gone down (OECD, 2016b). The main beneficiaries of the boom in the use of technologies in teaching and learning have been the producers of the hardware and software. Many of the biggest aid donors and contributors to international organisations are also countries with large technology industries. Countries have historically provided a significant portion of aid in a manner that favours their domestic industries, through export of goods and services to recipient countries (Nowak-Lehmann et al., 2009). Technologies for education are no exception; building of trust and acceptance that technologies will improve learning at an ultimately lower cost in aid-recipient countries brings a huge parallel benefit in terms of exports from donor countries.

4   Internationally Standardised Benchmarking of Education Processes

The SDGs quite rightly emphasise the need for data to facilitate informed monitoring and decision-making of progress toward the goals. Indeed, the Secretary General of the United Nations created a special group to look at the potential and need for data as part of the SDG processes (IEAG, 2014). The 232 global SDG indicators (UN DESA, 2018a), of which 11 pertain directly to education, are all national-level indicators that are useful for measuring progress overall but have shortcomings in identifying national and regional disparities, weak spots, and decentralised management tools. The need to generate and use robust data-based evidence at all levels of education is not in question. Nonetheless, all endeavours have both opportunity costs and perverse outcomes or side effects. In this case, the opportunity costs of developing and updating internationally comparable data are likely to be high in the poorest countries, effectively prioritising this information over both implementation and other needed indicators of quality, inequality, and groups with special needs.

Similarly, efforts to develop internationally comparable tools of measuring learning, such as the Programme for International Student Assessment (PISA) and now PISA for Development (PISA-D), the Learning Metrics Task Force, and the Early Grade Reading Assessment (EGRA), do not find unanimous favour with educators and scholars (Archer, 2014; Gorur, 2016; Sorensen, 2015) precisely because of what is seen by some as reductionist approaches that narrow curriculum, place heavy burdens on educators, and encourage ranking. Other criticisms stem from the top-down nature of the conception of international measurement systems, their lack of democratic accountability and pertinence in some situations, and finally the often-confidential way in which ranking criteria are developed (Andrews et al., 2014). The eye-catching nature of ranking has been demonstrated to influence education policies as governments publicly commit to moving up, but with unclear results on learning (Fischman et al., 2019).

Furthermore, the debate about ownership of large sets of data is not benign. Until recently, most internationally comparable data on learning outcomes have been publicly generated and publicly owned. However, the collaboration of Pearson in the conception and execution of the next round of PISA could be the first stage in an ominous development: private creation and ownership of international data about students, learning outcomes, and education processes. There is also a real danger that the indicators, pleasing as they may be internationally, cannot adequately inform policies and practice in national contexts (Ahmed, 2014).

Standardising assessment is only the first stage of internationally standardising learning that facilitates the generation of reliably comparable data. In the US, where standardised multiple-choice testing is both ubiquitous and the object of significant dissatisfaction among teachers and parents (Hagopian, 2014), such assessment has narrowed the curriculum so much that writing is barely taught, and an estimated 20% of first-year higher education students have to take remedial courses. Many never learn to write properly (Maguire, 2016). Teaching and learning through highly standardised and scripted methods, such as those developed in the US and used by Bridge Academies in Kenya, are proudly reported to mean that each child in each school is following an identical 'learning' process at any given time (Education International and Kenya National Union of Teachers, 2016).

The standardised testing market is lucrative, valued at US$1.7 billion annually in the US in 2012 (Chingos, 2012). While in financial terms this sum does not amount to more than several percentage points of education spending in the US, for developing countries widespread testing by commercial companies would obviously take a bigger proportion of budgets and a substantial financial outlay. Nevertheless, standardised testing and the corollary standardisation of the curriculum have huge commercial advantages that are now being widely pursued beyond OECD countries. The Bridge example is only one of many chains[3] that are now seeking to get footholds in places where demand for private education is high and public education is struggling to accommodate every child, let alone improve quality.

As already mentioned, standardised international data invite ranking, which has many possibly pernicious effects. The first is that ranking is the most eye-catching aspect of data, and so the one that gets the most public attention. As a consequence, it tends to take on priority status with decision-makers. Another is that ranking of schools and universities has the opposite effect of improving performance: those with information and means flock to the highly ranked institutions, reinforcing and often adding to inequality (Andrews, 2016).

5   Marketisation

All international agreements and bodies since the creation of the United Nations and Bretton Woods institutions followed the lead and direction of the Universal Declaration of Human Rights on education, directing school education to be not only free but a prime responsibility of governments.[4] However, about 30 years ago, a notion began to gain traction (Draxler, 2008) that the private sector, including corporations, has strong potential to contribute to education policy, management, and financing, and therefore to contribute to meeting the goals and targets of the Jomtien agreement (World Conference on Education for All, 1990) and now the SDGs. The entry point was the seemingly obvious requirement to diversify and amplify sources of financing to achieve universal education. Reinforcement came from neoliberal economics that revere market principles and excoriate government regulation and control. Meanwhile public-private partnerships (PPPs) in the public works of developing countries, essentially a disguised form of public borrowing (Hall, 2015), became widespread in OECD countries and was gradually promoted by bilateral and multilateral development financing institutions, in spite of the absence of evidence of their contribution to the public good (Utting & Zammit, 2006). Expanding programmatically from PPPs for infrastructure to include education as a legitimate area, the UN actively adopted collaboration with business as one mode of growing all facets of education (UN Global Compact, 2013; Global Compact, 2012).

In recent years, acceptance of PPP models has extended to the acceptance and welcoming of for-profit companies, often multinational, operating in developing countries at every level of education: policy, teacher training, creation and operation of institutions, and testing, always with the support of public sector resources. While philanthropy is certainly growing in volume and influence (van Fleet, 2012), net financial contributions to education by the for-profit private sector are so low that they are not being tracked. A new landscape of very wealthy philanthropic organisations has grown up during this period as well, often financed by the private fortunes of leaders of technology-based corporations in wealthy countries (Barkan, 2011). These philanthropists' approach to education mostly mirrors their views about the essential role of market forces in all things, and commitment to introducing private sector action into all spheres of public life. Private for-profit operators of education, even basic education, have found approval and even support from the World Bank (2013), bilateral donors (Right to Education Project [RTE] et al., 2015), and international think tanks (Education Commission, 2016; Ashley & Wales, 2015).

Although the proponents for marketisation of education claim it is necessary for expanded access, meeting SDGs, quality, and efficiency, it has not, and probably cannot be demonstrated to deliver those outcomes (Lewin, 2013; Sahlberg, 2013; RTE et al., 2015). As Lewin suggests, the reaffirmed promise that no country with a credible plan would lack resources to universalise primary education can appear to be sabotaged by the very parties that can ensure this promise is kept, namely donors (Lewin, 2013). More importantly, there is little evidence that educational investment, additional to that of governments and households, has been created.

This chapter's focus is on compulsory education, where until now the central role of government in ensuring access and regulation has been recognised. Nevertheless, for-profit higher education is not only expanding rapidly but also is more difficult to regulate because of its transborder nature. The development of for-profit higher education has been somewhat chaotic, underregulated, and with little discernible contribution to quality. Absent sufficient regulation, there have been problems of all sorts, ranging from unrecognised diplomas, high costs, low relevance to the job market, and outright fraud (United States Senate Health Education Labor and Pensions Committee, 2012). There are important lessons to be learned from the sometimes-disastrous expansion of unregulated for-profit higher education, such as predatory practices that lead to high drop-out rates, low-value or worthless degrees, and high costs that lead to individual debt (United States Senate Health Education Labor and Pensions Committee, 2012) as business expands its reach into other levels of education.

While the literature around the SDGs, and the SDGs themselves, often emphasise the importance of the public sector, in reality, international organisations have joined the march toward privatisation in the name of short-term fixes to long-term problems (Martens, 2017). A rich body of research is now available on both the concept of privatisation and concrete experiences (Verger et al., 2016; Draxler, 2012b; Ginsburg et al., 2012). Where there is robust research on comparative learning outcomes between the public and the for-profit sector, outcomes are inconclusive or favour the public sector (Aslam et al., 2017; Wulff, 2017). The comparative costs and results are hotly contested between critics and supporters. What is not contested is that teachers in the private sector are almost uniformly less qualified and paid less. Turnover of teachers is generally higher than in the public sector. The most marginalised or difficult-to-teach students are either not accepted or are eased out. And over time, leaching of resources from the public purse will damage education for the majority. In countries such as the US, the UK, Sweden, and Australia, where there has been a big shift toward private education, consequences are mixed, with positive effects principally accruing to higher socioeconomic groups, costs being lower only when teacher pay goes down and inequalities of achievement increase (Andrews, 2016; Carnoy, 1998; Reid, 2015).

6   Conclusions

The critical analysis above both is based on and joins a long series of cautions by researchers and civil society organisations about the profit-seeking actions that are contributing to weakening public sectors all over the world, and that can dilute, derail, and delay achievement of quality education for all (Martens, 2017). Public education is under threat in the face of determined efforts by private sector entities to capture public subsidies for profit. New philanthropists, with market-oriented philosophies of education, often steer their funding to support both policies and programmes that validate their own philosophies of marketisation (Walker, 2015). The arguments for privatising education simply do not stand up system-wide over time in any country. What does stand up is the overwhelming profit motive that sees a technology- and data-driven education, with educators as part of the gig economy and the public sector as the assumer of risks. There is no evidence that the confluence of education standardised in its delivery and evaluation, and driven by business interests, can contribute to meeting the aims of quality education for all. In my view, the international community is overly optimistic about the power relationships between the public and private sectors and thus may be dozing its way to another disastrous side-lining of its stated goal of free quality basic education for all.

The SDGs cannot succeed without strong governments, committed to the public good. The declaration preceding the goals is an affirmation of noble values signed by 'we', that is, the governments concerned (UNGA, 2015b). However, the implementation is described in terms of broad partnerships that may or may not emerge globally or more locally.

Indeed, there is strong demand by families for better education, often expressed as demand for private education in the absence of a sufficiently credible offering of public education. Even very poor people make huge, often untenable sacrifices to do what they see as best for their children. Not-for-profit private education is a long-standing part of the educational landscape and has existed, mostly harmoniously, alongside public education since the nineteenth century. For-profit education is a newer phenomenon, and although it is relatively small, except for higher education, it seems to be growing much more quickly than anyone could have imagined several decades ago. The desirable collective response is not to use public funds, either national or international, to assist in exacerbating the public-private divide but to invest more and more wisely in robust public systems. Both the economic and social health of societies depend on public goods. Measures that capture resources and capacity needed to build strong public sector responses to the education needs of the population may serve the few and the short term but will inevitably reduce service to many and damage the social fabric.

What is the way forward? I believe it lies in strong citizen pressure for democratic accountability, transparency about the use of public money to support private education – especially profit-making education – and an insistence that experimentation in education carried out with public money be firmly grounded in research, scalability, inclusivity, and transparency. It lies in bolder and more coordinated intentions and actions by development institutions to ensure that the for-profit entities with which they work are contributing to rather than draining from resources devoted to achieving SDG goals.

One of the perverse effects of pursuit of the EFA goals was arguably that the emphasis on school enrolments dimmed efforts to achieve equity and quality (Riddell & Niño-Zarazúa, 2016; Draxler, 2012a). A looming consequence of the SDGs in terms of education worldwide is the capture of public funds to support commercial interests, whose long-term effects could be deeply damaging to quality, equality, and the public good.

Notes

1 'By 2030, ensure that all girls and boys complete free, equitable and quality primary and secondary education leading to relevant and effective learning outcomes' (UNGA, 2015b).

2 The OECD report (2016) uses the word 'yet' 16 times to refer to the elusive promises of technology to improve learning at lower cost, that are, and have been for decades, just around the corner, but not 'yet' here.

3 E.g., APEC (Philippines), BRAC (Bangladesh), Omega (Ghana), GEMS Education (more than a dozen countries).

4 Article 26: (1) Everyone has the right to education. Education shall be free, at least in the elementary and fundamental stages. Elementary education shall be compulsory. Technical and professional education shall be made generally available and higher education shall be equally accessible to all on the basis of merit. (2) Education shall be directed to the full development of the human personality and to the strengthening of respect for human rights and fundamental freedoms. It shall promote understanding, tolerance and friendship among all nations, racial or religious groups, and shall further the activities of the United Nations for the maintenance of peace. (3) Parents have a prior right to choose the kind of education that shall be given to their children (UN, 1948).

CHAPTER 8

Financing SDG 4: Context, Challenges, and Solutions

David Archer and Tanvir Muntasim

1 Introduction

The new Sustainable Development Goal (SDG) on education establishes more ambitious targets than the past Millennium Development Goals (MDGS), moving beyond universal access to primary school and gender parity to include universalising primary and secondary education of good quality, ensuring access to early childhood care and education, advancing technical and vocational education, promoting youth and adult literacy within a framework of lifelong learning, as well as focusing on well-trained qualified teachers, improving equity, and ensuring safe learning environments. This is more ambitious even than the Education for All (EFA) framework. However, the commitment to resourcing has gone down from the MDG era (from the recommendation of 6% of gross domestic product [GDP] to a looser range of 4–6% and from 20% of national budget to 15–20%). This apparent mismatch between expanded targets and diminishing financing commitment is troubling education stakeholders. Current resources for education in developing countries are stretched. The effects of this include a decline in people's confidence in public education, an increasing fragmentation of provision and the spread of for-profit fee-charging schools, with worrying impacts on equity and quality. This presents serious challenges for those who believe in the fundamental equalising power of education. Parents living in poverty around the world see education as the ticket to social mobility for their children. This is often in tension with elites who are willing to invest large sums to give their own children an educational advantage in life. Seen in broader terms, it becomes clear that if more equal and fair societies are to be created, building more equal education systems is a fundamental bedrock. Today a radical shift is needed, requiring a renewed commitment from the international community and a rebuilding of confidence in the capacity of governments to finance public education that is of good quality for all, and that can only come from a substantial scaling up of taxation and investment.

Education is a global public good[1] and a fundamental human right ingrained in the social compact between the state and its citizens. It is a long-term investment that requires predictable financing. That financing should not only be contingent upon economic growth leading to more spending in the social sector, rather it should come from the political priority attached to education by the state as the duty-bearer for delivering on the right to education. In a world that is overly driven by a focus on economic returns, this is a challenge because investing in education does not bring short-term, one-off, quick wins. The major returns to investment in education accrue over 10 or more years (when children complete their education and enter adulthood). This is in tension with the pressures on governments to make short- and medium-term investment decisions, driven by Medium-Term Expenditure Plans, supported by the International Monetary Fund (IMF) and the World Bank, and the political demands of electoral cycles. For some ministries of finance, education seems like a bottomless pit of spending that yields no returns, as there is no mechanism in conventional finance projections to factor in longer-term returns on investment. Making the case for increased investment in education relative to other subsectors is thus closely linked to making the case for longer-term and more strategic thinking about sustainable development as a whole.

2   From EFA/MDGs to SDGs: The Financing Landscape

After failing to reach the EFA goals set out in the 1990 Jomtien Declaration, the international education community met again, in 2000, and agreed on the Dakar Framework for Action, to which 164 governments signed on with a lot of optimism. The Framework detailed an ambitious agenda around six EFA goals and outlined how those goals could be realised. Assurances were made that countries with credible education sector plans would not be allowed to fail for lack of resources (World Education Forum, 2000). Sadly, despite some tentative efforts, this bold commitment of external aid was not delivered in practice. The most concerted effort to support credible planning and harmonise education aid was the Fast Track Initiative (EFA-FTI), which later evolved into Global Partnership for Education (GPE). Whilst many developing country governments did develop credible plans, EFA-FTI/GPE failed to mobilise more than a small percentage of the estimated external resource gap, struggling to reach US$1 billion a year when the estimated annual gap is now at least US$39 billion (GPE, 2018). In comparison, the health sector mobilised significantly more in external aid, though not without some challenges, such as narrow targeting and reduced focus on system support.

The EFA agenda received its first setback when only an abbreviated version was incorporated within the MDGs, highlighting universal primary education (UPE) and gender parity, ignoring the need for action on quality, technical skills, early childhood education, and adult literacy. It ensured a disproportionate focus on UPE, narrowing the agenda of EFA, and diminishing financing beyond UPE. The rift between EFA and MDGs also became increasingly visible, with the education community becoming progressively isolated in their demand for the financing required for achieving the *full* EFA agenda from the wider development community. The World Bank, as host of the EFA-FTI, with support from key donors such as the UK Department for International Development (DFID) and the US Agency for International Development (USAID), played a particularly assertive role in reducing the EFA agenda to a focus on delivering the much narrower education MDG. The argument was made that more aid could be mobilised if targets were precise and achievable (like the MDGs) rather than more diffuse (like EFA).

As the Education Commission report points out, in fact, education's share of sector-allocable official development assistance (ODA) fell from 13% to 10% between 2002 and 2015. Similarly, nonconcessional loans for education decreased from a peak of US$2.7 billion in 2010 to US$1.6 billion in 2014; and much of this went to support higher rather than basic education. Even worse, the targeting of aid has been far from optimal: only 24% of education ODA was disbursed to low-income countries in 2014 and just 68% of that aid actually reached recipient countries (International Commission on Financing Global Education Opportunity [Education Commission], 2016). That occurred mainly because some bilateral donors, notably France, spend a large portion of their education aid to pay for scholarships to students studying in donor countries, thereby describing as 'aid' monies going to prop up their domestic higher education systems. Sadly, the new SDG 4 target on scholarships can be seen to reinforce such practices.

The failure to mobilise sufficient financing for education from ODA has had disturbing results. In the early years of the new millennium, inspired by the new goals and promises, developing countries made massive progress in terms of enrolment in primary schools, mostly following significant campaigns for the abolition of user fees (so parents could afford to send their children to school for the first time). However, few countries invested more domestic resources to match their rising enrolments, in part because ministries of finance were constrained by restrictive macroeconomic policies linked to IMF loans, which prevented any increases in the public-sector wage bill (Marphatia & Archer, 2005; Marphatia et al., 2007). This prevented the recruitment of more teachers and contributed to a situation in which overall government spending on education did not rise as a proportion of overall spending in the years since 2002 (Education Commission, 2016, p. 109). Aid was insufficient to fill the gaps and would have been inappropriate anyway for covering recurrent costs such as teacher salaries. So, in the absence of an expanded workforce of trained teachers, class sizes rose to impossible levels, particularly in rural schools and schools in marginal urban areas. Low-cost solutions were sought in many parts of Africa, notably through the hiring of paraprofessional or untrained teachers, a practice encouraged by the World Bank and some other donors. When the effect overall of this failure to invest in expanding systems was to damage the quality and reputation of public education, these same donors spearheaded a new narrative: Public systems are failing, and the only solution is to turn to non-state actors and privatisation. However, the narrative lacked any convincing evidence base and after two decades still fails to provide system-level examples of successful privatisation in low-income countries.

3   Shifting Terrain: Rise of the Private Sector in Public Education

While the narrative of public education in crisis continued to develop, policy-makers and thought leaders started looking for alternatives in the SDG era. In a desperate bid to increase financing for education, especially after the disillusionment about diminishing external aid, much attention was given to the private sector. One of the first inklings of expectation was visible in the UN Secretary General's report prior to SDG declarations, where the private sector was positioned firmly as an expected financier of development goals. The fundamental question – why the private sector, driven by the profit motive, would step into the arena of the public (not-for-profit) sector – was rarely asked, and never answered satisfactorily. A rise in Public-Private Partnerships (PPPS) started to become prominent in public service reforms of education and health, moving beyond more traditional PPPs in the area of infrastructure to include a fuller role in service delivery. The development banks in particular paved the way for the introduction of private players long before their prominence in the SDGs. A review of the Asian Development Bank's (ADB's) education portfolio revealed a striking note: between 2000 and 2009, 100 ADB-approved loans and grants in the education sector, covering 32 projects worth US$3 billion, had PPP components worth US$1.6 billion (ASPBAE, 2015). There is little evidence to suggest that private finance made any significant financial contribution to these PPPs.

There is a fundamental tension between the way the development sector has viewed the role of the private sector in education and the way the private sector has viewed itself playing a role. While development players expected the private sector to step into supporting public services with additional finances and investments (Lebada, 2017), many in the private sector identified education as a US$4.4 trillion industry (Komljenovic & Robertson, 2017) where big profits could be made by capturing public funds.

The emergence of commercially oriented, for-profit providers of basic education in developing countries occurred around the same time as negotiations were underway to define the future SDG framework (Srivastava, 2013; Walker et al., 2016). As a result, some actors focussed discussions in the buildup to the SDGs around the 'affordability' of education, in direct contradiction with the focus on 'free, quality basic education', as promised by the human rights laws enshrined in international covenants. The dramatic success of school fee abolition over just a decade was rapidly forgotten by those who wanted to reframe the debate, particularly the World Bank (Nielsen, 2006). The previously relatively uncontested notion of education as a right started to be gradually undermined by the notion of education as an affordable service. Private sector provision began to be seen as a 'solution' to the 'crises' of public education. Instead of bringing in new resources, the private sector counted on becoming education service providers, extracting profits both from charging fees and drawing down on public resources, and thus not generally making additional contributions to either the financing pot or to the strengthening of public provisions. At the same time, private sector actors in both developing and developed countries found new ways to avoid paying taxes and to spirit profits out of countries and into tax havens (ICIJ, 2018), thus further undermining public financing.

Alarmingly, some of the new resources coming in for education started to focus on financing multinational, for-profit, private education providers. This remains a small proportion of overall provisions, but it is growing aggressively and has powerful financial supporters. For example, the World Bank, through its private sector investment wing, the International Finance Corporation, invested US$10 million in Bridge International Academies, a low-fee, private school chain, whose practices are already being challenged by governments in Uganda and Kenya (Smith & Baker, 2017). Bilateral aid agencies and multilateral development banks are also investing in this sector and promoting this practice, along with philanthropic billionaires. These approaches have already been called into question by international human rights bodies, making renewed debate around the right to education timely, topical, and engaging (GI-ESCR, 2017). These phenomena have also seen education advocates and human rights organisations come together to challenge the privatisation and commercialisation of education with a strong consensus that public resources should not be channelled into subsidising private provision. Increasingly, links are being made between resisting privatisation and promoting tax justice (Ron Balsera, 2017).

One of the challenges in education financing has always been emergency and conflict situations, where the public system can be weakened. Humanitarian aid rarely addresses education in such times. Less than 3% of emergency aid is typically used for education (ECHO, 2018). True to the theory of 'disaster capitalism' (Klein, 2007), according to which the private sector steps in during times of disaster to make profits, the tendency toward privatisation has become more prominent in the education sector of humanitarian operations (Fontdevila, Verger, & Zancajo, 2017). For example, after many years of civil war followed by the Ebola crisis, Liberia initiated a pilot programme to hand over its public schools to private providers through the controversial Partnership Schools for Liberia programme. It was only through concerted challenges from teacher unions and civil society that a comprehensive plan was reduced to a smaller scale (Klees, 2017).

This increasingly prominent role of the private sector in education is a marked difference from the MDG and EFA era in terms of provision and financing. Whilst private provision remains for now a relatively small part of most systems, it is often larger in developing countries than developed ones. The tide toward privatisation in these contexts will only be reversed when there is adequate public financing for good quality public schools that can deliver fully on the promises of SDG 4.

4   Aid Architecture for Education Financing

One of the lessons from the MDG and EFA era was that there were not enough well-informed discussions around financing. The aid harmonisation agenda as originally articulated in Paris and later reinforced in Accra and Busan (OECD, 2005/2008) provided some momentum for education sector planning and donor coordination through in-country donor mechanisms. This informed the creation of the EFA-FTI (and its evolution into GPE) but relatively little changed in terms of broader development financing for education. The Financing for Development (FfD) discussions, which were held alongside SDG conversations, could have made a breakthrough in terms of influencing global financial reform. However, the outcomes in the Addis Ababa FfD Conference[2] in 2015 were disappointing, and the fact that the education constituency was not as strongly engaged as some others (e.g., health) was also a problem. Ultimately the FfD process did not deliver significant progress for education (see

Chapter 2 by Antonia Wulff for more details on this). Two follow-up meetings about FfD in the subsequent years also fizzled out, failing to follow through with substantial decisions. For example, the specific call, made by many civil society actors, for a new UN Tax Body that would be adequately resourced and empowered to set and enforce global tax rules was not taken up.[3]

In terms of the specific architecture for external aid to education, as noted above, the Education for All Fast Track Initiative (EFA-FTI) was set up after Dakar, evolving later into Global Partnership for Education (GPE), with the ambition of being the only multilateral partnership and fund dedicated exclusively to education in the world's poorest countries. In practice, EFA-FTI was initially limited only to primary education, but as GPE, it has now expanded its mandate in line with the SDG 4 agenda. It still focuses the majority of its resources on primary and secondary education, with early childhood education recently moving up on the agenda; but adult literacy, for example, is still largely ignored. An overall environment of diminishing education aid has affected GPE. The 2015–2018 replenishment of US$2.1 billion was 40% up on the first replenishment in 2011, but 40% short of its US$3.5 billion goal. GPE's ambition for a bold replenishment in February 2018 in Senegal also fell short, with just US$2.3 billion raised (short of its aspiration to mobilise US$2 billion per year by 2020). There have also been significant developments in mobilising more harmonised resources for education in fragile and emergency settings. Education Cannot Wait (ECW) was set up in 2016 and launched at the World Humanitarian Summit.[4] It is planning to raise a total of US$3.85 billion by 2020, but present commitments fall far short, and it is unlikely to achieve the levels of funding it seeks.

Realising the importance of education financing in the SDG era, the International Commission on Financing Global Education Opportunity, in short, the Education Commission, was set up in 2015 (with leadership from the Government of Norway and the UN Special Envoy for Global Education, Gordon Brown) to reinvigorate the case for investing in education and to chart a pathway for increased investment in education. It has published an impressive report 'The Learning Generation', making a compelling case for investment and providing some new research and ambitious targets. It has also, more controversially, recommended an 'International Financing Facility for Education' (IFFEd) that will mobilise loan-based resources for education in lower-middle-income countries from the multilateral development banks. There are concerns that this may lead to a proliferation of harmonised funds and new conditionalities as full alignment with GPE and ECW is not yet clear. There are also concerns about loan-based financing for education in the context of rising debt burdens (where debt servicing takes money out of national budgets that could otherwise be spent on education). There are particular concerns about whether IFFEd should lend to countries in moderate debt distress and whether empowering the multilateral development banks to lend more to education makes sense given their track record (including of supporting PPPs). There are also some uncertainties about whether IFFEd will be able to raise sufficient capital on the scale that it originally sought.

However much is mobilised in external resources for education, it will never be a substitute for governments in developing countries increasing their own domestic financing of education as a response to pressure from their own citizens. Even the Education Commission estimates that only 3% of required resources for SDG 4 are likely to come from external mechanisms, and the remaining 97% will need to be mobilised by the countries themselves. In this context, 97% of the Commission's attention – and everyone else's efforts – ought to be focussed on increasing domestic resource mobilisation for education. Sadly, this is not the case, and almost all international attention is focussed on finding external resources rather than the more strategic and significant challenge of supporting initiatives that will facilitate countries to better mobilise sustainable and predictable resources for themselves. In the next section, we look at what could be done to enhance domestic financing by increasing the size of budgets using progressive taxation and increasing the shares allocated to education.

5   Meeting the Financing Deficit: Domestic Resource Mobilisation

In addressing domestic financing of education, there has been a focus for many years on the share of national budgets being spent on education. Presently low-income countries spend an average of just 17% of their national budgets on education, and some countries with the biggest education challenges (such as Nigeria and Pakistan) fall dramatically short of that average. An indicative benchmark of good practice was set at 20% by EFA-FTI in 2002 and is now the measure of good practice used by the GPE. It is also referenced in the Incheon Framework, which (with clumsy grammar) calls for 'at least 15–20% of total public expenditure' (World Education Forum, 2015, p. 9) with an indication that the least developed countries (LCDs) are likely to need to exceed this. However, looking at the share of budgets spent on education in isolation of other factors, notably the overall size of governments budgets, is problematic.

Thankfully the discourse is shifting. Compared to the Jomtien (1990) and Dakar (2000) agreements, the Incheon Declaration and Framework for Action in 2015 was more explicit about the role of domestic financing and the particular role of action on tax, observing that to achieve the goals,

> countries will need to: Increase public funding for education: This requires widening the tax base (in particular, by ending harmful tax incentives), preventing tax evasion and increasing the share of the national budget allocated to education. (WEF, 2015, p. 67)

It is no coincidence that this focus on the overall size of government budgets and the need to address the tax base coincides with a renewed focus on quality and the need for teachers who are well-trained, qualified, and motivated. The biggest single costs for education are recurrent costs, especially for teacher salaries. To achieve the first target of the SDG – universalising access to primary and secondary education – will require the employment of millions more trained teachers, which requires a long-term, predictable source of financing. UNESCO estimates indicate that presently around half of teachers in Africa, for example, have had little or no training (UNESCO, 2015a), while other studies show that teacher salaries have approximately halved in real terms over recent decades (Lambert, 2004). Data show that in one-third of all countries, fewer than 75% of teachers have been trained according to national standards. In part this arises from the fact that untrained teachers can be paid lower salaries, so there is a disincentive to train. Yet multiple studies have demonstrated that teachers – and their level of knowledge about their subject – are the most important determinant of education quality (UNESCO, 2017b).

Not all potential sources of finance are suitable for addressing the challenge of training and deploying more teachers; for example, aid budgets rarely cover teacher salaries, except in the case of general or sector budget support, which has declined in recent years, following a peak in the post-Paris aid effectiveness era. In large part, this is because aid is both too short-term and too unpredictable. Governments are reluctant to employ a teacher with such funding as they are aware of the need to continue paying the salary long after the end of a particular aid project. This is also a problem with many other innovative financing mechanisms that may offer short-term funding but struggle to guarantee sustainable financing over decades. There are of course additional challenges that arise with any funding based on loans (given the renewed debt-repayment challenges faced by many developing countries) or funding that depends on charging fees (given the known impact these have on inequity and exclusion in education). The big education challenges need systemic solutions and sustainable financing – features that are most closely identified with taxation.

As it is, tax is already the major source of financing government's education plans, even in highly aid-dependent, low-income countries. Education campaigners have spent many years focussing on getting a rising share of the budget for education without paying much attention to the broader issues of the overall tax base. But a 20% slice of a small pie is small, and the biggest gains will come from increasing the size of the pie rather than adding an extra 1% share. Moreover, many countries are coming close to achieving the benchmark of 15–20% of public expenditure being devoted to education, and some exceed this but still lack sufficient revenue. It is thus time to pay more attention to the size of government budgets overall.

Tax-to-GDP ratios are a widely used measure of tax collection. A state that can credibly provide universal education is likely to require at least a ratio of 20%, which many low-income countries do not reach. Thomas Piketty describes states that raise less than 20% tax to GDP as 'regalian' states, having some superficial and ceremonial characteristics of a state, but not the means to become true 'social' states able to provide universal basic services (Piketty, 2014, pp. 473–481). UNCTAD agrees that 20% tax to GDP is a key benchmark for a state that is committed to development (UNCTAD, 2015).

Shifting focus from aid and budget shares and focussing more strongly on taxation as a source of revenue has other benefits: As well as raising predictable revenue, it is a key means of redistribution of resources and reducing inequality. There are also major benefits in terms of building accountability – strengthening relations between citizens and state – and encouraging better governance. When people are aware that they are taxpayers, as even the poorest landless labourers are, due to value-added tax (VAT), they are much more likely to feel confident to demand things from local government, rather than seeing services as arising from charitable benevolence.

There are many different types of taxation. Some are direct, such as corporate taxes and taxes on individuals' labour, investment income, or wealth. Some are indirect on transactions or sales, such as VAT, which are borne by the final consumer, or customs and excise linked to imports or exports. Another way of looking at this is that there are seven 'universal' types of taxation: on income, employment, consumption, profits, property, inheritance, and industrial processes. There are also important nontax revenues available to governments in some cases, particularly in natural resource-exporting countries, for example, royalties from mining.

Some forms of tax are progressive (put simply, where those with more pay more as a proportion of their income or wealth) and some regressive (where those with more pay less as a proportion of their income or wealth). An income tax that is set in different marginal bands (such that, for example, high earners pay 60%, mid-level 40%, and low earners pay 20%) is progressive. However, VAT, if there are no exemptions made for basic goods, tends to be regressive.[5] One might argue that any increase in tax, whether through progressive or regressive means, is acceptable, if the revenue is spent progressively on basic education that reaches people living in poverty. Indeed, expanding revenue through VAT might be considered acceptable if the increased revenue is then spent on basic education, as overall that would be powerfully redistributive. Indirect taxes such as VAT raise revenue much more quickly than direct ones. Not all spending on education can be seen as progressive in this way. Investment in higher education might benefit a privileged elite and thus be regressive, unless targeted to provide access to the poorest students. Ideally, progressive spending on education should be financed through progressive tax so there is a double dose of reducing inequality. This is particularly urgent given the growing concerns about the negative impact of inequality, expressed by a range of actors and institutions from the IMF to the Pope of the Roman Catholic Church to Oxfam. Economic inequality 'represents a major threat to the achievement of the SDGs, imposing costs across a whole range of outcomes: from poorer physical and mental health ... to worse prospects for sustained economic growth ... and worse outcomes for women and girls' (Cobham & Klees, 2016, p. 18).

The 'tax consensus' in developing countries for the last two to three decades has been dominated by advice provided by the IMF and the World Bank. These agencies have paid little regard to what is progressive or regressive. The policy trend since the 1990s has been to liberalise trade, and therefore reduce trade taxes. The economies of many low-income countries have been built on commodity exports, with a high ratio of exports to GDP, so trade taxes were previously an important source of revenue – sometimes yielding up to 30% of total government revenue. When customs and excise tariffs were removed, the IMF particularly recommended replacing the lost revenue by introducing indirect taxation, usually VAT, which is relatively easy to collect, partly because it depends on self-enforcement by traders and partly because it is less visible to those paying it. So, over the last few decades, VAT has been introduced rapidly in a large number of low-income countries as the quickest way to replace lost revenue, but one consequence of this has been to add to the regressive nature of many tax systems. Another unfortunate side effect arises from the relative invisibility of VAT. Many people paying VAT are not conscious of paying taxes, and this potentially affects people's relationship with the state and their confidence (as taxpayers) in holding public services to account. The IMF has not shown the same enthusiasm for expanding corporate tax or promoting progressive forms of income, property, or wealth taxes, although they have recently started to explore these areas more actively (IMF, 2014). The IMF and the World Bank do not pay corporate taxes, and their staff do not pay direct income taxes, which may affect their commitment to promoting these forms of taxation.

Perhaps the biggest single area where a breakthrough can be made to secure progressive tax for progressive spending on education concerns corporate taxation. This has become the focus of a lot of international attention in recent years as illustrated by the OECD's Base Erosion and Profit Shifting process and the G20 political impetus behind it, by the Africa Union's High Level Panel on Illicit Financial Flows, and by the growing popular movement calling for companies to pay a fair share of tax. This is also an area of taxation where there is a huge impact from tax avoidance strategies in developing countries, and which therefore represents a potentially significant means for scaling up financing of education. The US$39 billion annual resource gap for education could be more than filled by coordinated action in this one area!

Within corporate taxation, there are three main reasons to focus specifically on multinational corporations (MNCs) and large national companies. First, small- and medium-sized domestic businesses are not usually offered the same tax incentives or holidays, which are mostly used to attract foreign investment, as MNCs. Second, MNCs have particular opportunities to avoid taxation due to their international nature. Third, the amounts at stake are very large. A progressive intervention for greater tax justice should rightly start where the inequality is greatest, particularly for supporting education, given its powerful equalising potential.

Below we examine just four areas where action on taxation could make a massive difference to the financing of education in the coming years. The first is tax incentives – as vast revenue is foregone by governments under the illusion that they need to give tax breaks in order to attract investment. Second, looking at aggressive tax avoidance is crucial – as huge sums are lost to education and other public services by increasingly common but unethical practices.[6] Third, it is important to look at tax treaties – as many treaties are profoundly imbalanced, depriving developing countries of desperately needed resources. Fourth, there are opportunities to raise earmarked taxes linked to corporate practices. There are clearly many other areas of tax reform where additional work needs to be done, but we use these examples to illustrate the importance of taxation for transforming the financing of education.

5.1   *Tax Incentives*

Strategically targeted tax incentives can play a crucial role in supporting national development, but in developing countries many tax incentives cause far more harm than good. First, and most importantly, they can massively reduce government revenues by removing the requirement for companies to pay fair levels of tax. Second, they can encourage corruption and secrecy when negotiated in highly discretionary 'special deals' with individual companies. Third, they do not encourage stable long-term investments because they mainly attract 'footloose' firms that can move their investments from one country to another. Fourth, where they favour foreign investors, they can disadvantage domestic investors and deter them from entering markets or expanding. Finally, they often require large resources to administer and are rarely transparently implemented. The ostensible reason for governments providing tax incentives to business is to attract foreign direct investment (FDI), yet the evidence, including the academic literature, suggests that tax incentives are not needed to attract FDI (IMF, 2015). There are four types of incentives that are particularly problematic: discretionary incentives, tax holidays, tax incentives in free trade zones, and stability agreements.

There are no official estimates of global revenue losses from tax incentives but, in 2013, ActionAid estimated that developing countries lose US$139 billion a year just from corporate income tax exemptions, or nearly US$3 billion each week. In just over two months, if channelled to where it is most needed, this could fill the annual global finance gap for basic education. Reports published by the IMF, the African Development Bank, and other agencies have estimated revenue losses from tax incentives as exceedingly high as a proportion of GDP, for example in Ghana (6% – enough to double the education budget), Kenya (3.1% – enough to increase education budget by half), Uganda (2% – enough to double education spending), and Rwanda (4.7% – enough to double education spending). In Ethiopia, tax incentives amounted to around US$1.3 billion (4.2 per cent of GDP) in 2008–2009. If Ethiopia devoted just 10% of these revenues to basic education, then the country would have an additional US$133 million available, enough to get approximately 1.4 million more children into school (Archer, Curtis, and Pereira, 2016). There is a compelling case for governments to be much more targeted in the use of tax incentives to support specific strategic sectors where FDI might make a difference, to make specific pledges to end harmful incentives, and to invest the revenue that is gained in financing education and other national development priorities.

Some governments might fear that taking action on tax incentives would undermine FDI and give the impression they are 'not open for business', but the IMF argues there is little evidence to support this (IMF, 2015). Some education activists might argue there is no guarantee that increased revenue will be spent on education, but this will be true for all action on increasing the tax base (Walker et al., 2016). It will of course continue to be important to sustain pressure on governments to maintain (or increase) the share of spending on education. If this is achieved, then an expanded overall tax intake will lead to significant increases in spending on education.

5.2   *Tax Avoidance and Evasion*

Tax evasion occurs when individuals or companies break the tax law of any of the countries in which they operate. It relies fundamentally on concealing the existence of taxable income from the authorities, whether by nondisclosure or by active steps such as placing the proceeds in a secrecy jurisdiction. Tax avoidance is a term that is used to capture practices that, while not clearly violating the letter of the law, violate the spirit or intentions of the law. There is a strong case for placing less emphasis on the technical and often obscure distinction between tax evasion and tax avoidance, and to develop instead an ethical notion of tax compliance where individuals and companies actively work to ensure that they pay taxation in accordance with the spirit and intention of the law. There are various examples of approaches used to avoid tax compliance (Archer et al., 2016). They include the following:

– *Transfer pricing manipulation:* goods or services traded among different companies within the same group can be manipulated in order to shift money from one jurisdiction to another with lower tax rates.
– *Transfer mispricing:* deliberate and illegal steps are taken to artificially shift income and/or profits.
– *Excessive interest deductions and thin capitalisation:* guarantees are used to create excessive debt, or excessive interest rates are charged on intra-company loans.
– *Trade mis-invoicing:* deliberately misreporting the value of a commercial transaction on an invoice submitted to customs authorities.
– *Artificially channelling funds through tax havens:* attracted by low tax rates and high secrecy.
– *Hybrid mismatches:* these depend on differences in the tax treatment of an entity or instrument in two or more jurisdictions that, working together, result in double nontaxation.

It is generally agreed that tax evasion and avoidance have a significant impact in developing countries, but it is very difficult to provide a precise estimate. Lack of data and the opacity surrounding most of these mechanisms make it necessary to use approximations and indirect approaches to measure the problem. The very lowest estimated figure for tax losses is US$100 billion annually (UNCTAD, 2015), and if 20% of this were spent on education, it would be enough to cover half of the global resource gap to get all children into primary and lower secondary school, estimated at US$39 billion. Other estimates suggest as much as US$600 billion a year may be lost to avoidance and evasion globally (Kar & Spanjers, 2015). If a fair share of this amount went to education, this could have a transformative effect.

To achieve progress on addressing tax evasion and avoidance there is an urgent need to strengthen tax rules and systems in developing countries, change rules in developed countries where they affect developing countries, increase transparency and information exchange, and revamp corporate taxation at an international level. There is a strong case for using more aid money to strengthen national revenue authorities, so they can better enforce tax rules, but action is also needed at an international level to create fairer global tax rules (see later section on global reforms).

5.3   *Tax Treaties*

Tax treaties are bilateral or, less often, multilateral agreements that are ostensibly designed to prevent the double taxation of income that originates in one territory and is paid to residents, both individuals and companies, of another. Tax treaties are thus seen as an important piece in ensuring fair taxation of multinational companies and have become increasingly important with the surge of cross-border investments over the last few decades. The evidence that they attract investment into developing countries is unconvincing (ActionAid, 2016). While tax treaties are not explicitly designed to facilitate tax avoidance, that is nevertheless sometimes the effect they can have. Most often avoidance arises as a result of weaknesses in the agreement, outdated clauses, or biased negotiation processes. For example, some treaties are very old, which means they were not designed to deal with the increasingly globalised and digital economy and, in some cases, reflect a different balance of power at the time of negotiation (e.g., from colonial times). There are challenges that arise owing to the allocation of taxing rights, especially where 'resident-based taxation' (taxing a company where it is based) is preferred over 'source-based taxation' (tax paid where the economic activity occurs). Those challenges are due to reductions of withholding taxes and to the differences between treaties, for example, around definitions about what constitutes a taxable permanent establishment, which can be exploited for tax avoidance purposes. The lack of or inadequate anti-abuse clauses also create problems for developing countries.

The IMF has estimated that non-OECD countries lose around US$1.6 billion a year as a consequence of US treaty provisions in relation to dividend and interest payments alone. Similar research conducted in the Netherlands estimates losses of 770 million euros for developing countries in 2011 as a result of Dutch tax treaties. More recently, ActionAid has estimated that restrictions on Bangladesh's ability to levy withholding taxes on dividend payments alone results in an annual revenue loss of US$85 million. These estimates do not take into account the potential increase of tax avoidance and other indirect effects resulting from lower withholding taxes. The aggregated impact on developing countries could amount to much more than the IMF estimate of US$1.6 billion (ActionAid, 2016). However, any measure aimed at reducing the negative impacts of tax treaties on developing countries requires a cancellation or renegotiation of an existing treaty, which is not straightforward. Public pressure mobilised in both countries that highlights the egregious consequences of a treaty can help to create an environment in which this becomes possible.

5.4   *Earmarked Taxes*

Earmarking is the process of assigning revenue from specific taxes to particular objectives, in this case education. Under a full earmark, the earmarked revenue is the only source of finance for the programme, while a partial earmark means that other financing also contributes. Earmarking may also be broad, covering a whole spending programme, or narrow, for a specific project within the programme. A distinction can also be made between 'soft' earmarking, whereby government policy (but not legislation) determines allocation of certain taxes to education, and 'hard' earmarking, whereby such allocations are enshrined in law.

There are some examples of taxes earmarked for education, such as the Ghana Education Trust Fund (funded by 2.5% of VAT collections and mostly spent on higher education); the Nigeria Tertiary Education Trust Fund (to which national companies pay 2% of assessable profit, again spent on higher education); the Brazilian Fund for Maintenance and Development of Basic Education (partly financed by earmarking 15% of VAT revenues); China's Educational Surcharge levied on VAT taxpayers at 3% of Consumption and Business Taxes; and India's flagship education programme that is funded partly by an 'education cess' (a 'tax-on-tax' introduced on all Union taxes at a rate of 2 per cent). In any scenario in which earmarked taxes are used for education, there is a need to ensure that they are only one source of funding and that they are supplementary to existing allocations, generating genuinely additional revenue that would not otherwise be raised. One option here is setting a benchmark on existing tax allocations or spending on education, before introducing a new earmarked tax, so that it can be clearly seen (and tracked) that the earmarked tax is providing additional revenues.

The global agreement of an ambitious education SDG offers a particular moment when earmarked taxes for education may make sense. For example, many countries will need to ratchet up spending on education over the coming years to scale up public provision for early childhood education or to universalise access to secondary education. In such a case, even if there are concerns about permanent earmarking, a case could be made to introduce an earmarked tax initially with a limited (say 10-year) timeframe, on the understanding that the economic returns that emerge from such investment in education will, by the end of the period, have enabled the government to raise more revenue through normal forms of taxation. There will of course be challenges in making the case for any well-benchmarked earmarked tax, as other sectors such as health or roads might make equally powerful cases.

6 Global Reforms to Support Domestic Resource Mobilisation

6.1 *Global Taxes and Global Action on Tax*
There is a limit to what domestic tax reforms can achieve in the absence of global reforms to tax rules and regulations, as a report for the Education Commission points out (Cobham & Klees, 2016). The report notes that tax revenues in most lower-income countries have not seen convergence toward OECD country averages. In addition to domestic political issues, such as lack of elite willingness to support progressive tax policies, two main reasons for this international pattern can be identified. One, as noted previously, is the relatively consistent advice from international organisations (notably the IMF) following a 'tax consensus' that has overemphasised taxes on the sale of goods and services, while neglecting direct taxes on income, profits, assets, and capital gains. The other is the global failure to challenge tax havens' financial secrecy, which has grown as a cause and facilitating factor of international tax avoidance and evasion, and the driver of a wider regulatory and tax 'race to the bottom'.

Two main types of response can be considered: global reforms to support domestic tax reform and globally levied taxes. Of the former, reforms can help to address the major losses due to international evasion and avoidance. Revenue losses due to multinational corporate tax manipulation just by US-registered companies are estimated (including by IMF researchers) at or above US$650 billion, annually (Cobham & Jansky, 2015). Revenue losses on income taxes due to undeclared offshore wealth, meanwhile, are estimated to approach US$200 billion. Progress in these two areas, which will depend in large part on global countermeasures, can make a vital contribution to closing the domestic revenue gap.

Of globally levied taxes, a financial wealth tax, as suggested by Thomas Piketty, has major revenue potential. Levied at 0.01%, annually, revenues could cover the estimated requirement for additional public financing of the SDGs. Levied instead at 1%, revenues might plug the entire incremental financing gap for sustainable development. Finally, a global financial transactions tax could potentially contribute revenues in a range of US$60 billion to US$360 billion. In each case, international measures to ensure greater transparency could alternatively support the levying of such taxes at the national level (Piketty, 2014).

Crucial to global action on tax justice is the creation of a representative global body to set and enforce tax rules. At present the dominant actor is the OECD, which inevitably promotes reforms that are mostly in the interests of rich nations, giving little voice to the Global South. A more empowered international body, set up on democratic/representative principles inclusive of all nations, is needed to challenge the dominant corporate culture and the behaviour of the top 1% of earners, who by default tend to use tax havens to hide their money from revenue authorities. This can and must change, and public education around the world stands to be one of the greatest beneficiaries when it does.

6.2   *Linking Action on Aid and Action on Tax*

At present, few links are made between the call for more aid to education (and other sectors) and the call for reforms to global tax rules. Yet they should be intimately connected. Both are effectively calls for action by the rich countries in the OECD to shoulder a responsibility to support developing countries. Sometimes the case for aid is presented as a case for reparations – to redress historic injustices arising from colonialism and slavery. But in practice, most of the time, aid is presented as an act of generosity by rich countries to help those who are poorer. In making the case for tax reform, the argument is for action to stop injustices that are perpetuated every day, here and now, by the continuing plunder of resources from developing countries. The Mbeki Panel on illicit financial flows in Africa reported that at least US$50 billion is lost every year to illicit financial flows (over US$1 trillion in the past half-century) and probably much more, far exceeding the funds received in aid (High-Level Panel on Illicit Financial Flows from Africa, 2015, p. 13). The fear is that the apparently generous action of giving aid helps to cover up the calamitous inaction that allows tax avoidance and evasion to continue unchecked.

We need to see more action in both regards: to improve the flow of aid resources and to improve the global tax rules that effectively undermine or contradict that flow. Bilateral donors in OECD countries should be increasing the size of their aid budgets to hit the target of 0.7% of Gross National Product (GNP) and should be earmarking more toward basic education (a 20% share would make sense). They ought to be targeting aid to the countries where it is most needed, and they should provide that aid in a harmonised way in line with aid effectiveness principles, for which GPE has laid a reasonable foundation, supporting education sector plans in 65 countries. The very same OECD countries need to take action to reverse the outflows of resources from developing countries, recognising that global rules and regulations that have been put in place by OECD are not up to the job. These rules need an overhaul and that can only be properly done by a more democratic and representative body; so the OECD countries should be in the forefront of making the case for an empowered and resourced UN body that will take action to address the contradictions in the international system.

6.3   *The 4S Framework: Sensitivity and Scrutiny as Well as Size and Share*

This chapter has focused at length on how to increase the mobilisation of funding for education, but we are regularly told that the real issue is not about getting more money but making sure existing money is better spent (World Bank, 2018e). In fact, it is a case of both. Clearly there is a need for more money and for that money to be better spent! The 4S framework (Walker & Mowé, 2016) offers a useful structure for this analysis. In respect to domestic financing, we need to address:
– The *size* of the government revenue overall.
– The *share* of the national budget spent on education.
– The *sensitivity* of allocations within the education budget.
– The *scrutiny* of spending in practice to make sure money arrives.
This chapter has discussed the share of budgets but focussed mostly on the overall size. In practice, equal attention needs to be placed on the sensitivity of allocations within education, with a strong focus on ensuring that budgets seek to address educational inequalities. Girls and children from other marginalised groups, including children with disabilities and children affected by armed conflict and disasters, are more likely to be out of school. Their specific needs are rarely taken into account in education budgets. Increased sensitivity of the education budget will help to improve access to quality education for girls and children from other marginalised groups; and this tends to lead more reliably to overall systems improvements (Sahlberg, 2014).

Even with a combination of a good share, size, and sensitivity of spending, there can be serious problems if the money does not arrive in practice in the places where it is most needed. For this reason, there needs to be scrutiny of spending, particularly in the most disadvantaged areas, where funds are least likely to arrive. In many countries, budgets are not transparent, and inefficiency and corruption mean that money often doesn't reach the poorest schools. Increased analysis of education budgets and expenditure by civil society as well as greater transparency and accountability on the part of governments will help to ensure that money is properly spent where it is needed most.

This 4S framework was developed to provide a balanced overview of what kind of domestic financing is needed to deliver on the education SDG. It is in fact equally valid when considering international aid:

- The *size* of aid budgets overall should reach 0.7% of GNP. Currently, most countries fall short of this UN-endorsed target.
- The *share* of aid spent on basic education should reach 20% to match recommendations for developing country government spending. At present, only about 4% of global aid goes to basic education.
- The *sensitivity* of aid allocations should be focused on low-income countries and should provide harmonised support to system-wide reforms, rather than isolated projects, in line with aid effectiveness principles. Too much is currently spent on politically favoured countries, not those most in need.
- The *scrutiny* of aid budgets should seek to reinforce the accountability of governments to their own people, especially in the field of education, as donors cannot be present in every village. Too often aid money is linked with corruption or leads to governments feeling more accountable on education to external donors than to their own citizens.

7   Conclusions and Recommendations

7.1   *Mobilising Resources*

New ways must be pursued to raise both significant and sustainable financing to help countries achieve full implementation of all the targets in the education SDG. Short-term, one-off solutions will not represent a breakthrough. An extra billion or two will not make a lasting difference. Placing a strong focus on how to expand the tax base for the financing of education offers the best prospect for delivering what is urgently needed – tens of billions of dollars in sustainable funding, year after year. Crucially, this also offers a way to provide sustainable financing that deepens rather than undermines the accountability of national governments to deliver on the right to education. The sustainable financing that could potentially be raised includes startling sums:

- US$139 billion a year from persuading ministries of finance and revenue authorities to end harmful tax incentives.
- US$100 to US$600 billion a year from promoting effective action to end aggressive tax avoidance.

If education receives 20% of these sums (the present, widely accepted benchmark), then this will represent a dramatic breakthrough for financing the Education 2030 agenda.

How does this look at country level? Recent research published by ActionAid provides some striking figures. Pakistan, a country with one of the largest numbers of out-of-school children in the world, loses US$4 billion from harmful tax incentives. Even 20% of this amount would ensure a place in primary school for its 5.61 million out-of-school children, an extra 100,000 trained teachers, and free school meals for 1.8 million children (Ron Balsera, 2017). Of course, this will only happen if there is sustained pressure, particularly from Pakistani citizens and civil society. So, action to deepen mobilisation and accountability has to go hand in hand with this action on financing (see also Chapter 17 by Allyson Krupar and Anjela Taneja). There is also scope to raise many more billions through taxes earmarked for education linked, for example, to natural resource extraction or the profits of certain categories of companies.

This is an issue whose time has come. The outrage around the world following the Panama Papers and the Paradise Papers showed the widespread public and political support for reform, and showed that these issues are not going away. Education policymakers should champion action on taxation as the most effective single means to mobilise the tens of billions of dollars that are urgently needed. It is time for the negative cycle of lost revenue and low investment in education to be replaced by a positive cycle of expanding domestic tax revenue to invest sustainably in education that will yield long-term economic growth, which in turn will expand revenues further.

Building movements that link education and tax justice campaigners could help to make breakthroughs in this area, persuading national governments to stop offering harmful tax incentives, to strengthen their tax systems and capacities (including legal and regulatory frameworks), to renegotiate unsound tax treaties, and to raise new earmarked taxes for education. Such movements also need to sustain pressure for international reforms, for example, the formation of a new representative UN Tax body to take the setting and enforcing of tax rules away from the OECD club of rich nations. Pressure needs to be sustained on multinational companies themselves to commit to full transparency and pay taxes in the countries where they are invested. Any companies that want to play their role as private sector champions for education (such as those involved in the Global Business Coalition for Education) should first set an example in their own tax affairs, committing to high standards of tax transparency and country-by-country reporting of their profits. An active discussion is now taking place in the Global Partnership for Education about making progressive action on tax a requirement for private sector organisations working with the partnership, though it is anticipated that this will be a contentious discussion.

Donors also have a role to play in using aid to strengthen tax systems, including national revenue authorities. At present less than 0.1% of aid is spent in this way. Donors need to continue to coordinate and harmonise their efforts behind sector support to national education sector plans (e.g., through the GPE). The UN system also has a crucial role. A critical first step might be to end the archaic practice that makes UN, World Bank, and IMF salaries tax exempt. If international organisations are to become champions of tax justice, they cannot be compromised in their own practices.

6.3   *Allocating Resources*

Putting tax on the table does not mean other crucial dimensions of financing SDG 4 can be ignored, but it is an essential foundation. Pressure needs to be sustained for a fair share of national budgets to be spent on education, so every country reaches or exceeds the 20% benchmark of good practice. Moreover, budgets need to be sensitively and effectively spent, prioritising equity so as to ensure no one is left behind. Equitable allocation and spending must be a core principle in terms of education financing and costing equity should be a priority (Myers, 2016). Equal spending per child is not tantamount to equitable allocation. To be inclusive of the children still out of school and to reach this goal, variable allocation and spending that will factor in multiple aspects of marginalisation (e.g., gender, rural-urban divide, disability, ethnicity, remoteness, incidence of conflict, and disaster) and include relevant premiums necessary for achieving inclusion will be essential.

There is increasing interest in National Education Accounts that track household spending alongside government budgets spent on education. However, considered in the light of the arguments advanced in this chapter, high household expenditure for access to basic education should be treated as a regressive form of tax. Not only does it contradict the principle of free education, it also means the poor tend to be forced to spend more on education as a proportion of their income than the rich. It is indeed important to track this data, but it is problematic if high household spending, as occurs in some Asian countries, is celebrated as a sign of a population committed to education. In fact, such data should be used as evidence of the need for a more effective and progressive tax system.

6.4   *Systemic Issues*

Making progress toward achieving SDG 4 requires a systemic approach both to education reform and education financing. The level of change needed will not come about from pilots or short-term projects; rather efforts need to be harmonised behind the strengthening of systems over the medium and long term that can deliver inclusive and equitable education. National governments should play a pivotal role in developing nationally relevant education sector plans, though to be effective they need to ensure ongoing and systematic consultation with teachers, parents, civil society organisations, and parliaments to build the consensus necessary for sustaining reform.

Global actors can and must play a role but are most effective when they are reinforcing national-level processes and systems rather than imposing their own ideologies or solutions. The GPE, with its commitment to country leadership and consultative processes over education sector planning, sets a positive example, harmonising the efforts of most bilateral and multilateral agencies. There is a still a worrying disconnect between the theory of GPE and the practice at country level, where the World Bank is responsible for managing GPE grants in the role of a grant agent in most cases. However, a relatively representative board and decision-making process helps to sustain pressure for it to continue to improve.[7] There is a great danger that other global financing mechanisms, such as Education Cannot Wait or IFFEd, might lead to fragmentation or parallel efforts that undermine the focus on country-led reforms to education systems. This danger is becoming more alarming with the launch of even more new financing mechanisms (Education Outcomes Fund, Inclusive Education Initiative) without clear harmonisation in place (Edwards, S., 2018). Unfortunately, the global efforts to set up education financing mechanisms are not matched by efforts to promote fundamental reforms of tax rules and regulations or indeed to support countries to expand their own domestic resource mobilisation for education.

If SDG 4 is to be achieved, a comprehensive framework to transform the financing of education needs to be pursued. This means looking at the 4Ss – the size, share, sensitivity, and scrutiny of education budgets. A larger tax base is needed, along with a better share for education, sensitive allocations driven by equity, and effective scrutiny. The 2017–2018 Global Education Monitoring report highlights the crucial importance of accountability in successful education systems (UNESCO, 2017b). A key part of this is for citizens to know what money should be arriving in their local school and for them to be able to track this in practice and expose misuse or abuse. Civil society has a crucial role, sharing information, building capacity, and documenting practices in the most remote and disadvantaged communities, which are often the last to receive funds. As citizens become involved in tracking spending, they also build their confidence to engage in budget formulation processes, asking ever more strategic questions about the share, size, and sensitivity of education budgets.

The achievement of SDG 4 now hangs in the balance. If serious progress is to be made, some big breakthroughs in mobilising sustainable financing will be needed. The size of budgets, the share of budgets, the sensitivity of allocations, and the scrutiny of spending will need to be increased. The alternative scenario is frightening – one of continued underfunding of public education, increased dependency and conditionality of aid (e.g., through payment by results and ideologically driven PPPs), increased privatisation, and increasingly unequal education systems that exacerbate the inequality in the societies they serve.

The world in 2030 should not be lamenting once again the failure to mobilise the financing necessary to deliver on collectively agreed goals. A situation needs to be avoided where public education systems are further undermined, fragmented, and privatised for profit. The financing for delivering on the right to education can be ensured, thus making education a powerful force for delivering on all the other SDGs.

Notes

1   Of course, many see education also as a private good, yielding significant returns to the individual. It is the tension between these narratives of education that underlies many of the biggest disputes in education today.
2   See http://www.un.org/esa/ffd/ffd3/index.html
3   The UN and the World Bank are undermined as legitimate actors on tax justice by the fact that their own employees are tax exempt.
4   See http://www.educationcannotwait.org
5   Some exemptions can make VAT progressive. Education advocates might make a case for VAT exemptions to go beyond traditional items like food and fuel to include school equipment, sanitary pads, etc.
6   Such practices were highlighted in the vast troves of leaked documents known as the Panama Papers and the Paradise Papers. See the website of the International Consortium of Investigative Journalists: https://www.icij.org/tags/panama-papers/ and https://www.icij.org/tags/paradise-papers/
7   The authors acknowledge that they have relationships with GPE, one as a previous board member, the other as a current staff member and may be perceived to have their own biases.

CHAPTER 9

SDG 4 and the 'Education Quality Turn': Prospects, Possibilities, and Problems

Yusuf Sayed and Kate Moriarty

1   Introduction

The Sustainable Development Goals (SDGs) set the scene for an ambitious development framework in a global context of widening inequalities within and between countries, global economic crises, conflict, and climate change. Building on the Millennium Development Goals (MDGs), the SDGs propose a transformation of the existing economic, social, and environmental status quo across the world. If the ambition is taken at face value, it presents a radical political project that proposes to fundamentally alter human society by 2030 through the achievement of these goals and related targets. To achieve its ambition will require a level of political will, financing, and radical action never before seen. The consensus reached on SDG 4 reflects the value placed on education by people from diverse cultural and socioeconomic backgrounds around the globe, as well as by governments of different political persuasions. Despite the apparent consensus, tensions over quality and learning evident in the global policy formulation processes were not fully resolved in SDG 4 and have continued since the adoption of the SDGs in September 2015.

The year 2013 appears to have marked the explicit beginning of the struggle in which vision of education would prevail, with a key meeting organised by UNESCO and UNICEF held in Dakar, Senegal, and the launch of the High-Level Panel report (UN, 2013b). Between 2013 and 2015, different groups put forward their agendas; this included formal processes and extensive lobbying by a range of stakeholders. These can be categorised as two interrelated processes, the New York UN post-MDG process and the Paris post-EFA (Education for All) process. This included UNDP-led consultations on the post-2015 agenda, among which was a global on-line consultation on the 'World We Want' survey. These initiatives were complemented through face-to-face consultations and intergovernmental meetings such as in Dakar (2013), Muscat (2014), and Incheon (2015), as well as country-level dialogue fora ahead of the final agreement on the sustainable development agenda. The deliberations of the Open Working Group (OWG), which began its work at the Rio+20 conference (see

Chapter 2 by Antonia Wulff for details), were a major part of the process. Among the debates that characterised this process were the following:

– whether education would be a stand-alone goal;
– if it were a stand-alone goal, whether it would encapsulate a full agenda, that carried forward the broad scope of the EFA movement;
– contestation about the focus of learning and quality as well as access;
– contestation about which organisation would lead the global education agenda.

The two strands of debate and policy development – the education discussion and the UN process under the OWG – came together in the final text of the education goal. At face value, that text appears to offer a compromise between the earlier debates over quality and learning. However, a deeper reading of the text and of the global indicators for SDG 4 suggest that this is not the case. As one actor suggested, while the final SDG 4 is ambitious and there is 'beautiful language', it missed some important aspects, including any targets on financing of the education agenda (from an interview by K. Moriarty).[1]

This chapter will examine the vision of education and education quality that emerges from the SDG 4 process. It will specifically explore the significance of the 'quality turn', the renewed focus on quality not only as an overarching goal but embedded in the targets. It will consider whether the broad conceptualisations of quality that emerge from SDG 4 engage with the notion of quality as a dynamic process oriented toward social justice. In particular, it will bring into focus whether the promise of 'equitable and inclusive quality education and lifelong learning for all' advances social justice or whether it remains purely a symbolic policy.

The next section of the chapter discusses the methodology that underpins the analysis. This is followed by a brief contextualisation of the framing of the chapter. Subsequent sections examine SDG 4 in relation to what is meant by education quality and learning, how they are measured and some of the key conditions that are necessary for realising the global education agenda. The conclusion summarises the key arguments of the chapter.

2   Methodology

The analysis and arguments made in this chapter and our contribution to the wider debates on SDG 4 and quality are based on a view that 'not only is the world socially and historically constructed, but so are people and the knowledge they possess. We operate in and construct our world and our lives on a social, cultural and historical playing field' (Kincheloe, 2005, p. 2). We argue that the construction of SDG 4 is not neutral; it reflects a particular global social and political context and motivations in which differing social forces seek to make and remake the world.

The data on which this chapter draws includes a detailed engagement with the content, structure, and language of the key policy texts relating to education SDG 4, its targets, and indicators. In particular we focus on the final SDG document as agreed upon at the United Nations General Assembly in September 2015, as well as relevant education policy texts and statements that preceded that document. We follow Rizvi and Lingard (2010), seeing policy as intertextual. Thus, the analysis of the final SDG 4 document is complemented by analysing other relevant texts that have informed its construction and additional text, such as the global indicators that have shaped its meaning ever since. This includes the UNESCO reports and position papers on education, the consultation reports and documents on education published by UNESCO and UNICEF, and those of the OWG and the 2030 Framework of Education adopted in 2015. The chapter also includes insights selected from interviews with 'policy elites' directly engaged at senior levels in formulating the education SDG goal, targets, and indicators from both governmental and nongovernmental backgrounds (Moriarty, 2019). Additionally, reflections from our own separate professional engagement in these processes have also influenced our analysis and the arguments made. Collectively these data offer us an opportunity to deconstruct the beliefs, assumptions, values, and sociopolitical dynamics that have informed the development of SDG 4.

3   Situating the Analysis: Scope and Limits of the Policy Imagination

Policy responds to the cultural, social, political, and economic norms, and, in turn, is shaped by them. Policy is developed within a particular sociopolitical and economic environment, and is the result of political pressure to convert conflict over public goods, such as education, into 'an authorised course of action concerning their allocation' (Bell & Stevenson, 2006, pp. 8, 16).

Globalised ideas and ideologies play a fundamental role in the development of policy. Lingard and Rawolle (2011) point to an emergent global education policy field, which they refer to as a 'rescaling of politics' developed out of the interaction between global and national policy fields. They conceptualise this rescaling as the relocation of political authority beyond the nation state through a 'global education policy field' (Lingard & Rawolle, 2011, p. 490). Verger, Novelli, and Altinyelken (2012) argue that globalised ideas are now dominating to the extent that it is possible to identify a convergence of national policy directions in education that can be referred to as 'global education policy'. Robertson (2012) provides a very useful separation of the different ways in which global education policy can be understood. These include global as a condition of the world, as discourse, as project, as scale, and as reach. She considers the impact of neoliberalism and changes in technology, a particular social imaginary, as a way of framing education problems and their solutions. She cites EFA as an example, which today is replaced by SDG 4. She argues that these changes were not caused by 'a global steamroller; rather, the complex reworking, re/bordering and re/ordering of education spaces to include a range of scales of action' (Robertson, 2012, p. 18), highlighting the geographically situated nature of 'international' actors and organisations.

The idea of Westphalian sovereignty, a principle in international law whereby each nation state has exclusive sovereignty over its territory and domestic affairs, is rendered impotent in processes of policy determination by globalisation and the pervasiveness of the neoliberal economic model. Cultural theorist Mark Fisher suggested that neoliberalism is not only the dominant form of socioeconomic organisation but is in fact the only reality we can imagine (Fisher, 2009). This is the lens through which everything, including education policy, is now framed, as if this were somehow the only natural condition. There is a struggle over the control of this 'social imaginary' between 'a dominant neo-liberal imaginary underpinning educational policy' and 'a democratic alternative to it, conceived as a radically different way of interpreting the facts of global interconnectivity and interdependence' (Rizvi, 2006, p. 200). This struggle is evident in the formulation and content of SDG 4.

In undertaking this analysis, we thus conceive of policy as providing a normative framework to which the international community and nation states should aspire. Untangling the complex discourses and ideological influences shaping the policy decisions that produced SDG4 and its targets is therefore of particular importance to see how the struggles played out, not only in what was and what was not included, but in the conception of what quality education is, what it aims to do, and how it is achieved.

4   The Notion of Quality in SDG 4

There was no mention of quality education in the 1990 Jomtien World Declaration on Education for All, nor in the MDGs (World Conference on Education for All, 1990; UN, 2015a). Quality of education became a stronger focus in the EFA goals (World Education Forum, 2000). Yet the reality is that, in practice, there remained a significant gap. One of the primary reasons identified for this is that the emphasis on access has come at the expense of quality. A major barrier to delivering quality education has been resource constraints – financial, human, and infrastructural. For example, one of the gaps in previous educational goals was the lack of focus on teachers as an important factor for quality. Not only physical access and the number of schools matter but also the quality of the teaching and what people learn (Case & Deaton, 1999; Sayed & Ahmed, 2015). Qualified and motivated teachers are key agents in improving the quality of education (for more detail, see Chapter 10 by Stephanie Bengtsson, Mamusu Kamanda, Joanne Ailwood, and Bilal Barakat).

The notion of quality education gained further policy traction in discussions of the post-2015 framework, partly due to a growing recognition of the 'global learning crisis' identified by UNESCO in 2013 (UNESCO, 2013c, 2014f). The recognition of a 'learning crisis' was accompanied by an increasing concern in some quarters that what people learn matters and growing evidence that many who access school were not actually learning (Acedo, Adams, and Popa, 2012). We will now explore the theoretical foundation of education generally and educational quality specifically before analysing how quality education is conceptualised and constructed in SDG 4 and its associated targets.

4.1   Instrumentalist Versus Rights-Based Arguments for Education and Conceptions of Quality Education

Competing conceptions of quality were played out before the final iteration of the SDG 4 process. They have also continued, as discussed later in this chapter, in relation to the global and thematic indicators for SDG 4 developed under the auspices of the Inter-agency and Expert Group on Sustainable Development Goal Indicators (IAEG-SDGs) and the Technical Cooperation Group on the indicators for SDG 4, respectively.

A consistent line of criticism of the previous global education goals and the global development frameworks is that they were framed in an instrumentalist way, in which development generally and education quality more specifically were seen as a means to an end, most often growth in gross domestic product (GDP). This instrumentalist logic of education is rooted in ideas of human capital formation through education and in particular the influential analysis of 'rates of return' on educational investments undertaken by Psacharopoulos (1972), Mincer (1974), and McMahon and Wagner (1981). McMahon recently reiterated his assessment that not only do returns to education 'improve the life chances of individuals over their life cycles but in the aggregate are measures of the returns to education to broader regional and national development' (McMahon & Oketch, 2013, p. 79). These approaches stressed the economic value of education and were heavily promoted by the World Bank. This promotion of education motivated primarily on the basis of its economic value to the individual and society has had a substantial impact on education policy and expansion. The focus on the physical access to education in the MDGs (MDG 2 in particular) was driven by the argument that this gave the best rate of return for education to governments and the global education development community. Bennell (1996a) gave a trenchant critique of the justification for primary education based on rates of returns methodology. Although a large body of literature exists that supports education's potential to create economic benefits, the question remains: Whose interest does an education policy driven by economic imperatives alone really serve?

Critics of instrumentalist arguments (Sayed & Ahmed, 2015; Acedo et al., 2012) for education quality argue that a rights-based understanding of quality is not an idealist vision of education but rather a legally binding obligation that all countries have committed themselves to through the signing of at least one international human rights convention that has a provision on the right to education (Aubry & Dorsi, 2016). Quality education is a human right, as the Committee of the Rights of Child notes in its General Comment no. 1:

> Article 29 (1) not only adds to the right to education recognized in article 28 a *qualitative* dimension which reflects the rights and inherent dignity of the child; it also insists upon the need for education to be child-centered, child-friendly and empowering, and it highlights the need for educational processes to be based upon the very principles it enunciates. (UN Committee on the Rights of the Child, 2001, emphasis added)

Ignoring the right to quality education, in favour of a utilitarian model driven by a narrow rates-of-return imperative that reduces quality to literacy and numeracy, limits the ability of education to unlock a child's (or an adult's) full potential. While education can and does impact both individual income and wider economic indicators, the emphasis on the narrow instrumental value of education can be misleading as it does not necessarily end inequality. Further, such an emphasis might reinforce patterns of marginalisation for many disempowered children (Bivens, Moriarty, & Taylor, 2009). It also risks leaving groups behind or condemning them to cycles of exclusion that their families may have experienced for generations.

Viewed through a rights-based model of quality education, how and what children and adults learn is not only about content-knowledge but also about the experience they have and values of cooperation that education can help develop. Understanding rights and experiencing rights in practice in the classroom and wider school are critical for the sustainable societies proposed in the 2030 agenda. This type of rights-based education is 'a major building block in efforts to achieve social transformation towards rights-respecting societies and social justice' (UNESCO & UNICEF, 2007, p. 12). For further discussion of this theme, see Chapter 13 by Joel Westheimer on citizenship education and Chapter 14 by Hiraku Komatsu, Jeremy Rappleye, and Iveta Silova on education and sustainable development.

4.2   *Unpacking Conceptions of Education Quality and Learning in the Overarching SDG Education Goal and Targets*

While the SDG agenda makes a clear and obvious commitment to quality education and learning, as reflected in the overall goal, the struggle over the operationalisation of the conception of education quality lies at the heart of the SDG 4 debates. Although there are nuances in various positions, and a possibility for achieving compromise, in essence the divide falls between a vision of quality education creating more progressive social justice and of education serving an economic imperative.

Education quality is core to the overarching SDG 4 goal and is referred to directly in three of the 10 targets. The concept is embedded in other targets, without actual use of the word. There are several challenges in how the notion of education quality is operationalised in the targets, reflecting the tension about the understandings of education outlined in the preceding section. In particular, we analyse selected targets of SDG 4, namely, 4.1, 4.2, 4.3, 4.7, and 4.c, to consider the ways in which the 'quality turn' in SDG 4 is – or is not – addressed, and the competing notions of access and learning.

The inclusion of the notion of lifelong education in the overarching goal is reflected in a commitment to broaden what counts as a valid education provision. This is, for example, reflected in the following early childhood education (ECE) target:

> 4.2 By 2030, ensure that all girls and boys have access to quality early childhood development, care and pre-primary education so that they are ready for primary education. (UNGA, 2015b, p. 17)

The significance of investing in ECE, particularly for mitigating inequities, cannot be sufficiently emphasised (Heckman, 2008; Rose & Zubairi, 2017). However, this target does not include the word 'free', which risks leaving the most marginalised children excluded from its benefits. Currently 85% of children in low-income countries (LICS) are not accessing any form of preprimary education. There is a continuing low level of investment in this sector. LICS only spend just over 2 US cents per day for each child on preprimary education, and education donors collectively spent only 0.6% of total aid to education on preprimary schooling between 2012 and 2015, leading to a shortage of available public places (Rose & Zubairi, 2017). This leaves a massive gap in provision, which brings an increased burden to low-income households. That is likely to mean that these children are left behind. This target risks exacerbating the increasing privatisation of ECE provision in many low-income countries and ensuring the fact that it is mainly the middle and wealthy classes that benefit from such opportunities.

The wider vision of education provision in SDG 4 is also reflected in a clear commitment to expanding the focus away from primary education to encompass both secondary and higher education, as articulated in this target:

> 4.3 By 2030, ensure equal access for all women and men to affordable and quality technical, vocational and tertiary education, including university. (UNGA, 2015b, p. 17)

This reflects a clear commitment to expanding education provision. However, the risk is that targets 4.2 and 4.3 are weakly formulated and moreover tend to privilege access opportunities over meaningful epistemic access and completion. This effectively weakens the level of commitment to quality lifelong learning.

An important shift in the SDG 4 targets is toward the affective (Sayed et al., 2018). The previous MDG agenda adopted a fairly narrow and instrumentalist view of education, focussing on access to primary schooling. In SDG 4 the shift is toward learning outcomes, such as the acquisition of literacy and numeracy, as is made clear in the global indicators for Target 4.1 (see the following section). Whilst these are important, the fragile nature of nation states in the 21st century, increasing physical and symbolic violence, xenophobia, and the growing denial of the rights of groups such as LGBTIQ, migrants, and refugees have revealed a dire need for an 'affective turn' within education policies. Issues of social justice and social cohesion have taken on greater importance within the education quality agenda in recent times. An important shift in the SDG 4 targets is toward the affective (Sayed et al., 2018); however, this is only partial and poorly formulated. SDG 4 has a target on these issues:

> 4.7 By 2030, ensure that all learners acquire the knowledge and skills needed to promote sustainable development, including, among others, through education for sustainable development and sustainable lifestyles, human rights, gender equality, promotion of a culture of peace

and non-violence, global citizenship and appreciation of cultural diversity and of culture's contribution to sustainable development. (UNGA,
2015b, p. 17)

These affective learning objectives, grouped under Target 4.7, commit the signatories to a rights-based understanding of quality and would contribute to
rights-respecting societies and social justice. They offer a broader conception
of education quality. This includes the concept of global citizenship, which
gained prominence as the third priority of the UN Secretary General's Global
Education First Initiative (GEFI). Global citizenship sets out a vision of education that moves beyond the acquisition of knowledge to empathy and action
for other people and the environment (UNESCO, 2012a). However, while the
broadening of the affective is important, many of the processes and documents
that informed the final text of SDG 4 stress economic factors as the underpinning consideration for reaching sustainable development and an emphasis
on education's role in promoting economic growth. In the articulation of the
High-Level Panel report, for example, this function of education for human
capital appears to sit alongside ideas of rights and citizenship for social justice. However, the role of education in economic growth is predominant. This
brings to the fore the question of intention and discourse: Is the learner conceived as an 'economic global citizen' (Richardson, 2008) or a 'critical global
citizen' (Andreotti, 2011), and are the two – as the polarity of the debates sometimes suggests – irreconcilable?

While the inclusion of Target 4.7 is symbolically important, it is what can
be best described as a residual target, in which many of the learning needs
identified by diverse stakeholder groups are lumped together. This goal has
been described by one policy actor as 'too broad and too many concepts ... difficult for people to grasp, especially for politicians' (Moriarty, 2019, p. 132). This
lumping together means the target is seen as too complex and is likely to be
sidelined by governments as the policy is translated down to the nation level
for implementation (Moriarty, 2019).

Furthermore, the learning envisaged by targets 4.1 and 4.4 (see below) is
described as 'relevant', giving it increased and central value, whereas the learning outcomes listed in Target 4.7 are described as promoting and contributing to sustainable development. This suggests that they possibly add value but
are not essential. The separation of the learning outcomes into two categories
– 'relevant' and 'contributing' – implies that knowledge, skills, and values of
human rights, gender equality, and peace are not relevant to learners worldwide. It seems that Target 4.7 was conceived of as largely symbolic and likely
to be delegitimised and marginalised in its implementation, given its broad

scope and its vague and generic formulation. Of course, this cannot yet be known as national implementation of SDG 4, its monitoring, and evaluation are still in their infancy. However, as suggested in the discussion of indicators that follows, most policymakers are more likely to adopt an instrumentalist and narrow view of learning.

What is new, is a greater emphasis on skills for work and jobs, with Target 4.4 committing to 'substantially increase the number of youth and adults who have relevant skills, including technical and vocational skills, for employment, decent jobs and entrepreneurship' (UNGA, 2015b, p. 17), making explicit the role of education in developing skills for work. Vocational training is mentioned in three separate SDG4 targets. In this target we again see the use of the word 'relevant', reinforcing (albeit subtly) the role of education in the creation of human capital. Such a vision of education continues to be promoted in new global measures on human capital recently announced by the World Bank, which, it has been argued, undermine SDG 4 (Edwards, D., 2018).

There are several silences in the SDG 4 framework. Some are matters of policy neglect and inattention, but others are more substantive. Among these is lack of attention to teachers – their training, their support, their working conditions. Although Target 4.c does include the important recognition that teachers must be professionally qualified, the targets do not focus on the need for having well-supported, motivated teachers whose rights and responsibilities are recognised in policies and in working conditions. In the discussion that predated the final SDG 4 framework, there was a target for teachers:

> Target 6: By 2030, all governments ensure that all learners are taught by qualified, professionally-trained, motivated and well-supported teachers. (UNESCO, 2014a)

Yet disappointingly, the final SDG 4 reduces teachers and their work to the level of an input:

> 4.c By 2030, substantially increase the supply of qualified teachers, including through international cooperation for teacher training in developing countries, especially least developed countries and small island developing States. (UNGA, 2015b, p. 17)

Addressing inequality in learning is only possible if there is equity in access, as well as teacher distribution and training. In many education systems, well-qualified and experienced teachers are clustered in schools serving the advantaged (UNESCO, 2014f). To ensure equity in learning (which, at present, is mostly measured through testing), the target for teachers and the associated measures as proposed in various documents (Sayed & Ahmed, 2011) should also focus on equity. Learning does not occur in the absence of teachers and teaching; a commitment to equity in learning should therefore include a focus on teachers and teaching. Only through quality inputs will it be possible to have both quality outcomes. 'The quality of an education system cannot exceed the quality of its teachers' (Barber & Mourshed, 2007, p. 13). There is significant evidence to support the claim that teachers are key to improving education quality and learning outcomes (UIS, 2016c). This requires teachers who are not only qualified but understand and respect human rights and who reflect the diversity of the population at large – including female teachers and teachers with disabilities. This also implies a need for attention to teacher recruitment and deployment within national education systems to ensure that it is not only wealthy and urban schools which can, and do, attract the most qualified and motivated teachers. Consequently, measures of learning should have, at their heart, the improvement of teacher pedagogy and student learning. Yet SDG 4 falls short in addressing the wider issues of teacher motivation and rights.

The operationalisation of education quality in the 10 targets is likely to lead to a narrow and instrumentalist reading of what is to be achieved, and what is desirable and meaningful, for several reasons. First, a key conceptual limitation of the SDG 4 is how learning is defined and for what purpose(s). Among the factors influencing learning and quality is the curriculum, which is not mentioned in the text of SDG 4. The assumption underpinning the notion of curricula and knowledge in SDG 4 is that national governments have curricula that are consistent with the overarching goals and learning targets. Further, the notion of knowledge and learning that is articulated in the SDG 4 framework is that of learner outcomes in literacy and numeracy at the terminal phases of primary and secondary schooling; learner readiness for schooling; digital and literacy skills; and knowledge of environmental and geoscience (see the following section). Other affective areas of knowledge are not prominent in the global indicators of SDG 4. This raises the questions of whether this can be conceived as a holistic framework of knowledge and learning in which knowledge is valued.

Second, conceiving of quality education only as relevant and effective learning outcomes, limited to the narrow conception of learning as cognitive attainment, fails to address other important aspects of quality education. One of the SDGs, Goal 16, is to 'promote peaceful and inclusive societies' (UNGA, 2015b, p. 14). Simply having a high level of literacy and numeracy will not achieve this. Education must deliver learning that is 'relevant' to the challenge of overcoming intolerance and hatred. Failing to prioritise human rights and global citizenship as relevant and effective undermines this goal.

Finally, education quality is complex, and learning multifaceted. Quality education and learning involves many different inputs and processes, among which are the experience in the classroom, including rights-based participatory pedagogy; adequate numbers of trained teachers; the promise that children understand the language they are taught in; access to teaching and learning material that promotes diversity; a school environment that is safe and free from violence or attack; and the teaching of a broad and diverse set of knowledge and skills, along with the ability to reflect on, question, and create knowledge, rather than simply repeat it in examinations. Learning, if it is of quality, must therefore be a process, a set of skills, not measured only as definitive outcomes from standardised tests.

In summary, for the 2030 education agenda, a critical question must be whether education driven by the logic of the economy can lead to the ambitious change set out in *Transforming Our World: The 2030 Agenda for Sustainable Development* (UNGA, 2015b). The dominant discourses that have shaped SDG 4 may have limited its potential to contribute to a holistic vision of development from the outset. A model of education driven by a narrow and instrumentalist logic is likely to undermine an expansive view of quality education. Literacy and numeracy – the indicators for Target 4.1 – while key foundational skills, alone do not constitute a quality education. If education is not equitable, either in terms of access or in the way it is experienced, then it cannot be considered quality education. Creating equality of opportunity is not sufficient either, as challenges facing the most marginalised groups as a result of social class, gender, ethnicity, disability, sexual orientation, or other identities require targeted actions by governments and their international partners.

5   Turning Targets into Indicators: The Further Narrowing of the Education Quality Agenda and the Perils of Measurement

In the previous section, we examined conceptions of education quality and learning as they are reflected in the targets. In this section, we consider how indicators and the process of their development frame the ways in which education quality might be realised in the Education 2030 global agenda. We discuss the global shared monitoring frameworks for tracking education progress as these provide a sharper focus of policymakers' priorities of what success looks like. For details of the classification, see UN (2019).

The measurement of progress for the SDGs overall will theoretically be guided by four levels of indicators: global, regional, thematic, and national. Governments will be accountable to report only on the 11 global education indicators, which represent a boiling down of priorities. The thematic indicators, although broad and comprehensive, will not require the same level of international accountability as the global indicators, and governments will choose their priorities in relation to their national context.

While the development of the SDGs, including SDG 4, was a political process, the development of the global indicators is described as a technical process led by a group of country-level experts, the Inter-agency and Expert Group on SDG Indicators (IAEG-SDGs). While the work of the group has been heavily influenced by available data, to refer to the feasibility of data collection and other methodological considerations to portray this as a merely technical process is misleading. The 'scope and wording of global indicators will, without doubt, have real political significance' (Moriarty, 2016, p. 124). As with the MDGs, what is measured and reported on will undoubtedly drive action. These are the indicators to which governments will be held accountable; they constitute an 'agenda inside the agenda'. How these decisions on global indicators were made, by whom, and on what basis requires interrogation as, notwithstanding the challenges, the indicators were not purely derived from available data. One interview informant involved in these processes parodied the discussions thus:

> Oh, we can only have one global indicator for 4.1, it's going to be reading and maths as OECD would like it to be for end of lower secondary because that is what they measure. (Moriarty, 2019, p. 148)

The different levels of indicators proposed are problematic, signalling two parallel processes:

> At the moment there are no global indicators on children in or out of schools or completion, no indicator on numbers of children and personally I think this is wrong, we are missing something. ... Just as we had for the SDG process this is a parallel process on the indicators, where you have the IAEG that decides on global indicators and the education community that decides on the thematic ones. (Moriarty, 2019, p. 146)

Nevertheless, each technical sector does make inputs into the IAEG-SDGs. The comment above may reflect a sense of disconnection and/or internal divisions within nation states and/or between the two processes of indicator development.

Another policy actor expressed the view that it should be 'up to national context and resources of the national governments to put in place a system for monitoring this. ... [It] will come down to local political contexts (Moriarty, 2019, p. 145).

Developing indicators is not easy as the categorisation of the indicators themselves into three tiers, based on the availability of mechanisms and data for measuring progress highlights (see Chapter 1 by Antonia Wulff for more detail). In addition to the technical challenges, decisions on what indicators are used to measure and track progress are highly political choices, determined by particular views of education's purpose, and in turn, setting the direction of education, its aims, and functions.

The indicators that have been developed have enabled the prioritisation of some agendas over others. This is perhaps most starkly illustrated by the global indicator for Target 4.1. The global indicator does not attempt to capture key aspects of the target, such as completion of a full cycle of schooling and/or the percentage of those children in free public education. The choice to measure only the 'proportion of children and young people: (a) in grades 2/3; (b) at the end of primary; and (c) at the end of lower secondary achieving at least a minimum proficiency level in (i) reading and (ii) mathematics, by sex' (IAEG-SDGs, 2016) is a means to boil down the focus of the target only to learning to read, write, and count. This removes any measure of equity based on free education – a universal human right and central to a broader conception of education quality and learning. Limiting the measurement of learning in this way produces a notion of quantitative effectiveness, which relies on test results to verify effectiveness and quality (Bivens et al., 2009). Such a technicist approach runs the risk of losing sight of the idea that improving learning does not come about by assessment per se or by the frequency of assessment (Sayed & Kanjee, 2013). Children do not learn simply because they are assessed. They learn if assessment information results in changes and improvements in pedagogy. Measurement thus has limited policy purchase if it does not result in improvements in classroom practice. There is also a danger that, in stressing learning outcomes, teachers' professionalism is undermined by the highly structured learning that such an emphasis on testing often brings. Moreover, test results themselves do not necessarily reflect observed learning outcomes among students (Goldstein, 2004). A key problem with these sets of global indicators is that they do not deal with pedagogy and learning adequately. An exception may be the mainstreaming of the themes of Target 4.7, which are the heart of education quality.

Both the global and thematic indicators have a narrow and reductionist view of learning and pedagogy. For example, the thematic indicators for knowledge, skills, and learning readiness reduce these to the following:

1.   Readiness: stimulating home learning environment.
2.   Skills: digital literacy.
3.   Knowledge: environmental science and geoscience.

Alexander (2015, p. 257) has concerns about how education quality and learning are understood. He states:

> Education for the period post-2015 needs a radical and properly informed debate about indicators and measures in relation to the black box, or black hole, of teaching and learning, for classrooms are the true front line in the quest for educational quality. The proper sequence, surely, is not to make do with the odd measure that happens to have featured in a number of school effectiveness studies but to start with a rounded account of the educational process and the purposes it serves, then range comprehensively and eclectically across the full spectrum of relevant research and extrapolate what the evidence shows can safely be regarded as key indicators of quality, and only then proceed to the question of how those indicators that have been shown to have pre-eminent influence on the quality and outcomes of learning can be translated into measures.

Alexander (2015, p. 257) goes on to caution against 'a single global measure of the quality of teaching applied across all cultural and pedagogical contexts'. On the other hand, the International Commission on Financing Global Education Opportunity (Education Commission), established after the adoption of SDG 4 and reflecting a great diversity of actors, argued that 'to galvanize attention globally, a single global indicator of learning should be agreed on to complement national measures of learning' (Education Commission, 2016, p. 17).

Reflecting on the process of developing indicators, a senior policy actor interviewed by one of the authors of this chapter made a thoughtful observation: Those who felt that the overarching goal was too broad, and that it required a narrower learning goal, argued that this was achieved through the global indicator process, as 'certain groups didn't get the targets they wanted then they pushed for the indicators to pick the part of the target they want' (Moriarty, 2019, p. 149). Although that view could be regarded as partial, it expresses the sentiment that the choice of indicators was both highly political and hotly contested, especially over what quality education means in practice.

Measurement and assessment constitute a large global industry and perhaps the largest global market in education after textbook production. The assessment and measuring required to monitor progress in SDG 4 are likely to stimulate that industry. This begs the question of who controls the testing market and who stands to gain from an increased focus on the assessment of learning. It would, indeed, be unfortunate if the SDG 4 education agenda focussing on learning and its measurement created a scramble for market shares and deliberately or unwittingly intensified the current privatisation of assessment and testing.

Indicators, including the global indicators, are designed as measures of accountability. Such frameworks require the confidence and trust of those who are implementing them. National governments and, more fundamentally, teachers and schools should therefore be in the driver's seat in developing measures of accountability that are politically acceptable, professionally sound, and administratively manageable. However, as we noted previously, discussion about indicator development and measurement has been largely treated as a technical exercise and thus avoided discussion about the politics of measurement: who sets the agenda, who monitors, who collects data, who interprets the data, who is to be held accountable and for what. Neglecting such considerations runs the risk of disempowering national education actors (state and nonstate) and citizens who should, in the final instance, be leading the agenda. After all, policy traction and accountability provided by global targets only work if national governments use the information from monitoring progress to put in place education policy reforms to improve education quality.

Understandably, international agencies – and by implication, the national governments with whom they work – have a need to focus on clear, reliable, and measurable targets and indicators to measure learning. Parents and students alike also place value, for a variety of reasons, on measuring progress. This might be because of an understanding of education qualifications as a 'positional good' (Hirsch, 1977) or due to a more comprehensive understanding of the value that formative assessment can provide. But there is a real risk that the SDG 4 notion of learning is being narrowed and, like the MDG access agenda, becomes no more than a quest for quantitative measures to show progress. According to Bivens et al. (2009, p. 100), this 'narrow orientation of education towards the cognitive, the behavioural and ultimately the economistic, manifested through over-reliance on testing and measurement, is disabling its potential to bring about significant change within individuals and within society more widely'.

While SDG 4 in many ways embraces a more expansive education vision than did the MDGs, it remains limited within the confines of a social imaginary that perceives education as a vehicle for economic ends and imposes considerable data burdens on national governments. Moreover, the process of developing indicators reflects a false technicist approach that removes ownership from those who will be required to implement this ambitious agenda. The control of the indicator development agenda is likely to result in a process of monitoring and tracking progress that is outside the ownership of national governments.

6   The Challenge of Realising the Ambitious Global Education
        Agenda

The SDGs in general and SDG 4 in particular, unlike the previous global agenda, include a focus on implementation. SDG 4 contains targets (4.a, 4.b and 4.c), which are referred to as means of implementation (MOI). We have already referred to one of these relating to teachers in a previous section. In this section, we focus on Target 4.b and more generally the issue of financing, which we consider critical to support quality. We also discuss who or which organisation is to be held accountable for monitoring progress, as well as several conditions necessary for the attainment of SDG 4 and its 10 associated targets.

There is little attention devoted in the SDG 4 text to the international architecture for delivering and managing the process, except for the three 'means of implementation' targets. In particular, there is a remarkable silence about how this agenda is to be financed. The Education 2030 Framework for Action does offer this statement of intent:

> We emphasize that international public finance plays an important role in complementing the efforts of countries to mobilize public resources domestically, especially in the poorest and most vulnerable countries with limited domestic resources. An important use of international public finance, including official development assistance (ODA), is to catalyse additional resource mobilization from other sources, public and private. ODA providers reaffirm their respective commitments, including the commitment by many developed countries to achieve the target of 0.7 per cent of gross national income for official development assistance (ODA/GNI) to developing countries and 0.15 per cent to 0.2 per cent of ODA/GNI to least developed countries. (WEF, 2015, para. 43)

Despite strong advocacy leading up to the adoption of the SDG framework, there is no specific target or goal relating to financing SDG 4, unlike the EFA framework for action, which stated that 'no countries seriously committed to education for all will be thwarted in their achievement of this goal by a lack of resources' (WEF, 2000, p. 9). This omission speaks volumes about the declining commitment of the international community, which has driven the SDG process, to support national governments in achieving the goals and targets set.

The financing aspects of the sustainable development agenda were dealt with separately in the *Addis Ababa Action Agenda*, adopted shortly before the SDGs themselves in 2015 (UNGA, 2015a). Some may argue that SDG 4 did not need a target on financing, although the Addis Agenda contains very limited financing commitments to education. This however, is not the whole story. SDG Target 3.c, one of the health goals' MOI targets, does call on governments to 'substantially increase health financing' (UNGA, 2015b, p. 17).

The only references to financing education are in the MOI targets 4.b and 4.c, which refer to scholarships for higher education and financial support for teacher training. They fall short of a more robust commitment to education financing targets. They also ignore the call by the African Union for a specific higher education/university target, as opposed to scholarships, for higher education (Sayed & Ahmed, 2011).

The Education 2030 Framework for Action, adopted after the final SDG 4 text, does seek to address this weakness, and the World Education Forum in May 2015 also highlighted the need for education finance (World Education Forum, 2015). However, the absence of a financing target in SDG 4 can arguably be read alongside a policy discourse in the SDG framework as a whole, which constructs a positive role for the private sector in delivering public goods, from contributing resources to direct delivery. In its construction, the SDG policy framework intentionally or inadvertently elevates the private sector as an equal partner and stakeholder in realising and protecting human rights. The question that must be asked is whether the self-interest and utility-maximising behaviour of the private sector can be harnessed to the benefit of the public sector.

A key policy text, which provides guidance for the implementation of SDG 4 is the *Education 2030 Framework for Action*. That document spells out various approaches and strategies for implementing SDG 4. The Incheon Declaration, which promulgated the Framework for Action, states:

> We reaffirm that the fundamental responsibility for successfully implementing this agenda lies with governments. We are determined to establish legal and policy frameworks that promote accountability and transparency as well as participatory governance and coordinated partnerships at all levels and across sectors, and to uphold the right to participation of all stakeholders. (World Education Forum, 2015, p. 9)

While laying the central responsibility for accountability at the foot of government, it does beg the question of what the role of the various sectors and actors, including international agencies, is in monitoring progress. It leaves vague how different actors will be held to account and by whom.

Finally, the realisation of this education agenda requires an approach to implementation that emphasises historic and structural inequities in promoting education quality. SDG 4 discourse, which brings both education quality and equity to the fore, must be buttressed at the level of implementation by political will and financial investments.

7 Conclusion

This chapter focussed on how the global education agenda articulated in SDG 4 reflects education quality and learning. We have argued that this turn to education quality, while echoing earlier global agendas, represents a shift in focus and attention to learning as opposed to access to education.

We have pointed to some of the key conceptual limitations of how education quality is conceived in the SDG 4 goal and embedded in the 10 associated targets. In particular this chapter emphasises that the concept of quality education and learning is narrowed and reduced in instrumental ways that reduce its potential reach and impact. We argue that while a shift to the 'affective' is marked by the inclusion of Target 4.7, the lumping together of so many topics renders it inoperative, with the risk that it becomes a residual target. The failure to describe the learning in Target 4.7 as relevant or effective creates a hierarchy of learning, where human rights education – a legal obligation – is seen as less important than other areas. We argue that in SDG 4, the neglect of curricula and inclusion of teachers in the framework as a 'technical education input' reduces their agency and limits the potential of the 'quality turn'.

SDG 4 and its targets lead to a form of pseudo-technicism whereby a narrow set of indicators are axiomatically assumed to measure equitable and quality lifelong learning for all. In so doing, rights-based understandings of quality, including inclusive and child-centred pedagogy, interactive teaching and learning processes in the classroom, a curriculum that encourages critical thinking, and respect for and understanding of human rights, which many observers, including the authors, feel better measure quality and learning, are marginalised and delegitimised. Education quality is discursively constituted as instrumental and, once again, devoid of any understanding of the teaching and learning process.

Despite our critique, we do believe that the insertion of equity and education quality in the global development goals represents a welcome change in the global agenda and a sober response to a narrow focus on physical access that characterised the previous MDGs. However, for the 'quality turn' to be realised in practice, a set of necessary conditions is required that acknowledges a vision of education quality in which the focus on the affective is valued along with the cognitive. This education quality turn implies rethinking the indicators and refining the targets at the level of implementation such that a holistic, reflexive, and critical vision of education is promoted. Further this necessitates an approach to education financing and accountability that privileges the need of the poor and marginalised through quality public education. Such a vision of education is consistent with a rights-based approach to implementing SDG 4 (Moriarty, 2017). Only in this way can the 5P mantra of *People, Planet, Prosperity, Peace and Partnership,* articulated in the wider 2030 agenda for sustainable development, be realised. And only in fully embracing a rights-based vision of the 'quality turn' can SDG 4 contribute to social justice and redistribution of privilege and wealth in and through education. Without such a vision, the ideal of 'equitable and quality lifelong learning for all' will remain illusory and unattainable.

Note

1   This chapter draws on doctoral research of one of the authors.

CHAPTER 10

Teachers Are More Than 'Supply': Toward Meaningful Measurement of Pedagogy and Teachers in SDG 4

Stephanie Bengtsson, Mamusu Kamanda, Joanne Ailwood and Bilal Barakat

1   Introduction

The significant improvement in school access (particularly at the primary level) is one success story of the Education for All (EFA) movement and the Millennium Development Goals (MDGs). However, many already marginalised children were left further behind during the global mass enrolment drive of the 1990s and early 2000s, and today half of the world's children without basic skills in literacy or numeracy are actually *in* school, according to recent data from UNESCO (Rose, 2015). With the launch of the Incheon Declaration for Education 2030 in May 2015 and the Sustainable Development Goals (SDGs) later that year came a noticeable shift in the discourse, from an almost exclusive focus on expanding access to formal schooling to the improvement of the quality of education, specifically through the improvement of student learning outcomes. SDG 4 includes targets and corresponding indicators for basic literacy and numeracy achievement (Targets 4.1 and 4.6), for 'relevant skills ... for employment, decent jobs and entrepreneurship' (Target 4.4), and, finally, for 'the knowledge and skills needed to promote sustainable development' (Target 4.7). This emphasis on improving quality by improving learning outcomes has ignited an interest in teachers and teaching and, subsequently, has put teachers in a position of greater prominence on the SDG agenda in the form of a dedicated 'means of implementation' in Target 4.c: 'By 2030, substantially increase the supply of qualified teachers, including through international cooperation for teacher training in developing countries, especially least developed countries and small island developing States' (UNGA, 2015b).

While some might view it as a promising development that teachers are included in the SDGs, in this chapter, we argue that *how* teachers are included in the agenda is a cause for concern for educationists and for the international community as a whole. To elaborate, Target 4.c is the only one of the 10 education targets to explicitly mention teachers, and it does so in reductive terms, referring to them as a 'supply' and a 'means of implementation', rather than as active stakeholders in education (and as human beings in their own right, who may face discrimination and rights violations themselves). This view of teachers as merely a human resource input continues to dominate the discourse of international and national development policymakers and practitioners around the world. Such a view stands in contrast with the perspective of a burgeoning group of educationists who argue that teachers and teacher organisations should be included in the development of policies and agendas, and not just in the policies and agendas themselves (Ginsburg, 2012, 2017).

Our concerns are framed within a broader discussion around the measurement of progress in education. We engage with the emerging argument within the international educational discourse that it has become common practice to 'treasure what is easy to measure' (e.g., basic learning outcomes, enrolment rates, etc.), rather than to work toward ways to effectively 'measure what we treasure', no matter how challenging (Alexander, 2015). Looking at the current indicator framework intended to evaluate progress toward the SDGs at the global, thematic, regional, and national levels, we explore the extent to which the current SDG 4 indicator framework allows us to adequately measure progress relating to the role of teachers in the development agenda, and seek to understand the key barriers to and potential catalysts for effective measurement in this regard. We argue that, as the focus of the SDG agenda shifts from the global- and thematic-level toward regional- and national-level actors and action, a productive space has opened up for influencing the development of regional- and national-level indicators that conceptualise teachers as active stakeholders and rights-holders in education. Such indicators could focus on processes of teaching and learning, rather than the more easily quantifiable measures that have dominated the field to date. We contend that quality, inclusive, equitable education hinges on learning to treasure the world's teachers through measurement processes that build on the development of a range of quantitative and qualitative context-specific indicators.

2   Measuring Teachers

In order to contextualise our critical analysis of the measurement of teachers in SDG 4, we begin with a review of the scholarship on the measurement of educational progress, focusing on teacher performance and learning outcomes, and how this relates to the SDG agenda.

As 2015 – the target year for the MDGs and EFA – drew nearer, there was a growing realisation around the world that the overriding emphasis on access to and enrolment in primary education in these global agendas had sidelined education quality. The finding that children who had been attending school for years had in many cases still not mastered the basics of literacy and numeracy (Rose, 2015) drew particular attention, but the limitation of the singular focus on enrolment was also evident in the dire conditions and facilities of the schools that many children were enrolled in, among other problems. The Incheon Declaration and the launch of the SDGs heralded a welcome shift in focus in the international educational discourse toward quality and the improvement of student learning outcomes, in part through the improvement of teaching. Unfortunately, however, much of the new international policy literature examines teachers and teaching in a narrow sense, emphasising 'teacher qualification' and 'teacher performance' (which is commonly gauged by looking at student achievement on formal assessment), rather than attempting to understand the complexities of teachers' lives, experience, and ongoing education (Avalos & Barrett, 2013). As Alexander (2015, p. 255) points out, 'Preferred evidence is top-down. It reflects the world, the preoccupations, the priorities, and the experiences of policymakers rather than those of teachers and children'. As with the MDGs, these priorities and preoccupations are also focused on what is easily quantifiable (Barrett et al., 2015; King, 2017; Rose, 2015). This focus on what is most easily quantifiable tends to favour certain types of indicators, namely relatively straightforward input and output indicators rather than more complex process indicators (Alexander, 2015), and leads to mismatched proxy indicators, where, for example, student test scores are used as a proxy for teacher performance,[1] or the proportion of qualified teachers is used as a proxy for the quality of the teaching force.[2] Even the post-2015 agenda, then, is dominated by indicators such as student/teacher ratios, literacy rates, and enrolment rates, while 'non-quantifiable' indicators associated with quality such as citizenship, values, and/or sustainability are crowded into the omnibus Target 4.7 on education for sustainable development. Actual processes of teaching and learning are largely ignored.

There is a perceived capacity to measure learning as a direct output of teachers' work, and the subsequent emphasis on gauging the quality of the 'human capital' making up the teaching force, is one feature of a current neoliberal climate of global governance. This discourse of neoliberalism builds on free market–based ideals and economic principles to drive education improvement via blunt instruments of measurement (Ball & Olmedo, 2013). While the measurement tools employed within this governance regime – for example, standardised tests, teacher numbers and attendance/absenteeism, capital works, and student/teacher ratios – can provide some useful data (Bold et al., 2017), the positive and productive impact of neoliberal policies and evaluation measures on education, educational outcomes, and teacher capacity are limited.

Attempting to measure teacher quality through primarily quantitative proxy indicators is unlikely to build a deep picture of the conditions and circumstances under which teachers are working, including their personal and professional support networks, the extent of their own schooling, initial teacher training and their ongoing professional development, the availability of consumable resources, housing, contractual status, and reliable (and at least adequate) salaries, among many other factors. Also missing from current analyses of teaching quality are the perceptions and viewpoints of teachers themselves (see Akyeampong, Pryor, and Ampiah [2006] for a nuanced analysis of Ghanaian teachers' understandings of pedagogy, learning, and assessment, and a discussion of how active engagement and dialogue with teachers themselves can be used as a type of formative evaluation).

Rather than supporting education for a socially just and democratic society, neoliberal policies reproduce an economic market ideal of competition, one aspect of which is creating illusions of choice that contribute to a narrative of competitive educational systems. In such systems, with their educational 'winners' and 'losers'; parents are positioned as having a 'choice' to decide which school is most desirable for their child (Angus, 2015; Connell, 2013; Ndimande, 2016). This education 'market' plays out differently across the world. In many high-income countries, it is evident in the organisation of teacher appraisal around a performance goal structure, where teacher performance is evaluated based on student scores on standardised tests (Skaalvik & Skaalvik, 2017). This approach to teacher evaluation is often tied to performance pay schemes, where teachers' bonuses (and, in some cases, salaries) are awarded based on their 'value added' to student learning, which is measured by looking at student test scores, as, for example in the case of the recent Gates Foundation's Intensive Partnerships for Effective Teaching initiative (Stecher et al., 2018). It has been pointed out that it is actually not possible to objectively evaluate teacher performance, that it is unfair to hold only teachers accountable for student learning, and that teacher motivation and cooperation might be adversely affected as a result (Bramwell, Anderson, & Mundy, 2014).

Also typical in high-income countries is the use of international standardised testing, such as the Programme for International Student Assessment (PISA) and the Trends in International Mathematics and Science Study (TIMSS), in combination with national school comparison websites and reports, such as My School in Australia, and school league tables in the UK. Such websites tend to be populated with decontextualised, disembodied data from national standardised tests. Using standardised testing as a proxy for learning or school quality while apportioning blame for poor outcomes to individual schools and teachers rather than systemic ills or injustices perpetuates, and can even increase, schooling inequalities (Gable & Lingard, 2013).

In low-income countries, educational gaps have been further emphasised, in part through the neoliberal structural adjustment programmes of the 1980s and 1990s, where international loans were disbursed only if certain conditions were met by receiving governments (Connell, 2013). These structural adjustment policies aimed to achieve macroeconomic stabilisation by downsizing public expenditure, privatising public utilities, and liberalising markets. Educational changes instituted as a result of structural adjustment included a concentration of public investment at the primary level, cuts to the number of civil servants, the fostering of a climate more receptive to private education provision, the decentralisation of education systems, and increased contributions by parents to offset the costs of educational infrastructure and resources (Mundy and Verger, 2015). Subsequently, and in keeping with the development agendas of the time, education spending was directed at promoting educational expansion at the primary education level, with enrolment rates used as the primary indicator of progress. This emphasis on expansion masked significant inequalities in education provision, as wealthier families were in a better position to ensure the quality of their children's schooling, and children from poorer families left to attend underresourced and overstretched government schools, where qualified teachers were not guaranteed, if they attended at all. This legacy of inequality continues today.

It should be noted that neoliberalism, with 'its central dynamic not within the metropole, but in the *relation* between metropole and periphery' (Connell, 2013, p. 101), has had another consequence for the international education development agenda: Knowledge and expertise on education and development tend to flow from high-income to low- and middle-income countries, regardless of their relevance and quality, and rarely in the opposite direction (Akyeampong et al., 2006; Connell, 2007; Pence & Ashton, 2016). In fact, despite the problems associated with teacher evaluation based on performance goal structures and value-added models that is currently favoured by many high-income countries, a recent rigorous review of the political economy of education systems in so-called developing countries recommends 'formal examinations of students to provide a basis for assessing school performance' and 'serious performance-based evaluations of teachers' as part of the structural changes needed to bring about positive educational reform (Kingdon et al., 2014, p. 52). In other words, the chances that low- and middle-income countries will be given adequate space and resources to sustain their own locally sustainable programmes without facing competition from imported solutions from high-income countries are slim (Masko & Bosiwah, 2012), and the chances that high-income countries will look to low- and middle-income countries for ideas are even slimmer.

Marginalising the systemic and institutional realities of teachers' personal and professional lives through restrictive measurement does the classic neoliberal work of shifting focus from the social and organisational structures, cultures, and resources teachers need to do their work effectively, to individual teachers and their perceived individual and autonomous commitment and capacity. In other words, while the blunt neoliberal measurement tools may provide some useful evidence for 'big picture' outcomes, they are unlikely to provide much in the way of evidence for what forms of support teachers need to improve student learning. For this information, teachers, teacher educators, and governments need to work together to collaborate/research and build locally sustainable programmes for capacity building and change. However, as has been alluded to earlier, teachers are very rarely asked for input as active participants in educational processes, even when it would seem appropriate to do so. A case in point is a recent World Bank report, entitled *What Do Teachers Know and Do? Does It Matter? Evidence from Primary Schools in Africa*. The authors used 'data derived from direct observations, unannounced visits, and tests' (Bold et al., 2017, p. 2) to determine how much time teachers spend teaching, if they have relevant content knowledge and skills, if they have pedagogical knowledge and skills, and the extent to which these knowledge and skills bases matter. However, at no point do they actually ask teachers for input or seem to consider the impact their evaluations are having on the teachers in question. As Schweisfurth (2015, p. 259) notes, 'Classroom interactions are at the heart of pedagogy, and any effort to improve or to evaluate the outcomes of these processes generates its own set of interactions, and shapes the priorities and identities of teachers and learners'. In the UK, Ball (2003) and Ball and Olmedo (2013) argued that performing 'teaching' within an environment of surveillance and measurement entails personal and professional costs for teachers. In other words, when the processes of teaching and learning are ignored in evaluations, and teachers are treated as inputs/resources to be assessed 'objectively' for quality by external experts, their ability to do their jobs well is significantly constrained. This performance culture has led to a 'controlled or compliant professionalism' among teachers, who tend to be more conservative and risk-averse, and are unlikely to view themselves as active agents of development, able to 'contribute to the production and co-production of new knowledge about practice in order to improve it' (Sachs, 2016, p. 424).

Paragraph 9 of the Incheon Declaration, which replaced the 2000 EFA Declaration and attempted to shape the SDG on education, makes an important step forward in this regard, resolving to 'ensure that teachers and educators are empowered, adequately recruited, well-trained, professionally qualified, motivated and supported within well-resourced, efficient and effectively governed systems' (WEF, 2015, p. 8). This is a particularly noteworthy improvement given that, while teachers were mentioned a number of times in the 2000 EFA Declaration, for example, in the framing document, where 'governments, organisations, agencies, groups and associations represented at the World Education Forum' pledged to 'enhance the status, morale and professionalism of teachers' (WEF, 2000, p. 8), there were no explicit references to teachers and teaching in the main text of the six EFA goals.[3] However, teachers are still relatively marginalised in the overall SDG agenda. The scant attention paid to teachers in both past and current agendas is puzzling even from a more neoliberal perspective that *does* treat teachers purely as inputs, given that they are – by far – the costliest input. After all, it is not uncommon for staff salaries to account for 90% of recurrent education expenditure or around 70% of overall expenditure.

Within the global education research community, the role of teachers is much more highly recognised and valued, as captured in the work of Akyeampong et al. (2006), Ball and Olmedo (2013), Schweisfurth (2015), and others. In the words of Alexander (2015, p. 254), 'Without teachers there is no teaching, and without good teachers the learning potential of many children will remain untapped'. In recent years, we have seen significant innovations within scholarship demonstrating the effectiveness of student-centred pedagogy, or 'learner-centred education', in a range of contexts around the world. Yet, ironically, 'pedagogy continues to be a neglected priority in discussions on the post-2015 agenda for education' (Schweisfurth, 2015, p. 259) and the actual relationship between students and teachers is largely ignored.

Based on the research demonstrating the effectiveness of learner-centred education, policymakers and practitioners have tended to oversimplify learner-centred education as meaning the polar opposite of 'teacher-centred education', which has further contributed to a 'learner-centric' measurement of education and a failure to recognise the importance of teacher-centred planning and the key role for teachers as active 'facilitator[s] of learning' (Di Biase, 2019, p. 569). Further, while learner-centred approaches do important work in drawing attention to the rights of students (Schweisfurth, 2015) (see Chapter 16 by Luke Shore and Viktor Grønne), there is significantly less educational programming that is based on a view of teachers as rights-holders (Tao, 2013).

3   A Global Snapshot of the Current Status of the 'Supply of Teachers' Target

We now turn to an analysis of the current status of the 'supply of teachers' target and its corresponding indicators to provide a global snapshot. As previously mentioned, Target 4.c is one of the three means of implementation targets presented for SDG 4. It represents a commitment to 'substantially increase the supply of qualified teachers' by 2030, focusing particularly on so-called 'least developed countries' and 'small island developing States'. Broadly speaking, recent data on teacher availability suggest a huge demand for teachers in order to meet Target 4.c. In 2016, almost 70 million new teachers were projected to be required to reach the 2030 education goals. Over 24 million teachers are needed at the primary school level, of which at least 21 million will be needed to cope with staff attrition, which is discussed in the following paragraphs. The remaining 3.4 million primary school teachers will be required to reduce the student/teacher ratio to 40:1. The additional number of teachers needed for secondary education is almost double that for primary. By 2030, at least 44.4 million teachers will be needed in secondary education: 27.6 million of these new recruits will replace teachers who will leave the workforce and 16.7 million will be needed to work with increased numbers of students projected to attend secondary schools while reducing the student/teacher ratio to 25:1 (UIS, 2016c, p. 1).

For both of these levels of education, teacher shortage is most acute in sub-Saharan Africa and Southern Asia. At the primary level, 26% of the total teachers needed are for sub-Saharan Africa, and 17% for Southern Asia. At the secondary school level, 25% of the 44.4 million needed are for Southern Asia and 24% for sub-Saharan Africa. In spite of the apparent shortage in both regions, there is a significant difference in the demand for teachers. That is, in sub-Saharan Africa, 38% of the 6.3 million teachers required for primary education will be recruited to staff new classrooms and the remaining 62% will be recruited as replacement for attrition. By comparison, in Southern Asia, over 90% of teacher demand for primary education is attributed to staff attrition and only 6% of new recruits will be used to staff new classrooms. For secondary education, 66% of teachers will be needed to staff new staff classrooms in sub-Saharan Africa relative to the 45% projected for Southern Asia (UIS, 2016c, p. 15).

Teacher shortage and attrition are not restricted to low- and middle-income countries. According to a recent European Commission report on teaching careers in Europe, most countries report shortages of teachers and an ageing teaching workforce (Eurydice, 2019). Further, some European countries faced challenges with insufficient numbers of students enrolling in initial teacher education and teachers leaving the profession.

Seven indicators have been developed to monitor progress toward Target 4.c. Four levels of indicators have been proposed to measure progress toward each SDG: global, thematic, regional, and national (Sachs-Israel, 2016). The global level indicators are a small set of globally comparable indicators developed by the Inter-Agency Expert Group on SDG Indicators and to be used for monitoring all the goals. Eleven of these indicators are listed under the education goal SDG 4. The thematic indicators are a broader set of indicators developed by the Technical Advisory Group on Education Indicators (TAG), a multistakeholder group that includes teacher representation, which was connected with the EFA Steering Committee. The thematic indicators are based on five criteria: relevance, alignment with target concepts, regular data collection feasibility across countries, ease of communication, and interpretability. There are 43 thematic indicators for education, of which the 11 global indicators are a subset (Sachs-Israel, 2016).

Both global and thematic indicators are predominantly quantitative in nature and focus on inputs and outputs, rather than the key processes of teaching and learning. While discussions around the indicators occurred alongside the development of the 17 SDGs and 169 accompanying targets (and, to some extent had been going on long before the development of the SDG agenda), the global and thematic indicators were formally proposed and decided only after the launch of the goals and targets, and the regional and national ones are still in various stages of development across the world.

Of the seven indicators developed to monitor Target 4.c, one is global and six are thematic. The precise wording of these indicators has evolved over time. By October 2015, those developing and negotiating the indicators had expressed them in terms of percentages of teachers who were 'qualified, trained, motivated, and supported' (UNESCO & UIS TAG, 2015, p. 10; see Table 10.1). That formulation was repeated in the SDG 4 Framework for Action (FFA), published in December 2015 (WEF, 2015, pp. 74, 81).

By October 2016, at the second meeting of the Technical Cooperation Group for SDG 4 held in Madrid, the present formulation of SDG 4 indicators emerged (UIS, 2017j, pp. 16, 56). That formulation is reproduced in authoritative guidance issued by UIS in February 2018 (UIS, 2018e, p. 43; see Table 10.2). The process of indicator development was, frankly, messy, with technically sound concepts sometimes subordinated to the need to achieve political agreement. For example, the original concept of percentages of qualified, trained, motivated, and supported teachers, is not explicitly addressed by the resulting, current indicators.

The global indicator for Target 4.c is Indicator 4.c.1, formerly 39 (see Tables 10.2 and 10.1, respectively), a stand-alone indicator that is to be used to evaluate progress at the global level. The remaining thematic indicators for Target 4.c are also intended to be comparable across countries, but they broaden the scope of what is being considered, aiming to assess multiple aspects of the teaching profession.

TABLE 10.1   Indicators to monitor Target 4.c, October 2015. 4.c. By 2030, substantially increase the supply of qualified teachers, including through international cooperation for teacher training in developing countries, especially least developed countries and small island developing states

Concept	No.	Indicator	Equity	Sex	Location	Wealth	Available	Coverage	Proposed global indicators	Comments
Qualified	37	Percentage of teachers qualified according to national standards by education level and type of institution	Yes	X	X		Yes			Common standards will need to be agreed that can be applied to both public and private institutions Qualified teachers have at least the minimum academic qualifications required by national standards for teaching a specific subject
	38	Pupil/qualified teacher ratio by education level	No				Yes			

(cont.)

TABLE 10.1   Indicators to monitor Target 4.c, October 2015. 4.c. By 2030, substantially increase the supply of qualified teachers, including through international cooperation for teacher training in developing countries, especially least developed countries and small island developing states. (cont.)

Concept	No.	Indicator	Equity	Sex	Location	Wealth	Available	Coverage	Proposed global indicators	Comments
Trained	39	Percentage of teachers in (i) pre-primary; (ii) primary; (iii) lower secondary; and (iv) upper secondary who have received at least the minimum organised and recognised teacher (i.e. pedagogical) training pre-service and in-service required for teaching at the relevant level in a given country, by type of institution	Yes	X	X		Yes		TAG UN	Common standards will need to be agreed that can be applied to both public and private institutions Trained teachers have received at least the minimum pedagogical training required by national standards to become a teacher
	40	Pupil-teacher ratio by education level	No				Yes			
Motivated	41	Average teacher salary relative to other professions requiring a comparable level of education qualification	No				1–3 years			A methodology will be developed based on labour force data
	42	Teacher attrition rate by education level	No	X			1–3 years			The coverage of current data collections will be extended to all countries

(cont.)

TABLE 10.1 Indicators to monitor Target 4.c, October 2015. 4.c. By 2030, substantially increase the supply of qualified teachers, including through international cooperation for teacher training in developing countries, especially least developed countries and small island developing states. (cont.)

Concept	No.	Indicator	Equity	Sex	Location	Wealth	Available	Coverage	Proposed global indicators	Comments
Supported	43	Percentage of teachers who received in-service training in the last 12 months by type of training	No	X			3–5 years			A tool to assess the incidence, duration and content of training will be developed

Notes:

Column 1 lists the four concepts relevant to Target 4.c – qualified, trained, motivated, and supported – to which each indicator corresponds.

As part of the focus on equity, columns 4–7 indicate whether only the national average or aggregate value of an indicator can be tracked or whether, as in the majority of cases, the indicator can be disaggregated by particular individual characteristics (sex, location or wealth).

Column 8 indicates whether an indicator is currently available and, if not, how long it might take for an indicator to be developed. If an indicator is currently available, column 9 indicates the current extent of country coverage.

Column 10 identifies those indicators that were proposed by the un system to the IAEG-SDGS as potential global reporting indicators and identifies the two cases where the tag recommends an alternative selection.

Finally, column 11 offers some initial thoughts on outstanding, indicator-specific issues, which have been taken into account and need to be addressed.

SOURCE: UNESCO AND UIS TAG (2015, P. 10)

TABLE 10.2   Indicators to monitor Target 4.c, October 2016 onwards

---

Target 4.c By 2030, substantially increase the supply of qualified teachers,
including through international cooperation for teacher training in developing
countries, especially least developed countries and small island developing States

---

4.c.1	Proportion of teachers in: (a) pre-primary education; (b) primary education; (c) lower secondary education; and (d) upper secondary education who have received at least the minimum organised teacher training (e.g., pedagogical training) pre-service or in-service required for teaching at the relevant level in a given country, by sex
4.c.2	Pupil-trained teacher ratio by education level
4.c.3	Percentage of teachers qualified according to national standards by education level and type of institution
4.c.4	Pupil-qualified teacher ratio by education level
4.c.5	Average teacher salary relative to other professions requiring a comparable level of qualification
4.c.6	Teacher attrition rate by education level
4.c.7	Percentage of teachers who received in-service training in the last 12 months by type of training

---

SOURCE: UIS (2018E, P. 43)

The four concepts are still covered by these seven indicators: qualification
(4.c.3 and 4.c.4, formerly 37 and 38), training (4.c.1 and 4.c.2, formerly 39 and
40), motivation (4.c.5 and 4.c.6, formerly 41 and 42), and support (4.c.7, formerly 43), but not as explicitly. Despite the changed wording, it is clear that
some care has been taken to look beyond the notion of an adequately qualified
'supply' of teachers, as called for in the target: Not only does this set of indicators draw a distinction between 'qualification' and 'training', where the former
refers to the academic qualification and the latter to pedagogical preparation,
but it includes measures of teacher 'motivation' and 'support' in recognition
of the fact that good teaching is not just dependent on having qualified and
trained teachers but also on whether or not those teachers feel motivated and
have adequate support in the form of in-service teacher education. In fact, the
2016 UNESCO Global Education Monitoring (GEM) Report provides an explanation for this broadened monitoring scope:

> There has been dissatisfaction that the SDGs treat teachers as a 'means
> of implementation', which risks underestimating the profession's

fundamental contribution to the provision of good quality education and an enabling learning environment. The formulation of the target is weak, with a limited conception of key teacher issues.

The GEM Report addresses the monitoring implications of the more general commitment, expressed in the Education 2030 Framework for Action, to 'ensure that teachers and educators are empowered, adequately recruited, well-trained, professionally qualified, motivated and supported'. (UNESCO, 2016b)[4]

To assess the level of qualification among teachers, two indicators are proposed (4.c.3 and 4.c.4): Indicator 4.c.3 measures the percentage of teachers that are qualified, and Indicator 4.c.4 measures the ratio of pupils to qualified teachers. Two indicators are also proposed to assess the level of training (4.c.1 and 4.c.2). Subtle changes to the wording were introduced between 2015 and 2016: The former Indicator 39 referred to both 'organised and recognised' training. The current Indicator 4.c.1 mentions only 'organised' training. The loss of recognition as a feature of desirable teacher training is unfortunate. On the other hand, the training was described as 'teacher (i.e., pedagogical) training' in Indicator 39; by 2016 this morphed into 'teacher training (*e.g.*, pedagogical training)' in Indicator 4.c.1 [emphasis added]. This represents an acknowledgement that teacher training includes pedagogical training but is much more than that, which is a positive development. The current Indicator 4.c.1 requires measurement of teacher training 'by sex' rather than 'by type of institution', which demands at least a minimal examination of gender concerns.

The last two concepts – motivation and support – are measured by teacher salary (Indicator 4.c.5, formerly 41) and attrition rate (Indicator 4.c.6, formerly 42) in the case of motivation, and in-service training (Indicator 4.c.7, formerly 43) in the case of support. The feasibility of accurately measuring these indicators has been subject to much debate.

Interestingly, as the UNESCO GEM Report for 2016 highlighted, while Target 4.c focuses on 'qualified' teachers (which traditionally refers to teachers who have the minimum academic qualifications, regardless of the field of study, expected for the education level to be taught), the corresponding global indicator focuses on 'trained' teachers (which traditionally refers to professional training in education). This has led to some confusion in the international education community, though a choice to emphasise professional teacher training rather than educational attainment in monitoring the 'supply' of teachers seems a logical one.

Although data are increasingly available on teacher training, there are concerns as to the extent to which this indicator can be truly comparable across countries (UNESCO, 2017b). That is, there is yet not a standard level of training, pre-service or in-service, that is demanded by the international community. Countries determine their own standards of teaching, prerequisites for teacher training, and pathways into teaching, and these can also vary within countries, for example, depending on whether teachers will be entering the public or the private education sector. When it comes to refugee education, a meaningful measure seems even more out of reach: In her global review of the state of refugee education, Dryden-Peterson (2011) notes that, at the time, refugee teachers were defined as 'trained' if they had had at least 10 days of training.

With such differences in policy and practice, there is doubt as to whether it is feasible for the international community to derive a meaningful comparison between countries in this regard. As the 2017/18 UNESCO GEM Report puts it: 'Even the concept of a common definition of training requirements seems too ambitious, given the varied challenges teachers face worldwide' (UNESCO, 2017b, p. 244). In fact, it could be argued that teacher training *should* look different in different parts of the world, precisely because of these contextual variations, and that, therefore, attempting to agree on a rigid common global definition of requirements for teacher training would seem counterproductive.

A similar reservation can be expressed about the indicator that measures qualification. This too is based on standards set in each country and, as such, presents heterogeneous definitions of what constitutes a 'qualified' teacher (UIS, 2017h). There are wide variations between countries in the process of qualification to be a teacher. Differences exist, for instance, in the admission requirements, duration of a programme, curriculum content, delivery modality, amount of school-based practice, and forms of assessment (UIS, 2017h). A further problem that compounds this complexity is that not all countries have a clear distinction between 'trained' and 'qualified', as alluded to in the previous paragraph. Some countries combine both the academic qualification with the professional training while others treat the two pathways as separate. Evidence from the UIS database shows that 81 countries reported data on both qualified and trained teachers for primary education and 61 countries reported data for the same indicators for secondary education (UIS, 2017h, p. 1). Of these 81 and 61 countries, 31 and 15, respectively, defined qualified teachers as being the same as trained teachers. Discrepancies between the supply of trained and qualified teachers are most prevalent in low-income countries. In Jamaica, for example, 15% of secondary school teachers are categorised as 'qualified' compared to 85% of teachers that are categorised as 'trained' (UNESCO, 2017b).

This contrasts with Niger where 100% of teachers are 'qualified', and 15% are 'trained'.

According to Table 10.1, all of the indicators for training and qualification (4.c.1 to 4.c.4, formerly 37 to 40) are technically available. However, according to the 2017 GEM Report, which has as its mandate to monitor progress on all of the SDG 4 targets, not all countries report data for qualified classroom teachers. The report found that from 2016 to 2017 the number of countries reporting data for qualified classroom teachers had increased from 40 to 48% at the primary level and from 29 to 38% at the secondary level. The number of countries reporting data for trained teachers changed only modestly between the two years: data were available for 47% of the 209 countries in 2017, relative to 46% in 2016 at the primary level; for trained teachers at the secondary level, data availability was slightly lower in 2017 than in 2016 (dropping from 36 to 35%). Limitations in data availability make it difficult to present a reliable estimate of global, regional, or subregional averages. Because of the earlier emphasis on primary education in the MDGs, data availability on indicators related to primary education is greater than for preprimary or secondary education. Though perhaps not consistently measured, data for the global indicator on improving the supply of 'trained teachers' (4.c.1) is more readily available because this had been previously reported under the MDG/EFA Framework by some countries, particularly in terms of the ratio of pupils to trained teacher at the primary level. Thus, in the new GEM Report, it has been possible to generate a global average for trained teachers for primary education but not the other levels of education. Globally, according to available data, primary school teachers are more likely to have been trained (86%) than those at the preprimary (36%) and secondary levels (45%) (UNESCO, 2017b, p. 244).

When it comes to teacher training and qualification, the indicators for Target 4.c only measure the supply of qualified teachers at the early childhood, primary, and secondary levels: there is no indicator on qualified teachers at the higher education level and for TVET and adult education (see Chapter 6 by Stephanie Allais, Elaine Unterhalter, Palesa Molebatsi, Lerato Posholi and Colleen Howell and Chapter 15 by Stephanie Allais and Volker Wedekind). Crucially, there is no indicator on qualified and trained teacher educators, even though in many countries teacher educators lack adequate preparation to be training future teachers (Akyeampong, 2017; Iwakuni, 2017). Nor are there any indicators on the quality of teacher education institutions and programmes, despite the fact that there is a strong link between the quality of initial teacher education and the health of the education system (Livingston, 2016). Further, despite the fact that it is also listed as a means of implementation, Target 4.b makes no special mention of scholarships for teacher education, focusing instead on information communications technology (ICT), engineering, and science:

> By 2020, substantially expand globally the number of scholarships available to developing countries, in particular least developed countries, small island developing States and African countries, for enrolment in higher education, including vocational training and information and communications technology, technical, engineering and scientific programmes, in developed countries and other developing countries. (UNGA, 2015b)

This latter point is particularly problematic, as the mass expansion of ECE, secondary education, adult education, and higher education implied by the rest of SDG 4 will require a significant increase in the number of qualified teachers, especially if quality education is to be ensured.

It is even more difficult to show what the current state of progress is on the indicators for motivation (4.c.5 and 4.c.6) and support (4.c.7). There is a paucity of data since many countries do not regularly and systematically collect data on remuneration packages (4.c.5), attrition/turnover (4.c.6), and in-service training (4.c.7). The OECD is the only organisation worldwide that systematically collects data on teacher salaries. Even so, out of the 35 OECD countries, recent data shows that only 24 reported data on teacher salaries for primary and secondary education, and only 21 reported data on teacher salaries for preprimary education. From the available evidence, teacher salaries increase with the level of education at which they teach. However, overall, their income is significantly lower than other workers who hold commensurate qualifications (UNESCO, 2017b, p. 245). Similar observations have been made in Latin America, where between 1997 and 2007, teacher salaries were found to be significantly lower than in other professions (Mizala & Nopo, 2016, p. 20). Collecting data on 'average' teacher salaries relative to other professions requiring similar educational qualifications may not prove useful in the long term, given the typically large disparities in pay between beginning teachers and senior teachers (Crehan, 2016), and between teachers working in the private and public sectors.

Data availability for teacher attrition (Indicator 4.c.6) is also limited, largely because teacher attrition is a complex, nonlinear phenomenon that will look different in different country contexts. Currently, this indicator is only available as an indirect estimate. Specifically, it is derived from comparing the reported number of teachers in successive years, as well as new entrants into the teaching force. Again, countries are more likely to report on this phenomenon in primary education, although only 26 of 209 countries reported data, according to the 2017 GEM Report (UNESCO, 2017b, p. 25). Among the countries reporting data on attrition, it is unclear whether the data submitted distinguish between temporary and permanent exit from the teaching profession. Further, attrition data are generally not disaggregated according to teacher background characteristics such as age, sex, or location. Finally, this indirect estimate does not allow for the potentially important distinction between teachers leaving the profession due to retirement (which plays a key role in teacher attrition), death, emigration, family commitments, further study, or a change of profession. In Sweden, for example, many teachers leave the profession temporarily and return years later after undertaking individual efforts to improve their teaching abilities (Lindqvist, Nordänger, & Carlsson, 2014). With respect to this question, there is practically no internationally comparable data available. In contrast to some other indicators, however, there are data available at some level of every education administration on public school teachers who quit and stop drawing a government salary, which typically distinguish between retirement and resignation. While this leaves some measurement issues unresolved, such as the differentiation between those who emigrate but do not leave the profession, consolidating these available data would go a considerable way toward developing a model for global attrition flows, especially since these potentially follow one of the more predictable patterns in education planning.

Crucially, teacher recruitment often follows a cyclical pattern. This means that retirements go up and down, reflecting ebbs and flows in recruitment 30 to 40 years earlier. Even without administrative data on actual retirements, there appears to be an unexploited opportunity to examine the overall age profile of teachers in international databases of censuses and/or large-scale household surveys. The same applies to other important characteristics of teachers, such as their family status. Studies from low- and middle-income countries have shown that the background characteristics of teachers as well as their working conditions can have a significant bearing on whether they remain in or exit the teaching profession (Akyeampong & Stephens, 2002; Avalos & Valenzuela, 2016). Being able to predict attrition flow and a greater availability of more detailed data, therefore, would be important to determine future teacher recruitment needs (to replace retiring teachers) and to understand other reasons for teacher attrition, which could then be addressed through policy solutions.

An issue that relates to both Indicator 4.c.1 (trained teachers) and Indicator 4.c.6 (attrition) is the complete absence of data on individuals who trained as teachers in the past, including those who are not currently in the profession. This figure would include both individuals who failed to secure a teaching post during a trough in the recruitment cycle mentioned previously, as well as others who eventually left the profession. Such a figure would be relevant not only because it would provide a more accurate basis for an extrapolation of the potential teacher training capacity than the actual growth rate in the teaching force does, but also because, where this capacity is insufficient to meet the demand for teachers implied by universal primary and secondary schooling by 2030, at least some of this dormant pool of teachers may be reactivated. Broadly speaking, in global educational databases, data coverage relating to teachers is very limited, even when it comes to more straightforward, quantitative indicators. The basic indicators available are the number of teachers by education level, and the percentage of teachers that are female, trained, qualified, and leaving the teaching profession each year (i.e., the attrition rate), respectively. Even among these elementary pieces of information, there are significant gaps in coverage, as discussed above. The most detailed and nuanced data are available for Africa and, more recently, a handful of countries in East and South West Asia, for which UIS in 2014 included additional queries in its standard country questionnaires. For Africa, this includes the possibility of identifying new recruits as well as new teacher training graduates. For East and South West Asia, in addition to these data, information is also available about contract type and average years of teaching experience.

The ability to monitor such indicators would be crucial to examining the implications of estimates of the need for new teachers to meet all the targets for SDG 4 (UIS, 2016c). Not least, a massive recruitment drive may substantially change the balance of experienced to novice teachers, but may also be used to justify the practice of increasing the share of contract teachers, both potentially detrimental developments that call for close monitoring.

In sum, there is a historic dearth of systematic global data collection on key dimensions of teachers' roles within the education system, and next to none on their characteristics as people. There are some promising steps toward more detailed data collection. However, this has been limited to a small number of countries so far and is still severely restricted in terms of the variables covered.

4   Discussion

The global and thematic indicators proposed to monitor progress on Target 4.c broadened the scope of what was seen as a weakly formulated, narrowly defined target on teachers, by attempting to address more complex teacher issues beyond training and qualification, including motivation and support (UNESCO, 2016b). However, these seven indicators are all quantitative and are insufficient on their own to serve as proxy indicators, particularly in the case of the indicators for the concepts of motivation and support. Anyone who has spent any time in a classroom will attest that to determine whether or not teachers feel sufficiently motivated and supported is dependent on more than an understanding of teacher salary (Indicator 4.c.5), attrition rate (Indicator 4.c.6), and access to in-service training (Indicator 4.c.7). For example, when it comes to in-service training, research suggests that teachers are often reluctant to participate in the most common continuing professional development (CPD) activities, including workshops and short courses, as they take up time in an already overcrowded schedule with very little pay-off (Geldenhuys & Oosthuizen, 2015). According to the research, the opportunity to work with an experienced mentor is often much more highly valued by beginning teachers than more formally organised CPD (Avalos & Valenzuela, 2016). Improved motivation and adequate support are also dependent on teachers' relationships with other key education support personnel who make up the complex social fabric of schools, including principals, administrative staff, school counsellors, teaching assistants, school management committee members, cooks, cleaners, and bus drivers, to name a few. These key education support personnel are noticeably absent from the SDG agenda.

The data required to track progress according to these seven indicators are not always readily accessible in the majority of country contexts, and even where they are, often they are not disaggregated (or disaggregated only by sex and location, but not by wealth). Finally, none of the indicators take national hiring processes into account, when, as discussed in a recent review of the literature on alternative teacher hiring practices in low- and middle-income countries (Chudgar, Chandra, & Razzaque, 2014), teacher staffing policies in many of these contexts are in flux. While many 'contract teachers' who work in these contexts are undertrained or underqualified, there is little reliable information about these teachers and their impact on learning outcomes. This adds a further level of complexity to the process of data collection on teachers. For a small number of years and some African countries, UIS collected and published data on the proportion of teachers who were newly recruited and their training status, but this exercise has not been updated recently.

The trend toward casualisation may also have an impact on the attractiveness of teaching as a profession for potential future recruits, and hence on future learning, and raises important questions about the status of teaching as a profession and about teachers' labour rights, issues that have been raised previously in the international community, though not sufficiently represented (cf. the ILO/UNESCO *Recommendation Concerning the Status of Teachers* [ILO and

UNESCO, 1966]). Rather than focusing solely on teachers as a system input – or means of implementation – to achieving education for all, a direct link must be made between the role of teachers and SDG 8, which calls for 'full and productive employment and decent work for all' (UNGA, 2015b). We noted at the beginning of this chapter that Target 4.c is the only one of the 10 SDG 4 targets to mention teachers. Further, outside of the seven indicators for Target 4.c, teachers/teaching are only mentioned once in the remaining 36 indicators for Target 4.7. Global Indicator 4.7.1 aims to measure the extent to which (i) global citizenship education and (ii) education for sustainable development, including gender equality and human rights, are mainstreamed at all levels in: (a) national education policies, (b) curricula, (c) *teacher education*, and (d) student assessment (UIS, 2018e, p. 42, emphasis added).

In other words, in spite of the attempts to broaden the scope of measurement for the dedicated teachers target, there appears to be no scope for measuring what teachers actually do – i.e., teaching[5] – and their relationship to education quality (Alexander, 2015; Rose, 2015). This highlights a significant problem raised by Faul in her analysis of global policy actors' narratives of EFA in relation to the post-2015 agenda, that while there is 'seeming consensus that access to school should be complemented with quality there is ongoing competition as to what "quality" may mean'. Faul further argues that 'policy actors can mobilise the metanarrative of "quality" to legitimise and justify their policy preference' (Faul, 2014, p. 16). In fact, targets 4.1, 4.2, and 4.3 all call for ensuring 'quality' education at various levels, and yet, despite burgeoning evidence demonstrating that teachers and teaching are fundamental to ensuring education quality (Mendenhall et al., 2015), the corresponding indicators are all to do with student participation rates and student learning outcomes, with a heavy emphasis on the cognitive dimensions of learning (especially literacy and numeracy). There are no corresponding indicators related to teachers or teaching.

While there are some regional and national initiatives and research underway that attempt to capture data on teachers and teaching, including teacher absenteeism, number of teaching hours and content knowledge, the data collection methods employed often involve observation of teachers, rather than interaction with them (see the research by Bold et al. [2017] discussed earlier, for example). These surveillance-style evaluations have led Schweisfurth and others to call for a more 'interactionist perspective' to education (Schweisfurth, 2015, p. 262), one which recognises that teachers are shaped not only by their teacher education programmes, as well as their interactions with each other and with their students, but also by how they are observed and evaluated by the administration, the community, and researchers. A case in point is research conducted by Akyeampong and others involving Ghanaian teachers. They described how teachers admitted to 'dubbing' (recycling lesson notes) or 'computation' (imputing missing marks) to meet strict inspection requirements given time and other constraints, when unexpected visits were made by school inspectors. They note that, while these practices can be viewed as 'abuses of the system and evidence of incompetence ... if instead one works with the premise that teachers are potentially competent, but struggling to cope with difficult circumstances, [these practices] can instead be seen [as] a rational response to a burdensome and counterproductive system' (Akyeampong et al., 2006, p. 170).

Three points are worth noting here. First, some forms of evaluation and surveillance can actually lead to poor teaching practices. Second, qualitative data relating to the standards and processes of teaching within countries provide important context for quantitative measures. Third, teachers have a potentially powerful role to play in monitoring SDG 4 themselves, particularly as they were instrumental in work with the EFA Steering Committee, OWG deliberations, and TAG, as discussed by Antonia Wulff in Chapter 2. After all, the Ghanaian teachers actually admitted to these poor teaching practices but were then able to explore the reasons for this together with the researchers. In other words, the international community should include 'members of the teaching profession', not just in the language of their declarations but also in practice. It would be important to ensure meaningful inclusion by reaching out to teacher unions and other representative organisations.

5   Conclusion: Learning to Treasure the World's Teachers and Measure Accordingly

We have argued that teachers are a central and human part of the education system, that they are rights-holders and require ongoing professional communities and development. The current focus on quantifiable inputs and outputs – and attempts to find easily quantifiable proxy indicators – marginalise the human work of education, silencing teachers' need for an inclusive work environment, adequate resourcing, opportunities for collaboration and continuing professional development, and other forms of support (Sachs, 2016). As Sayed and Ahmed suggest, 'The post-2015 education agenda, whilst containing a welcome target on teachers that represents, at some level, a substantive advance in the current global education discourse, needs to pay more attention to ... [the d]ynamic process-oriented models of teaching and learning, the continued foregrounding of pedagogy, and substantive engagement with diversity and context' (Sayed & Ahmed, 2015, p. 337).

SDG 4 and the Incheon Declaration represented a welcome shift in the development discourse, with potentially transformative language, foregrounding inclusion, equity, and quality. For Rose (2015, p. 290),

> Successful goals and targets are easily communicated, such that they capture public concerns and provide a focal point for global mobilization and action. … They should not be seen as an end in themselves but rather a trigger for action, spurring governments to identify and implement contextually relevant strategies that can achieve universal rights. An important advantage of internationally agreed goals and targets is that they transcend national politics, and so avoid shifting in priorities according to which party is in power.

As a whole, the SDGs do represent a powerful focal point for such global action, but the success of the agenda is dependent on the capacity of governments to identify and implement those 'contextually relevant strategies' that Rose highlights.

Now that the focus of the SDG agenda has begun to shift from the global- and thematic-level toward regional- and national-level actors and action, a productive space has opened up for influencing the development and implementation of these 'contextually relevant strategies', and, subsequently, the regional- and national-level indicators required to evaluate them. Burford, Tamás, and Harder (2016) discuss one promising model of engaging with local civil society organisations to improve the design of indicators for the complex SDGs. They describe how the conventional model employed by the UN process led to the development of 'rigid global-level indicator[s] with unclear local value'. Drawing from and synthesising the experience and expertise of a broad base of local-level stakeholders can lead to the development of a more meaningful 'reference "fuzzy framework" of slightly generalised proto-indicators suited for deep contextualisation locally' (Burford et al., 2016, p. 1). We would argue that a similar approach could be taken to developing indicators on the role of teachers and effective teaching in the SDGs.

Despite the transformative language used to articulate the overarching SDG 4 (Brisset & Mitter, 2017), Target 4.c and its corresponding indicators describe teachers from a purely utilitarian perspective, as a means to an end. As discussed extensively in this chapter, they are not even considered an active means to an end: not only are they referred to merely as 'supply', but there are no indicators designed to measure what teachers actually do in the classroom.

If we instead view teachers not only as a means to an end but as rights-holders and active partners in education, it allows us to take a more nuanced approach to further indicator development at the regional and national level. For example, a target such as Target 4.a, to 'build and upgrade education facilities that are child, disability and gender sensitive and provide safe, non-violent, inclusive and effective learning environments for all' could include indicators measuring how the learning environment is experienced by teachers, and, in so doing, ensure that 'inclusive, equitable, and quality education' extends to teachers as well (UNGA, 2015b).

Notes

1   See, for example, the Intensive Partnerships for Effective Teaching initiative, which used student test scores to determine how much a teacher has improved students' academic growth through a form of value-added modelling (Stecher et al., 2018).

2   As is the case with Target 4.c of the SDGs and its corresponding indicators.

3   The six EFA goals were as follows: Goal 1: Expand early childhood care and education. Goal 2: Provide free and compulsory primary education for all. Goal 3: Promote learning and life skills for young people and adults. Goal 4: Increase adult literacy by 50%. Goal 5: Achieve gender parity by 2005, gender equality by 2015. Goal 6: Improve the quality of education.

4   See http://gem-report-2016.unesco.org/en/chapter/target-4-b-teachers/

5   Not only are there challenges associated with collecting these data, but Target 4.7 significantly expands the remit of what teachers are expected to teach without providing much guidance, thus putting teachers under additional stress.

CHAPTER 11

Reshaping Quality and Equity: Global Learning Metrics as a Ready-Made Solution to a Manufactured Crisis

Aaron Benavot and William C. Smith

1   Introduction

Ranking countries on a global scale of learning has become a top priority in the education world. The introduction of global learning metrics (GLM) effectively transforms 'conventional' discussions of education progress, which have focussed on enrolment or completion rates, gender parity, and out-of-school children. While there is no common definition of a GLM, it typically refers to a single global scale in which measures of learning from different standardised assessments are placed (Hanushek & Edwards, 2017). The UNESCO Institute for Statistics (UIS) discusses, in theory, an ideal GLM based on a perfectly equated learning assessment programme (UIS, 2018g). It is unlikely that such an ideal GLM will ever come into existence. Meanwhile, UIS is developing guiding tools and definitions to support the alignment and comparability of results from different assessments in relevant domains and at different education levels. This would mean that nationally representative assessment programmes would begin to use shared definitions and linking methodologies to create a common format of reporting (a global scale or metric) in a transparent way (UIS, 2018g). The Australian Council for Educational Research (2019) refers to a GLM as a 'universal learning progression' in which student achievement on any national, regional, or international learning assessment can be converted into universal learning progression units.

The fascination with GLMs shifts the focus to the outcomes of schooling and embraces the mantra of results-oriented policymaking. GLMs also enable countries to report progress on the Sustainable Development Goal on Education (SDG 4), specifically the first target (4.1), which calls on countries to 'ensure that all girls and boys complete free, equitable and quality primary and secondary education *leading to relevant and effective learning outcomes*' (WEF, 2015, p. 20, emphasis added).

The effort to compare national learning outcomes on a universal scale has been spearheaded by UIS in its official capacity to collect cross-nationally comparable data to measure SDG 4 targets. Supported by major bilateral and multilateral donors, UIS has been working overtime to construct and report global, regional, and national estimates of the percentages of children/young people who achieve a minimum proficiency level in reading and mathematics in primary and secondary education (the global indicator of Target 4.1). For example, UIS currently reports reading proficiency data for students at the end of lower secondary education (typically grade 8 or 9) for almost 90 countries.[1] Such global coverage of learning levels would have been unthinkable two decades ago.

There is no consensus on the technical procedures to combine information from different assessment platforms.[2] Nevertheless, the overall message is crystal clear: first, all countries in the world should conduct nationally representative learning assessments of children and youth, preferably by participating in international assessments, in order to determine learner proficiency levels in reading and mathematics; and second, it is desirable to combine select results from such assessments and map them onto a global learning scale. In effect, learning should be seen as independent of national context – for example, independent of education structure, curricular policy, language of instruction, and level of development.

This chapter critically interrogates on-going efforts to establish and legitimate global learning metrics. It highlights how and why the massive push to ensure that all students worldwide demonstrate measurable proficiencies in reading and mathematics has emerged, and with what consequences for the broader SDG 4 agenda, especially equity issues. Drawing on the growing rhetoric of a 'global learning crisis' and informed by innovative yet problematic technical work, we argue that the powerful movement to construct GLMs has several 'unintended' outcomes. These include the effective narrowing of the comprehensive global agenda on education (SDG 4), the undermining of a carefully negotiated country-led process to promote lifelong education opportunities for all, the devaluing of learning that is not measurable or comparable, and the weakening of the principle of educational equity.

2 The Rise of Large-scale Comparative Assessment and the Quantification of Education Outcomes

Since the 1960s standardised learning assessments have seen a dramatic upswing in usage. In 1961, the International Association for the Assessment of Educational Achievement (IEA) completed its first pilot study, concluding that cross-nationally comparable results were possible (Pettersson, Popkewitz,

& Lindblad, 2016). Momentum for comparison grew in the 1970s and 1980s as more researchers believed education systems could be systematically compared with each other (Kamens, 2013). Between 1960 and 1989, 43 international surveys of academic achievement were conducted (Heyneman & Lee, 2014). During the 1990s and 2000s, participation in regional and national assessments increased rapidly (Kamens & Benavot, 2011). Fuelling the motivation for standardised testing was an assumption that 'the quality of educational practices can be unambiguously quantitatively measured and that such measures are sufficiently precise and robust to be aggregated into policy-relevant rankings' (Meyer, 2017, p. 17).

The establishment of the OECD's Programme for International Student Assessment (PISA) in 1999 provided a robust platform for the comparison of student learning. Between 1999 and 2012, participation in PISA and other international assessments increased by 50% (Smith, 2014). Overall, by 2008 nearly three-quarters of developing countries had participated in at least one national, regional, or international assessment (Kamens & Benavot, 2011).

Beyond the unprecedented increase in the number of tests conducted, there has been a shift in the intention and ownership of such assessments. Pizmony-Levy (2013) highlights the relative decline in the number of researchers participating in the IEA's General Assembly, replaced by individuals affiliated with, or officially representing, national governments. Some have also pointed to the changing purposes of testing, with greater emphasis on using outcomes for accountability (Smith, 2014). The pattern of increased government involvement made clear that national education policymakers viewed the assessment of learning as 'an important, perhaps a key, strategy for improving educational quality' (Chapman & Snyder, 2000, p. 457).

The rise of learning assessments mirrored an increased reliance on quantitative measurement rather than qualitative judgement. Buttressed by a belief in meritocracy and positivism, and an imperative to avoid subjective value judgements and perceptions of discrimination, some trusted that 'the only hierarchy that can be accepted is based on meritocratic ideas aggregated from evaluations of the performance of individuals' (Pettersson et al., 2016, p. 180). Positivism suggests that true levels of merit can be objectively measured (Abraham, 1994). Numbers are seen as 'technical, objective, and calculable and embodying the idea of giving all equal chances and representation' (Pettersson et al., 2016, p. 184) with comparable data replacing personal judgement (Muller, 2018). The efficiency movement in the early 20th century brought positivism into education, advocating for a scientisation of education with standardised and quantified best practices replacing teachers' intuition (Meyer, 2017). In the past thirty years, economic globalisation has pressured countries to assess the competitiveness of their education systems and labour forces (Kamens & Benavot, 2011). More broadly, formal institutions are 'increasingly ... subjected to performance measurements that define success or failure according to narrow and arbitrary metrics' (Muller, 2018).

Increased country participation in learning assessments reflects a global environment in which education policies are increasingly diffused, borrowed, and contextualised (Steiner-Khamsi, 2004). Indeed, countries more integrated into world society are more likely to test students (Kamens & McNeely, 2010). In addition, in what some describe as the 'global education compact' (Daun & Mundy, 2011; Mundy, 2006), formerly ideologically opposed institutions, such as the World Bank and UNESCO, are working together toward a merging of agendas. This convergence can be seen in the *Education 2030 Framework for Action* (WEF, 2015), where certain guidelines such as fair and inclusive education are more aligned with humanist approaches supported by UNESCO, while others, such as defining education quality through testing, derive from an instrumental or neoliberal paradigm commonplace in the World Bank (Akkari, 2018). Sahlberg (2011) refers to a 'global education reform movement' that reinforces neoliberal principles and reforms such as increased decentralisation, standardisation, and privatisation. Learning assessments, drawing on the 'global testing culture', derive from and further encourage such education reforms (Smith, 2016a). This testing culture draws scripts and models of expected behaviour for all education stakeholders, which shape how education is understood and valued. It thus becomes common sense that 'testing is synonymous with accountability, which is synonymous with education quality' (Smith, 2016b, p. 7).

3   Debating the Post-2015 Agenda for Education

As discussions over post-2015 priorities were held, two overarching camps – with different foci and underlying ideologies – sought to influence the direction of the global education goal and targets (see Chapter 9 by Yusuf Sayed and Kate Moriarty). The humanistic camp pushed strongly for education that was fee-free and inclusive (Unterhalter, 2019). Based on a rights-based approach that placed government as the primary duty bearer, this camp focussed on issues related to equity, social justice, and nondiscrimination (Brissett & Mitter, 2017). By contrast, the economic camp, undergirded by human capital theory, highlighted education's role in economic development and tied education quality to labour force demands and occupational opportunities. The main purpose of education, according to the camp, is utilitarian: 'preparing children to work within an established socio-economic order with the ultimate goal of achieving economic growth' (Brissett & Mitter, 2017, p. 195).

In the consultation process over the emergent global goal on education, debates between the two camps ensued. In 2013, at the Thematic Consultation on Education in Dakar, Senegal, the outcome document advanced a limited view of quality as meeting minimum standards in reading, writing, and counting at the primary level with an overarching emphasis on learning outcomes (UNESCO, 2013d; Unterhalter, 2019). Subsequently, as Unterhalter (2019) found in her review of the lead-up to SDG 4, expert-led consultations tended to emphasise links between inadequate learning and poor economic growth. Wider consultations initiated by the Open Working Group viewed education more comprehensively, emphasising provision at all levels and providing broader definitions of quality that included enabling conditions and diverse learning outcomes, including for sustainable development and global citizenship. The humanistic approach illustrated through the Open Working Group was, in part, fuelled by the active participation of civil society organisations (for more details, see Chapter 2 by Antonia Wulff).

4   Key Concerns of the Two Camps: Equity and Learning

Equity and learning represent core concerns in both camps. Where they differ is how the issues are framed and to what purposes. The utilitarian view of education emphasises a narrower array of school-based learning outcomes, typically foundational skills, measured rigorously and assessed frequently, which serve as the basis of evidence-based reforms. The humanistic camp emphasises equity and rights-based approaches in education and a broader conception of quality, including inputs, processes, and outcomes. Assessing learner experiences and an array of learning outcomes, both inside and outside of formal schooling, as well as the provision of qualified, prepared, and duly compensated teachers, are key to this view.

For the utilitarian camp, education for all had become 'learning for all', an (some would say 'the') overarching policy priority in which the measurement and assessment of learning took centre stage. Assessments, especially those that lent themselves to cross-national comparison, would enable policymakers to identify policies that improve the skills and competencies of current students and enhance future workers' competitiveness in the global economy. The humanistic camp had a more ambivalent attitude toward assessments, since it shifts the focus from enabling conditions and quality teaching to test scores as the privileged criteria for policy formulation. That said, disaggregated data from learning assessments might be beneficial insofar as they shine a light on the distinct learning challenges facing marginalised and excluded children.

To effectively address the learning challenges faced by the least advantaged populations, assessments would need to collect detailed information about multiple disadvantaged groups. Concerns were voiced as to which groups to include in assessments and which to leave out (Doble, 2015). For example, should assessments be school-based (thereby excluding children not enrolled in school) or household-based (thereby excluding those not living in a household)? Should they go beyond households and sample orphans or those living in institutionalised settings? Should they include 'unregistered' children or those living in 'illegal' refugee or migrant settlements? For equity purposes the sampling frame and sample size of learning assessments are critical issues since they determine the (non)representation of at-risk groups. This is especially true for learners with intersecting disadvantages – for example, girls with disabilities or linguistic minorities who live in rural villages (Lockheed & Wagemaker, 2013). Furthermore, disadvantage is often context-specific, requiring country input and attention to salient groups (Benavot, 2018b).

A longstanding critique of cross-national assessments is their inability to capture meaningful differences among learners who score at the lower end of a learning scale (Lockheed & Wagemaker, 2013). In PISA, for example, two-thirds of countries that scored below the OECD average in 2009 were low- and middle-income countries. In Peru, 82% of students fell below the 400-point mark. Such students were deemed illiterate, which means that the assessment provided little useful policy information (Lockheed & Wagemaker, 2013). Results from the 2015 PISA indicated that the reading score of the typical poor country was below the fifth percentile of OECD countries. This percentile is considered close to 'special needs' (Crouch, 2017). This suggests that the lowest levels in assessments like PISA or Trends in International Mathematics and Science Study (TIMSS) are too high for most students in low-income countries (Winthrop and Anderson Simons, 2013). Given this lack of detailed information at the lower end of the skills spectrum, analyses to identify associated factors may be inaccurate (Lockheed & Wagemaker, 2013). The IEA suggests that accuracy declines when students score less than 30% correct (Crouch, 2017). Lengthening the assessment could provide useful information about students scoring at the bottom, but this may not be a feasible, or complete, solution (Crouch, 2017).

In addition to detailed information on lower learning levels, understanding the determinants of learning among disadvantaged learners requires extensive background information (Klemenčič & Mirazchiyski, 2018). This is usually accomplished through companion surveys completed by students, teachers, school administrators, and/or parents. Unfortunately, this information gets little attention in public policy discussions, thereby missing the context-specific obstacles facing marginalised groups (Winthrop and Anderson Simons, 2013). Using data for equity purposes also entails that teachers and school leaders have access to data in a format they understand and can use (Rose, 2016). Summative assessments, especially those linked with accountability measures, assume that all students start at the same development level and thus make it difficult to tailor interventions to specific groups of learners (Ahsan & Smith, 2016). Furthermore, it is erroneous to believe, as many decisionmakers do, that policies found to be effective for the 'average' or typical learner will be equally effective in addressing the needs of learners from marginalised groups (Benavot, 2018b). Detailed data and specialised analyses are critical for identifying more or less effective policies for marginalised learners.

4.1   *Manufacturing a 'Crisis' in Learning and the Push for Reform*

The language and narrative employed to frame the results of learning assessments also distinguishes the two camps. Words like 'crisis' and 'shock' have been used in the past to describe the 'appalling' state of affairs in education. In the 1960s and again in the 1980s, Philip Coombs wrote extensively about conditions fostering a 'world educational crisis', especially in the Global South (Coombs, 1968, 1985). In 1983, *A Nation at Risk* garnered extensive media attention in the US, claiming 'a rising tide of mediocrity [in education] that threatens our very future as a nation and a people' (US National Commission on Excellence in Education, 1983, p. 1) and touched off a wave of local, state, and national reforms. In 1993, Alan Rogers referred to the 'world crisis' in adult education, especially in relation to adult literacy (Rogers, 1993). In 2000, the results of the first PISA assessment revealed a lacklustre performance of German students. The public 'shock' then triggered intensive public discussion and scholarly debates about the need for extensive education reform. The 2013 EFA Global Monitoring Report highlighted 'the global learning crisis', estimating that, regardless of whether they have ever attended school, 250 million children could not read, write, or count well and that 775 million adults lacked basic reading and writing skills (UNESCO, 2014c, p. 191). In short, while the crisis hyperbole has a long history in education circles, its prevalence appears to be increasing.

Among those who employ a 'crisis' narrative in reference to learning, the diverse contexts in which learning deficits are created and fostered are often minimised. The purported existence of a 'global learning crisis' leaves little room for nuance. It reduces the issue into a simple dichotomy: some education systems are successfully producing students who achieve high average test scores on assessments, while most systems are ineffective, failing, or both, and in need of significant restructuring. Such narratives are commonly mobilised by those concerned with economic growth or global competitiveness. They tend to overlook deeper conditions that contribute to low or unequal learning levels and would need to be addressed if real improvements were to be realised.

In many contexts, the media latch onto and amplify the crisis narrative. They flash ominous headlines with country rankings on television and radio. Driven by directives that require the rapid production of simplified, newsworthy material (Yasukawa, Hamilton, and Evans, 2017), media reports on education tend to be overly negative and emphasise quality or excellence over equity (Baroutsis & Lingard, 2017). Results from international large-scale assessments, especially PISA, have garnered growing media attention. Often presented in international league tables or country rankings (see following paragraphs), the stories 'reduce the complexity of PISA findings to simple messages that are aimed at changing or reinforcing particular perceptions of education and influencing the decisions of policy-makers' (Sellar, Thompson, & Rutkowski, 2017, p. 25). The OECD and the World Bank have encouraged the use of such 'catalyst data' (Sellar et al., 2017, p. 19) to 'spur action' (World Bank, 2017b, p. 93). The naming and shaming approach of countries through league tables has been described as PISA shock. Reform efforts following the release of PISA results have been documented in countries like Denmark, Germany, Japan, and Portugal (Rey, 2010; Volante, 2015).

Media presentations of country comparisons not only reinforce the notion that education quality can be reflected in a single test score, but often identify who is to blame. Responsibility for poor quality (i.e., low test scores) is laid at the feet of schools and teachers, whereas little consideration is given to either systemic problems (e.g., insufficient funding, substandard school structures, and inappropriate instructional materials) or uneven policy implementation (Kumashiro, 2012). In Turkey, following back-to-back poor performances on the 2003 and 2006 PISA, the Ministry of National Education overlooked structural and systemic issues and placed blame predominantly on teachers and their inability to implement the new curriculum (Gür, Celik, & Özoğlu, 2012). Research on media representation of teachers in Australia, Bangladesh, Oman, Saudi Arabia, and South Africa reinforced a one-sided portrayal of teachers as lazy, unprofessional, and often engaged in misconduct (Alhamdan et al., 2014). This may be shaped in part by the absence of educator voices as experts in media reports on education (Yasukawa et al., 2017).

5   The Role of League Tables in Manufacturing Calls for Reform

Whether the learning crisis is real or manufactured, it has taken on a new complexion in the post-2015 era as league tables have gone global. David Edwards, the General Secretary of Education International, suggests that poor learning outcomes are not a shock for those on the front line; teachers are keenly aware of poor learning levels since they labour in overcrowded classrooms and underresourced schools (Hanushek & Edwards, 2017). What is damaging in recent years is how learning challenges and the learning crisis are presented. Global league tables serve as a mechanism by which assessments enact hierarchical control. Country rankings on international assessments become part of an international struggle for developing (and securing) talent (Volante & Ritzen, 2016). Media outlets assume that rankings contain adequate information to draw conclusions about education quality: rankings are 'often the only evidence used in policy debates on education' (Klemenčič & Mirazchiyski, 2018, p. 1). This is despite the limited and relatively uninformative information provided (Klemenčič & Mirazchiyski, 2018) and the consistent misrepresentation or misinterpretation of assessment results (Sellar, Thompson, & Rutkowski, 2017).

One of the concerns with global metrics and minimum benchmarks is how results will impact poor-performing countries (UIS, 2018h). League tables often lead to bifurcated reactions, heaping praise on high-performing countries while casting a dark shadow on low-achieving ones (Lockheed & Wagemaker, 2013). Countries near the bottom of an international ranking have reacted in various ways, including ceasing their participation in the assessment (Winthrop & Anderson Simons, 2013); withholding certain, less favourable results (Sellar et al., 2017); narrowing curricular policy to focus on tested subjects and question types (Heyneman and Lee, 2014); and attempting to 'emulate' practices believed to be prevalent in high-performing countries (Volante, 2015). The dangers of using a single measure to initiate or reform education policies have actually been highlighted by some of the biggest proponents of GLMs. The World Bank, for example, has cautioned that 'when a single metric becomes the sole basis for big policy triggers, the corresponding stakes may become dangerously high' (World Bank, 2017b, p. 93).

6   Assessments as Ready-Made Solutions

It is thus not a coincidence that as learning assessments expand at an unprecedented pace worldwide, rhetoric referring to the 'global learning crisis' reaches new heights. Assessments not only provide a concrete gauge of the extent of the crisis, they also suggest solutions. For some, there is no difference between measuring the problem and solving the problem. As Pettersson and colleagues note, numbers on education can 'be transformed from representations of education into education per se' (Pettersson et al., 2016, p. 177). Test scores can be considered rationalised myths (Booher-Jennings, 2005). Abiding by an institutionalised, impersonal, and rationalised myth legitimates the behaviour of actors (Meyer & Rowan, 1977). In this sense, 'tests become a virtue *in and of themselves*' (Akkari, 2018, p. 10); all actors in education are expected to adapt their behaviour in response to, or for the sake of, improving test results.

Large-scale assessments both prompt the search for ready-made solutions and act as ready-made solutions themselves. Assessments can easily transform into simplified, prepackaged reforms that speed up the process of policy adoption and implementation (Lewis & Hogan, 2016). Access to ready-made solutions helps reassure the public that pressing learning problems are being addressed and resolved. The choice of a solution frequently aligns with already established cultural beliefs or views on education, often complimenting an ongoing intervention (Rosen, 2009).

In Chapter 12 of this volume, Clara Fontdevila recognises that assessments act as 'the policy *solution* to an institutionalized *problem* ... the learning crisis'. This is in part due to the perceived alignment between assessment and common values in education that prioritise some types of knowledge over others and a belief that the process of participating in a robust standardised assessment denotes a modern education system that is reflective, willing to learn, and based in science. Assessments capitalise on the prioritised position of academic intelligence. Subjects understood to require metacognitive skills are given more weight in assessments, while supposedly less cognitively demanding subjects like visual arts, ecology, or social studies are minimised (Baker, 2014). This is evident in the rise of sciences and mathematics as subjects for all students at the end of the 20th century (Kamens & Benavot, 1991; Kamens, Meyer, & Benavot, 1996).

Additionally, the application of assessments speaks to the widespread faith in science. The view of education 'as a "technical" science that can be studied, rationalized, and quantified' (Wiseman, 2010, p. 18) makes it difficult for policymakers to question the scientific results emanating from assessments (Rosen, 2009). Quantitative results are considered more accurate and trustworthy than summative pronouncements on the state of education or 'subjective' evaluations by teacher associations or school leaders (Wiseman, 2010). Cross-national assessments, which are considered a technically robust, valid scientific measure of academic knowledge, are perfectly positioned for countries seeking to gain international legitimacy and demonstrate their commitment to quality education.

7   International Organisations and the Post-2015 Education Agenda

The view that internationally comparable learning assessments are the necessary means to both identify and remedy the learning crisis is bolstered by international agencies, regional organisations, and many NGOs (Boli & Thomas, 1999; see also Chapter 12 by Clara Fontdevila). Organsations such as the IEA, World Bank, OECD, UNESCO, and UNICEF have historically competed for supremacy in the global policy arena (Mundy, 1999). In the post-2015 landscape, the World Bank and the OECD have used their perceived technical expertise to solidify their position.

The World Bank's Education Sector Strategy 2020, *Learning for All* (World Bank, 2012b), illustrates the dominance of outcome over input in the organisation's thinking. In comparing this strategy, released in 2011, with the prior strategy from 1999, Joshi and Smith (2012) find a near 100% increase in terms associated with a testing culture. In practice, the World Bank spent the time between the two strategies adding assessment programmes to their funding packages. Between 1998 and 2009, the World Bank funded 166 projects with an assessment focus across 90 countries. In a quarter of the countries, the Bank funded participation in an international assessment. By organising the 166 projects into three-year periods equated with PISA assessment cycles, participation in international assessments grew from 7.1% (1998–2000) to 27.3% (2004–2006). See Figure 11.1 (World Bank, 2012a).

World Bank support for learning assessments can also be seen in the Systems Approach for Better Education Results (SABER) tool. Developed in 2011, SABER is designed to capture comparable information on education policies to drive institutional change through the creation of a national education report card. As part of their overall grade, countries are judged against their participation and implementation of learning assessments. Those that do not participate in international assessments receive lower marks (Bruns, Filmer, & Patrinos, 2011). Although voluntary in nature, the public shaming and increasing link between participation and funding opportunities suggests SABER acts as a normative guide to the 'right' kind of reform (Smith, 2014).

Similarly, the OECD has created a platform in which statistics are viewed as objective and, therefore, the results of their assessments (PISA and the Programme for the International Assessment of Adult Competencies [PIAAC]) produce indisputable scientific evidence (Martens, 2007). Through PISA, the

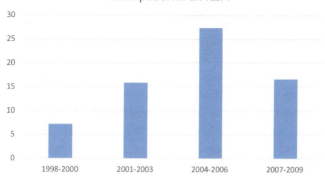

FIGURE 11.1   Changing inclusion of International Large-Scale Assessments (ILSAS) in World
Bank projects, 1998–2009 (Source: World Bank, 2012a)

OECD promoted a performance culture (Bieber & Martens, 2011), which rede-
fines competence and mastery in education. In the OECD's long-term strategy
for PISA, 'the yardstick for educational success is no longer simply improvement against national standards, but against the best-performing education
systems worldwide' (OECD, 2013, p. 4). In the run-up to SDG 4, OECD representatives sought ways to promote PISA as a global learning metric and expand
its reach worldwide. To foster the participation of developing countries, the
OECD piloted PISA for Development (PISA-D), which was designed to promote
more robust national assessments through institutional capacity building. As
one of PISA's six long-term objectives, efforts are underway to align national
assessments with PISA scales. This has included workshops at the national level
to develop PISA-like assessment instruments. To date, evidence that national
assessments have been adapted to follow PISA proficiency levels can be found
in China, Norway, Canada, Ecuador, and Paraguay (Addey, 2017). Although
PISA was not ultimately endorsed as the global metric for measuring SDG Target 4.1, the OECD aspires for universal participation in PISA by 2030 (Ward,
2016). Signing India to PISA in 2021 is a step in that direction. In the meantime,
the OECD is tracking progress on most SDG 4 targets of its own member states
by repositioning various OECD indicators, including PISA results, as measures
of SDG 4 targets (OECD, 2017a).

7.1   *Assessment Funded as Quality in Development Projects*
As noted above, assessment results are increasingly used as a proxy for quality in aid projects (Kamens & McNeely, 2010), reinforcing the testing culture
and increasing low- and middle-income country participation in assessments

(Akkari, 2018). Donors are making funding decisions based on whether measurable impact can be identified (Winthrop and Anderson Simons, 2013). All too often, education is compared with the health sector, with donors demanding an easily implemented and communicated indicator (Hanushek & Edwards, 2017). However, unlike having children vaccinated or using bed nets to reduce the spread of malaria, education interventions are not easily packaged and implemented, nor can they be universally applied in every context (Snilstveit et al., 2016). Pressure to comply with the 'common sense' belief in assessment can be high. For example, in 2011 a major donor of the Global Campaign for Education (GCE) pulled its financial support when GCE failed to support a single, early-grade reading metric and instead continued its focus on rights-based education (Edwards, 2016).

Aid agencies are playing an influential role in the creation and legitimation of global learning metrics. The UK Department for International Development's (DFID's) funding for the 'Best Education Statistics for Improved Learning (BEST)' is an illustrative case. Running from 2013 to the end of 2017, the £6.4 million programme supported UIS's production of global learning outcomes, the OECD's PISA for Development, and the Global Education Monitoring (GEM) Report with an aim 'to help ensure education policies and programmes that are evidence based, with a greater focus on learning and ultimately contribute to disadvantaged girls and boys achieving improved learning outcomes' (UK DFID, 2016). In its 2016 review, DFID commended UIS for 'publishing data on learning outcomes for the first time', and with the establishment of the Global Alliance to Monitor Learning (GAML) and concept papers for universal learning scales, concluded that UIS 'exceeded expectations for work towards a global learning metric', although the planned work on equity was 'slightly behind schedule' (UK DFID, 2016). DFID recommended that it 'should track and support UIS's work on taking forward the Education Financing Commission's recommendation to develop a global lead indicator for education' (UK DFID, 2016).

To further intensify the link between assessment results and funding, some aid agencies have started to implement results-based financing in education. Many of the largest global donors, including the Asian Development Bank, the European Commission, Global Partnership for Education (GPE), DFID, and the World Bank, support some form of results-based financing, in which funding is released in proportion to the level of results attained (UNESCO, 2017b). Results-based financing is meant to spur progress by rewarding improvements in learning (Savedoff, 2016). Results-based financing using test scores typically provides funds to the national government, although this is not always the case. In Bangladesh and Chile, private providers were allocated funding for students who passed tests (Savedoff, 2016). This represents an increasing trend toward local performance-based pay, shifting resources away from government provision (Savedoff, 2016).

The World Bank formally adopted a Program for Results (PforR) instrument in 2012 (Savedoff, 2016), after which it committed to doubling its results-based financing in the education sector to US$5 billion between 2015 and 2020 (World Bank, 2015b). As of April 2016, the World Bank had initiated 37 PforR programmes, only two of which were in education. The largest education programme – the multi-donor 'Big Results Now in Education' programme in Tanzania – included a dedicated US$122 million through the World Bank's PforR instrument. In the Tanzania programme, six disbursement-linked indicators trigger the release of payment. The sixth indicator is improvement in student learning as demonstrated through a reading assessment. If this indicator were fully met, US$16 million, or 13% of the total World Bank loan, would be released (Savedoff, 2016).

DFID piloted payment for results programmes in Ethiopia and Rwanda, which focussed on taking and passing competency tests (Savedoff, 2016). The programme in Ethiopia, to which DFID committed £30 million, continued a tradition in other sectors of linking British aid to results (Perakis & Savedoff, 2015). Launched in 2012 it rewarded the government for increasing the number of students sitting for the lower secondary exam and the number of students passing. Greater amounts were paid for girls sitting and passing the exam and for students from poorer regions. Tying payments to results at the end of lower secondary education was based on the assumption that sitting for the exam would be 'a good proxy for completion, and resulting test scores provide information about the quality of the education' (Perakis & Savedoff, 2015, p. 28).

The fund was expected to release £10 million per year for three years (Savedoff, 2016). In the first year £900,000 was released, in the second year £5.6 million, and in the third year £9 million. Poor performance in the first year was a challenge for DFID as the Ethiopian government treated the unreleased funds as lost revenue and a form of punishment (Perakis & Savedoff, 2015). Following the project's conclusion, a DFID-commissioned evaluation found that the observed outcomes could not be attributed to the programme, which was not continued (Perakis & Savedoff, 2015).

8   SDG 4: The Global Goal on Education

8.1   *Creating and Then Undercutting an Ambitious Global Agenda in Education*

Since the SDGs came into force in January 2016, there appears to be a growing disjuncture between the espoused broad principles of the SDG agenda – namely, equity, inclusion, and quality, which countries and institutions of widely differing ideological inclinations agreed to – and how these principles compete for supremacy during local policy creation and resource allocation (Clark et al., 1999; Smith, 2018). For example, SDG 4 calls on schools to develop multidimensional learners with wide-ranging knowledge and skills, but in practice, the content of education that countries are asked to assess is narrowly defined. The logic behind the process of delimiting the purposes of education appears reasonably sound: one cannot focus on all things at all times, and it makes sense to allow political and practical considerations to determine which principles gain traction and which do not.

And yet, there appears to be more than political expediency and pragmatism at work. In the run up to the new 2030 Agenda, representatives of particular education stakeholders were encouraged, sometimes forcefully, to jettison contentious proposals and strive toward consensus. During the SDG negotiations, different groups from the humanistic camp proposed targets and indicators that were later dropped or altered. In 2014, the Muscat Agreement proposed goals for both education financing and provision of trained teachers (UNESCO, 2014a). The draft Goal 7, requiring all countries to dedicate 4–6% of their GDP or 15–20% of their public expenditure to education, was subsequently discarded. Draft Goal 6, ensuring all learners are taught by 'qualified, professionally-trained, motivated and well-supported teachers', was eventually downgraded to a means of implementation and reworded to 'substantially increase the supply of qualified teachers'. Supporters of adult education were told to get under the big tent idea of 'lifelong learning' and were left without any explicit mention of adult education in the targets (Benavot, 2018a).

Although it may not have been apparent at the time, the technical and political processes of operationalising targets and identifying indicators began to undercut the collective vision of an ambitious, holistic global agenda in education (McGrath & Nolan, 2016). Extensive consultation and consensus-building gave way to specialised experts leading technical discussions in which powerful and vocal international actors became more actively involved (Unterhalter, 2019). In meeting the 'requirement' for internationally comparable, quantifiable indicators (King, 2017), most of the proposed indicators in education were weakly aligned with the intended scope of the targets (Johnston, 2016). Among the 43 SDG 4 indicators that were proposed, only 11 came to be defined as global indicators with important measurement and reporting implications. Monitoring progress on SDG 4, as reflected in the UN's annual SDG report, was limited to data on the 11 global indicators (King, 2017). Countries were not required to collect or report data on the 32 thematic indicators.[3] This suggests that, in practice, more countries are likely to pay closer attention and allocate more resources to the monitoring and reporting of the global indicators (Smith, 2019), even though the UN Secretary General recognised that such indicators are 'unlikely to fully satisfy the needs of communities' (UIS, 2018h, p. 11).

8.2   *Capturing Quality in the sDG 4 Agenda*

As the results of international assessments are increasingly valued as objective measures of education quality, it should come as no surprise that the principle of quality is narrowly tied to assessments results. A pronounced utilitarian turn has taken root. As a result, discussions of sDG 4 targets, once they are operationalised and implemented, give minimal attention to equity and inclusion, and place the latter two in competition for scarce sources. After securing desirable formulations of sDG targets, the more humanistic approach voiced by civil society is being marginalised in practice (Doble, 2015). The instrumental view that strong test results, narrowly construed as proficiency in reading and mathematics, promote economic competitiveness continues to gather steam, thereby undermining the original intent of sDG 4 and the role of education as a driver of progress in other sDGs (Brissett & Mitter, 2017; King, 2017; Unterhalter, 2019; see also Chapter 9 by Yusuf Sayed and Kate Moriarty).

It is true that Target 4.7 captures a more humanistic, rights-based understanding of quality. However, that target includes multiple, often contested themes like global citizenship, sustainable development, human rights, gender equality, and cultural diversity, each of which embodies unique measurement challenges. For these and other reasons, the importance and value of Target 4.7 relative to other targets are being undermined (Brissett & Mitter, 2017). Unlike Target 4.1, which benefited from well-established measurement instruments, at least for the end of lower secondary education, approaches to measuring Target 4.7 themes have been few, uneven, and lacking consistent definitions (Unterhalter, 2019; UNESCO, 2016b).

Central to the remaking of the quality principle in sDG 4 is the role played by uIs. Due to several factors, including funding priorities and the divide between global and thematic indicators, uIS has focussed squarely on measuring the global indicator for Target 4.1 (Smith, 2019). Armed with a mandate to provide comparable data on sDG 4 indicators and establish robust methodologies for measuring each indicator, uIS has been the key player in creating consensus on learning metrics (see Chapter 12 by Clara Fontdevila in this book). Pushing to expand country coverage on sDG Indicator 4.1.1, uIS estimated that by 2017 only one third of countries had participated in a cross-national assessment of sufficient quality to allow for reporting (UIS, 2017b). To support and provide legitimacy for the measurement of SDG 4 targets and indicators, UIS led the establishment of several expert groups.

The GAML constitutes the largest and most active group. It focusses on SDG 4 targets with learning outcomes – namely, targets 4.1, 4.2, 4.4, 4.6, and 4.7 (UIS, 2016b) – and includes many of the same actors that participated in the Learning Metrics Task Force. As membership in the GAML is based on self-funded participation, donors dominate meetings and have played a significant role in directing the focus toward Target 4.1. At their May 2017 meeting, the GAML concluded that a global reporting scale should be developed by mapping national, regional, and international assessments to a common metric (UIS, 2017b). To take advantage of the wave of international assessments planned for 2018 and 2019, UIS and the GAML made the production of the necessary methodology, global reporting scale, and metadata an urgent priority to be met by December 2018 (UIS, 2017b).

Contrasting the activity of the GAML with the Inter-Agency Group on Educational Inequality Indicators (IAG-EII; originally the Inter-Agency Group on Disaggregated Education Indicators) helps highlight the prioritisation of learning assessments. The IAG-EII was developed 'in response to the call for a greater focus on equity in the global post-2015 education agenda and for more efficient use of available information' (UIS, 2016a, p. 3) and counted UIS, UNICEF, and the World Bank as its founding members. Compared to the GAML, the members of the IAG-EII appear to be taking a more relaxed approach to meeting their relatively fewer goals. The concept note for the group states that over a three- to five-year period they seek to harmonise the definition of individual characteristics such as sex, location, and wealth. The group aims 'to summarize periodically (if possible, annually) the main findings on the key indicators in a report' (UIS, 2016a, p. 4). However, the first report, originally targeting a December 2017 publication date, has yet to be published on the group's website.

In comparison, the GAML Results Framework outlines ambitious production with 31 separate outputs planned around assessment between February 2017 and the end of 2018 (UIS, 2017f). One could argue that it makes little sense to compare these two entities: GAML is larger and includes more self-funded members. That, however, is precisely the point. The energy and resources connected to the GAML demonstrate the prioritisation of learning assessments – assumed to be a measure of quality – over disaggregated equity indicators. Finally, one may argue that Target 4.1 is not all that the GAML covers. Yet, in evaluating the GAML's Results Framework, the combined targets directly tied to 4.2, 4.4, 4.6, and 4.7 total just less than one-third of the more general outputs on learning assessment (10 relative to 31).

9   What Does This Mean for Equity and a GLM?

The enormous time and effort expended to operationalise SDG 4, primarily by assessing reading and mathematics proficiency levels on a GLM, means that many quality and equity issues have taken a back seat. Improving equity in tested reading and mathematics levels does little to improve broader quality and equity concerns in education. As Slee (2013, p. 6) pointed out, more humanist values of education, such as inclusion and equity, are often 'inaudible when located amid more strident educational discourses', such as standards and performance rankings. One obvious example of this is the inattention to stalled out-of-school numbers – the premier access measure under EFA (Hanushek & Edwards, 2017). As learning outcomes are prioritised, some argue that 'enrollment is no longer the main issue' (Savedoff, 2016); instead countries are expected to focus on the low level of learning taking place in schools. Learning is narrowly understood in this context as school-based knowledge captured through comparative learning assessments. According to UIS and others, 'learning goals and targets in the post-2015 agenda *will only be meaningful* if they are underpinned by empirically derived common numerical scales that accommodate results from a range of different assessments of learning outcomes' (UIS et al., 2014, p. 1, emphasis added). This helps explain the concentrated, almost relentless efforts to develop GLMs that measure the global indicator for Target 4.1, while measurement strategies for other SDG 4 indicators – even those connected to learning – languish by comparison.

   While quantitative experts continue to tinker with alternative methods to map results from different learning assessments onto a single global metric, we raise a final issue: what might be the impact or possible unintended consequences of GLMs on the global education agenda, especially in relation to equity and quality. We begin by noting that in 2017, for the first time, UIS estimated that over 617 million children and adolescents around the world were not meeting minimum proficiency levels in reading and mathematics (UIS, 2017i). Supported by DFID and the work of the GAML, this top-line number is, in part, UIS's response to a recommendation from the International Commission on Financing Global Education (Education Commission, 2016)[4] and a reflection of UIS's desire to meet donor demands and drive advocacy. This figure seeks to provide a snapshot of the percentage of children and youth who have not acquired basic foundational skills, worldwide and by geographic region. UIS further drew attention to responsibility at the local level. In identifying three potential causes for the 'fact' that globally 58% and 56% of the relevant age group will not reach minimum proficiency levels in reading and mathematics, respectively, blame was squarely placed on schools and in class-rooms (Montoya, 2018).

The World Bank introduced an updated global dataset on education quality in January 2018. The full database contains data from 163 countries spanning the years 1965–2015. It illustrates one potential iteration of a global learning metric by calibrating international and regional assessments to an overall metric through doubloon countries – countries that participated in both an international and a regional assessment. Over time, the United States is used as an anchor country, as it is the only country that has participated in the full set of assessments since 1964. Results can be disaggregated by gender, loca-tion, immigrant status, and home language (Altinok, Angrist, & Patrinos, 2018). Harmonised test scores from the global dataset on education quality consti-tute one of five components used by the World Bank to calculate their newly launched Human Capital Index (HCI) (World Bank, 2018a).

The abovementioned examples demonstrate that as figures derived from GLMs take centre stage, the needs of marginalised groups of children are likely to go unnoticed and underappreciated. Consider out-of-school children, who are no longer highlighted as one of the most pressing policy concerns. In 2016, 263 million school-age children remained out of school (UIS, 2018d). At the primary level, about 40% of the 61 million out-of-school children are never expected to enter school (UNESCO, 2016b). Furthermore, providing access for the most marginalised is more expensive; without consistent focus and fund-ing, these children are likely to remain excluded (Smith, 2019).

Most large-scale assessments are not designed to address the learning chal-lenges faced by out-of-school children or youth. Nearly all international and regional assessments omit out-of-school children from their sampling frames (Winthrop & Anderson Simons, 2013). As Sellar et al. (2017) suggest, not only does this disadvantage those out of school, but it can also lead to a misinter-pretation of results. For example, PISA tests 15-year-olds with results usually generalised to the entire age cohort. However, in their examination of 16 coun-tries that participated in the 2012 PISA, out-of-school rates meant that one in five 15-year-olds were not included in the sampling frame. In Costa Rica, nearly 50% of 15-year-olds were not in school, and thus their learning levels were not captured by the PISA assessment.

The learning measure included in the aforementioned HCI is based on results from regional and international assessments without concern for those out of school. This means that in national contexts where out-of-school lev-els are relatively high, the index overestimates a major component. Some approaches to constructing GLMs seek to overcome this issue by mapping household surveys and citizen-led assessments to the global scale (Montoya &

Hastedt, 2017). However, unless all countries take part in surveys that capture children both in and out of school, true measures of out-of-school children, including their learning levels, will be biased. In the end, GLMs simply do not provide the country-specific information needed by policymakers to understand the nature of the learning challenges facing marginalised children and thus identify potentially effective policies.

Interestingly, in its calculation of the global number of children and youth who will not meet minimum proficiency levels, UIS includes estimates of those out of school (UIS, 2017i). However, the presentation of the global figures almost entirely focusses on learning deficits and not on identifying effective policies to ensure access and completion of the most vulnerable and marginalised populations (Smith, 2019). One report estimates that the world's out-of-school population constitutes about 15% of the total number of children lacking sufficient literacy and numeracy skills (UIS, 2017i). Breaking this global number down by region, a recent UIS blog illustrates that among children not meeting minimum proficiency, the percentage that are out-of-school is lower in Asia, Latin America, and Sub-Saharan Africa than in Europe and North America (Montoya, 2018). In looking at how these numbers are represented, there are concerns that to address the 'learning crisis' policymakers may focus attention on the group representing the largest percentage of children and youth contributing to the 'crisis', such as those in school in Sub-Saharan Africa. This would diminish attention on the still severe out-of-school issue, especially in regions where the challenge is most pressing.

Another critical implication stems from the fact that current learning assessments capture a limited range of learning domains. Education has always valued the knowledge of some learners over others. Assessments tend to privilege academic knowledge and cognitive skills in a few subject domains: language, mathematics, social and natural sciences (Benavot, 2018b). These tendencies undergird 'a meritocratic ideology' that 'has not only brought about assessment practices that enable and promote some, but not other, educational activities' but also 'sustains and legitimizes educational distribution of life chances for different individuals' (Pettersson et al., 2016, p. 197). The cultural knowledge and competencies of learners from ethnic, religious, or linguistic minorities, who are frequently among those excluded from school or unable to complete a full cycle, are often unrecognised, untested, or both. There is little information in current GLMs that would provide policymakers and educators with information about the challenges faced by such learners.

GLMs favour knowledge conveyed in school during the initial phases of life-long learning. The diverse types of knowledge and skills, which are learned or reinforced over the life course both in and out of school, are not assessed

(Benavot, 2018b). For example, the World Bank's dataset relies on regional and international assessments of school-based knowledge. While the UIS top-line number includes out-of-school children, it makes a false and highly problematic assumption that no learning takes place outside the confines of school. All out-of-school children are assumed, by definition, to be lacking minimum proficiencies in foundational skills.

This discussion raises a deep concern as to the purposes of assessment: what is being prioritised in assessment results and who benefits from such assessments? Countries have defined different educational purposes and curricular priorities, which should be taken into account in assessment frameworks (Winthrop and Anderson Simons, 2013). Not all assessments can and should be used for the same purpose (Benavot & Köseleci, 2015). And yet, among large scale assessments that benchmark proficiency levels, UNESCO's Technical Cooperation Group (UIS, 2018h) suggests there are two main purposes: improved learning and hierarchical control. Some have debated these purposes of GLMs, questioning the utility of a simple tool or benchmark for improving student performance or whether they serve as instruments to punish countries through rankings (Winn & Goebel, 2017). Eric Hanushek suggests that GLMs help us 'think about judging the education' in different countries (Cavanagh, 2018); the World Bank supports GLMs as a form of cross-country comparison that helps 'generate accountability for learning' (World Bank, 2017b, p. 97).

Well-designed learning assessments should guide policy interventions to improve quality and student learning. However, while global rankings may drive policy or identify 'stages at which policy interventions may be required', they provide preciously little information to guide potential interventions or improve the quality of instruction (UIS et al., 2014, p. 12). This is especially true in those countries near the bottom of the league tables that tend to focus 'only on their rankings rather than on using the results to stimulate reflection on how they might improve their system' (Lockheed & Wagemaker, 2013, p. 297). Even for willing systems, the decontextualised piecemeal information contained in rankings is insufficient for effective action. Of the results available, they are not provided in a timely manner to stakeholders who can make use of them (World Bank, 2017b). As Edwards suggests, if 'it was about improvement then the information would feed its way back into the hands of the people that are best positioned to make decisions to improve' (Hanushek & Edwards, 2017).

Adapting international learning assessments to the national context potentially enhances their ability to address learning needs. 'Not aligning metrics to national policy and curricula will reduce their use and usefulness in informing policy development and supporting classroom interventions as they diverge from countries' needs and priorities' (UIS, 2018h, p. 45). National and, to a lesser extent, regional assessments are more likely than international assessments to capture context-specific factors that foster or impede learning. National assessments are less expensive to administer, less likely to lead to shallow calls for wholesale reform, and more likely to capture the implemented curriculum in a country and its role in student learning (Kamens & Benavot, 2011). Unfortunately, the current vision for GLMs relies, almost exclusively, on international and regional assessments. If a guiding principle in the push for GLMs is to establish no new tests (UIS, 2017b), then it remains unclear if developing countries will have the expertise, funds, and capacities needed to strengthen national assessments to acceptable quality.

If the prevailing purposes of assessments are neither feasible nor desirable, why do developing countries participate? For many, participation acts as a visual marker of a serious commitment to improving the education system. For example, the post-Pinochet government in Chile decided to participate in international assessments, thus demonstrating a functioning government to its citizens (Kijima & Leer, 2016). For other countries, external pressure to be included in the global wave of assessments is strong. As one official in Paraguay stated when asked about his country's participation in PISA-D, 'Not being on the information map in the 21st century is unbearable' (Addey & Sellar, 2018). Developing countries, as latecomers to international assessments, tend to participate to establish legitimacy by 'doing what is expected of them by their individual and institutional peers' (Wiseman, 2010, p. 2). And, as previously mentioned, participation is increasingly an integral component of aid packages. The promise that country participation in GLMs will be voluntary (Motivans, 2014) rings hollow, given these many pressures on developing countries.

10   Conclusion

This chapter focussed on the construction and legitimation of global learning metrics in the context of SDG 4. It argued that learning assessments are being promoted as a ready-made solution with a viable methodology to measure a simplified notion of quality – namely, whether students achieve minimum proficiency levels in reading and mathematics in primary and secondary education. This abiding faith in measurement as a pathway to solving the 'global learning crisis' is rooted in a culture in which tests are seen as objective measures of individual and national effort, and higher test scores are associated with increased economic prosperity.

Currently, the global scales for monitoring proficiency levels have yet to be finalised. In the interim, early versions of GLMs raise concerns as to their impact on equity issues: Will the obsession over measuring and monitoring learning diminish the importance of, or effectively marginalise, equity concerns in SDG 4? Will GLMs undermine support and funding for the 263 million children and youth who are excluded from school? Will country efforts to improve foundational skills in literacy and numeracy undercut innovative policies and practices to ensure that all out-of-school children and youth gain access to a full and rich education and enjoy its benefits?

The dramatic depiction of a world in which hundreds of millions of children and youth are not learning, and the implications of this for future prosperity, downplays whether countries are taking concrete steps to universalise completion of primary and secondary education and ensure that 12 years of schooling are free (specifically, fee-free). Paradoxically, the global figure of more than 600 million not acquiring foundational skills is itself based on out-of-school figures for children and youth who are *assumed* to not be learning. This suggests that the 'learning crisis' in regions like Sub-Saharan Africa is driven in no small measure by those not attending school and those not completing a full cycle of schooling. Similarly, the World Bank's global dataset on education quality draws from international and regional surveys on children in school, altogether omitting those out of school.

This chapter also raises concerns about the relevance and utility of GLMs to countries and education professionals. Countries have been the movers and shapers of the 2030 Agenda for Sustainable Development. Country representatives led discussions over the formulation and scope of the SDGs, and they committed their governments to implementing this ambitious vision and comprehensive set of targets. The policies and actions they have and will put in place, and the partnerships they empower, will determine, in the final analysis, how much progress will be realised in the coming years. Of concern is whether GLMs meet the specific needs of countries: do they provide useful, contextualised information for feasible reform efforts? And when countries find themselves at the bottom or near the bottom of the new league tables, what steps will they take? Narrow the curriculum or teacher preparation? Exclude poor achievers from the assessments? Weaken the more challenging multilingual approaches to teaching and learning?

The intense focus on outcomes, especially learning outcomes, in the broad SDG 4 agenda is quite clear. Many of the 10 SDG 4 targets and the 11 global indicators emphasise important outcomes of schooling – specifically, foundational skills, employability skills, youth and adult literacy, knowledge and skills for global citizenship and sustainability, and more. These results-oriented indicators serve as an accountability framework for determining country progress. Though a broad range of actors contributed to the formulation of goals and targets, in developing indicators, it has been experts, international agencies, and donors, all legitimate actors, whose voices are the strongest. The views of country leaders, civil society representatives, and educators, who typically support a more humanistic understanding of education, have taken a back seat. The dialogue and decisions around putting SDG 4 into action seems to be dominated by those supporting an economic-oriented, utilitarian role for education. Given the time, collective effort, and funding needed to consider and pilot alternative measurement strategies, the longer-term impact of these actors and their actions should not be minimised. Consciously or not, their decisions as to which concrete procedures should be employed to reflect education realities on the ground have effectively prioritised which targets and indicators will gain visibility and which will not.

As the SDG era progresses, the issues outlined in this chapter are unlikely to be attenuated. The tensions between different camps and viewpoints, especially at the country and regional levels, are likely to become more palpable. Simplifying quality education to the lowest common denominator – namely, minimum proficiencies in foundational skills – and using this measure to dominate the policy discourse and donor priorities, GLMs threaten to broaden existing inequalities, valuing some forms of knowledge over others, and benefiting those already invested in large-scale assessments.

Notes

1   These proficiency levels are reported for at least one data point since 2012 (see http://data.uis.unesco.org/). To access these data, look under 'SDG4', 'Target 4.1', and 'Indicator 4.1.1', entitled 'Achieving at least minimum proficiency level in reading at the end of lower secondary education'.

2   Three approaches are currently being considered: statistical recalibration, social moderation, and the Rosetta stone approach (Gustafsson, 2018).

3   Strictly speaking, reporting on both global and thematic indicators is voluntary, although more attention is paid to the former than the latter.

4   From Recommendation 1: 'To galvanize attention globally, a single global indicator of learning should be agreed on to complement national measures of learning. The international community should track, rank, and publicize countries' progress in getting all children learning' (Education Commission, 2016, p. 17).

CHAPTER 12

Learning Assessments in the Time of SDGs: New Actors and Evolving Alliances in the Construction of a Global Field

Clara Fontdevila

1 Introduction

Large-scale learning assessments feature prominently in the indicator framework associated with the SDG 4 agenda as key data sources to monitor progress on this area, particularly given measurement challenges relative to comparability and data availability. While the assessment of student learning has been a practice on the rise since the mid-1990s (Benavot & Tanner, 2007; Heyneman & Lee, 2016; Kamens & Benavot, 2011; Pizmony-Levy, 2013), the adoption of the SDG 4/Education 2030 agenda represents a milestone in the consolidation of such a trend. Both the global and the thematic indicator frameworks established for the monitoring of Education 2030 are unambiguous on the need for countries to adopt or participate in some form of learning assessment so that student achievement can be reported on an internationally comparable scale. Up to five targets in SDG 4 include one or more learning-related indicator, and five out of 11 global indicators require reporting on student learning, skills, or knowledge. These measurement needs turn the adoption and use of large-scale assessments (LSAs) into an essential condition for tracing and tracking progress in the new education goals.

The magnitude of the changes and the new dynamics brought about by the SDG 4/Education 2030 agenda lend themselves to a productive enquiry on the relationship between the different organisations involved in the promotion, administration, or use of LSA. The shift entailed by the new education agenda is not only likely to have a direct and positive impact on the centrality and legitimacy of assessment. More importantly, this push is likely to penetrate the agendas of these organisations and to affect the interrelationships among the different actors with a role in LSA.

So far, the relationships among these organisations have received limited attention. Particularly when it comes to developing countries, the links between international large-scale assessments (ILSAS) and national large-scale assessments (NLSAS) have rarely been explored in depth. To some extent, this could be the result of a particular division of labour within the scholarly analysis of LSAS. However, even the relationship among different ILSAS remains only partially explored, and most of the work has focussed on the role, evolution, and influence of major 'players', including the OECD and the International Association for the Evaluation of Educational Achievement (IEA) (e.g., see Grek [2009] and Pizmony-Levy [2013], respectively). In short, the global learning assessment landscape has been explored only to a limited extent. Changes brought about by SDG 4 constitute a useful entry-point to understand both its structure and recent changes.

2   Key Concepts

In this chapter, I inquire into the reconfiguration or reshaping of the global assessment field as entailed by the negotiation and adoption of SDG 4 in order to gain a better understanding of the composition and structure of this community of practice. To this aim, I examine changes both in the institutional agendas of the different organisations involved in the promotion and administration of LSAS, and in the relationship among these agencies.

The working hypothesis that orients this chapter is that the negotiation of SDG 4 targets and indicators has decisively contributed to the consolidation, integration, and diversification of a global field of assessment. The notion of *field* is here used in the sense advanced by Bourdieu (1983) – a structured and differentiated social space of specialised practice revolving around distinctive beliefs and institutions, and in which different actors struggle and compete for the preservation or transformation of their own relative positions.

More specifically, the degree and impact of the SDG 4 agenda are examined in relation to the key dimensions of field autonomy put forward by Buchholz (2016) in her discussion of global fields. These mechanisms include (a) the establishment of a distinctive set of institutions (i.e., the articulation of an institutional infrastructure in which the field-specific principles become objectified); (b) the existence of an distinctive 'form of belief', which construes a specific sphere of practice as distinctive, independent, and valuable in its own right; and (c) the emergence of autonomous and field-specific principles of hierarchisation. Later sections of the chapter, dedicated to presentation of the main findings, are structured around these three subprocesses.

Methodologically, this chapter builds on the combination of three methods. First, the research draws on the analysis of documentary data derived from the main reports, policy briefs, and presentations prepared by the main organisations involved in the different consultation and coordination mechanisms described (see Table 12.1). The analysis aimed to identify frequent themes and foci of debate within these documents, as well as the positions, priorities, and framings mobilised by the different stakeholders.

Second, semi-structured interviews were conducted with 41 key informants, experts, and representatives of these organisations (see Table 12.1). The interviews were transcribed and correspondingly anonymised in order to guarantee the confidentiality of the information. The purpose of the interviews was to gain an understanding of the different motivations and incentives driving different organisations' engagement in the SDG 4 process, as well as to identify supporting frameworks, normative beliefs, and main areas of contention.

Finally, the research benefited also from the observation of one of the meetings convening and fostering debate and discussion among these actors, the third meeting of the Global Alliance to Monitor Learning (GAML), in Mexico City, May 2017. The main focus of observation was on the informal and formal relationships and communication patterns among different actors within

TABLE 12.1   List of interviewees

Group 1	Bilateral and multilateral development agencies and banks; multistakeholder partnerships	WB, IADB, USAID, GPE, DFID	7
Group 2	UN system agencies	UIS, UNESCO, UNICEF, UN-Women, GEMR	11
Group 3	Private sector organisations (research institutes, foundations, think tanks)	RTI, Pearson, CUE-Brookings, Hewlett Foundation, ACER	9
Group 4	NGOs and civil society organisations	Save the Children, ActionAid, GCE	7
Group 5	Regional assessment networks; agencies and organisations in charge of ILSAs, citizen-led assessments	OECD, IEA, ASER Centre, PASEC	4
Group 6	Others	University-affiliated experts, UN-related or UN-supported initiatives (e.g., Education Commission)	3

the field, as well as the procedures and mechanisms of decision-making and consensus-building.

3 The Institutionalisation of a Global Assessment Infrastructure

In this section, I focus on the first of the mechanisms described by Buchholz in the construction of a field, that is, is the 'establishment of an institutional infrastructure for the worldwide circulation of ideas, persons, and goods across borders' (2016, p. 14). The establishment of forums and spaces that enable regular exchange (and competition), and help connect the different players in the field, is instrumental in ensuring the global outlook of the different stakeholders. These organisations and events play an integrative and unifying role, crucial for the construction of a field as a space of specialised practice, and an arena in which organisations position themselves vis-à-vis other stakeholders involved in a given sphere of activity.

From the outset, the many national, regional, and international assessments established in the mid-1990s have been connected, especially through their relationships with international agencies, nongovernmental organisations, regional organisations, and professional networks. In fact, some scholars have identified international organisations, nongovernmental organisations (NGOs), and regional associations as the main carriers and agents of diffusion of both national and international assessment (Chabbott, 2003; Kamens & Benavot, 2011; Kamens & McNeely, 2010; Lockheed, 2013). However, these promotion and diffusion efforts seem to occur in a disorganised or highly decentralised way. Hence, the general interconnectedness has not translated into the articulation of an institutional infrastructure in which the field-specific principles become objectified. The following section will describe some of the mechanisms and spaces that have contributed to some degree of integration and institutionalisation.

3.1 *The Learning Metrics Task Force Initiative: Laying the Foundations for a Global Debate*

Early stages of the run-up to the articulation of SDG 4 prompted some key changes in a scarcely institutionalised community of practice. As early as 2012, the establishment of the Learning Metrics Task Force (LMTF)[1] laid the foundations for the construction of a global infrastructure able to foster a minimal integration of the different efforts in place. More specifically, the socialisation and familiarisation effect brought about by LMTF meetings played an important role in constructing new and shared meanings and the legitimation of the assessment programme.

The LMTF was envisaged as a multistakeholder partnership co-convened by the Center for Universal Education (CUE) at the Brookings Institution and the UNESCO Institute for Statistics (UIS). The taskforce kicked off in the early years of the post-2015 global education debate, and in its first phase, it explicitly focussed on 'catalyzing global dialogue and developing a series of recommendations on learning assessments' (Anderson & Ditmore, 2016, p. 4). To this end, the taskforce organised three open consultations and launched three thematic reports and a summary report. Beyond the specific recommendations that resulted from the discussion (a question to which I will return later in this chapter), the impact of the LMTF was central in creating a sense of community and common purpose among different agents involved with assessment and monitoring activities. A UN staff member (Group 2) interviewed for this study stated:

> If you look at the work of the LMTF you will see that the discussion of indicators was already there and was quite influential. Of course, the LMTF was launched in 2012, and the agenda evolved. ... But the technical work involved the same people, or more, that were involved later in the GAML. There was a natural link between the two ... so you can see a political agenda on learning ... on the technical seminal work of the LMTF ... and then of course the SDG 4 itself. So, I do really think the LMTF was quite a rich experience because of the diversity of people involved.

It is also important to take into account that, while the LMTF was formally a collaboration between CUE and the UIS, different interviewees suggest that CUE was always far more in control of the agenda than the UIS. The fact that the UIS joined these efforts only at a subsequent stage (and, apparently, in a rather accidental way) suggests that, during this early phase, the Institute had a rather limited political clout. A private sector representative (Group 3) commented:

> It's interesting because the LMTF was co-led by the UIS and the Brookings Institution ... but all the networking, consultation ... was done by the Brookings Institution. So the UIS was doing things related to mandate ... but really, the Brookings Institution was instrumental.

3.2   *From the LMTF to the LMP and GAML: The UIS in the Driving Seat?*

The constitution of the Learning Metrics Partnership (LMP) and, later on, of the GAML, emerged to some extent as a continuation of the LMTF effort. Most of the interviewees for this study regard them as a sort of prolongation of the LMTF. However, these new spaces proved a key opportunity for UIS to regain a position of authority. Particularly in the GAML, the guidance and ascendancy exerted by the Institute have been clearer and stronger than in the LMTF. According to different interviewees, this was a deliberate move prompted to a large extent by a change in the leadership of the Institute. According to an interviewee from a development agency (Group 1):

> I think the first thing Silvia Montoya [the current director of UIS] did when she came, she stopped the partnership. Because she wanted to understand all the moves, and why we were engaging and why they were driving this. Because Brookings was driving the LMTF, and in the work that was done, UIS was not contributing much. We convened meetings and contributed to the publications, but we didn't really contribute a lot to this. And it was not participatory, in essence. And UIS wanted something participatory. That's why GAML was created, it's more participatory.

There is a certain consensus among the interviewees that one of the key factors explaining the repositioning of UIS in the debate and the progress in the 'global assessment conversation' was the appointment of a new Director of UIS whose motivation and leadership capacity would differ notably from her predecessor's. However, the leading position enjoyed by UIS from mid-2015 also owes much to a series of external changes not directly connected to the agency exerted by UIS. In particular, it is largely the result of the formal recognition of the Institute as the custodian agency for the reporting of global indicators (UIS, 2016b), and as the main source of cross-comparable data on education (WEF, 2015).

It is however unclear to what extent UIS was prepared or willing to assume this leading position and whether other agencies in the development field regarded UIS in these terms. In this sense, it is important to take into account that UNESCO-led production of statistics was in fact subjected to heavy criticism during the 1990s, a situation that the creation of UIS in 1999 could only partially reverse. The legitimacy and authority enjoyed by UIS have thus tended to be limited and subject to strong competition from other international organisations, including the World Bank and the OECD (Heyneman, 1999; Cussó & D'Amico, 2007).

The LMP was conceived as a joint initiative of the UIS and the Centre for Global Education Monitoring of the Australian Council for Educational Research (ACER-GEM),[2] in partnership with the Australian Government's

Department of Foreign Affairs and Trade (DFAT). The LMP was oriented to 'develop a set of nationally and internationally-comparable learning metrics in mathematics and reading, and to facilitate and support their use for monitoring purposes in partnership with interested countries' (UIS-ACER, 2014, p. 1). The flagship products of the initiative included advances in the UIS Catalogue and Database of Learning Assessments, and the Learning Assessment Capacity Index database. These two products, in fact, were to some extent the embryonic version of the work that would be further developed by the GAML. In any case, and beyond the more tangible outputs of that effort, the LMP contributed to the development of an institutional structure enabling and furthering the circulation of ideas and people within the field of assessment.

The GAML, in turn, was originally defined as an 'umbrella initiative to monitor and track progress towards all learning-related Education 2030 targets' (UIS, 2016b) and has been characterised by an evolving structure as well as by its changing composition. The singularity of the GAML lies in the fact that it constitutes a space of debate separate from the Technical Cooperation Group (TCG), a platform convened by both UIS and the UNESCO Education Sector's Division of Education 2030 Support and Coordination. While the TCG has a political mandate to develop and debate the SDG 4 thematic indicators, the UIS decided to keep the debate on learning outcomes within GAML, an ad hoc platform.

The separate existence of the GAML has major implications, particularly given the initially limited presence of country representatives, compared to TCG. According to the last note on its governance structure (UIS, 2017d), its membership is open to any individual willing to contribute to the work of GAML, with members typically falling under nine different categories: international organisations, development partners, regional organisations, regional development banks, civil society organisations, UIS technical partners, assessment organisations, scholars and academics, and representatives of UN member states (who remain however a very limited fraction of the total).

In terms of governance, the management of the platform (defined as coordination, support, and logistic functions) is handled by a Secretariat hosted by UIS, while its general oversight and guidance on priorities is the responsibility of a Strategic Planning Committee. The latter is composed of the UIS Director, a chair, and several vice co-chairs, including representatives of international organisations, civil society, teachers' unions, regional assessments, global assessments, and country representatives. Decisions are to be endorsed by the GAML plenary during in-person meetings, which it assumed all the members will attend. In this sense, GAML is by definition an inclusive and accountable space. The decision-making procedures, however, remain relatively underdeveloped, unspecified, or unclear to most of the interviewees for this study. The protocol and procedures for invitation, as well as the channels used to encourage participation, also remain rather unclear at the time of writing.

3.3   *A First-of-Its-Kind Initiative?*

As noted above, the GAML has not by any means been the first global space to serve socialisation purposes within the learning assessment community. For example, the unifying or brokering role played by the PISA for Development (PISA-D), which parallels the efforts described in this section, should not be underestimated. The PISA-D project was devised as an extension of PISA to lower- and middle-income countries (Addey, 2017) and relies to an important extent on the funding provided by bilateral and multilateral donors who have also been involved in the GAML efforts.

In this sense, the assessment field has never been a fully 'balkanised' or fragmented realm. On the contrary, the different professionals and organisations concerned with assessment (as promoters, designers, funders, and so on) have nurtured informal ties and formalised relations of cooperation for years. However, the specificity and novelty of the efforts described previously related to the *global* perspective they foster – the fact that they are not organisation- or region-specific. In addition, the coordination efforts under way are likely to ensure a greater legitimacy of the global assessment field within its broader environment, the global education policy field. Because democratisation is increasingly regarded as a key element when it comes to securing legitimacy in the context of globalisation (Buchanan & Keohane, 2006), the inclusive and accountable nature of the UIS-promoted platforms is likely to ensure high levels of social acceptance.

However, the distribution of roles and power is far from settled; it is in fact continuously negotiated and built by a variety of actors and forces. On the one hand, the GAML has contributed to ensure a much more central and leading role for UIS (especially in comparison to the LMTF initiative). However, the limited authority and normative capacity enjoyed by UIS make such a position rather vulnerable. Also, UIS is considered a latecomer in the learning assessment landscape and has long focussed on the adult literacy field through the LAMP programme (Literacy Assessment and Monitoring Programme), which has been affected by resource and prestige challenges since its inception (Addey et al., 2017). Some of the interviewees for this study referred to the limited financial capacity of UIS, noting that it could put in jeopardy both the success of the global reporting effort and UIS's leadership or steering capacity. A staff member of a development agency (Group 1) expressed this view:

> I think there's a problem of strategic orientation of UNESCO. UNESCO is simply incapable of prioritising. This is a massive area of public good where UNESCO has a comparative advantage from its position to provide. ... The financial situation of UIS is ... a sign ... that UNESCO actually does not understand that. ... And that's sad, because it leaves the door open to another organisation that may be less well-placed to guarantee minimum standards for such a process to be beneficial for the world. Of course, UIS is trying and they will get some funding for that ... but it's not the way it should be.

In fact, much of the work of the GAML appears to be highly dependent on the funding of UIS and a very limited group of agencies and organisations – the UK Department for International Development (DFID), the Australian Department of Foreign Affairs and Trade (DFAT), and the Hewlett Foundation (UIS, 2017d). While these financial contributions do not necessary translate into higher levels of influence, the overreliance on such a limited number of partners could have an impact on UIS's image of neutrality and impartiality, especially given the limited formalisation regarding decision-making and invitation procedures.

The relatively limited technical expertise on LSAS currently available within UIS tends to perpetuate a certain relation of dependence on external partners such as consultancy firms, university-affiliated scholars, or independent research organisations. While such collaboration ensures a certain degree of sophistication in the execution of the objectives, it may also pose significant risks in terms of sustainability, and even of legitimacy if not accompanied by the necessary levels of public scrutiny and institutional capacity-building.

4   A New Vision for a New Agenda: The Imperative of Assessment

This section considers a second key mechanism in the articulation of a social field, that is, the existence of a distinctive 'form of belief' that construes a specific sphere of practice as distinctive, independent, and valuable in its own right (Buchholz, 2016). The formation of a field does not arise out of the establishment of institutionalised spaces in a *mechanical* way. Another crucial dimension of field autonomy is thus the articulation of an autonomous ideology or vision which, crucially, defines and legitimatises a sphere of practice as singular and valuable in its own right, superior in some way to other practices (Bourdieu, 1983; Buchholz, 2016; Gorski, 2013).

The emergence of a relatively integrated global assessment field has revolved around the identification of assessment as the policy *solution* to an institutionalised *problem* (i.e., one that has entered institutional agendas). The problem identified is the learning crisis. Such a coupling has been very much enabled and fostered by the particular framing of the post-2015 debate.

As early as in 2006, three economists connected to the World Bank and the Center for Global Development proposed to replace the education-related Millennium Development Goal (MDG) with a Millennium Learning Goal so that education systems would be judged and held accountable by their learning outcomes (Filmer, Hasan, & Pritchett, 2006). These scholars were vocal in their criticism of an inputs-based approach to school quality, and portrayed learning outcomes (as measured by regional or international assessments) as a proxy for education quality (Filmer et al., 2006; see also Barrett, 2011). A similar focus on student achievement was also embraced in the World Bank Education Strategy 2020 (World Bank, 2011).

Such an approach raised a variety of concerns, particularly regarding the possibility of unintended consequences, such as standardisation of the curriculum, diversion of attention from other less easily measurable purposes of education, or lack of attention to the quality of the process (Barrett, 2011; Bonal, Verger, & Zancajo, 2015; Klees, 2013; Rose, 2015). Eventually, the final wording and formulation of the goals and targets avoided such pitfalls by including learning targets with other quality-related targets related to inputs and processes (Bonal et al., 2015; Rose, 2014).

However, most of the debate in the run-up to the formulation of SDG 4 continued to revolve around the so-called 'learning agenda'. The increasing availability of data evidencing low levels of learning despite global progress in enrolment, contributed significantly to the growing visibility and centrality of the learning/quality binary. The 'global learning crisis' spotlighted by the EFA Global Monitoring Report (UNESCO, 2012b, 2014f) and its equity-oriented framework were instrumental in giving currency to the issue and fostered an alignment of a variety of stakeholders around the need to pay greater attention to quality and/or learning outcomes. The negotiation and adoption of SDG 4, as well as the development of monitoring mechanisms, contributed greatly to secure and disseminate the 'quality turn' within the global discourse on education, understood as an effort to transcend a focus on schooling and enrolment figures as key indicators of progress. (For further discussion of this transformation, see Chapter 9 by Yusuf Sayed and Kate Moriarty; Sachs-Israel, 2017; Sayed, Ahmed, & Mogliacci, 2018.)

The coupling of the learning/quality problem with the 'assessment solution' and their rise in the global agenda are the consequence of a wide range of predisposing and precipitating factors (whose complexity is beyond the scope of this chapter; for more detail, see Chapter 11 by Aaron Benavot and William C. Smith). The run-up to SDG 4 contributed decisively to securing this connection and making it visible. Such intertwining is particularly clear in the first works produced by the LMTF.[3] Indeed, most of its activity revolved in fact around measurement-related interventions. According to three promoters of the LMTF initiative, 'The real debates now center on how to conceptualise and assess learning within a global framework' (Winthrop, Anderson, & Cruzalegui, 2015, p. 298). The different reports produced and resulting from the LMTF consultations tended to emphasise measurement as an essential and necessary (although not sufficient) part of the policy solution to the learning problem.

The importance attributed to measurement as a key part of the equation is explicit in Winthrop et al. (2015, p. 300):

> [MDG] goals and indicators were chosen over other EFA goals because they were easier to measure at the global level (Winthrop and Anderson, 2013). Robust data were available in a majority of countries and comparability across national contexts was possible. ... Availability of metrics has especially driven funding from donors who choose funding priorities based on areas where they perceive their external support can have a measurable impact.

This interpretation of the comparatively poor traction of the EFA agenda and the limited progress of the education-related MDGs (as opposed to other areas, including health) appears to have inspired to a large extent the quest for globally comparable learning and its framing as a key part of the solution. Given the high levels of visibility of the LMTF, one of the unintended effects of the initiative could be what has been described as a 'conflation' between quality and benchmarking (Soudien, 2013). Assessment thus became a key policy route to address the quality and equity imperatives, making it a priority area for most bilateral and multilateral aid agencies or lending programmes.

5   Principles of Hierarchisation: An Improbable Agreement?

This section examines the third mechanism described by Buchholz (2016) as key in the articulation of a field, that is, emergence of autonomous and field-specific principles of hierarchisation. In fact, the emphasis on the existence of a *common vision* of the prior section risks obscuring the existence of contending approaches and visions within a field. Similarly, theories of the global diffusion of assessment risk eliding the existence of competition dynamics (or power relations) within a given sphere of practice.

The assessment field is far from a unified bloc. Rather, like most social fields, it is an arena of struggle about the kind of knowledge that is valued and of competition for dominant positions (Go & Krause, 2016). Far from being equal partners in a flat world, the different agencies and organisations involved in the debate strive and compete for global legitimacy. In that sense, the nascent global field of assessment is far from being settled, that is to say, one that 'has reached a higher degree of consolidation, being characterised by a "robust social order" and established "rules of the game"' (Fligstein & McAdam, 2012, p. 92).

5.1   Divisive Issues and Classification Struggles

Most areas of disagreement were identified at an early stage by some of the leaders within the LMTF. Taking stock of the different debates fostered by the LMTF activity, Winthrop et al. (2015) summarised the areas with a lack of consensus as follows: a narrow versus broad scope of learning measurement, globally comparable versus nationally defined goals and targets, universal versus country-determined benchmarks, measuring learning for all versus only those who are in school, and top-down versus bottom-up implementation.

While not necessarily constituting fault lines, these different positions emphasise and value different aspects of assessment and suggest two more general positions, confirmed in interviews for this study. In general terms, an opposition or divisive line emerges between those who value scientific sophistication and a particular variety of expertise cultivated in highly specialised agencies with a proven record, and those who prioritise the value of local relevance, context-sensitivity, or country ownership. To some degree, this struggle intersects with (but does not completely equate with) the different value attributed to cross-country comparability and, more generally, to the ultimate purpose given to assessment. While some agents expect that assessment will trigger change by providing domestic governments with better or more reliable information necessary to improve policy formulation and planning, others emphasise the value of cross-comparability or the 'disciplining' effect of national assessments within the global arena, that is, cross-accountability pressures resulting from global reporting. Hence, although these theories are not incompatible, they necessarily end up placing a different value on comparability. A UN staff member (Group 2) interviewed for this study noted:

> The two logics are the two ends of the spectrum. If you are sitting at the international global level, the internationally comparable – that's how you see things. And if you are at the other end of spectrum, you're looking at ... you want some kind of assessment that is easy to design, which

doesn't take long, which is cheap. ... You need, in your context, to improve your interventions, to better inform yourself, to better design or to read-just interventions.

These 'classification struggles' are more likely to become visible as some organ-isations face the need to privilege a particular approach by means of providing financial aid, policy recommendations, technical support, etc. This is clearly the case of the GAML, whose participants are expected to reach consensus on the most appropriate tools for the reporting of global indicators, and to pro-vide countries with guidance to improve learning assessments. The GAML and other SDG 4 fora are not exactly interest-free realms – as different organisations are likely to use them to promote and disseminate their own vision or prod-ucts. Some of the representatives of the most reputable and/or long-standing assessment programmes have indeed been particularly vocal in asserting the superiority of cross-comparable assessments. Remarkably, these are strategi-cally framed as appropriate not only given their readiness for global and the-matic reporting but also as a fast track to build capacity at a national level. Representatives from the OECD and the IEA not only emphasise the technical superiority and cost-efficiency of their flagship programmes but also portray them as learning and training opportunities for participant countries.

5.2   A Balancing Act

At the time of writing, it is still unclear which (if any) approach will be privi-leged. On the one side, and at least in relation to Target 4.1,[4] the GAML has unequivocally encouraged the expansion and strengthening of national assess-ments, emphasising ownership as well as the logics of assessment as a public good. These are to be plotted or anchored against a global reporting scale, after an assessment of its quality. While in the short term, global monitoring will be based on these cross-national assessments, this is not the approach privileged in the long term (Montoya, 2017; UIS, 2017e, 2017g). A development agency staff member (Group 1) argued:

> You cannot make progress in this work without involving organisations with high capacity ... but then the question is how do you make sure that the outputs of that do not privilege a particular organisation. ... It's a really delicate balancing exercise. ... But they also need to satisfy certain standards in terms of how they collaborate, and what they make public, and what their agenda is ... and [it] is not that easy ... but from that point of view, I think the GAML is trying to accommodate as many players as possible.

Much of the GAML effort has been recently directed at the construction of reporting scales expected to enable a solid and rigorous linking of both national and cross-national assessments to a common scale of performance levels (UIS, 2017l). Those efforts seem to avoid a zero-sum approach and to accommodate the use of different assessments.

The possibility of using national assessments for global reporting purposes represents a significant shift in learning assessment practices. While cross-national assessments had been long considered useful for international comparisons and as a means to inform national policy, the same was not true for national assessments, in that NLSAs were deemed far less appropriate for global reporting. As noted by Benavot and Koseleci (2015, p. 19), 'National learning assessments are not designed for comparing learning outcomes across education systems'[5]. Scholars had given some thought to this possibility and worked on theorising its requirements (e.g., Lockheed, 2016). This seemed more of a technical feasibility than a ready-to-be-implemented approach. To some extent, the conversation fostered by the LMTF opened the door or created the conditions for the coordination efforts that such a goal would require.

Such a shift represents a change in the relationship between dominant players, who historically monopolised visibility in relation to large-scale assessments as monitoring tools, and 'pretenders', who may be seeking a more visible and central position as new market niches unfold. The disruptive potential of such an approach lies in the fact that ILSAs have precisely constructed their authority by way of emphasising their potential for cross-comparability purposes. According to Martens (2007), the 'comparative turn' (or 'governance by comparison') was one the main drivers of OECD success. Similarly, as Grek (2009, p. 25) noted, 'the OECD has created a niche as a technically highly competent agency for the development of educational indicators and comparative educational performance measures'. The construction of a universal scale, against which any national assessment can be anchored or plotted, puts into question the comparative advantage of the IEA or OECD in that regard.

Ultimately, the privileging of any particular approach (cross-national vs. national; open-source vs. licensed models of assessment, etc.) does not depend solely on GAML, let alone UIS, guidance. The advice or support of aid and lending agencies is going to be a determinant in consolidation or spread. Through financial and technical assistance, initiatives like the Global Partnership for Education, as well as bilateral aid agencies and multilateral development banks, are likely to have a crucial impact in fostering specific models of their preference. Most interviewees for this study noted the ambivalent, divided, or evolving attitude of most of these organisations, or do not agree about the direction of their preferences. Existing assessment programmes are free to continue advancing their own agenda, regardless of the direction that the GAML is taking. Efforts from OECD to advance the PISA-D are likely to proceed even if they are not necessarily the sole or priority approach favoured by GAML discussions.

6   Final Remarks

Most of the processes described previously are still in progress and so is the scholarship exploring them. The empirical basis informing and supporting this chapter is limited. The chapter aims only to propose some tentative explanations that will require further elaboration. Nonetheless, some preliminary conclusions can be drawn at this point.

First, evidence suggests that there is a global field of learning assessment in the making, although this is very much in a nascent stage and with little integration. The establishment of an incipient infrastructure and the development of a shared language is partly due to the growing interdependence of different types of organisations involved in assessment-related work. The existence of different and competing criteria for the categorisation of LSAs suggests that the field is in an emerging and evolving stage with its boundaries and organising principles open to (re)definition.

In fact, the articulation and unfolding of a field should not be equated to the emergence of a complete consensus among the multiple actors populating this social space. Different actors in the assessment field tend to emphasise different purposes of NLSAs and, consequently, place a different value on cross-comparability, efforts to develop domestic capacity, etc. The fact that no assessment programme enjoys a hegemonic position at the moment leaves the space open to competitive dynamics among concerned organisations. The same applies to the international organisations in charge of collecting and harmonising this data. While UIS attempts to regain a central role, the lead is likely to be disputed by other organisations, which are better resourced and enjoy even higher reputations.

Second, the field seems to be increasingly diverse in its composition, and the production of metrics and harmonisation of data is not by any means the remit of international organisations. Paradoxically, the growing integration and consolidation of the assessment field have been accompanied by its opening to a wider range of stakeholders. The negotiation and early implementation of SDG 4 have increased the number further. Certain private actors, including think tanks and research institutes, seem to have deployed considerable influence in the configuration of the field.

The self-ruling nature of these organisations raises some concerns regarding accountability and transparency. While this 'private' status does not preclude the possibility of productive exchanges, it is very likely to generate conflicts of interests in the medium- and long-term, or to make public scrutiny increasingly difficult. It is thus important to develop mechanisms to hold these actors accountable, as well as to ensure that their contributions are guided by democratic and transparency principles. The emerging institutional architecture of the field should be equipped with a clear and well-defined governance structure. While the GAML has the potential to fulfil the role, its convening capacity and its normative and scientific authority are far from consolidated. Uncoordinated efforts on the part of lending agencies or assessment programmes may reinforce the centrifugal dynamics and fragmentation referred to previously. At this stage, it is unclear if the monitoring structures implemented as a result of the SDG 4 agenda will be able to counter these dynamics.

Third, the emergent nature of the field risks having a diverting effect in relation to other areas that also require improved measurement, especially in terms of political and technical attention. The assessment needs associated with the new agenda could create a perverse incentive for organisations involved in the collection of education indicators and even for other organisations in the development field, not traditionally engaged in data collection. As a global 'assessment market' unfolds, the prestige and visibility gains associated with its central positions may motivate some organisations to put additional effort into this area. As a consequence, other education dimensions that are indeed central to the SDG 4 agenda may remain underdeveloped or underscrutinised in practice.

Other challenges created by the push for LSA concern the ultimate potential of assessment and monitoring as levers for change. However, more empirical work is needed to better understand whether LSAs can live up to their promise, and, especially, under which circumstances. It is not clear, for instance, how to ensure that countries' *participation* in LSAs translates into greater capacity to make use of data or to eventually develop their own assessment capacity. Similarly, risks associated with the narrowing of curriculum, conflicts of interest among providers, or countries' dependence on external support should not be underestimated. While this is not necessarily the case, and while capacity-building and technical programmes projected by the SDG agenda could play a central role as enablers of an effective and balanced use of such tools, those risks constitute an empirical question that can only be addressed through research and accurate monitoring.

Finally, and in spite of the abovementioned limitations, the preliminary results of this research suggest some possible future research lines.

First, while this research focussed on assessment programmes for basic education (primary and lower secondary), learning assessments cover a range of educational sectors (early years, adult education, higher education, etc.). Each of these engages a different combination of interest groups and presents different trajectories that could be tracked empirically.

Second, the past and future development of the assessment field could be explored with a clearer emphasis on its relationship with its broadest environment, that is, the global education policy field (Jakobi, 2009) as well as extra-educational structures, events, and processes (Dale, 2005). The links between LSAS and SDG 4 and wider SDG processes are obvious starting points. The relative autonomy of this global field in relation to national assessment fields should be also examined in more depth in order to understand how different national assessment cultures (or education policy dynamics) are reflected in the global context.

Finally, it would be worth exploring the impact and recontextualisation of this global assessment agenda at national or subnational levels in order to understand which local processes are advanced or affected by the evolution of the global field.

Notes

1 Sometimes referred to as LMTF 1.0, to contrast it with a second phase, which I discuss below.
2 ACER is an Australian-based, not-for-profit, research-oriented organisation with a focus on education. ACER depends financially on research and consultancy contracts commissioned by education administrators as well as private, non-governmental, and international organisations. Historically, ACER has played a key role in the implementation and administration of cross-country, large-scale assessments including Programme for International Student Assessment (PISA), Trends in International Mathematics and Science Study (TIMSS), and Progress in International Reading Literary Study (PIRLS).
3 This is not to suggest such coupling was the direct result of LMTF. Before its creation, the assessment programme had already entered the political agenda of different organisations in the development field, after having been gathering momentum for a while.

4 Some interviewees suggest that efforts in relation to Target 4.2 (related to early childhood development, care, and preprimary education) could be headed in the opposite direction. However, this debate appears to still be developing and falls beyond the scope of this specific section of the chapter.

5 Similarly, the emergence of hybrid assessments combining elements from LSAs with household-based educational surveys (Wagner, 2011) would have had comparable 'diluting' effects.

CHAPTER 13

Can Education Transform Our World? Global Citizenship Education and the UN's 2030 Agenda for Sustainable Development

Joel Westheimer

> To refuse to face the task of creating a vision of a future ... immeasurably more just and noble and beautiful than ... today is to evade the most crucial, difficult, and important educational task.
>
> GEORGE COUNTS (1932)

∴

1 Introduction

Belief in the fundamental importance of education for improving society has been long-standing. Across more than a century of school reform around the world, the idea that young people must learn to be good stewards of their communities has concerned scholars and policymakers alike (Dewey, 1916; Educational Policies Commission, 1940; Gutmann, 1987; Soder, 1996; Parker, 2003; Walling, 2004; Noddings, 2015; Apple, 2018). So, it is not entirely surprising that the United Nations' Sustainable Development Goals (SDGs) see education as a key element of global transformational change (UNGA, 2015b).

SDG 4 seeks inclusive, equitable, quality education for all children and young adults, and aims to reach a set of 10 targets for education worldwide by 2030 (UNGA, 2015b, pp. 19–20). Other chapters in this book address a diverse set of aims represented in these targets, including, for example, adequate financing (Chapter 8 by David Archer and Tanvir Muntasim), gender equality (Chapter 3 by Naureen Durrani and Anjum Halai), disability (Chapter 4 by Christopher Johnstone, Matthew Schuelka, and Ghada Swadek), assessment (Chapter 12 by Clara Fontdevila), and the rights of students to receive an education that is free of a profit motive (Chapter 7 by Alexandra Draxler). These are all important parts of pursuing equity and access to quality education for all children. My focus in this chapter is on the role of global citizenship education in pursuing those and other similar aims. While policymakers have often looked to schools to provide students with the knowledge and skills they need to secure productive employment and flourish economically, I will be concerned with a different lever for change: the potential for education to foster a more just and sustainable society for all by preparing students to be civically and politically engaged citizens.

School is not only a vehicle for the transmission of knowledge but also a place where children learn about the society in which they are growing up, how they might engage productively, how they can fight for change when change is warranted, and how to know when it is warranted. For that reason, the goals, content, and methods of educational programmes are highly contested. How a country schools its children is a reflection of its collective principles and ideals. In particular, to speak of citizenship education (global and otherwise) is to speak not only of the world as we see it, but also, and more importantly, of the global society that we hope the next generation will help to create. Ideas about what makes a 'good' citizen are a proxy for a vision of the good society, and agreeing on common elements of a good society is a challenging undertaking for even one nation state. To extend that challenge to a quest for a common vision among all the earth's nations invites certain contention, and yet is an essential element of any agenda for global change. This chapter, then, has implications well beyond SDG 4. As I argue in what follows, if we seek the kind of lasting progress called for by the 2030 Agenda for Sustainable Development, educators must be empowered to engage youth and young adults in a vision of change and equip them with the tools they need to get there.

Are we teaching children to unquestioningly preserve social, political, and economic norms and behaviours, or to imagine and pursue new and better ones? Do we teach them only the importance of following the rules or also to question when the rules are not worth following? Do we teach students to mobilise in support of policies that promote only their own self-interest, or to think more broadly about their ethical obligations to others? If today's youth are to participate in political decision-making and in efforts to move toward more sustainable social, political, and economic arrangements, schools must ensure that they are sufficiently well-informed to do so effectively.

John Dewey (1916) described schools as miniature communities and noted that the school is not only a preparation for something that comes later but also a community with values and norms embedded in daily experiences. Transforming the way we teach citizenship (local, national, and global) then, is not only the purview of the civics and social studies classroom, but a journey into all classrooms, all subjects, and the entire school experience. Schools teach lessons in citizenship regardless of whether or not they follow a citizenship education curriculum. How classrooms are set up, who gets to talk when, how adults conduct themselves, how decisions are made, how lessons are enacted – all these inevitably serve as lessons in citizenship. Whether teachers explicitly 'teach' lessons in citizenship or not, students learn about community organisation, the distribution of power and resources, rights, responsibilities, and of course, justice and injustice.

SDG 4, in its broadest sense, is about worldwide equity and access to quality education. But its specific target goals reach further and are tied to all 17 goals for a sustainable world. By 2030, Target 4.7 declares, all learners should 'acquire the knowledge and skills needed to promote sustainable development, including, among others, through education for sustainable development and sustainable lifestyles, human rights, gender equality, promotion of a culture of peace and non-violence, global citizenship and appreciation of cultural diversity' (UNGA, 2015b, p. 17). Global citizenship education, as illustrated in Target 4.7, is a central part of SDG 4, but it is also a precondition for many of the other goals and targets in the 2030 Agenda. SDG 4 seeks to promote well-being for all at all ages; SDG 10 calls for reducing inequality between and within countries; SDG 13 seeks action on climate change; SDG 16 aims to foster peaceful and inclusive societies, provide access to justice for all, and build effective, accountable, and inclusive institutions at all levels. These goals are far-reaching, and in addition to political will, they require the kinds of social and cultural paradigm shifts that come from shared educational ideals.

Are the SDGs achievable? How can research on global citizenship education inform education policy and practice that aligns with, supports, and moves us further along the path toward the ambitious agenda the SDGs propose? What knowledge, skills, and behaviours must students learn in order to create a world that cultivates and defends human rights, gender equality, environmental sustainability, peace, and diversity?

2   A Common Vocabulary

Before delving into specifics about the potential of global citizenship education to contribute to the 2030 Agenda, I would like to note the complexity of the vocabulary associated with these kinds of educational approaches and goals. Scholars, policymakers, and practitioners employ a variety of terms to describe education that aims to improve society broadly and, more specifically, to do so by fostering local, national, or global citizenship. Some discourses focus on individual citizens and seek to improve behaviour and 'character'. Others include collective efforts to pursue social, political, economic, and environmental justice. Just a sampling of relevant terms includes character education, citizenship education, civic education, democratic education, education for democratic citizenship, education for sustainable development, environmental justice education, global citizenship education, human rights education, moral education, service learning, and social justice education. The many terms carry with them different assumptions, emphases, and priorities, and – to make matters more confusing – are often used interchangeably.

So why do I choose to use the term 'global citizenship education' in this chapter? First, global citizenship education is a term often used in international policy documents, along with human rights education, education for sustainable development, and more targeted terms such as gender equality, anti-poverty strategies, and peace (see, for example, UNESCO, 2014b, 2015c, 2016a, 2018d). It has also become a common term among teachers, professors of education, and policymakers interested in citizenship education in both national and international contexts (Ellis, 2016; Gaudelli, 2016; Goren & Yemini, 2017; Noddings, 2005; Oxley & Morris, 2013; Schultz, 2017).

Second, a notion of global citizenship education draws attention to the global scope of societal issues such as climate change, economic inequality, or immigration. Global citizenship invokes a kind of pluralistic, multi-ethnic, and multinational ideal – what Martha Nussbaum (2002) calls cosmopolitan citizenship. This ideal, according to Robert Scott (2018, p. 1), emphasises that 'one's identity transcends, even as it respects, geographical and national borders; that one's social, political, environmental and economic actions occur in an interdependent world'. As a universal educational goal, global citizenship education, much like human rights education, seeks to find common ground, despite the various political systems and climates in which students live.

Finally, global citizenship tends toward a more expansive rather than purely legal notion of citizenship. As Meira Levinson (2014a, p. 135) notes, legal citizens 'have rights and privileges accorded or protected by the state, as well as duties toward the state'. Rights, Levinson argues, might include the right to vote, to seek political office, to travel freely, and to be protected by the state from physical harm. At the same time, legal citizens have obligations to the state such as paying taxes and military or jury service. Global citizenship, on the other hand, carries no legal meaning or status, which means one can easily distinguish programmes that teach global citizenship from efforts to prepare youth and adults to pass a national citizenship test or requirement. Among K-16 educators, teaching children, youth, and young adults to be 'good citizens' is most often understood as teaching the knowledge, skills, and social dispositions consistent with living in a community, where people not only get along but also shape the practices, norms, and institutions that define it. Global citizens, in this sense, refers not only to those with legal or political status but to all residents of the local, national, and global community.

Although there is some consensus about the broad applicability of the term 'global citizens', there remains a notably broad (and sometimes contradictory) set of related goals and education practices. If educators can agree that schools have an essential role to play in preparing students for informed engagement in civic and political life, they cannot seem to agree on what that requires. The very same efforts that are applauded by some are viewed as misguided by others. The result for school children has been a mostly watered-down notion of citizenship education that emphasises good character and patriotism over critical thinking and engaging with multiple perspectives.

3   What Kind of Citizens?

Partly in response to the indistinct definitions I describe above, a significant body of education scholarship is concerned not only with *whether* students should learn citizenship (global and otherwise) or even *how*, but also with the range of goals and ideological assumptions underpinning the approaches (Banks, 2008, 2017; Parker, 2003; Ross, 2017; Stitzlein, 2017). It was in that vein of inquiry that colleagues and I began studying programmes and policy in the United States and Canada to better understand what kind of citizens practitioners and policymakers were imagining schools might produce, and the political implications of resulting programme and policy choices (see, for example, Westheimer & Kahne, 2004; Kahne & Westheimer, 2006; Westheimer, 2015, 2017).

Our research led us to create a typology of three conceptions or visions of the 'good' citizen to better understand the aims and effects of various programmatic approaches. Since we first proposed the original typology, it has been used by scholars and practitioners in education, political science, sociology, social work, environmental studies, journalism, and public policy, and it has been translated into a dozen languages. Colleagues and other scholars working independently have used this framework to examine educational programmes in, for example, Australia, Canada, England, Hong Kong, Ireland, Israel, Japan, Malawi, Mexico, the Netherlands, New Zealand, Scotland, Singapore, South Korea, and the United States (for example, see Peterson and Bentley, 2017; Ng & Yuen, 2016; Kennedy, 2007; Grossman & Cogan, 2012; Mallon, 2018; Zamir & Baratz, 2013; Namphande et al., 2017; de Groot, Goodson, & Veugelers, 2014; Wood, Taylor, & Atkins, 2013; Biesta, 2008; Sim, 2006). Although our work has been conducted primarily (although not exclusively) in North America, it seems that the desire to clarify and make sense of the underlying aims of educational programs – including those implemented in response to the SDGs – is global.

Three visions of what it means to be a 'good' citizen emerged from our studies (Westheimer & Kahne, 2004; Kahne & Sporte, 2008; Westheimer, 2015): the *Personally Responsible Citizen*; the *Participatory Citizen*; and the *Social Justice-Oriented Citizen* (see Table 13.1). I describe these here as a framework for discussing the interrelationship between global citizenship education and the objectives and vision of a better world represented by the UN's 2030 Agenda.

Personally Responsible Citizens contribute to food or clothing drives when asked and volunteer to help those less fortunate, whether in a soup kitchen or a senior centre. They might contribute time, money, or both to charitable causes. Both those in the character education movement and those who advocate community service emphasise this vision of good citizenship. They seek to build character and personal responsibility by emphasising honesty, integrity, self-discipline, and hard work. Or, they nurture compassion by engaging students in volunteer community service.

Participatory Citizens participate in the civic affairs and social life of the community at local, state/provincial, national, and sometimes global levels. Educational programmes designed to support the development of participatory citizens focus on teaching students about how government works, and, in democratic countries, the importance of voting. They also highlight the role of other institutions (e.g., community-based organisations, churches) and encourage students to plan and participate in organised efforts to care for those in need. While the personally responsible citizen would contribute cans of food for the homeless, the participatory citizen might organise the food drive.

The *Social Justice-Oriented Citizen* is an individual who knows how to critically assess multiple perspectives, examine social, political, and economic structures, and explore strategies for change that address root causes of problems. These are critical thinkers, and this vision of citizenship is the least commonly pursued. Programmes that encourage this form of citizenship emphasise the ability to think about issues of fairness, equality of opportunity, and political engagement (some of the very issues highlighted in the UN's 2030 Agenda). They share with the participatory citizen an emphasis on collective work related to the life and needs of the community. However, they make critical engagement a priority and encourage students to become informed about a variety of complex social issues and look for ways to improve society. These programmes are less likely to emphasise the need for charity and volunteerism as ends in themselves and more likely to teach about ways to effect systemic

TABLE 13.1   Three kinds of citizens

	Personally responsible citizen	Participatory citizen	Social justice-oriented citizen
Description	Acts responsibly in the community Works and pays taxes Picks up litter, recycles, and gives blood Helps those in need, lends a hand during times of crisis Obeys laws	Active member of community organisations and/or improvement efforts Organises community efforts to care for those in need, promote economic development, or clean up environment Knows how government agencies work Knows strategies for accomplishing collective tasks	Critically assesses social, political, and economic structures Explores strategies for change that address root causes of problems Knows about social movements and how to effect systemic change Seeks out and addresses areas of injustice
Sample action	Contributes food to a food drive	Helps to organise a food drive	Explores why people are hungry and acts to solve root causes
Core assumptions	To solve social problems and improve society, citizens must have good character; they must be honest, responsible, and law-abiding members of the community	To solve social problems and improve society, citizens must actively participate and take leadership positions within established systems and community structures	To solve social problems and improve society, citizens must question and change established systems and structures when they reproduce patterns of injustice over time

SOURCE: WESTHEIMER (2015)

and lasting change. If participatory citizens are organising the food drive and personally responsible citizens are donating food, social justice-oriented citizens are asking why people are hungry and acting on what they discover to address root causes of hunger (for example, poverty, inequality, or structural impediments to self-sufficiency).

4   Personal Responsibility Is Not Enough

More than a decade of studies by scholars in a broad variety of geographical, political, economic, and social contexts (see Westheimer, 2015 for review) come to similar conclusions: The kinds of goals and practices commonly represented in citizenship education programmes usually have more to do with volunteering, charity, and obedience (*personally responsible citizenship*) than with social action, social change, or sustainability (*participatory* and *social justice-oriented citizenship*). In other words, good citizenship – to many educators and policymakers – means listening to authority figures, dressing neatly, being nice to neighbours, and helping out at a soup kitchen, rather than grappling with the kinds of social policy decisions needed to build a more sustainable and just world.

Many school-based programmes that take the time to teach citizenship are the kind that emphasise either good character – including the importance of helping those in need – or technical knowledge of legislatures and how government works. Far less common are school programmes that teach students to think about root causes of problems or challenge existing social, economic, and political norms as a way of improving society. When we deny students the opportunity to consider paths for change that involve a critical examination of collective social, political, and economic questions (and not just individual character), we also betray important principles of good governance (see, for example, the UN's 2030 Agenda [UNGA, 2015b, paras. 9, 20, 35, and 44], political participation [paras. 19 and 20], and the need for citizens to be able to engage as critical agents with informed critique to make collective choices [para. 51]).

The 2030 Agenda's call for transformative change requires that educators engage students in efforts to understand structural change and not just personal responsibility. Although the sustainable development goals are rightly ambitious, I see at least three vulnerabilities that place at risk their transformative potential: the preference for apolitical conceptions of citizenship in global citizenship education programs (citizenship without politics); calls for youth empowerment with little attention to issues of control and authority (empowerment without power); and a vision of sustainable development unmoored from norms of representative governance (sustainability without democracy).

4.1   Citizenship without Politics

There is a parable about a small village by a river. One day the villagers were working in fields by the river when a woman notices a baby floating down-stream. She yells out and someone runs into the river and rescues the baby. One neighbour provides clothes, another food, and so on. The next day, the same villagers are working by the river. They see two babies floating down-stream and rescue them. The following day it is four babies and after that eight. Within a short time, practically the entire village is wading into the water, res-cuing babies, clothing them, feeding them, trying to find others who will house them, and then returning to rescue more. After a week of rescuing hundreds of babies, one villager yells out, 'Hey! Why don't we go upstream and find out how all these babies are falling into the river?' The others quickly reject the sugges-tion, saying that there are too many babies in the river, and everyone should continue rescuing them lest they drown.

The moral of the story? Volunteering and providing services for those in need is important. But providing those services without also looking at the root causes of the problem – looking upstream – makes little sense. Personal responsibility and even participating with others to organise a response to a social problem is admirable but inadequate if we do not also look at the struc-tural causes that are creating the need for direct service in the first place. Char-acter traits such as honesty, integrity, and responsibility for one's actions are certainly valuable for becoming good neighbours and citizens. But, on their own, they have little to do with the unique requirements of the kind of com-munity and global citizenship engagement that promotes the types of struc-tural and sustainable changes that underpin the UN's 2030 agenda. Some programmes actually promote volunteering and charity as an *alternative* to social policy and organised government action. For example, former US Presi-dent George H. W. Bush famously promoted community service activities for youth by imagining a 'thousand points of light', representing charitable efforts to respond to those in need (Bush, 1988). But if young people understand these actions as a kind of *noblesse oblige* – a private act of kindness performed by the privileged – and fail to examine the deeper structural causes of social ills, then the thousand points of light risk becoming a thousand points of the sta-tus quo. The kind of global citizen that can work with others to 'transform our world' as envisioned in the 2030 Agenda (UNGA, 2015b) may be a kind and decent person, but will also need to be significantly more; an overemphasis on kindness might even discourage challenges to the status quo so as not to ruffle feathers.

Education that teaches students to follow the rules, obey authority figures, be honest, help others in need, clean up after themselves, try their best, and be team players is rarely controversial. But without an analysis of power, politics, and one's role in local and global political structures – and without showing students how they can work with others toward fundamental change – students will be unlikely to become effective citizens who can transform their communities and the world by addressing issues identified by the 2030 Agenda such as poverty, hunger, and inequality. Through an examination of inequities, both historical and extant, programmes that emphasise participatory and social justice-oriented visions of the 'good' citizen can also enable reflection on the ways overlapping and intersecting categories such as race, class, gender, and sexuality can constrain and enable social action for the collective benefit of all.

Although any approach to SDG 4 must be broad enough to account for global political diversity, if we are to take seriously the transformative aspirations of the 2030 Agenda, we must consider teaching and learning activities that make participation and the quest for social justice possible. Programmes that privilege individual acts of compassion and kindness often neglect the importance of social action, political engagement, and the pursuit of just and equitable policies. The vision promoted is one of citizenship without politics or collective action – a commitment to individual service, but not to social justice.

4.2   Empowerment without Power

I opened this chapter with a quotation from George Counts's famous 1932 speech before the Progressive Education Association, *Dare the School Build a New Social Order?* In that same speech, Counts went on to argue that capitalism is cruel and inhumane, and that it 'has exploited our natural resources without the slightest regard for the future needs of our society; it has forced technology to serve the interests of the few rather than the many' (Counts, 1932, p. 47). His speech and subsequent publication carefully spelled out political, economic, and social forces that had to be challenged through education if society were to be improved or 'transformed'. It addressed directly the power relations at play in any serious effort to realign those forces. For example, zeroing in on economic power differentials, Counts spoke of a democratic tradition of governance that had run up against a kind of industrial feudalism marked by massive inequality. 'Unless the democratic tradition is able to organize and conduct a successful attack on the economic system', Counts argued, 'its complete destruction is inevitable. If democracy is to survive, it must seek a new economic foundation' (Counts, 1932, p. 45).

Transforming Our World: The 2030 Agenda for Sustainable Development was penned at a time of rising economic inequality at levels not seen since the Great Depression, which was when Counts delivered his 1932 speech. Yet, while the word 'power' appears 28 times in Counts's 11,000-word pamphlet, it appears exactly once in the 15,000-word UN's 2030 Agenda (UNGA, 2015b). The ways in which politics and inequality might affect efforts toward sustainable development are similarly absent. 'Empower', on the other hand, appears at least 15 times. Empowerment without a discussion of power, politics, or inequality is an incomplete discussion at best, an insidious one at worst. For sustainable development education and goals to flourish, education reform will need to promote a conception of global citizenship that furthers not only personal responsibility and participation but also the ability to grapple with conflicting interests, social movements, and social change. The historical answer to Counts's *Dare the Schools Build a New Social Order?* has mostly been 'no'. But I want to take the aspirational goal of transformation seriously. The promise to *Transform Our World*, in part through education, will require grappling with the competing ideological agendas inherent in unconstrained economic growth, neoliberal concentrations of wealth and poverty, nonrepresentative forms of government, and instrumental visions of education that privilege economic competitiveness, high stakes assessments, and rule-following over critical thinking and human development.

4.3   *Sustainability without Democracy*

Early in the 2030 Agenda, the authors note that 'democracy, good governance and the rule of law ... are essential for sustainable development' (UNGA, 2015b, p. 5). It is the one and only use of the word 'democracy' or any of its variants in the 15,000-word document. The only other reference to the right of self-governance appears in SDG 16, which calls for ensuring 'responsive, inclusive, participatory and representative decision-making at all levels' (UNGA, 2015b, p. 28). The reasons for the decoupling of the right to self-governance from more universal notions of human rights and sustainability are a matter of political compromise. The SDGs are universal and are intended to be implemented by and in all countries whether democratic, totalitarian, theocratic, or otherwise. That makes an explicit demand for democratic governance impossible. Yet, even a more elastic conception of democratic principles is difficult to square with the well-known limits of international standards. But if the 2030 Agenda must necessarily fall short of a call for democracy as a prerequisite for sustainability, equality, and justice, it could support participatory and social justice-oriented education through a more robust exploration of the power that democratic representation, in its ideal form, represents.

A vision of citizenship that makes little or no reference to political representation risks relegation to liberal platitude. This could explain the preference in United Nations documents for the term 'global citizenship education' over 'citizenship education' or 'education for democratic citizenship'. Global citizens, after all, do not vote. They do not set social, economic, or political policy or have any representation on any local, national, or global governing body. The predilection for a notion of citizenship unmoored from a pesky need for representation is especially worthy of concern in a time of threats to even established democratic countries of the Global North. In a widely circulated 2017 report, the Pew Research Center raised considerable alarm among those who have generally assumed that Western democracies enjoy relative stability amidst an entrenched culture of democratic governance. Although the report was entitled *Globally, Broad Support for Representative and Direct Democracy*, commentators, civic educators, and political scientists highlighted a number of findings that challenged the rosier title. In the United States, for example, 22% of respondents thought that a political system in which a leader could make decisions without interference from Congress or the courts would be a good way of governing. Almost half of US millennials thought the same (globally, that figure was 26%) (Wike et al., 2017).

In another study released a few months earlier, Harvard lecturer Yascha Mounk and Australian political scientist Roberto Stefan Foa examined longitudinal data from the World Values Survey and found that between 1995 and 2014, the number of people who reported a preference for a government leader who did not need to bother with elections increased in almost every developed and developing democracy. Again, the growth has been greatest among youth and young adults (Mounck & Foa, 2016; Foa & Mounk, 2016). Social media echo chambers further entrench antidemocratic tendencies and pollute genuine social and political discourse (Bonikowski, 2017; Kahne & Bowyer, 2017; UN, 2016). Yoichi Funabashi, chairman of the Rebuild Japan Initiative (dedicated to strengthening democratic ideals in Japan) summarises the risks succinctly: 'If society becomes characterized by intolerant divisions, in which people immediately select their allies and dismiss others as foes based on such criteria as race, ethnicity, religion or lifestyle, then democracy's foundational principles, rooted in careful deliberation and compromise, will be rendered inoperable' (Funabashi, 2017).

5   What Do We Do Now?

In the remaining space, I highlight three successful approaches that encourage students to imagine a more just and sustainable world and give them the tools to achieve it. Although I use classroom examples to better ground my arguments in the context of classroom life for students and teachers, I hope these descriptions clarify for policymakers, reformers, government and civil society actors, and others the conditions required for teachers to effect meaningful change. The inevitably loose coupling between broad vision statements such as those represented in the sDGs and on-the-ground education reform can be made tighter only through the demonstration of real-world examples.

5.1   *Teach Students to Question*
Citizens who do not question cannot be stewards of the kind of socially, politically, and economically just society that the 2030 Agenda envisions. One hallmark of a vulnerable society is the notion of one single 'truth' (one history, one policy choice, one leader, and so on). In some places, questioning that truth may be discouraged; in others, it may be illegal. But education for global citizenship teaches students how to ask challenging questions, the kind of uncomfortable queries that challenge tradition (Giroux, 2017). Although most of us would agree that traditions are important, history demonstrates that progress often comes only from questioning the way things are. Dissent – feared and suppressed in closed societies – is the engine of progress in free ones. International standards and global school reform efforts should do everything possible to ensure that teachers and students have opportunities to ask these kinds of questions.

For example, Bob Peterson, a one-time Wisconsin Elementary Teacher of the Year, worked with his students at La Escuela Fratney in Madison, Wisconsin, to examine the full spectrum of ideological positions that emerged following the September 11, 2001, terrorist attacks. Instead of avoiding his fifth-grade students' challenging questions, Peterson encouraged them. He placed a notebook prominently at the front of the classroom labelled 'Questions That We Have'. As the students discussed their questions and the unfolding current events, Peterson repeatedly asked students to consider their responsibilities to one another, to their communities, and to the world (Westheimer, 2015).

5.2   *Expose Students to Multiple Perspectives*
Much as Darwin's theory of natural selection depends on genetic variation, any theory of robust global citizenship education depends on encouraging a multiplicity of ideas, perspectives, and approaches to exploring solutions to

issues of widespread concern. Mechouat (2017), for example, writing about citizenship education in Morocco, argues that in order to strengthen society, in particular with regard to gender equality, civic education must encourage students' freedom of expression, which in turn increases their engagement with diverse ideas. Students need practice in entertaining multiple viewpoints on issues that affect their lives (Bruen et al., 2016; Campbell, 2008; Lin, Lawrence, & Snow, 2015). These issues – sustainability versus economic growth, for example – might be controversial. But improving society requires embracing that kind of controversy so citizens can engage in dialogue and work together toward understanding and enacting sensible policies.

Why would we expect adults, even politicians, to be able to intelligently and compassionately discuss different viewpoints in the best interests of their constituents if schoolchildren never or rarely get that opportunity? In schools that further the kinds of goals represented by the SDGs, teachers engage young people in deep historical, political, social, economic, and even scientific analysis. They also challenge children to imagine how their lived experiences are not universal and how issues that may seem trivial to them could matter deeply to others. They have students examine multiple perspectives not only to know that their (or their parents') views may not be shared by everyone but also to engender a critical empathy for those with competing needs. Perspective-taking also introduces students to intersectionality and the ways in which people's diverse experiences shape their worldviews and priorities. Teaching students that their experience is not universal – and is in fact very specifically situated by race, class, gender, economic status, and so on – allows them to consider and encourage efforts to protect all members of a community, rather than just those who look and live like them. This is the kind of teaching that encourages future citizens to leverage their civic skills for the greater social good, rather than their own particular interests, thus working to challenge social inequities.

For example, teachers might be encouraged to present newspaper articles from around the world (easily accessed through the internet) that examine the same event. Which facts and narratives are consistent? Which are different? Why? Textbooks from several different countries could provide another trove of lessons on multiple viewpoints and the role of argument and evidence in deliberation. For instance, in the English-language context, schools in Canada, the United Kingdom, and the United States present strikingly different perspectives on the War of 1812. Why not also ask students to research who wrote their textbook? Was it one person or a committee? Why were those people chosen? What kind of author was *not* invited to participate? The idea that a person or group actually *wrote* a textbook reminds us that the words are not sacrosanct but represent the views of a particular time, place, and group of authors. These approaches help demonstrate to students that 'facts' are less stable than is often thought.

Students should also examine multiple perspectives on controversial *contemporary* issues. Students are frequently exposed to past historical controversies, such as slavery, Nazism, or laws denying voting rights to women, that are already settled in the minds of all but a small fringe minority. But those same students are too often shielded from matters that require thoughtful engagement with *today's* competing ideas. That kind of engagement is exactly what global citizenship requires.

5.3   *Focus on the Local*

Despite the global ambitions of SDG 4, teachers should be encouraged to have students consider their specific surroundings and circumstances for meaningful education on sustainable development. It is not possible to teach civically engaged thinking that could lead to transformative change without providing a specific context and environment to think about. For that reason, among many others, nationally or internationally standardised tests are difficult to reconcile with in-depth critical thinking about issues that matter to students in a particular time and place. In many jurisdictions, ever more narrow curriculum frameworks emphasise preparing students for standardised assessments in mathematics and literacy at the same time that they short-change the social studies, history, and even the most basic citizenship education (Au, 2007; Koretz, 2017). Not only do children learn less, what they learn tends to follow prescriptive formulas that match the standardised tests. In the process, more complex and difficult-to-measure learning outcomes are left behind. These include creativity and emotional and social development but also the kinds of thinking skills associated with robust civic engagement. Teachers' ability to teach critical thinking and students' ability to think and act critically are diminished as the uniformity demanded inhibits the possibilities of using localised knowledge (Meier & Gasoi, 2018; Blankstein & Noguera, 2016; Strauss, 2012). Similarly, Pineda's (2010) study of standardised testing in Mexico and Argentina demonstrates the ways in which such tests ignore local and indigenous knowledge, stifle creativity, and exacerbate social inequality by locking students in particular tracks in the labour economy. Curricular approaches that spoon-feed students to succeed on narrow academic tests teach students that broader critical thinking is optional.

Although the overall international reform context may limit in-depth, critical analysis, a significant number of teachers continue to teach those skills. As the important work of Kahne and Middaugh (2008) has demonstrated for the US, however, it tends to be higher-achieving students, often from wealthier neighbourhoods, who are receiving a disproportionate share of the kinds of citizenship education that sharpen students' thinking about issues of public debate and concern. This demographic divide or 'civic opportunity gap' results in unequal distribution of opportunities to engage civically and in thoughtful ways.

One way to provide experiences with participation in civic and political life is to engage students in community-based projects that encourage the development of personal responsibility, participation, and critical analysis. Community-based service activities (Kahne & Westheimer, 2001; Evans, 2015) can foster the knowledge, skills, and dispositions of engaged, global citizens. Similarly, recent work on action civics is a particularly powerful and thoughtful way to foster civic participation that transcends community service to also include a focus on government, politics, and policy (Blevins, LeCompte, & Wells, 2016; Levinson, 2014b). When students have the opportunity to engage with civics education through direct action in their own local context, the impacts of their work are integrated with their lived experience and can teach fundamental lessons about the power of citizen engagement (Facing History and Ourselves, 2018; Obama, 2018).

Of course, choosing to be explicitly political in the classroom can cause friction for teachers – with students, parents, and administrators. Teachers have been disciplined, suspended, and fired for engaging students in discussions of controversial issues (Journell, 2017; Stitzlein, 2013; Westheimer, 2007). Even when teachers avoid expressing their own political views, encouraging discussion, controversy, and action in the classroom can be daunting. Students may express views that make classmates uncomfortable; they may engage in political acts that concern their parents; or they may choose to challenge their own school's policies. Education aimed at transformation can be messy. Rather than let fear of sanction and censorship dictate pedagogical choices, however, local, national, and global policymakers should support and protect teachers and enable them to use debates and controversy as 'teachable moments' in civic discourse.

6   Can Education Transform Our World?

In her influential book, *The Way We Argue Now* (2006), literary theorist Amanda Anderson argued that questions about how we should live should be central to literary criticism. I find the same to be true for education. Schools can serve to promote peace, equality, sustainability, public health, and many if not all of the remaining sustainable development goals over the long term.

But to do so, educators must be enabled to include those goals in the fabric of the school curriculum and broader mission; education must be seen as more than an engine of the economy; and teachers must be allowed to build school cultures that impel students to envision a better world and to learn the knowledge, skills, and dispositions required to make that world possible. At a time when national borders and identities are increasingly blurred, contested, and crossed, a transnational or cosmopolitan civic identity is also needed. We are sustainable only to the extent that we learn to sustain one another.

Citizenship education is not a new idea. For as long as there has been public education, schools have taught lessons in citizenship, moral values, good behaviour, and 'character' (Dewey, 1909; Draper, 1858; Fahey, 1916; Mosier, 1965; Tyack & Hansot, 1982). Even before there was formal schooling, informal education was replete with such goals (Heater, 2015; Spring, 2018). Today's schools, regardless of country, inevitably teach these lessons as well. For example, schools teach children to follow rules, to wait their turn, and (ideally) to cooperate with others. Schools (again, ideally) teach children how to acquire and process information and how to articulate their ideas to others – all necessary skills for civic participation. Some schools also help students consider whether being a 'good' citizen ever requires questioning rules, or what might be the proper balance between rule-following and thinking about the origins and purposes of rules. Global citizenship education that aims to foster just and sustainable societies will require that students learn to think critically, ask questions about the world around them, and engage with multiple ways of seeing and perceiving. Public policies – local, national, and global – that support these efforts are the key to making SDG 4 effective.

At a time of rising economic inequality and widespread fear, xenophobia, attacks on a free press, and dangerous forms of populism, teaching and learning that helps young people understand and respond to these phenomena is essential. The UN's 2030 Agenda for Sustainable Development outlines bold goals that universal education can help meet. Basic skills like literacy and numeracy are, perhaps, the first important step, but they are not enough. A sustainable and just global society requires that children and youth gain the knowledge, capacities, and dispositions associated with a robust, civically engaged life.

CHAPTER 14

Will Education Post-2015 Move Us toward Environmental Sustainability?

Hikaru Komatsu, Jeremy Rappleye and Iveta Silova

> Every year the problems are getting worse. We are at the limits. If I may use a strong word I would say that we are at the limits of suicide.
>
> POPE FRANCIS, SPEAKING AT THE COP21 PARIS CLIMATE CHANGE CONFERENCE (2015)

∙ ∙

1 Introduction: Education at the Limits[1]

Developing sustainable societies is now recognised as the foremost challenge of the 21st century. In 2015, United Nations member states ratified the Sustainable Development Goals (SDGs), a set of targets that purported to place the global community on the path toward a sustainable future. The SDGs sought to extend the previous Millennium Development Goals (MDGs), but also incorporate new domains that, since the 1990s, had been widely recognised as pressing global challenges. Foremost among these new challenges is the stark reality of climate change. The 2015 ratification of the SDGs coincided with the historic UN Climate Change Conference, held in Paris (COP21) – the global community's most ambitious attempt to date to keep global warming below the 2°C threshold. Failure to do so, the Paris Agreement warned, would lead to 'catastrophic' consequences.

The SDGs feature targets for education, with SDG 4 explicitly seeking to achieve 'quality education for all' through a combination of increasing access to education, raising quality, equalising existing inequalities (e.g., in gender), and ensuring that 'all learners acquire knowledge and skills needed to promote sustainable development, including among others through education for sustainable development and sustainable lifestyles, human rights, gender equality, promotion of a culture of peace and non-violence, global citizenship, and appreciation of cultural diversity and of culture's contribution to sustainable development' (UNGA, 2015b, p. 17; see also Appendix 1). SDG 4 is also promoted as essential for achieving sustainability.

Nonetheless, some scholars and practitioners have been critical about the purported effectiveness of SDG 4 for the achievement of sustainability. First, it has been pointed out that the SDG 4 'emphasises education in terms of its potential economic and social benefits' rather than its environmental consequences (Sterling, 2015, 2016). Second, the overall logic of the SDGs is that 'the goals depend on each other – but no one has specified exactly how' (Nilsson, Griggs, & Visbeck, 2016, p. 320). This becomes even more problematic when considering that national 'policymakers lack tools to identify which interactions are the most important to tackle, and evidence to show how particular interventions and policies help or hinder progress towards the goals'. That is, 'if countries ignore the overlaps [between SDGs] and simply start trying to tick off targets one by one, they risk perverse outcomes' (Nilsson et al., 2016, pp. 320–321). Third, and in support of the point made above, extensive analyses of major United Nations and World Bank reports revealed 'weak coverage of linkages between education and SDGs 12–15' (Vladimirova & Le Blanc, 2016; see also Le Blanc, 2015). Those latter four goals are directly related to the environment and target sustainable consumption and production, climate change, oceans and marine resources, and terrestrial ecosystems.

The Agenda 2030 framework refers to 'interlinkages' between the 17 SDGs (UNGA, 2015b, pp. 2, 31, 34). However, those interlinkages remain implicit and poorly articulated in SDG statements (Nilsson et al., 2016). The United Nations agencies, such as UNESCO, and other international organisations seek to encourage interlinkages between education and other SDGs, at least to some extent. However, our argument herein is that when interactions between different SDGs are earnestly considered by these actors, they are nearly always imagined as exclusively positive, that is, reflecting the assumption that *improving existing forms of education will positively impact environmental sustainability*.

However, we find this core assumption surprising and highly problematic, given that the world is the most 'educated' it has ever been and yet the nearest to environmental breakdown (Randers, 2012; Turner, 2012; UNGA, 2015b; Rappleye & Komatsu, in press; Silova, Komatsu, & Rappleye, 2018). At the heart of the problem is a de facto endorsement of and a continued reliance on modern mass schooling, one rooted in the 'modernist Western paradigm' (Sterling, Dawson, & Warwick, 2018, p. 5; Silova, Komatsu, & Rappleye, 2019). Most international development efforts thus far, including education initiatives associated with the MDGs and SDGs, have consistently prioritised Western education models that focus on economic growth, technocratic determinism, human exceptionalism, and liberal individualism over environmental concerns. Yet, for decades now, many scholars have underscored that education in its current form is a central part of the environmental problem (e.g., Schumacher, 1973; Bowers, 1995, 2002; Orr, 2004, 2009). Orr (2009, p. 176) wrote:

> Education has long been a part of the problem, turning out graduates who were clueless about the way the world works as a physical system or why that knowledge was important to their lives and careers, while at the same time promoting knowledge of the sort that has fuelled the destruction of ecologies and undermined human prospects.

What is problematic is not simply that the United Nations does not accept the fact that education in its current form is a central part of the environmental crisis. Rather the problem is that this possibility has not even been seriously considered by the world's most powerful 'development' actors, as we review in detail in the pages that follow.

Against this backdrop, the objective of this chapter is threefold. First, we confirm that potentially negative interactions between education and other SDGs are largely missed and/or dismissed in SDG-related policy and analytical work by major international organisations, such as UNESCO, the OECD, and the World Bank. This dismissal of negative interactions between education and other SDGs means that the current education paradigm remains unquestioned, resulting in the continued prioritisation of economic growth and social equity over the environment. Second, we present empirical evidence of the possibility that promoting education based on the current paradigm can have negative impacts on the achievement of other SDGs. For this purpose, we use one example: analysing the potentially negative interaction between promoting education access and quality (SDG 4) and alleviating climate change (SDG 13). Third, we then shift to spotlight a missing component within the existing analyses of the current education paradigm – culture. We suggest that culture, which encodes our attitudes and values, strongly affects our environmental impacts on the Earth.[2] Through these interlocking three steps, we underscore the pressing need to reflect deeply on the consequences of the current education paradigm, one rooted in the 'modernist Western paradigm' for climate change (Sterling et al., 2018). Our purpose is to initiate a different sort of conversation than the one that currently surrounds SDG 4: one that helps researchers, practitioners, and policymakers alike imagine something beyond the current education paradigm and gives the next generation a chance to shift off our current trajectory of environmental catastrophe.

2   The Existing Educational Paradigm: Should We Leave It
       Unquestioned?

Within the existing literature, potentially negative interactions between education and other SDGs are largely overlooked or dismissed, leaving the current education paradigm unquestioned. Here we analyse the SDG targets
themselves and their interpretation as presented in major reports published
by UNESCO, the OECD, and the World Bank. Although implementation of the
SDGs is officially envisaged as being led by national policymakers and plan-
ners, research has consistently shown that these international organisations
have strong influence on the contours of national policymaking (e.g., Edwards,
2012; Verger, Edwards, & Altinyelken, 2014; Auld, Rappleye, & Morris, 2019). In
some cases, the influences can be decisive for developing countries that have
limited policymaking capacity or funding (Rahman & Quadir, 2018; Rappleye
& Un, 2018; Auld et al., 2019). This section confirms that the negative interactions between education and other SDGs go unquestioned, resulting in a de
facto prioritisation of business-as-usual in education (i.e., continued prioritisation of economic growth and social equity over the environment).

2.1   SDG Targets

SDG 4 comprises seven targets (4.1–4.7) and three means of implementation
(4.a, 4.b, and 4.c) (for details, see Appendix 1). The first six targets (4.1–4.6)
primarily focus on the improvement of access and quality of education. As
such, these six targets do not require reconsideration of current approaches
and policy preferences, but instead call for more thoroughgoing implementation. This dominance of the current education paradigm in the SDGs seems to
imply that contemporary problems are largely the result of incomplete implementation, rather than one cause of our current condition.

This strong belief in continuity with past approaches is clearly expressed in
the United Nations' announcement of the SDGs (UNGA, 2015b). The Preamble
states:

> We recognize that eradicating poverty in all its forms and dimensions,
> including extreme poverty, is the greatest global challenge and an indis-
> pensable requirement for sustainable development. (UNGA, 2015b, p. 1)

It then continues:

> The 17 Sustainable Development Goals and 169 targets which we are
> announcing today … seek to build on the Millennium Development Goals

and complete what they did not achieve. They seek to realize the human rights of all and to achieve gender equality and the empowerment of all women and girls. (UNGA, 2015b, p. 1)

Here we see the SDGs are viewed as an extension of the MDGs, and the effort is to expand the current development and education paradigm via more thorough implementation, rather than affecting a change of course.

In contrast with the first six, the last target (4.7) suggests that the current education paradigm itself has negative interactions with other SDGs. It includes the phrase 'education for sustainable development and sustainable life styles' (UNGA, 2015b, p. 17). For some this might suggest an approach to education that goes beyond the current education paradigm, questioning the role of education in contributing to and reproducing the economic growth logic. Unfortunately, it is left unclear whether this reading is possible due to the simplicity and ambiguity of the wording of Target 4.7. We shall return to this issue later when we analyse reports published by international organisations.

Beyond SDG 4, several targets in other SDGs do mention education (e.g., Targets 3.7, 8.6, 12.8, and 13.3). For this reason, it could be argued that different SDGs and associated targets must be viewed as not independent but interlocking. Yet what is striking here is that education is *always* deemed to be in the service of progress toward other SDGs. For example, SDG Target 13.3 states:

Improve education, awareness-raising and human and institutional capacity on climate change mitigation, adaptation, impact reduction and early warning. (UNGA, 2015b, p. 23)

Improvement of education is automatically assumed to lead to mitigation of the damages caused by climate change. We do not object to this possibility. But we find it problematic that the SDGs do not address the possibility that education in its current form is not the solution but instead one cause of climate change and other related environmental problems.

2.2   UNESCO

UNESCO has recently published several major reports focussing on the SDGs. In reviewing these reports here, we sought to understand how much UNESCO recognises potentially negative interactions between education and other SDGs. We found that negative interactions are almost never discussed.

Education 2030: Incheon Declaration and Framework for Action for the Implementation of Sustainable Development Goal 4 discusses the interaction between education and other SDGs as follows:

Education can accelerate progress towards the achievement of all of the SDGs and therefore should be part of the strategies to achieve each of them. (WEF, 2015, p. 24)

In contrast to this wholly positive but terse appraisal, a subsequent 2017 report entitled *Education for Sustainable Development Goals: Learning Objectives* elaborates a bit more deeply. The report admits that 'not all kinds of education support sustainable development' (UNESCO, 2017c, p. 7), perhaps a sign of UNESCO's awareness of the need to pursue a different educational paradigm. However, the report unexpectedly continues that the education for achieving sustainability (i.e., Education for Sustainable Development, ESD) is 'now well-established', describing it as follows:

ESD is holistic and transformational education that addresses learning content and outcomes, pedagogy and the learning environment. Thus, ESD does not only integrate contents such as climate change, poverty and sustainable consumption into the curriculum; it also creates interactive, learner-centred teaching and learning settings. What ESD requires is a shift from teaching to learning. (UNESCO, 2017c, p. 7)

Disappointingly, these 'interactive learner-centred teaching and learning settings' are what the current global education paradigm already valorises (and has valorised for the past several decades). The report assumes that such education practices based on the current paradigm 'make possible the development of the key competencies needed for promoting sustainable development' (UNESCO, 2017c, p. 7). It is not difficult to find similar examples dotted around other UNESCO reports. For example, the UN Decade of Education for Sustainable Development (DESD) Report states:

ESD is influencing learning pedagogies and advancing approaches that help learners to ask questions, analyse, think critically and make decisions in collaboration with others. ... Participatory learning processes, critical thinking and problem-based learning are proving particularly conducive to ESD. (UNESCO, 2014d, p. 30)

Here, ESD and learner-centred pedagogy are depicted as virtually synonymous. Furthermore, UNESCO has suggested that the methodologies outlined in the DESD report should become part of the mechanisms to assess the progress toward Target 4.7 (UIS, 2018e, p. 37), underscoring that UNESCO shows little intent to reflect more deeply on the current education paradigm.

What does this 'current education paradigm' entail? One way to describe it is by referring to UNESCO's explanation of key competencies for achieving the SDGs:

> As societies around the world struggle to keep pace with the progress of technology and globalization, they encounter many new challenges. These include increasing complexity and uncertainty. ... A rapidly pro-liferating amount of information is available to them. All these conditions require creative and self-organized action because the complexity of the situation surpasses basic problem-solving processes that go strictly according to plan. People must learn to understand the complex world in which they live. They need to be able to collaborate, speak up and act for positive change. ... We can call these people 'sustainability citizens'. (UNESCO, 2017c, p. 10)

There are two implicit assumptions in this statement. First, 'sustainability citizens' must be able to process and analyse much information to understand the world around them. Second, 'sustainability citizens' must organise their own behaviours rationally based on their own understanding, rather than react to and interact with the environments around them. In the following paragraphs, we discuss the OECD, but here it is worth highlighting how closely its vision of 'key competencies' aligns with that of UNESCO:

> Key competencies assume a mental autonomy, which involves an active and reflective approach to life. They call not only for abstract thinking and self-reflection, but also for distancing oneself from the socializing process. ... This means being self-initiating, self-correcting, and self-eval-uating rather than dependent on others to frame the problems, initiate adjustments, or determine whether things are going acceptably well. (OECD, 2000, p. 13)

Here the valorisation of abstract thought and independence is striking: all problems are ultimately problems of the self. Both this and UNESCO's 'sus-tainability citizens' conceptualisation turn out to be almost indistinguishable from the ideal 'man' of the Western Enlightenment, which emphasises the use of rationality and individual autonomy to improve the conditions of human beings (Duignan, 2018). The Western Enlightenment provides the conceptual foundations for progressive education (Thomas, 2012). Progressive education in turn is the origin and driver of student-centred pedagogy, in which students are expected to rationally organise their actions, learn from the outcomes of those actions, and eventually achieve success through self-directed projects (for a critique of this approach, see Komatsu & Rappleye, 2017c).

In contrast with the UNESCO reports reviewed here, the web pages of UNESCO go one step further in a critical direction (UNESCO, 2018a, 2018c). These pages address the necessity of 'reorienting education' to 'transform society' mainly through SDG Target 4.7 and to 'help people develop knowledge, skills, values and behaviours needed for sustainable development' (UNESCO, 2018a). This statement implies that the current education paradigm needs to be reoriented. However, nowhere in these web pages are the problems of the current education paradigm explicitly discussed, probably due to space limitations.

To our knowledge, the only material describing explicitly the problem of the current education paradigm in any substantial depth is the 2016 Global Education Monitoring Report (GEMR). GEMRs are editorially independent of UNESCO and cannot be used to argue for UNESCO's official opinion. Still, they may give us some sense of the thinking among those working in close proximity to the organisation. In its first chapter, the 2016 GEMR explicitly admits that 'the Millennium Development Goals failed to ensure environmental sustainability'. Citing the final MDG review, the GEMR points out that 'the cost to future generations of environmental damage during development was not evaluated, as it was commonly believed that countries could grow now and clean up later' (UNESCO, 2016b, p. 5). Indeed, in 1997, about three years before the MDGs were launched, the signatories of the United Nations Framework Convention on Climate Change agreed to the Kyoto Protocol introducing legally binding emission reduction targets for developed countries. Not only did the Kyoto Protocol fail to find its way into the MDGs, but global CO_2 emissions have been continuously rising since 1997.

Recognising the failure of the MDGs on this front, the 2016 GEMR tried to propose fundamental changes to the current education paradigm. Chapter 1 appears to reject the high-modern assumptions of the past, that is, the faith that science, technology, human rationality, and individual creativity will make a transition to a sustainable society. Instead, the chapter directs attention beyond the usual 'modern solutions', highlighting divergent development trajectories and 'pre-modern' or 'non-modern' conceptual resources. Indeed, the chapter depicts several countries outside the European high-modern cultural orbit as being successful in reconciling environmental sustainability and human well-being:

> Countries struggle to find balance between human development and sustainable practices. Some, including Cuba, Georgia, the Republic of

> Moldova and Sri Lanka, have begun to find it, managing to keep produc-
> tion and consumption within sustainable bounds. (UNESCO, 2016b, p. 22)

The report goes on to list other successful countries including Jamaica, Colombia, the Dominican Republic, Indonesia, and the Philippines (UNESCO, 2016b,
p. 23, figure 1.2B).

The report contrasts these cases with the relatively unsuccessful countries
of Europe, North America, and the Asian Tigers, all areas that have led the
world in economic growth over the past three decades:

> The countries with the largest ecological footprints are mostly in Europe
> and Northern America. Countries that have experienced rapid increases
> in education, health and living standards, including the Republic of
> Korea and Singapore, have seen their ecological footprint nearly double
> as domestic consumption has expanded. (UNESCO, 2016b, p. 22)

Particularly in its critique of South Korea and Singapore, this report seems to
signal a radical departure from its previous views of education. Instead of a
positive evaluation of the 'development success' of East Asian economic systems through education (e.g., OECD, 2011; World Bank, 2018e), we find this
more negative evaluation precisely because the environment is considered to
be equally as important as economics and education.

2.3   *The OECD*

Reviewing the official OECD web page about the SDGs and two major reports
recently published there, *Better Policies for 2030: An OECD Action Plan on the
Sustainable Development Goals* (OECD, 2016a) and *Measuring Distance to the
SDG Targets: An Assessment of Where OECD Countries Stand* (OECD, 2017a), we
found no explicit interpretation of the SDGs. Instead, the OECD exclusively
focusses on more thorough implementation of the existing education paradigm. The OECD web page states that 'the OECD supports the United Nations
in ensuring the success of the 2030 Agenda for Sustainable Development by
bringing together its existing knowledge, and its unique tools and experience'
(OECD, 2018b).

The OECD evinces virtually no reflection on the effectiveness of SDGs vis-à-
vis the environment. Instead, it suggests that its contribution to the achievement of SDGs will be providing 'measures and systems for monitoring' the
progress (OECD, 2018b). Similarly, *Better Policies for 2030* states that the OECD
aims to 'support countries as they identify where they currently stand in
relation to the SDGs' (OECD, 2016a, p. 3). The primary purpose of *Measuring*

Distance is monitoring. The report 'uses the latest information on various indicators available in OECD databases to establish countries' distance from individual targets' (OECD, 2017a, p. 1).

Interestingly, a new report published by the OECD, entitled *The Future of Education and Skills: Education 2030*, implies there are potentially negative impacts of education on society and the environment. The report states that 'the rapid advance of science and technology may widen inequities, exacerbate social fragmentation and accelerate resource depletion' (OECD, 2018a, p. 3). However, the forms of education the OECD envisages as necessary to combat these negative impacts are exactly those based on the current education paradigm (i.e., emphasis on basic literacy and numeracy skills, student-centred pedagogy directed toward cognitive 'gains', individualised instruction accelerated with technology, etc.). The report asserts that future education needs to have 'a personalised learning environment that supports and motivates each student to nurture his or her passions, make connections between different learning experiences and opportunities, and design their own learning projects and processes in collaboration with others', as well as building a solid foundation that includes 'literacy and numeracy' and 'digital literacy and data literacy' (OECD, 2018a, p. 4). Here the commitment to the Western Enlightenment paradigm seems obvious: personalised, passionate, experience-based, and technologically mediated.

2.4   *The World Bank*

As with our analysis of the OECD, we reviewed the official World Bank web pages that discuss the SDGs and three major reports recently published by the Bank. The World Bank simply interprets the SDGs as already aligned with its existing goals. The web page states that 'the SDGs are aligned with the World Bank Group's twin goals of ending extreme poverty and boosting shared prosperity' (World Bank, 2018c). The same interpretation of the SDGs is echoed in other reports (World Bank, 2016, 2017a). For example, the Bank's 2015/2016 Global Monitoring Report states that 'the two sets of goals [the SDGs and the World Bank's existing goals] can be seen as very similar' (World Bank, 2016, p. 99).

Considering this interpretation of the SDGs, it makes sense that the World Bank repeatedly declares its intention to improve access to and quality of education without finding it necessary to contemplate possible negative impacts of the current form of education on the environment (e.g., World Bank, 2016, p. 8; 2017a, p. 21). It seems obvious that the World Bank has not seriously reflected on the current education paradigm but sees it as universally valid in both space and time. For example, the 2018 *World Development Report* emphasises South

Korea's 'successful economic development' through education (World Bank, 2018d, p. xi) but mentions none of the environmental caveats that were raised in the 2016 GEMR.

The absence of serious reflection on the current education paradigm is evident both in the overall conceptualisation of the role of education in the SDGs and its operationalisation by major international agencies in the field of education, including UNESCO, OECD, and the World Bank. Such unreflective acceptance of the current education paradigm has resulted in a de facto endorsement of business-as-usual in education, in other words, continued prioritisation of economic growth and social equity over the environment, further reinforced by a narrow range of data used to monitor achievement of the SDGs. Perhaps this also explains why major reports by the OECD (2017a) and the World Bank (2018e) focus on how *their* data (e.g., Programme for International Student Assessment [PISA]) will contribute to monitoring achievement of SDGs, ensuring value-for-money in implementing predetermined policy decisions, and identifying the most efficacious mechanisms for financing and implementing the existing education paradigm, instead of radically reevaluating its impact vis-à-vis environmental sustainability.

3   Potentially Negative Interaction between Education and the Environment

We have thus far demonstrated that official statements by leading international organisations largely lack contemplation about possible negative interactions between current forms of education and the environment. This section uses empirical data to highlight the presence of such negative interactions, focussing on the relations between improvement of education access and quality, on the one hand, and climate change, on the other.

3.1   *Data and Methods*
We examine the relationships between the lower-secondary completion rate and CO_2 emissions per capita, as well as between the percentage of students having a 'fixed level of proficiency' in literacy and numeracy skills according to the OECD's definition and CO_2 emissions per capita for various countries. The OECD defines the 'fixed level of proficiency' in literacy and numeracy skills as being identical to Level 2 or higher in PISA (Hanushek & Woessmann, 2015; OECD, 2017a). Our analysis excluded data from major oil exporters (e.g., Bahrain, Iran, Kuwait, Oman, Qatar, Saudi Arabia, Trinidad and Tobago, and United Arab Emirates) because the CO_2 emissions of these countries did not

follow the general relationship between education and CO_2 emissions (i.e., CO_2 emissions for these countries were much higher than expected from the education indicators).

Although SDG 4 has a large number of indicators, we decided to use the lower-secondary enrolment rate and the percentage of students having a fixed level of proficiency as proxy indicators for the general level of education of any given population. Indeed, these indicators are widely used or recommended in major reports concerning the SDGs (e.g., UNESCO, 2016b; World Bank, 2016; OECD, 2017a). We are fully aware that these indicators do not fully represent or cover the whole scope of SDG 4. But the two proxy indicators selected represent the current education paradigm and its twofold aim of enhancing access as well as quality, as also captured in SDG 4, and are appropriate to the primary purpose of our analysis. That purpose is to detect the presence of interactions between education and the environment, not to assess the total impact of education on the environment. Our focus on the abovementioned indicators is primarily due to the availability of data. However, the fact that so much data are available for these indicators suggests the magnitude of attention and political power they have.

Our analysis of the relationships between education and CO_2 emissions per capita is based on simple correlation analysis. The relationships are assessed using the Pearson's correlation coefficient (r). Since an r value is highly affected by outliers, we calculate 95% confidence intervals (CI) to examine the stability of the correlation using the bootstrapping method (Diadonis & Efron, 1983; Komatsu & Rappleye, 2017c). We do not conduct statistical testing of any relationships and differences because such an approach is quite often deeply misleading, particularly in the field of education.[3]

Since we use simple correlation analysis, we do not attempt to evaluate a direct impact of education on CO_2 emissions. We are rather interested in understanding the impact of accelerating the implementation of the dominant educational paradigm, including the improvement of education access, on CO_2 emissions. Our focus in the analysis is whether or not there are countries with a high enrolment rate and percentage of students with a fixed level of proficiency, but at the same time with low CO_2 emissions per capita. If there are no countries satisfying these conditions, education in its current form would potentially have negative interactions with the environment.

3.2   *Results and Discussion*
We observed positive correlations between the lower-secondary completion rate and per capita CO_2 emissions, with r being .749 (CI = [.649; .828]) (Figure 14.1a) and between the percentage of students with the fixed level of proficiency

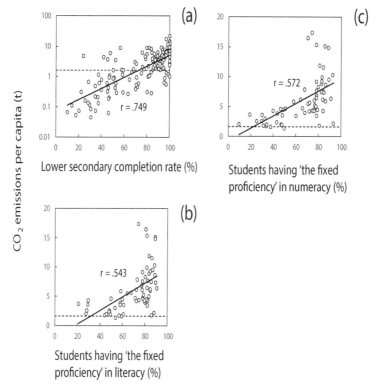

FIGURE 14.1   Relationship of (a) the lower-secondary completion rate with CO_2 emissions per capita. Relationships between the ratios of 15-year-old students with (b) basic literacy and (c) numeracy and CO_2 emissions per capita. A dotted line denotes the CO_2 emission per capita in 2050 in the IPCC scenario leading to 1.3 to 2.1°C temperature increases (van Vuuren et al., 2011). Data for the lower-secondary completion rate were derived from the World Bank Open Data (World Bank, 2018d). Data for the ratios of students with basic literacy and numeracy were derived from PISA 2015 (OECD, 2016c)

and per capita CO_2 emissions with r being .543 (CI = [.418; .667]) for reading and .572 (CI = [.442; .708]) for math (Figures 14.1b and 14.1c). That is, countries with 'better' education tended to have more detrimental impacts on climate change. These positive correlations would probably be even more pronounced if we considered international trades in foodstuffs and industrial products. That is, rich countries tend to have 'better' education and also externalise their CO_2 emissions through international trade. For example, some of the CO_2 emissions generated by American consumption are attributed to China, which serves as one of many 'factories' for the production of American goods and therefore absorbs much of the pollution associated with it (Komatsu, Rappleye, & Silova, 2019b).

What is important from the climate change perspective is that few countries with 'good' education satisfied the Intergovernmental Panel on Climate Change (IPCC) target to limit the global mean temperature increase to less than 2°C relative to preindustrial levels (van Vuuren et al., 2011; Houghton, 2015). If we assume only the current global population and no future population growth,[4] per capita CO_2 emissions need to be reduced to 1.61 t (dotted lines in Figure 14.1) or lower by 2050 to meet the target.[5] Only seven countries among the 61 with a high lower-secondary completion rate (>90%) had per capita CO_2 emissions lower than 1.61 t (Figure 14.1a). Furthermore, no countries with a high percentage of students with the fixed proficiency (>70%) had per capita CO_2 emissions lower than 1.61 t (Figures 14.1b and 14.1c).

It is true that improvement in education (particularly education of girls and women) usually leads to lower fertility rates, resulting in the alleviation of population growth (Martin, 1995; Osili and Long, 2008) and this, in turn, may lead to a reduction in CO_2 emissions. However, we assumed no change in the world population between the present and 2050 in the prior discussion to account for such possible effects. Yet our data suggest that the current per capita CO_2 emissions are too high to be offset by the reduction in the population growth rate through education alone.

Advocates for the SDGs might further argue that our analysis ignores the interrelated nature of the SDGs and their targets, and mistakenly assesses the impact of selected targets of SDGs on the environment. This argument is understandable, but our analysis did not intend to assess the impact of education on the environment as a whole. Rather, the primary purpose is to highlight the presence of potentially negative interactions between targets in SDG 4 and the environment, which are largely ignored in the discussion about SDGs. Our analysis thus should be viewed as a necessary first step to understand how SDG 4 targets are (or are not) interrelated with other targets.

In fact, what we show here is not without precedent. It has been widely known for over two decades that improvement in education accompanies the rise of economic output and CO_2 emissions (Hotz-Eakin & Selden, 1995).[6] Sceptical readers might argue that although this might be the case for developing countries, developed countries are now reducing CO_2 emissions. It is true that several developed countries were successful in reducing CO_2 emissions *per economic output*, which might be related to the improvement of education. However, most of these countries have been and still are unsuccessful in reducing the *total* CO_2 emissions (Raupach et al., 2007; Jackson, 2009),[7] suggesting that improvement in education quality would not lead to the alleviation of climate change. Our findings in this section thus complement these previous studies in environmental economics and sciences.

What then is the novelty of our analysis? It lies in connecting the issue of negative interactions between education and the environment with the current debates over the SDGs. As we underscored in the previous section, virtually no reports by international organisations mention such negative interactions. Recognising interactions (including negative ones) among different SDGs is a prerequisite for effective policymaking in the future.

4   What Is Missing from the Current Education Paradigm?

The above two sections suggest that at least some parts of current education practices have negative interactions with the environment. It is thus unreasonable to continue promoting reforms based on the belief that a thoroughgoing expansion and achievement of the current education paradigm will lead to sustainability, particularly environmental sustainability. Our previous analysis suggested that the dominant education paradigm assumes, true to Western Enlightenment logic, that if people are equipped with the skills to reason and the knowledge about the problems they face, they will act to solve the problems. Against this backdrop, this section suggests the possibility that knowledge and skills alone would not be sufficient to achieve environmental sustainability. Instead, we suggest that culture, which encodes our attitudes and values, strongly affects human impacts on climate.

4.1   Data and Methods

We examine the relationships between awareness and risk perception of climate change and CO_2 emissions for various countries. Data for awareness and risk perception of climate change were derived from the Gallup Poll 2007–2008 (Pugliese & Ray, 2009). The Gallup Poll included data for the percentages of people who were aware of climate change and who viewed climate change as a personal threat. Concerning the first issue, respondents were asked, 'How much do you know about global warming or climate change?' and allowed to select one option among the four: (1) have not heard of it, (2) know something about it, (3) know a great deal about it, and (4) don't know/refused. The percentage of those who selected the second or third options was used in the analysis. Concerning the second issue raised by the poll, respondents were asked, 'How serious of a threat is global warming to you and your family?' and allowed to select one option among the four: (1) very/somewhat serious, (2) not very/not serious at all serious, (3) don't know/refused, and (4) not aware. The percentage of those who selected the first option was used in the analysis.

We then examine the relationship between one of Hofstede's cultural dimensions (i.e., the individualism vs. collectivism dimension; Hofstede, Hofstede, & Minkov, 2010). The degree of individualism was represented by the individualism score derived from the 2010 version dataset for Hofstede's cultural dimensions (Hofstede et al., 2010). This dataset assesses characteristics of national culture for various countries and has been used widely (e.g., Park, Russell, & Lee, 2007; Peng & Lin, 2009; Onel & Mukherjee, 2014). An individualism score, which represents the degree of individualism for a given country, ranges between 0 and 100 with higher values indicating more individualistic.

In our analysis, we use data only for countries having a sufficiently long life expectancy (i.e., no less than 75.5 years). This threshold of 75.5 years allowed us to include all the core members of the OECD and to eliminate potential arguments about the trade-offs between long life and environmental sustainability. This treatment is necessary because countries with lower awareness and risk perception of climate change may lack basic conditions for life and have low per capita CO_2 emissions. The threshold of 75.5 years' life expectancy thus captures countries with large contributions to the global ecological footprint (EF): 61.7% of global EF relative to their population, which is 39.2% of the world's total (see Komatsu, Rappleye, & Silova, 2019a).[8]

4.2   Results and Discussion

We did not observe a negative correlation between awareness and CO_2 emissions (Figure 14.2a). Rather, the correlation was positive (r = .625 with CI being [.451; .773]). Similarly, we did not observe a clear negative correlation between risk perception and CO_2 emissions (r = −.07 with CI being [−.417; .241], Figure 14.2b). That is, countries whose people are aware of climate change and perceive the potential risks of climate change did not always have lower per capita CO_2 emissions.

These findings suggest that knowledge alone would not be sufficient to achieve environmental sustainability. It is true that many previous studies found that people with more knowledge of environmental science tend to have higher concern for environmental problems (Meyer, 2015; Chankrajang & Muttarak, 2017). Joel Westheimer addresses a similar point concerning civic education in Chapter 13. But our findings call into question whether this higher concern will lead people to successfully reduce their *actual* environmental impacts.

Figure 14.2c shows the relationship between individualism scores and CO_2 emissions. The correlation was clear and positive (r = .556 with CI being [.213; .774]). That is, countries where individualism is stronger tended to have higher per capita CO_2 emissions. Inversely, countries where interdependence

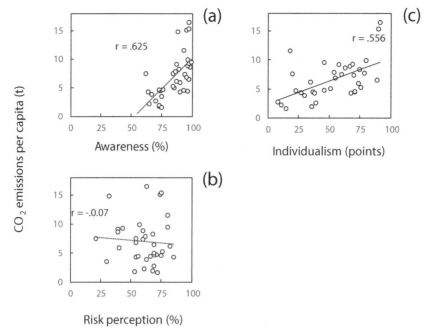

FIGURE 14.2   Relationships of (a) awareness and (b) risk perception of climate change and
individualism scores with CO_2 emissions per capita. This analysis used data only
for countries whose life expectancy is no less than 75.5 years. Data were derived
from the Gallup Poll (Pugliese & Ray, 2009), the World Bank Open Data (World
Bank, 2018d), and Hofstede et al. (2010)

(collectivism) is stronger tended to have lower per capita CO_2 emissions. We
are fully aware that correlation does not prove causation. Our exploratory argument needs further examination and elaboration. Still these results suggest the
possibility that culture affects actual human impacts on climate.

Our findings align with previous studies in environmental psychology
(Arnocky, Stroink, & DeCicco, 2007; Adger et al., 2013; Chuang, Xie, & Liu,
2016). This last-cited study reported that the interdependent self, which is
more prevalent in interdependent (collectivist) cultures, is more effective in
controlling one's own desire for the sake of collective social benefit and consequently willing to engage in pro-environmental behaviour. In addition,
Arnocky et al. (2007) reported that interdependent selves cooperated more
effectively with others than independent selves under hypothetical conditions
of resource constraints. This finding also supports the idea that interdependent selves control (regulate) their behaviour more effectively than independent selves when they are faced with environmental problems or dilemmas.
The novelty of our findings is thus that a specific dimension of culture concerning the concept of selfhood could be a major factor explaining not only

within-country but between-country variations in people's environmental attitudes.[9] More importantly, our analysis revealed that cultural dimensions are strongly related to actual human impacts on the Earth. To date, this point has not been sufficiently addressed in environmental psychology (e.g., Schultz, 2001; Gifford, 2014; Chuang et al., 2016). Readers interested in details of a large study we conducted are referred to Komatsu et al. (2019a).

We then asked whether or not the variation in per capita CO_2 emissions with the cultural dimension is large enough to affect the possibility of meeting the IPCC target. If per capita emissions for the world population's equal those for Costa Rica (whose per capita CO_2 emissions and individualism score were low), the global CO_2 emission is estimated to be 3.23 Gt [gigatonnes = 10^{10} tonnes] carbon, which is equivalent to 11.84 Gt CO_2 (see Figure 14.3). This value is 33% of current global emissions and almost equivalent to the global emission needed by 2050 to meet the IPCC 2°C target (3.19 Gt carbon). What then happens if we assume that the per capita CO_2 emissions for the world population equals those for the mean per capita CO_2 emissions for individualistic societies (i.e., the mean per capita CO_2 emissions for countries having individualism scores higher than 75)? All those countries are located in Europe or North America (Figure 14.4). The global CO_2 emission under this assumption is estimated as 19.7 Gt carbon. That value is close to the global emission in 2050

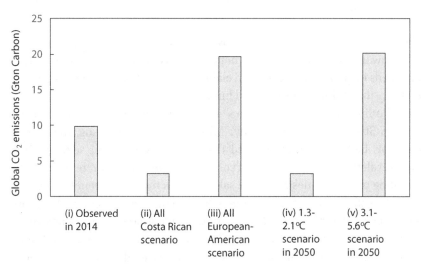

FIGURE 14.3   Global CO_2 emissions for different cases. (i) actual emissions in 2014; emissions assuming that CO_2 emissions for the world population equal (ii) those of Costa Rica; (iii) those of Europe and America; and emissions in 2050 in the IPCC scenarios leading to (iv) 1.3 to 2.1 and (v) 3.1 to 5.6°C temperature increases, respectively. Data for the IPCC scenarios were derived from van Vuuren et al. (2011) and Meinshausen et al. (2011)

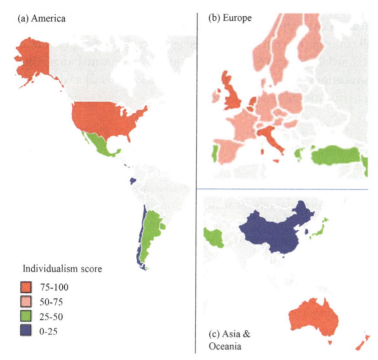

FIGURE 14.4   Countries classified by the individualism score. Countries lacking individualism
scores and whose life expectancy is short (i.e., < 75.5 years) are not coloured.
Data for individualism scores were derived from Hofstede et al. (2010)

in the scenario assuming a 3.1 to 5.6°C temperature increase (20.2 Gt carbon).
If the correlation in Figure 14.2c does represent causality, the effect of cultural
factors would be quite large from an environmental standpoint.

The results described above have serious implications for SDG 4. Although
SDG 4 and related discussions occasionally mention the need to change behaviours and underlying cultural patterns, a much stronger emphasis on knowledge and skills is everywhere apparent. It is true that ESD is assumed to play
the role of changing people's behaviours and culture. However, the current
conceptualisation of ESD narrowly promotes one form of education, which is
anchored in Western modernist schooling and privileges human exceptionalism and liberal individualism over other values. Yet such an approach promotes
independent rather than interdependent selfhood (Rappleye & Komatsu, 2017;
Rappleye et al., 2020). This notion of independent selfhood is a very explicit
goal of leading international organisations, as reviewed above. That makes
sense when considering that student-centred education has its origin in the
West where independent selfhood is the de facto assumption (Thomas, 2012,
Siedentop, 2014). If interdependent selfhood is one key for achieving sustainability, it is questionable whether ESD as currently practised, emphasising

forms of education characterised by independence, rationality, and the atom-ised 'self', will contribute to our collective recognition of and progress toward environmental sustainability. We understand this is a provocative suggestion, but more provocations are necessary to avoid business-as-usual as the planet moves closer to catastrophic consequences.

5   Conclusions

We began this chapter by confirming that negative interactions between edu-cation and other SDGs are largely dismissed in SDG statements and their inter-pretations by major international organisations. This dismissal means that the current education paradigm remains unquestioned, resulting in the continued prioritisation of economic growth and social equity over the environment. We then suggested the presence of such negative interactions by taking an example of the interaction between education and climate change. Finally, we pointed out that cultural dimensions concerning the concept of selfhood might be a factor strongly affecting human environmental impacts on the Earth, although culture and the concept of selfhood are not even recognised within the cur-rent education paradigm, let alone central to current debates on education and environmental sustainability.

Based on these findings, we make the following three recommendations for scholars, practitioners, and policymakers:
– Policymakers and practitioners should be duly cautious about the effective-ness of ESD as currently proposed.
– Scholars and practitioners need to become aware of the deeper assump-tions underlying different education practices.
– Scholars and international organisations should rethink the relevance of universal scales of sustainability.

The following describes each of these recommendations as invitations for future research and debate.

5.1   *Caution about the Effectiveness of ESD*
Although ESD has been proposed as one of the central mechanisms of achiev-ing sustainability by major actors, including international organisations, our findings suggest that national policymakers and practitioners should be duly cautious about the effectiveness of the ESD in its current form. While it is true that the current approach to ESD initiates some movement in the direction

of sustainability, the underpinning assumptions about subjectivity and self-hood of the ESD approach are largely indistinguishable from, and too easily fall into complementarity with, the currently dominant education paradigm. Those who question the effectiveness of the currently proposed ESD are not only critical scholars, such as Bowers (1995, 2002), Orr (2004, 2009), Sterling (2016), and Sterling et al. (2018), but in fact thinkers who once subscribed to the approach themselves (UNESCO, 2014d, p. 184).

5.2   Becoming Aware of Different Assumptions Underlying Education Practices

Because the effectiveness of ESD as currently practised is uncertain, scholars and practitioners need to look for educational practices based on different assumptions than those of the 'modernist Western paradigm' (Sterling et al., 2018). One promising means to do so is to look to non-Western countries and indigenous cultures where the current education paradigm has not been fully internalised. Indeed, the IPCC's October 2018 Special Report on Climate Change explicitly mentions that 'education, information, and community approaches, including those informed by indigenous knowledge and local knowledge, can accelerate the wide scale behavior changes consistent with adapting to and limiting global warming' (IPCC, 2018: section D.5.6). Yet, while there is some awareness of the importance of non-Western education practices among some policy stakeholders, it is disappointing that major international organisations, such as the World Bank and the OECD, are now seeking to replace remaining elements of indigenous systems in non-Western countries with those based on the current education paradigm, often through the creation of international large-scale assessments and related competency-based curricular changes (Takayama, 2008; Gorur, 2016; Addey, 2017; Auld et al., 2019). For a fuller discussion of these ideas, see Silova et al. (2018) and the subsequent response by Vickers (2018).

We believe that some critical distance from Western modes of thinking and education – a particular cultural arrangement, not a universal phenomenon – is a crucial step for locating alternatives *beyond* the Western education paradigm as we face the climate change catastrophe. As this chapter has illustrated, the education paradigm promoted by major international agencies reflects not only the economic growth logic of these organisations but also the 'subjectivity' projects they try to enact globally, e.g., a focus on abstract thinking (cognition alone); and the reduction of 'society' to an agglomeration of atomised (neo)liberal individuals competing for rapidly shrinking resources on Earth.

We seek to open space for questioning whether such approaches are conducive to sustainable lifestyles, not necessarily provide answers. We are requesting that scholars and policymakers reimagine education on a much wider scale, considering alternatives *beyond* the Western education paradigm that can contribute to the collective effort to think in new ways.

One very promising, school-based alternative is the Japanese Food for Education programme (Komatsu & Rappleye, 2018). At the same time, experimental attempts to go beyond the current education paradigm are also available in Western contexts, for example, the overall curriculum approach of Schumacher College in the United Kingdom (Sterling et al., 2018).[10] Similarly, many indigenous practices aim to reintegrate alternative ways of coexisting with nature and the Earth within the modern school curriculum (Masuku van Damme & Neluvhalani, 2004; Glasson et al., 2010; Shukla, Barkman, & Patel, 2017). These initiatives work under the assumption that the individual is not independent but fully embedded in social and natural networks (Sterling et al., 2018), offering alternative resources for thinking about sustainability of environment and culture.

There is an urgent need to set up an arena to exchange information about such experiments. Several academic journals (e.g., *Journal of Transformative Education*) have been playing a limited role in this regard. Yet this means the exchange is still restricted to very narrow academic circles, usually working on the periphery of mainstream research and facing considerable obstacles in a Western-dominated linguistic and publishing world. This work has now a far more urgent priority than monitoring education access and quality in pursuit of the 'modernist Western paradigm'. Is there any reason that international organisations could not help facilitate such information exchange?

5.3   *Rethinking the Relevance of Universal Scales of Sustainability*

We are highly sceptical about the effectiveness of establishing a 'universal scale' to measure progress to sustainability, although several international organisations seem to be intent on doing so. Using scales in such a way implicitly assumes that the current world lacks something important and therefore it should be achieved by *progress*. This assumption, which is in fact a globally dominant worldview, and its policy impacts, are exactly what led us to our current world: increasingly dire environmental challenges met only with continued economic growth, technological innovations, and extension of 'progress' targets (Uchiyama, 2010). Readers might argue that the most critical contemporary problem is runaway capitalism rather than our ontology (i.e., fundamental building blocks of a worldview). Our position is that runaway capitalism is one consequence of our current ontology. We cannot thus solve the problem without rewriting our ontology.

If we still believe in the effectiveness of having a scale, it should rather be organised to measure how much we have forgotten. This is exactly opposite to the direction in which the OECD and other international agencies are moving. Humans potentially have (and perhaps originally had) various relationships, including religious and spiritual ones, with nature. But modern people tend to forget this fact and see nature as merely a standing reserve of commodities, such as water, timber, and minerals. Like others, we too see excessive consumption as correlated with what has been forgotten; capitalist excesses and catastrophic consumption run freest where the amnesia about other ways of being is most acute (Mita, 2018). Thus, relevant scales should be redirected to 'measuring' ontological and psychological dimensions. This is clearly not an easy task, but fortunately various subfields of psychology, including environmental, social, and cultural psychology, have already accumulated useful knowledge and preliminary tools to guide us in the task (e.g., Frantz et al., 2005; Arnocky et al., 2007; Stroink & DeCicco, 2011; Amerigo, Aragones, & Garcia, 2012; Gifford, 2014; Chuang et al., 2016). Connecting approaches found in cultural psychology with education policies and actual embodied practice are an urgent task for education scholars and international organisations alike.

We opened this chapter with the unprecedented pessimism of the Pope over the current 'suicide' trajectory. 'People no longer seem to believe in a happy future', he wrote in the more extended Encyclical Letter on the environmental problem published six months before the Paris Climate Talks, suggesting, 'If we want to bring about deep change, we need to realize that certain mindsets really do influence our behavior. Our efforts at education will be inadequate and ineffectual unless we strive to promote a new way of thinking about human beings, life, society, and our relationship with nature' (Francis, 2015, p. 157). And what precisely is to be the crux of that education-led renewal, that crucial shift in 'mindset'? The move away from individualism: 'Isolated individuals can lose their ability and freedom to escape the utilitarian mindset. ... Social problems must be addressed by community networks and not simply the sum of individual good deeds' (Francis, 2015, p. 160). 'Networks' mean precisely *relations* over atomised entities. How might education foster those? What new pedagogies are needed? Would those education systems that never had the Western-turned-modern ideology of individualism so deeply entrenched have resources for us to learn from (Dumont, 1986; Bellah et al., 1985; Taylor, 1989)?

'There needs to be a distinctive way of looking at things, a way of thinking, policies, an educational programme, a lifestyle and a spirituality which together generate resistance to the assault of the technocratic paradigm', wrote Pope Francis. 'To seek only a technical remedy to each environmental problem which comes up is to separate what in reality [is] interconnected' (Francis, 2015, p. 84). In this chapter, we have expressed our pessimism over current

SDG 4 discussions that explore mere technical solutions and neglect changes in mindset. We deplore the almost total disregard for environmental issues. More constructively, we suggest that we can learn from sources that sit outside the Western tradition precisely because the deepest issues are cultural. The Pope's passion and problématique are laudable, but we would depart from him over where to go looking for 'new ways of thinking'. Becoming aware of those alternatives and then connecting to them helps mitigate the pessimism wrought by the illusion of isolation.

Notes

1   All authors contributed equally to this chapter.
2   This perspective has been repeatedly put forth by leading philosophers, historians, sociologists, and others over the past several decades (e.g., White, 1967; Maki, 1977[2003]; Naess, 1989; see also Komatsu & Rappleye, 2017b). However, very few education scholars and practitioners show any awareness of this discussion unfolding over the past 50 years.
3   The primary reason for not conducting statistical testing is that even very weak relationships or very small differences can be statistically significant if sample sizes are sufficiently large. For example, a relationship having r of .00620 is statistically significant if the sample size exceeds 100,000. This problem has already been identified for decades (Berkson, 1938; Bakan, 1966; Carver, 1978) and echoed by many contemporary researchers (Thompson, 1996, 2002; Nuzzo, 2014; Komatsu & Rappleye, 2017a). For this reason, many researchers have shifted to reporting confidence intervals and effect sizes (e.g., r, Spearman's rho, Cohen's d, and Glass' $delta$) to avoid the problems of statistical significance (Johnson, 1999; Thompson, 2002; Komatsu, Shinohara, & Otsuki, 2015).
4   In truth, this is an impossibly optimistic starting point. Currently the projection for global population by 2050 is 9–11 billion (depending on the model utilised). This is an increase of 2–4 billion since 2012.
5   Even these difficult-to-reach estimates are likely overly optimistic. A recent study published in *Nature* (Resplandy et al., 2018) argues that previous research had underestimated ocean heat uptake due to methodological constraints and that, in fact, to achieve the Paris target of 2ºC warming, emissions will need to be reduced by more than previously thought. That is, the original estimates underestimated the extent and speed of the coming catastrophe.
6   Education is not only a cause but a result of economic growth. Furthermore, the contribution of education to economic growth is not decisive as commonly advocated by proponents of extreme human capital theory (Komatsu & Rappleye, 2017a).

7 This is also the case when using a more comprehensive indicator (i.e., Ecological Footprint of Consumption) instead of CO_2 emissions (York, Rosa, & Dietz, 2004, 2009; Dietz, Rosa, & York, 2012). Not only developing countries, but developed countries are unsuccessful in reducing Ecological Footprint of Consumption.

8 In our analysis, we do not use multiple linear regression analysis, although it is widely used particularly by social scientists. Using that method would have included untested assumptions in the analysis (see Komatsu, et al., 2019a). One problematic assumption of multiple linear regression analyses is that all independent variables affect the dependent variable in a linear way. But those relationships are quite often nonlinear (e.g., Komatsu et al., 2014). Another problematic assumption is that different independent variables affect the dependent variable in an additive manner. Different factors actually quite often affect dependent variables in a multiplicative manner, as widely acknowledged by natural scientists (e.g., Komatsu et al., 2014). Owing to these problems, we do not use multiple linear regression analysis in this study.

9 In particular, a specific concept of self interacts with its specific social environments, e.g., institutions, practices, products, and others (Markus & Kitayama, 2010; Komatsu et al., 2019a). The relationship between individualism scores and EF would stem not only from differences in patterns of personal consumption, but from social institutional arrangements. For example, collectivistic societies may be more prone to establishing institutions to promote pro-environmental behaviour (UNESCO, 2016b, p. 27).

10 Nevertheless, it is dangerous and counterproductive to seek to identify 'best practices' for sustainability without awareness of the complex contexts within which such practices occur and without attunement to different assumptions underlying such education practices. One major reason for this is fundamental differences in the underpinning assumptions of self, others, time, and space among societies (e.g., Markus & Kitayama, 1991, 2010; Nisbett, 2003; Rappleye & Komatsu, 2016, 2017, in press; Rappleye et al., 2020; Silova, 2019). It may be more productive to learn from practices of other societies to consciously realise the underlying assumptions of one's own.

CHAPTER 15

Targets, TVET and Transformation

Stephanie Allais and Volker Wedekind

1   Introduction

The explicit inclusion of technical and vocational education and training (TVET) in the United Nations Sustainable Development Goals was greeted with excitement by advocates for this sector. For a sector that is generally neglected and has low status (Fooks, 1994), ensuring that the SDGs included a focus on TVET was a hard-fought accomplishment. Vocational education was once again a visible part of the international discourse on the role of education in development and would be taken seriously.

We know from the Education for All (EFA) campaign and the Millennium Development Goals (MDGs) that goals and their associated targets have real effects on education systems, with attention and resources following commitments to targets. There can be little doubt that the international targets for achieving universal primary education affected education systems across the globe. Arguably, many more young people are at school because of the focussed attention that these goals and targets generated. However, in this chapter we argue that the incorporation of TVET in SDG 4 and the explicit quantifiable targets associated with it may be something of a pyrrhic victory for the sector. We consider why this education sector in particular is not easily amenable to international targets, and why target-setting for TVET may have perverse or unintended consequences. While our argument applies across all contexts, we are particularly interested in the implications for TVET systems in developing countries where decisions to allocate scarce resources often have greater consequences.

We first outline in broad terms the shifts in the discourses and focus on TVET in international and national policy processes and provide an overview of the key targets and indicators of the SDGs and other regional and national strategies. We then consider why TVET is inherently not amenable to international target-setting – partly because of how heterogenous TVET systems are, and partly because of the ways in which they are embedded in specific contexts and structured by them. In the third section, we draw on experiences as researchers and in policy processes, primarily in South Africa. We problematise the use of targets and indicators by looking at three issues: the nature of quantifiable targets; the tendency for target-setting that results in policy posturing; and the difficulty of applying simple indicators to complex systems.

2   TVET in Development Discourses and the Emergence of Targets and Indicators

The status of TVET in development strategies has had a chequered history (King, 2009). In the decades after World War II, TVET and skills development were part of the orthodoxy of human capital development approaches that were championed by the World Bank and other international agencies. By the early 1990s, based on rates-of-return analyses and various other critiques, donors prioritised basic education, and the emphasis on TVET was reduced (Ashton et al., 1999; Bennell, 1996a, 1996b; Bennell & Segerstrom, 1998; Gill, Fluitman, & Dar, 2000; Wolf, 2004).

In recent years, as participation rates in schooling have improved, the World Bank, a long-time critic, has started advocating for building TVET systems. Developing vocational skills has, again, become the focus of national policies and donor agency agendas (King, 2013b). This reemergence of a focus on TVET promotion is attributed to a range of factors. Zeelen (2015) argues that as countries reached near universal primary enrolment, so attention shifted to the very high levels of drop-out, opt-out, or push-out from the schooling system that left large numbers of young adults neither in education nor work. Vocational education is viewed as providing a solution to a perceived mismatch between the school curriculum and the workplace. A second line of argument looked to vocational education as a mechanism for better aligning local economic skills needs with supply. This is particularly pressing in the context of the changing nature of work, with technological and social changes requiring more complex and specific skills.

The phenomenon of setting goals and targets at a global level emerged with the rise, in the 1970s, of project management approaches linked to performativity, measurability, and accountability, which continue to dominate management discourses (Boltanski & Chiapello, 2006). In order to accurately compare, report, and evaluate, these approaches hold that it is necessary to first define goals, and then set measurable targets and indicators. This marked a shift in the way in which interventions and policies were conceptualised and articulated, with increasing emphasis on restricted lists and clearly developed targets rather than complex, open-ended, and multifaceted processes, which had shaped many of the earlier approaches to development.

The EFA initiative adopted in 1990 at the Jomtien Conference set the pattern within the education sector. While the EFA movement advocated for quality education and improved outcomes, much of the focus remained on access and enrolment, catalysing governments in developing countries, aid agencies, and nongovernmental organisations (NGOs) around a single target. Schooling systems were expanded, teachers trained and employed, and infrastructure built in order to achieve the goal. Countries were compared and 'shamed' if they were not progressing. Significant strides toward meeting the targets were made. The Dakar World Education Forum of 2000 renewed the commitment to achieving EFA, albeit acknowledging that a greater focus on quality was needed, and advocating for a broader conception of basic education. While there were a handful of references to vocational education in the Dakar Framework, they largely emphasised skills development, career guidance, and vocationalisation of aspects of the schooling system. More than 10 years after the Dakar Framework was adopted, the 2012 *Education for All Global Monitoring Report* focussed for the first time on youth and skills, although even then the stress was mainly on school-and-skill (UNESCO, 2012b). In its summary, it argues, 'Most advocates now see skills training not as separate from, but as integral to, general education, offering foundation and transferable skills at the same time as job skills' (UNESCO, 2012b, p. 27). TVET as a distinct focus remained absent.

The MDGs, adopted in 2000, ran in parallel to the EFA initiative but had a wider development remit. Goal 2, devoted to education, was essentially a narrower version of the EFA commitment, focussing again primarily on access to basic education. Adult, higher, and vocational education could at best be indirectly inferred in some of the five other goals, but were not targeted. Aid money and technical assistance committed to TVET from a variety of international organisations have subsequently increased – although at the same time, policy focus has shifted from traditional notions of building technical skills to entrepreneurship and transferable skills, and to competence-based training and national qualifications frameworks (Allais, 2014).

The debates about the SDGs marked a significant moment for advocates for TVET. They won agreement on the inclusion of a right to all forms and levels of education, explicitly including vocational education. In the Education 2030 Framework for Action, vocational education is seen as an important part of broader educational goals, as well as key to supporting equitable and sustainable economic and social development, contributing to the realisation of human rights, and developing the productive capacity of people, their societies, and their economies (WEF, 2015). These broad goals are translated into two specific targets: 4.3, which focusses on equal access to affordable quality technical, vocational, and tertiary education; and 4.4, which says that by 2030, we need to have substantially increased the number of youth and adults who have 'relevant skills, including technical and vocational skills, for employment, decent jobs, and entrepreneurship'. However, the agreed indicators, which measure the achievement of the target, are very narrowly and inappropriately framed: Indicator 4.4.1 reads: 'Proportion of youth and adults with information and communications technology (ICT) skills, by type of skill' (see Appendix 2).[1]

The approach of setting goals as a policy tool is not restricted to the United Nations and its agencies. For example, the African Union (AU) has followed up with its own commitments. On 31 January 2016, the AU adopted the Continental Education Strategy for Africa as the framework for a transformative education and training system in Africa (AU, 2016). The strategy aims to shape the policies of African countries along similar lines to the SDGs, including expanding TVET opportunities at both secondary and tertiary levels and strengthening linkages between the world of work and education and training systems. This follows an earlier 2014 AU resolution that adopted a continental TVET Strategy, calling on member states to (i) enhance support and investment for TVET as it is fundamental for skill development for the youth and to promote employability and entrepreneurship through innovation; and (ii) to align their national TVET strategies to the AU Continental TVET Strategy for effectiveness. Clearly at the level of the African continent, TVET is seen as being key to education and development (AU, 2018). The expansion of TVET is seen as solving apparent skills shortages, enhancing productivity, and absorbing a major youth unemployment problem, among many other goals.

At the national level, governments throughout the world have adopted similar approaches in national development plans and national education and skills strategies. Vocational and skills education is highlighted as an important strand of development agendas, and goals and targets are specified to concretise the commitments made under the plans.

This section has shown that there is a confluence of both a new commitment to TVET globally, regionally, and nationally, and that this commitment is expressed at various levels through the process of goal setting, usually coupled with targets and indicators that need to be measurable and achievable. In the next section, we explore three issues that separately and in combination convince us that, for TVET systems at least, there are real dangers in this new TVET gospel, as well as in the attempt to set goals and targets at such high levels. The issues are interlinked but are separated for the purpose of presenting the arguments. We start by considering the inherent heterogeneity of TVET internationally, which is problematic for target setting. We then reflect on our experiences working in the South African policy terrain, and the ways in which goals and targets took away policy attention from the important task of building institutional capacity. Finally, we argue that goals like SDG 4 can have the effect of focussing attention on reform only *within* education and training systems, while TVET is shaped by economic, political, and social factors to a greater degree than the rest of the education and training system.

3   Complicated and Complex Systems

TVET systems are not easily amenable to international targets for the same reason that there is no strong comparative education research tradition in this sector: national TVET systems are very heterogeneous (Cedefop, 2017) and idiosyncratic (Bosch, 2017). The heterogeneity arises from the fact that how TVET is defined and bounded within each country varies, and so there is little agreement on what is included or excluded under the term. Vocational education straddles formal, informal, and nonformal education as well as the public and private sectors. It can take place in school-like institutions such as colleges, in workplaces, or in hybrid spaces. It can be undertaken before entry into an occupation or afterward (or in a liminal time/space such as an internship or apprenticeship where one is neither fully student nor fully worker). It can occur at various levels of education from very basic or primary through to higher levels, and the points and manner in which it splits from 'general' education differ across countries. There are differences in terms of when specialisation starts, whether learning is primarily in workplaces or education institutions, and what the pathways are to other education and training programmes (Bosch, 2017). Different types of labour markets (internal labour markets, occupational labour markets, tournaments) all have very different implications for training and skills because education pays off very differently in all of them (Marsden, 2009; van de Werfhorst, 2011). All of these factors mean that the configuration of TVET varies across and within contexts and is idiosyncratic because the internal and external factors shaping the system (the nature of the economy; the regulatory context, including regulation of the labour market; the cultural and historical antecedents) vary greatly.

This alone would suggest that setting common goals and objectives for TVET should be approached with caution. How can there be targets and indicators that make sense in such heterogeneous systems?[2] Furthermore, TVET systems are also complicated (they have many and diverse component parts) and, more importantly, complex (the parts are interconnected in ways that feedback within the system unpredictably).[3]

This complexity is in no small part a consequence of the fact that vocational programmes emerged in different ways in different economic sectors within countries. Programmes are often related to the very specific needs of particular industrial sectors in smoothing the transition from school to work and attempting to improve the skills of job applicants, or ensuring that the particular needs of employers are met. All of this means that *within* countries, let alone *between* countries, a wide range of different types of programmes, providers, and award systems exist. This is in sharp contrast with schooling and university systems, which may differ from country to country, but which have had stronger traditions of nationally recognised certificates and award bodies, and share many similarities across national boundaries. In many countries today TVET systems are described as fragmented, and as having a proliferation of qualifications, which is one reason why qualifications frameworks have been such a focus of reform for TVET systems (Allais, 2017a). Countries that have adopted the British qualification model have often seen further fragmentation and proliferation of TVET qualifications through the very policies aimed at streamlining them (Allais, 2014).

The strongest comparative research tradition focussed on TVET comes from political science, and what has been labelled as comparative capitalism, following Hall and Soskice's *Varieties of Capitalism* (Hall & Soskice, 2001). There is much debate within and about comparative capitalism: Does it remain empirically useful? Is it merely additive (Ashman & Fine, 2013)? Is it of any use in thinking about developing countries and development and, in particular, in African countries (Breckenridge, 2018)? Researchers have drawn attention to its inadequate account of power relations (Streeck, 2012) and the inherent limits of methodological nationalism (Lauder, Brown, & Ashton, 2017). But it is clear from the body of literature that has developed in this tradition that TVET systems are shaped by their social, political, and economic context in ways that are different from school and university systems. Institutional political economy demonstrates that factors such as labour market regulation; unionisation; the nature and extent of employer organisation; the role of industry peak bodies; the broader political, institutional, and cultural context; the degree of federalism in a country; and the relative powers of national governments and states/provinces all affect how people are educated for different occupations, and how the relationships between education and training systems and labour markets function (Iverson & Stephens, 2008; Martin, 2017; Streeck, 2012; Thelen & Busemeyer, 2012). These factors interact with each other in complex ways, such as how incentives to learn are shaped by labour market opportunity structures (Keep, 2012).

The changing structure of labour markets adds further pressure. In wealthy countries there is increased casualisation, rising youth unemployment, and a trend toward 'hourglass' economies – where the middle-level skills section of the labour market for which traditional TVET systems predominantly prepare learners is shrinking, and employment opportunities are mainly for those with high- and low-level skills and unskilled labour. In African countries, the numbers of people employed in formal, well-paid jobs have always been very small. Stagnant economies and deindustrialisation, with some exceptions, make it increasingly difficult to build TVET systems. In the regulated sector of the labour market, professions are sometimes protected, but there are few well-remunerated, protected, and stable employment opportunities beneath them, other than in the civil service. It is hard to improve vocational education because it does not, in fact, lead to many good labour market opportunities (Allais, 2018b).

Clearly the 'problem' with skills is more complex than the deficit-based approaches within supply-side policy that blame educational institutions for being inflexible and unresponsive, and for not producing the right kind of graduate with the right skill set for work. Governments in wealthy liberal market economies have been trying to 'fix' TVET for decades, without paying attention to the structure of the labour market, the way in which demand for skills is articulated, and the role that workplaces need to play in supporting the development of skills (Keep, 2005; Raffe, 2015; Wheelahan, Buchanan, & Yu, 2015; Wolf, 2002).

The massification of higher education in many countries aggravates the difficulties faced by TVET systems, because anyone who can access higher education will rather do so than enrol for a TVET alternative. All of this reinforces the ways in which TVET is expected to play a highly compensatory role, which in turn makes it particularly difficult to introduce specialised knowledge, and very complex to take decisions about what should be prioritised in the sequencing and selection of knowledge in the curriculum.

This is exacerbated by other factors that are more common in Africa and other post-colonial contexts than other parts of the world. In many African countries, formal TVET systems are tiny, low in status, and fraught with crises:

> Although some countries have invested in the development of greater access to technical and vocational training (Egypt, South Africa, Morocco and Tunisia, for example), most still have training systems that cater for only a very small minority (between 1% and 6%) of the young people in education. (ICQN/TVSD Ministerial Conference, 2014)

A study of southern African countries' TVET systems commissioned by UNE-SCO found that while Southern African Development Community (SADC) countries placed significant emphasis on TVET in their public commitments, the (rather limited) data available highlighted a number of weaknesses in the systems. These included poor management information systems, a lack of a common definition of what is meant by TVET between and within countries, uneven or weak quality assurance systems, policy incoherence, complex governance and funding arrangements, and generally low levels of employer participation (McGrath et al., 2013).

The UNESCO SADC report highlights a problem we face as researchers interested in TVET – lack of system level data:

> It is evident that TVET Management Information Systems (MIS) are often absent or weak. This was by far the worst ordinal indicator in the national monitoring reports. There are huge data gaps and weaknesses for several indicators. ... Even getting basic data and ensuring their accuracy is [sic] beyond some systems, and the ability to disaggregate for target group, to compare public and private provision or to do any forecasting are beyond the horizon for several countries. It is difficult to see how TVET systems can be successfully transformed when there is a lack of feedback data at both institutional and national levels. (McGrath et al., 2013, p. 17)

Historical factors have worked against building strong formal TVET systems in many developing countries. Despite the variations (shaped to some extent by different colonial legacies), most countries place a high value on TVET in policy pronouncements as a vehicle for addressing economic and other social challenges, but the societies generally do not place a high value on TVET, with academic routes being viewed as the preferred educational pathway by the general public (Zeelen, 2015). The reasons for this are many and complex. Foster (1965) advanced the classic thesis that young people's preference for general education is rational despite policymakers' attempts to guide them into vocational education. Nherera (2000) pointed out that the state has always been the major employer in African countries, and that the state has always favoured general education. Another explanation is that African countries have not been able to catch up with industrialisation (Amsden, 2007). Even those countries in Africa with stronger TVET systems tend to be primarily centre- or school-based rather than apprenticeship- or internship-based. TVET programmes thus often have quite weak linkages to employers, and the data around youth transitions from TVET to work is often poor. Thus, there are high expectations for one of the least respected and resourced parts of the education system.

None of this means that there are no successes for TVET in Africa. There are certainly examples of good practice as well as innovation in many institutions, and some pockets of excellence exist. And international policy focussed on building access to high quality technical education is important. But the capacity to respond to the demands of high-level goals or targets imposed from outside the education system is limited. International and national targets tend to lead to an emphasis on policy reform *within* the sector for which the targets are set. These high-level targets do not take account of the complex relationships the education system has to factors outside itself. This could be very damaging for TVET systems, especially in poor countries, and especially those where formal TVET systems have historically been very weak. It places high expectations on weak institutions, whose weaknesses are in many instances shaped by their context: what Busemeyer and Iverson (2014, p. 242) call the 'institutional context which shapes the level and composition of skills'.

The second problem with targets, which is more acute for poor countries and for TVET than the rest of the education and training system, is that targets focus too narrowly on one factor, such as access, which can be dangerous and destructive. This is widely argued to have been one of the problems with EFA – simply flooding schools with learners without changing anything else in the system and claiming that the targets have been met (UNESCO, 2015b). In countries as diverse as South Africa, Uganda, and Ethiopia, one of the things that has undermined quality and completion rates in both university and TVET systems over the past decade has been dramatic expansion in order to meet targets, but with insufficient accompanying financial expansion. Educational expansion implies not just scaling up (which in many cases has not happened) but also the adding of more resources per student than was the case before, because the expansion of numbers often means expansion to student populations with weaker educational backgrounds.

Pressure to expand access to TVET invariably means that the expansion focusses on the formal state system and takes the form of increasing the number of colleges or expanding their capacity to enrol more students. This college model of TVET is driven by a school logic and does not mean that students graduating from those colleges will have access to the world of work or genuine labour market opportunities upon completion. Instead, often this type of expansion is about signalling certain messages that have little to do with TVET. In addition, because of the particular colonial, neocolonial, and Bretton Woods institutions' influences, the organisational forms and the policies that regulate educational processes (curriculum, assessment, pedagogy) tend to mimic systems that have been developed for different contexts. This mimicry takes various forms, either through symbolic policies that signal high-level intentions without clear procedural or resource specification, borrowing of policies and strategies that are inappropriate to the context, or focussing on form over function and scale over quality (Fuller, 1991; Harley & Wedekind, 2004; Jansen, 2002; Mattson & Harley, 2003; Phillips & Ochs, 2003; Steiner-Khamsi & Waldow, 2012).[4] This has resulted in education systems with uneven or generally fragile institutions with limited capacity to respond to the pressures to address the high-level intentions and targets that are imposed through international political processes and the influence of international development agencies.

The SDG indicator for TVET (4.4.1) currently reduces the whole of TVET to ICT skills. While such a narrow target is problematic, another problem is created when targets are too broad. Within TVET reform, there is a tendency for academic scholars, policymakers, and civil society actors to emphasise a broad role for TVET. We are not arguing for narrow and overspecified TVET; in fact TVET, particularly in today's labour market and particularly in contexts where many learners have weak school education, should contain substantial components of general education (Gamble, 2013). So UNESCO, for example, argues for the importance of a wider lifelong learning perspective informed by a human development perspective (UNESCO, 2016c). The SDGs oblige TVET to include education for human rights, sustainable development, and citizenship. This sounds desirable at face value. But in practice, it places yet another obstacle in front of weak institutions trying to offer courses that are not highly valued, often to poorly prepared students. Actual policy modalities are difficult in TVET; it is really not easy for governments to figure out what to do. And, as we discuss in the following pages, this often leads to government posturing.

In summary, we have discussed a number of ways in which targets can be particularly problematic for TVET. If they are overspecified by focussing on, for example, expanding enrolment or measuring access to information technology without recognising the constraints on the system to do so, they can result in unintended consequences such as pockets of excellence being weakened or destroyed, and resources being allocated for one part of the curriculum rather than another. If they are too broad, they can result in TVET systems being expected to take on more functions than their capacity allows. Because goals are almost always divorced from the TVET system's internal dynamics, they can potentially damage the system that they are supposed to be strengthening. And because goals are also focussed on TVET as a system, they ignore the ways in which the broader economic and social context shapes the possibilities of improving TVET.

4   Reform and Policy Posturing

In this section, we draw on our joint experience working as academic researchers focussed on knowledge, curriculum, pedagogy, and political economy, but
also as participants involved with national policy at the highest levels since the
democratic transition in South Africa, with a considerable focus on policy for
TVET.[5]

   In our experience, the SDGs have not been a major factor driving policy
development or implementation in South Africa, and there is little evidence
that they have been anything more than additional reporting obligations for
people in the Ministry of Foreign Affairs and statistical offices. The same can
be said for national target-setting. Our experience of working in and with government in education policy development and implementation, particularly
in TVET, is that there is enormous pressure on government officials to engage
in posturing rather than actually changing things. There are many forces that
push governments toward 'playing at doing government' – being engaged in
activities that are essentially posturing, or busywork.

   Michael Fielding playfully suggested, '[Target-setting] is, in one sense, the
viagra of economic and educational under-performance: set some targets and
you'll feel better, be seen to get something done and satisfy the prurience of
an increasingly promiscuous accountability' (1999, p. 277). Spreen captured a
similar idea, arguing that stating something in a policy document tends to create the impression that it will happen:

> My own experience in educational reform in the United States has made
> me susceptible to the argument that when policies are put on paper with
> a coherent logic we are deluded into thinking fundamental change is
> taking place. Observers of policy reform often do not take into account
> what it takes to truly alter the structure of society or its institutions nor
> do they consider important distinctions made on the ground by those
> implementing the policies. (Spreen, 2001, p. 17)

This is even more likely to be the case with a goal such as SDG 4, which has
a number of systemic implications that may be at odds with each other. The
inclusion of education and skills at all levels – at the survivalist level, at the
mid-level of occupations, and at the level of complex professional work – may
sound straightforward but it is unhelpful for policymakers who have limited
resources.

   Target-setting has a particular allure when the modalities of actually making things happen, and making things work, are not obvious or easy to create;

and TVET systems are examples where policy decisions are complicated and difficult. Some examples of poorly planned policy modalities include a recent decision, in both Zimbabwe and South Africa, to link vocational programmes more closely to employers by making it compulsory that students are attached to work places. The net effect in both countries has been either to reduce enrolment dramatically, or to allow people to enrol, but then never be awarded their qualification, because they are never able to complete the workplace component. This problem was discussed in many national planning meetings in which we participated.

Another example relates to the introduction of a new TVET certificate, which was formally phased into South African TVET colleges in 2007. This was a qualification that was far broader than its predecessors, such that it resembled the broad kind of TVET for which academic researchers have been advocating (McGrath, 2012; Wheelahan et al., 2015). On paper it looked good. In practice, employers were unfamiliar with it, and graduates found that it had little purchase in the market place. Colleges did not have the capacity (both in terms of infrastructure and teachers) to deliver the programme as the curriculum designers had intended, and the students who entered the programme were not eager young people interested in exploring a particular occupational field, but in the main were either high school drop-outs/push-outs or high school graduates with no access to other study or work opportunities. These students more often than not had experienced difficulties studying mathematics at school and were hoping for something more practical. The curriculum, however, was demanding. So, the system did not have the capacity, and the society did not have the understanding, to make this qualification worthwhile or productive (Wedekind, 2018).

South Africa is a good example of a country with a penchant for high-level plans and targets. The country has a National Development Plan (NDP); a Human Resource Development Council with its own strategy; a National Skills Agency with a National Skills Development Strategy; and national plans for parts of the system such as the post-school system, industrial development strategies and plans, and economic and sector-specific plans and strategies. Each strategy or plan has targets or goals or initiatives that have a direct impact on the institutions that need to deliver the education and skills part of that plan.[6] For example, the NDP proposes expanding the system of training artisans to 30,000 graduates per annum by the target year of 2030. This aspirational target, set with no clear justification, has become something of a mantra in the skills system, with much of that system working toward achieving a target that is not based on any explicit rationale. In South Africa the term *artisan* refers to a very limited set of trades in the engineering field and does not take account of the shifts in South Africa's economy (the financial services sector is now the largest) or any clear analysis of what the mining and manufacturing sectors actually require. While we do not take issue with the potential benefits of having greater numbers of qualified artisans, the point is rather that a relatively arbitrary target has been elevated to a holy grail. The achievement of this target is one of the primary drivers shaping the TVET system, potentially to the detriment of training provision for other sectors and occupations. Indeed, the recently announced vocational stream within the schooling system is justified primarily in terms of meeting this 30,000-artisan target, despite the fact that there has been no discussion about how this school track actually articulates with apprenticeships and the qualification of artisans. Once again, the target seems to develop a life of its own without account being taken of the complexity of the institutional arrangements.

An example of perverse outcomes can be seen at the level of policy and strategy. Because of a concern about TVET and skills development funding being channelled into short skills courses (of varying quality), and a wider critique of narrow training, the third iteration of the South African National Skills Development Strategy placed high priority on the funding of full qualifications that would supposedly ensure that workers would be able to progress into higher or other forms of work. While not referring directly to international goals, the rationale for this in the strategy aligns with the notion of lifelong learning – that education should not just focus on efficiencies and productivity training, but empower people to develop and grow within the occupation and articulate into other careers or higher learning.

This high-level goal was then translated through the funding mechanisms of the various Sector Education and Training Authorities and resulted in a major shift away from short course training to supporting students in full-time qualifications at public TVET colleges. The problem with this focus on qualifications was that existing employees tended to be excluded as neither they nor the employers were willing or able to commit to extended periods of study in order to get qualifications that were not highly regarded in the industry. Furthermore, in some sectors (such as ICT for example) the majority of employees already had appropriate qualifications, and short courses to update knowledge or introduce new technologies were the most appropriate intervention; yet, the commitment to a national strategy meant that they could not be prioritised. The consequence was that some employers funded their own training, and there was a weakening of the link between the public provision of training and employers.

Each of the above examples is more complex than presented here, but the overarching point is this: whether at global level such as the MDGs and SDGs, or at regional or continental level such as AU and SADC, or at national level in plans and strategies, setting well-intentioned and ambitious targets has two effects. Either they force compliance with the form without achieving the intended outcome, or more often than not, they create distortions that have unintended but serious consequences, particularly in further weakening the TVET system by expecting it to do things that it was not designed to do. This creates a vicious cycle in which institutions that have low status in society are further undermined, and thus the prejudices are confirmed.

A major problem with targets is fake target-meeting or gaming. For example, governments commit to creating jobs and then release lists of 'job opportunities' that have been created. There is much research on the fact that targets are proxies, and focus on meeting the proxy often displaces the meaningful activity to which it was supposed to lead (Elton, 2004; McNay, 1999; Campbell, 1979). Of course this is a general problem, as Goodhart's Law[7] suggests, not a TVET- or even education-related one.

Our experiences in South Africa suggest that policy posturing and target-setting do little to strengthen and develop the TVET system and in many instances have weakened it. We suggest that target-setting and internationally comparative measures should be treated with great caution.

5   Conclusions

TVET has drawn increasing attention from international donors and national policymakers; its explicit incorporation into SDG 4 can be seen as part of that. We argue that a general problem with target-setting for social policy is that setting goals for a specific system creates the illusion that the system itself can achieve those goals – that policies and actions endogenous to the system under consideration are required, even when some lip-service is paid to context or interconnectedness.

TVET offers a particularly stark reminder about why that is not the case. Economic factors, labour markets, and the nature of school and university systems largely shape the possibilities and difficulties experienced in TVET systems. This reinforces the tendency of governments toward posturing, which is most likely in areas where it is hard to figure out the actual policy modalities required to change something or make something happen. There are many forces that push governments toward activities that are essentially posturing, or busywork. This has manifested in serial reforms in all aspects of education systems, but particularly, in TVET. Where progress has been made – and despite the extreme fragility of TVET there are pockets of progress – it is often in spite of, not because of, grand target-setting.

We suggest that the focus on TVET and skills in the SDGs has done little to improve TVET, and may weaken it, because vocational education in developing countries can only make a limited contribution to equity in the context of substantial labour market reform and industrial development. National and international targets in the main get in the way of building TVET systems in Africa that can make this limited contribution.

Target-setting for TVET tends to lead to the designing of TVET systems for labour markets that do not exist and for student populations that countries do not have. There are vastly inflated ideas of what TVET can and should do, and by expecting too much from TVET we make it very difficult for it to do almost anything. Governments take fragile institutions and give them impossible tasks, and then create the illusion that the reasons for the failure of TVET systems are reformable by changing TVET policy.

Does this mean that there should be no international commitments and goals that shape aspirations for national systems? We believe that the SDGs can serve a useful purpose in focussing attention on a sector that has been poorly understood. However, we would suggest that narrow indicators such as enrolment, throughput, or provision of ICT should be avoided. Instead, countries could be asked to account for the extent to which there are policies in place to support the development of a TVET system in its full complexity. These policies must be related to TVET, and not subsumed within a general education framework. Such policies should address the specific contextual conditions of the TVET system, the labour market, and social and political interactions, because this complexity has to be tackled by governments, which want to improve skills levels and productivity. Governments should be asked to report on what policies are in place, what resources are committed to the implementation of those policies, and how they will be monitored and evaluated. Because of this context-oriented approach, a qualitative process of peer review rather than a technical evaluation may then be a more appropriate mechanism, as substantive, contextually sensitive judgements need to be made.

We noted earlier that there is a paucity of data and research on TVET in many developing contexts. In part, this is related to weaknesses in administrative capacity, but also the fact that vocational education has a very weak research base in universities. In order to develop and monitor the policies proposed above, and deepen the insights into the dynamics of the system, this research capacity needs to be strengthened at universities. A concrete measure on which governments could report would therefore be the degree to which they are supporting the development of this critical capacity.

TVET work has always been, and will continue to be, extremely difficult in poor countries. What is needed is dedicated energy, resources, time, creativity, and experimentation. TVET systems are never going to solve large-scale educational or social problems in the absence of major structural economic and labour market reform. The corollary of this is that the more pressure there is on TVET to solve such problems, the less it will succeed even on a modest scale.

Acknowledgement

Stephanie Allais gratefully acknowledges support from the South African National Research Foundation, through the South African Research Chairs Initiative and specifically the Skills Development Research Chair, which supported her in the writing of this chapter.

Notes

1   How this came about and its consequences are discussed in detail by King (2017).
2   In contrast, primary education does have significant commonality in purpose and structures across contexts, and setting targets for levels of literacy or numeracy may be legitimate.
3   For a discussion on the distinction between 'complicated' and 'complex' social systems see Poli (2013).
4   Fuller argued that schools function primarily as signals of modernity on the African landscape that 'display [W]estern symbols and advance modern expectations and promises' (Fuller, 1991, p. xix) because 'looking modern brings affection from larger [W]estern states and spurs the arrival of foreign capital. And by signalling the coming of economic growth, real or illusory, the fragile state strengthens its own domestic position' (Fuller, 1991, pp. 19–20).
5   One author of this chapter was special advisor to a previous South African Minister of Higher Education and Training; we have both worked on a recent national plan for the whole post-school education system in South Africa; we have written policy documents such as Green and White papers for the post-school system, served on many Ministerial Task teams under three different ministers, and engaged formally and informally with government officials in many processes, as well as with international organisations, in particular the International Labour Organisation and UNESCO.

6 While some of these planning processes can be viewed as attempts to do state-led modern planning in the mode critiqued by James C. Scott (1998), our argument is different. Unlike the projects Scott described that massively intervene in society and the natural world, many of the South African plans have very little coordinated purchase and tend to impact in ad hoc ways.

7 Goodhart's Law: 'When a measure becomes a target, it ceases to be a good measure' (Elton, 2004). See also Campbell's Law: 'The more any quantitative social indicator is used for social decision-making, the more subject it will be to corruption pressures and the more apt it will be to distort and corrupt the social processes it is intended to monitor' (Campbell, 1979).

CHAPTER 16

Between Tokenism and Inclusion: The Student Movement in the Post-2015 Process

Luke Shore and Viktor Grønne

1   Introduction

Students at all levels of education are one of the central constituencies, along with teachers, parents, and families, of the global education community. As the recipients of teaching, students have a direct interest in the design, implementation, and evaluation of education policy and practice. As participants in the educational process, they have experience that can inform the improvement of policy and practice. Students have long organised themselves into associations and unions that struggle for their interests to be recognised at institutional, local, and national levels. Students have also brought their unions together into confederations at the international level in order to represent these interests in the relevant processes of international and intergovernmental organisations. In negotiations to adopt the post-2015 Agenda, which culminated with the 2030 Agenda for Sustainable Development and its 17 Sustainable Development Goals (SDGs), national unions and regional platforms represented the interests of the student constituency, with varying results. This chapter documents the involvement of students in the post-2015 process in order to record that experience and build on it, identifying lessons that can be learned for the implementation and monitoring of SDG 4, and, more broadly, for future global processes.

The chapter is based on the claim that students, as a central constituency in education, are entitled to be actively involved at every stage of education governance. It is a claim that is based on the principle that people should be involved in decision-making processes to the extent that those decisions affect their lives. In order to realise this, students, along with teachers and parents, should be allowed to associate into unions or other forms of representative organisations. In processes of education governance, these associations should then be granted a seat at the table and decisions codetermined between them, invited experts, and the relevant authority, which could be an educational institution, local authority, or state or international institution, according to the level of the decision-making process. To be considered as legitimate representatives of the constituency, the associations must have an extensive membership base and adhere to the highest standards of democracy and accountability in their internal processes.

Such student participation in a system of education governance can bring a number of benefits. First, it can remedy inequalities in resources and representation by empowering the groups directly involved to participate in processes that affect them. Second, it can function as a means of citizenship education by socialising large numbers of people into processes of democratic governance and accountability, both in the internal processes of organisations and in codetermination with the authorities. Third, it can solve information asymmetries and failures by providing a mechanism for educational constituencies to continuously draw attention to problems about which the centralised authority would not otherwise be aware. Fourth, it can solve collective problems by providing a means for the various actors in education to discuss complex issues and explore, decide, and implement strategies for addressing them together (Cohen & Rogers, 1995, pp. 42–44).

Student participation is a conception of education governance broadly accepted by the entirety of the student movement, as well as by teacher and parent representatives, with the exception of small groups of activists from the autonomist and anarchist traditions that reject incorporation in favour of decentralised and nonhierarchical self-organisation. This corporatist approach, rooted in ideas of associational democracy, ensures that education reflects the interests of those directly involved, and of society more broadly, and that it optimises education as a public service. When we write of the student constituency, we refer to the corporatist approach outlined above, as represented by student movements, unions, guilds, and the like. The student constituency can be understood to overlap with the broader youth constituency on a range of issues but has a more legitimate claim to representation when it comes to education policy. It is also important to make a distinction between two types of student institutions. On the one hand, there are *student movements*, student unions, and student guilds, which embody the corporatist approach (e.g., a university student union, which is open to and mandated to represent all students on campus, who in turn direct its work). On the other hand, there are *student organisations*, which are student-led and often work with student issues but do not have the same standards of representativeness (e.g., a conservative or a radical students' organisation, open only to those who sympathise with its cause, and which promotes that ideology on campus and in broader society [Klemenčič, 2014]). In this chapter, however, we use organisations to describe both student unions and organisations.

As authors, we write from a European vantage point, which reflects the fact that European student organisations took a lead in representing the student constituency in the post-2015 negotiations. In constructing this narrative and analysis, we have consulted with actors from all world regions. We have endeavoured to ensure that this account faithfully reflects the experiences of the student constituency from around the world, while at the same time recognising this chapter to be a shared personal reflection. Although we reference published works where possible, one of the purposes of this chapter is to document knowledge that exists within the global student movement, but which has never been recorded in the literature.

2   State of the Global Student Movement in 2014

As the process to agree on the education component of the post-2015 agenda got underway, the global student movement found itself fragmented and uncoordinated. Although the Occupy movement and antiglobalisation movements, which were partly student led, had swept across the world in recent years, the same has not been the case for the student movement based around schools, campuses, and education issues.

The global student movement peaked during the Cold War, when the International Union of Students (IUS), aligned to Moscow, and the International Student Conference (ISC), aligned to Washington, were at their height. Both attracted thousands of national student representatives to their global meetings, coordinated student solidarity across the world, and, in the case of IUS in particular, represented students' interests toward global bodies such as the UN. IUS and ISC were, however, funded by the KGB and CIA, respectively. In 1967, the CIA's covert funding of ISC was exposed, which prompted a furious reaction from European members and soon precipitated the organisation's bankruptcy in 1969 (Paget, 2003). With the collapse of the Soviet Union, IUS faltered too. Its funding dried up in the early 1990s and the organisation eventually became entirely dormant following a final conference in Ghana in 2003 (Deca, 2012). The history of IUS and ISC has taught students that they can organise successfully at the global level. At the same time, it reveals the challenges involved, in particular, mediating the ideological positions of participating organisations, which tends to be further complicated by geopolitical considerations (Altbach, 1970). While students essentially agreed on education policy and practice, it was their language and tone as well as their interest in and perceived mandate to speak about broader social issues that have, historically, proved divisive (Grønne, 2017).

During the Cold War, in the 1960s and 1970s, students were not only well organised globally, but also regionally. The *Organización Continental Latinoamericana y Caribeña de Estudiantes* (OCLAE) united students across the Latin American continent from its headquarters in Havana and wielded significant influence in IUS (Altbach, 1989). The Western European Students' Information Bureau (WESIB), later the European Students' Information Bureau (ESIB) and now the European Students' Union (ESU), was created in 1982 against the backdrop of the ISC bankruptcy 13 years earlier. It empowered national student unions at the tertiary level across Europe through information sharing (Sundström, 2012). The Organising Bureau of European School Student Unions (OBESSU) was founded in an effort to bring together school students from both sides of the Iron Curtain and came to play an important role in building capacity among existing national school student unions, representing students in secondary and vocational education, and helping to establish them where they did not yet exist.[1] The All-African Students' Union (AASU) was at its peak during this period, successfully uniting student movements that had played a crucial role in independence movements across the continent. In the 1990s, students in Asia established the Asia Students' and Youth Association (ASA). Until 2003, these regional movements maintained regular contact, even though IUS was perceived as communist and was then financially disabled (Deca, 2012).

In subsequent years, however, a number of factors eroded what remained of the global student movement. Out of many possible reasons, we highlight two. First, there was a lack of global education issues around which student organisations could organise. The MDGs did not include tertiary education, although some organisations attempted to make a case for 'Higher Education in Education for All'. The majority of student organisations were, and remain, focussed on tertiary education. Second, developing preoccupations with regional issues such as Latin American economic integration and the European integration of higher education systems meant student organisations turned their attention away from the global arena.

In Europe through the 2000s, ESIB slowly but steadily shifted its focus from information sharing and technical reporting to representation in policymaking processes. This development was a consequence of the Bologna Process (European Commission, 2019), in which ESIB had become the sole representative of the European student constituency. ESIB adapted its structure and changed its name to the European Students' Union to reflect its new foci (Klemenčič, 2012). Between 2008 and 2012, ESU had a working group on international cooperation, which initially made great headway, bringing together North American, African, Arab, and Asian student representatives, and applying for an international EU-funded Youth in Action project. The project application was, however, unsuccessful and deeper cooperation never materialised. The UK National Union of Students (NUS-UK) organised an international student summit in conjunction with their 90th anniversary in 2012, but there was no agreement on shared policies or a strategy for cooperation going forward. Meanwhile, OBESSU was focussing its energy on supporting the establishment of school student unions in Central and Eastern Europe. It attempted to build connections with school student unions in other regions, but most countries did not have such organisations, student representation being restricted to universities and other tertiary-level institutions. While there is a strong tradition of school student unionism in Latin America, OBESSU struggled to establish stable contact with these organisations, its interactions depending on the mediation of its Spanish member organisation, the *Confederación Estatal de Asociaciones de Estudiantes* (CANAE).

In Africa, AASU, which was based in Accra and had previously been highly successful, ran into a major leadership crisis, which it only began to overcome in 2012.[2] A number of unions had grown increasingly dissatisfied with the Ghanaian government's attempts to influence AASU, which had allegedly, in some cases, extended to rigging elections. Some of AASU's strongest member organisations had also been weakened with implementation of the World Bank's Structural Adjustment Policies across the continent. Others had been co-opted by their respective governments as partisan organisations (Luescher-Mamashela & Mugume, 2014). In Latin America, OCLAE continually attempted to revive IUS, within which it had been one of the most influential groups, but most of its member organisations were focussing on opposing the Latin American economic integration process, which had picked up pace around this time (Grugel & Singh, 2015).

It was in this context that UNESCO developed an interest in building momentum for a global student movement, holding the World Conference on Higher Education (WCHE) in 2009, at which students had their own parallel forum that fed into the plenary. Students had also been present at WCHE +5 in 2003, in larger numbers, in fact, but the forum did not present serious opportunities on which they could build. In preparation for the 2009 WCHE, UNESCO reached out to both national and regional student unions, the corporate representatives of the student constituency, as well as issue-based and party-aligned student organisations such as the *Association des Etats Généraux des Etudiants de l'Europe* (AEGEE) and the European Democrat Students (EDS) (UNESCO, 2009; Deca, 2012). The different backgrounds of the participating organisations, particularly their different attitudes to representativeness and partisanship, meant that the students were off to a bad start. It was hard to establish consensus about exactly what the students wanted, and how it could be achieved, given the significant differences in how the organisations were structured. As a result, the participants, who had not been extensively consulted in preparations for the forum, did not feel ownership of the process, resulting in a vague outcome document and little follow-up (Grønne, 2017).

Nevertheless, UNESCO was determined to continue its involvement with students. Among other things, it became engaged in a partnership between European and Asian students in an effort to build ASA's capacity, and supported ESU's working group on international cooperation to organise international student meetings at UNESCO headquarters in Paris during 2009 and 2010, in an attempt to offer a 'neutral' ground for the meetings. UNESCO also improved its connections with OCLAE through its regional office in Santiago (ESU, 2010). Despite UNESCO making headway, much if not all of this work was lost when its Higher Education Section was cut substantially in 2011, following the United States' decision to suspend funding for UNESCO. Consequently, students also turned their back on UNESCO, as there were no concrete projects, actions, or policies in which to engage.

About the same time, the Commonwealth nations launched the Commonwealth Students Association (CSA). Launched in 2012, CSA brings together student leaders from across the Commonwealth to advocate for student interests and strengthen the extent and quality of student representation. Backed by the expertise and resources of the Commonwealth Secretariat, CSA soon established itself as a strong platform, despite its lack of a formal governance structure (Day et al., 2016).

This was the backdrop against which students entered the debates around education in the post-2015 process. Student movements were well functioning at national level in much of the world, with the exceptions of Asia, the Middle East, and some parts of Africa, but there were almost no avenues of communication between the regions, nor was there any deeper understanding of the common struggles shared by students around the world. Despite UNESCO's involvement having peaked as recently as 2009/10, much of the experience had been lost by the time the post-2015 process had begun, not only in UNESCO, but in student organisations as well, due to their high turnover of activists, representatives, and staff members, and the disappearance of financial support for global cooperation. Finally, students were occupied with responding to the fallout from the 2008 economic crisis, in the aftermath of which sweeping changes were made to national education systems across the world.

3   Making an Impact on SDG 4

The Global EFA meeting held in Muscat in May 2014 represented a significant step in the process to agree on SDG 4, which culminated later at the World

Education Forum (WEF) in Incheon in May 2015 and at the United Nations General Assembly in New York in September 2015. At this early stage, the student constituency was not engaged in the discussions, and their absence was reflected in the Muscat Agreement. Aside from a brief mention of learners alongside other stakeholders such as families and communities, there was nothing in the document about the interests of students, their distinct place in education governance, or their role in negotiating and implementing the post-2015 agenda.

Over the next few months, the student constituency became more engaged. CSA, ESU, and OBESSU led the way, participating in discussions about the post-2015 agenda with UNESCO, the Commonwealth Secretariat, the European Union, and the Council of Europe. At its general assembly in May 2014, ESU established a working group on the topic, which was led by the National Union of Students in Norway (NSO), with student unions from Austria, Denmark, Latvia, Spain, and the United Kingdom also participating. It was only because NSO had been approached by the Norwegian government for its inputs to the negotiations that the process had caught the attention of ESU, which otherwise had not taken much note of the process.

ESU took part in the 2014 World Conference on Youth in Sri Lanka, which gathered almost 1,500 youth from across the world to deliberate on youth in the post-2015 process. The conference took place within the framework of the United Nations World Programme of Action for Youth and was the first time that ministers adopted a declaration together with youth representatives. Although the conference was hailed as a success by a number of organisations in the broader youth constituency and ministers, it largely proved a failure. Participants were selected on criteria that were not transparent, with some participants representing nobody but themselves and most participants coming from Southeast Asia or Africa, with the remaining regions poorly represented. The conference, which could have ignited a global wave of representative youth engagement in the post-2015 process, ended up as a footnote that never attracted notice outside the United Nations Economic and Social Council (ECOSOC). The conference's deliberations were never brought into the Open Working Group (OWG) on SDGs.

Following the World Conference on Youth, ESU engaged more proactively from the beginning of 2015, but by then the overarching framework for education 2030 was already in place. OBESSU engaged with the process in its own way. One of its board members was selected to be part of the Youth Advocacy Group of the Global Education First Initiative (GEFI). OBESSU actually had a mandate to speak on behalf of students, although this was not a criterion for GEFI, which was a group of hand-picked individuals. Through its resulting acquaintance with the United Nations system, OBESSU started to contribute to the positions of the UN Major Group for Children and Youth (UN MGCY).[3]

GEFI was not an initiative owned or spearheaded by student organisations, but since it was led by the UN Secretary General, it provided a certain level of access to the UN system for those selected to be involved. OBESSU also took a lead in developing the educational positions of the European Youth Forum, which was strongly involved in the OWG process through the UN MGCY. In its inputs, OBESSU supported the emerging focus on equal access to quality education, pushed for the inclusion of vocational and technical education, and highlighted the need for education to be safe, inclusive, and free of fees and hidden costs. ESU, OBESSU, and CSA followed the OWG proceedings with interest, occasionally participating in the consultations, but they did not have a strategy behind their advocacy. Without a permanent presence in New York, they had a limited ability to lobby member states, precluding a more sophisticated involvement with the process.

As Antonia Wulff points out in Chapter 2, at this stage it was also unclear from exactly which inputs the education agenda would be developed. Students focussed their attention on UNESCO, the institution with which they already had some familiarity. Looking back, had students had a better understanding of how the process would develop, it is fair to speculate they would have devoted more attention to the New York process. CSA had perhaps the greatest access to member states as their participation in the post-2015 process was supported by the Commonwealth Secretariat. As Commonwealth member states have some of the largest numbers of young people as a proportion of their population, the Secretariat had been pushing for a focus on youth in the post-2015 agenda and, in particular, for a specific youth goal. CSA lent its support to these positions but was not able to leverage its access to further the student agenda.

SDG 4 turned out to be relatively uncontroversial in the OWG process, although there was some debate about the extent to which education should be free as opposed to affordable. In these discussions, student organisations, like many other civil society actors, supported the language of universality and the language of rights, and advocated for free education. Perhaps the most contentious point on the student agenda was the inclusion of tertiary education. Most opposition on this point came from member states that wanted to reduce the number of targets, particularly the United Kingdom and Japan. Much of civil society did not push back: the basic education community tended to ignore tertiary education, while youth representatives were divided on the point. Actors from the Global North tended to support its inclusion, while those from the South felt it would be too much to take on in SDG 4. Some actors, such as GCE, did not focus on tertiary education in their initial position but came to embrace its inclusion later in the process.

Despite these reservations, both member states and civil society eventually came together to support a much broader education agenda than the MDGs had contained. For CSA, ESU, and OBESSU, the priority was to have their issues reflected in the targets: for CSA the mainstreaming of youth; for ESU higher education; for OBESSU secondary and vocational education; and for the three of them, a focus on access, quality, and inclusion. As the OWG process approached its conclusion, it seemed clear that these issues would indeed be reflected in the OWG proposal for the SDGs, and so CSA, ESU, and OBESSU did not attempt to intensify their involvement in the process. Although they were not as involved as other educational stakeholders or youth organisations, CSA, ESU, and OBESSU regarded themselves, and the student movement as a whole, as among the most important stakeholders in SDG 4. Still, each organisation was restricted for its own reasons: CSA because, as a newly founded organisation, they had not established channels of institutional access beyond those provided by the Secretariat; and ESU and OBESSU because they did not have much spare capacity to engage in United Nations processes in addition to their day-to-day advocacy with the European institutions. For ESU and OBESSU in particular, there was also the problem that their member organisations, which dictated their strategic direction and priorities, had, with a few exceptions, little awareness of or interest in the post-2015 process, regarding it as distant, abstract, and peripheral to their concerns.

As the OWG process drew to a close, student organisations attempted to bring the post-2015 agenda closer to the grassroots through International Students Day. Observed on 17 November every year, the date commemorates the Nazi storming of Czech universities in 1939 and the subsequent internment and execution of students. It was observed for many years, especially in Central and Eastern Europe, but after the collapse of the Berlin Wall and the subsequent crisis within IUS, commemorations became sporadic and uncoordinated. It was not until the 2004 World Social Forum in Mumbai that International Students Day was relaunched, with ESU and OBESSU providing international coordination ever since.

In the summer of 2014, OBESSU, in consultation with ESU, decided to launch a global call for action, which, on the 10th anniversary of the Mumbai forum, aimed to bring together students on every continent behind a common agenda. It was an ambitious project given the disconnect between student movements around the world. ESU and OBESSU worked together regularly, they had contacts with the North American unions and had recently started to work with CSA on the post-2015 agenda, but there was little communication between them, OCLAE, AASU, and the member organisations of those platforms. It was decided that the call for action should focus on the post-2015 agenda, as a process in which student organisations around the world shared a common interest.

A call for action was launched, which included the demands for education to be free of costs and fees, free of discrimination, and free of fear, and called on the United Nations to prioritise free, equal access to quality education and safe learning environments in the post-2015 agenda. The call was initially signed by ESU, OBESSU, the United States Student Association (USSA), and the Canadian Federation of Students (CFS). Over the following weeks, more than 30 organisations, representing students from 97 countries across every continent, signed the call, with nonstudent organisations such as Education International (EI) also declaring their support.

On 17 November 2014, hundreds of thousands of students mobilised, with demonstrations and commemorations in over 40 countries. Students from secondary, higher education, and vocational systems participated in actions related to issues as diverse as rising tuition fees, changes to student evaluation, and the militarisation of schools and campuses. The scale and scope of these events took OBESSU and ESU by surprise. With this commemoration, the student constituency asserted that they are indeed an active stakeholder in global education and, in the post-2015 process, that they have common interests across the world, which they expected to be recognised and reflected in the Agenda. It was also a moment for the student movement to reassert the fundamental principles of access, quality, inclusion, and equity for which it stands, and to demonstrate its strength and unity. A few weeks later, UN Secretary-General Ban Ki-Moon released his Synthesis Report, which broadly accepted the proposals of the OWGs. ESU and OBESSU were pleased about the inclusion of higher education, secondary, and vocational education, while CSA was disappointed but unsurprised by the absence of a youth goal.

Student organisations continued to participate in the process through the Regional Ministerial Meetings during the spring of 2015. The meetings were organised by UNESCO and aimed at collecting input to and building consensus around the outcome document of the WEF that was hosted in Incheon, South Korea, in May of that year. CSA was given an opportunity to provide input into the Commonwealth's shared position for the African Regional Meeting in Kigali, as well as to the national position of Kenya, the latter owing to the then-Interim President working in the UNESCO National Commission. For CSA, the highest priority was now student mobility, specifically a strong draft of Target 4.b on scholarships. Student participation at the actual meeting was, however, completely lacking. It has been claimed that this was because certain states worked actively to prevent students from entering the space, as well as there being a lack of funding for them to participate. At the Europe and North America Regional Ministerial Conference in Paris, the ministers assembled included the most significant mention of students in the official documents to date. In the 'Education for Sustainable Development and Global Citizenship Education' section of the Paris Statement was the following:

> We recognise that the participation of children, students and young people in education governance, can help develop skills such as problem solving, critical thinking, and decision making, and strengthen the behavioural capacities required to effectively engage in society. We commit to strengthen existing and emerging education governance processes in formal and non-formal contexts and ensure the active involvement of children, students and young people, parents, families and communities and work with them to monitor the quality of educational services. (UNESCO, 2015d, p. 4)

This was an important commitment to the participation of students in education governance and, by extension, to the involvement of students in implementing, monitoring, and evaluating the Agenda. European governments had previously demonstrated their commitment to student participation in education governance in documents of the European Commission and the Bologna Process, the passage on students in the Paris Statement was successfully advocated by ESU, which was present at the meeting. It helpfully provided official support for including students in the Framework for Action (FFA).

The Paris Statement was also the first time that the notion of 'learner-centred learning' was introduced into the process. The notion has since become contested, in that private providers argue it refers to free school choice, but ESU had advocated a flipping of the classroom, with the teacher making learners and their needs the centre of attention. Other important issues addressed during the Regional Conference from the perspective of students included an entire rewrite of the paragraph relating to the labour market, traditionally a point of contention between student unions and governments, and as well as committing to ensuring that draft Target 4.b should not lead to a brain-drain effect from the Global South to the Global North, which, it was thought, would ultimately hold back sustainable development.

In many ways, the Paris meeting proved groundbreaking for ESU's involvement in the process. EI and ESU had only ever cooperated on European policy, and due to the limited scope of the MDGs, ESU had also never come into contact with the GCE. The overlapping interests of ESU and GCE were, however, realised in Paris, and ESU's involvement developed largely thanks to the support from EI and GCE, which would later prove students' only point of access to the negotiating table. Nevertheless, ESU's late involvement with EI and GCE goes to show how little insight into global processes it had from the outset of the negotiations.

By the time of the WEF in Incheon, in May 2015, the goals and targets of SDG 4 had taken shape. UNESCO actively encouraged student participation at the meeting but at this point, it was too late for them to have a meaningful impact. While the NGO Forum offered some space for students to influence the discourse of the gathering, most of the policy developments took place in the drafting committee of the main forum, which was limited to the EFA Steering Committee, and saw neither student, nor youth, representation. Member states were reluctant to discuss the issues dealt with in the drafting committee, and as a result, students relied on representatives from EI and GCE to carry their voice into that committee. Student representatives were also absent from the plenary sessions. While GEFI participated in one plenary session, no elected student representative ever took the plenary stage, which once again shows a lack of recognition. Student representatives were not helped by their lack of coordinated representation.

The WEF mirrored the WCHE failure to meaningfully engage students. To make things worse, the UNESCO Youth Forum a few months later repeated this failure: students and youth were given a dedicated space out of a genuine interest to engage them, but since this space to build capacity and ideas was not followed by a genuine chance to impact the main conference, for example, by discussing the outcome in plenary, putting forward motions, or having a seat at the table where the main outcome was drafted, the Youth Forum remained a tokenistic attempt at inclusion.

4   Getting the Implementation Framework Right

After the SDGs were adopted, students and the rest of the education community slowly started shifting their focus to the FFA. The drafting of the FFA was done in a closed drafting committee carried over from the WEF without any student representation.

At this late stage in the process, discussions had also shifted to financing and indicators. It was at this point that student participation in the post-2015 process reached its limits. While student organisations were aware of the Inter-Agency Expert Group on SDG Indicators (IAEG-SDGs), the Financing for

Development, and other processes that would come to shape the actual implementation of the SDGs, they did not have the access or technical expertise to engage in them.

In these processes, students had a strong claim to participation, both as the recipients of education, and as partners in the formulation, implementation, and monitoring of the Agenda. But students were not invited, despite requests to be included. These experiences point to one of the student movement's central challenges: had it been a national process, students could have protested, staged media events, metaphorically kicked in the door to the meeting room, and made their voices heard. Yet all these 'traditional' strategies fall short because when the discussions go global there are hardly any meaningful places to protest. International media are not concerned with the student voice, and with limited funding, students cannot justify paying their own way to meetings, only to be refused entrance at the door. The experience shows the need for students to rethink how they engage in international negotiations. From the European side, ESU attempted to mobilise their national members around the national discussions on SDG indicators and in that way influence the IAEG-SDG, but lack of technical capacity and the complex nature of the process meant the students could not make themselves relevant. Ultimately, student influence was limited to providing inputs to EI and GCE, which those organisations then carried into the closed EFA Steering Committee, directly or in the case of EI also through the Workers and Trade Unions Major Group.

The failure to develop effective lobbying strategies points to a challenge of paramount importance: If students want to succeed in the global arena in the future, they must build a better understanding of the international and intergovernmental bureaucracies, and learn how to both influence the system from the outside, for example by writing formal letters to the UNESCO Director-General, or from the inside, by putting forward a legitimate claim to student representation in all these processes.

UNESCO offered a small gesture of recognition to students when it gave ESU the opportunity to address the Special High-Level Meeting on the FFA for Education 2030, but as youth delegates rather than student representatives. UNESCO insisted the seat be given to a participant from the UNESCO Youth Forum, which in itself had placed more emphasis on individuals than democratic representation. It was only because ESU's representative had also participated at the forum as a national expert, nominated by the National Union of Students (Denmark), that UNESCO agreed. This experience highlights UNESCO's continued problems with recognising the distinct differences between the youth and student constituencies.

It is difficult to account for this change in UNESCO's approach to youth and students between 2011 and 2015. A possible explanation is that the coordination of the process was handled by a dedicated EFA team within UNESCO's Education Sector, which did not have the same understanding of the student constituency or experience in cooperating with students as UNESCO's former Higher Education Section. Another possible explanation is that the UNESCO Youth Strategy simply does not recognise students. It focusses solely on youth as a homogeneous group, in line with the broader UN Youth Strategy. Unfortunately, this means it does not recognise the differences that exist within the youth demographic with regards to educational status, a distinction of particular importance in UNESCO's area of work. Students are a distinct and central educational stakeholder, with democratically accountable and representative organisations. UNESCO's failure to recognise this demands continued attention and eventual resolution.

Whilst the post-2015 process has been widely described as the most extensive UN consultation in history, as well as one of the most participatory and open intergovernmental negotiation processes, the failure of institutions to engage the student constituency on SDG 4 indicates a fundamental problem with their approach to consultation. In order to elucidate the criticism, we believe it is instructive to establish a distinction between an inclusive process and a democratic process. In an inclusive process, there is an extensive consultation in which the institutions welcome inputs from every organisation that claims to have an interest in the process and considers those inputs to have more or less equal weight. In a democratic process, there is a similarly extensive consultation, but in addition, the representatives of the constituencies concerned have a seat on the relevant committees and working groups so that decisions can be codetermined between the authorities and the representatives of the constituencies affected.

In their approach to negotiating SDG 4, the institutions betrayed a conceptual confusion, operating an inclusive process with sporadic elements of a democratic process. In the EFA Steering Committee, the teacher constituency was afforded representation but the student constituency was not. In justifying their inclusion, the institutions argued that teachers are integral to the educational process and should be welcomed as partners in the development, implementation, and monitoring of SDG 4. Yet students are similarly central to the educational process and to include teachers without including these other constituencies is inconsistent. It is an oversight that has consequences for the legitimacy of the consultative process and for the prospects for successful implementation. It created a process that prioritised organisations with the most resources. Further, in neglecting to consider students as equal partners, the institutions missed an opportunity to harness the grassroots force of their civil society networks to mobilise behind the agenda. While the special consideration given to teachers partly reflects their greater strategic engagement with the process and their having a global confederation of unions, which students do not have, it also conveys a certain ignorance in the institutions concerning the role of students in education policy and practice.

5   Engaging Students Globally in SDG 4

By 2016, member states had agreed to the most ambitious education goal the world had seen. Students had some success: tertiary education as well as vocational and technical education had been included in the goal; the language around labour market involvement had been softened; the right to free quality education had been reaffirmed, although still only progressively at tertiary level; scholarships had been included in a more sustainable way; and the distinct position of students in monitoring and implementing the goal had, to some extent, been recognised in the FFA. Yet, these victories did not come simply because of student advocacy. In fact, students were not primarily responsible for achieving these victories, with broader civil society organisations playing a larger role. Still, there is no doubt that student involvement, though limited to just a few actors, bolstered the move toward a broad and progressive agenda and pushed SDG 4 in a student-friendly direction, while also affirming students as vanguards of equitable access to quality education that takes a whole-learner approach and rejects narrow definitions of learning.

As the focus shifted from negotiating the goals to actually realising them, students once again had to reframe the work within their own movements in order to make it relevant to the struggles that students face at the grassroots level. An example of this was OBESSU, ESU, EI, and initially the European University Association developing 'A Joint Vision for Secondary and Higher Education for All in Europe', outlining how SDG 4 could be implemented in Europe in the area of secondary and tertiary education. For instance, it linked Target 4.5 on ensuring equal access to education with the need to develop National Access Plans that was already agreed upon in the Bologna Process. But despite external funding, ESU still struggled to convince the national unions to embrace the SDGs. There is a general consensus among them that the SDGs are important, and some unions like NUS-UK and the National Union of Students in Denmark have engaged actively with them in their policy work. Still, there is a long way to go before the SDGs are fully integrated and utilised in student advocacy at the national level, as well as through the local initiatives in which they engage, including quality assurance, curriculum development, and extra-curricular activities.

In terms of the other regional platforms of student organisations, OCLAE has taken the opposite approach in Latin America to the Europeans. View-ing the SDGs as an attempt to mainstream capitalist development around the world, OCLAE, an avowedly socialist platform, continues to refrain from engaging directly in SDG 4. The irony, though, is that much of OCLAE's work is aligned with the goal: they emphasise a universal right to free education; they highly prioritise active citizenship education, even if it does not necessarily have a global dimension, and they view education as a way of empowering people to develop themselves and their societies.

Suffering from limited capacity to participate during the negotiations, AASU is now focussed on working proactively with the SDGs. The Secretary-General elected in 2016 has established a unit to work solely with the SDGs.

Meanwhile in North America, CFS and USSA have followed the SDG process from the sidelines. CFS seems keen to mainstream all 17 SDGs across their work and has a broad mandate to engage in societal discussions. Combined with a strong representation of indigenous students, many of whom still face major obstacles to accessing education and basic rights in general, CFS has also sig-nalled its intentions to engage with other areas such as SDG 6 on water and sanitation, and SDG 13 on climate action.

Coordinating these efforts globally remains difficult for students. The latest attempt came in May 2016, when tertiary-level students from 16 countries met in Bergen, Norway, for the Global Student Voice meeting organised by NSO. They adopted the Bergen Declaration, which not only outlines the representa-tives' priorities for education but also aims to establish the meetings as a tra-dition. Although the Bergen Declaration does not mention the SDGs, due to opposition from OCLAE, it reaffirms the students' commitment to implement-ing SDG 4, such as when it discusses the existing development model:

> Further, we also claim that education is one of the most important tools for providing global citizens with the necessary skills and opportunities to fight climate change, empowering individuals and building resilient communities that will challenge the current development model which is causing harm to the planet and its people. (Global Student Voice, 2016, p. 4)

The National Union of Students in Brazil (UNE) volunteered to host a 2nd Stu-dent Voice Meeting in 2017. It was postponed twice due to a lack of funding. At the time of writing, discussion about a potential 2nd Meeting still regularly surfaces between national student unions, but it remains to be seen who will be able to gather all the different student unions and organise the event. As this demonstrates, students themselves are usually in no position to cover travel costs, as they are already burdened by student debt, and their organisations often have limited resources, too, being unable to collect substantial membership dues directly from students. This stands in stark contrast to teacher, head teacher, and rector conferences, which tend to enjoy reliable financial backing from their members. Thus, if there is a genuine desire to better include students at the global level, financial resources must be mobilised. But it remains to be seen if students can manage to unite behind one shared set of principles. The SDGs offer a common narrative, but as shown above, differences in the unions' support for the SDGs mean it is highly unlikely.

The FFA did leave the possibility for students to take on a role in the global governance of SDG 4 through a youth seat in the Education 2030 Global Steering Committee, though the process around the selection of the youth representative was unclear. Ultimately, a participant from the 2015 UNESCO Youth Forum was selected to sit on the Steering Committee, without a mandate from students anywhere in the world, yet another failure to recognise the distinction between youth and students, and a prioritisation of individuals over representative organisations. It is worth noting that UNESCO frames the Youth Forum as the democratic body through which youth can influence the organisation, but in reality, the past fora have tended to emphasise personal excellence above democratic organisations. Coupled with an unclear decision-making process when drafting, adopting, and presenting the Forum's recommendations, it cannot be taken as democratic, nor in any way representative of youth globally. As the Steering Committee composition rotated at the beginning of 2018, UNESCO once again selected an individual participant from the 9th UNESCO Youth Forum in 2015, although this time the person did represent an organisation working on education. That organisation, however, was founded by the individual herself, and does not have any democratic avenues through which members can seek to influence it.

UNESCO continues to argue that the failure of students to organise on the global level means that no one can legitimately claim the seat on behalf of the constituency. Although partially true, the explanation opens up a discussion about the standard of representativeness to which student organisations are held. Four representative regional bodies exist globally across three regions (ESU, AASU, OCLAE, and OBESSU), not counting USSA and CFS in North America, which do not have a formal partnership, yet rather than offer the seat to one of these, or mediate an ad hoc solution such as a system of rotating the seat or establishing a consultative council, it was decided to offer the seat to an individual young person. This decision shows how meaningful involvement of students suffers from a UN-wide attempt at mainstreaming youth, which is often more concerned with the age of the individuals, than with whether they have a mandate from the constituency on behalf of whom they claim to speak. This narrow focus is not only undemocratic but also significantly reduces the quality of the youth input, thereby missing out on essential insights from a constituency with firsthand expertise. It is a practice that is completely at odds with that applied to other stakeholders, such as trade unions and indigenous people, and calls for reconsideration in the future. Allowing students into the Steering Committee would have positive implications for UNESCO and the broader SDG 4 agenda as the student movement would become more deeply invested in the success of the agenda, and thereby more effectively engaged at the grassroots level, too. It is a genuine problem in international politics that young people are not viewed as equal stakeholders who should be afforded a seat at the table where decisions about their lives and future are made. The intentions to offer youth a dedicated space are good and should not be discouraged, but what matters the most is that young people's democratic organisations are given the same voice in decision-making as those of their older peers.

For now, this leaves students to structure their engagement with the SDGs on their own. One possible approach, which was aired by Southern African and Canadian students, and which is likely to find support in Europe, too, is for students to provide shadow data and reportage on the implementation of SDG 4. While students were effectively unable to engage in the development of the indicators, they still have a proud tradition of reporting on the actual developments at ground level. This expertise can be leveraged at all levels – national, regional, and global – to challenge the positive framing on their progress that states will inevitably present at the High-Level Political Forum on Sustainable Development (HLPF), the apex body for the follow-up and review of the implementation of the 2030 Agenda, and other similar fora, like the Regional Forum for Sustainable Development (RFSD). The Global Education Monitoring Report (GEMR) Secretariat has already taken a step in this direction, by inviting European and South African student representatives to contribute to the GEMR 2017 and publishing a dedicated youth report with support from student unions as well as other education ambassadors (UNESCO, 2017b), but the involvement can, and should, be developed further. Students themselves could benefit from publishing their own comprehensive reports.

That said, students do not yet seem to be in a position where developing these reports independently is feasible. The issue is not as much about resources, though this is a challenge to students, as about the structure and culture of the student movement. Historically, education policy has always been a domestic responsibility. Europe has moved beyond this slightly with the Bologna and Copenhagen Processes. This reality is also reflected in how students are organised, the strategies they deploy, and in their analytical lens. Increasingly though, education policy is being globalised, not only because of SDG4, but through global conventions, trade agreements, and the like. In Chapter 12, Clara Fontdevila describes an example of this development. The student movement needs to reconfigure itself to be better attuned to the international dimension of contemporary education policy. No radical change is demanded, but students must embed the global perspective into their existing argumentation and activities. The existence of international education agendas is, however, not just a challenge, for it can also offer students increased leverage with governments by giving them a new range of tools to hold governments to account.

For all the reasons just given, it is evident that there is a genuine need for students to come together globally and claim a voice, if they want to retain influence over the education systems in which their members find themselves. From our interviews with student leaders and coordinators of wider youth-led platforms, it is clear that there is support across the board for organising students globally. However, it is also clear that there continue to be major ideological differences between students, just as old misconceptions continue to breed distrust, particularly between the Latin American and European representatives. As such, any future attempt at organising must be sufficiently flexible that everyone can see themselves represented in it, while also being sufficiently strong that student unions will see the added value. There are two primary ways in which this can be achieved: either students start off with technical cooperation, building a platform that is devoid of policies, focussed on exchanging information, statistics, and common positions that benefit all members of the platform, or they focus their attention on universal student struggles around which they can achieve consensus, forming a more political sort of association. Having reviewed student-formulated documents, the most likely topics around which they might find consensus are the cost of education, students as equal stakeholders in education governance, and equity in education systems. The existing regional student bodies function as gatekeepers to the national unions, and any future platform must win support from the regional bodies but be centred around the national unions.

Even if a global student platform is limited to technical cooperation or to the three topics listed previously, it will still be able to engage with the SDGs. For the first part, the increased technical capacity, stemming from technical cooperation, will allow students to better follow and impact the global agenda through their governments. Should the students successfully manage to organise around a political union, the three topics outlined above all have major implications for the SDGs, and in particular SDG targets 4.1 and 4.3, which are of relevance to the entire student constituency.

Failing to mobilise globally will have serious ramifications for student engagement in the implementation of SDG 4 and leave students exposed to future global processes that might be outright hostile to students. A process without the corporate influence of the student constituency may, by forgoing the positive influences on policymaking mentioned in our introduction, lead to less efficient resource distribution and management, and to outcomes antithetical to student interests such as reduced access, increased fees, poorer quality, the closing off of avenues for students to influence on the national level, and so on. As our account shows, the primary reason given by UNESCO and the broader UN system for excluding representative student voices, is the fact that no single organisation can legitimately claim to be representative of all the world's students. While this holds students to a higher level of representativeness than other constituencies, we also have to acknowledge that establishing a platform of cooperation, even if initially fragile or superficial, would mean that students have a stronger claim to participation.

6   Lessons for the Student Constituency

A number of different lessons can be drawn from the student constituency's participation in the post-2015 process, both for student unions and for the institutions. It became clear during the OWG process that if AASU, CSA, ESU, OBESSU, and OCLAE do not participate in meetings at the UN in New York, then other individuals and organisations, which though not actually representative of the constituency, will claim the mantle of the student representatives. It is not helped by the UN not recognising, and seemingly not understanding, the distinction between the student and youth constituencies, the composition of the student constituency, and the differing representativeness of different organisations. Nor is it helped by the UN's tendency to select individual advocates rather than representative organisations to participate in its processes, which undermines proper democratic representation. The UN and UNESCO in particular should make an active effort to engage independent, democratic, and representative student unions, and to ensure their deep and continued involvement throughout the monitoring, implementation, and evaluation of the SDGs, as well as in all stages of future sustainable development processes. This is important not only to improve the scope, diversity, and representativeness of the UN's inputs from civil society but to harness the reach, capacity,

and influence of student organisations around the world to promote education and sustainable development.

Had students had more meaningful ways of engaging in the post-2015 negotiations, or, for that matter, other international standard-setting instruments
in the education sphere, we would be looking at a different global education
landscape today. Students' dream of a free and accessible education system
that empowers its learners and prepares them to engage with their society all
too often suffers because of agendas narrowly aimed at developing a skilled
labour force, which neglect the role of education in building an open society.

The student movement also has lessons to learn. AASU, CSA, ESU, OBESSU,
and OCLAE understand that they are broadly united behind the same values,
but their attitude toward, and capacity to engage in, institutional processes
differs considerably. AASU has an impressive history but continues to suffer
in the aftermath of its recent leadership crisis. It requires support from other
actors in terms of membership development, capacity building, and financing
in order to take its place at the table. ESU and OBESSU have years of experience engaged in institutional processes, those of the European Union and the
Council of Europe especially, but their capacity to engage in United Nations
processes is lacking. In order to improve their engagement, they need to dedicate resources to improving their understanding of the actors, issues, and processes, and to developing an advocacy strategy and to proactively intervening
in discussions; they would benefit from support and advice from organisations with similar values and objectives in doing this. CSA needs to continue to
strengthen its membership base, and thus bolster its own representativeness,
and to engage more strategically in the interactions with member states, which
its relationship to the Commonwealth Secretariat affords them the opportunity to do. With the formal establishment of the organisation, and the election
of a new Executive Committee in February 2018, which includes experienced
student activists, CSA seems to have taken a leap forward. OCLAE may have
chosen to reject the SDGs, but it would be beneficial if they engaged in dialogue about their concerns with the other regional platforms. In fact, all of the
regional platforms need to improve their communication and coordination
with each other to share information and, where there is an appetite to do so,
to develop shared policy positions and a shared advocacy strategy. This would
help student unions break out of the cycle of neglecting and rebuilding their
international contact over and over again.

Before entering global negotiations, students need to have clearer objectives and a strategy for how to achieve them. In the post-2015 process, students
worked primarily through their regional platforms, which led to bottlenecks
in their influence, particularly when those platforms were not given sufficient

recognition. While negotiations took place at the global level, students should have leveraged their national connections to influence the priorities of member states and ultimately the global agenda (see Chapter 2 by Antonia Wulff for a discussion of the OWG and member states' failure to involve national CSOs in determining their country positions). NSO in Norway remains the only national union to have done so in the post-2015 process. European students especially have extensive experience with coordinating national advocacy to influence international negotiations, as their strong influence on the Bologna Process testifies, and they should do the same in UN processes. Achieving such success requires not only cooperation from national governments but also that students establish, early in the negotiations, a shared understanding of how the process will impact students, and thus how it should be shaped.

7   Looking Ahead to Implementation

In the decade following the 2008 financial crisis, students have once again come to the fore as activists in their education systems and societies. Students in Chile and Colombia successfully waged protests against their governments to combat privatisation and a narrow focus on the needs of the labour market. Across the US, students are mobilising against tuition fee increases, which cause a debt burden that crushes young people. Students at the University of Cape Town led protests for a decolonised education system, as represented by their opposition to the statue of Cecil Rhodes, and then again later when students at the University of the Witwatersrand sparked national demonstrations against proposed fee increases. In Burma, students marched to the capital when new legislation severely limited their right to self-government and imposed restrictions on academic freedom. And the list goes on: in Denmark, Zimbabwe, Burkina Faso, UK, Japan, South Korea, Brazil, Mexico, and Bangladesh students have been standing up to injustices in the education system and broader society (Grønne, 2017).

These grassroots struggles for access, quality, and equity continue, far removed from considerations of SDG 4. The adoption of that agenda has not given direction to their struggles or even to the language of their struggles, and it has not led to more cooperative attitudes from government. It certainly does not seem to have any bearing on the subjects of students' own struggles, which are determined by the corporate interests of their constituency, but more importantly, by their vision of education as a human right, a public good, and a means to personal and social emancipation. For many education activists, those values are at the heart of what SDG 4 is, or at least should be, about.

Nevertheless, most student activists are unaware that SDG 4 exists or do not see SDG 4 as useful to their causes. While many SDG activists are young people, they seem to be focussed on goals other than SDG 4. From a global perspective, the SDGs continue to struggle to establish themselves as a global standard. Young activists from the Global North working to implement the SDGs are still primarily occupied with devising and implementing projects in the Global South, rather than with their own local constituencies.

It would be easy then to dismiss SDG 4 as a bureaucratic exercise, more for administrators and statisticians than for students, parents, and teachers, but that would be a mistake. It matters at the grassroots level. It represents a commitment made by states in front of the international community. It provides civil society with a standard against which to hold their governments to account. Young people, and students in particular, have a vital role to play in campaigning for the SDGs and ensuring they are mainstreamed across the institutions in which students find themselves. There is no reason why schools and universities would not commit to the SDGs; integrate them into their curricula; adapt their operations to support the realisation of the agenda; and become SDG laboratories, whereby campuses are opened up to the surrounding community to experiment with the SDGs, and where research expertise can be offered on how to advance their implementation. Campaigning for this would give students a strong voice in how their education systems are shaped. Diving deeper into the FFA and the 2030 Agenda text, it becomes clear that the SDGs can also guide practical actions, such as creating new modes of learning; breaking down barriers to education; investing in education and research; and ensuring a vibrant institutional democracy – issues around which student movements have traditionally campaigned.

Students also have to recognise their privileged position in society vis-à-vis less educated members of society and make efforts to implement the broader 2030 Agenda. After all, the SDGs are interconnected, and SDG 4 can only facilitate the implementation of the remaining 16 goals if students develop their capacity, familiarise themselves with the goals and efforts to realise them and help to implement the entire agenda at the local level. Even if some student movements are not mandated by their members to work outside questions of education, there is no reason why student activists could not engage themselves outside the student movement itself and build a parallel SDG movement led by students.

Given the fact that regional platforms are only as strong as their members, it is perhaps too much to expect the SDGs to filter down from the regional platforms to local level. Instead, the success of student efforts to guide the implementation of SDG 4 starts with the local and national movements picking up the baton themselves. Peer-learning, and indeed activists and organisations inspiring each other, will be key in ensuring broader student action on the SDGs. We do see some movements starting to take action, such as the NUS-UK, which has implemented an ambitious sustainability strategy rooted in the SDGs. Yet more movements will have to come forward and showcase the tangible change created through the SDG framework in order for that framework to gain traction among students.

Student action now shapes students' ability to influence future development processes, something which they should be concerned about as education policies are increasingly decided at international level. This development poses new challenges to student movements, as they must reinvent their activism and advocacy to make an impact in the global arena, from which it has otherwise been absent for many years. Ultimately, engaging students in SDG 4 and beyond should concern the education community as a whole. The member states should be held accountable to the 2030 Agenda for Sustainable Development at the grassroots level, as the amalgam of local struggles and actions, rather than only in rarefied meetings in New York. If this is to happen, students will have to fulfil their role.

8   Recent Developments

At its 6th World Assembly, the GCE at long last elected its first ever student-led organisation to its board. In 2015, the GCE had already recognised the need to include the constituency for whom it worked to make a positive difference in its decision-making processes. The result was that two seats on the board were reserved for youth- and student-led organisations. As GCE at the time did not have an eligible member, the seats were occupied by representatives from organisations working with youth and students rather than youth- and student-led organisations.

In 2018, the GCE still only had one full member eligible to be designated youth- or student-led: the European Students' Union. The GCE had recognised that they could not build a youth and student movement around one organisation. With support from ActionAid and Plan International, they organised a youth caucus side event at the World Assembly, where national and regional coalitions were encouraged to send youth delegates identified within their networks. The members of the youth caucus were largely given freedom to organise the side event themselves, which presented an opportunity to discuss shared struggles and, not least, wishes for the global movement. The caucus also unanimously put forward ESU as a representative for the youth and student caucus during elections. *Studentenes og Akademikernes Internasjonale Hjelpefond* (Students' and Academics' International Assistance Fund – SAIH), a Norwegian student NGO working to develop higher education and protect academic freedom, was also elected, but for the seat of the Northern Coalition.

The election of ESU and SAIH to the GCE Board testifies to a movement that recognises that it is accountable toward those same people on whose behalf they claim to be acting. But the way GCE approached the election is also interesting, because, in realising that no legitimate youth or student union with a global mandate existed, and would not come into existence any time soon, GCE chose to create its own constituency at the global level, based on the idea that representatives would at least face some degree of accountability.

In many ways, the GCE student and youth caucus does respond to many of the issues raised throughout this chapter. It seeks to ensure legitimate representation through some sort of elections open to everyone, aggregating opinions of the constituency, and it attempts to balance the Global North's stronger unions with participation from activists from the Global South.

That said, the current structure of the youth caucus is problematic. It faces challenges of representativeness, because many of its participants are either from youth sections of, or closely associated with and dependent on, GCE's existing members. As such, there is a risk that the representatives in the youth caucus simply end up carrying the policies of their 'adult' NGOs into the youth caucus.

Similarly, several of the participants in the youth caucus did not hold any sort of elected position but were instead chosen by existing GCE members based on their personal merits. While participants selected in this way can certainly bring forward novel and constructive ideas, the fact remains that they are not accountable to anyone. This way of selecting participants also has the unfortunate side effect of blurring the distinction between the youth and student constituencies.

While GCE at global level has at last acted justly with its youth constituency, the change has not taken root among all of its national and regional coalitions. Some youth and student participants are not welcome in their own coalitions, due to a range of issues, such as not being able to pay the membership fees or not being recognised by all members of the coalitions. This obviously also weakens GCE's global efforts to increase their own accountability.

Still, with its youth caucus, GCE and the youth and students involved exemplify the difficulty of walking the fine line between tokenism and genuine inclusion. Despite the challenges briefly outlined above, the youth caucus remains an initiative that should be applauded and followed with great interest. Many of its challenges can be worked out, and a group of participants in the caucus are already working to set up structures that promise to increase its independence and representativeness. These ambitions, however, will require additional support from GCE and its international non-governmental organisation members if they are to succeed.

Notes

1   https://obessu.org/about/about-us/
2   Information about AASU is taken from a document entitled *History of* AASU, which formerly appeared on the AASU website (www.aasuonline.org), which is no longer available on the Internet.
3   The Major Group for Children and Youth is a space for the children and youth constituency to organise within United Nations sustainable development processes.

CHAPTER 17

The Right to Education and SDG 4: Lessons from the Field and Next Steps for Civil Society Monitoring

Allyson Krupar and Anjela Taneja

1   Introduction

To fulfil Sustainable Development Goal 4 (SDG 4), governments have committed to work toward specific targets using agreed-upon monitoring indicators and processes. A core principle of SDG 4 is that 'education is a fundamental human right and an enabling right' (UNESCO, 2016d, p. 2). SDG 4 reiterates governments' commitments to uphold and respect the right to education, as codified in international law. This codification and associated rights-based approaches to achieving SDG 4 help civil society organisations (CSOs) hold governments accountable for their obligations. More than three years into the SDG period, it is time to revisit the extent to which rights-based approaches inform CSO-led SDG 4 monitoring. Monitoring undertaken by civil society and citizens at large can make a valuable contribution toward creating a bottom-up push for SDG 4 implementation. This chapter seeks to understand the emerging civil society practices used to monitor SDG 4 implementation by drawing on rights-based approaches, to evaluate such approaches in CSO-led SDG monitoring, and to identify possible best practices. Findings can support CSOs and national monitoring bodies to integrate rights-based approaches in SDG 4 monitoring.

Implementation of the SDGs has been slow, partly as a result of the design of the 2030 Agenda. The SDGs' low level of obligation and weak enforcement mechanisms allowed member states to agree to the framework and resulted in the agenda's universal endorsement, but credible follow-up, review, and monitoring mechanisms are critical to ensuring the SDGs' long-term impact. Civil society can undertake policy monitoring by identifying areas in which current policies fall short of SDG 4 commitments. CSOs can also participate in SDG 4 review processes, initiate their own reviews, and generate evidence on implementation. CSOs' evidence can be used for to enforce formal accountability and redress mechanisms through existing state and international channels, to support the filing of complaints, and to provide information for human rights

© KONINKLIJKE BRILL NV, LEIDEN, 2020 | DOI: 10.1163/9789004430365_017

reviews. This chapter explores how civil society is undertaking these functions early in SDG 4 implementation.

The SDGs constitute a new development regime built on the Millennium Development Goals (MDGs) and for SDG 4 on the Education for All (EFA) movement (Tikly, 2017). In turn, the SDGs affect, and are affected by, other closely aligned regimes, including aid, trade, security, and human rights. International regimes encompass a range of 'implicit or explicit principles, norms, rules, and decision-making procedures around which actors' expectations converge' (Krasner, 1982, p. 186; Tikly, 2017). Each of these regimes, consequently, provide for additional accountability structures, needs, and entry points for SDG monitoring. This proliferation of spaces where aspects of the SDGs are monitored, combined with weak accountability for their implementation, creates challenges for nonstate actors seeking to monitor and support their implementation.

We first situate current efforts and past experiences using rights-based approaches to monitor national commitments to achieve international benchmarks. We also present methods to monitor SDG 4 fulfilment, drawing on diverse experiences from civil society. We specifically discuss the Right to Education Index (RTEI) and related advocacy strategies as a potential resource to enhance monitoring and inform implementation. Drawing on civil society engagement, we highlight advocacy implications and data gaps in existing SDG 4 monitoring tools and practices. To do so, we drew on evidence from operations reported by 26 individuals surveyed from diverse CSOs working worldwide, with four follow-up, in-depth interviews. We also conducted a qualitative meta-analysis of CSO-published reports and online content related to rights-based approaches and SDG 4 monitoring. We conclude that national-level advocacy in collaboration with international networks and partnerships, building on strategies such as those implemented by CSOs surveyed here, are key to rights-based approaches to SDG 4 monitoring.

2   Background to Rights-Based Approaches

This research supports integrating human rights in SDG implementation and national policy development (OHCHR, 2017a). The OHCHR defines a human rights-based approach as a conceptual framework that is based on international human rights standards and directed to promoting and protecting human rights. It seeks to analyse inequalities and redress discriminatory practices and unjust distributions of power that impede development (OHCHR,

2006). Tangible human rights-based approaches in development have been defined as:

- Assessment and analysis to identify human rights claims and duty-bearers' obligations as well as the immediate, underlying, and structural causes of the nonrealisation of rights.
- Assessment of the capacity of rights-holders to claim their rights and of duty-bearers to fulfil their obligations and to develop strategies to build these capacities.
- Monitoring and evaluation of outcomes and processes guided by human rights standards and principles through recommendations from international human rights bodies and mechanisms (adapted from UNICEF, 2003, pp. 91–93).

We focus here on the last aspect described above, emphasising rights-based monitoring of SDG 4 achievement, with additional definitions identified in CSOs' programming discussed in more depth below.

2.1   *Official Mechanisms for SDG Monitoring and Potential CSO Spaces within Them*

The SDGs, despite their wide endorsement, are a political declaration and not legally binding. Instead, the SDGs exert influence indirectly to determine global planning benchmarks, provide standards for performance evaluation by member states, and identify broad norms that determine what 'ought to be done' and how (Fukuda-Parr, 2014, p. 120). Regular monitoring, reporting, and tracking national performance forms a critical component framing how SDGs exert influence. The SDG outcome document, Agenda 2030 (UNGA, 2015b), provides guiding principles[1] for the review process, describes an overarching accountability architecture, reiterates that the process must be state-led, and stresses its voluntary nature. The next section details how CSOs can officially engage in rights-based SDG monitoring to establish the background for CSO-led reporting operations detailed in our findings below.

2.2   *Official SDG Monitoring: Structures for CSO Engagement*

Official SDG accountability mechanisms have two main tracks: quantitative indicators to track progress, and qualitative follow-up and review processes at national, regional, and global levels to measure, track, and support progress.

2.2.1   Quantitative Indicators

The targets and indicators under SDG 4 have been thoroughly debated. There is some ongoing refinement; for instance, four potential additional indicators are under consideration to be included by 2020 (IAEG-SDGs, 2017). CSOs are also engaged in developing alternative indicators and rights-based monitoring tools and reports (e.g., Action for Sustainable Development [Action4SD], 2016; Right to Education Initiative [RTE], 2015). Conversely, some educational researchers and civil society members are calling for fewer indicators (e.g., Anderson, 2015). Disagreement on indicators and their measurement methodology affects CSOs' ability to effectively monitor national progress, particularly when they are not aware of or involved in these debates, negotiations, or decisions.

Many countries are experiencing challenges satisfying current data collection needs for SDG indicators. For example, the 2017 Asia-Pacific SDG progress report identified that only 25% of the global SDG indicators have available data (United Nations Economic and Social Commission for Asia and the Pacific [ESCAP], 2018). In response, ongoing efforts aim to strengthen national data systems, providing advocacy opportunities for national education data to be openly available, transparent, and collected regularly for effective social accountability (High-level Group, 2017; UIS, 2017a). The absence of official SDG monitoring data makes it difficult for CSOs to develop shadow reports, reports that parallel official governmental reports about SDG fulfilment, or to conduct social audits of relevant data.

2.2.2   Qualitative Reviews

The High-Level Political Forum on Sustainable Development (HLPF), the apex body for SDG monitoring, is a global convening space for governments, intergovernmental organisations with SDG mandates, and CSOs working on SDGs to discuss progress and present findings. Voluntary National Review (VNR) reports, the formal space for national monitoring, and reports by UN regional commissions, UN bodies, civil society, and the private sector are submitted to the HLPF. All Major Groups and Other Stakeholders (UN, 2014a), including the new Education and Academia Stakeholder Group (UN, 2017), submit reports on the SDGs, including SDG 4, to the HLPF to draw attention to implementation.[2] Every year, the HLPF focusses special attention on a couple of the goals. In 2019, for the first time, SDG 4 will be among those reviewed by the HLPF.

UN regional commissions also undertake regional monitoring and reviews that feed into the global process. CSO networks and coordination mechanisms are emerging to shadow these spaces (e.g., Asia Pacific Regional CSO Engagement Mechanism, 2017; SDG Watch Europe, 2016). However, the extent to which education is reflected in regional mechanisms varies. CSOs working on education have not been actively engaged in many of these processes and instead focus on thematic processes (UIS, 2018b). The UN Economic and Social Commission for Asia and the Pacific has a Thematic Working Group on

Education 2030+ co-chaired by UNESCO and UNICEF and including other UN agencies to support regional implementation of the Education 2030 Agenda and other targets impacting education (UNAPRCM, 2016).

A consistent civil society demand has been to strengthen civil society participation in regional coordination mechanisms, mirroring the HLPF Coordination Mechanism for the SDGs globally, to ensure greater transparency in the process of reviewing progress and ensuring accountability (UN, 2018d). Regional SDG reviews and peer review mechanisms undertaken by the regional commissions, such as the New Partnership for Africa's Development, may offer an opportunity to strengthen accountability. OECD country assessments, peer reviews, and peer learning mechanisms may also strengthen SDG mutual accountability in OECD countries (OECD, 2018b). The current follow-up and review architecture unfortunately fails to provide concrete modalities for independent civil society monitoring, data collection, and reporting that may aid social accountability. Submission of shadow reports to the VNRs or as part of regional review is not currently in place but may assist in making the process more rights-based.

Human rights organisations and advocates call for stronger SDG accountability mechanisms through explicit connections between human rights and SDG monitoring (Center for Economic and Social Rights [CESR], 2015; Donald, 2016; McGrath & Nolan, 2017). Another civil society request has been the inclusion of alternative, non-official sources of statistics as sources of evidence for SDG monitoring (Tap Network, 2017). Such inclusion could strengthen accountability by providing complementary evidence to official statistics. However, there has been little interest from governments in the inclusion of alternative data sources as data sources for measuring progress on the SDGs.

UNESCO is the lead agency for the implementation of SDG 4. The Education 2030 Framework for Action (FFA) outlines a multistakeholder mechanism for global coordination with the SDG 4 Education 2030 Steering Committee. Regionally and nationally, engagement frameworks and mechanisms include regional progress reviews and national government-led, system-wide approaches that build on existing national structures. The official role of SDG 4 monitoring is held by the Global Education Monitoring Report (GEMR) (UNESCO, 2017b). Although this mechanism provides opportunities for CSOs' participation and provision of inputs, CSOs do not formally submit reports, and there are no formal mechanisms for CSO engagement on the GEMR with the national government within country. Comprehensive peer review mechanisms at the regional level may allow for more rigorous analysis but are not currently in place.

Finally, the Sustainable Development Solutions Network (SDSN) has created monitoring tools for SDG 4 through the SDG Index and Dashboards. The

SDG Index indicators include expected years of schooling, literacy rates, net primary school enrolment, population with tertiary education, Programme for International Student Assessment (PISA) scores, and population with upper secondary and post-secondary nontertiary education (Sachs et al., 2016, p. 29). These indices are, however, not rooted in official SDG indicators and are voluntary.

2.3   SDG *Monitoring Mechanisms*

SDG implementation creates additional monitoring challenges that go beyond the space provided by the SDG follow-up and review architecture. SDG targets are aligned with human rights law (Winkler & Williams, 2017), opening avenues for rights-based monitoring through submissions of shadow reports highlighting the status of education, individual (OHCHR, 2017b), and collective complaints (OHCHR, 2017c); complaints to the office of the UN Special Rapporteur on the right to education; and engagement with the Universal Periodic Review (UPR) process. UNESCO also has a confidential complaints procedure to receive complaints about the right to education (UNESCO, 2010). Regional African, European, and Inter-American human rights frameworks (RTE, 2017) also provide additional reporting avenues that could be used to highlight overall progress toward SDG 4 implementation. At the same time, some CSOs have requested that recommendations issued by UN human rights mechanisms, including the UPR and special procedures and conclusions of human rights treaty bodies, could further inform HLPF reviews.

A rights-based approach, according to UNICEF, is explicitly grounded in guidance provided by treaty bodies, including UN General Comments and concluding observations about education (UNICEF, 2007). Rights-based monitoring includes quantitative data. However, there has been a shift in recent years toward a greater focus on qualitative data involving input from more stakeholders, including students, parents, teachers, school administrators, as well as official national data collection bodies. While the specific targets and indicators are embedded in existing human rights commitments, the overwhelming reliance on quantitative indicators for monitoring raises intriguing questions about the extent of compatibility between official SDG monitoring and rights-based monitoring.

In sum, SDG monitoring processes provide for clear entry points for participation of civil society. CSOs have begun to use some, but not all, of these monitoring mechanisms. In the next section, we present our analysis of civil-society-led SDG 4 monitoring in the early stages of implementation.

3   Methodology

Based on human rights research approaches (e.g., Coomans, Grünfeld, & Kamminga, 2010; McClintock, 2013), this section presents a qualitative meta-analysis of rights-based approaches in organisational documents and secondary sources, survey and interview data from practitioners working on the right to education, and a case of one CSO-led rights-based monitoring tool, the RTEI.

3.1   *Data Sources*

Data was gathered in 2017 in a survey of the wider community of practice affiliated with the right to education[3] (n=27), complemented by a qualitative meta-analysis of organisational reports through a search for organisations that defined rights-based approaches, had a rights-based monitoring example, or had an SDG 4 monitoring example on their website or in public reports. We identified ten large CSOs and networks that published information about rights-based SDG 4 monitoring on their websites. The survey was not representative and convenience sampling resulted in potential selection bias. By including a qualitative meta-analysis of available organisational reports and online content, we hoped to minimise selection and response bias. The meta-analysis is also limited, however, due to the lack of publicly available reports and a succinct searchable database of practitioners' work.

This chapter particularly draws on the experience of the RTEI, a CSO-led education monitoring tool managed by RESULTS Educational Fund, presenting it as a case study. RTEI seeks to monitor the right to education based on the international right to education framework, a non-exhaustive list of human rights laws and agreements.[4] This case was selected because it highlights CSOs' practices, research, and action in advocating for the full satisfaction of the right to education. We focussed on identified indicators and advocacy strategies proposed in the RTEI project that used or reflected a rights-based approach to SDG 4 monitoring as defined in the literature above and through the meta-analysis. Data was drawn from reports from two organisations participating in RTEI and conducting SDG 4 monitoring domestically. This case is included as an additional resource in surveying the field of rights-based approaches, without suggesting it is necessarily a 'best practice', which remains to be proven. Rather, RTEI is a useful example of a rights-based SDG 4 monitoring tool with which we have had personal experience developing.

4   Surveying the Field: Rights-Based Approach to SDG Monitoring

Data we collected defined rights-based approaches in monitoring SDG 4 as an overarching principle in organisational programming. We identified three themes in human rights-based advocacy and monitoring definitions: (i) holding the state accountable, (ii) addressing marginalisation, and (iii) raising awareness about the right to education. These themes add to the definition of rights-based approaches identified from UNICEF above.

For CSOs that participate in rights-based advocacy and SDG monitoring, holding the state accountable includes:
– Identifying rights-holders and duty-bearers;
– Identifying the state's responsibility to guarantee and deliver the right to education;
– Using commitments made by the state to its citizens as key leverage points; and
– Promoting an environment in which rights-holders can claim their rights and duty-bearers can meet their obligations.

Interestingly, respondents frequently cited their work in addressing marginalisation, whether ethnic, gender based, dis/ability based, or based on some other group identity, as an example of their rights-based approach. Addressing marginalisation is both a component of rights-based programming and advocacy, but we focus specifically on elements related to advocacy here. Rights-based advocacy and monitoring activities that address marginalisation reported by respondents include:
– Focussing on marginalised, disadvantaged, and excluded groups;
– Identifying disparities to address underlying causes of poverty;
– Ensuring that all marginalised groups, particularly persons with disabilities and their families, are central to advocacy;
– Prioritising people living in poverty; and
– Focussing on women and girls' access to education.

It is not clear from the data, however, the extent to which marginalised peoples are involved in advocacy, or if advocacy is more focussed on addressing marginalisation without inclusion.

Finally, survey respondents and meta-analysis data identified participatory awareness raising activities as key to rights-based advocacy and monitoring. For instance, a rights-based awareness raising approach includes:
– Sensitising society and decision-makers on why the right to education should be implemented fully and uniformly by the state;
– Building CSOs' capacity to influence decision-making processes;

- Empowering rights-holders to claim their rights and work toward social transformation through action-oriented educational activities; and
- Focussing on the barriers impeding rights-holders' access to education or benefitting from a quality education equally.

Local ownership and participation are essential in rights-based approaches, recognising citizens as key actors in their own development and not as passive recipients.

4.1   Civil Society Initiatives toward SDG 4 Monitoring

Twenty-two of 27 survey respondents participated in SDG monitoring activities in some way. Twenty-three reported using rights-based approaches, as defined above. Specific SDG 4 work focussed mostly on early childhood development (Target 4.2, 59%), primary and secondary education (Target 4.1, 52%), and equity, especially gender equality in education (Target 4.5, 44%). CSOs were active in creating enabling conditions for official SDG monitoring to take place. The most frequently reported types of engagement included advocating with governments or intergovernmental bodies for rights-based SDG reviews, advocating for the inclusion of marginalised communities in SDG monitoring, and working with official data or monitoring systems (59%).

4.1.1   Monitoring Strategies

Strategies in SDG 4 monitoring emphasised contributing (individually or organisationally) to regional or global CSO reports (44%), informally tracking progress toward SDG 4 but not engaging in formal reporting (41%), participating in CSO-led monitoring (37%), and participating in government-led monitoring (37%). In contrast, no respondent took part in a formal VNR process, but these processes do not occur annually in all countries and only about half of UN member states would have conducted theirs at the time of the research. These strategies signify that, although CSOs may be engaging with stakeholders in other sectors to contribute to the development of broad CSO reports, SDG 4 monitoring is still in its infancy, focussing on informal tracking and collective CSO contributions rather than formal reporting mechanisms. This is also partly structural as there are no clear and consistent processes for VNRs at the national level. In contrast, some other sectors (e.g., SDG 16) are moving toward regular reports on SDG implementation. Seven respondents did report engaging in official regional or global monitoring or follow-up and review processes by UNESCO, the UN Regional Commissions, or the UN, but did not specify the type of formal review.

Interestingly, 44% of respondents reported engaging with learning assessments for SDG 4 monitoring, signifying the importance of the testing architecture. SDG 4 is the first international framework to include learning outcome indicators and global testing as integral parts of monitoring achievement internationally. Processes are underway to refine and coordinate existing international assessments and strengthen governments' capacities to undertake national assessments. CSOs participated in these processes through advising on national learning assessments and international assessment development groups such as UNESCO's Global Alliance to Monitor Learning (GAML). For more information on GAML, see Chapter 12 by Clara Fontdevila. In addition, the People's Action for Learning Network, a South-South collaboration across organisations in nine countries, has conducted nationwide, household-based learning assessments that collectively assess over one million children annually. The focus on learning assessments could accelerate test-based accountability, a controversial feature of the 'global educational reform movement' (You, 2017; Sahlberg, 2010; Smith, 2017) and narrow the Education 2030 Agenda to a focus on literacy and numeracy, steering countries away from a holistic, rights-based vision of education (UN, 1989). Due to the emphasis on testing in SDG 4 implementation, CSOs may find more avenues to engage in national, regional, and international learning assessment monitoring or may distance their advocacy from standardised assessments that could hide discrimination or inequality.

4.1.2   Beyond SDG 4

For activities that encompassed other SDGs beyond SDG 4, respondents described work on implementation and planning, using rights-based approaches through avenues similar to those described above. Specific strategies reported included using letters to the media, drawing on international law, including views of people with disabilities in reporting and activities, increasing citizens' awareness of the SDGs, and building international, regional, and national networks with other CSOs to persuade policymakers of SDG relevance. Survey respondents also described how they contributed to other SDG-related activities, such as implementation and planning. The most common CSO role reported was creating citizens' awareness about the SDG agenda (56%), followed by participating in sector planning for SDG implementation (33%), and advocating with the UN to strengthen coordination related to the SDGs between states (33%). In interviews, one civil society representative described how education and training were used in SDG monitoring, as a tool to raise public awareness about the SDGs and governmental obligations in schools, particularly focussing on inclusive education. Another respondent emphasised that SDG monitoring was enhanced by training when organisations worked with government officials on SDG 4 implementation planning.

Given the recency of SDG implementation, it is not surprising that respondents in 2017 were still identifying where and how they would contribute to monitoring. Those that have produced monitoring materials share them with civil society (59%) most frequently, followed by local media (33%), and the governmental education ministry (30%). Examples were provided, such as media and organisational reports focussing on national issues related to SDG implementation. Supranational engagement reportedly occurred infrequently with UNESCO or GPE (26%) and through formal regional reviews (11%). Engagement with formal accountability spaces created under the new SDG architecture is still weak. One respondent also mentioned contributing to UIS monitoring, although not in a formal report. In an interview, one respondent described drafting a national shadow report that monitors the implementation of the new national strategic plan in line with SDG 4. Civil society representatives can contribute to formal monitoring as well as conducting their own monitoring to offset formal systems that may not be using a rights-based approach.

4.1.3   Working with Networks
The Education and Academia Stakeholder Group coordinates inputs and contributions from the education and academic communities, especially on SDG 4. Several CSOs working on SDG 4 implementation and monitoring likewise work through other major groups that generate SDG reports. Regional education networks affiliated with the Global Campaign for Education (GCE) also track SDG 4 progress and support CSOs. *Campaña Latinoamericana por el Derecho a la Educación* (Latin American Campaign for the Right to Education) (CLADE) uses the *Observatorio Regional de Educación Inclusiva* (Regional Observatory of Inclusive Education) to monitor SDG 4. The observatory gathers information, documentation, and opinions on education systems through the lenses of inclusion and nondiscrimination. Documents include normative frames, national curriculum, education policy, and opinions from the education community such as teachers, students, and parents. CLADE has participated in regional planning and construction of monitoring mechanisms (UNESCO, 2017a) and plans to submit a 'E2030 Monitoring Report' on Latin America in the 2017 HLPF.

Several national networks affiliated with GCE have produced national SDG reports. The Campaign for Popular Education's (CAMPE) report (Ahmed et al., 2016) is a quantitative study contributed to by CSOs, governments, and academics, looking especially at SDG 4 progress in Bangladesh related to literacy, skills development, and lifelong learning initiatives, and their interactions with socioeconomic indicators (Nath & Chowdhury, 2016). In addition, GCE member networks in countries such as Nepal (NGO Federation of Nepal, 2017), Bangladesh (Ahmed et al., 2016), the Netherlands, Peru, and Denmark participated in researching and drafting national CSO shadow reports and engaging with formal national VNR processes. Another coalition, *Foro SocioEducativo* (*Foro*) promotes citizen monitoring of the execution of education policies by the Ministry of Education in the Dominican Republic. *Foro* promotes education monitoring through the *Guia para la Veeduria Social de las Politicas Educativas* (Guide for Social Oversight of Educational Policies) (Orti, Maldonado, & Solano, 2015). Their report introduces monitoring in the Dominican Republic's political and legal context and provides guidance and tools for citizen monitoring.

Further regional collaboration is evident in the emphasis of the Asia South Pacific Association for Basic and Adult Education (ASPBAE) on the role of civil society in national, regional, and international dialogues about development goals; creating networks between organisations; and contributing to intergovernmental policy design related to the SDGs (Khan, 2016). Specifically, ASPBAE calls on CSOs to monitor goal satisfaction by working with government officials and policymakers, learners, and teachers, and other civil society groups. This monitoring is the responsibility of the government but supported by CSOs who advocate for government attention to at-risk populations and provide oversight to identify gaps in existing governmental monitoring plans. Other initiatives such as the ACT Alliance provide examples of CSO network-building by seeking to increase 'civil society engagement and coalition' (ACT Alliance, 2016, p. 6) around SDG indicators that are integral to their campaigns, although not focussed on education.

Wider coalition-building around the SDGs is underway, frequently with monitoring at its heart. For example, Action4SD is a global civil society platform to monitor progress toward sustainable development through working groups. Their Working Group on Monitoring and Accountability helps share citizen-generated reports on the progress on the SDGs at national and regional levels (Action4SD, 2017).

Another type of civil society engagement, citizen-generated evidence and use, provides opportunities to amplify citizen voices and influence implementation. This, however, remains an underused approach despite efforts by organisations like Civicus and their Datashift project to coordinate engagement among the various producers of citizen-generated data (Civicus, 2017). Absence of clear spaces for inclusion of unofficial data sources in formal mechanisms of SDG monitoring is a critical lost opportunity.

Challenges to SDG 4 monitoring identified in survey responses include the state's lack of commitment to monitoring (37%), weak information and data systems for reporting (37%), lack of awareness among policymakers about the right to education in the SDGs (26%), and a lack of clarity about reporting discrimination (36%). Data availability and validity are perennial challenges in monitoring, whether coordinated by CSOs or the state. To overcome data availability issues, especially related to the right to education, monitoring tools can draw on indicators and indices such as RTEI, the Sustainable Development Solutions Network's (SDSN) index, RTE, and others that aggregate relevant data.

4.2   *Right to Education Index (RTEI) Case Study*
Here we explore RTEI as one case of a rights-based CSO-developed data collection and indicator identification tool. RTEI seeks to monitor the right to education based on the international right to education framework, a non-exhaustive list of human rights laws and agreements. It was developed through a participatory process with civil society partners in the Global South and North. It includes data collected biennially and was not originally developed for the SDGs. The RTEI framework emphasises a more robust analysis than the SDSN's tool and SDG Index, but does not include all SDG 4 targets. Some SDG 4 indicators are not reflected in international human rights law, such as early childhood education, and are thus not part of RTEI. RTEI has two advocacy purposes related to SDG 4 monitoring: (i) mapping the data collected against SDG indicators and (ii) supporting national civil society campaigns that may aim to monitor SDG 4. RTEI is CSO-led and flexible, allowing national CSO interpretation and direction of advocacy. It collects qualitative data on right-to-education indicators through a questionnaire (RESULTS Educational Fund, 2016) that can further support specific campaigns, such as SDG 4 monitoring, and is often lacking in official review processes.

4.2.1   Accountability through Indicators
The data collected in RTEI in 2016 were assembled by national CSO-led research teams in 15 countries.[5] SDG 4 indicators were used in this analysis to construct an SDG 4 rights-based monitoring tool and identify baselines of SDG 4 satisfaction for longitudinal study and further analysis (see Table 17.1). The data from the RTEI indicators listed in Table 17.1 are analysed briefly below to understand CSO-led projects that used RTEI in their rights-based approaches.[6] RTEI includes indicators for SDG Target 4.1, which focusses on free and equitable education, such as the percent of traditional-age learners in primary and secondary schools (removing overage learners), the net enrolment and completion rates for primary and secondary school, and the legal protection of free and compulsory education. However, national passing score data was

unavailable due to too many missing responses. These data limitations highlight challenges in using solely quantitative methods to monitor SDG 4 implementation because data may be unavailable, biased, or incomparable across
countries. In 2016, national assessment data were only available in six of the
countries presented. In addition, the diversity of national assessments in RTEI
countries highlights the challenge in this metric to adequately monitor the
'proportion of children and young people: (a) in grades 2/3; (b) at the end of
primary; and (c) at the end of lower secondary achieving at least a minimum
proficiency level in (i) reading and (ii) mathematics, by sex' (UN, 2018c). Using
national assessments that vary widely, RTEI creates indicators that clearly
represent the national context but are weak in international comparison.
However, enrolment and completion rates recorded in RTEI are particularly
relevant in national Target 4.1 monitoring.

Using RTEI data as a lever for Target 4.1 monitoring and accountability can
influence national assessment paradigms and efforts to increase enrolment
and completion rates. This example can also show comparisons between
countries (see Figure 17.1).

Figure 17.1 presents how the 15 countries in RTEI in 2016 performed on indicators related to SDG Target 4.1, which aims to ensure that 'all girls and boys
complete free, equitable, and quality primary and secondary education leading to relevant and effective learning outcomes' (see Table 1.1 in Chapter 1).
Canada has the highest score because it has the highest reported passing rate
on national assessments, the lowest out-of-school rates and overage learner
rates, and the highest enrolment rates, in addition to laws protecting free and
compulsory education. The subindex could inform national advocates and

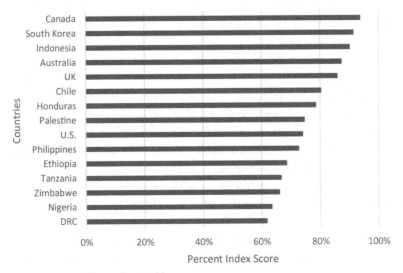

FIGURE 17.1   4.1 Free and equitable RTEI scores

policymakers seeking to identify where gaps in policy exist. This aggregated score represents one example of how RTEI micro-indices and overall scores can show comparative accountability across select SDG 4 indicators. After calculating SDG 4 subindex scores and comparing outcomes nationally, CSOs can direct advocacy toward increasing government monitoring and transparency. Scores can also provide background and overarching examples in national and international CSO-led reports, including shadow reports. As one CSO-led tool for SDG 4 accountability, RTEI has potential but its influence and accountability depend on national CSOs engaging in formal SDG monitoring processes.

4.2.2   RTEI in Advocacy

One example of an RTEI-associated project, which was conducted in 2017 and focussed on rights-based approaches to SDG 4 monitoring, was the Teacher Creativity Center (TCC) in Palestine. TCC used RTEI to focus broadly on raising awareness of SDG 4 amongst policymakers and citizens. TCC's activities conducted public outreach and engaged citizens in the generation and use of education data, such as quality, equity, financing, and system reform. They included workshops with national stakeholders, data training sessions, meetings with policymakers, and additional data collection with trained citizens and CSOs. In addition, they met with partners and stakeholders to discuss plans to reach SDG 4. TCC also undertook shadow reporting, with the hopes of submitting to UNESCO, the UN Special Rapporteur on the Right to Education, the Palestinian Ministry of Education and Higher Education, and local media. TCC intends to engage with formal and national monitoring mechanisms both at national and international levels. Their project, described in organisational documentation, adds data collection strategies to the rights-based monitoring strategies identified in our survey and meta-analysis. Using RTEI, and developing further data collection to supplement the indicators monitored, represents an innovative CSO-led quantitative strategy.

RTEI is one tool among many that can be used for a variety of advocacy purposes. TCC survey respondents also reported plans to use RTEI for research on the right to education and tangentially, health, to identify indicators for monitoring national plans, and using country reports and results for national advocacy.

5   Conclusions

Effective monitoring and follow-up are critical for the SDG agenda's success. This chapter suggests that effective rights-based monitoring approaches are based on three prerequisites: (i) international and national governmental accountability; (ii) civil society-led accountability, especially related to marginalisation; and (iii) capacity development and human rights education. Each of these present strategies and challenges for civil society engagement with the SDGS.

5.1   *International and National Accountability*

Monitoring of SDG 4 must rely on a balance of qualitative with quantitative measures. Overall, international accountability mechanisms are state-focussed, with CSOs contributing shadow reports and conducting parallel monitoring to ensure successful implementation.

CSOs have multiple avenues for SDG monitoring but are only beginning to become familiar with the new formal SDG monitoring, follow-up, and review architecture. Stronger mechanisms for state accountability, more organic mechanisms for peer-learning, and connections between the various accountability spaces could support greater civil society engagement. National accountability mechanisms to be submitted to international monitoring bodies should draw on CSO and coalition experiences and provide space for the participation of marginalised communities in processes of SDG monitoring.

Data must inform advocacy efforts nationally and engage with the overarching international SDG monitoring architecture described above. With the SDGs progressively becoming the dominant framework for global development discourse, the evidence generated by CSOs to monitor progress on the SDGs could be used for multiple other purposes. For instance, with increasing emphasis on learning assessments in SDG 4 implementation, CSOs can both promote larger quality learning indicators beyond assessments and monitor implementation of assessments that may have deleterious or discriminatory effects. One finding from the data collected and the RTEI case study is that organisations can develop their own core lists of SDG indicators that draw upon SDG 4, the Education 2030 FFA, human rights law, and regional or national policy frameworks and supplement them with qualitative data to address specific reporting needs.

5.2   *Civil Society-Led Accountability*

CSOs represented in this study highlighted how citizen participation, focus on addressing marginalisation, strengthening national advocacy, supporting coalition building, and supplementing official monitoring with alternative perspectives were critical to make SDG 4 monitoring rights-based. Citizens' participation, especially with marginalised communities, such as persons with disabilities and women and girls, was particularly emphasised in rights-based approaches. The focus on equity in rights-based approaches to SDG 4 monitoring can be strengthened to better identify discrimination within countries that impede fulfilment of the goals. Despite the SDG agenda's inclusion of Target 4.5 with a specific focus on equity, CSOs currently have difficulty identifying data about discrimination. This was evident in RTEI and in survey responses. When data are available, CSOs are unsure where to report discrimination in official SDG 4 monitoring mechanisms.

While working on official reporting, CSOs can engage with accountability institutions, such as statistics and education ministries, to strengthen data collection and emphasise specific avenues for government attention that may be relevant in strengthening respect for human rights and fulfiling SDG 4. Given that survey respondents highlighted the lack of official understanding of the relationship between the right to education and SDG 4, referencing specific national obligations to international law can clarify this relationship and advance rights-based monitoring and implementation. These efforts are already underway as interviewees and the RTEI case study presented awareness-raising with state officials and other stakeholders as key to early stages of SDG 4 monitoring.

5.3 *Capacity Development*

Data availability is a critical problem for both the state and CSOs undertaking monitoring. CSOs can work to strengthen data systems and generate their own reports and evidence, either through national-level questionnaires like RTEI's or local- and school-based data collection. The state is ultimately responsibility for collecting the requisite data to monitor SDG 4 implementation and may reject alternative data sources. The most frequent type of monitoring reported in this chapter related to official data monitoring systems, and the largest challenge was weak information systems that complicated reporting. Survey respondents and interviewees identified working with national accountability institutions directly as one example of rights-based SDG 4 monitoring. At the same time, respondents felt that both CSOs and state officials lacked adequate understanding of the SDG framework and aspects of monitoring. Consequently, to increase the likelihood that SDG monitoring and implementation are successful, stronger investment in capacity building for both state and civil society is warranted.

Although only mentioned briefly in survey responses, CSOs can engage in SDG monitoring by identifying additional indicators to supplement international benchmarks and localise national advocacy. Focussing on assessments, CSOs can use national assessments and disaggregated data to identify equity and discrimination concerns across regions, marginalised groups, and income levels, among other factors. TCC's development of further data collection

TABLE 17.1   Comparison of SDG 4 indicators with RTEI indicators

SDG Target 4.1: By 2030, ensure that all girls and boys complete free, equitable, and quality primary and secondary education leading to relevant and effective learning outcomes.

SDG indicators	RTEI indicator
Percentage of children/young people (i) in grades 2/3; (ii) at the end of primary; and (iii) at the end of lower secondary achieving at least a minimum proficiency level in (a) reading and (b) mathematics	4.3.3: What percent of students received a passing score on the national assessment/exam? a. Overall primary b. Reading primary c. Math primary d. Overall secondary e. Reading secondary f. Math secondary
Administration of a nationally representative learning assessment (i) in grades 2/3 (ii) at the end of primary and (iii) at the end of lower secondary	
Gross intake ratio to the last grade (primary, lower secondary)	3.3.2: What is the net enrolment rate aa. For primary schools? (Overall) ba. For secondary schools? (Overall)
Completion rate (primary, lower secondary, upper secondary)	3.3.3aa: What is the school completion rate? aa. Overall primary ba. Overall secondary
Out-of-school rate (primary, lower secondary, upper secondary)	One minus the net enrolment rate (measured in 3.3.2)
Percentage of children over-age for grade (primary, lower secondary)	Not available
Number of years of (i) free and (ii) compulsory primary and secondary education guaranteed in legal frameworks	3.1.1: Do national laws provide for free and compulsory education?

SDG Target 4.3: By 2030, ensure equal access for all women and men to affordable and quality technical, vocational, and tertiary education, including university.

SDG indicators	RTEI indicator
Participation rate of youth and adults in formal and non-formal education and training in the previous 12 months, by sex	Unavailable

(cont.)

TABLE 17.1   Comparison of SDG 4 indicators with RTEI indicators (*cont.*)

Gross enrolment ratio for tertiary education	3.3.1ca What is the gross enrolment rate for technical and vocational training? (Overall) 3.3.1da What is the gross enrolment rate for tertiary schools?
Participation rate in technical-vocational education programmes (15- to 24-years old)	Unavailable

SDG Target 4.5: By 2030, eliminate gender disparities in education and ensure equal access to all levels of education and vocational training for the vulnerable, including persons with disabilities, indigenous peoples, and children in vulnerable situations.

SDG indicators	RTEI indicator
Parity indices (female/male, rural/urban, bottom/top wealth quintile and others such as disability status, indigenous peoples and conflict-affected, as data become available) for all education indicators on this list that can be disaggregated	3.3.2: What is the net enrolment rate for primary schools? – For females divided by the rate for males – In rural areas divided by the rate in urban areas – For people with lower income divided by higher income, or – For people with disabilities divided by the overall rate. 3.3.2: What is the net enrolment rate for secondary schools? – For females divided by the rate for males – In rural areas divided by the rate in urban areas – For people with lower income divided by higher income, or – For people with disabilities divided by the overall rate.

(*cont.*)

TABLE 17.1   Comparison of SDG 4 indicators with RTEI indicators (*cont.*)

Percentage of students in primary education whose first or home language is the language of instruction	5.2.3: What percent of students are not taught in their mother tongue?
Extent to which explicit formula-based policies reallocate education resources to disadvantaged populations	Unavailable
Education expenditure per student by level of education and source of funding	1.5.1: What is the current public expenditure per pupil as a percentage of GDP per capita?
Percentage of total aid to education allocated to low income countries	Unavailable

SDG Target 4.6: By 2030, ensure that all youth and a substantial proportion of adults, both men and women, achieve literacy and numeracy.

SDG indicators	RTEI indicator

Percentage of population in a given age group achieving at least a fixed level of proficiency in functional (a) literacy and (b) numeracy skills, by sex	4.3.4: What is the literacy rate
	  ab. For male youth?
	  ac. For female youth?
	  bb. For male adults?
	  bc. For female adults?

Youth/adult literacy rate	4.3.4: What is the literacy rate?
	  aa. Youth Overall?
	  ba. Adult Overall?

Participation rate of youth/adults in literacy programmes	3.1.6 Is basic education publicly provided for adults who have not completed primary education?

(*cont.*)

TABLE 17.1   Comparison of SDG 4 indicators with RTEI indicators (*cont.*)

SDG Target 4.7: By 2030, ensure that all learners acquire the knowledge and skills needed to promote sustainable development, including, among others, through education for sustainable development and sustainable lifestyles, human rights, gender equality, promotion of a culture of peace and non-violence, global citizenship and appreciation of cultural diversity and of culture's contribution to sustainable development.

SDG indicators	RTEI indicator
Extent to which (i) global citizenship education and (ii) education for sustainable development, including gender equality and human rights, are mainstreamed at all levels in: (a) national education policies, (b) curricula, (c) teacher education, and (d) student assessment	4.1.1: Do national laws or policies direct education towards the following aims? And 4.1.2: Does the national curriculum direct education towards the following aims? And 4.3.1 Do national assessments or exams attempt to evaluate pupils progress towards the following aims? – The development of respect for human rights and fundamental freedoms – The development of respect for the child's parents, cultural identity, language, and values, as well as respect for the values of the child's country and other civilisations – The development of the child's responsibilities in a free society, including understanding, peace, tolerance, equality, and friendship among all persons and groups – The development of respect for the natural environment 4.1.5b Does national curriculum include the following topic? Human rights 4.3.2b Do national assessments or exams evaluate pupil's understanding of the following topic? Human Rights

(*cont.*)

TABLE 17.1   Comparison of SDG 4 indicators with RTEI indicators (*cont.*)

Percentage of students by age group (or education level) showing adequate understanding of issues relating to global citizenship and sustainability	Unavailable
Percentage of 15-year-old students showing proficiency in knowledge of environmental science and geoscience	Unavailable
Percentage of schools that provide life skills-based HIV and sexuality education	Unavailable
Extent to which the framework on the World Programme on Human Rights Education is implemented nationally	Unavailable

SDG Target 4.a: Build and upgrade education facilities that are child, disability, and gender sensitive and provide safe, non-violent, inclusive, and effective learning environments for all.

SDG indicators	RTEI indicator

Proportion of schools with access to: (a) electricity; (b) the Internet for pedagogical purposes; (c) computers for pedagogical purposes; (d) adapted infrastructure and materials for students with disabilities; (e) basic drinking water; (f) single-sex basic sanitation facilities; and (g) basic handwashing facilities (as per the WASH indicator definitions)	2.2.4: What is the percentage of schools with potable water?
	    a. For primary schools?
	    b. For secondary schools?
	5.1.2: Are reasonable accommodation measures available for children with disabilities in mainstream schools?

Percentage of students experiencing bullying, corporal punishment, harassment, violence, sexual discrimination, and abuse	4.2.4: Does corporal punishment occur in practice?
Number of attacks on students, personnel, and institutions	Unavailable

(*cont.*)

TABLE 17.1   Comparison of SDG 4 indicators with RTEI indicators *(cont.)*

SDG Target 4.c: By 2030, substantially increase the supply of qualified teachers, including through international cooperation for teacher training in developing countries, especially least developed countries and small island developing states.

SDG indicators	RTEI indicator
Percentage of teachers qualified according to national standards by education level and type of institution	2.3.1 What is the percentage of teachers that are appropriately trained
Pupil/qualified teacher ratio by education level	2.3.2 What is the minimum standard pupil-trained teacher ratio? b. Primary school d. Secondary school
Percentage of teachers in: (a) pre-primary; (b) primary; (c) lower secondary; and (d) upper secondary education who have received at least the minimum organised teacher training (e.g. pedagogical training) pre-service or in-service required for teaching at the relevant level in a given country	Unavailable
Pupil/trained teacher ratio by education level	Unavailable
Average teacher salary relative to other professions requiring a comparable level of education qualification	2.3.4: What is the mean teacher salary relative to the national mean salary?
Teacher attrition rate by education level	Unavailable
Percentage of teachers who received in-service training in the last 12 months by type of training	Unavailable

SOURCES: UN (2015B); RESULTS EDUCATIONAL FUND (2016)

strategies and its training of citizens and policymakers to collect rigorous data for SDG monitoring presents one potential path for CSO monitoring. However, primary data collection and coordination for SDG monitoring remains the responsibility of the state, and CSOs may not be equipped to rigorously collect or analyse nationwide assessment data without national infrastructure and statistics. Although school- and local-based monitoring can often provide valuable insights, national ministries and organising bodies must bring data to one place, rather than require CSOs to collect and analyse primary data themselves.

Organisational and practitioners' experiences show how CSOs can contribute to SDG accountability by using rights-based approaches that policymakers may overlook. This includes informal monitoring with communities most directly affected by SDG 4 implementation and creating networks of organisations and policymakers to enhance national capacity to monitor SDG 4. As SDG 4 monitoring develops, CSOs can continue and enhance monitoring mechanisms by presenting rights-based approaches and highlighting what mechanisms have the most impact on national actors. Given the role that CSOs have played in shaping the SDG agenda, they also have a critical role in ensuring that governments are held to account for its implementation.

Notes

1   These include universality, transparency, equity, participation, and action-orientation (Together 2030, 2016).

2   The annual reports submitted by Major Groups and Other Stakeholders do not constitute comprehensive monitoring reports.

3   This included the online RTEI community, the Right to Education Project's community, the Global Campaign for Education community, the Global Partnership for Education community, and the Economic, Social, and Cultural Rights email lists. All surveys were conducted via email and Survey Monkey and analysed using Microsoft Excel for frequencies. Qualitative questions were analysed using a content analysis of repeated themes. Staff from 12 different national organisations in 10 countries, one regional organisation, and two global organisations completed the survey. Twelve respondents skipped the organisational demographic questions. Of survey respondents, four participants provided further follow-up in interviews.

4   The tool was developed in consultation with civil society organisations from 2013 to 2015, piloted in five countries, and completed the first round of data collection in 2016. It includes indicators monitoring governance, availability, accessibility, acceptability, and adaptability to the right to education (Tomaševski, 2006).

5   In 2016, CSO participants in RTEI were from Australia, Canada, Chile, the Democratic Republic of Congo, Ethiopia, Honduras, Indonesia, Nigeria, Palestine, the Philippines, South Korea, Tanzania, the United Kingdom, the United States, and Zimbabwe. RTEI CSO partners identified data from national governmental sources,

prioritising most recent data. When national data was unavailable, organisations identified international governmental data, then national research organisation data, and finally news reports and other sources.

6 Due to the small sample in RTEI 2016, only 15 countries' data were analysed by imputation when fewer than three countries were missing data. This was done by calculating a given indicator's mean values for only the region and income group to which the country with missing data belongs, then replacing the missing values with the smallest value between those two means.

SDG 4 Targets

Antonia Wulff

Goal 4. Ensure inclusive and equitable quality education and promote lifelong learning opportunities for all

4.1 By 2030, ensure that all girls and boys complete free, equitable and quality primary and secondary education leading to relevant and effective learning outcomes.

4.2 By 2030, ensure that all girls and boys have access to quality early childhood development, care and pre-primary education so that they are ready for primary education.

4.3 By 2030, ensure equal access for all women and men to affordable and quality technical, vocational and tertiary education, including university.

4.4 By 2030, substantially increase the number of youth and adults who have relevant skills, including technical and vocational skills, for employment, decent jobs and entrepreneurship.

4.5 By 2030, eliminate gender disparities in education and ensure equal access to all levels of education and vocational training for the vulnerable, including persons with disabilities, indigenous peoples and children in vulnerable situations.

4.6 By 2030, ensure that all youth and a substantial proportion of adults, both men and women, achieve literacy and numeracy.

4.7 By 2030, ensure that all learners acquire the knowledge and skills needed to promote sustainable development, including, among others, through education for sustainable development and sustainable lifestyles, human rights, gender equality, promotion of a culture of peace and non-violence, global citizenship and appreciation of cultural diversity and of culture's contribution to sustainable development.

4.a Build and upgrade education facilities that are child, disability and gender sensitive and provide safe, non-violent, inclusive and effective learning environments for all.

4.b By 2020, substantially expand globally the number of scholarships available to developing countries, in particular least developed countries, small island developing States. and African countries, for enrolment in higher education, including vocational training and information and communications technology, technical, engineering and scientific programmes, in developed countries and other developing countries.

4.c   By 2030, substantially increase the supply of qualified teachers, including through international cooperation for teacher training in developing countries, especially least developed countries and small island developing States.

(Source: UNGA, 2015b)

SDG 4 Targets and Indicators

Antonia Wulff

Goal 4. Ensure inclusive and equitable quality education and promote lifelong learning opportunities for all

Target 4.1 By 2030, ensure that all girls and boys complete free, equitable and quality primary and secondary education leading to relevant and effective learning outcomes	
4.1.1	Proportion of children and young people (a) in Grade 2 or 3; (b) at the end of primary education; and (c) at the end of lower secondary education achieving at least a minimum proficiency level in (i) reading and (ii) mathematics, by sex
4.1.2	Administration of a nationally-representative learning assessment (a) in Grade 2 or 3; (b) at the end of primary education; and (c) at the end of lower secondary education
4.1.3	Gross intake ratio to the last grade (primary education, lower secondary education)
4.1.4	Completion rate (primary education, lower secondary education, upper secondary education)
4.1.5	Out-of-school rate (primary education, lower secondary education, upper secondary education)
4.1.6	Percentage of children over-age for grade (primary education, lower secondary education)
4.1.7	Number of years of (a) free and (b) compulsory primary and secondary education guaranteed in legal frameworks
Target 4.2 By 2030, ensure that all girls and boys have access to quality early childhood development, care and pre-primary education so that they are ready for primary education	
4.2.1	Proportion of children under 5 years of age who are developmentally on track in health, learning and psychosocial well-being, by sex
4.2.2	Participation rate in organised learning (one year before the official primary entry age), by sex

4.2.3   Percentage of children under 5 years experiencing positive and stimulating home learning environments

4.2.4   Gross early childhood education enrolment ratio in (a) pre-primary education and (b) early childhood educational development

4.2.5   Number of years of (a) free and (b) compulsory pre-primary education guaranteed in legal frameworks

Target 4.3 By 2030, ensure equal access for all women and men to affordable quality technical, vocational and tertiary education, including university

4.3.1   Participation rate of youth and adults in formal and non-formal education and training in the previous 12 months, by sex

4.3.2   Gross enrolment ratio for tertiary education by sex

4.3.3   Participation rate in technical-vocational programmes (15- to 24-year-olds) by sex

Target 4.4 By 2030, substantially increase the number of youth and adults who have relevant skills, including technical and vocational skills, for employment, decent jobs and entrepreneurship

4.4.1   Proportion of youth and adults with information and communications technology (ICT) skills, by type of skill

4.4.2   Percentage of youth/adults who have achieved at least a minimum level of proficiency in digital literacy skills

4.4.3   Youth/adult educational attainment rates by age group, economic activity status, levels of education and programme orientation

Target 4.5 By 2030, eliminate gender disparities in education and ensure equal access to all levels of education and vocational training for the vulnerable, including persons with disabilities, indigenous peoples and children in vulnerable situations

4.5.1   Parity indices (female/male, rural/urban, bottom/top wealth quintile and others such as disability status, indigenous peoples and conflict-affected, as data become available) for all education indicators on this list that can be disaggregated

4.5.2   Percentage of students in primary education whose first or home language is the language of instruction

4.5.3   Extent to which explicit formula-based policies reallocate education resources to disadvantaged populations

4.5.4   Education expenditure per student by level of education and source of funding

4.5.5   Percentage of total aid to education allocated to least developed countries

Target 4.6 By 2030, ensure that all youth and a substantial proportion of adults, both men and women, achieve literacy and numeracy

4.6.1   Proportion of population in a given age group achieving at least a fixed level of proficiency in functional (a) literacy and (b) numeracy skills, by sex

4.6.2   Youth/adult literacy rate

4.6.3   Participation rate of illiterate youth/adults in literacy programmes

Target 4.7 By 2030, ensure all learners acquire knowledge and skills needed to promote sustainable development, including among others through education for sustainable development and sustainable lifestyles, human rights, gender equality, promotion of a culture of peace and non-violence, global citizenship, and appreciation of cultural diversity and of culture's contribution to sustainable development

4.7.1   Extent to which (i) global citizenship education and (ii) education for sustainable development, including gender equality and human rights, are mainstreamed at all levels in: (a) national education policies, (b) curricula, (c) teacher education and (d) student assessment

4.7.2   Percentage of schools that provide life skills-based HIV and sexuality education

4.7.3   Extent to which the framework on the World Programme on Human Rights Education is implemented nationally (as per the UNGA Resolution 59/113)

4.7.4   Percentage of students by age group (or education level) showing adequate understanding of issues relating to global citizenship and sustainability

4.7.5   Percentage of 15-year-old students showing proficiency in knowledge of environmental science and geoscience

Target 4.a Build and upgrade education facilities that are child, disability and gender sensitive and provide safe, non-violent, inclusive and effective learning environments for all

4.a.1   Proportion of schools with access to: (a) electricity; (b) Internet for pedagogical purposes; and (c) computers for pedagogical purposes; (d) adapted infrastructure and materials for students with disabilities; (e) basic drinking water; (f) single-sex basic sanitation facilities; and (g) basic handwashing facilities (as per the WASH indicator definitions)

4.a.2   Percentage of students experiencing bullying in the last 12 months

4.a.3   Number of attacks on students, personnel and institutions

Target 4.b By 2020, substantially expand globally the number of scholarships available to developing countries, in particular least developed countries, small island developing States and African countries, for enrolment in higher education, including vocational training, information and communications technology, technical, engineering and scientific programmes in developed countries and other developing countries

| 4.b.1 | Volume of official development assistance flows for scholarships by sector and type of study |
| 4.b.2 | Number of higher education scholarships awarded by beneficiary country |

Target 4.c By 2030, substantially increase the supply of qualified teachers, including through international cooperation for teacher training in developing countries, especially least developed countries and small island developing States

4.c.1	Proportion of teachers in: (a) pre-primary education; (b) primary education; (c) lower secondary education; and (d) upper secondary education who have received at least the minimum organised teacher training (e.g., pedagogical training) pre-service or in-service required for teaching at the relevant level in a given country, by sex
4.c.2	Pupil-trained teacher ratio by education level
4.c.3	Percentage of teachers qualified according to national standards by education level and type of institution
4.c.4	Pupil-qualified teacher ratio by education level
4.c.5	Average teacher salary relative to other professions requiring a comparable level of qualification
4.c.6	Teacher attrition rate by education level
4.c.7	Percentage of teachers who received in-service training in the last 12 months by type of training

Note: Global indicators are presented in coloured shading.
(Source: UIS, 2018e)

References

Abraham, J. (1994). Positivism, structurationism and the differentiation-polarisation theory. *British Journal of Sociology of Education, 15*, 231–241.

Acedo, C., Adams, D., & Popa, S. (Eds.). (2012). *Quality and qualities: Tensions in education reforms.* Rotterdam, The Netherlands: Sense Publishers.

Ackerman, X., & Scott, K. (2017). Gains and gaps in girls' education. *Compare: A Journal of Comparative and International Education, 47*(1), 133–136.

ACT Alliance. (2016). *ACT Alliance advocacy strategy.* Geneva: ACT Alliance. Retrieved January 26, 2019, from http://actalliance.org/wp-content/uploads/2016/07/ACT-Advocacy-Strategy-May-2016.pdf

Action4SD. (2016). *Learning by doing: Civil Society engagement in the high-level political forum's national review process.* N.p.: Action4SD. Retrieved January 21, 2019, from http://www.civicus.org/images/CivilSociety.HLPF.NationalReviewProcess.pdf

Action4SD. (2017). *Monitoring and accountability working group planning meeting notes.* Retrieved January 26, 2019, from http://action4sd.org/wp-content/uploads/2017/02/Action4SDMonitoringAccountabilityWGNotes.pdf

ActionAid International. (2016). *Mistreated: The tax treaties that are depriving the world's poorest countries of vital revenue.* Johannesburg: ActionAid International. Retrieved November 9, 2018, from http://www.actionaid.org/sites/files/actionaid/actionaid_-_mistreated_tax_treaties_report_-_feb_2016.pdf

Adams, A. (1999). Language planning in the European Union and the Republic of South Africa: Parallel cases? In L. Limage (Ed.), *Comparative perspectives on language and literacy.* Selected papers from the work of the Language and Literacy Commission of the 10th World Congress of Comparative Education Societies held in Cape Town, 1998 (pp. 533–542). Dakar: UNESCO.

Addey, C. (2017). Golden relics & historical standards: How the OECD is expanding global education governance through PISA for development. *Critical Studies in Education, 58*(3), 311–325.

Addey, C., & Sellar, S. (2018). Why do countries participate in PISA? Understanding the role of international large-scale assessments in global education policy. In A. Verger, H. Altinyelken, & M. Novelli (Eds.), *Global education policy and international development: New agendas, issues and policies* (2nd ed., pp. 97–118). New York, NY: Bloomsbury.

Addey, C., Sellar, S., Steiner-Khamsi, G., Lingard, B., & Verger, A. (2017). The rise of international large-scale assessments and rationales for participation. *Compare, 47*(3), 443–452.

Adger, W., Barnett, J., Brown, K., Marshall, N., & O'Brien, K. (2013). Cultural dimensions of climate change impacts and adaptation. *Nature Climate Change, 3*(2), 112–117.

Adu-Yeboah, C. (2015). Mature women students' experiences of social and academic support in higher education: A systematic review. *Journal of Education and Training, 2*(2), 145–162.

African Union. (2016). *Continental education strategy for Africa 2016–2025: CESA 16–25.* Addis Ababa: AU. Retrieved April 5, 2019, from https://au.int/sites/default/files/documents/29958-doc-cesa_-_english-v9.pdf

African Union. (2018). *Continental strategy for Technical and Vocational Education and Training (TVET): To foster youth employment.* Addis Ababa: AU. Retrieved April 9, 2019, from https://au.int/sites/default/files/pressreleases/35308-pr-tvet-english_-_final_2.pdf

Ahmed, M. (2014). Squaring the circle: EFA in the post-2015 global agenda. *International Journal of Educational Development, 39,* 64–69.

Ahmed, M., Haque, K., Rahaman, M. M., & Quddus, M. (2016). *Framework for action: Education 2030 in Bangladesh: A civil society perspective.* Dhaka: Campaign for Popular Education and Citizens' Platform for SDGs, Bangladesh. Retrieved January 26, 2019, from http://bdplatform4sdgs.net/2017/05/04/education-2030-bangladesh-civil-society-perspective/

Ahsan, S., & Smith, W. (2016). Facilitating student learning: A comparison of classroom and accountability assessment. In W. Smith (Ed.), *The global testing culture: Shaping educational policy, perceptions, and practice* (pp. 131–152). Oxford: Symposium.

Ainscow, M., & Miles, S. (2008). Making education for all inclusive: Where next? *Prospects, 38*(1), 15–34.

Akkari, A. (2018). International agenda education 2030: An uncertain consensus or a tool to mobilize education actors in the 21st century? *International Journal of Educational Studies, 5*(2), 59–70.

Akyeampong, K. (2017). Teacher educators' practice and vision of good teaching in teacher education reform context in Ghana. *Educational Researcher, 46*(4), 194–203.

Akyeampong, A., Lussier, K., Pryor, J., & Westbrook, J. (2013). Improving teaching and learning of basic maths and reading in Africa: Does teacher preparation count? *International Journal of Educational Development, 33*(3), 272–282.

Akyeampong, K., Pryor, J., & Ampiah, J. (2006). A vision of successful schooling: Ghanaian teachers' understandings of learning. Teaching and assessment. *Comparative Education, 42*(2), 155–176.

Akyeampong, K., & Stephens, D. (2002). Exploring the backgrounds and shaping of beginning student teachers in Ghana: Toward greater contextualisation of teacher education. *International Journal of Educational Development, 22*(3–4), 261–274.

Alexander, R. (2015). Teaching and learning for all? The quality imperative revisited. *International Journal of Educational Development, 40*(C), 250–258.

Alhamdan, B., Al-Saadi, K., Baroutsis, A., Du Plessis, A., Hamid, O. M., & Honan, E. (2014). Media representation of teachers across five countries. *Comparative Education, 50*(4), 490–505.

Allais, S. (2014). *Selling out education: National qualifications frameworks and the neglect of knowledge.* Rotterdam, The Netherlands: Sense Publishers.

Allais, S. (2017a). Labour market outcomes of national qualifications frameworks in six countries. *Journal of Education and Work, 30*(5), 457–470.

Allais, S. (2017b). Towards measuring the economic value of higher education: Lessons from South Africa. *Comparative Education, 53*(1), 147–163.

Allais, S. (2018a). Analysis must rise: A political economy of falling fees. In G. Khadiagala, S. Mosoetsa, D. Pillay, & R. Southall (Eds.), *New South African review 6: The crisis of inequality* (pp. 152–166). Johannesburg: Wits University Press.

Allais, S. (2018b, September 12–14). *Skill formation in African countries: Insights from Ethiopia, Ghana and South Africa.* Presentation to the International Initiative for Promoting Political Economy, Pula, Croatia.

Altbach, P. (1970). The international student movement. *Journal of Contemporary History, 5*(1), 156–174.

Altbach, P. (Ed.). (1989). *Student political activism: An international reference handbook* (1st ed.). Westport, CT: Greenwood Press.

Altinok, N., Angrist, N., & Patrinos, H. (2018). *Global data set on education quality (1965–2015)* (Policy Research Working Paper 8314). Washington, DC: World Bank.

Altman, B. (Ed.). (2016). *International measurement of disability: Purpose, method and application.* Cham: Springer.

Aly, J. (2007). *Education in Pakistan: A white paper: Revised: Document to debate and finalize the national education policy.* Retrieved December 19, 2018, from http://planipolis.iiep.unesco.org/sites/planipolis/files/ressources/pakistan_national_education_policy_review_whitepaper.pdf

Amerigo, M., Aragones, J., & Garcia, J. (2012). Exploring the dimensions of environmental concern: An integrative proposal. *Psychology, 3*(3), 353–365.

Amsden, A. (2007). *Escape from empire: The developing world's journey through heaven and hell.* Cambridge, MA: MIT Press.

Anastasiou, D., & Keller, C. (2014). Cross-national differences in special education coverage: An empirical analysis. *Exceptional Children, 80*(3), 353–367.

Anderson, A. (2006). *The way we argue now: A study in the cultures of theory.* Princeton, NJ: Princeton UP.

Anderson, B. (1991). *Imagined communities: Reflections on the origins and spread of nationalism.* London: Verso.

Anderson, K. (2015). We have SDGs now, but how do we measure them? *Education Plus Development.* Washington, DC: Brookings Institution. Retrieved January 26, 2019, from https://www.brookings.edu/blog/education-plus-development/2015/11/03/we-have-sdgs-now-but-how-do-we-measure-them/

Anderson, K., & Ditmore, T. (2016). *Champions for learning: The legacy of the learning metrics task force.* Montreal & Washington, DC: UIS/CUE-Brookings. Retrieved

January 11, 2019, from https://www.brookings.edu/wp-content/uploads/2016/11/global_111516_lmtf.pdf

Andreotti, V. de O. (2011). The political economy of global citizenship education. *Globalisation, Societies and Education, 9*(3–4), 307–310.

Andrews, J. (2016). School performance in multi-academy trusts and local authorities – 2015. In *Research area: School performance and leadership*. London: Education Policy Institute.

Andrews, P. et al. (2014, May 6). OECD and PISA tests are damaging education worldwide – Academics. *The Guardian*. Retrieved January 17, 2019, from https://www.theguardian.com/education/2014/may/06/oecd-pisa-tests-damaging-education-academics

Angus, L. (2015). School choice: Neoliberal education policy and imagined futures. *British Journal of Sociology of Education, 36*(3), 395–413.

Apple, M. (2018). *The struggle for democracy in education: Lessons from social realities*. New York, NY: Routledge.

Archer, D. (2014). *Critical reflections on the learning metrics task force*. Act!onAid. Retrieved November 26, 2018, from http://www.actionaid.org/2014/02/critical-reflections-learning-metrics-task-force

Archer, D., Curtis, M., & Pereira, J. (2016). *Domestic tax and education* (Background paper for the learning generation). New York, NY: Education Commission. Retrieved November 9, 2018, from http://curtisresearch.org/wp-content/uploads/domestic_tax_and_education_final_report.pdf

Arnocky, S., Stroink, M., & DeCicco, T. (2007). Self-construal predicts environmental concern, cooperation, and conservation. *Journal of Environmental Psychology, 27*(4), 255–264.

Ashley, L., & Wales, J. (2015). *The impact of non-state schools in developing countries: A synthesis of the evidence from two rigorous reviews* (Education rigorous literature review). London: Overseas Development Institute. Retrieved February 22, 2019, from https://assets.publishing.service.gov.uk/government/uploads/system/uploads/attachment_data/file/486417/imact-non-state-schools-dev-countries.pdf

Ashman, S., & Fine, B. (2013). Neo-liberalism, varieties of capitalism, and the shifting contours of South Africa's financial system. *Transformation, 81/82*, 144–178.

Ashton, D., Green, F., James, D., & Sung, J. (1999). *Education and training for development in East Asia: The political economy of skill formation in newly industrialised economies*. London: Routledge.

Asia Pacific Regional CSO Engagement Mechanism. (2017). *What is RCEM?* Retrieved January 23, 2019, from http://asiapacificrcem.org/

Asia South Pacific Association for Basic and Adult Education (ASPBAE). (2015). *Education PPPs in Asia Pacific*. Unpublished research paper.

Aslam, M., & Kingdon, G. (2008). Gender and household education expenditure in Pakistan. *Applied Economics, 40*(20), 2573–2591.

Aslam, M., & Kingdon, G. (2012). Can education be a path to gender equality in the labour market? An update on Pakistan. *Comparative Education, 48*(2), 211–229.

Aslam, M., Rawal, S., & Saeed, S. (2017). *Public-private partnerships in education in developing countries: A rigorous review of the evidence.* London: Ark Education Partnerships Group.

Assan, J., & Walker, L. (2012). The political economy of contemporary education and the challenges of switching formal language to English in Rwanda. In P. Noack & M. Campioni (Eds.), *Rwanda fast forward: Social, economic, military and reconciliation prospects* (pp. 176–191). London: Palgrave Macmillan.

Au, W. (2007). High-stakes testing and curricular control: A qualitative metasynthesis. *Educational Researcher, 36*(5), 258–267.

Aubry, S., & Dorsi, D. (2016). Towards a human rights framework to advance the debate on the role of private actors in education. *Oxford Review of Education, 42*(5), 612–628.

Auld, E., Rappleye, J., & Morris, P. (2019). PISA for development: How the OECD and World Bank shaped educational governance post-2015. *Comparative Education, 55*(2), 197–219.

Australian Council for Educational Research (ACER). (2019). *Centre for global education monitoring.* Canberra: ACER. Retrieved April 1, 2019, from https://www.acer.org/au/gem/learning-progression-explorer#faq-2

Avalos, B., & Barrett, A. (2013). Teacher professionalism and social justice. In L. Tikly & A. Barrett (Eds.), *Education quality and social justice in the global south: Challenges for policy, practice and research* (pp. 75–90). London: Routledge.

Avalos, B., & Valenzuela, J. (2016, July). Education for all and attrition/retention of new teachers: A trajectory study in Chile. *International Journal of Educational Development, 49*, 279–290.

Bakan, D. (1966). The test of significance in psychological research. *Psychological Bulletin, 66*(6), 423–437.

Baker, D. (2014). *The schooled society: The educational transformation of global culture.* Stanford, CA: Stanford UP.

Balagopalan, S. (2012). Does 'gender' exhaust a feminist engagement with elementary education? *Contemporary Education Dialogue, 9*(2), 319–325.

Ball, J. (2010). *Enhancing learning of children from diverse language backgrounds: Mother tongue-based bilingual or multilingual education in the early years.* Paris: UNESCO. Retrieved February 22, 2019, from http://unesdoc.unesco.org/images/0021/002122/212270e.pdf

Ball, S. (2003). The teacher's soul and the terrors of performativity. *Journal of Education Policy, 18*(2), 215–228.

Ball, S., & Olmedo, A. (2013). Care of the self, resistance and subjectivity under neoliberal governmentalities. *Critical Studies in Education, 54*(1), 5–96.

Bamgbose, A. (1991). *Language and the nation: The language question in Sub-Saharan Africa*. Edinburgh: Edinburgh University Press.

Bamiro, O. (2016). Sustainable financing of higher education in Nigeria: Funding models. In M. Faborode & O. Edigheji (Eds.), *The future and relevance of Nigerian universities and other tertiary institutions* (pp. 48–80). Abuja & Dakar: Committee of Vice-Chancellors of Nigerian Federal Universities and Trust Africa.

Banks, J. (2008). Diversity, group identity, and citizenship education in a global age. *Educational Researcher, 37*(3), 129–139.

Banks, J. (2017). Failed citizenship and transformative civic education. *Educational Researcher, 46*(7), 366–377.

Barber, M., & Mourshed, M. (2007). *How the world's best-performing school systems come out on top*. New York, NY: McKinsey & Company. Retrieved December 3, 2018, from https://www.mckinsey.com/~/media/mckinsey/industries/social%20sector/our%20insights/how%20the%20worlds%20best%20performing%20school%20systems%20come%20out%20on%20top/how_the_world_s_best-performing_school_systems_come_out_on_top.ashx

Barkan, J. (2011). Got dough? How billionaires rule our schools. *Dissent, 58*(1), 49–57. Retrieved from https://www.dissentmagazine.org/article/got-dough-how-billionaires-rule-our-schools

Barkan, J. (2018). Death by a thousand cuts: Privatizing public education in the USA. In G. Steiner-Khamsi & A. Draxler (Eds.), *The state, business and education: Public-private Partnerships Revisited*. Cheltenham: Edward Elgar.

Baroutsis, A., & Lingard, B. (2017). Counting and comparing school performance: An analysis of media coverage of PISA in Australia, 2000–2014. *Journal of Education Policy, 32*(4), 432–449.

Barr, N. (2004). Higher education funding. *Oxford Review of Economic Policy, 20*(2), 264–283.

Barrett, A. (2011). A millennium learning goal for education post-2015: A question of outcomes or processes. *Comparative Education, 47*(1), 119–133.

Barrett, A., Sayed, Y., Schweisfurth, M., & Tikly, L. (2015). Learning, pedagogy and the post-2015 education and development agenda. *International Journal of Educational Development, 40*, 231–236.

Becker, G. (1993). *Human capital: A theoretical and empirical analysis, with special reference to education*. Chicago, IL: University of Chicago Press.

Beisheim, M. (2018). *UN reforms for the 2030 agenda: Are the HLPF's working methods and practices "fit for purpose"?* (SWP Research Paper 9). Berlin: Stiftung Wissenschaft und Politik. Retrieved December 5, 2018, from https://www.swp-berlin.org/fileadmin/contents/products/research_papers/2018RP09_bsh.pdf

Bell, L., & Stevenson, H. (2006). *Education policy: Process, themes and impact.* London & New York, NY: Routledge.

Bellah, R., Madsen, R., Sullivan, W., Swinder, A., & Tipton, S. (1985). *Habits of the heart: Individualism and commitment in American life.* Berkeley, CA: University of California Press.

Benavot, A. (2018a). The invisible friend: Adult education and the sustainable development goals. *Adult Education and Development, 85,* 4–9.

Benavot, A. (2018b). 'Learning at the bottom of the pyramid' and the global targets in education. In D. Wagner, S. Wolf, & R. Boruch (Eds.), *Learning at the bottom of the pyramid: Science, measurement and policy in low-income countries* (pp. 215–229). Paris: IIEP-UNESCO.

Benavot, A., & Koseleci, N. (2015). *Seeking quality in education: The growth of national learning assessments, 1990–2013* (Background paper prepared for the Education for All Global Monitoring Report 2015). Paris: UNESCO. Retrieved January 28, 2019, from https://unesdoc.unesco.org/ark:/48223/pf0000233733

Benavot, A., & Tanner, E. (2007). *The growth of national learning assessments in the world, 1995–2006* (Background paper prepared for the Education for All Global Monitoring Report 2008). Retrieved January 11, 2019, from https://unesdoc.unesco.org/ark:/48223/pf0000155507

Bennell, P. (1996a). Rates of return to education: Does the conventional pattern prevail in Sub-Saharan Africa? *World Development, 24*(1), 183–199.

Bennell, P. (1996b). Using and abusing rates of return: A critique of the World Bank's 1995 education sector review. *International Journal of Educational Development, 16*(3), 235–248.

Bennell, P., & Segerstrom, J. (1998). Vocational education and training in developing countries: Has the World Bank got it right? *International Journal of Educational Development, 18*(4), 271–287.

Benson, C. (2005). *Girls, educational equity and mother tongue-based teaching.* Bangkok: UNESCO. Retrieved February 22, 2019, from http://unesdoc.unesco.org/images/0014/001420/142049e.pdf

Benson, C. (2011). *Evaluation of the state of bilingual education in Cambodia.* Undertaken November 2010 to March 2011 for MoEYS with UNICEF support. Unpublished report. Phnom Penh: UNICEF.

Benson, C. (2016). *Addressing language of instruction issues in education: Recommendations for documenting progress.* Background paper commissioned by UNESCO for the Global Education Monitoring Report 2016. Paris: UNESCO. Retrieved February 22, 2019, from http://unesdoc.unesco.org/images/0024/002455/245575E.pdf

Benson, C., & Elorza, I. (2015). Multilingual Education for All (MEFA): Empowering non-dominant languages and cultures through multilingual curriculum development.

In D. Wyse, L. Hayward, & J. Zacher Pandya (Eds.), *The Sage handbook of curriculum, pedagogy and assessment* (pp. 557–574). London: Sage.

Benson, C., & Wong, K. (2017). Effectiveness of policy development and implementation of L1-based multilingual education in Cambodia. *International Journal of Bilingual Education and Bilingualism, 22*(2), 250–265.

Berkson, J. (1938). Some difficulties of interpretation encountered in the application of the chi-square test. *Journal of the American Statistical Association, 33*(203), 526–536.

Bhambra, G., Gebrial, D., & Nisancioglu, K. (2018). *Decolonising the university.* London: Pluto Press.

Bhattacharya, A., & Kharas, H. (2015, April 8). Worthy of support. *The Economist.*

Bieber, T., & Martens, K. (2011). The OECD PISA study as a soft power in education? Lessons from Switzerland and the US. *European Journal of Education, 46*(1), 101–116.

Biesta, G. (2008). What kind of citizen? What kind of democracy? Citizenship education and the scottish curriculum for excellence. *Scottish Educational Review, 40*(2), 38–52.

Biffl, G., & Issac, J. (2002). Should higher education students pay tuition fees? *European Journal of Education, 37*(4), 433–455.

Bivens, F., Moriarty, K., & Taylor, P. (2009). Transformative education and its potential for changing the lives of children in disempowering contexts. *IDS Bulletin, 40*(1), 97–108.

Blankstein, A., & Noguera, P. (2016). *Excellence through equity: Five principles of courageous leadership to guide achievement for every student.* Washington, DC: Association for Supervision and Curriculum Development.

Blevins, B., LeCompte, K., & Wells, S. (2016). Innovations in civic education: Developing civic agency through action civics. *Theory & Research in Social Education, 44*(3), 344–384.

Bold, T., et al. (2017). *What do teachers know and do? Does it matter? Evidence from primary schools in Africa* (Policy Research Working Paper 7956). Washington DC: World Bank Group.

Boli, J., & Thomas, G. (1999). *Constructing world culture: International nongovernmental organizations since 1875.* Stanford, CA: Stanford UP.

Boltanski, L., & Chiapello, E. (2006). *The new spirit of capitalism.* London: Verso.

Bonal, X., Verger, A., & Zancajo, A. (2015). *Indicators for a broad and bold post-2015 agenda: A comprehensive approach to educational development.* London: OSF.

Boni, A., Lopez-Fogues, A., & Walker, M. (2016). Higher education and the post-2015 agenda: A contribution from the human development approach. *Journal of Global Ethics, 12*(1), 17–28.

Bonikowski, B. (2017). Ethno-nationalist populism and the mobilization of collective resentment. *British Journal of Sociology, 68*(S1), S182–S213.

Booher-Jennings, J. (2005). Below the bubble: 'Educational triage' and the texas accountability system. *American Education Research Journal, 42*(2), 231–268.

Booth, T., & Ainscow, M. (2016). *Index for inclusion: Developing learning and participation in schools* (4th ed.). Bristol: Centre for Studies on Inclusive Education.

Bosch, G. (2017). Different national skill systems. In C. Warhurst, K. Mayhew, D. Finegold, & J. Buchanan (Eds.), *The Oxford handbook of skills and training* (pp. 424–443). Oxford: Oxford University Press.

Bothwell, E. (2018, September 6). THE developing rankings based on sustainable development goals. *THE World University Rankings.* Retrieved May 3, 2019, from https://www.timeshighereducation.com/news/developing-ranking-based-sustainable-development-goals

Bourdieu, P. (1983). The field of cultural production, or: The economic world reversed. *Poetics, 12*(4–5), 311–356.

Bourdieu, P., & Passeron, J.-C. (1970). *La reproduction: éléments pour une théorie du système d'enseignement.* Paris: Les Editions de Minuit.

Bous, K. (2019). *False promises: How delivering education through public-private partnerships risks fueling inequality instead of achieving quality education for all.* Oxford: Oxfam International. Retrieved May 7, 2019, from https://oxfamilibrary.openrepository.com/bitstream/handle/10546/620720/bp-world-bank-education-ppps-090419-en.pdf

Boutieri, C. (2016). *Learning in Morocco: Language politics and the abandoned educational dream.* Bloomington, IN: Indiana UP.

Bowers, C. (1995). *Educating for an ecologically sustainable culture: Rethinking moral education, creativity, intelligence, and other modern orthodoxies.* Albany, NY: State University of New York Press.

Bowers, C. (2002). Towards an eco-justice pedagogy. *Environmental Education Research, 8*(1), 21–34.

Bramwell, D., Anderson, S., & Mundy, K. (2014). *Teachers and teacher development: A rapid review of the literature.* Toronto: Ontario Institute for Studies in Education. Retrieved March 14, 2019, from https://www.oise.utoronto.ca/cidec/UserFiles/File/Website/Rapid_Review-teacher_development_June_30_final_2.pdf

Breckenridge, K. (2018, March 5). *What happened to the theory of African capitalism?* Presentation to the Wits Institute for Social and Economic Research Seminar, WISER, Johannesburg. Retrieved April 5, 2019, from https://wiser.wits.ac.za/content/what-happened-theory-african-capitalism-13042

Breier, M. (2010). From 'financial considerations' to 'poverty': Towards a reconceptualisation of the role of finances in higher education student drop out. *Higher Education, 60*(6), 657–670.

Brissett, N., & Mitter, R. (2017). For function or transformation? A critical discourse analysis of education under the sustainable development goals. *Journal for Critical Education Policy Studies, 15*(1), 181–204.

Brock-Utne, B. (2010). Research and policy on the language of instruction issue in Africa. *International Journal of Educational Development, 30*, 636–645.

Brock-Utne, B., Desai, Z., & Qorro, M. (Eds.). (2003). *Language of Instruction in Tanzania and South Africa (LOITASA)*. Dar es Salaam: E&D Vision.

Brock-Utne, B., Desai, Z., & Qorro, M. (Eds.). (2004). *Researching the Language of Instruction in Tanzania and South Africa*. Cape Town: African Minds.

Brock-Utne, B., Desai, Z., & Qorro, M. (Eds.). (2005). *LOITASA research in progress*. Dar es Salaam: KAD Associates.

Brock-Utne, B., Desai, Z., & Qorro, M. (Eds.). (2006). *Focus on fresh data on the language of instruction debate in Tanzania and South Africa*. Cape Town: African Minds.

Brock-Utne, B., Desai, Z., Qorro, M., & Pitman, A. (Eds.). (2010). *Language of Instruction in Tanzania and South Africa: Highlights from a Project*. Rotterdam, The Netherlands: Sense Publishers.

Brown, K. (2016, October). *From MDGs to SDGs, the case of gender*. IPID Invited Lecture, University of Minnesota.

Bruen, J., Crosbie, V., Kelly, N., Loftus, M., Maillot, A., McGillicuddy, A., & Péchenart, J. (2016). Teaching controversial topics in the humanities and social sciences in Ireland: Using structured academic controversy to develop multi-perspectivity in the learner. *Journal of Social Science Education, 15*(3), 18–25.

Bruns, B., Filmer, D., & Patrinos, H. (2011). *Making schools work: New evidence on accountability reforms*. Washington, DC: World Bank.

Brzyska, B. (2018). Trends in exclusion rates for students with special educational needs within PISA. *Oxford Review of Education, 44*(5), 633–650.

Buchanan, A., & Keohane, R. (2006). The legitimacy of global governance institutions. *Ethics and International Affairs, 20*(4), 405–437.

Buchholz, L. (2016). What is a global field? Rethinking Bourdieu's field theory beyond the nation-state. *Sociological Review, 64*(2), 31–60.

Burford, G., Tamás, P., & Harder, M. (2016). Can we improve indicator design for complex sustainable development goals? A comparison of a values-based and conventional approach. *Sustainability (Switzerland), 8*(9), 861.

Busemeyer, M., & Iverson, T. (2014). The political economy of skills and inequality. *Socio-Economic Review, 12*, 241–243.

Bush, G. H. W. (1988). *1988 republican national convention acceptance address*. Delivered 18 August 1988, New Orleans, LA. Retrieved November 22, 2018, from https://www.americanrhetoric.com/speeches/georgehbush1988rnc.htm

Butler, J. (1990). *Gender trouble: Feminism and the subversion of identity*. London & New York, NY: Routledge.

Butler, J. (2004). *Undoing gender*. New York, NY: Routledge.

Campbell, D. (1979). Assessing the impact of planned social change. *Evaluation and Program Planning, 2*(1), 67–90.

Campbell, D. (2008). Voice in the classroom: How an open classroom fosters political engagement among adolescents. *Political Behavior, 30*(4), 437–454.

Cappa, C., Petrowski, N., & Njelesani, J. (2015). Navigating the landscape of child disability measurement: A review of available data collection instruments. *ALTER-European Journal of Disability Research/Revue Européenne de Recherche sur le Handicap, 9*(4), 317–330.

CARE. (2010). *Rapid policy and institutional analysis with reference to CARE's Marginalized Ethnic Minorities (MEM) Impact Group.* Phnom Penh: CARE International.

Carnoy, M. (1998). National voucher plans in Chile and Sweden: Did privatization reforms make for better education? *Comparative Education Review, 42*(3), 309–337.

Carver, R. (1978). The case against statistical significance testing. *Harvard Educational Review, 48*(3), 378–399.

Casale, D., & Posel, D. (2011). English language proficiency and earnings in a developing country: The case of South Africa. *The Journal of Socio-Economics, 40*(4), 385–393.

Case, A., & Deaton, A. (1999). School inputs and educational outcomes in South Africa. *Quarterly Journal of Economics, 114*(3), 1047–1084.

Cavanagh, S. (2018, February 16). World Bank's 'global dataset' offers new way for comparing countries' educational performance. *EdWeek Market Brief.* Retrieved March 17, 2019, from https://marketbrief.edweek.org/marketplace-k-12/world-bank-unveils-new-tool-for-measuring-countries-ed-performance-and-economic-growth/

Cedefop. (2017). *The changing nature and role of vocational education and training in Europe: Conceptions of vocational education and training: An analytical framework* (Vol. 1, Cedefop Research Paper No. 63). Luxembourg: Publications Office of the European Union. Retrieved 5 April 2019, from https://publications.europa.eu/en/publication-detail/-/publication/d43d2858-deee-11e7-9749-01aa75ed71a1/language-en

Center for Economic and Social Rights. (2015). *Human rights in sustainable development.* New York, NY: CESR. Retrieved January 23, 2019, from http://www.cesr.org/human-rights-sustainable-development

Center for Universal Education at the Bookings Institution, Save the Children, and Women Thrive Worldwide. (n.d.). *Equitable learning for all in the post-2015 development agenda.* Retrieved June 12, 2019, from https://www.savethechildren.org/content/dam/global/reports/advocacy/EQUITABLE-LEARNING.PDF

Centre for Bhutan Studies and GNH Research. (2016). *A compass towards a just and harmonious society: 2015 GNH survey report.* Thimphu: Centre for Bhutan Studies and GNH Research. Retrieved February 23, 2019, from http://www.bhutanstudies.org.bt/wp-content/uploads/2017/05/2015-Survey-Results.pdf

Chabbott, C. (2003). *Conducting education for development: International organizations and education for all.* New York, NY: Routledge.

Chambers, R., & Conway, G. (1991). *Sustainable rural livelihoods: Practical concepts for the 21st century* (IDS Discussion Paper 296) Brighton: Institute of Development Studies. Retrieved February 23, 2019, from https://opendocs.ids.ac.uk/opendocs/bitstream/handle/123456789/775/Dp296.pdf?sequence=1

Chankrajang, T., & Muttarak, R. (2017). Green returns to education: Does schooling contribute to pro-environmental behaviours? Evidence from Thailand. *Ecological Economics, 131*(C), 434–448.

Chapman, D., & Snyder, C. (2000). Can high stakes national testing improve instruction? Re-examining conventional wisdom. *International Journal of Educational Development, 20,* 457–474.

Chatterjee, P. (1989). Colonialism, nationalism, and colonialized women: The contest in India. *American Ethnologist, 16,* 622–633.

Chingos, M. (2012). *Strength in numbers: State spending on K-12 assessment systems.* Washington, DC: Brookings Institution. Retrieved November 27, 2018, from https://www.brookings.edu/wp-content/uploads/2016/06/11_assessment_chingos_final_new.pdf

Chisamya, G., DeJaeghere, J., Kendall, N., & Khan, M. (2012). Gender and education for all: Progress and problems in achieving gender equity. *International Journal of Educational Development, 32*(6), 743–755.

Chuang, Y., Xie, X., & Liu, C. (2016). Interdependent orientations increase pro-environmental preferences when facing self-interest conflicts: The mediating role of self-control. *Journal of Environmental Psychology, 46,* 96–105.

Chudgar, A., Chandra, M., & Razzaque, A. (2014). Alternative forms of teacher hiring in developing countries and its implications: A review of literature. *Teaching and Teacher Education, 37,* 150–161.

Civicus. (2017). *All citizen-generated data initiatives tagged with (4) quality education.* Retrieved January 26, 2019, from https://network.thedatashift.org/sdg/quality-education

Clark, C., Dyson, A., Millward, A., & Robson, S. (1999). Theories of inclusion, theories of schools: Deconstructing and reconstructing the 'inclusive school'. *British Educational Research Journal, 25*(2), 157–176.

Clarke, J. (2015, September 26). 7 reasons the SDGs will be better than the MDGs. *The Guardian.*

Cloete, N. (2016). The ideology of free higher education in South Africa: The poor, the rich and the missing middle. *Kagisano, 10,* 115–124.

Cobham, A., & Jansky, P. (2015). *Measuring misalignment: The location of US multinationals' economic activity versus the location of their profits* (ICTD Working Paper 42). Brighton: ICTD. Retrieved November 9, 2018, from https://opendocs.ids.ac.uk/opendocs/bitstream/handle/123456789/11202/ICTD_WP42.pdf

Cobham, A., & Klees, S. (2016). *Global taxation: Financing education and the other sustainable development goals* (Background paper for The Learning Generation). New York, NY: Education Commission. Retrieved October 26, 2018, from http://www.taxjustice.net/wp-content/uploads/2016/11/Global-Taxation-Financing-Education.pdf

Cohen, J., & Rogers, J. (1995). *Associations and democracy* (The Real Utopias Project, Vol. 1). New York, NY & London: Verso.

Cohen, S. (2005). *The idea of Pakistan*. Lahore: Vanguard.

Colclough, C. (1996). Education and the market: Which parts of the neoliberal solution are correct? *World Development, 24*, 589–610.

Coleman, J. (1986). The idea of the developmental university. *Minerva, 24*(4), 476–494.

Committee on the Rights of Persons with Disabilities, United Nations Human Rights Council. (2015). *Consideration of reports submitted by states parties under article 35 of the convention: Initial reports of states parties due in 2011: Morocco* (CRPD/C/MAR/1). Retrieved February 23, 2019, from https://tbinternet.ohchr.org/_layouts/treatybodyexternal/Download.aspx?symbolno=CRPD%2FC%2FMAR%2F1&Lang=en

Connell, R. (1995). *Masculinities*. Cambridge: Polity Press.

Connell, R. (2007). *Southern theory: The global dynamics of knowledge in social science*. Sydney: Allen & Unwin.

Connell, R. (2013). The neoliberal cascade and education: An essay on the market agenda and its consequences. *Critical Studies in Education, 54*(2), 99–112.

Coomans, F., Grünfeld, F., & Kamminga, M. (2010). Methods of human rights research: A primer. *Human Rights Quarterly, 32*, 180–187.

Coombs, P. (1968). *The world educational crisis: A systems analysis*. New York, NY: Oxford University Press.

Coombs, P. (1985). *The world crisis in education: The view from the eighties*. New York, NY: Oxford University Press.

Cornu, C., & Liu, Y. (2018). *TCG4: Development of SDG thematic indicator 4.b.2*. Paris: UNESCO. Retrieved November 8, 2018, from http://tcg.uis.unesco.org/wp-content/uploads/sites/4/2018/08/TCG4-41-Development-of-Indicator-4.a.2.pdf

Counts, G. (1932). *Dare the school build a new social order?* Carbondale, IL & Edwardsville, IL: Southern Illinois University Press. (Republished 1979 by Arcturus Books)

Crehan, L. (2016). *Exploring the impact of career models on teacher motivation* (Management of Teachers). Paris: IIEP-UNESCO. Retrieved March 14, 2019, from http://unesdoc.unesco.org/images/0024/002462/246252e.pdf

Crouch, L. (2017, March 2–3). *Single universal assessment? Or scales for comparison?* Abridged version of presentation given at Penn Invitational Working Conference on 'Learning at the Bottom of the Pyramid', Philadelphia, PA.

Cummins, J. (1980). The cross-lingual dimensions of language proficiency: Implications for bilingual education and the optimal age issue. *TESOL Quarterly, 14*(2), 175–187.

Cummins, J. (2006). Identity texts: The imaginative construction of self through multiliteracies pedagogy. In O. Garcia, T. Skutnabb-Kangas, & M. E. Torres-Guzman (Eds.), *Imagining multilingual schools: Languages in education and glocalization* (pp. 51–68). Clevedon: Multilingual Matters.

Cummins, J. (2009). Fundamental psycholinguistic and sociological principles underlying educational success for linguistic minority students. In T. Skutnabb-Kangas, R. Phillipson, A. K. Mohanty, & M. Panda (Eds.), *Social justice through multilingual education* (pp. 19–35). Bristol: Multilingual Matters.

Cussó, R., & D'Amico, S. (2007). From development comparatism to globalization comparativism: Towards more normative international education statistics. *Comparative Education, 41*(2), 199–216.

Dale, R. (2005). Globalisation, knowledge economy and comparative education. *Comparative Education, 41*(2), 117–149.

Darvas, P., Gao, S., Shen, Y., & Bawany, B. (2017). *Sharing higher education's promise beyond the few in Sub-Saharan Africa*. Washington, DC: World Bank.

Daun, H., & Mundy, K. (2011). *Education governance and participation with focus on developing countries*. Stockholm: Stockholm University, Institute of International Education.

Davis, O. (2016). *No test left behind: How pearson made a killing on the US testing craze*. Talking Points Memo (TPM) (Online). Retrieved November 27, 2018, from http://talkingpointsmemo.com/features/privatization/four/

Day, M., Stuart, R., McVitty, D., & Francis, D. (2016). *The state of student governance in the Commonwealth*. London: Commonwealth Secretariat. Retrieved January 3, 2019, from http://thecommonwealth.org/sites/default/files/inline/STATE%20OF%20 STUDENT%20GOVERNANCE%20REPORT_FINAL%20PRINT%20VERSION.pdf

de Groot, I., Goodson, I., & Veugelers, W. (2014). Dutch adolescents' narratives of their citizenship efficacy: 'Hypothetically, I could have an impact'. *Educational Review, 66*(2), 148–167.

de Leeuw, S. (2009). 'If anything is to be done with the Indian, we must catch him very young': Colonial constructions of Aboriginal children and the geographies of indian residential schooling in British Columbia, Canada. *Children's Geographies, 7*(2), 123–140.

Dean, M. (2007). *Governing Societies: Political perspectives on domestic and international rule*. Maidenhead: Open University Press.

Dearden, J. (2014, April). *English as a medium of instruction: A growing global phenomenon: Phase 1* (Interim report). Oxford: University of Oxford and the British Council.

Deca, L. (2012). ESU and the temptation of going global. In V. Ivosevic et al. (Eds.), *ESU turns 30! Fighting for student rights since 1982* (pp. 29–36). Limassol: ESU.

Retrieved January 3, 2019, from https://www.esu-online.org/wp-content/uploads/2016/07/30th-Anniversay-Online.pdf

DeJaeghere, J. (2015). Reframing gender and education for the post-2015 agenda: A critical capability approach. In S. McGrath & Q. Gu (Eds.), *Routledge handbook of international education and development* (pp. 63–77) Abingdon: Routledge.

Desai, Z. (1999). Enabling policies, disabling practices. *Per Linguam, 15*(1), 42–53.

Desai, Z. (2000). Mother tongue education: The key to African language development? A conversation with an imagined South African Audience. In R. Phillipson (Ed.), *Rights to language: Equity, power and education* (pp. 174–178). Mahwah, NJ: Lawrence Erlbaum Associates.

Desai, Z. (2010). Reflections on the LOITASA project in South Africa: Three years later. In B. Brock-Utne, Z. Desai, M. Qorro, & A. Pitman (Eds.), *Language of instruction in Tanzania and South Africa: Highlights from a project* (pp. 207–213) Rotterdam, The Netherlands: Sense Publishers.

Desai, Z. (2013). Local languages: Good for the informal marketplace but not for the formal classroom? *Education as Change, 17*(2), 193–207.

Desai, Z. (2016). Learning through the medium of English in multilingual South Africa: Enabling or disabling learners from low income contexts? *Comparative Education, 52*(3), 343–358.

Desai, Z., Qorro, M., & Brock-Utne, B. (Eds.). (2010). *Educational challenges in multilingual societies.* Cape Town: African Minds.

Desai, Z., Qorro, M., & Brock-Utne, B. (Eds.). (2013). *The role of language in teaching and learning science and mathematics.* Cape Town: African Minds.

Deumert, A., Inder, B., & Maitra, P. (2005). Language, informal networks and social protection. *Global Social Policy, 5*(3), 303–328.

Dewey, J. (1909/1975). *Moral principles in education.* Carbondale, IL: Southern Illinois University Press.

Dewey, J. (1916/1944). *Democracy and education.* New York, NY: Macmillan.

Di Biase, R. (2019). Moving beyond the teacher-centred/learner-centred dichotomy: implementing a structured model of active learning in the Maldives. *Compare: A Journal of Comparative and International Education, 49*(4), 565–583.

Diadonis, P., & Efron, B. (1983). Computer-intensive methods in statistics. *Scientific American, 248*, 116–131.

Dietz, T., Rosa, E., & York, R. (2012). Environmentally efficient well-being: Is there a Kuznets curve? *Applied Geography, 32*(1), 21–28.

Doble, R. (2015, March). *Post-2015 education negotiations update for GCE UK.* Unpublished document.

Donald, K. (2016). Promising the world: Accountability and the SDGs. *Health and Human Rights Journal.* Retrieved January 23, 2019, from https://www.hhrjournal.org/2016/01/promising-the-world-accountability-and-the-sdgs/

Dorji, R., & Schuelka, M. (2016). Children with disabilities in Bhutan: Transitioning from special educational needs to inclusive education. In M. Schuelka & T. Maxwell (Eds.), *Education in Bhutan: Culture, schooling, and gross national happiness* (pp. 181–198). Singapore: Springer.

Draper, L. (1858). 'Moral and religious instruction in public schools'. In *The sixth annual report on the condition and improvement of the common schools and educational interests of the state of Wisconsin for the year 1858*. Madison, WI: Artwood and Rublee.

Draxler, A. (2008). *New partnerships for education: Building from experience*. Paris & Geneva: UNESCO and World Economic Forum.

Draxler, A. (2012a). *Baking the cake after 2015: Do the EFA goals have the right ingredients?* NORRAG Blog (Online). Retrieved November 27, 2018, from http://www.norrag.org/baking-the-cake-after-2015-do-the-efa-goals-have-the-right-ingredients/

Draxler, A. (2012b). International PPPs in education: New potential or privatizing public goods? In S. Robertson, K. Mundy, A. Verger, & F. Menashy (Eds.), *Public private partnerships in education: New actors and modes of governance in a globalizing world*. Northampton, MA: Elgar.

Draxler, A., & Haddad, W. (Eds.). (2002). *Technologies for education: Potentials, parameters, and prospects*. Paris & Washington, DC: UNESCO and Academy for Educational Development.

Dryden-Peterson, S. (2011). *Refugee education: A global review*. Geneva: UNHCR. Retrieved March 14, 2019, from http://www.unhcr.org/4fe317589.pdf

Dryden-Peterson, S. (2015). *The educational experiences of refugee children in countries of first asylum*. Washington, DC: Migration Policy Institute.

Duchêne, A., & Heller, M. (2012). Multilingualism and the new economy. In M. Martin-Jones, A. Blackledge, & A. Creese (Eds.), *The Routledge handbook of multilingualism* (pp. 369–383). London: Routledge.

Duignan, B. (2018). Enlightenment. *Encyclopedia Britannica*. Retrieved December 11, 2018, from https://www.britannica.com/event/Enlightenment-European-history

Dumont, L. (1986). *Essays on individualism: Modern ideology in anthropological perspective*. Chicago, IL: University of Chicago Press.

Dunne, M. (2007). Gender, sexuality and schooling: Everyday life in junior secondary schools in Botswana and Ghana. *International Journal of Education Development*, 27(5), 499–511.

Dunne, M. (2009). *Gender as an entry point for addressing social exclusion and multiple disparities in education*. New York, NY: UNGEI Global Advisory Committee.

Dunne, M., Durrani, N., Fincham, K., & Crossouard, B. (2017). *Troubling muslim youth identities: Nation, religion, gender*. Basingstoke: Palgrave Macmillan.

Durrani, N. (2008). Schooling the 'other': Representation of gender and national identities in Pakistani curriculum texts. *Compare: A Journal of Comparative and International Education*, 38(5), 595–610.

Durrani, N., & Halai, A. (2018). Dynamics of gender justice, conflict and social cohesion: Analysing educational reforms in Pakistan. *International Journal of Educational Development, 61*, 27–39.

Durrani, N., Halai, A., Kadiwal, L., Rajput, S.K., Novelli, M., & Sayed, Y. (2017). *Education and social cohesion in Pakistan*. New York, NY: UNICEF. Retrieved July 11, 2018, from http://sro.sussex.ac.uk/67152/

Easterly, W. (2015, September). The SDGs should stand for senseless, dreamy, garbled. *Foreign Policy, 26*.

Education International. (2013). *Equitable quality education: A precondition for sustainable development* (Statement submitted to OWG 4, 18 June 2013). Brussels: EI. Retrieved December 5, 2018, from https://sustainabledevelopment.un.org/content/documents/3721education2.pdf

Education International and Kenya National Union of Teachers. (2016). *Bridge vs. reality: A study of bridge international academies' for-profit schooling in Kenya*. Brussels & Nairobi: EI and KNUT. Retrieved May 7, 2019, from https://download.ei-ie.org/Docs/WebDepot/Bridge%20vs%20Reality_GR%20Report.pdf

Educational Policies Commission. (1940). *Education and the defense of American Democracy*. Washington, DC: National Education Association of the United States and the American Association of School Administrators.

Edwards, D. (2012). International processes of education policy formation: An analytic framework and the case of plan 2021 in El Salvador. *Comparative Education Review, 57*(1), 22–53.

Edwards, D. (2016). *Are global learning metrics desirable? That depends on what decision they are attempting to inform*. Paper from Conference 'The Possibility and Desirability of Global Learning Metrics', Mary Lou Fulton Teachers College, Arizona State University, Glendale, AZ. Retrieved March 16, 2019, from https://education.asu.edu/sites/default/files/ps_david_edwards.pdf

Edwards, D. (2018). What's wrong with the World Bank's human capital index? *Education International* (Online). Retrieved December 3, 2018, from https://worldsofeducation.org/en/woe_homepage/woe_detail/16022/what's-wrong-with-the-world-bank's-human-capital-index-by-david-edwards

Edwards, S. (2018). Is the global education sector heading toward fragmentation? *Devex*. Retrieved October 27, 2018, from https://www.devex.com/news/is-the-global-education-sector-heading-toward-fragmentation-93270

EFA Global Monitoring Report Team. (2015). *Investing in teachers is investing in learning: A prerequisite for the transformative power of education*. Oslo Summit on Education for Development. Oslo: UNESCO.

Ellis, M. (2016). *The critical global educator: Global citizenship education as sustainable development*. New York, NY: Routledge.

Elton, L. (2004). Goodhart's law and performance indicators in higher education. *Evaluation & Research in Education, 18*(1–2), 120–128.

Espinoza, O. (2008). Solving the equity-equality conceptual dilemma: A new model for analysis of the educational process. *Educational Research, 49*(4), 343–363.

Essack, S. (2012). Translating equitable access into retention and success in African higher education: The role and responsibility of individual institutions. *Journal of Higher Education in Africa/Revue de l'enseignement Supérieur en Afrique, 10*(2), 47–62.

Eurodad. (2018). *History RePPPeated: How public private partnerships are failing.* Brussels: Eurodad. Retrieved December 5, 2018, from https://eurodad.org/files/pdf/1546956-history-repppeated-how-public-private-partnerships-are-failing-.pdf

European Civil Protection and Humanitarian Aid Operations (ECHO). (2018). *Education in emergencies.* Retrieved October 25, 2018, from https://ec.europa.eu/echo/what/humanitarian-aid/education-emergencies_en

European Commission. (2019). *The Bologna process and the European higher education area.* Retrieved February 19, 2019, from https://ec.europa.eu/education/policies/higher-education/bologna-process-and-european-higher-education-area_en

European Students' Union. (2010, January 20). *Global student movement sets priorities for future work.* European Students' Union. Retrieved February 12, 2019, from https://www.esu-online.org/?news=global-student-movement-sets-priorities-for-future-work

Eurydice. (2019). *Teaching careers in Europe: Access, progression and support.* Brussels: European Commission. Retrieved March 30, 2019, from https://eacea.ec.europa.eu/national-policies/eurydice/content/teaching-careers-europe-access-progression-and-support_en

Evans, H. (2015). Service-learning and political engagement, efficacy, and apathy: A case study at Sam Houston State University. *Education, Citizenship and Social Justice, 10*(2), 107–117.

Evans, R., & Cleghorn, A. (2012). *Complex classroom encounters: A South African perspective.* Rotterdam, The Netherlands: Sense Publishers.

Facing History and Ourselves. (2018). *Choosing to participate* (Rev. ed.). Brookline, MA: FHAO.

Fahey, S. H. (1916). Moral education: What the schools can do. In *National education association journal of addresses and proceedings 1916.* Ann Arbor, MI: The Association.

Faul, M. (2014). Future-perfect/present-imperfect: Contemporary global constraints on the implementation of a post-2015 education agenda. *International Journal of Educational Development, 39*, 12–22.

Feiring, B., & Hassler, A. (2016). *Human rights in follow-up and review of the 2030 agenda for sustainable development.* Copenhagen: Danish Institute for Human Rights.

Fielding, M. (1999). Target setting, policy pathology and student perspectives: Learning to labour in new times. *Cambridge Journal of Education, 29*(2), 277–287.

Filmer, D., Hasan, A., & Pritchett, L. (2006). *A millennium learning goal: Measuring real progress in education* (Working Paper 97). Washington, DC: Center for Global Development.

Fischman, G., Topper, A. M., Goebel, J., & Holloway, J. L. (2019). Examining the influence of international large-scale assessments on national education policies. *Journal of Education Policy, 34*(4), 1–30. https://doi.org/10.1080/02680939.2018.1460493

Fisher, M. (2009). *Capitalist realism: Is there no alternative?* Winchester: Zero Books.

Fleisch, B. (2008). *Primary education in crisis: Why South African children underachieve.* Cape Town: Juta.

Fligstein, N., & McAdam, D. (2012). *A theory of fields.* Oxford: Oxford University Press.

Foa, R., & Mounk, Y. (2016). The danger of deconsolidation: The democratic disconnect. *Journal of Democracy, 27*(3), 5–17.

Fontdevila, C., Verger, A., & Zancajo, A. (2017). Taking advantage of catastrophes: Education privatization reforms in contexts of emergency. In T. Koinzer, R. Nikolai, & F. Waldow (Eds.), *Private schools and school choice in compulsory education. Global change and national challenges* (pp. 223–244). Basel: Springer VS. Retrieved October 25, 2018, from https://www.researchgate.net/publication/318184496_Taking_Advantage_of_Catastrophes_Education_Privatization_Reforms_in_Contexts_of_Emergency

Fooks, D. (1994). The life and times of cinderella. In P. Kearns and W. Hall (Eds.), *Kangan: 20 years on: A commemoration: TAFE 1974–1994* (pp. 29–43). Adelaide: NCVER. Retrieved April 5, 2019, from https://www.voced.edu.au/content/ngv%3A28383

Foster, P. (1965). The vocational school fallacy in development planning. In J. Karabel & A. Halsey (Eds.), *Power and ideology in education* (pp. 356–365). New York, NY: Oxford University Press.

Foulds, K. (2013). The continua of identities in postcolonial curricula: Kenyan students' perceptions of gender in school textbooks. *International Journal of Educational Development, 33*(2), 165–174.

Francis (Pope). (2015). *Laudato Si: On care for our common home* (Encyclical letter). Vatican City: Libreria Editrice Vaticana. Retrieved December 12, 2018, from http://w2.vatican.va/content/francesco/en/encyclicals/documents/papa-francesco_20150524_enciclica-laudato-si.html

Frantz, C., Mayer, F., Norton, C., & Rock, M. (2005). There is no 'I' in nature: The influence of self-awareness on connectedness to nature. *Journal of Environmental Psychology, 25*(4), 427–436.

Freire, P. (1970). *Pedagogy of the oppressed.* New York, NY: Herder and Herder.

Fukuda-Parr, S. (2014). Global goals as a policy tool: Intended and unintended consequences. *Journal of Human Development and Capabilities: A Multi-Disciplinary Journal for People-Centered Development, 15*(2–3), 118–131.

Fuller, B. (1991). *Growing-up modern: The western state builds third-world schools.* London: Routledge.

Funabashi, Y. (2017, January 17). Trump's populist nationalism. *Japan Times.* Retrieved November 22, 2018, from https://www.japantimes.co.jp/opinion/2017/01/17/commentary/japan-commentary/trumps-populist-nationalism/

Gaad, E. (2011). *Inclusive education in the middle east.* New York, NY: Routledge.

Gable, A., & Lingard, B. (2013). NAPLAN and the performance regime in Australian schooling: A review of the policy context (UQ Social Policy Unit, Research Paper No. 5). Brisbane: University of Queensland.

Gamble, J. (2013). Why improved formal teaching and learning are important in Technical and Vocational Education and Training (TVET). In *Revisiting global trends in TVET: Reflections on theory and practice* (pp. 204–238). Bonn: UNESCO-UNEVOC. Retrieved April 5, 2019, from https://unevoc.unesco.org/print.php?q=Revisiting+global+trends+in+TVET+Reflections+on+theory+and+practice

García, O. (2009). *Bilingual education in the 21st century: A global perspective.* Chichester: Wiley-Blackwell.

Gaudelli, W. (2016). *Global citizenship education.* New York, NY: Routledge.

Geldenhuys, J., & Oosthuizen, L. (2015). Challenges influencing teachers' involvement in continuous professional development: A South African perspective. *Teaching and Teacher Education, 51*, 203–212.

Gellner, E. (1983). *Nations and nationalisms.* Oxford: Basil Blackwell.

Gifford, R. (2014). Environmental psychology matters. *Annual Review of Psychology, 65*, 541–579.

Gill, I., Fluitman, F., & Dar, A. (2000). *Vocational education and training reform: Matching skills to markets and budgets.* Washington, DC: Oxford University Press/World Bank.

Ginsburg, M. (2012). Teachers as learners: A missing focus in 'learning for all'. In S. Klees, J. Samoff, & N. Stromquist (Eds.), *The World Bank and education: Critiques and alternatives* (pp. 83–94). Rotterdam, The Netherlands: Sense Publishers.

Ginsburg, M. (2017). Teachers as human capital or human beings? USAID's perspective on teachers. *Current Issues in Comparative Education, 20*(1), 6–30.

Ginsburg, M., Brady, K., Draxler, A., Klees, S., Luff, P., Patrinos, H., & Edwards, D. (2012). Public-private partnerships and the global reform of education in less wealthy countries: A moderated discussion. *Comparative Education Review, 56*, 155–175.

Giroux, H. (2017). The scourge of illiteracy in authoritarian times. *Contemporary Readings in Law and Social Justice, 9*(1), 14–27.

Glasson, G., Mhango N., Phiri, A., & Lanier, M. (2010). Sustainability science education in Africa: Negotiating Indigenous ways of living with nature in the third space. *International Journal of Science Education, 32*(1), 125–141.

Glewwe, P., & Krafft, C. (2014). *Benefits and costs of the education targets for the post-2015 development agenda* (Education Perspective Paper). Copenhagen: Copenhagen Consensus Center.

Global Compact. (2012). *Business, the millennium development goals, the post-2015 development framework and the UN Global Compact.* New York, NY: The Global Compact.

Global Initiative for Economic, Social and Cultural Rights (GI-ESCR). (2017). *Human rights bodies statements on private education September 2014–November 2017* (Synthesis paper version 9). Retrieved November 9, 2018, from https://www.gi-escr.org/privatisation-synthesis

Global Partnership for Education. (2018). *Education challenges.* Washington, DC: GPE. Retrieved October 24, 2018, from https://www.globalpartnership.org/education/education-challenges

Global Student Voice. (2016, May 11). *The Bergen declaration: Uniting for a global student voice* (pp. 1–4). Bergen: GSV. Retrieved January 3, 2019, from https://www.esu-online.org/wp-content/uploads/2016/07/The-Bergen-Declaration-Uniting-for-a-global-student-voice.pdf

Go, J., & Krause, M. (2016). Fielding transnationalism: An introduction. *Sociological Review, 64*(2), 6–30.

Gogolin, I. (2009). Linguistic habitus. In J. L. Mey (Ed.), *Concise encyclopedia of pragmatics* (pp. 535–537). Oxford: Elsevier.

Goldstein, H. (2004). Education for all: The globalization of learning targets. *Comparative Education, 40*(1), 7–14.

Goren, H., & Yemini, M. (2017). Global citizenship education redefined – A systematic review of empirical studies on global citizenship education. *International Journal of Educational Research, 82*(C), 170–183.

Gorski, P. (2013). *Bourdieu and historical analysis.* New York, NY: Duke University Press.

Gorur, R. (2016). Seeking like PISA: A cautionary tale about the performativity of international assessments. *European Educational Research Journal, 15*(5), 598–616.

Government of Khyber Pakhtunkhwa, Department of Elementary and Secondary Education (GoKP). (2012). *Education sector plan 2010/11 to 2015/16.* Peshawar: Department of Elementary and Secondary Education. Retrieved December 16, 2018, from http://www.kpese.gov.pk/Downloads/Education%20Sector%20Plan.pdf

Government of Khyber Pakhtunkhwa, Department of Elementary and Secondary Education. (2015). *Education sector plan 2015/16–2019/2020* (2nd Draft). Unpublished document.

Government of Pakistan, Ministry of Education (GoP, MoE). (2006). *National curriculum for pakistan studies grades IX – X 2006.* Islamabad: MoE. Retrieved December 19, 2018, from http://bisep.com.pk/downloads/curriculum/Grades-IX-X/PAKISTAN%20STUDIES%20IX-X.pdf

Government of Pakistan, Ministry of Education. (2009). *National education policy 2009*. Islamabad: MoE. Retrieved December 19, 2018, from http://planipolis.iiep.unesco.org/sites/planipolis/files/ressources/pakistan_national_education_policy_2009.pdf

Government of Pakistan, Ministry of Federal Education and Professional Training (GoP, MFEPT). (2017). *National education policy 2017–2025*. Islamabad: GoP, MFEPT. Retrieved December 19, 2018, from http://planipolis.iiep.unesco.org/sites/planipolis/files/ressources/pakistan_national_education_policy_2017-2025.pdf

Government of Sindh, Education and Literacy Department (GoS). (2014). *Sindh education sector plan 2014–18*. Karachi: Education and Literacy Department. Retrieved December 19, 2018, from http://www.sindheducation.gov.pk/Contents/Menu/Final%20SESP.pdf

Grek, S. (2009). Governing by numbers: The PISA 'effect' in Europe. *Journal of Education Policy, 24*(1), 23–37.

Griggs, D. (2013). Sustainable development goals for people and planet. *Nature, 495*, 305–307.

Groce, N., & Mont, D. (2017). Counting disability: Emerging consensus on the Washington group questionnaire. *The Lancet Global Health, 5*(7), 649–650.

Grønne, V. (2017). *Global student cooperation: Prospects for Increased cooperation*. Mountain View, CA: Creative Commons. Retrieved January 3, 2019, from https://drive.google.com/file/d/0Bwwfla_XUa-MVmhod1RPY25pMEE/view

Grossman, D., & Cogan, J. (Eds.). (2012). *Creating socially responsible citizens: Cases from the Asia-Pacific region*. Charlotte, NC: Information Age.

Grugel, J., & Singh, J. (2015). Protest, citizenship and democratic renewal: The student movement in Chile. *Citizenship Studies, 19*(3–4), 353–366.

Gupta, J., & Vegelin, C. (2016). Sustainable development goals and inclusive development. *International Environmental Agreements, 16*, 433–448.

Gür, B., Celik, Z., & Özoğlu, M. (2012). Policy options for Turkey: A critique of the interpretation and utilization of PISA results in Turkey. *Journal of Education Policy, 27*(1), 1–21.

Gustafsson, M. (2018). *Costs and benefits of different approaches to measuring the learning proficiency of students (SDG Indicator 4.1.1)* (Information Paper No. 53). Montreal: UIS. Retrieved March 17, 2019, from http://gaml.uis.unesco.org/wp-content/uploads/sites/2/2018/12/4.1.1_26_The-costs-and-benefits-of-different-approaches-to-the-SDG-indicator-on-the-proficiency-of-school-students.pdf

Gutstein, D. (2012). *Pearson's plan to control education: Report to the B.C. teachers' federation*. Burnaby: Donald Gutstein. Retrieved August 25, 2019, from https://bctf.ca/uploadedFiles/Public/Issues/Privatization/PearsonGutsteinReport.pdf

Guttman, A. (1987). *Democratic education*. Princeton, NJ: Princeton University Press.

Hadidi, M., & Al Khateeb, J. (2015). Special education in Arab countries: Current challenges. *International Journal of Disability, Development and Education, 62*(5), 518–530.

Hagopian, J. (Ed.). (2014). *More than a score: The new uprising against high-stakes testing.* Chicago, IL: Haymarket.

Halai, A., & Durrani, N. (2018). Teachers as agents of peace? Exploring teacher agency in social cohesion in Pakistan. *Compare: A Journal of International and Comparative Education, 48*(4), 535–552.

Hall, D. (2015). *Why public-private partnerships don't work: The many advantages of the public alternative.* Greenwich: Public Services International Research Unit, University of Greenwich.

Hall, P., & Soskice, D. (Eds.). (2001). *Varieties of capitalism: The institutional foundations of comparative advantage.* Oxford: Oxford University Press.

Hanushek, E., & Edwards, D. (2017). *Global learning metrics: Debate* (IIEP Learning Portal). Retrieved March 17, 2019, from https://learningportal.iiep.unesco.org/en/blog/global-learning-metrics

Hanushek, E., & Woessmann, L. (2015). *Universal basic skills: What countries stand to gain.* Paris: OECD.

Harley, K., & Wedekind, V. (2004). Political change, curriculum change and social formation, 1990 to 2002. In L. Chisholm (Ed.), *Changing class: Education and social change in post-apartheid South Africa* (pp. 195–220). Cape Town: HSRC Press.

Harriss-White, B. (2006). Poverty and capitalism. *Economic and Political Weekly, 41*(13), 1–7.

Hazelkorn, E. (2012). Striving for excellence: Rankings and emerging societies. In D. Araya & P. Marbert (Eds.), *Emerging societies.* London & New York, NY: Routledge.

Hazelkorn, E. (2015). *Rankings and the reshaping of higher education: The battle for world-class excellence.* London: Palgrave Macmillan.

Hazelkorn, E., Coates, H., & McCormick, A. (2018). *Research handbook on quality, performance and accountability in higher education.* Cheltenham: Edward Elgar.

Heater, D. (2015). *A history of education for citizenship.* New York, NY: Routledge.

Heckman, J. (2008). The case for investing in disadvantaged young children. In *Big ideas for children: Investing in our nation's future* (pp. 49–58). Washington, DC: First Focus. Retrieved December 3, 2018, from https://firstfocus.org/wp-content/uploads/2014/06/Big-Ideas-2008.pdf

Heugh, K. (2009). Literacy and bi/multilingual education in Africa: Recovering collective memory and expertise. In T. Skutnabb-Kangas, R. Phillipson, A. K. Mohanty, & M. Panda (Eds.), *Social justice through multilingual education* (pp. 103–124). Bristol: Multilingual Matters.

Heugh, K., Benson, C., Bogale, B., & Gebre Yohannes, M. (2012). Implications for multilingual education: Student achievement in different models of education in

Ethiopia. In T. Skutnabb-Kangas & K. Heugh (Eds.), *Multilingual education and sustainable diversity work from periphery to centre* (pp. 239–262). London: Routledge.

Heyneman, S. (1999). The sad story of UNESCO's education statistics. *International Journal of Educational Development, 19,* 66–74.

Heyneman, S., & Lee, B. (2014). The impact of international studies of academic achievement on policy and research. In L. Rutkowski, M. von Davier, & D. Rutkowski (Eds.), *Handbook of international large-scale assessment: Background, technical issues, and methods of data analysis* (pp. 37–72). London: CRC Press.

Heyneman, S., & Lee, B. (2016, May). International organizations and the future of education assistance. *International Journal of Educational Development, 48,* 9–22.

Hickel, J. (2015). *Five reasons to think twice about the UN's sustainable development goals.* Africa at LSE. Retrieved December 6, 2018, from http://blogs.lse.ac.uk/africaatlse/2015/09/23/five-reasons-to-think-twice-about-the-uns-sustainable-development-goals/

Hickel, J. (2019). The contradiction of the sustainable development goals: Growth versus ecology on a finite planet. *Sustainable Development, 27*(1), 1–12.

High-Level Group for Partnership, Coordination and Capacity-Building for Statistics for the 2030 Agenda for Sustainable Development. (2017). *Cape Town global action plan for sustainable development data.* New York, NY: United Nations. Retrieved January 23, 2019, from https://unstats.un.org/sdgs/hlg/Cape-Town-Global-Action-Plan/

High-Level Panel on Illicit Financial Flows from Africa. (2015). *Illicit financial flows.* Addis Ababa: UNECA. Retrieved October 27, 2018, from https://www.uneca.org/sites/default/files/PublicationFiles/iff_main_report_26feb_en.pdf

Higher Education Commission (HEC). (2010). *Curriculum of education: B.Ed. 4-year degree program (elementary & secondary), associate degree in education, MS/M.Ed. education (Revised 2010).* Islamabad: HEC. Retrieved December 19, 2018, from http://www.nacte.org.pk/Download/Education-2010.pdf

Hinchy, J. (2017). The eunuch archive: Colonial records of nonnormative gender and sexuality in India. *Culture, Theory and Critique, 58*(2), 127–146.

Hirsch, F. (1977). *The social limits to growth.* London: Routledge & Kegan Paul.

Hofstede, G., Hofstede, G. J., & Minkov, M. (2010). *Cultures and organizations: Software of the mind* (3rd ed.). New York, NY: McGraw Hill.

Holmarsdottir, H., Møller Ekne, I., & Augestad, H. (2011). The dialectic between global gender goals and local empowerment: Girls' education in Southern Sudan and South Africa. *Research in Comparative and International Education, 6*(1), 14–26.

Hook, T. (2017). *Partnership schools for Liberia: A critical review.* Brussels: Education International. Retrieved June 12, 2019, from https://download.ei-ie.org/Docs/WebDepot/LIBERIA18julyv7.pdf

Hotz-Eakin, D., & Selden, T. (1995). Stoking the fires? CO_2 emissions and economic growth. *Journal of Public Economics, 57*(1), 85–101.

Houghton, J. (2015). *Global warming: The complete briefing* (5th ed.). Cambridge: Cambridge University Press.

Hovens, M. (2002). Bilingual education in West Africa: Does it work? *International Journal of Bilingual Education and Bilingualism, 5*(5), 249–266.

Howie, S., et al. (2017). *PIRLS literacy 2016: South African highlights report.* Pretoria: Centre for Evaluation and Assessment. Retrieved February 22, 2019, from https://repository.up.ac.za/bitstream/handle/2263/66185/Combrinck_Pirls_2017.pdf?sequence=1&isAllowed=y

Hüfner, K. (2017). The financial crisis of UNESCO after 2011: Political reactions and organizational consequences. *Global Policy, 8*(Suppl. 5), 96–101. Retrieved December 5, 2018, from https://onlinelibrary.wiley.com/doi/epdf/10.1111/1758-5899.12459

Human Rights Watch. (2015). *Morocco: Flawed draft disability rights law.* Retrieved February 23, 2019, from https://www.hrw.org/news/2015/10/26/morocco-flawed-draft-disability-rights-law

Humphreys, S., Undie, C., & Dunne, M. (2008). Gender, sexuality and development: Key issues in education and society in Sub-Saharan Africa. In M. Dunne (Ed.), *Gender, sexuality and development* (pp. 7–38). Rotterdam, The Netherlands: Sense Publishers.

IAEG-SDGs. (2017). *Plenary meeting: 5th meeting of the Inter-agency and Expert Group on Sustainable Development Goal Indicators (IAEG-SDGs).* Ottawa: IAEG-SDGs. Retrieved January 23, 2019, from https://unstats.un.org/sdgs/files/meetings/iaeg-sdgs-meeting-05/15.Proposal%20for%20additional%20indicators%20and%20comprehensive%20reviews_plenary.pdf

Ibourk, A. (2016). *Learning achievement in Morocco: A status assessment.* Rabat: Policy Center for the New South. Retrieved February 23, 2019, from http://www.ocppc.ma/publications/learning-achievement-morocco-status-assessment

ICQN/TVSD Ministerial Conference. (2014). *Summary conclusions on the ICQN/TVSD country reports on 'providing Africa's youth with skills and training for jobs'.* Abidjan: ICQN/TVSD. Retrieved April 6, 2019, from http://www.adeanet.org/pqip-dctp/sites/default/files/documents/summary_conclusions_on_the_country_reports.pdf

Illich, I. (1971). *Deschooling society.* London: Calder & Boyars.

Independent Expert Advisory Group on a Data Revolution for Sustainable Development (IEAG). (2014). *A world that counts.* New York, NY: IEAG.

Ingstad, B., & Whyte, S. (Eds.). (2007). *Disability in local and global worlds.* Berkeley, CA: University of California Press.

Inter-Agency and Expert Group on Sustainable Development Goal Indicators (IAEG-SDGs). (2016). *Final list of proposed sustainable development goal indicators* (E/CN.3/2016/2/Rev.1). New York, NY: United Nations. Retrieved December 3, 2018, from https://sustainabledevelopment.un.org/content/documents/11803Official-List-of-Proposed-SDG-Indicators.pdf

Intergovernmental Panel on Climate Change (IPCC). (2018). *Global warming of 1.5°C: Summary for policymakers.* Retrieved December 12, 2018, from http://report.ipcc.ch/sr15/pdf/sr15_spm_final.pdf

International Commission on Financing Global Education Opportunity (Education Commission). (2016). *The learning generation: Investing in education for changing world.* New York, NY: Education Commission. Retrieved March 16, 2019, from https://report.educationcommission.org/downloads/

International Consortium of Investigative Journalists. (2018). *Offshore leaks database.* Retrieved November 10, 2018, from https://offshoreleaks.icij.org

International Labour Organization and UNESCO. (1966). *Recommendation concerning the status of teachers.* Paris: ILO/UNESCO. Retrieved March 14, 2019, from https://unesdoc.unesco.org/ark:/48223/pf0000160495

International Monetary Fund (IMF). (2014). *Spillovers in international corporate taxation.* Washington, DC: IMF. Retrieved October 26, 2018, from https://www.imf.org/external/np/pp/eng/2014/050914.pdf

International Monetary Fund. (2015). *Options for low income countries' effective and efficient use of tax incentives for investment: Report to the G-20 development working group by the IMF, OECD, UN and World Bank.* Washington, DC: IMF. Retrieved November 9, 2018, from https://www.imf.org/external/np/g20/pdf/101515.pdf

Iverson, T., & Stephens, J. (2008). Partisan politics, the welfare state, and three worlds of human capital formation. *Comparative Political Studies, 45*(4–5), 600–637.

Iwakuni, S. (2017). Impact of initial teacher education for prospective lower secondary school teachers in Rwanda. *Teaching and Teacher Education, 67*, 538–549.

Jackson, T. (2009). *Prosperity without growth: Economics for a finite planet.* New York, NY: Earthscan.

Jakobi, A. (2009). Global education policy in the making: International organisations and lifelong learning. *Globalisation, Societies and Education, 7*(4), 473–487.

Jansen, J. (2002). Political symbolism as policy craft: Explaining non-reform in South African education after apartheid. *Journal of Education Policy, 17*(2), 199–215.

Jansen, J. (2017). *As by fire: The end of South African universities.* Cape Town: Tafelberg.

Johnson, D. (1999). The insignificance of statistical significance testing. *Journal of Wildlife Management, 63*(3), 763–772.

Johnston, B. (2004). The economics and politics of cost sharing in higher education: Comparative perspectives. *Economics of Education Review, 23*, 403–410.

Johnston, B. (2016, November 15). *SDG indicators must match the ambition of the goals.* Devex. Retrieved March 17, 2019, from https://www.devex.com/news/opinion-sdg-indicators-must-match-the-ambition-of-the-goals-89168

Johnstone, C., Lazarus, S., Lazetic, P., & Nikolic, G. (2018). Resourcing inclusion: Introducing finance perspectives to inclusive education policy rhetoric. *Prospects*, 1–21.

Jones, P. W. (1997). On World Bank education financing. *Comparative Education, 33*(1), 117–130.

Joshi, D., & Smith, W. (2012). Education and inequality: Implications of the World Bank's education strategy 2020. In C. Collins & A. Wiseman (Eds.), *Education strategy in the developing world: Revising the World Bank's education policy* (pp. 173–202). Bradford: Emerald.

Journell, W. (2017). *Teaching politics in secondary education: Engaging with contentious issues*. New Paltz, NY: SUNY Press.

Kadiwal, L., & Durrani, N. (2018). Youth negotiation of citizenship identities in Pakistan: Implications for global citizenship education in conflict-contexts. *British Journal of Educational Studies, 66*(4), 537–558.

Kahne, J., & Bowyer, B. (2017). Educating for democracy in a partisan age: Confronting the challenges of motivated reasoning and misinformation. *American Educational Research Journal, 54*(1), 3–34.

Kahne, J., & Middaugh, E. (2008). *Democracy for some: The civic opportunity gap in high school* (Working Paper 59). Washington, DC: Center for Information and Research on Civic Learning (CIRCLE).

Kahne, J., & Sporte, S. (2008). Developing citizens: The impact of civic learning opportunities on students' commitment to civic participation. *American Educational Research Journal, 45*(3), 738–766.

Kahne, J., & Westheimer, J. (2001). Social justice, service learning, and higher education: A critical review of research. *School Field, 7*(5–6), 31–42. Retrieved December 4, 2018, from https://www.academia.edu/1159140/Social_justice_service_learning_and_higher_education_A_critical_review_of_research

Kahne, J., & Westheimer, J. (2006). The limits of efficacy: Educating citizens for a democratic society. *PS: Political Science and Politics, 39*(2), 289–296.

Kamens, D. (2013). Globalization and the emergence of an audit culture: PISA and the search for 'best practices' and magic bullets. In H-D. Meyer & A. Benavot (Eds.), *PISA, power, and policy: The emergence of global educational governance* (pp. 117–140). Oxford: Symposium.

Kamens, D., & Benavot, A. (1991). Elite knowledge for the masses: The origins and spread of mathematics and science education in national curricula. *American Journal of Education, 99*(2), 137–180.

Kamens, D., & Benavot, A. (2011). National, regional and international learning assessments: Trends among developing countries, 1960–2009. *Globalisation, Societies and Education, 9*(2), 285–300.

Kamens, D., & McNeely, C. (2010). Globalization and the growth of international educational testing and national assessment. *Comparative Education Review, 54*(1), 5–25.

Kamens, D., Meyer, J., & Benavot, A. (1996). Worldwide patterns in academic secondary education curricula. *Comparative Education Review, 40*(2), 116–138.

Kar, D., & Spanjers, J. (2015). *Illicit financial flows from developing countries: 2004–2013.* Washington, DC: Global Financial Integrity. Retrieved November 9, 2018, from https://financialtransparency.org/wp-content/uploads/2015/12/IFF-Update_2015-Final.pdf

Keep, E. (2005). Reflections on the curious absence of employers, labour market incentives and labour market regulation in English 14–19 policy: First signs of a change in direction? *Journal of Education Policy, 20*(5), 533–553.

Keep, E. (2012). *Youth transitions, the labour market and entry into employment: Some reflections and questions* (SKOPE Research Paper No. 108). Cardiff: SKOPE, Cardiff University.

Kennedy, K. (2007). Student constructions of 'active citizenship': What does participation mean to students? *British Journal of Educational Studies, 55*(3), 304–324.

Khan, M. L. A. (2016). ASPBAE plans 2016 – Priorities towards the right to education and lifelong learning in the sustainable development goals. In H. Hinzen & S. Schmitt (Eds.), *Agenda 2030 – Education and lifelong learning in the sustainable development goals* (pp. 25–33). Bonn: DVV International. Retrieved January 26, 2019, from https://www.dvv-international.de/fileadmin/files/Inhalte_Bilder_und_Dokumente/Materialien/IPE/IPE_75_EN_web.pdf

Khan, S. (2017). Khwaja sara, hijra, and the struggle for rights in Pakistan. *Modern Asian Studies, 51*(5), 1283–1310.

Khoja-Moolji, S. (2015). Suturing together girls and education: An investigation into the social (re)production of girls' education as a hegemonic ideology. *Diaspora, Indigenous, and Minority Education, 9*(2), 87–107.

Khoja-Moolji, S. (2017). The making of humans and their others in and through transnational human rights advocacy: Exploring the cases of Mukhtar Mai and Malala Yousafzai. *Signs: Journal of Women in Culture and Society, 42*(2), 377–402.

Khoja-Moolji, S. (2018). *Forging the ideal educated girl: The production of desirable subjects in muslim South Asia.* Oakland, CA: University of California Press.

Khokhar, F. (2013). *Pakistan studies for classes IX and X.* Jamshoro: Sindh Textbook Board. Retrieved December 19, 2018, from http://bachatdukan.com/product/pakistan-studies-for-class-ix-x-sindh-textbook-jamshoro/

Kijima, R., & Leer, J. (2016). Legitimacy, state building and contestation in education policy development: Chile's involvement in cross-national assessments. In W. Smith (Ed.), *The global testing culture: Shaping educational policy, perceptions, and practice* (pp. 43–62). Oxford: Symposium.

Kincheloe, J. (2005). *Critical constructivism primer.* New York, NY: Peter Lang.

King, K. (2009). Education, skills, sustainability and growth: Complex relations. *International Journal for Educational Development, 29*, 175–181.

King, K. (2013a). Editorial: Post-1990, post-2000, post-2015 – Education and skills – North & South. *NORRAG News, 49*, 3–6.

King, K. (2013b). *The year of global reports on TVET, skills & jobs. Consensus or diversity?* Geneva: NORRAG.

King, K. (2017). Lost in translation? The challenge of translating the global education goal and targets into global indicators. *Compare: A Journal of Comparative and International Education, 47*(6), 801–817.

Kingdom of Bhutan, Ministry of Education (MoE). (2012). *National policy on special educational needs.* Thimphu: Policy and Planning Division, MoE. Retrieved February 23, 2019, from http://planipolis.iiep.unesco.org/sites/planipolis/files/ressources/bhutan_special_needs_policy.pdf

Kingdom of Bhutan, MoE. (2015). *Annual education statistics.* Thimphu: Policy and Planning Division, MoE.

Kingdom of Bhutan, MoE. (2018). *Thirty-second education policy guidelines and instructions.* Thimphu: Policy and Planning Division, MoE.

Kingdom of Cambodia, Ministry of Education, Youth and Sport (MoEYS). (2013). *Prakas on identification of languages for Khmer national learners who are Indigenous people.* Phnom Penh: MoEYS. (Unofficial translation from Khmer into English)

Kingdom of Cambodia, MoEYS. (2015). *Multilingual education national action plan 2015–2018.* Phnom Penh: MoEYS. (Unofficial translation from Khmer into English)

Kingdom of Morocco. (2012). *Sustainable development in Morocco: Achievements and perspectives from Rio to Rio +20.* Retrieved February 23, 2019, from https://sustainabledevelopment.un.org/content/documents/1010file.pdf

Kingdom of Morocco. (2016). *Rapport du Royaume du Maroc concernant les premières mesures en matière de mise en œuvre de l'Agenda 2030 pour le Développement Durable* [*Report of the Kingdom of Morocco on the first steps in the implementation of the 2030 agenda for sustainable development*] (*Voluntary National Review-Morocco*). Retrieved February 26, 2019, from https://sustainabledevelopment.un.org/content/documents/10560NVR (Morocco).pdf

Kingdom of Morocco, High Commissioner for Planning. (2015). *Morocco between the millennium development goals and the sustainable development goals: Achievements and challenges.* Retrieved February 26, 2019, from https://www.hcp.ma/file/174386/

Kingdom of Morocco, High Council for Education, Training, and Scientific Research (HCETSR). (2015). *For a school of equity, quality and promotion: A strategic vision for reform 2015–2030: Abstract.* Rabat. Retrieved February 26, 2019, from http://www.csefrs.ma/wp-content/uploads/2015/05/Résumé-vision-Anglais-AR.pdf

Kingdom of Morocco, HCETSR. (2019). *The right to inclusive education: Conceptual shift, changes in practice and evaluation results* (Unofficial translation from Arabic). Retrieved from https://www.csefrs.ma/الحق-في-التربية-الدامجة-الانتقال-المف/

Kingdom of Morocco, Ministry of National Education, Vocational Training, Scientific Research and Higher Education (MNEVT). (2016a). *Localization of priority actions within projects for the 2015–2030 strategy* (unofficial translation from Arabic). Retrieved February 26, 2019, from https://www.men.gov.ma/Fr/Documents/DomMP-projetsstrategiquesV25025016.pdf

Kingdom of Morocco, MNEVT. (2016b). *Projects of the strategic vision 2015–2030* (unofficial translation from Arabic). Retrieved February 26, 2019, from https://www.men.gov.ma/Fr/Documents/ProjetstratAF17022016.pdf

Kingdom of Morocco, MNEVT. (2018, May 23). *The accommodation of the baccalaureate examination for students with disabilities* [Memorandum]. Rabat: MNEVT.

Kingdom of Morocco, MNEVT. (2019). *Details of the report: Consultative meeting with a representative group active in the field of disabilities* (unofficial translation from Arabic). Retrieved February 3, 2019, from https://www.men.gov.ma/Ar/Pages/DetailActualite.aspx?ActuID=LNhbd2fBxHc

Kingdom of Morocco, MNEVT, Directorate of Curriculum. (2017a). *Presentation of inclusive programs for application of the strategic vision 2015–2030* (unofficial translation from Arabic). Retrieved February 26, 2019, from https://www.men.gov.ma/Ar/Documents/visionstrategique1530/Visionstrategique1530-P3-7.pdf?TSPD_101_R0=621d4482b2b01380c06b08ddoce8254dw300000000000000000224484bc4ffff0o00000000000000000000000005bc0e876001c92443d

Kingdom of Morocco, MNEVT, Directorate of Curriculum. (2017b). *Reference framework for curriculum design for the benefit of children with disabilities in the inclusive classroom.* Sale, Morocco: Directorate of Curriculum (unofficial translation from Arabic). Retrieved February 26, 2019, from https://www.men.gov.ma/Ar/Documents/C-ref_curricu-enfanten_situhand141217.pdf

Kingdom of Morocco, MNEVT, Regional Academy for Education and Vocational Training. (2017). *Work program for the year 2017* (unofficial translation from Arabic). Retrieved February 26, 2019, from http://aref-rsk.men.gov.ma/ar/Documents/plan%20d%27action%202017.pdf

Kingdom of Morocco, National Human Rights Council. (2015). *Protection and promotion of the rights of persons with disabilities.* Rabat: CNDH. Retrieved February 26, 2019, from https://www.cndh.org.ma/sites/default/files/protection_and_promotion_of_the_rights_of_persons_with_disabilities.pdf

Kingdon, G., et al. (2014). *A rigorous review of the political economy of education systems in developing countries: Final report* (Education Rigorous Literature Review). London: DFID. Retrieved March 14, 2019, from https://eppi.ioe.ac.uk/cms/Portals/0/PDF%20reviews%20and%20summaries/Political%20economy%202014Kingdon.pdf?ver=2014-04-24-141259-443

Klees, S. (2013, July 18). Whither post-2015? A critique of the post-2015 high level panel's education and economic goals. *NORRAG Blog.* Retrieved January 13, 2019, from https://www.norrag.org/whither-post-2015-a-critique-of-the-post-2015-high-level-panel-education-and-economic-goals/

Klees, S. (2017). *Liberia's experiment with privatizing education* (Working Paper 235, National Center for the Study of Privatization in Education). New York, NY: Teachers College, Columbia University. Retrieved October 25, 2018, from http://ncspe.tc.columbia.edu/working-papers/WP235.pdf

Klein, N. (2007). *The shock doctrine: The rise of disaster capitalism.* Toronto: Random House of Canada.

Klemenčič, E., & Mirazchiyski, P. (2018). League tables in educational evidence-based policy-making: Can we stop the horse race, please? *Comparative Education, 54*(3), 309–324.

Klemenčič, M. (2012). How ESIB got into the Bologna process. In V. Ivosevic et al. (Eds.), *ESU turns 30! Fighting for student rights since 1982* (pp. 17–28). Limassol: ESU. Retrieved January 3, 2019, from https://www.esu-online.org/wp-content/uploads/2016/07/30th-Anniversay-Online.pdf

Klemenčič, M. (2014). Student power in a global perspective and contemporary trends in student organising. *Studies in Higher Education, 39*(3), 395–411.

Komatsu, H., et al. (2014). A model relating transpiration for Japanese Cedar and Cypress plantations with stand structure. *Forest Ecology and Management, 334,* 301–312.

Komatsu, H., & Rappleye, J. (2017a). A new global policy regime founded on invalid statistics? Hanushek, Woessmann, PISA, and economic growth. *Comparative Education, 53*(2), 166–191.

Komatsu, H., & Rappleye, J. (2017b). Incongruity between scientific knowledge and ordinary perceptions of nature: An ontological perspective for forest hydrology in Japan. *Journal of Forest Research, 22*(2), 75–82.

Komatsu, H., & Rappleye, J. (2017c). A PISA paradox? An alternative theory of learning as a possible solution for variations in PISA scores. *Comparative Education Review, 61*(2), 269–297.

Komatsu, H., & Rappleye, J. (2018). *Will SDG4 achieve environmental sustainability? Center for Advanced Studies in Global Education (CASGE)* (Working Paper No. 4). Tempe, AZ: Mary Lou Fulton Teachers College Arizona State University and CASGE. Retrieved February 15, 2019, from https://education.asu.edu/sites/default/files/working_paper_4_final.pdf

Komatsu, H., Rappleye, J., & Silova, I. (2019a). Culture and the independent self: Obstacles to environmental sustainability? *Anthropocene, 26.* Retrieved August 28, 2019, from https://www.sciencedirect.com/science/article/pii/S2213305419300098

Komatsu, H., Rappleye, J., & Silova, I. (2019b, January 16). Facing the climate change catastrophe: Continuing an urgent conversation. *ASU Mary Lou Fulton Teachers College Blog.* Retrieved February 13, 2019, from https://blog.global.education.asu.edu/facing-the-climate-change-catastrophe-continuing-an-urgent-conversation/

Komatsu, H., Shinohara, Y., & Otsuki, K. (2015). Models to predict changes in annual runoff with thinning and clearcutting of Japanese Cedar and Cypress plantations in Japan. *Hydrological Processes, 29*, 5120–5134.

Komljenovic, J., & Robertson, S. (2017). Making global education markets and trade. *Globalisation, Societies and Education, 15*(3), 289–295.

Koretz, D. (2017). *The testing charade: Pretending to make schools better.* Chicago, IL: University of Chicago Press.

Kosonen, K. (2013). The use of non-dominant languages in education in Cambodia, Thailand and Vietnam: Two steps forward, one step back. In C. Benson & K. Kosonen (Eds.), *Language issues in comparative education: Inclusive teaching and learning in non-dominant languages and cultures* (pp. 39–58). Rotterdam, The Netherlands: Sense Publishers.

Kosonen, K. (2017). *Language of instruction in Southeast Asia.* Paper commissioned for the 2017/8 Global Education Monitoring Report "Accountability in Education: Meeting our Commitments", UNESCO, Paris. Retrieved February 22, 2019, from http://unesdoc.unesco.org/images/0025/002595/259576e.pdf

Krasner, S. (1982). Structural causes and regime consequences: Regimes as intervening variables. *International Organization, 36*(2), 185–205.

Kumashiro, K. (2012). *Bad teacher! How blaming teachers distorts the bigger picture.* New York, NY: Teachers College Press.

Kumi, E., Arhin, A., & Yeboah, T. (2014). Can post-2015 sustainable development goals survive neoliberalism? A critical examination of the sustainable development – Neoliberalism nexus in developing countries. *Environment, Development and Sustainability, 16*, 539–554.

Laitin, D., Ramachandran, R., & Walter, S. (2016, June 6–7). *Language of instruction and student learning: Evidence from an experimental program in Cameroon.* Paper presented at the WIDER Development Conference on Human Capital and Growth, Helsinki, Finland. Retrieved February 22, 2019, from https://www.wider.unu.edu/sites/default/files/Events/PDF/Papers/Ramachandran.pdf

Lambert, S. (2004). *Teachers' pay and conditions: An assessment of recent trends in Africa.* Background paper prepared for the Education for All Global Monitoring Report 2005, UNESCO, Paris.

Langa, P. (2017, October 15). New dictionaries to help preserve SA's language heritage. *News24* (Johannesburg). Retrieved October 25, 2018, from https://www.news24.com

Langenhoven, K. (2010). Mother tongue instruction and understanding of natural science concepts in a South African primary school. In B. Brock-Utne, Z. Desai, M. Qorro, & A. Pitman (Eds.), *Language of instruction in Tanzania and South Africa: Highlights from a project* (pp. 133–144). Rotterdam, The Netherlands: Sense Publishers.

Lauder, H., Brown, P., & Ashton, D. (2017). Theorizing skill formation in the global economy. In C. Warhurst, K. Mayhew, D. Finegold, & J. Buchanan (Eds.), *The Oxford handbook of skills and training* (pp. 401–423). Oxford: Oxford University Press.

Laurillard, D., & Kennedy, E. (2017). *The potential of MOOCs for learning at scale in the global south* (Centre for Global Higher Education working paper series). London: Economic & Social Research Council.

Le Blanc, D. (2015). Towards integration at last? The sustainable development goals as a network of targets. *Sustainable Development, 23*(3), 176–187.

Le Grange, L. (2013). Ubuntu, Ukama and the healing of nature, self and society. *Educational Philosophy and Theory, 44*(Suppl. 2), 56–67.

Leach, F. (2008). The education of girls in early 19th century Sierra Leone. In M. Dunne (Ed.), *Gender, sexuality and development* (pp. 41–54). Rotterdam, The Netherlands: Sense Publishers.

Lebada, A. (2017). *Where are we in financing the SDGs?* Winnipeg: IISD. Retrieved November 10, 2018, from http://sdg.iisd.org/commentary/policy-briefs/where-are-we-in-financing-the-sdgs/

Lee, S., Watt, R., & Frawley, J. (2015). Effectiveness of bilingual education in Cambodia: A longitudinal comparative case study of ethnic minority children in bilingual and monolingual schools. *Compare: A Journal of Comparative and International Education, 45*(4), 526–544.

Letseka, M. (2012). In defence of Ubuntu. *Studies in Philosophy and Education, 31*(1), 47–60.

Levinson, M. (2014a). Citizenship and civic education. In D. Phillips (Ed.), *Encyclopedia of educational theory and philosophy* (pp. 135–138). Thousand Oaks, CA: Sage.

Levinson, M. (2014b). *No citizen left behind.* Cambridge, MA: Harvard University Press.

Lewin, K. (2013). *Making rights realities: Does privatising educational services for the poor make sense?* Lewes: Centre for International Education, University of Sussex.

Lewin, K. (2015). *Goals and indicators for education and development: Consolidating the architectures.* New York, NY: OSF. Retrieved May 6, 2019, from https://www.opensocietyfoundations.org/sites/default/files/lewin-goals-indicators-edu-dev-20150515.pdf

Lewis, S., & Hogan, A. (2016, September 12). Fast policy: When educational research morphs into quick fixes and 'silver bullets'. *AARE EduResearch Matters.* Retrieved March 17, 2019, from https://www.aare.edu.au/blog/?p=1755

Lin, A., Lawrence, J., & Snow, C. (2015). Teaching Urban youth about controversial issues: Pathways to becoming active and informed citizens. *Citizenship, Social and Economics Education, 14*(2), 103–119.

Lindqvist, P., Nordänger, U., & Carlsson, R. (2014). Teacher attrition the first five years: A multifaceted image. *Teaching and Teacher Education, 40*, 94–103.

Lingard, B., & Rawolle, S. (2011). New scalar politics: Implications for education policy. *Comparative Education, 47*(4), 489–502.

Livingston, K. (2016). Teacher education's role in educational change. *European Journal of Teacher Education, 39*(1), 1–4.

Lockheed, M. (2013). Causes and consequences of international assessments in developing countries. In H.-D. Meyer & A. Benavot (Eds.), *PISA, power, and policy: The emergence of global educational governance* (pp. 163–183). Oxford: Symposium.

Lockheed, M. (2016). *Measures that matter: Learning outcome targets for sustainable development goal 4: An examination of national, regional and international learning assessments.* Background paper prepared for the 2016 Global Education Monitoring Report. Retrieved January 16, 2019, from https://unesdoc.unesco.org/ark:/48223/pf0000245842

Lockheed, M., & Wagemaker, H. (2013). International large-scale assessments: Thermometers, whips or useful policy tools? *Research in Comparative and International Education, 8*(3), 296–304.

Lomas, L. (2002). Does the development of mass education necessarily mean the end of quality? *Quality in Higher Education, 8*(1), 71–79.

Luescher-Mamashela, T., & Mugume, T. (2014). Education student representation and multiparty politics in African higher education. *Studies in Higher Education, 39*(3), 500–515.

Lusiani, N., & Muchhala, B. (2015). *Universal rights, differentiated responsibilities: Safeguarding human rights beyond borders to achieve the sustainable development goals.* New York, NY & Penang: Center for Economic and Social Rights and Third World Network. Retrieved December 5, 2018, from http://cesr.org/sites/default/files/CESR_TWN_ETOs_briefing.pdf

MacFeely, S. (2018). *The 2030 agenda: An unprecedented statistical challenge.* Berlin: Friedrich-Ebert-Stiftung. Retrieved December 5, 2018, from http://library.fes.de/pdf-files/iez/14796.pdf

Maguire, J. (2016). *Why many college students never learn how to write sentences.* The James G. Martin Center for Academic Renewal (Online). Retrieved November 30, 2018, from https://www.jamesgmartin.center/2016/04/why-many-college-students-never-learn-how-to-write-sentences/

Maki, Y. (1977[2003]). *Kiryuno naru oto [The sound of air flow].* Tokyo: Chikuma.

Mallon, B. (2018). *The impact and evaluation of development education in irish primary schools.* Dublin: Development and Intercultural Education within Initial Teacher Education.

Mangenot, M., Giannecchini, L., & Unsi, A. (2019). *What education activists say and do about the privatization of education.* Washington, DC: Global Partnership for Education. Retrieved May 7, 2019, from https://www.globalpartnership.org/blog/what-education-activists-say-and-do-about-privatization-education

Marginson, S. (2016). The worldwide trend to high participation higher education: Dynamics of social stratification in inclusive systems. *Higher Education, 72*(4), 413–434.

Markus, H., & Kitayama, S. (1991). Culture and the self: Implications for cognition, emotion, and motivation. *Psychological Review, 98*(2), 224–253.

Markus, H., & Kitayama, S. (2010). Cultures and selves: A cycle of mutual constitution. *Perspectives in Psychological Science, 5*(4), 420–430.

Marphatia, A., & Archer, D. (2005). *Contradicting commitments: How the achievement of education for all is being undermined by the international monetary fund.* London: ActionAid International and Global Campaign for Education. Retrieved October 25, 2018, from http://www.right-to-education.org/resource/contradicting-commitments-how-achievement-education-all-being-undermined-international

Marphatia, A., Moussié, R., Ainger, A.-M., & Archer, D. (2007). *Confronting the contradictions: The IMF, wage bill caps and the case for teachers.* Johannesburg: ActionAid International. Retrieved October 25, 2018, from http://www.actionaid.org/publications/confronting-contradictions

Marsden, D. (2009, July 8–10). *The decline of occupational labour markets and the spread of prolonged entry tournaments: Labour market segmentation in Britain.* Presentation at the ILO Conference on Regulating for Decent Work – Innovative Labour Regulation in a Turbulent World, Geneva. Retrieved April 6, 2019, from https://www.ilo.org/legacy/english/protection/travail/pdf/rdwpaper_pl3a.pdf

Martens, J. (2017). Reclaiming the public (policy) space for the SDGs. In *Spotlight on sustainable development 2017* (Reflection Group on the 2030 Agenda for Sustainable Development, ed.). New York, NY: Reflection Group.

Martens, K. (2007). How to become an influential actor: The 'comparative turn' in OECD education policy. In K. Martens, A. Rusconi, & K. Lutz (Eds.), *Transformations of the state and global governance* (pp. 40–56). London: Routledge.

Martin, C. (2017). Skill builders and the evolution of national vocational training systems. In C. Warhurst, K. Mayhew, D. Finegold, & J. Buchanan (Eds.), *The Oxford handbook of skills and training* (pp. 36–53). Oxford: Oxford University Press.

Martin, T. (1995). Women's education and fertility: Results from 26 demographic and health surveys. *Studies in Family Planning, 26*(4), 187–202. Retrieved December 11, 2018, from http://gsdl.ewubd.edu/greenstone/collect/admin-mprhgdco/index/assoc/HASH50d0.dir/P0014.pdf

Masko, A., & Bosiwah, L. (2012). Teacher accountability and student responsibility: A cross-cultural comparison of American and Ghanaian schooling practices, policies and a reflection on NCLB. *Curriculum and Teaching Dialogue, 14*(1–2), 39–51.

Masuku van Damme, L., & Neluvhalani, E. (2004). Indigenous knowledge in environmental education processes: Perspectives on a growing research arena. *Environmental Education Research, 10*(3), 353–370.

Mattson, E., & Harley, K. (2003). Teacher identities and strategic mimicry in the policy/ practice gap. In K. Lewin, M. Samuel, & Y. Sayed (Eds.), *Changing patterns of teacher education in South Africa: Policy, practice and prospects* (pp. 284–305). London: Heinemann.

Mawdsley, E. (2018). 'From billions to trillions': Financing the SDGs in a world 'beyond aid'. *Dialogues in Human Geography, 8*(2), 191–195.

May, S. (2004). Maori-medium education in Aotearoa/New Zealand. In J. Tollefson & A. Tsui (Eds.), *Medium of instruction policies: Which agenda? Whose agenda?* (pp. 21–41). Mahwah, NJ: Lawrence Erlbaum Associates.

Mazrui, A., & Mazrui, A. (1998). *The power of babel: Language and governance in the African Experience.* Oxford: James Currey.

Mboti, N. (2015). May the real Ubuntu please stand up? *Journal of Mass Media Ethics, 30*(2), 125–147.

McClintock, M. (2013). A basic approach to human rights research. *Human Rights Advocacy and the History of International Human Rights Standards.* Ann Arbor, MI: University of Michigan. Retrieved January 26, 2019, from http://humanrightshistory.umich.edu/research-and-advocacy/basic-approach-to-human-rights-research/

McCowan, T. (2016a). Three dimensions of equity of access to higher education. *Compare: A Journal of Comparative and International Education, 46*(4), 645–665.

McCowan, T. (2016b). Universities and the post-2015 development agenda: An analytical framework. *Higher Education, 72*(4), 505–523.

McCowan, T. (2018). The university as engine of development? *Philosophical Inquiry in Education, 25*(2), 118–204.

McGrath, S. (2012). Vocational learning for development: A policy in need of a theory? *International Journal for Educational Development, 32*(5), 623–632.

McGrath, S., Lugg, R., Papier, J., Needham, S., & Neymeyer, S. (2013). *Status of TVET in the SADC region: Assessment and review of Technical and Vocational Education and Training (TVET) in the Southern African development community region and of the development of a regional strategy for the revitalisation of TVET.* Paris: UNESCO. Retrieved April 6, 2019, from http://unesdoc.unesco.org/images/0022/002256/225632e.pdf

McGrath, S., & Nolan, A. (2016). SDG4 and the child's right to education. *NORRAG News, 54*, 122–123. Retrieved March 17, 2019, from https://pure.au.dk/ws/files/108443910/NORRAG_News_54.pdf

McGrath, S., & Nolan, A. (2017). *SDG 4 and the child's right to education.* Retrieved January 23, 2019, from http://www.right-to-education.org/blog/sdg-4-and-child-s-right-education

McMahon, W., & Oketch, M. (2013). Education's effects on individual life chances and on development: An overview. *British Journal of Educational Studies, 61*(1), 79–107.

McMahon, W., & Wagner, A. (1981). Expected returns to investment in higher education. *Journal of Human Resources, 16*(2), 274.

McNay, I. (1999). The paradoxes of research assessment and funding. In M. Henkel & B. Little (Eds.), *Changing relations between higher education and the state* (pp. 191–203). London: Jessica Kingsley.

Mechouat, K. (2017). Approaching and implementing civic education pedagogies and engagement values in the Moroccan classrooms: Gender-based perspectives. *European Scientific Journal, 13*(7), 259–276.

Mégret, F. (2008). The disabilities convention: Human rights for persons with disabilities or disability rights? *Human Rights Quarterly, 30*(2), 494–516.

Meier, D., & Gasoi, E. (2018). *These schools belong to you and me: Why we can't afford to abandon our public schools.* Boston, MA: Beacon Press.

Meier, G. (2000). Ideas for development. In G. Meier & J. Stiglitz (Eds.), *Frontiers of development economics: The future in perspective* (pp. 1–12). Oxford: Oxford University Press and World Bank.

Meinshausen, M., et al. (2011). The RCP greenhouse gas concentrations and their extension from 1765 to 2300. *Climatic Change, 109*(1–2), 213–241.

Mendenhall, M., et al. (2015). Quality education for refugees in Kenya: Pedagogy in Urban Nairobi and Kakuma refugee camp settings. *Journal on Education in Emergencies, 1*(1), 92–130.

Metz, T., & Gaie, J. (2010). The African ethic of Ubuntu/Botho: Implications for research on morality. *Journal of Moral Education, 39*, 273–290.

Meyer, A. (2015). Does education increase pro-environmental behavior? Evidence from Europe. *Ecological Economics, 116*(C), 108–121.

Meyer, H.-D. (2017). The limits of measurement: Misplaced precision, phronesis, and other aristotelian cautions for the makers of PISA, APPR, etc. *Comparative Education, 53*(1), 17–34.

Meyer, J., & Rowan, B. (1977). Institutionalized organizations: Formal structure as myth and ceremony. *American Journal of Sociology, 83*(2), 340–363.

Miles, S., & Singal, N. (2010). The education for all and inclusive education debate: Conflict, contradiction or opportunity? *International Journal of Inclusive Education, 14*(1), 1–15.

Milligan, L. (2014). 'They are not serious like the boys': Gender norms and contradictions for girls in Rural Kenya. *Gender and Education, 26*(5), 465–476.

Milligan, L., Clegg, J., & Tikly, L. (2016). Exploring the potential for language supportive learning in English medium instruction: A Rwandan case study. *Comparative Education, 52*(3), 328–342.

Milligan, L., & Tikly, L. (2016). English as a medium of instruction in postcolonial contexts: Issues of quality, equity and social justice. *Comparative Education, 52*(3), 277–280.

Milligan, L., Tikly, L., Clegg, J., & Mukama, I. (2014). *Baseline report: Improving learner outcomes through language supportive textbooks and pedagogy.* Unpublished report.

Mincer, J. (1974). *Schooling, experience, and earnings.* New York, NY: National Bureau of Economic Research.

Mita, M. (2018). *Gendaishakaiha dokohe mukaunoka: Kogen no misuburashisa wo kirhiraku koto [Where is the contemporary society headed? Opening to the breath-taking view from the Plateau].* Tokyo: Iwanami Shoten.

Mizala, A., & Nopo, H. (2016). Measuring the relative pay of school teachers in Latin America 1997–2007. *International Journal of Educational Development, 46,* 20–32.

Mkandawire, T. (2001). *Social policy in a development context* (Social Policy and Development Programme Paper No. 7). Geneva: United Nations Research Institute for Social Development.

Mohamedbhai, G. (2014). Massification in higher education institutions in Africa: Causes, consequences and responses. *International Journal of African Higher Education, 1*(1), 59–83.

Mohanty, A. (2009). Multilingual education: A bridge too far. In T. Skutnabb-Kangas, R. Phillipson, A. K. Mohanty, & M. Panda (Eds.), *Social justice through multilingual education* (pp. 3–15). Bristol: Multilingual Matters.

Monkman, K., & Hoffman, L. (2013). Girls' education: The power of policy discourse. *Theory and Research in Education, 11*(1), 63–84.

Montoya, S. (2017, April 24). The cost of ignorance revisited: A reply by Silvia Montoya. *NORRAG Blog.* Retrieved January 15, 2019, from https://www.norrag.org/cost-ignorance-revisited-reply/

Montoya, S. (2018). *The learning crisis is causing a skills crisis. Here's why.* Montreal: UIS. Retrieved March 17, 2019, from https://sdg.uis.unesco.org/2018/08/27/the-learning-crisis-is-causing-a-skills-crisis-heres-why/

Montoya, S., & Hastedt, D. (2017). *News from Hamburg: Big steps forward towards reliable metrics to harmonise learning assessment data globally.* Montreal: UIS. Retrieved March 17, 2019, from http://uis.unesco.org/en/blog/news-hamburg-big-steps-forward-towards-reliable-metrics-harmonise-learning-assessment-data

Moriarty, K. (2016). Rewriting the ambition of SDG4: The risk of narrow global indicators. *NORRAG News, 54,* 124–125. Retrieved December 3, 2018, from https://pure.au.dk/ws/files/108443910/NORRAG_News_54.pdf

Moriarty, K. (2017). *Achieving SDG4 through a human rights based approach to education: World development report 2018* (Background paper). Washington, DC: World Bank. Retrieved December 3, 2018, from https://openknowledge.worldbank.org/bitstream/handle/10986/28869/121118-WP-PUBLIC-WDR18-BP-Achieving-SDG4-MORIARTY.pdf?sequence=1&isAllowed=y

Moriarty, K. (2019). *Developing a transformative vision of global education? Unpacking quality and learning in the policy formation and content of SDG4* (Doctoral thesis). Brighton: University of Sussex.

Morley, L. (2014). Inside African private higher education: Contradictions and challenges. *International Higher Education, 76*, 14–15.

Morley, L., Leach, F., & Lugg, R. (2009). Democratising higher education in Ghana and Tanzania: Opportunity structures and social inequalities. *International Journal of Educational Development, 29*(1), 56–64.

Moroccan Press Agency Ecology. (2017, April 5). *OECD: Morocco highlights its action plan for SDGs implementation.* Rabat: MAP Ecology. Retrieved February 26, 2019, from http://mapecology.ma/en/slider-en/oecd-morocco-highlights-its-action-plan-for-sdgs-implementation/

Morrow, W. (1993). Epistemological access in the university. *AD Issues, 1*(1), 3–5. Academic Development Centre, University of the Western Cape: Bellville, South Africa.

Mosier, R. (1965). *Making the American mind: Social and moral ideas in the McGuffey readers.* New York, NY: Russell & Russell.

Mosse, D. (2010). A relational approach to durable poverty, inequality and power. *Journal of Development Studies, 46*(7), 1156–1178.

Motala, E., Vally, S., & Maharaj, R. (2018). Education, the state and class inequality: The case for free higher education in South Africa. In G. Khadiagala, S. Mosoetsa, D. Pillay, & R. Southall (Eds.), *New South African review 6: The crisis of inequality* (pp. 167–182). Johannesburg: Wits University Press.

Motivans, A. (2014, October 14). *The post-2015 global education agenda and learning measurement.* Presentation at IEA GASS, Vienna. Retrieved March 17, 2019, from https://www.iea.nl/sites/default/files/fileadmin/user_upload/General_Assembly/55th_GA/Other_presentations/GA55_post-2015_education_agenda.pdf

Mounk, Y., & Foa, R. (2016, December 8). Yes, people really are turning away from democracy. *Washington Post.* Retrieved December 4, 2018, from www.washingtonpost.com/news/wonk/wp/2016/12/08/yes-millennials-really-are-surprisingly-approving-of-dictators/

Muhanguzi, F., Bennett, J., & Muhanguzi, H. (2011). The construction and mediation of sexuality and gender relations: Experiences of girls and boys in secondary schools in Uganda. *Feminist Formations, 23*(3), 135–152.

Muller, J. (2000). *Reclaiming knowledge: Social theory, curriculum and education policy.* London & New York, NY: Routledge Falmer.

Muller, J. (2018, March 16). The metric god that failed. *Project Syndicate.* Retrieved from https://www.project-syndicate.org/onpoint/the-metric-god-that-failed-by-jerry-z--muller-2018-03?barrier=accesspaylog

Mullis, I., Martin, M., Foy, P., & Hooper, M. (2017). *PIRLS 2016: International results in reading.* Chestnut Hill, MA: TIMSS & PIRLS International Study Center, Lynch School of Education, Boston College, and International Association for the Evaluation of Educational Achievement. Retrieved February 22, 2019, from https://files.eric.ed.gov/fulltext/ED580353.pdf

Mundy, K. (1999). Educational multilateralism in a changing world order: UNESCO and the limits of the possible. *International Journal of Educational Development, 19*(1), 27–52.

Mundy, K. (2006). Education for all and the new development compact. *Review of Education, 52,* 23–48.

Mundy, K., & Verger, A. (2015). The World Bank and the global governance of education in a changing world order. *International Journal of Educational Development, 40,* 9–18.

Murdoch, R. (2011). *Education: The last Frontier.* e-G8 Forum Paris. Retrieved November 27, 2018, from https://edu.blogs.com/files/blog---murdoch-education---the-last-frontier-may-2011.pdf

Murgatroyd, S., & Sahlberg, P. (2016). The two solitudes of educational policy and the challenge of development. *Journal of Learning for Development – JL4D, 3,* 9–21.

Murray, S. (2002). Language Issues in South African Education: An overview. In R. Mesthrie (Ed.), *Language in South Africa* (pp. 434–438). Cambridge: CUP.

Musset, P. (2012). *School choice and equity: Current policies in OECD countries and a literature review* (OECD Working Paper No. 66). Paris: OECD. Retrieved November 30, 2018, from http://www.google.fr/url?sa=t&rct=j&q=&esrc=s&source=web&cd=1&cad=rja&ved=0CCwQFjAA&url=http%3A%2F%2Fwww.oecd-ilibrary.org%2Feducation%2Fschool-choice-and-equity_5k9fq23507vc-en&ei=oRrRUdq9GIHa4AT_o4HIAQ&usg=AFQjCNHy1Kb8QFICcv3zedvs_v6MyEsbGQ&bvm=bv.48572450,d.bGE

Myers, J. (2016). *Costing equity: The case for disability-responsive education financing.* Brussels: International Disability and Development Consortium and Light for the World. Retrieved October 27, 2018, from https://iddcconsortium.net/sites/default/files/resources-tools/files/iddc-report-short_16-10-17.pdf

Myers, J., Pinnock, H., & Suresh, S. (2017). *#Costing Equity: The case for disability-responsive education financing.* London: Open Society Foundations and International Disability and Development Consortium. Retrieved February 26, 2019, from https://www.iddcconsortium.net/sites/default/files/resources-tools/files/iddc-report-short_16-10-17.pdf

Naess, A. (1989). The environmental crisis and the deep ecological movement. In A. Naess (Ed.), *Ecology, community and lifestyle* (pp. 23–34). Cambridge: Cambridge University Press.

Namphande, P., Clarke, L., Farren, S., & McCully, A. (2017). Education for democratic citizenship in Malawian Secondary Schools: Balancing student voice and adult privilege. *Compare: A Journal of Comparative and International Education, 47*(5), 703–721.

Naseem, M. (2006). The soldier and the seductress: A post-structuralist analysis of gendered citizenship through inclusion in and exclusion from language and social studies textbooks in Pakistan. *International Journal of Inclusive Education, 10*(4–5), 449–467.

Nath, S., & Chowdhury, A. M. (2016). *Literacy, skills, lifelong learning: SDG 4 in Bangladesh: Where we are* (Education Watch 2016). Dhaka: CAMPE. Retrieved January 26, 2019, from http://www.campebd.org/Files/EW_Report_2016_Full_Web.pdf

Ndimande, B. (2016). School choice and inequalities in post-apartheid South Africa. *Global Education Review, 3*(2), 33–49.

NEMIS-AEPAM. (2017). *Pakistan education statistics 2015–16.* Islamabad: National Education Management Information System – Academy of Educational Planning and Management, Ministry of Federal Education and Professional Training, Government of Pakistan, Islamabad. Retrieved December 15, 2018, from http://library.aepam.edu.pk/Books/Pakistan%20Education%20Statistics%202015-16.pdf

NEPI. (1992). *National Education Policy Investigation: Language.* Cape Town: Oxford University Press/NECC.

NEPI. (1993). *National Education Policy Investigation: The framework report.* Cape Town: Oxford University Press/NECC.

Ng, S. W., & Yuen, G. (2016). Hong Kong: Social justice and education for justice-oriented citizens in a politicized era. In A. Peterson, R. Hattam, M. Zembylas, & J. Arthur (Eds.), *The Palgrave international handbook of education for citizenship and social justice* (pp. 411–413). London: Palgrave Macmillan.

NGO Federation of Nepal. (2017). *Nepal SDGs forum: Civil society report on implementation of SDGs in Nepal, 2017.* Kathmandu: NGO Federation of Nepal. Retrieved January 26, 2019, from http://action4sd.org/wp-content/uploads/2017/07/CSO-SDGs-Report-Final.pdf

Nherera, C. (2000). Globalisation, qualifications and livelihoods: The case of Zimbabwe. *Assessment in Education: Principles, Policy, and Practice, 7*(3), 335–362.

Nielsen, H. D. (2006). *From schooling access to learning outcomes: An unfinished agenda: An evaluation of World Bank support to primary education.* Washington, DC: World Bank. Retrieved January 31, 2019, from http://documents.worldbank.org/curated/en/370901468154169343/pdf/372650SchoolingoAccess01PUBLIC1.pdf

Nigeria, National Universities Commission. (2019). *Private universities.* Retrieved May 4, 2019, from http://nuc.edu.ng/nigerian-univerisities/private-univeristies/

Nilsson, M., Griggs, D., & Visbeck, M. (2016). Mapping the Interactions between sustainable development goals. *Nature, 534,* 320–322.

Nisbett, R. (2003). *The geography of thought: How Asians and Westerners think differently ... and why?* New York, NY: Free Press.

Nkomo, M., & Sehoole, C. (2007). Rural-based universities in South Africa: Albatrosses or potential nodes for sustainable development. *International Journal of Sustainability in Higher Education, 8*(2), 234–246.

Noddings, N. (2005). *Educating citizens for global awareness*. New York, NY: Teachers College Press.

Noddings, N. (2015). *Education and democracy in the 21st century*. New York, NY: Teachers College Press.

Nomlomo, V. (2008). IsiXhosa as a medium of instruction in science teaching in primary education in South Africa: Challenges and prospects. In M. Qorro, Z. Desai, & B. Brock-Utne (Eds.), *LOITASA: Reflecting on phase 1 and entering phase 2* (pp. 81–101). Dar es Salaam: E&D Vision.

Nomlomo, V. (2009). *Science teaching in English and isiXhosa: Languages of instruction*. Saarbrucken: VDM Verlag.

Nowaczyk, M. (2015). *Advocating for multilingual education in Cambodia*. Phnom Penh: CARE.

Nowak-Lehmann D. F., Martínez-Zarzoso, I., Klasen, S., & Herzer, D. (2009). Aid and trade: A donor's perspective. *Journal of Development Studies, 45*(7), 1184–1202.

Nussbaum, M. (2002). Patriotism and cosmopolitanism. In J. Cohen (Ed.), *For love of country* (pp. 2–17). Boston, MA: Beacon.

Nuzzo, R. (2014). Scientific method: Statistical errors. *Nature, 506*, 150–152.

Oanda, I., & Jowi, J. (2012). University expansion and the challenges to social development in Kenya: Dilemmas and pitfalls. *Journal of Higher Education in Africa/Revue de l'enseignement supérieur en Afrique, 10*(1), 49–71.

Oanda, I., & Sall, E. (2016). From peril to promise: Repositioning higher education for the reconstruction of Africa's future. *Future: International Journal of African Higher Education, 3*(1), 51–78.

Obama, B. (2018). Cameron Kasky, Jaclyn Corin, David Hogg, Emma Gonzalez, and Alex Wind. The 100 most influential people of 2018: Parkland students. *Time Magazine*. Retrieved from http://time.com/collection/most-influential-people-2018/5217568/parkland-students/

OECD. (2000). *Definition and selection of key competencies – A contribution of the OECD program definition and selection of competencies: Theoretical and conceptual foundations*. Paris: OECD. Retrieved December 11, 2018, from https://www.orientamentoirreer.it/sites/default/files/materiali/2000%20 deseco%20contributo.pdf

OECD. (2005/2008). *The Paris declaration on aid effectiveness and the Accra agenda for action*. Paris: OECD. Retrieved October 25, 2018, from http://www.oecd.org/dac/effectiveness/parisdeclarationandaccraagendaforaction.htm

OECD. (2011). *Lessons from PISA for the United States: Strong Performers and Successful Reformers in Education*. Paris: OECD.

OECD. (2013). *Beyond PISA 2015: A longer-term strategy for PISA*. Paris: OECD.

OECD. (2016a). *Better policies for 2030: An OECD action plan on the sustainable development goals*. Paris: OECD.

OECD. (2016b). *Innovating education and educating for innovation: The power of digital technologies and skills.* Paris, OECD.

OECD. (2016c). *PISA 2015 results: Excellence and equity in education, PISA* (Vol. 1). Paris: OECD.

OECD. (2017a). *Measuring distance to the SDG targets: An assessment of where OECD countries stand.* Paris: OECD.

OECD. (2017b). *Sustainable development goals and public governance* (Online). Paris: OECD. Retrieved November 30, 2018, from http://www.oecd.org/gov/sustainable-development-goals-and-public-governance.htm

OECD. (2018a). *The future of education and skills: Education 2030.* Paris: OECD.

OECD. (2018b). *OECD and the sustainable development goals: Delivering on universal goals and targets.* Retrieved January 23, 2019, from http://www.oecd.org/development/sustainable-development-goals.htm

OHCHR. (2006). *Frequently asked questions on a human rights-based approach to development cooperation.* New York, NY & Geneva: United Nations. Retrieved January 21, 2019, from http://www.ohchr.org/Documents/Publications/FAQen.pdf

OHCHR. (2017a). *United Nations human rights appeal 2017.* Geneva: OHCHR. Retrieved January 21, 2019, from http://www.ohchr.org/Documents/AboutUs/UNHumanRightsAppeal2017.pdf

OHCHR. (2017b). *Submission of information and individual complaints.* Geneva: OHCHR. Retrieved January 23, 2019, from https://www.ohchr.org/EN/Issues/Education/SREducation/Pages/IndividualComplaints.aspx

OHCHR. (2017c). *Human rights council complaint procedure.* Geneva: OHCHR. Retrieved January 23, 2019, from https://www.ohchr.org/EN/HRBodies/HRC/ComplaintProcedure/Pages/HRCComplaintProcedureIndex.aspx

Oketch, M. (2016). Financing higher education in Sub-Saharan Africa: Some reflections and implications for sustainable development. *Higher Education, 72*(4), 525–539.

Olowu, D. (2012). University-community engagement in South Africa: Dilemmas in benchmarking. *South African Review of Sociology, 43*(2), 89–103.

Omoeva, C., Moussa, W., & Hatch, R. (2018). *From concept to practice: Five steps to measure education equity.* Data for Sustainable Development: UIS blog. Montreal: UIS. Retrieved July 3, 2019, from https://sdg.uis.unesco.org/2018/05/21/from-concept-to-practice-five-steps-to-measure-education-equity/

Onel, N., & Mukherjee, A. (2014). The effects of national culture and human development on environmental health. *Environment, Development and Sustainability, 16*(1), 79–101.

Open Working Group (OWG) 4. (2013, June 17–19). *Fourth session of the open working group on sustainable development goals.* Retrieved December 5, 2018, from https://sustainabledevelopment.un.org/processes/post2015/owg/session4

Open Working Group (OWG) 9. (2014, March 3–5). *Ninth session of the open working group on sustainable development goals.* Retrieved January 18, 2019, from https://sustainabledevelopment.un.org/processes/post2015/owg/session9

Open Working Group (OWG) 10. (2014, *March 31–April 4*). *Tenth session of the open working group on sustainable development goals.* Retrieved December 6, 2018, from https://sustainabledevelopment.un.org/processes/post2015/owg/session10

Open Working Group (OWG) 11. (2014, May 5–9). *Eleventh session of the open working group on sustainable development goals.* Retrieved January 18, 2019, from https://sustainabledevelopment.un.org/processes/post2015/owg/session11

Open Working Group (OWG) 12. (2014, June 16–20). *Twelfth session of the open working group on sustainable development goals.* Retrieved December 6, 2018, from https://sustainabledevelopment.un.org/processes/post2015/owg/session12

Orr, D. (2004). *Earth in mind: On education, environment, and the human prospect.* Washington, DC: Island Press.

Orr, D. (2009). *Down to the wire: Confronting climate collapse.* New York, NY: Oxford University Press.

Orti, A., Maldonado, C., & Solano, G. (2015). *Guia para la Veeduria Social de las Politicas Educativas.* Santo Domingo: Foro Socioeducativo. Retrieved January 26, 2019, from http://www.forosocioeducativo.org.do/phocadownload/guia%20veeduria%20social%20nov%202015%20final.pdf

Osili, U., & Long, B. (2008). Does female schooling reduce fertility? Evidence from Nigeria. *Journal of Development Economics, 87*(1), 57–75.

Oviawe, J. (2016). How to rediscover the ubuntu paradigm in education. *International Review of Education, 62*(1), 1–10.

Oxley, L., & Morris, P. (2013). Global citizenship: A typology for distinguishing its multiple conceptions. *British Journal of Educational Studies, 61*(3), 301–325.

Paget, K. (2003). From Stockholm to Leiden: The CIA's role in the formation of the international student conference. *Intelligence and National Security, 18*(2), 134–167.

Pakistan Bureau of Statistics. (2017a). *Provisional summary results of 6th population and housing summary – 2017.* Islamabad: PBS. Retrieved December 19, 2018, from http://www.pbs.gov.pk/content/provisional-summary-results-6th-population-and-housing-census-2017-0

Pakistan Bureau of Statistics. (2017b). *Population by religion.* Islamabad: PBS. Retrieved December 25, 2018, from http://www.pbs.gov.pk/sites/default/files//tables/POPULATION%20BY%20RELIGION.pdf

Pakistan Studies for Class 10th. (n.d.) Peshawar: Leading Books Publishers.

Park, H., Russell, C., & Lee, J. (2007). National culture and environmental sustainability: A cross-national analysis. *Journal of Economics and Finance, 31*(1), 104–121.

Parker, W. (2003). *Teaching democracy: Unity and diversity in public life.* New York, NY: Teachers College Press.

Pence, A., & Ashton, E. (2016). Early childhood research in Africa: The need for a chorus of voices. In S. Farrell, E. Kagan, & M. Tisdall (Eds.), *The Sage handbook of early childhood research* (pp. 380–397). London: Sage.

Peng, Y. S., & Lin, S. S. (2009). National culture, economic development, population growth and environmental performance: The mediating role of education. *Journal of Business Ethics, 90*(2), 203–219.

Perakis, R., & Savedoff, W. (2015). *Does results-based aid change anything? Pecuniary interests, attention, accountability and discretion in four case studies* (CGD Policy Paper 052). Washington, DC: Center for Global Development.

Peters, S. (2007). 'Education for all?' A historical analysis of international inclusive education policy and individuals with disabilities. *Journal of Disability Policy Studies, 18*(2), 98–108.

Peterson, A., & Bentley, B. (2017). Education for citizenship in South Australian public schools: A pilot study of senior leader and teacher perceptions. *Curriculum Journal, 28*(1), 105–122.

Pettersson, D., Popkewitz, T., & Lindblad, S. (2016). On the use of educational numbers: Comparative constructions of hierarchies by means of large-scale assessments. *Espacio, Tiempo y Educación, 3*(1), 177–202.

Phakeng, M. (2016). Mathematics education and language diversity: Past present and future. In A. Halai and P. Clarkson (Eds.), *Teaching and learning mathematics in multilingual classrooms: Issues for policy, practice and teacher education* (pp. 11–23). Rotterdam, The Netherlands: Sense Publishers.

Phakeng, M., & Moschkovich, J. (2013). Mathematics education and language diversity: A dialogue across settings. *Journal for Research in Mathematics Education, 44*(1), 119–128.

Phillips, D., & Ochs, K. (2003). Processes of policy borrowing in education: Some explanatory and analytical devices. *Comparative Education, 39*(4), 451–461.

Piketty, T. (2014). *Capital in the twenty-first century* (A. Goldhammer, Trans.). Cambridge, MA: Belknap Press.

Pillay, P., Woldegiorgis, E., & Knight, J. (2017)). Higher education finance: Implications for regionalization. In J. Knight & E. Tadesse (Eds.), *Regionalization of African higher education: Progress and prospects* (pp. 175–187). Leiden: Brill Sense.

Pineda, M. F. (2010). Standardized tests in an era of international competition and accountability. *International Perspectives on Education and Society, 13*, 331–353.

Pizmony-Levy, O. (2013). *Testing for all: The emergence and development of international assessment of student achievement, 1958–2012* (PhD dissertation), Indiana University. Ann Arbor, MI: ProQuest. Retrieved March 17, 2019, from https://eric.ed.gov/?id=ED562896

Poli, R. (2013). A note on the difference between complicated and complex social systems. *Cadmus, 2*(1), 6.

Prah, K., & Brock-Utne, B. (Eds.). (2009). *Multilingualism: An African advantage: A paradigm shift in African language of instruction policies*. Cape Town: CASAS.

Psacharopoulos, G. (1972). Rates of return to investment in education around the world. *Comparative Education Review, 16*(1), 54–67.

Pugliese, A., & Ray, J. (2009). *Top-emitting countries differ on climate change threat*. Retrieved December 12, 2018, from http://news.gallup.com/poll/124595/Top-Emitting-Countries-Differ-Climate-Change-Threat.aspx#2

Pullella, P. (2015, November 30). World headed toward 'suicide' if no climate agreement: Pope. *Reuters*. Retrieved December 7, 2018, from https://www.reuters.com/article/us-climatechange-summit-pope/world-headed-toward-suicide-if-no-climate-agreement-pope-idUSKBN0TJ2FY20151130

Purewal, N. (2015). Interrogating the rights discourse on girls' education: Neo-liberalism, neo-colonialism, and the Beijing platform for action. *IDS Bulletin, 46*(4), 47–53.

Qorro, M., Desai, Z., & Brock-Utne, B. (Eds.). (2008). *LOITASA: Reflecting on phase I and entering phase II*. Dar es Salaam: E&D Vision.

Qorro, M., Desai, Z., & Brock-Utne, B. (Eds.). (2012). *Language of instruction: A key to understanding what the teacher is saying*. Dar es Salaam: KAD Associates.

Raffe, D. (2015). First count to five: Some principles for the reform of vocational qualifications in England. *Journal of Education and Work, 28*(2), 147–164.

Rahman, M., & Quadir, F. (2018). The civil service's 'fast food approach' to development policy-making in Bangladesh: Critique and agenda for reform. *Asia Pacific Journal of Public Administration, 40*(3), 159–174.

Randers, J. (2012). *2052: A global forecast for the next forty years*. White River Junction, VT: Chelsea Green.

Rappleye, J., & Komatsu, H. (2016). Living on borrowed time: Rethinking temporality, self, nihilism, and schooling. *Comparative Education, 52*(2), 177–201.

Rappleye, J., & Komatsu, H. (2017). How to make lesson study work in America and worldwide: A Japanese perspective on the onto-cultural basis of (teacher) education. *Research in Comparative and International Education, 12*(4), 398–430.

Rappleye, J., & Komatsu, H. (in press). Towards comparative educational research for a finite future. *Comparative Education*.

Rappleye, J., Komatsu, H., Uchida, Y., Krys, K., & Markus, H. (2020). Happiness, self, pedagogy: Constructive critique of the OECD's (mis)measure of student well-being. *Journal of Education Policy, 35*(2), 258–282. doi: 10.1080/02680939.2019.1576923.

Rappleye, J., & Un, L. (2018). What drives failed policy at the World Bank? An inside account of new aid modalities to higher education: Context, blame, and infallibility. *Comparative Education, 54*(2), 250–274.

Raupach, M., Marland, G., Ciais, P., Le Quéré, C., Canadell, J., Klepper, G., & Field, C. B. (2007). Global and regional drivers of accelerating CO_2 emissions. *Proceedings of the National Academy of Sciences, 104*(24), 10288–10293.

Ravitch, D. (2013). *Stop blaming schools for inequality.* Diane Ravitch's Blog. Retrieved November 30, 2018, from http://dianeravitch.net/2013/04/29/stop-blaming-schools-for-inequality/

Regmi, K. (2015). Can lifelong learning be the post-2015 agenda for the least developed countries? *International Journal of Lifelong Education, 34*(5), 551–568.

Reid, A. (2015). *Building our nation through public education.* Melbourne: Australian Government Primary Principals Association. Retrieved November 30, 2018, from http://apo.org.au/system/files/60542/apo-nid60542-17016.pdf

Reimer, E. (1971). *School is dead.* New York, NY: Doubleday.

Republic of South Africa (RSA). (1996). *The constitution of the republic of South Africa, 1996. Act 108 of 1996.* Pretoria: Government Printers.

Republic of South Africa, Department of Basic Education (DBE). (2010a). *National policy pertaining to the programme and promotion requirements of the national curriculum statement grades R-12 including Curriculum Assessment Policy Statements (CAPS).* Pretoria: DBE.

Republic of South Africa, DBE. (2010b). *The status of the Language of Learning and Teaching (LoLT) in South African public schools: A quantitative review.* Pretoria: DBE.

Republic of South Africa, Department of Education (DoE). (1997). *Language-in-education policy* (Government Notice No. 383, Vol. 17997). Pretoria: DoE.

Resplandy, L., et al. (2018). Quantification of ocean heat uptake from changes in atmospheric O_2 and CO_2 composition. *Nature, 563*, 105–108.

RESULTS Educational Fund. (2016). *Right to education index: 2016 RTEI questionnaire.* Washington, DC: RESULTS. Retrieved January 26, 2019, from https://www.rtei.org/documents/16/RTEIquestionaire.pdf

Rey, O. (2010). The use of external assessments and the impact on education systems. In S. Stoney (Ed.), *Beyond Lisbon 2010: Perspectives from research and development for education policy in Europe* (pp. 137–157). Slough: National Foundation for Educational Research.

Richardson, G. (2008). Conflicting imaginaries: Global citizenship education in Canada as a site of contestation. In M. Peters, A. Britton, & H. Blee (Eds.), *Global citizenship education: Philosophy, theory and pedagogy* (pp. 115–131). Rotterdam, The Netherlands: Sense Publishers.

Ricketts, E. (2013). *Women's access to secondary education in colonial and postcolonial Tanzania and Rwanda* (Master's theses. Paper 1472). Loyola University, Chicago, IL. Retrieved November 24, 2018, from http://ecommons.luc.edu/luc_theses/1472

Riddell, A. (2007). *Education Sector-Wide Approaches (SWAps): Background, guide and lessons.* Paris: UNESCO.

Riddell, A., & Niño-Zarazúa, M. (2016). The effectiveness of foreign aid to education: What can be learned? *International Journal of Educational Development, 48*, 23–36.

Riep, C., & Machacek, M. (2016). *Schooling the poor profitably: The innovations and deprivations of bridge international academies in Uganda.* Brussels: Education International. Retrieved July 3, 2019, from https://download.ei-ie.org/Docs/WebDepot/DOC_Final_28sept.pdf

Right to Education. (2015). *Applying right to education indicators to the post-2015 education agenda.* London: Right to Education Project. Retrieved January 26, 2019, from http://www.right-to-education.org/sites/right-to-education.org/files/resource-attachments/RTE_Applying_RTE_Indicators_to_the_Post_2015_Agenda_2015.pdf

Right to Education. (2017). *Regional human rights mechanisms.* Retrieved January 24, 2019, from http://www.right-to-education.org/page/regional-human-rights-mechanisms

Right to Education Project et al. (2015). *The UK's support of the growth of private education through its development aid: Questioning its responsibilities as regards its human rights extraterritorial obligations.* Retrieved November 30, 2018, from https://tbinternet.ohchr.org/Treaties/CESCR/Shared%20Documents/GBR/INT_CESCR_ICO_GBR_21740_E.pdf

Rizvi, F. (2006). Imagination and the globalisation of educational policy research. *Globalisation, Societies and Education, 4*(2), 193–205.

Rizvi, F., & Lingard, B. (2010). *Globalizing education policy.* London & New York, NY: Routledge.

Robertson, S. (2012). Researching global education policy: Angles In/On/Out ... In A. Verger, M. Novelli, & H. Altinyelken (Eds.), *Global education policy and international development: New agendas, issues and practices.* New York, NY: Continuum.

Rogers, A. (1993). The world crisis in adult education: A case study from literacy. *Compare, 23*(2), 159–175.

Ron Balsera, M. (2017). *Tax, privatisation and the right to education: Influencing education financing and tax policy to transform children's lives.* Johannesburg: ActionAid International. Retrieved October 26, 2018, from http://www.actionaid.org/sites/files/actionaid/tax_privatisation_report_online.pdf

Rose, P. (2014, June 10). *New proposals on post-2015 education goals: How do they compare?* Global Partnership for Education. Retrieved January 28, 2019, from https://www.globalpartnership.org/blog/new-proposals-post-2015-education-goals-how-do-they-compare

Rose, P. (2015). Three lessons for educational quality in post-2015 goals and targets: Clarity, measurability and equity. *International Journal of Educational Development, 40*(C), 289–296.

Rose, P. (2016). *1, 2, 3 testing: Assessing learning of what, for what and for whom? Breaking down the debate on learning assessments and a global learning metric.* Washington, DC: GPE. Retrieved March 17, 2019, from https://www.globalpartnership.org/blog/1-2-3-testing-assessing-learning-what-what-and-whom

Rose, P., & Zubairi, A. (2017). *Bright and early: How financing pre-primary education gives every child a fair start in life.* London: Theirworld. Retrieved November 15, 2018, from http://www.ungei.org/Theirworld-Report-Bright-and-Early-June-2017_2.pdf

Rosen, L. (2009). Rhetoric and symbolic action in the policy process. In G. Sykes, B. Schneider, & D. Plank (Eds.), *Handbook on education policy research* (pp. 267–285). New York, NY: Routledge.

Rosendal, T. (2011). *Linguistic landshapes: A comparison of official and non-official language management in Rwanda and Uganda, focusing on the position of African languages.* Cologne: Rüdiger Köppe Verlag.

Ross, E. (2017). *Rethinking social studies: Critical pedagogy in pursuit of dangerous citizenship.* Charlotte, NC: Information Age.

RTI International. (2016). *EdData II task order 15: Data for Education Programming in Asia and the Middle East (DEP/AME) situation and needs assessment for students who are blind/low vision or deaf/hard of hearing in Morocco.* Washington, DC: USAID. Retrieved February 26, 2019, from https://www.globalreadingnetwork.net/sites/default/files/eddata/R1-026_Morocco_Inclusion_Study_Report_ENGLISH_FINAL.pdf

Sachs, J. (2012). From millennium development goals to sustainable development goals. *The Lancet, 379,* 2206–2211.

Sachs, J. (2016). Teacher professionalism: Why are we still talking about it? *Teachers and Teaching: Theory and Practice, 22*(4), 413–425.

Sachs, J., Schmidt-Traub, G., Kroll, C., Durand-Delacre, D., & Teksöz, K. (2016). *SDG index and dashboards: A global report.* New York, NY: Bertelsmann Stiftung and SDSN. Retrieved January 23, 2019, from http://www.sdgindex.org/assets/files/sdg_index_and_dashboards_compact.pdf

Sachs-Israel, M. (2016). The SDG 4-education 2030 agenda and its framework for action: The process of its development and first steps in taking it forward. *Bildung und Erziehung, 69*(3), 269–290.

Sachs-Israel, M. (2017). The SDG4-education 2030 agenda and its framework for action: The process of its development and first steps in taking it forward. *Bildung und Erziehung, 69*(3), 269–290.

Sahlberg, P. (2010). Rethinking accountability in a knowledge society. *Journal of Educational Change, 11*(1), 45–61.

Sahlberg, P. (2011). The fourth way of Finland. *Journal of Educational Change, 12*(2), 173–185.

Sahlberg, P. (2013, December 8). The PISA 2012 scores show the failure of 'market based' education reform. *The Guardian* (online). Retrieved November 30, 2018, from http://www.theguardian.com/commentisfree/2013/dec/08/pisa-education-test-scores-meaning

Sahlberg, P. (2014). *Finnish lessons 2.0: What can the world learn from educational change in Finland?* New York, NY: Teachers College Press.

Salamanca Statement and Framework for Action on Special Needs Education. (1994, June 7–10). Adopted by the world conference on special needs education: Access and quality. Salamanca, Spain. Salamanca: UNESCO and Ministry of Education and Science, Spain. Retrieved February 26, 2019, from http://www.unesco.org/education/pdf/SALAMA_E.PDF

Samoff, J., & Carrol, B. (2003). *From manpower planning to the knowledge era: World Bank policies on higher education in Africa* (UNESCO forum on higher education, research and knowledge). Paris: UNESCO.

Samuelson, B., & Freedman, S. (2010). Language policy, multilingual education and power in Rwanda. *Language Policy, 9*(3), 191–215.

Savedoff, W. (2016). *A Global Offer for Learning (GOL): Based on experience with paying for results* (CGD Policy Paper 095). Washington, DC: Center for Global Development.

Sayed, Y., & Ahmed, R. (2011). Education quality in post-apartheid South African policy: Balancing equity, diversity, rights and participation. *Comparative Education, 47*(1), 103–118.

Sayed, Y., & Ahmed, R. (2015). Education quality, and teaching and learning in the post-2015 education Agenda. *International Journal of Educational Development, 40*(C), 330–338.

Sayed, Y., & Ahmed, R. (2018). The 2030 global education agenda and the SDGs: Process, policy and prospects. In A. Verger, H. Altinyelken, & M. Novelli (Eds.), *Global education policy and international development: New agendas, issues and policies* (pp. 185–207). New York, NY: Bloomsbury.

Sayed, Y., Ahmed, R., & Mogliacci, R. (2018). The 2030 global education agenda and the SDGs: Process, policy and prospects. In A. Verger, M. Novelli, & H. K. Altinyelken (Eds.), *Global education policy and international development* (2nd ed., 185–208). London: Bloomsbury.

Sayed, Y., et al. (2018). *Engaging teachers in peacebuilding in post-conflict contexts: Rwanda and South Africa synthesis report.* Brighton: Centre for International Education, University of Sussex. Retrieved December 3, 2018, from http://sro.sussex.ac.uk/76123/

Sayed, Y., & Kanjee, A. (2013). Assessment in Sub-Saharan Africa: Challenges and prospects. *Assessment in Education: Principles, Policy & Practice, 20*(4), 373–384.

Schendel, R., & McCowan, T. (2016). Expanding higher education systems in low- and middle-income countries: The challenges of equity and quality. *Higher Education, 72*(4), 407–411.

Schuelka, M. (2013a). Excluding students with disabilities from the culture of achievement: The case of the TIMSS, PIRLS and PISA. *Journal of Education Policy, 28*(2), 216–230.

Schuelka, M. (2013b). Inclusive education in Bhutan: A small state with alternative priorities. *Current Issues in Comparative Education, 15*(1), 145–156.

Schuelka, M. (2015). The evolving construction and conceptualization of disability in Bhutan. *Disability and Society, 30*(6), 820–833.

Schuelka, M. (2018). The cultural production of the 'disabled' person: Constructing student difference in Bhutanese schools. *Anthropology and Education Quarterly, 49*(2), 183–200.

Schultz, L. (2017). *International youth white paper on global citizenship.* Edmonton: The Centre for Global Citizenship Education and Research.

Schultz, P. (2001). The structure of environmental concern: Concern for self, other people, and the biosphere. *Journal of Environmental Psychology, 21*(4), 327–339.

Schultz, T. (1961). Investment in human capital. *American Economic Review, 51*, 1–17.

Schumacher, E. F. (1973). *Small is beautiful: A study of economics as if people mattered.* London: Blond & Briggs.

Schweisfurth, M. (2015). Learner-centred pedagogy: Towards a post-2015 agenda for teaching and learning. *International Journal of Educational Development, 40*, 259–266.

Scott, J. (1998). *Seeing like a state: How certain schemes to improve the human condition have failed.* New Haven, CT: Yale University Press.

Scott, R. (2018). Global citizenship: Imagined destiny or improbable dream. *UN Chronicle, 54*(4). Retrieved November 21, 2018, from https://unchronicle.un.org/article/global-citizenship-imagined-destiny-or-improbable-dream

SDG Watch Europe. (2016). *About us.* Retrieved January 23, 2019, from https://www.sdgwatcheurope.org/about-us/

Sellar, S., & Hogan, A. (2019). *Pearson 2025: Transforming teaching and privatising education data.* Brussels: Education International. Retrieved June 12, 2019, from https://issuu.com/educationinternational/docs/2019_ei_gr_essay_pearson2025_eng_24

Sellar, S., Thompson, G., & Rutkowski, D. (2017). *The global education race: Taking the measure of PISA and international testing.* Edmonton: Brush Education.

Sherab, K., Dorji, K., Dukpa, D., Lhamo, K., Thapa, R., & Tshomo, S. (2015). *Opportunities and challenges of implementing inclusive education in Bhutanese schools: A case study.* Thimphu: UNICEF-Bhutan. Retrieved February 23, 2019, from https://www.researchgate.net/publication/303661279_Title_Opportunities_and_Challenges_of_Implementing_Inclusive_Education_in_Bhutanese_Schools_A_Case_Study

Shukla, S., Barkman, J., & Patel, K. (2017). Weaving Indigenous agricultural knowledge with formal education to enhance community food security: School competition as a pedagogical space in rural anchetty, India. *Pedagogy, Culture & Society, 25*(1), 87–103.

Siedentop, L. (2014). *Inventing the individual: The origins of western liberalism.* Cambridge, MA: Harvard University Press.

Silova, I. (2019). Toward a wonderland of comparative education. *Comparative Education, 55*(4), 444–472.

Silova, I., Komatsu, H., & Rappleye, J. (2018, October 12). Facing the climate change catastrophe: Education as solution or cause? *NORRAG Highlights.* Retrieved December 12, 2018, from https://www.norrag.org/facing-the-climate-change-catastrophe-education-as-solution-or-cause-by-iveta-silova-hikaru-komatsu-and-jeremy-rappleye/

Silova, I., Rappleye, J., & Komatsu, H. (2019). Measuring what really matters: Education and large-scale assessments in the time of climate crisis. *ECNU Review of Education, 2*(3), 342-346. https://doi.org/10.1177/2096531119878897

Sim, J. (2006). *Social studies and citizenship education: Teacher knowledge and practice in Singapore secondary schools* (Doctoral dissertation). Faculty of Education and Social Work, University of Sydney, Sydney.

Simons, G., & Fennig, C. (Eds.). (2017). *Ethnologue: Languages of the world* (20th ed.) Dallas: SIL International. Retrieved February 22, 2019, from https://www.ethnologue.com/ethnoblog/gary-simons/welcome-20th-edition

Simpson, J. (2013). *Baseline assessment of English language proficiency of school Teachers in Rwanda.* Kigali: British Council.

Simpson, J. (2017). *English language and medium of instruction in basic education in low- and middle-income countries: A British Council perspective.* London: British Council.

Skaalvik, E., & Skaalvik, S. (2017). Motivated for teaching? Associations with school goal structure, teacher self-efficacy, job satisfaction and emotional exhaustion. *Teaching and Teacher Education, 67,* 152–160.

Skelton, C., & Francis, B. (2009). *Feminism and the schooling scandal.* London: Routledge.

Slee, R. (2013). Meeting some challenges of inclusive education in an age of exclusion. *Asian Journal of Inclusive Education, 1*(2), 3–17.

Smith, M. (2011). Which in- and out-of-school factors explain variations in learning across different socio-economic groups? Findings from South Africa. *Comparative Education, 47*(1), 79–102.

Smith, W. (2014). The global transformation toward testing for accountability. *Education Policy Analysis Archives, 22*(116), 1–34.

Smith, W. (Ed.). (2016a). *The global testing culture: Shaping educational policy, perceptions, and practice.* Oxford: Symposium.

Smith, W. (2016). An introduction to the global testing culture. In W. Smith (Ed.), *The global testing culture: Shaping educational policy, perceptions, and practice* (pp. 7–24). Oxford: Symposium.

Smith, W. (2017). National testing policies and educator based testing for accountability: The role of selection in student achievement. *OECD Journal: Economic Studies, 2016*(1), 131–149.

Smith, W. (2018). Quality and inclusion in the SDGs: Tension in principle and practice. In C. Ydesen, A. Morin, & B. Hamre (Eds.), *Testing and inclusive schooling* (pp. 89–104). Oxford: Routledge.

Smith, W. (2019). One indicator to rule them all: How SDG 4.1.1 dominates the conversation and what it means for the most marginalized. *Annual Review of Comparative and International Education*. Bradford: Emerald.

Smith, W., & Baker, T. (2017). *From free to fee: Are for-profit, fee-charging private schools the solution for the world's poor?* Washington, DC: RESULTS Educational Fund. Retrieved October 25, 2018, from https://www.results.org/uploads/files/From_Free_to_Fee.pdf

Snilstveit, B., Stevenson, J., Menon, R., Phillips, D., Gallagher, E., Geleen, M., ... Jimenez, E. (2016). *The impact of education programmes on learning and school participation in low- and middle-income countries: A systematic review summary report* (3ie Systematic Review Summary 7). London: 3ie. Retrieved March 17, 2017 from https://www.3ieimpact.org/sites/default/files/2019-05/SR24-education-review_2.pdf

Soder, R. (1996). *Democracy, education, and the schools*. New York, NY: Jossey-Bass.

Sorensen, T. (2015). *Review of Early Grade Reading Assessment (EGRA)*. Brussels: Education International.

Soudien, C. (2013). What's being overlooked in the post-2015 agenda for education? *Compare, 43*(6), 838–842.

South Africa, Council on Higher Education. (2013). *A proposal for undergraduate curriculum reform in South Africa: The case for a flexible curriculum structure* (Report of the task team on undergraduate curriculum structure). Pretoria: CHE. Retrieved May 2, 2019, from https://www.che.ac.za/sites/default/files/publications/Full_Report.pdf

Spivak, G. (1988). Can the subaltern speak? In C. Nelson and L. Grossberg (Eds.), *Marxism and the interpretation of culture* (pp. 271–313). Chicago, IL: University of Illinois Press.

Spreen, C. (2001). *Globalization and educational policy borrowing: Mapping outcomes-based education in South Africa* (PhD thesis). Teachers College Columbia University, New York, NY. Retrieved April 6, 2019, from https://www.researchgate.net/publication/35490203_Globalization_and_educational_policy_borrowing_mapping_outcomes-based_education_in_South_Africa

Spring, J. (2018). *The American school: From the puritans to the trump era*. New York, NY: Routledge.

Sprunt, B., Deppeler, J., Ravulo, K., Tinaivunivalu, S., & Sharma, U. (2017). Entering the SDG era: What do Fijians prioritise as indicators of disability-inclusive education? *Disability and the Global South, 4*(1), 1065–1087.

Sprunt, B., Hoq, H., Sharma, U., & Marella, M. (2017). Validating the UNICEF/ Washington Group Child Functioning Module for Fijian schools to identify seeing, hearing and walking difficulties. *Disability and Rehabilitation, 41*(2) 201–211.

Srivastava, P. (Ed.). (2013). *low-fee private schooling: aggravating equity or mitigating disadvantage?* Oxford: Symposium.

Stecher, B., et al. (2018). *Improving teaching effectiveness: The intensive partnerships for effective teaching through 2015–2016: Final report.* Santa Monica, CA: Rand Corporation and American Institutes for Research. Retrieved March 14, 2019, from https://www.rand.org/pubs/research_reports/RR2242.html

Steiner-Khamsi, G. (2004). *The global politics of educational borrowing and lending.* New York, NY: Teachers College Press.

Steiner-Khamsi, G., & Draxler, A. (Eds.). (2018). *The state, business, and education: Public-private partnerships revisited.* Cheltenham: Edward Elgar.

Steiner-Khamsi, G., & Waldow, F. (2012). *World yearbook of education 2012: Policy borrowing and lending in education.* Oxford and New York, NY: Routledge.

Sterling, S. (2015). Goal 4. In *Review of the sustainable development goals: The science perspective* (pp. 27–30). International Council for Science (ICSU) and International Social Science Council (ISSC). Paris: ICSU.

Sterling, S. (2016). A commentary on education and sustainable development goals. *Journal of Education for Sustainable Development, 10*(2), 208–213.

Sterling, S., Dawson, J., & Warwick, P. (2018). Transforming sustainability education at the creative edge of the mainstream: A case study of schumacher college. *Journal of Transformative Education, 16*(4), 323–343.

Stevenson, H., & Wood, P. (2013). Markets, managerialism and teachers' work: The invisible hand of high stakes testing in England. *The International Education Journal: Comparative Perspectives, 12,* 42–61.

Stiglitz, J. (1999). Knowledge as a global public good. In I. Kaul, I. Grunberg, & M. Stern (Eds.), *Global public goods: International cooperation in the 21st century* (pp. 308–325). Oxford: Oxford University Press.

Stiglitz, J. (2018, August 20). Meet the 'change agents' who are enabling inequality. *New York Times* (online). Retrieved November 30, 2018, from https://www.nytimes.com/2018/08/20/books/review/winners-take-all-anand-giridharadas.html

Stitzlein, S. (2013). *Teaching for dissent: Citizenship education and political activism.* New York, NY: Routledge.

Stitzlein, S. (2017). *American public education and the responsibility of its citizens: Supporting democracy in the age of accountability.* Oxford: Oxford University Press.

Strauss, V. (2012, July 9). Texas GOP rejects 'critical thinking' skills. Really. *Washington Post*. Retrieved from http://www.washingtonpost.com/blogs/answer-sheet/post/texas-gop-rejects-critical-thinking-skills-really/2012/07/08/gJQAHNpFXW_blog.html

Streeck, W. (2012). Skills and politics: General and specific. In M. Busemeyer & C. Trampusch (Eds.), *The political economy of collective skill formation* (pp. 317–352). Oxford and New York, NY: Oxford University Press.

Stroink, M., & DeCicco, T. (2011). Culture, religion, and the underlying value dimensions of the metapersonal self-construal. *Mental Health Religion & Culture, 14*(9), 917–934.

Sundström, B. (2012). How it all began. In V. Ivosevic, A. Päll, R. Primožič, M. Slegers, & M. Vukasovic (Eds.), *ESU turns 30! Fighting for student rights since 1982* (pp. 5–12). Limassol: ESU. Retrieved January 3, 2019, from https://www.esu-online.org/wp-content/uploads/2016/07/30th-Anniversay-Online.pdf

Swanson, D. (2015). Ubuntu, indigeneity, and an ethic for decolonizing global citizenship. In A. Abdi, L. Shultz, & T. Pillay (Eds.), *Decolonizing global citizenship education* (pp. 27–38). Rotterdam, The Netherlands: Sense Publishers.

Syed, J., & Ali, F. (2011). The White woman's burden: From colonial civilisation to third world development. *Third World Quarterly, 32*(2), 349–365.

Takayama, K. (2008). The politics of international league tables: PISA in Japan's achievement crisis debate. *Comparative Education, 44*(4), 387–407.

Tan, Y., & Goh, S. (2014). International students, academic publications and world university rankings: The impact of globalisation and responses of a Malaysian public university. *Higher Education, 68*(4), 489–502.

Tao, S. (2013). Investigating teacher capabilities in Tanzanian primary schools. In B. Moon (Ed.), *Teacher education and the challenge of development: A global analysis* (pp. 129–149). London: Routledge.

Tap Network. (2017). *Expanding the data ecosystem: The role of 'non-official' data for SDG monitoring and review*. Retrieved January 23, 2019, from http://tapnetwork2030.org/wp-content/uploads/2015/04/Non-OfficialDataforSDGMonitoringandAccountability_FINAL.pdf

Taylor, C. (1989). *Sources of the self: The making of modern identity*. Cambridge, MA: Harvard University Press.

Technical Cooperation Group on the Indicators for SDG 4. (2017). *Sustainable Development Goal (SDG) 4 country profile Morocco*. Retrieved February 26, 2019, from http://tcg.uis.unesco.org/wp-content/uploads/sites/4/2018/08/MA.pdf

Technical Support Team [TST] to the Open Working Group on Sustainable Development Goals. (2013). *TST issues brief: Education and culture*. New York, NY: TST. Retrieved December 5, 2018, from https://sustainabledevelopment.un.org/content/documents/18290406tstisuesedcult.pdf

Teferra, D. (2013). *Funding higher education in Sub-Saharan Africa*. Dordrecht: Springer.

Teferra, D. (2016). African flagship universities: Their neglected contributions. *Higher Education, 72*(1), 79–99.

Thelen, K., & Busemeyer, M. (2012). Institutional change in German vocational training: From collectivism toward segmentalism. In M. Busemeyer & C. Trampusch (Eds.), *The political economy of collective skill formation* (pp. 68–100). Oxford and New York, NY: Oxford University Press.

Thomas, G. (2012). *Education: A very short introduction*. Oxford: Oxford University Press.

Thompson, B. (1996). AERA editorial policies regarding statistical significance testing: Three suggested reforms. *Educational Research, 25*(2), 26–30.

Thompson, B. (2002). "Statistical," "practical," and "clinical": How many kinds of significance do counselors need to consider? *Journal of Counseling & Development, 80*(1), 64–71.

Thorbecke, E. (2006). *The evolution of the development doctrine: 1950–2005* (UNU-WIDER Discussion Paper 2006/155). Helsinki: UNU-WIDER.

Tikly, L. (2017). The future of education for all as a global regime of educational governance. *Comparative Education Review, 61*(1), 22–57.

Together 2030. (2016). *From ambition to implementation: Ensuring that no one is left behind*. Retrieved January 21, 2019, from https://sustainabledevelopment.un.org/content/documents/10116Together%202030%20Written%20Inputs%20to%20the%20HLPF%20April%202016.pdf

Tomaševski, K. (2006). *Human rights obligations in education: The 4-A scheme*. Tilburg: Wolf Legal Publishers.

Topdar, S. (2015). Duties of a "good citizen": colonial secondary school textbook policies in late nineteenth-century India. *South Asian History and Culture, 6*, 417–439.

Turner, G. (2012). On the cusp of global collapse? Updated comparison of the limits to growth with historical data. *Gaia, 21*(2), 116–124.

Tyack, D., & Hansot, E. (1982). *Managers of virtue: Public school leadership in America, 1820–1980*. New York, NY: Basic Books.

Uchiyama, T. (2010). *Kyodotaino kisoriron* [Basic theory of community]. Tokyo: Nobunkyo.

UN Women. (2018). *Turning promises into action: Gender equality in the 2030 agenda for sustainable development*. New York, NY: UN Women. Retrieved December 19, 2018, from http://www.unwomen.org/-/media/headquarters/attachments/sections/library/publications/2018/sdg-report-gender-equality-in-the-2030-agenda-for-sustainable-development-2018-en.pdf?la=en&vs=4332

UNCTAD. (2015). *World investment report 2015: Reforming international investment governance*. New York, NY & Geneva: United Nations. Retrieved November 11, 2018, from https://unctad.org/en/PublicationsLibrary/wir2015_en.pdf

UNESCO. (2009). Global student statement to the world conference on higher education 2009. In *World conference on higher education 2009: Final report (Annex V – Other reports)* (pp. 123–127). Paris: UNESCO. Retrieved February 12, 2019, from https://docplayer.net/57520982-World-conference-on-higher-education-2009-final-report-paris-unesco-headquarters-5-to-8-july-2009.html

UNESCO. (2010). *Claiming human rights: Guide to international procedures available in cases of human rights violations in Africa.* Retrieved January 24, 2019, from http://www.claiminghumanrights.org/unesco_procedure.html

UNESCO. (2011). *Report on the role for UNESCO as global coordinator and leader of Education for All (EFA)* (187 EX/8 Part 1). Paris: UNESCO. Retrieved December 6, 2018, from http://unesdoc.unesco.org/images/0021/002111/211172e.pdf

UNESCO. (2012a). *About the global education first initiative.* Retrieved December 3, 2018, from http://www.unesco.org/new/en/gefi/about

UNESCO. (2012b). *Youth and skills: Putting education to work* (EFA global monitoring report 2012). Paris: UNESCO. Retrieved April 6, 2019, from https://unesdoc.unesco.org/ark:/48223/pf0000218003

UNESCO. (2013a). *Concept note on the post-2015 education agenda.* Paris: UNESCO. Retrieved December 5, 2018, from http://www.unesco.org/new/fileadmin/MULTIMEDIA/HQ/ED/ED_new/pdf/UNESCOConceptNotePost2015_ENG.pdf

UNESCO. (2013b). *Education transforms lives.* Paris: UNESCO. Retrieved April 18, 2019, from https://unesdoc.unesco.org/ark:/48223/pf0000223115

UNESCO. (2013c). *The global learning crisis: Why every child deserves a quality education.* Paris: UNESCO. Retrieved February 21, 2019, from https://unesdoc.unesco.org/ark:/48223/pf0000223826?posInSet=1&queryId=47eeea87-8ce2-4c85-af79-6e9ab1b9999a

UNESCO. (2013d). *Thematic consultation on education in the post-2015 development agenda 18–19 March 2013, Dakar, Senegal: Summary of outcomes.* Retrieved April 10, 2019, from http://www.unesco.org/new/fileadmin/MULTIMEDIA/HQ/ED/pdf/post-2015-summaryoutcomes.pdf

UNESCO. (2014a). *2014 GEM final statement: The Muscat agreement.* Muscat: UNESCO. Retrieved March 17, 2019, from https://unesdoc.unesco.org/ark:/48223/pf0000228122

UNESCO. (2014b). *Global citizenship education: Preparing learners for the challenges of the 21st century.* Paris: UNESCO. Retrieved January 27, 2019, from https://unesdoc.unesco.org/ark:/48223/pf0000227729

UNESCO. (2014c). *Morocco: Education for all 2015 national review.* Paris: UNESCO. Retrieved February 26, 2019, from http://unesdoc.unesco.org/images/0023/002317/231799e.pdf

UNESCO. (2014d). *Shaping the future we want: UN decade of education for sustainable development (2005–2014) final report.* Paris: UNESCO.

UNESCO. (2014e). *Sustainable development begins with education: How education can contribute to the proposed post-2015 goals.* Paris: UNESCO. Retrieved February 22, 2019, from http://unesdoc.unesco.org/images/0023/002305/230508e.pdf

UNESCO. (2014f). *Teaching and learning: Achieving quality for all* (EFA global monitoring report 2013/4). Paris: UNESCO. Retrieved April 6, 2019, from https://unesdoc.unesco.org/ark:/48223/pf0000225660

UNESCO. (2015a). *The challenge of teacher shortage and quality: Have we succeeded in getting enough quality teachers into classrooms?* (EFA GMR Policy Paper 19). Paris: UNESCO. Retrieved November 9, 2018, from http://unesdoc.unesco.org/images/0023/002327/232721E.pdf

UNESCO. (2015b). *Education for all 2000–2015: Achievements and challenges* (Global Education Monitoring Report 2015). Paris: UNESCO. Retrieved May 7, 2019, from https://unesdoc.unesco.org/ark:/48223/pf0000232205

UNESCO. (2015c). *Global citizenship education: Topics and learning objectives.* Paris: UNESCO. Retrieved January 27, 2019, from https://unesdoc.unesco.org/ark:/48223/pf0000232993

UNESCO. (2015d). *Regional ministerial conference on education post-2015 European and North American States: 19–20 February 2015: Paris statement.* Paris: UNESCO. Retrieved February 12, 2019, from http://www.unesco.org/new/fileadmin/MULTIMEDIA/HQ/ED/ED_new/Paris-Statement.pdf

UNESCO. (2016a). *The ABCs of global citizenship education.* Paris: UNESCO. Retrieved January 27, 2019, from https://unesdoc.unesco.org/ark:/48223/pf0000248232

UNESCO. (2016b). *Education for people and planet: Creating sustainable futures for all* (Global Education Monitoring Report 2016). Paris: UNESCO. Retrieved December 19, 2018, from https://unesdoc.unesco.org/ark:/48223/pf0000245752

UNESCO. (2016c). *Strategy for Technical and Vocational Education and Training (TVET) (2016–2021).* Paris: UNESCO.

UNESCO. (2016d). *Unpacking sustainable development goal 4 education 2030: Guide.* Paris: UNESCO. Retrieved January 21, 2019, from http://unesdoc.unesco.org/images/0024/002463/246300E.pdf

UNESCO. (2017a). *8th Collective Consultation of NGOs (CCNGO) on education 2030: Implementing SDG 4 – Education 2030: Meeting report.* Siem Reap: UNESCO. Retrieved January 26, 2019, from http://www.worldomep.org/file/Final_CCNGO_8th_Global_Meeting_Report.pdf

UNESCO. (2017b). *Accountability in education: Meeting our commitments* (Global Education Monitoring Report 2017/8). Paris: UNESCO. Retrieved January 23, 2019, from http://gem-report-2017.unesco.org/en/home/

UNESCO. (2017c). *Education for sustainable development goals: Learning objectives.* Paris: UNESCO.

UNESCO. (2018a). *Education for sustainable development.* Retrieved December 11, 2018, from https://en.unesco.org/themes/education-sustainable-development

UNESCO. (2018b). *GEM report summary on disabilities and education.* Paris: UNESCO. Retrieved February 26, 2019, from http://unesdoc.unesco.org/images/0026/002653/265353e.pdf

UNESCO. (2018c). *Global action programme on education for sustainable development.* Retrieved December 11, 2018, from https://en.unesco.org/gap

UNESCO. (2018d). *Preparing teachers for global citizenship education: A template.* Bangkok: UNESCO. Retrieved January 27, 2019, from https://unesdoc.unesco.org/ark:/48223/pf0000265452

UNESCO. (n.d.-a). *Inclusion in education.* Paris: UNESCO. Retrieved February 26, 2019, from https://en.unesco.org/themes/inclusion-in-education

UNESCO. (n.d.-b). *World inequality database on education.* Retrieved December 15, 2018, from https://www.education-inequalities.org

UNESCO Institute for Statistics. (2015). *Thematic indicators to monitor the education 2030 agenda: Technical advisory group proposal.* Montreal: UIS. Retrieved December 5, 2018, from http://uis.unesco.org/sites/default/files/documents/thematic-indicators-to-monitor-the-education-2030-agenda-technical-advisory-group-proposal-2015-en.pdf

UNESCO Institute for Statistics. (2016a). *Inter-Agency Group on Disaggregated Education Indicators (IAG-DEI): Concept note.* Montreal: UIS. Retrieved March 17, 2017 from http://uis.unesco.org/sites/default/files/documents/iag-eii-concept-note-march-2016.pdf

UNESCO Institute for Statistics. (2016b). *Sustainable development data digest. Laying the foundation to measure sustainable development goal 4.* Montreal: UIS. Retrieved January 12, 2019, from http://uis.unesco.org/sites/default/files/documents/laying-the-foundation-to-measure-sdg4-sustainable-development-data-digest-2016-en.pdf

UNESCO Institute for Statistics. (2016c). *The world needs almost 69 million new teachers to reach the 2030 education goals* (UIS Fact Sheet No. 39). Montreal: UIS. Retrieved December 4, 2018, from http://unesdoc.unesco.org/images/0024/002461/246124e.pdf

UNESCO Institute for Statistics. (2017a). *The data revolution in education* (Information Paper No. 39). Retrieved January 21, 2019, from http://uis.unesco.org/sites/default/files/documents/the-data-revolution-in-education-2017-en.pdf

UNESCO Institute for Statistics. (2017b). *Expanding coverage for global indicator 4.1.* Montreal: UIS. Retrieved March 17, 2017 from http://gaml.uis.unesco.org/wp-content/uploads/sites/2/2018/08/Expanding_Coverage4.1.-UIS_Draft_Proposal_for_Discussion002.pdf

UNESCO Institute for Statistics. (2017c). *The global alliance to monitor learning: Concept paper.* Montreal: UIS. Retrieved June 14, 2019, from http://gaml.uis.unesco.org/wp-content/uploads/sites/2/2018/10/gaml-concept_paper-2017-en2_0.pdf

UNESCO Institute for Statistics. (2017d). *The global alliance to monitor learning: Governance and organization.* Montreal: UIS. Retrieved January 12, 2019, from http://uis.unesco.org/sites/default/files/documents/gaml-governance-organization-2017-en.pdf

UNESCO Institute for Statistics. (2017e). *The Global Alliance to Monitor Learning: Log frame and operational plan.* Montreal: UIS.

UNESCO Institute for Statistics. (2017f). *The Global Alliance to Monitor Learning (GAML): Result framework.* Montreal: UIS. Retrieved March 17, 2017 from http://uis.unesco.org/sites/default/files/documents/gaml-result-framework-2017-en.pdf

UNESCO Institute for Statistics. (2017g). *The Global Alliance to Monitor Learning: Third meeting concept note.* Mexico City: UIS. Retrieved 15 January 2019, from http://uis.unesco.org/sites/default/files/documents/gaml-may-2017-meeting-concept-note.pdf

UNESCO Institute for Statistics. (2017h). *Improving the global measurement of teacher training* (Background paper prepared for the 2017/8 Global Education Monitoring Report). Paris: UNESCO.

UNESCO Institute for Statistics. (2017i, September). *More than one-half of children and adolescents are not learning worldwide* (UIS Fact Sheet No. 46). Montreal: UIS. Retrieved March 17, 2017 from http://uis.unesco.org/sites/default/files/documents/fs46-more-than-half-children-not-learning-en-2017.pdf

UNESCO Institute for Statistics. (2017j). *The quality factor: Strengthening national data to monitor sustainable development goal 4* (SDG 4 Data Digest 2017). Paris: UIS. Retrieved March 14, 2019, from http://uis.unesco.org/sites/default/files/documents/quality-factor-strengthening-national-data-2017-en.pdf

UNESCO Institute for Statistics. (2017k). *Report of the director on the activities of the institute.* Montreal: UIS. Retrieved December 5, 2018, from http://uis.unesco.org/sites/default/files/documents/report-of-director-on-activities-of-the-institute-2017.pdf

UNESCO Institute for Statistics. (2017l). *SDG 4 reporting: Linking to the UIS reporting scale through social moderation: GAML 4th meeting.* Madrid: UIS.

UNESCO Institute for Statistics. (2018a). *The investment case for SDG 4 data.* Montreal: UIS. Retrieved December 5, 2018, from http://uis.unesco.org/sites/default/files/documents/investment-case-sdg4-data.pdf

UNESCO Institute of Statistics. (2018b). *Metadata for the global and thematic indicators for the follow-up and review of SDG 4 and education 2030.* Montreal: UIS. Retrieved November 8, 2018, from http://uis.unesco.org/sites/default/files/documents/metadata-global-thematic-indicators-sdg4-education2030-2017-en_1.pdf

UNESCO Institute of Statistics. (2018c). *Morocco: Education and literacy.* Retrieved February 26, 2019, from http://uis.unesco.org/en/country/ma?theme=education-and-literacy

UNESCO Institute for Statistics. (2018d, February). *One in five children, adolescents and youth is out of school* (UIS Fact Sheet No. 48). Montreal: UIS. Retrieved March 17, 2017, from http://uis.unesco.org/sites/default/files/documents/fs48-one-five-children-adolescents-youth-out-school-2018-en.pdf

UNESCO Institute of Statistics. (2018e). *Quick guide to education indicators for SDG 4.* Retrieved February 26, 2019, from http://uis.unesco.org/sites/default/files/documents/quick-guide-education-indicators-sdg4-2018-en.pdf

UNESCO Institute of Statistics. (2018f). *SDG 4 data book: Global education indicators 2018.* Montreal: UIS. Retrieved February 26, 2019, from http://uis.unesco.org/sites/default/files/documents/sdg4-data-book-2018-en.pdf

UNESCO Institute for Statistics. (2018g). *SDG 4 data digest: Data to nurture learning.* Montreal: UIS. Retrieved March 17, 2017, from http://uis.unesco.org/sites/default/files/documents/sdg4-data-digest-data-nurture-learning-2018-en.pdf

UNESCO Institute for Statistics. (2018h). *TCG4: SDG4 benchmarking – Background paper.* TCG4/33, Presented on 16–18 January 2018 in Dubai, UAE. Retrieved March 17, 2017, from http://tcg.uis.unesco.org/wp-content/uploads/sites/4/2018/08/TCG4-33-Benchmark-Background-Paper.pdf

UNESCO Institute for Statistics and Australian Council for Educational Research. (2014). *Learning metrics partnership.* UIS, Australian Aid, DFAT and ACER. Retrieved January 12, 2019, from http://uis.unesco.org/sites/default/files/documents/learning-metrics-partnership-a-capacity-support-and-policy-strengthening-initiative-to-develop-and-use-common-learning-metrics-mathematics-reading-2014-en_1.pdf

UNESCO Institute for Statistics, Australian Aid, Australian Government Department of Foreign Affair and Trade, and Australian Council for Educational Research. (2014). *Learning metrics partnership: A capacity support and policy strengthening initiative to develop and use common learning metrics for mathematics and reading.* Montreal: UIS. Retrieved March 17, 2017, from https://unesdoc.unesco.org/ark:/48223/pf0000230939

UNESCO & Mahatma Gandhi Institute of Education for Peace and Sustainable Development (MGIEP). (2017). *Rethinking schooling for the 21st century: The state of education for peace, sustainable development and global citizenship in Asia.* New Delhi: UNESCO and MGIEP.

UNESCO & UIS Technical Advisory Group. (2015). *Thematic indicators to monitor the education 2030 agenda: Technical advisory group proposal.* Paris: UNESCO and UIS. Retrieved March 13, 2019, from https://unesdoc.unesco.org/ark:/48223/pf0000235172

UNESCO & UNICEF. (2007). *A human rights-based approach to education for all.* Paris: UNESCO. Retrieved December 4, 2018, from http://unesdoc.unesco.org/images/0015/001548/154861e.pdf

UNICEF. (2003). *The state of the world's children 2004.* New York, NY: UNICEF. Retrieved January 23, 2019, from https://www.unicef.org/sowc04/files/SOWC_O4_eng.pdf

UNICEF. (2007). *A human rights-based approach to education for all.* New York, NY: UNICEF. Retrieved January 24, 2019, from http://unesdoc.unesco.org/images/0015/001548/154861e.pdf

UNICEF. (2012). *Two-stage child disability study among children 2–9 years: Bhutan 2010–2011.* Thimphu: National Statistics Bureau. Retrieved February 26, 2019, from http://www.nsb.gov.bt/publication/files/pub9er1152un.pdf

UNICEF. (2014). *UNICEF annual report 2014 Morocco.* Rabat: UNICEF. Retrieved February 26, 2019, from https://www.unicef.org/about/annualreport/files/Morocco_Annual_Report_2014.pdf

UNICEF. (2015). *Case study on inclusive education development: Capacity building and mobilization to improve access and quality education for disabled children.* Retrieved February 26, 2019, from http://www.oosci-mena.org/uploads/1/wysiwyg/Case_study_on_inclusive_education_Morocco.pdf

UNICEF. (2016). *UNICEF annual report 2016 Morocco.* Retrieved February 26, 2019, from https://www.unicef.org/about/annualreport/files/Morocco_2016_COAR.pdf

United Kingdom, Department for International Development. (2016). *Annual review – Summary sheet. Better Education Statistics for Improved Learning (BEST)* (Programme Code: 203295). London: DFID. Retrieved March 17, 2019, from iati.dfid.gov.uk/iati_documents/5701626.odt

United Nations. (1948). *Universal declaration of human rights.* New York, NY: UN.

United Nations. (1989). *Convention on the rights of the child.* New York, NY: UN. Retrieved January 26, 2019, from https://www.ohchr.org/en/professionalinterest/pages/crc.aspx

United Nations. (2000). *United nations millennium declaration* (A/RES/55/2). New York, NY: UN. Retrieved February 26, 2019, from http://unstats.un.org/unsd/mdg/Host.aspx?Content=Indicators/About.htm#Declaration

United Nations. (2006). *Convention on the rights of persons with disabilities.* Retrieved February 23, 2019, from https://www.un.org/development/desa/disabilities/convention-on-the-rights-of-persons-with-disabilities/convention-on-the-rights-of-persons-with-disabilities-2.html

United Nations. (2011). *Realizing the millennium development goals for persons with disabilities towards 2015 and beyond* (A/RES/65/186). New York, NY: UN.

United Nations. (2012a). *My world: The united nations global survey for a better world.* Retrieved December 5, 2018, from http://vote.myworld2015.org

United Nations. (2012b). *The secretary-general's high-level panel of eminent persons on the post-2015 development agenda.* Retrieved December 5, 2018, from https://www.un.org/sg/en/management/hlppost2015.shtml

United Nations. (2013a). *A million voices: The world we want.* New York, NY: UN. Retrieved December 5, 2018, from https://www.undp.org/content/dam/undp/library/MDG/english/UNDG_A-Million-Voices.pdf

United Nations. (2013b). *A new global partnership: Eradicate poverty and transform economies through sustainable development: The report of the high-level panel of eminent persons on the post-2015 development agenda.* New York, NY: United Nations. Retrieved November 15, 2018, from https://www.un.org/sg/sites/www.un.org.sg/files/files/HLP_P2015_Report.pdf

United Nations. (2014a). *About major groups and other stakeholders.* Sustainable Development Goals Knowledge Platform. Retrieved January 23, 2019, from https://sustainabledevelopment.un.org/aboutmajorgroups.html

United Nations. (2014b). *Focus area document (24 February 2014).* Sustainable Development Goals Knowledge Platform. Retrieved December 6, 2018, from https://sustainabledevelopment.un.org/content/documents/3276focusareas.pdf

United Nations. (2014c). *Focus area document (19 March 2014).* Sustainable Development Goals Knowledge Platform. Retrieved December 6, 2018, from https://sustainabledevelopment.un.org/content/documents/3402Focus%20areas_20140319.pdf

United Nations. (2014d). *Introduction and Proposed Goals and Targets on Sustainable Development for the Post2015 Development Agenda.* Sustainable Development Goals Knowledge Platform. Retrieved December 6, 2018, from https://sustainabledevelopment.un.org/content/documents/4528zerodraft12OWG.pdf

United Nations. (2014e). *Working document for 5–9 May session of open working group.* Sustainable Development Goals Knowledge Platform. Retrieved December 6, 2018, from https://sustainabledevelopment.un.org/content/documents/3686WorkingDoc_0205_additionalsupporters.pdf

United Nations. (2015a). *The millennium development goals report 2015.* New York, NY: UN. Retrieved June 12, 2019, from https://www.un.org/millenniumgoals/2015_MDG_Report/pdf/MDG%202015%20rev%20(July%201).pdf

United Nations. (2016). *Racism, xenophobia increasing globally, experts tell third committee, amid calls for laws to combat hate speech, concerns over freedom of expression.* Retrieved December 4, 2018, from www.un.org/press/en/2016/gashc4182.doc.htm

United Nations. (2017). *Education and academia stakeholder group.* Sustainable Development Goals Knowledge Platform. Retrieved January 23, 2019, from https://sustainabledevelopment.un.org/index.php?page=view&type=30022&nr=746&menu=3170

United Nations. (2018a). *Extreme poverty and human rights: Note by the secretary-general* (Report of the Special Rapporteur on Extreme Poverty and Human Rights. A/73/396). New York, NY: UN. Retrieved December 5, 2018, from https://undocs.org/A/73/396

United Nations. (2018b). *IAEG-SDGs: Tier classification for global SDG indicators.* Retrieved December 3, 2018, from https://unstats.un.org/sdgs/iaeg-sdgs/tier-classification/

United Nations. (2018c). *Indicator 4.1.1. SDG indicators: Metadata Repository.* Retrieved January 26, 2019, from https://unstats.un.org/sdgs/metadata/

United Nations. (2018d). *Major groups and other stakeholders.* Sustainable Development Goals Knowledge Platform. Retrieved February 19, 2019, from https://sustainabledevelopment.un.org/mgos

United Nations. (2018e). *Sustainable development goal 4.* Retrieved March 14, 2019, from https://sustainabledevelopment.un.org/sdg4

United Nations. (2018f). *Sustainable development goal 8.* Retrieved March 14, 2019, from https://sustainabledevelopment.un.org/sdg8

United Nations. (2019). *IAEG-SDGs: Tier classification for global SDG indicators.* New York, NY: UN DESA. Retrieved April 16. 2019, from https://unstats.un.org/sdgs/iaeg-sdgs/tier-classification/

United Nations Asia-Pacific Regional Coordination Mechanism (UNAPRCM). (2016). *Terms of reference: Thematic Working Group on Education 2030+ (TWG-EDU).* Retrieved January 23, 2019, from http://www.unaprcm.org/sites/default/files/twgattachment/Terms%20of%20Reference%20-%20TWG%20Education%20 2030%2B.pdf

United Nations Committee of the Right of the Child. (2001). *General comment No. 1 (2001) article 29 (1): The aims of education.* New York, NY: United Nations. Retrieved December 3, 2018, from https://www.ohchr.org/EN/Issues/Education/Training/Compilation/Pages/a)GeneralCommentNo1TheAimsofEducation(article29)(2001).aspx

United Nations Department of Economic and Social Affairs. (2018a). *SDG indicators: Global indicator framework for the sustainable development goals and targets of the 2030 agenda for sustainable development.* Retrieved November 30, 2018, from https://unstats.un.org/sdgs/indicators/indicators-list/

United Nations Department of Economic and Social Affairs. (2018b). *Voluntary national reviews: Synthesis report 2018.* High-Level Political Forum on Sustainable Development. New York, NY: UN DESA. Retrieved April 19, 2019, from https://sustainabledevelopment.un.org/content/documents/210732018_VNRs_Synthesis_compilation_11118_FS_BB_Format_FINAL_cover.pdf

United Nations Economic and Social Commission for Asia and the Pacific (ESCAP). (2018). *Asia and the Pacific SDG progress report 2017.* Bangkok: UN ESCAP. Retrieved

February 21, 2019, from https://www.unescap.org/sites/default/files/Asia-Pacific-SDG-Progress-Report-2017.pdf

United Nations General Assembly (UNGA). (1992). *Report of the United Nations conference on environment and development (Rio de Janeiro, 3–14 June 1992): Annex 1: Rio declaration on environment and development* (A/CONF.151/26. Vol. I). New York, NY: UNGA. Retrieved April 17, 2019, from https://www.un.org/documents/ga/conf151/aconf15126-1annex1.htm

United Nations General Assembly (UNGA). (2012). *The future we want. Resolution adopted by the General Assembly on 27 July 2012.* (A/RES/66/288). New York, NY:UN. Retrieved December 5, 2018, from http://www.un.org/ga/search/view_doc.asp?symbol=A/RES/66/288&Lang=E

United Nations General Assembly (UNGA). (2013). *Open working group of the general assembly on sustainable development goals.* Resolution adopted by the General Assembly on 15 January 2013 (A/RES/67/555). New York, NY: UN. Retrieved December 5, 2018, from https://undocs.org/A/67/L.48/Rev.1

United Nations General Assembly (UNGA). (2014). *Report of the open working group on sustainable development goals established pursuant to general assembly resolution 66/288. Resolution adopted by the General Assembly on 10 September 2014* (A/RES/68/309). New York, NY: UN. Retrieved December 5, 2018, from https://undocs.org/A/RES/68/309

United Nations General Assembly (UNGA). (2015). *Addis ababa action agenda of the third international conference on financing for development (Addis ababa action agenda).* New York, NY: UN. Retrieved November 27, 2018, from http://www.un.org/ga/search/view_doc.asp?symbol=A/RES/69/313&Lang=E

United Nations General Assembly (UNGA). (2015b). *Transforming our world: The 2030 agenda for sustainable development.* Resolution adopted by the General Assembly on 25 September 2015 (A/RES/70/1). Retrieved November 27, 2018, from https://sustainabledevelopment.un.org/post2015/transformingourworld

United Nations General Assembly (UNGA). (2017). *Right to education: Note by the secretary-general. Report of the special rapporteur on the right to education* (A/72/496). New York, NY: UN. Retrieved December 5, 2018, from https://undocs.org/A/72/496

United Nations Global Compact. (2013). *UN-business partnerships: A handbook.* New York, NY: UN Global Compact.

United States Agency for International Development (USAID). (2013). *USAID Morocco country development cooperation strategy 2013–2017.* Retrieved February 26, 2019, from https://www.usaid.gov/sites/default/files/documents/1883/CDCS%20Morocco%202013-2017%20FINAL%20Public.pdf

United States Department of Education Office of Planning Evaluation and Policy Development. (2010). *Evaluation of evidence-based practices in online learning: A meta-analysis and review of online learning studies.* Washington, DC: Department of Education. Retrieved November 30, 2018, from https://www2.ed.gov/rschstat/eval/tech/evidence-based-practices/finalreport.pdf

United States, National Commission on Excellence in Education. (1983). *A nation at risk: The imperative for educational reform: A report to the nation and the secretary of education, united states department of education.* Washington, DC: The Commission.

United States, Senate Health Education Labor and Pensions Committee. (2012). *For profit higher education: The failure to safeguard the federal investment and ensure student success.* Retrieved November 30, 2018, from https://www.gpo.gov/fdsys/pkg/CPRT-112SPRT74931/pdf/CPRT-112SPRT74931.pdf

Unterhalter, E. (2005). Fragmented framework? Researching women, gender, education, and development. In S. Aikman & E. Unterhalter (Eds.), *Beyond access: Transforming policy and practice for gender equality in education* (pp. 15–35). Oxford: Oxfam GB.

Unterhalter, E. (2012). Mutable meanings: Gender equality in education and international rights frameworks. *The Equal Rights Review, 8,* 67–84.

Unterhalter, E. (2017). Negative capability? Measuring the unmeasurable in education. *Comparative Education, 53*(1), 1–16.

Unterhalter, E. (2019). The many meanings of quality education: Politics of targets and indicators in SDG4. *Global Policy, 10*(Suppl. 1), 39–51. Retrieved May 7, 2019, from https://onlinelibrary.wiley.com/doi/epdf/10.1111/1758-5899.12591

Unterhalter, E., & Carpentier, V. (Eds.). (2010). *Global inequalities and higher education: Whose interests are you serving?* London: Macmillan.

Unterhalter, E., Allais, S., Mcowan, T., Howell, C., Oanda, I. & Oketch, M. (2018). *Conceptualising higher education and the public good in Ghana, Kenya, Nigeria, and South Africa.* Paper presented at the CIES 2018 Annual Conference, CIES, Mexico City, Mexico. Retrieved May 10, 2019, from http://discovery.ucl.ac.uk/10050089/1/Howell_Conceptual%20paper%20April%202018%20revised2.pdf

Unterhalter, E., Vaughan, R., & Smail, A. (2013). Secondary and higher education in the post 2015 framework. *Compare, 43*(6), 817–822.

Utting, P., & Zammit, A. (2006). *Beyond pragmatism: Appraising UN-business partnerships: What drives the public private partnership phenomenon?* Geneva: UNRISD. Retrieved November 30, 2018, from http://citeseerx.ist.psu.edu/viewdoc/download?doi=10.1.1.610.8974&rep=rep1&type=pdf

van de Werfhorst, H. (2011). Skills, positional good or social closure? The role of education across structural-institutional labour market settings. *Journal of Education and Work, 24*(5), 521–548.

van Fleet, J. (2012). *Private philanthropy & social investments in support of education for all.* Background paper prepared for the Education for All Global Monitoring Report 2012, Youth and Skills: Putting Education to Work. Paris: UNESCO.

van Vuuren, D., Stehfest, E., Elzen, M., Kram, T., Vliet, J., Deetman, S., ... Ruijven, B. (2011). RCP2.6: Exploring the possibility to keep global mean temperature increase below 2°C. *Climatic Change, 109*, 95–116.

Vanderdussen Toukan, E. (2017). Expressions of liberal justice? Examining the aims of the UN's sustainable development goals for education. *Interchange, 48*, 293–309.

Verger, A., Edwards, D., & Altinyelken, H. (2014). Learning from all? The World Bank, aid agencies and the construction of hegemony in education for development. *Comparative Education, 50*(4), 381–399.

Verger, A., Fontdevila, C., & Zancajo, A. (2016). *The privatization of education: A political economy of global education reform.* New York, NY: Teachers College Press.

Verger, A., Lubienski, C., & Steiner-Khamsi, G. (2016). *World yearbook of education 2016: The global education industry.* New York, NY: Routledge.

Verger, A., Novelli, M., & Altinyelken, H. (Eds.). (2012). *Global education policy and international development: New agendas, issues, and policies.* New York, NY: Continuum.

Vickers, E. (2018, December 7). Education and climate change: Is blaming 'western modernity' the answer? *NORRAG Highlights.* Retrieved December 23, 2018, from https://www.norrag.org/education-and-climate-change-is-blaming-western-modernity-the-answer-by-edward-vickers/

Vinjevold, P. (1999). Language issues in South African classrooms. In N. Taylor & P. Vinjevold (Eds.), *Getting learning right: Report of the president's education initiative research project* (pp. 205–226). Johannesburg: Joint Education Trust.

Vladimirova, K., & Le Blanc, D. (2016). Exploring links between education and sustainable development goals through the lens of UN flagship reports. *Sustainable Development, 24*(4), 254–271.

Volante, L. (2015). The impact of PISA on education governance: Some insights from highly reactive policy contexts. *International Studies in Educational Administration, 43*(2), 103–117.

Volante, L., & Ritzen, J. (2016). The European Union, education governance and international education surveys. *Policy Futures in Education, 14*(7), 988–1004.

Waghid, Y. (2018). On the educational potential of Ubuntu. In E. Takyi-Amoako & N. Assié-Lumumba (Eds.), *Re-visioning education in Africa* (pp. 55–65). New York, NY: Palgrave Macmillan.

Wagner, D. (2011). *Smaller, quicker, cheaper: Improving learning assessments for developing countries.* Paris & Washington, DC: IIEP-UNESCO and EFA-FTI.

Walker, D. (2015). *Toward a new gospel of wealth.* Equals Change Blog (Online). Retrieved November 30, 2018, from https://www.fordfoundation.org/ideas/equals-change-blog/posts/toward-a-new-gospel-of-wealth/

Walker, J., & Mowé, K. (2016). *Financing matters: A toolkit on domestic financing for education.* Cape Town: Global Campaign for Education, Education International and ActionAid. Retrieved October 27, 2018, from http://www.campaignforeducation.org/docs/resources/GCE%20Financing_Matters_EN_WEB.pdf

Walker, J., Taneja, A., Abuel-Ealeh, S., & Pearce, C. (2016). *Private profit, public loss: Why the push for low-fee private schools is throwing quality education off track.* Johannesburg: Global Campaign for Education. Retrieved November 9, 2018, from http://www.right-to-education.org/sites/right-to-education.org/files/resource-attachments/GCE_Private_Profit_Public_Loss_2016_En.pdf

Walling, D. (2004). *Public education, democracy, and the common good.* Washington, DC: Phi Delta Kappa Educational Foundation.

Walter, S. (2008). The language of instruction issue: Framing an empirical perspective. In B. Spolsky & F. Hult (Eds.), *The handbook of educational linguistics* (pp. 129–146). Malden, MA: Blackwell.

Walter, S., & Dekker, D. (2011). Mother tongue instruction in Lubuagan: A case study from the Philippines. *International Review of Education, 57*(5–6), 667–683.

Wangenge-Ouma, O. (2011). Managing resource dependence difficulties in African higher education: The case of multiple exchange relationships. *Higher Education Policy, 24*(3), 167–184.

Ward, M. (2016). *PISA for development* (PowerPoint presentation). Paris: OECD. Retrieved March 17, 2019, from http://www.unescobkk.org/fileadmin/user_upload/epr/Quality/NEQMAP/1-1.PISA_for_Development_Michael_Ward.pdf

Wedekind, V. (2018). The idealisation of apprenticeship. In S. Allais & Y. Shalem (Eds.), *Knowledge, curriculum, and preparation for work* (pp. 104–126). Leiden: Brill Sense.

Westheimer, J. (2007). *Pledging allegiance: The politics of teaching about patriotism in America's classrooms.* New York, NY: Teachers College Press.

Westheimer, J. (2015). *What kind of citizen? Educating our children for the common good.* New York, NY: Teachers College Press.

Westheimer, J. (2017). What kind of citizens do we need? *Educational Leadership, 75*(3), 12–14.

Westheimer, J., & Kahne, J. (2004). What kind of citizen? The politics of educating for democracy. *American Educational Research Journal, 41*(2), 237–269.

Wheelahan, L., Buchanan, J., & Yu, S. (2015). *Linking qualifications and the labour market through capabilities and vocational streams.* Adelaide: NCVER. Retrieved April 6, 2019, from https://www.ncver.edu.au/__data/assets/file/0018/9261/linking-quals-and-labour-market.pdf

White, L. (1967). The historical roots of our ecologic crisis. *Science, 155*(3767), 1203–1207.

Wike, R., Simmons, K., Stokes, B., & Fetterolf, J. (2017). *Globally, broad support for representative and direct democracy: But many also endorse nondemocratic alternatives.* Washington, DC: Pew Research Center.

Wilson, K. (2012). *Race, racism and development: Interrogating history, discourse and practice.* London: Zed Books.

Winkler, I., & Williams, C. (2017). The sustainable development goals and human rights: A critical early review. *International Journal of Human Rights, 21*(8), 1023–1028.

Winn, K., & Goebel, J. (2017). *Measuring the un-measurable.* Mary Lou Fulton Teachers College, Arizona State University. Retrieved March 17, 2019, from https://blog.global.education.asu.edu/measuring-the-un-measureable/

Winthrop, R., & Anderson Simons, K. (2013). Can international large-scale assessments inform a global learning goal? Insights from the learning metrics task force. *Research in Comparative and International Education, 8*(3), 279–293.

Winthrop, R., Anderson, K., & Cruzalegui, I. (2015). A review of policy debates around learning in the post-2015 education and development agenda. *International Journal of Educational Development, 40*, 297–307.

Wisbey, M. (2016). *Mother tongue-based multilingual education: The key to unlocking SDG4: Quality education for all.* Bangkok: Asia-Pacific Multilingual Education Working Group and UNESCO Bangkok.

Wiseman, A. (2010). The uses of evidence for educational policymaking: Global contexts and international trends. *Review of Research in Education, 34*, 1–24.

Wolf, A. (2002). *Does education matter? Myths about education and economic growth.* London: Penguin.

Wolf, A. (2004). Education and economic performance: Simplistic theories and their policy consequences. *Oxford Review of Economic Policy, 20*(2), 315–333.

Wood, B., Taylor, R., & Atkins, R. (2013). Fostering active citizenship through the New Zealand social studies curriculum: Teachers' perceptions and practices of social action. *New Zealand Journal of Educational Studies, 48*(2), 84–98.

World Bank. (2011). *Learning for all: Investing in people's knowledge and skills to promote development.* Washington, DC: World Bank.

World Bank. (2012a). *List of education projects* (Database). Retrieved March 17, 2019, from http://datatopics.worldbank.org/education/files/EducationProjects/EducationProjectList.xlsx

World Bank. (2012b). *World Bank education sector strategy 2020: Learning for all.* Washington, DC: World Bank. Retrieved March 15, 2019, from http://siteresources.worldbank.org/EDUCATION/Resources/ESSU/EducationStrategyUpdate_April2012.pdf

World Bank. (2013). *Using low-cost private schools to fill the education gap: An impact evaluation of a program in Pakistan: From evidence to policy.* Washington, DC: World Bank.

World Bank. (2015a). *From billions to trillions: Transforming development finance.* Washington, DC: World Bank. Retrieved December 5, 2018, from http://siteresources.worldbank.org/DEVCOMMINT/Documentation/23659446/DC2015-0002(E)FinancingforDevelopment.pdf

World Bank. (2015b, May 18). *World Bank Group doubles results-based financing for education to US$5 billion over next 5 years* (Press release). Retrieved March 17, 2019, from http://www.worldbank.org/en/news/press-release/2015/05/18/world-bank-group-doubles-results-based-financing-for-education-to-us5-billion-over-next-5-years

World Bank. (2016). *Development goals in an era of demographic change* (Global Monitoring Report 2015/2016). Washington, DC: World Bank.

World Bank. (2017a). *Implementing the 2030 agenda: 2017 update*. Washington, DC: World Bank.

World Bank. (2017b). *World development report 2018: Learning to realize education's promise*. Washington, DC: World Bank.

World Bank. (2018a). *The human capital project*. Washington, DC: World Bank.

World Bank. (2018b). *Morocco data*. Retrieved February 26, 2019, from https://data.worldbank.org/country/morocco?view=chart

World Bank. (2018c). *Sustainable Development Goals (SDGs) and the 2030 agenda*. Retrieved December 11, 2018, from http://www.worldbank.org/en/programs/sdgs-2030-agenda#1

World Bank. (2018d). *World Bank open data*. Retrieved December 12, 2018, from https://data.worldbank.org/

World Bank. (2018e). *World development report 2018: Learning to realize education's promise*. Washington, DC: World Bank.

World Bank Group (WBG). (2015). *World Bank Group gender strategy (FY16-23): Gender equality, poverty reduction and inclusive growth*. Washington, DC: World Bank. Retrieved December 17, 2018, from https://openknowledge.worldbank.org/handle/10986/23425

World Bank Group. (2018). *Kingdom of Morocco governing towards efficiency, equity, education and endurance: A systematic country diagnosis*. Retrieved February 26, 2019, from https://openknowledge.worldbank.org/bitstream/handle/10986/29929/123653.pdf?sequence=5&isAllowed=y

World Conference on Education for All. (1990). *World declaration on education for all and framework for action to meet basic learning needs*. Jomtien: UNESCO. Retrieved November 15, 2018, from http://unesdoc.unesco.org/images/0012/001275/127583e.pdf

World Conference on Higher Education (WCHE). (2009). *The new dynamics of higher education and research for societal change and development* (Communiqué. 2009 World Conference on Higher Education). Paris: UNESCO. Retrieved May 3, 2019, from https://www.inqaahe.org/sites/default/files/UNESCO%20communique.pdf

World Education Forum (WEF). (2000). *The Dakar framework for action: Education for all: Meeting our collective commitments*. Paris: UNESCO. Retrieved October 29, 2018, from http://unesdoc.unesco.org/images/0012/001211/121147e.pdf

World Education Forum (WEF). (2015). *Education 2030: Incheon declaration and frameworkforactionfortheimplementationofsustainabledevelopmentgoal4*. Paris: UNESCO. Retrieved October 29, 2018, from http://unesdoc.unesco.org/images/0024/002456/245656E.pdf

Wulff, A. (2017). Cashing in on SDG 4. In *Spotlight on sustainable development 2017* (Reflection Group on the 2030 Agenda for Sustainable Development, ed.). New York, NY: Reflection Group.

Yamada, S. (2016). *Post-education-for-all and sustainable development paradigm: Structural changes with diversifying actors and norms* (International Perspectives on Education and Society, Vol. 29). Bingley: Emerald.

Yasukawa, K., Hamilton, M., & Evans, J. (2017). A comparative study of national media responses to the OECD survey of adult skills: Policy making from the global to the local? *Compare, 47*(2), 271–285.

York, R., Rosa, E., & Dietz, T. (2004). The ecological footprint intensity of national economies. *Journal of Industrial Ecology, 8*, 139–154.

York, R., Rosa, E., & Dietz, T. (2009). A tale of contrasting trends: Three measures of the ecological footprint in China, India, Japan, and the United States, 1961–2003. *American Sociological Association, 15*(2), 134–146.

You, Y. (2017). Comparing school accountability in england and its East Asian sources of 'borrowing'. *Comparative Education, 53*(2), 224–244.

Young, M. (2008). *Bringing knowledge back in: From social constructivism to social realism in the sociology of knowledge.* London & New York, NY: Routledge.

Yuval-Davis, N., & Anthias, F. (Eds.). (1989). *Woman-nation-state.* Basingstoke: Macmillan.

Zamir, S., & Baratz, L. (2013). Educating 'good citizenship' through bilingual children literature Arabic and Hebrew. *Journal of Education and Learning, 7*(4), 223–230.

Zeelen, J. (2015). *Bowling together: Lifelong learning as a collective challenge in the north and the south.* Inaugural Lecture, Groningen: Rijksuniversiteit Groningen.

Ziegler, R. (2013). The role of language in shaping learner self-concept. In Z. Desai, M. Qorro, & B. Brock-Utne (Eds.), *The role of language in teaching and learning science and mathematics* (pp. 103–112). Cape Town: African Minds.

Index

Printed in the United States
By Bookmasters